TRADITIONS
OF SOCIAL CHANGE

a
reader
for
the
seventies

Joyce Gelb
The City College of the City University
of New York

Marian Lief Palley
University of Delaware

NEW YORK CHICAGO **Holt, Rinehart and Winston, Inc.**
SAN FRANCISCO ATLANTA DALLAS MONTREAL TORONTO LONDON SYDNEY

**TO
ANDREW,
STEPHEN,
AND
ELIZABETH**

Copyright © 1971 by Holt, Rinehart and Winston, Inc.
All Rights Reserved

Library of Congress Catalog Card Number: 73–136556
SBN: 03–085309–5
Printed in the United States of America

1 2 3 4   090   9 8 7 6 5 4 3 2 1

PREFACE

Most frequently, American politics has been considered from the vantage point of what Morris Janowitz has identified as *middle majority politics*. That is, the conventional wisdom has identified in the American political tradition a tendency toward a convergence of political orientations resulting in a "narrowing of party differences" and, by implication, a reinforcement of political integration.[1] Traditionally, the collective perception of Americans has been consonant with the tenets of middle majority politics. More recently, however, the applicability of such tenets to contemporary American politics has been called into question by an increasing number of observers. To many students of American politics, underlying the apparent tendencies toward middle majority politics are the signs of countervailing if not contradictory forces—forces more characteristic of an alternative model of "consensus and cleavage politics." This alternative model of politics assumes the existence of "sources of rigid ideological orientation and political extremism in social change and political leadership" . . . "it is therefore oriented toward the detection of new sources of resistance to political integration."[2]

[1] Morris Janowitz, *Political Conflict* (Chicago: Quadrangle Books, 1970), pp. 89–90.
[2] Janowitz, *Political Conflict*, p. 91.

Preface

In our political science classes at the Newark College of Rutgers University, the University of Delaware, and the City College of New York, students have begun to question traditional notions and models of American politics. They sense in the contemporary American political system tendencies in conflict with the conventional wisdom. They are asking questions that traditional approaches either fail to address or have failed in answering. This collection of articles will, we hope, stimulate consideration of such questions as well as provoke a search for answers. It is intended as a step toward filling a void in the literature of American politics: to recast traditional concerns in the light of compelling contemporary issues. Our general purpose has been to compile materials that contribute to an understanding of the currents of change in the American political system. We are concerned not only with identification of the components of change, but also with comprehension of the roots of change and with fostering informed thinking about implications.

A number of people have assisted us in the development of this volume. First, we should like to thank the editors at Holt, Rinehart and Winston, who were always willing and eager to provide assistance and encouragement. Daniel Rich of the Political Science Department of the University of Delaware read and provided valuable comments on sections of this book, as did Jerrold Schneider, then of the Brookings Institution. Lillian Kimberg, Gladys Hartman, and Marjorie Pritsky all provided invaluable assistance in typing drafts of the manuscript. Finally, we must thank our husbands, Joseph Gelb and Howard Palley, for the assistance they provided in the editing of this volume, as well as for the encouragement and moral support they have given us during the time we spent working on this book.

New York, New York J.G.
Newark, Delaware M.L.P.
January 1971

CONTENTS

Preface iii

Introduction: The Politics of Social Change 1

PART I
TRADITIONAL FORMS OF POLITICAL ARTICULATION AND AGGREGATION 7

chapter one   PERSPECTIVES ON CONTEMPORARY POLITICS   10

1. The Power Structure *Arnold Rose*   10
2. New Political Alignments in the Great Society *Peter F. Drucker*   18

chapter two   POLITICAL PARTIES   31

3. The Political Party *Frank J. Sorauf*   31
4. Political Parties in Western Democracies: Some Skeptical Reflections *Anthony King*   41
5. The End of American Party Politics *Walter Dean Burnham*   61

chapter three   PRESSURE GROUPS   74

6. American Hybrid *Robert A. Dahl*   74
7. Tolerance *Robert Paul Wolff*   79
8. Statement of Ralph Nader, Attorney, Washington, D.C., April 4, 1966 *Ralph Nader*   86

PART II
TOWARD ISSUE-ORIENTED POLITICS   95

chapter four   THE THIRD-PARTY SOLUTION   98

9. On the Politics of Conscience and Extreme Commitment *Seymour Martin Lipset*   98
10. Strategies for a New Politics: New Party or New Democratic Coalition *Arnold S. Kaufman*   104
11. The Wallace Whitelash *Seymour Martin Lipset and Earl Raab*   112

chapter five THE POLITICS OF THE LEFT   125

    12. Student Protest *Jerome Skolnick*   125
    13. You Have to Grow Up in Scarsdale to Know How Bad Things Really Are *Kenneth Keniston*   145
    14. The Agony of the Campus *Irving Howe*   157

chapter six THE POLITICS OF THE RIGHT   167

    15. The Republican Radical Right *Sheilah Koeppen*   167
    16. The Righteous Rightist *Ira S. Rohter*   177
    17. The Radical Right *Eugene V. Schneider*   188

PART III
NEW SOCIAL FORCES: SOCIAL SCIENCE AND COMMUNICATIONS   195

chapter seven THE MEDIA AND POLITICS   198

    18. Television: The Timid Giant *Marshall McLuhan*   198
    19. Television and Voting Turnout *William A. Glaser*   209
    20. Has Television Reshaped Politics? *Angus Campbell*   223
    21. The Late Vote: Summary of Findings and Their Implications *Kurt Lang and Gladys Engel Lang*   228
    22. The Times They Are A-Changin': The Music of Protest *Robert A. Rosenstone*   242

chapter eight THE USES OF SOCIAL SCIENCE   255

    23. Polling in 1968 *Archibald M. Crossley and Helen M. Crossley*   255
    24. The Cybernetic State *Allen Schick*   269

PART IV
ETHNIC AND CLASS TENSIONS   283

chapter nine THE DISPOSSESSED   286

    25. "La Raza": Mexican Americans in Rebellion *Joseph L. Love*   286
    26. Renaissance and Repression: The Oklahoma Cherokee *Albert L. Wahrhaftig and Robert K. Thomas*   297
    27. Blacks, Blocs and Ballots: The Relevance of Party Politics to the Negro *Joyce Gelb*   305
    28. Subcommunity Leadership in a Black Ghetto: A Study of Newark, New Jersey *Marian Lief Palley, Robert Russo, and Edward Scott*   325

chapter ten THE WORKING CLASS 342

29. The Forgotten American *Peter Schrag* 342
30. Organized Labor in Electoral Politics: Some Questions for the Discipline *Harry M. Scoble* 354
31. The Pluralist Period: The AFL until the New Deal *J. David Greenstone* 374

chapter eleven THE AFFLUENT MIDDLE CLASS 386

32. Politics and Reform in American Cities *James Q. Wilson* 386
33. Wallace and the Middle Class: The White Backlash in Wisconsin *Michael Rogin* 400
34. The Scar of Wallace *Edward Schneier* 409

PART V
NEW FORMS OF POLITICAL ARTICULATION 415

chapter twelve COMMUNITY ORGANIZATION 417

35. Reveille for Radicals *Saul Alinsky* 417
36. Social Science and Social Policy *Daniel Patrick Moynihan* 425
37. The Price of Community Control *David K. Cohen* 435

chapter thirteen PROTEST AND VIOLENCE 451

38. Violence in America *Hugh Davis Graham and Ted Robert Gurr* 451
39. Disruptive Tactics *Harry Specht* 472
40. Protest as a Political Resource *Michael Lipsky* 484

INTRODUCTION

**THE POLITICS
OF SOCIAL CHANGE**

It is clear that "tendencies to change are inherent in all human societies because they face basic problems to which no overall continuous solutions exist. These problems include uncertainties of socialization, perennial scarcity of resources relative to individual aspirations, and different contrasting types of social orientation or principles of social organization." [1]

In the past, the American political system has provided reasonably viable alternatives to the ever-changing problems that have confronted the nation. As environmental stresses have caused new conflicts, political parties and interest groups—acting as "inputs" into the political system—have, traditionally, been able to assimilate, if not actually solve, the problems that have arisen. In other words, the input process has been able to function as part of the "tension-management system" [2] which exists in this nation—and in any nontraditional society.[3]

Traditionally, the political parties in the American system have acted as

---

[1] S. N. Eisenstadt, "Social Change, Differentiation and Evolution," *American Sociological Review*, 29 (June 1964), 376.
[2] Wilbur Moore, *Social Change* (Englewood Cliffs, N.J.: Prentice-Hall, 1964), pp. 10–11.
[3] On the sole occasion that the American political system was unable to prove itself adaptive to the conflicting tensions of society, the Civil War resulted.

"power brokers" for the system. They have provided the arena through which groups with conflicting interests could meet, reach consensus and coalition, and elect representatives to governmental office. The general (and often vague) agreements that have emerged from party forums have been offered as "alternative" approaches to the problems of the American polity. The parties have represented the multitude of opinions which prevail in this nation in the form of aggregate opinions.[4] The voters have chosen the candidates of one of the two major parties and, in doing so, have directed solutions to the problems of the day. It appears that voter choice in the United States has *not* usually, in the past, been essentially "issue-oriented." To date, the most salient influence on American voters has been "party," based on family, habit, and socioeconomic status.

In fact, as it is evident from an examination of the data in Table 1, party iden-

TABLE 1

Percentage of Party Identification, 1952–1968

Identification	1952	1954	1956	1958	1960	1962	1964	1966	1968
Strong Democrat	22	22	21	23	21	23	26	18	19.7
Weak Democrat	25	25	23	24	25	23	25	27	24.9
Independent Democrat	10	9	7	7	8	8	9	9	9.9
Independent	5	7	9	8	8	8	8	12	10.0
Independent Republican	7	6	8	4	7	6	6	7	9.2
Weak Republican	14	14	14	16	13	16	13	15	14.9
Strong Republican	13	13	15	13	14	12	11	10	10.1
Apolitical	4	4	3	5	4	4	2	2	1.3
Total	100	100	100	100	100	100	100	100	100.0

Source: Survey Research Center, University of Michigan; furnished through the Inter-University Consortium for Political Research, and quoted by Nelson W. Polsby, "An Emerging Republican Majority," *Public Interest,* 17 (Fall 1969), 125.

tification has been highly constant over time.[5] Of course there are other influences on the voting behavior of the American public. In addition to party influence, there have been the more transient influences of issues and particular candidates. Thus Dwight Eisenhower's presidential victories in 1952 and in 1956 were in large part a response to his appeal as a candidate, and were not due to his Republican party affiliation. This is especially clear if one notes that the total percentage of Republican party identifiers in 1952 totaled only 34 percent of the voters.[6]

---

[4] See Robert A. Dahl, *A Preface to Democratic Theory* (Chicago: University of Chicago Press, 1956), p. 128.
[5] It should be noted that while party identification figures appear constant over time, they may conceal a good deal of net change. Gerald Pomper has shown that over one-fifth of the electorate in each election from 1952 to 1964 had changed its party loyalty at some time before the election. See Pomper, *Elections in America* (New York: Dodd, Mead, 1968), p. 120 (Table 5.1).
[6] Quoted by Polsby (see footnote to Table 1).

The data in Table 1 indicate that, as recently as 1964, 51 percent of American voters identified as either "Strong Democrats" or "Weak Democrats." In other words, a clear majority of the American voting public preferred the Democratic party. By 1970, however, this clear-cut preference of the American polity for the Democratic party had ceased. In July 1969, a Gallup Poll reported that 42 percent of the American public then expressed a preference for the Democratic party, 30 percent of the voters expressed a preference for the Republican party, and an unprecedented 28 percent of the voters claimed "independence" of political party affiliations.[7] The most obvious question we must ask in the light of these electoral preference changes is: What has led to this decline in Democratic party affinity among the American voters, and the resultant increase in self-professed electoral "independence"? Are we witnessing a period of party realignment,[8] customarily associated with periods of national crisis and turmoil, or, as Walter Dean Burnham suggests in "The End of American Party Politics," are the pressures of change so unique and so great that the traditional party system will disappear? Whatever the outcome, "change, not continuity, seems evident." [9]

Regardless of the political party affiliation of successful candidates, it is clear that individuals who do succeed in gaining election to political office—generally executive or legislative office—are influenced at least as much by powerful "interests" in their districts, such as labor, business, and professional organizations, as they are by party and wide constituency claims.[10] In a broader sense, both the theory and the reality of politics in the United States have been noted for their reliance on "pluralism" or "interest group liberalism." Robert Dahl has suggested that, dating from the days of Madison's *Federalist* No. 10, "a great many questions of policy (have been) placed in the hands of private, semipublic, and local governmental organizations . . ." [11] and "there is a high probability that an active and legitimate group in the population can make itself heard effectively at some crucial stage in the process of decision." [12] Robert Paul Wolff, in his article "Tolerance," seeks to demonstrate that such pluralism often has operated at the expense of the general public, and, more particularly, the unorganized poor.

On balance, it appears that direct access to the decision makers—both elected and appointive—in the American political system is limited, for both individuals and noninstitutionalized groups, by virtue of traditional institutional patterns and power relationships. Recognizing this as a fact of American political life, new groups that lack economic and other resources have attempted recently to reach the loci of power through protest tactics, including violence, and the development of new forms of political organization.

---

[7] According to Gallup's figures, this indicated a shift, since 1960, of −5 percent (from 47 percent) for the Democratic party, and +5 percent (from 23 percent) for independents. Printed with permission of the American Institute of Public Opinion, 1969.
[8] See V. O. Key, Jr., "A Theory of Critical Elections," *Journal of Politics*, 17 (February 1955), 3–18.
[9] Pomper, *Elections in America*, p. 122.
[10] Louis Anthony Dexter, "The Job of the Congressman," in Raymond Wolfinger (ed.), *Readings in American Political Behavior* (Englewood Cliffs, N.J.: Prentice-Hall, 1966), pp. 5–26.
[11] Robert A. Dahl, *Pluralistic Democracy in the United States* (Chicago: Rand McNally, 1967), p. 23.
[12] Dahl, *Pluralistic Democracy in the United States*, p. 145.

POLITICS AND SOCIAL CHANGE

In the past decade in the United States, many social pressures for change have been accentuated as a result of

1. The intensification of group consciousness among ethnic and racial minorities and youth, and perhaps, too, among class-based groupings
2. The increasing "issue orientation" of a segment of the American population, including a significant portion of the affluent middle class, expressed as dissatisfaction with national priorities established by the national government
3. The increased availability of information and the nationalization of social movements due to the mass media (especially television) and to new techniques of social research (particularly public opinion polls)
4. The search for new types of political expression—from community-action organizations to violent protest—to enable hitherto powerless groups to gain a voice in the decision-making process

Today the impetus for change seems to occur more rapidly than it did a hundred or even ten years ago. This is due especially to the increased speed and tension of American political life, accentuated by mass transit and the mass media. Impatient people are unwilling to go through the travail of attaining consensus through traditional, gradual political channels. It appears to some that, in any case, no consensus may be possible on such issues as race and poverty. Also, since participation in the established political processes often requires compromising one's own positions in order to develop a consensus acceptable to a broad coalition of supporters, groups excluded from meaningful participation in the political system—either by design or by virtue of their unwillingness to participate in the "system"—have created new political organizations to articulate their demands. Antipoverty groups, welfare rights groups, issue-oriented groups of the left and right, ethnic blocs, and revolutionary youth groups seek, through a combination of traditional and nontraditional tactics, to press their claims for rapid change.

Protest and violence appear to be the most effective means at the disposal of these marginal groups to make their positions known to the decision makers and to the public, and to force policy changes. In the past, such groups as farmers, suffragettes, and trade unionists successfully utilized these techniques of protest and violence in order to bring their grievances to public attention. Today, due in large measure to the mass media, which tends to give extensive coverage to disruptions in society, the use of disruptive tactics as alternative means of gaining rapid access to the political system may be reinforced.

The media have also profoundly influenced the political system by focusing attention on the personality and visual appeal of a candidate for public office, rather than on his partisan identification. Technological innovations such as television and opinion polling may have transformed substantially the nature of politics in the twentieth century; in an age of instant visual communication and advanced predictive techniques, the slow-moving political process may become obsolescent. Private organizations (such as the major broadcasting networks and survey research companies) appear to have a greater impact upon the political process than many of the traditional institutions.

The demands placed upon the political system by those who seek to gain a greater role in decision making have brought to the surface tensions that are racial and class-oriented in nature. While the role of the political party in the past was one of conciliating the positions of groups with contradictory or even hostile attitudes and demands, today the "politics of confrontation" seemingly has made group tensions more overt and perhaps less susceptible to traditional processes of compromise and negotiation.

Today issue orientation seems to be playing a greater role among all groups in American society than party affiliation. This does not mean necessarily that voters have developed full-blown ideologies. Rather, it seems to indicate that when timely issues such as race and war do arise, issue orientation may play a major role in political behavior.[13] The results of the 1969 mayoralty races in Los Angeles, Detroit, and Minneapolis indicated strongly issue-oriented responses by the voters of those cities—since in those cities "law and order" candidates won elections on the basis of issue-focused campaigns.[14] In New York City, a similar mayoral contest, based on "conservative" versus "liberal" principles, appeared to shatter traditional party coalitions.

Some advocates of "left" and "right" political positions speak in terms of organizing third parties on the local and national level; the showing of third party candidate George Wallace in the 1968 presidential campaign indicated that significant numbers of voters could be wooed away from the two major parties. Other "ideologues" talk of a significant realignment of the Democratic and Republican parties, resulting in a greater polarization that could render the American political system unworkable. Finally, passionate proponents of the "New Left" and the "Radical Right" have sought to abandon the traditional political system entirely, in the hope of substituting a new order for the existing order they claim to detest.

CONCLUSIONS

The question that we must ask as students of American politics, in the light of these changes in the social milieu, is: *Is the American political process adequate to cope with the conflicting pressures of a rapidly changing postindustrial society?*

We may conclude that unless political parties and powerful interest configurations welcome newly articulated interests into their midst, as they have usually been able to do in the past, and hasten their pace of adaptation to changing conditions and problems, they will be left behind, and new forms and methods will replace them as meaningful brokers of power in the future.

Graham Wallas noted in 1910 in *Human Nature and Politics* that citizens require "something simpler and more permanent, something which can be loved

---

[13] See Angus Campbell, Philip Converse, Warren Miller, and Donald Stokes, *The American Voter* (New York: Wiley, 1960), chap. 10, for a discussion of the nonideological nature of American voting.
[14] While no exact data are available, it appears that voter attitudes polarize largely along class lines. In Los Angeles, for example, lower-middle-class and middle-class Jews who lived in black-Jewish border areas, where a fierce debate over bussing raged, demonstrated surprisingly strong pro-Yorty sentiment. Canvassers and campaign organizers placed the blame for the switch from a normally "liberal" vote on one issue: "school unrest." See James Q. Wilson and Harold Wilde, "The Urban Mood," *Commentary*, 48 (October 1969), 59.

and trusted and which can be recognized at successive elections as being the same thing that was loved and trusted before; the party is such a thing." [15] If the political party is viewed as an essential tool of the democratic governmental process, then it is clear that the party's possible demise may have profound implications for every aspect of our political system.

The pluralistic political process, based as it has been on group interactions, negotiations, and peaceful resolution of conflict, can survive only if it can broaden the extent of popular participation and the scope of its policy making. If these accommodations are not made, it appears that the American political environment will remain "warlike," tense, and increasingly divided, and the ever-changing demands of an ever-changing American public will go unheeded.

[15] (New York: Appleton-Century-Crofts, 1921), pp. 103–104.

TRADITIONAL FORMS OF POLITICAL
ARTICULATION AND AGGREGATION

It has been acknowledged generally that the major political parties and interest groups—the latter including business, finance, and agriculture—strongly influence the bulk of decision making in the United States. For almost three hundred years, the individuals who have asserted influence through parties and interest groups have been able to maintain an American political system which has been widely regarded as responsive to the multitude of articulated interests represented in the American population. Political scientists have pointed to both two party politics and interest group pluralism as effective techniques for producing consensus and stability for the American political system. Equally as important, parties and interest groups have been seen as providing essential "linkages" between the citizen and his government.

However, the apparent massive upsurge in aggregated and articulated interest group activity in the United States in the past decade has led some to reevaluate the adequacy of these traditional political institutions. Can the traditional party mechanisms and long-lived interest group configurations, which have for so long influenced decision making, continue to maintain their powerful positions? Or will new accommodations and concessions have to be made to groups previously *out* of the "influence business," if social stability and consensus are again to become meaningful realities? Finally, if newly aggregated and articulated interests—such as racial minorities and the unorganized poor—are successful in altering the fundamentally conservative nature of the American political process, will this simply broaden the political spectrum or will new political forms develop to replace the parties and interest groups which have ruled the United States for so many generations?

The articles included in Chapter One, by Arnold Rose and Peter Drucker, both address themselves to the question of who governs. The excerpt from Rose's *The Power Structure* examines the role of traditional elites in American society. Drucker suggests that new forces in American society appear to be causing realignment and change.

The selections in Chapter Two attempt to analyze the theory and practice of the traditional forms of political organization. First, three perspectives on the role of the major political parties are presented. In the chapter reprinted from *Political Parties in the American System,* Frank Sorauf presents an overview of the functions, roles, and structure of political parties in the American system of government. Next, Anthony King registers a sharp dissent to the "conventional wisdom" that political parties are central to the American political system. King contends that parties are less important in the political scheme of things than political scientists believe. The final selection by Walter Dean Burnham provides evidence for the argument that political parties are "withering away" in American politics, and that the future policy consequences of a "politics without parties" will be disastrous.

Included in Chapter Three are articles concerned with the importance of interest groups as articulators of specific policy demands in American government. Robert Dahl analyzes the theory that elites control the American government and concludes that multiple influences—or pressure groups—are actually dominant. Robert Paul Wolff provides an indictment of the fundamentally conservative nature of interest group pluralism in American politics; while Ralph Nader provides a specific example of the great pressure wielded by one major interest group, the automotive industry, in the governmental decision-making process—and perhaps also an example of the ability of a dedicated individual to use the system to obtain a redistribution of values.

CHAPTER ONE

**PERSPECTIVES
ON CONTEMPORARY POLITICS**

1

The Power Structure

Arnold Rose

Political power in the United States, like any other social phenomenon, is changing its locus of concentration, its distribution, and its manifestations constantly.[1] Some of the observations and generalizations made in this book will be out of date by the time the reader is able to analyze and criticize them. Recent changes, for example, have occurred in the rural-urban distribution of power in state legislatures, in the strength of the Republican–Southern Democratic "coalition" in Congress, and in the extent to which businessmen are to be found in key positions in the national Administration. Nevertheless, most aspects of power have remained sufficiently stable for a student of the power structure to draw generalizations and to note slow-moving trends. In contrast to the major theses of C. Wright Mills and Floyd Hunter—that there is a secret, hierarchical, and unified power structure in the United States headed by an economic elite, that the political elite occupies only a secondary position in the power structure, and that

"Conclusion" from *The Power Structure: Political Process in American Society* by Arnold M. Rose. Copyright © 1967 by Oxford University Press, Inc. Reprinted by permission.

[1] Even from the time the present study was begun, in 1960, until it was sent to the publishers, in 1966, there were so many significant changes that additions, corrections, and qualifications had to be made regularly in the manuscript.

the masses are apathetic and act in terms of false consciousness of their interests—we would assert the following propositions. Most of them are based on studies reported or summarized in this book; others are based merely on general or participant observation.

1. There is a power structure in every organized activity of American life and at every level—national, regional, state, and local. Power is the major means used by a large, heterogeneous society to effect or to resist change, and—except in simple face-to-face relations—power is structured, which is to say that there are different roles and role relationships, and a pattern into which these roles and relationships fit.

2. There are varying degrees of relationship and agreement among these varied power structures. They are certainly not unified into a simple power structure, even *within* the categories of the economic and the political, although occasionally semi-permanent liaisons develop among them. Nor are they usually countervailing, because each operates primarily within its own sphere of influence, although countervailing (or check-and-balance) relationships occasionally do occur. The political party power structures—there are at least four major ones on the national level alone—probably have the largest number of relationships with other power structures, both because one of their specific roles is to mediate conflicts and because they have a large degree of control over the bureaucratic machinery of government, which—in turn—monopolizes most of the instruments of organized physical force.

3. Within each power structure, a small number of persons hold the largest amount of power. In community studies, this has been estimated to constitute less than 1 per cent of the population, but such estimates refer to those who lead in community-wide political decisions, and not to power *within* the spheres of business, unions, voluntary associations, schools, churches, etc. While in any sphere of activity there are "leaders," who constitute a tiny proportion of all those affected by the activity, this does not mean that the others have no power whatsoever. Opposition groups occasionally form, and sometimes succeed in overturning the existing elite. In all cases where there are elections, the rank-and-file voters exercise some restraining and modifying power over the elite. Their power is a function of the extent to which they have interacted to create a public opinion, the extent to which the election machinery is honest, and the extent to which voters are equal. Under these criteria, most governmental elections accord a good deal of power to the electorate, most business corporation elections accord practically no power to the electorate, and labor union and voluntary association elections vary between these two poles. But even in government and in actively democratic trade unions, there is an ever-changing elite which exercises most of the power at any given moment.

4. Each elite manifests its power mainly within its own domain. That is, the strongest powers of businessmen are exercised within their own businesses, and the strongest powers of politicians and public administrators are exercised within government. But particularly the political and economic elites, among all the elites, influence each other's spheres. Especially since the 1930s the government has set various restrictions and controls on business, and has heavily taxed business and the public to carry out purposes deemed to be for the general good—welfare programs, education programs, highways, war and military defense activi-

ties, etc. Business leaders use lobbyists, "business representatives" in legislatures, contributions to campaign funds, publicity designed to influence public opinion, the "political strike," and other lesser techniques to influence government. Businessmen influence government more effectively than most non-businessmen—not only because they can afford lobbyists, advertisements and other costly techniques—but also because they are more educated, more knowledgeable, more articulate, and more activist than average citizens. The latter qualities give them an advantage quite compatible with a democratic society.

5. The economic elite has its greatest success in influencing government where there are no counter-pressures—from other sectors of the economic elite, from other non-economic elites, and from public opinion. The result has been that the economic elite has been relatively successful in influencing government purchasing agents and the independent regulatory commissions. This is not quite an accurate way of stating the facts, however, since individual businesses often compete strongly with each other in influencing these factors of government, and there is a considerable turnover in the individual businesses benefited by these sectors of government. In pressuring or appealing to the top levels of the federal administration, to the Congress, or even to many state legislatures (especially outside the South), businessmen have been much less successful since the 1930s. In fact, as far as general legislation is concerned, they have had an almost unbroken series of defeats, although they have succeeded in *delaying* the passage of certain bills for years. Thus, while businessmen have gained certain economic benefits from government, their typical ideology—in favor of businessman leadership in the society and of a minimum of government activity for the benefit of other segments of the population—has made no progress.[2]

6. While the federal government has been gaining ascendancy over the state and local governments, and while the office of the President has been gaining power at the expense of Congress, it is far from true that the state governments and the Congress are powerless. Rather, it could be said that the "balance of power" doctrine envisaged in the Constitution has come into operation only since 1933, because the federal government (except for military activities) and the presidency (except in wartime) were relatively weak institutions before then. These two trends in political power have reduced the influence of the economic elite, for the federal government is less susceptible to influence from businessmen than are most of the state governments, and the presidency is less susceptible to such influence than are many of the congressmen.

7. In the early 1960s a coalition of several decades' duration between two major political power structures—the conservative leadership of the Republican party and the Democrats in power in most of the Southern states—largely broke down. The Southern Democrats, changing in membership and reduced in number by Republican inroads on their constituencies, drew closer to the Northern Democrats, except publicly over the issue of civil rights. The South was rapidly becoming like the North—in its industrialization, urbanization, patterns of race rela-

---

[2] It has been argued that this businessman's ideology represents a "false consciousness" —that is, it claims to represent an economic interest, but is in fact, contrary to the economic interest of businessmen. The factual argument is that businessmen gain most economic benefits when the government actively promotes the welfare and education of even its poorest citizens, when it maintains a regularly unbalanced budget, and when it reduces tariffs—all policies which most businessmen oppose.

tions permitted by Negro voting, and development of a two-party system.[3] The Republican party was sharply divided between its conservatives and liberals, on the one hand, and a smaller group of right-wing extremists with a vigorous ideology who seized control of the party's grass-roots structures in the majority of states. The extremists—while occasionally ideologically supportive of business— were not as willing to make political compromises in behalf of business or as willing to trust leading businessmen, as had been the previous conservative leaders of the Republican party. All these developments, coupled with the political skill of President Lyndon B. Johnson, permitted the passage of a great deal of "liberal" legislation in the 1964–65 sessions of Congress—including "Medicare" for the elderly, . . . federal aid to education, the anti-poverty program, tax reduction without a balanced budget, a comprehensive civil rights act, a voting rights act, elimination of national quotas for immigrants, creation of a new Department of Housing and Urban Development, aid to urban mass-transit programs and to highway and city beautification efforts, and a National Foundation on the Arts and Humanities. Further, the President had an unofficial price control policy which worked for a few years to keep major industries from raising prices.

8. In the passage of the above-mentioned legislation, interested economic elite pressure groups were mostly defeated. On the other hand, the major legislation sought by organized labor—repeal of Section 14(b) of the Taft-Hartley Act—was also defeated in the Senate. The one economic elite group that continued to reap major economic benefits from government activity was the armaments and space-exploration supply industries, although the Secretary of Defense made certain decisions on procurement—such as in favor of competitive bidding rather than cost-plus contracts—even in this area which were not favored by the leading manufacturers.

9. Through the Voting Rights Act of Congress and the *Baker* v. *Carr* and *Reynolds* v. *Sims* decisions of the United States Supreme Court—including the giving of permission to the Attorney General to seek a Court review of the poll tax (which was consequently outlawed by the Supreme Court)—a major democratization of voting for state legislatures was occurring in many states. Both state and local government activities were increasingly influenced by standards set by federal aid programs that covered ever wider spheres.

10. The pattern of legislation at both federal and state levels revealed the emergence of new popular pressure groups with considerable power, partly because of demographic shifts and partly because of growing political consciousness among these groups. These groups are the elderly, a portion of whom are now organized into many associations, the most politically active of which is the National Association of Senior Citizens; the Negroes, possibly a majority of whom are organized into various civil rights associations and activist churches; and the "resentful disaffecteds," practically all organized into a variety of leftist and rightist extremist organizations, of which the John Birch Society is the largest and the wealthiest. The political organization of voluntary associations representing these three categories of the "masses" provides increasing evidence of a thesis expounded in an earlier section on "Reactions against the Mass Society."

---

[3] The decline in the number of "safe" Democratic House seats has been documented by Raymond E. Wolfinger and Joan Heifetz, "Safe Seats, Seniority, and Power in Congress," *American Political Science Review*, 59 (June 1965), 337–349.

11. The major area of small-group control of national policy remaining in the country was that of foreign policy. The most powerful arm of this small group—namely the President and his official advisers—are quite exposed to the public. But there are secret decision-makers operating in this area also—secret in that their influence and processes of decision-making are not accessible to the public. These decision-makers are the CIA, the foreign policy "experts" in the universities and in such organizations as the Foreign Policy Association and the Council on Foreign Relations, and the military supplies industrialists who exert their influence mainly through the military leaders. The last-named are the ones whom Mills placed at the pinnacle of the power elite in the United States; we identify them rather as one influence among several affecting the nation almost exclusively in the area of foreign policy. We are entirely skeptical about Mills's contention that the other "members" of the economic elite—say, for example, those organized in the Chamber of Commerce—have more influence on foreign policy than the workers organized into trade unions, especially when they engage in shipping boycotts.

12. Despite the fact that the Republican party's ideological move to the right after 1962 left the Democrats securely in command of the center, the program of the Democratic party remained as liberal as it had ever been. This can be seen not only by comparing national party platforms over the years, but by reviewing the legislation supported (and usually passed) by the majority of Democrats in Congress and by the Democratic Presidents Kennedy and Johnson. This can be explained either as a long-run trend—in terms of the increasing strength of voters who favor liberal measures and generally support the Democratic party as the instrument to achieve them—or as part of a structural cycle. Lipset specifies a version of the latter theory: [4] Republican Presidents seek center support and so force Republican congressmen from safe conservative seats to behave in a more liberal fashion. When a Republican holds the presidency, the Southern contingent of conservative Democrats have more power in their party. Thus, in a Republican presidency, the two congressional parties are not so far apart. But when a Democrat holds the presidency, he pulls his congressmen to the left, to respond to the needs of the greater number of voters there, while the Republican congressmen are free to follow their ideological inclination toward the right, and the two parties are quite far apart. It is difficult to judge from the facts which theory is correct, but this author tends to regard the former theory as more persuasive, especially in view of the decline of differences between South and North. In any case, there has been a significant difference between the platforms and policies of the two national parties at least since 1932,[5] and the difference in the mid-1960s was as great as could be found between democratic political parties anywhere in the Western world. The increasing number of differences between the two major political parties, and the growing ideological framework for those differences, will probably have profound implications for the political future of the United States

---

[4] Seymour Martin Lipset, *Political Man* (New York: Doubleday, 1960), pp. 306–307.

[5] The basic ideological difference between the leadership of the two parties, on the average, has been demonstrated by Herbert McClosky, Paul J. Hoffman, and Rosemary O'Hara, "Issue Conflict and Consensus Among Party Leaders and Followers," *American Political Science Review*, 54 (June 1960), 406–427. The public, also, sees ideological differences between the two parties. See, for example, the report of the Minnesota Poll in the *Minneapolis Sunday Tribune*, November 3, 1963, p. UM2.

—but it is still too early to foresee the future development. Nevertheless, from the standpoint of the thesis of this book, we can say that there is little evidence that business is playing any significant role in the development of these trends. Business is a declining influence on the political power structures, except in the narrow area of its relationship to government procurement officials and the independent regulatory commissions—largely because business exerts its strongest efforts on these and because there are few countervailing influences on them. . . .

13. The public's and the formal leadership's image of the power structure—if we can generalize from a study of the one state of Minnesota—does not include many people as seeing the economic elite as all-powerful, although the extent to which they do see business as influential may be somewhat exaggerated in terms of the facts. Judging from their public pronouncements, it is the political extremist—of both the right and the left—whose image of the American power structure includes a conspiratorial and all-powerful role for the economic elite. The extremist groups have different names for this "all-powerful group" but they refer to the same business elite: The "lunatic fringe" rightists call them "the hidden group behind the communists," the more rational extreme rightists call them "the Establishment"; the more rational extreme leftists also call them "the Establishment" or "Wall Street," but are more likely to use the Mills-Hunter terms "the power elite" or "the power structure," while the less rational extreme leftists either use the same terms or refer bluntly to "the big business conspiracy." While it is of considerable interest that the political extremists of both right and left—apparently along with many non-extremist intellectuals influenced by Mills and Hunter—have the same image of the top business elite as being all-powerful, it is of greater importance to note that the majority of the people and of the positional leaders of American organized society do not have this image. We have adduced much evidence in . . . that the top business elite are far from having an all-powerful position; that power is so complicated in the United States that the top businessmen scarcely understand it, much less control it; and that since 1933 the power position of businessmen has been declining rather than growing.

14. Because the spheres of their organizations have grown in recent decades, the elites of the federal administration (including the military), of the federal courts, of certain voluntary associations, and of certain education and scientific institutions, have grown more powerful. While on rare occasions they supersede in power the top political elites—as when the United States Supreme Court ordered the state governments to end racial segregation and to reapportion their legislatures in accord with population, or when the same Court declares unconstitutional a federal statute, or when the civil rights associations pressure Congress into voting for a statute as sweeping as the Civil Rights Act of 1964, or when the labor and old-age groups pressure Congress into voting for a statute as sweeping as the Medicare Act of 1965 (although both these statutes had the full support of that significant political elite—the President)—the political elites are usually ascendant over them. The political elites control the agencies of force and the instruments of legislation, have considerable access to the mass media, and have the support of public opinion. The political elites—the two major parties, the President, the factions in the houses of Congress, the executives and legislatures of the states and large cities—are not unified of course, and they check-and-balance each other to a considerable extent.

15. While the two major political parties are listed by us as among the most

powerful groups in the United States, their structures are quite generally misunderstood by the public and by nonspecialized intellectuals and other leadership groups. They are structured mainly as voluntary associations, with grass-roots elections that range from being wholly democratic to being "controlled" from a self-perpetuating group at the top. In some states (e.g. Texas) they are highly fractionated and schismatic. They are structured on the layer principle: ward or county, municipality, district, and state. They scarcely exist as voluntary associations at the national level—except for the quadrennial national nominating conventions—but they exist in the caucuses of Congress, where they are the most important single influence on congressmen's voting behavior despite the bifurcation within both political parties.

16. While money in the hands of rich people opens special opportunities to democratic political processes—such as through the use of lobbyists, advertisements, and campaign contributions—these processes are by no means closed to poor people. A volunteer campaign worker for a congressman will have more influence on him than most lobbyists, and as much influence on him as a campaign contribution equivalent to the voluntary labor, roughly speaking. The fact that the political party in most states is an open, if not entirely democratic, voluntary association, and the fact that it is the single most important influence on most elected officials, also gives the non-wealthy citizen access to political power often greater than that of the wealthy, but not politically active, citizen. In this context it should be understood that most elected officials, especially at higher levels, are only partially open to pressures of any kind. Practically all congressmen, and probably most state legislators, vote for bills in accord with their own personal convictions—when they have convictions with regard to specific bills—most of the time. Where they do not have convictions regarding a specific bill, the most important influence on them are the caucus leaders or committee chairmen of their own political party who are representing the party leadership's position. The "personal convictions" factor suggests that the *initial* selection of candidates and the means which they use to get elected to Congress are the two most important links in the chain leading to the passage of bills where influence can be most effectively applied. It is for this reason that we say that voluntary campaign labor, participation in the grass-roots party (as voluntary association), and monetary campaign contributions are the most powerful instruments to influence a legislator (or probably any other elected official).

In sharper summary, the conclusions of this book—in contrast with those of Mills and Hunter—are that power structure of the United States is highly complex and diversified (rather than unitary and monolithic), that the political system is more or less democratic (with the glaring exception of the Negro's position until the 1960s), that in political processes the political elite is ascendant over and not subordinate to the economic elite, and that the political elite influences or controls the economic elite at least as much as the economic elite controls the political elite. To arrive at such conclusions we must in part have a contrast conception: What should the American political power structure be compared to? We believe that Mills has implicitly compared the existing American power structure to some populist or guild socialist ideal, which has never existed and which we believe could never exist considering basic sociological facts—such as the existence of culture, of the value of money to most people, etc. Our implicit comparison in this book has been to any known other society—past or present (with the possible exception of the contemporary Scandinavian countries). We do not say that the multi-influence hypothesis is entirely the fact, or that the United States is completely democratic; we simply say that such statements are more correct for the United States today than for any other society.

. . . (We) wish merely to repeat in conclusion the statement of the multi-influence hypothesis which has guided the studies reported . . . : Segments of the economic elite have violated democratic political and legal processes, with differing degrees of effort and success in the various periods of American history, but in no recent period could they correctly be said to have controlled the elected and appointed political authorities in large measure. The relationship between the economic elite and the political authorities has been a constantly varying one of strong influence, co-operation, division of labor, and conflict, with each group influencing the other in changing proportion to some extent, and each operating independently of the other to a large extent. Today there is significant political control and limitation of certain activities of the economic elite, and there are also some significant processes by which the economic elite use their wealth to help elect some political candidates and to influence other political authorities in ways which are not available to the average citizen. Further, neither the economic elite nor the political authorities are monolithic units which act with internal consensus and co-ordinated action with regard to each other (or probably in any other way): in fact, there are several economic elites, which only very rarely act as units within themselves and among themselves, and there are at least two (we prefer to think of them as four) political parties which have significantly differing programs with regard to their actions toward any economic elite and each of these parties has only a partial degree of internal cohesion.

The power structure of the United States is indeed so complex that this book only touches on certain aspects of it, rather than providing full empirical evidence for these aspects. We believe, however, that enough empirical documentation has been provided to give basic support to the multi-influence hypothesis as a general statement about what is true of the power structure of the United States.

2
New Political Alignments in the Great Society

Peter F. Drucker

The objective realities to which American politics must address itself have been changing drastically in the last fifteen years or so:

- in population structure
- in social and political structure
- in respect to the power centers in American society
- and in the international environment

As a result, fundamental assumptions accepted as near axioms in both our domestic and our foreign policies are becoming increasingly untenable.

The issues around which American politics is tending to organize itself will increasingly be both new and different from those of the last half century. Long-accepted issues—or at least their traditional formulations—will increasingly come to appear unreal if not meaningless.

Above all, the new realities are rapidly obsoleting traditional political alignments.

Excerpted from Chapter 7 of *A Great Society?* edited by Bertram M. Gross, © 1966, 1967, 1968 by Basic Books, Inc., Publishers, New York.

Alignments that have molded the American political process for most of the last hundred years—the "bridge" role of the "Solid South" and its political power; the strategic role of economic blocs; and so on—are likely to lose their significance. This process is just beginning to be visible—above all the turmoil and agony of the Republican Party. It is likely to change both parties, however, if not to revise the accepted polarization of American politics around "non-ideological" interests and around domestic affairs. It is also quite unlikely that foreign policies can continue to be "bi-partisan"; they are more likely to become the center of major political controversy.

President Johnson's "Great Society" represents a first response to some of the new issues, both at home and abroad. But it approaches these new issues largely within the old framework. It appeals primarily to the old values and it employs mostly the traditional rhetoric. It is thus essentially a transitional phase—and one would guess that the President is highly conscious of this. The emphasis on "consensus" is above all an attempt, both highly constructive and politically very dangerous, to accomplish some of the most important of the new tasks *before* they have become political issues. Even at its most successful, the era of "consensus," like any earlier "Era of Good Feeling," can therefore only be a prelude to a—probably prolonged—period of vocal dissent, violent political ferment, and sudden political landslides.

New Domestic Realities

The recent past—the two decades since the end of World War II, or the fifteen years since the Korean War—has produced clearly visible shifts in the political, social, and economic realities at home and abroad.

In bald statement, the changes that appear most significant to me are:

i. Within the last fifteen to twenty years, the United States has become a *Metropolitan Society* in which the great majority of the people live in a fairly small number of large, densely-populated metropolitan areas, dependent upon common services, each an intricate system of great technical and political complexity.

ii. The center of gravity of the American work force has been shifting from manual worker—skilled or unskilled, on the farm or in workshop or factory—to *The Knowledge Worker* with a very high degree of formal schooling. For the knowledge worker, and for an economy based on knowledge work, poverty ceases to be the general condition of mankind. Not that the "knowledge worker" is "rich," but his income tends to be so high as to remove the constant anxiety about the next meal in which mankind as a whole has always lived. Above all, the knowledge worker enjoys a job security unknown to history.

As a further result of this shift to knowledge work, there is in process a radical change in the position of the manual worker. Neither his job security nor his income deteriorates. But he tends to be seen as economically "non-productive" and as socially "marginal." He is no longer seen as essential. In his stead the employed educated middle class is increasingly becoming the *New Majority*.

iii. Within these last fifteen years, the United States has become a society of big, semi-autonomous, and tightly-organized institutions. There is not only "big government"—Federal as well as state and municipal (within which the Civil

Services and the Armed Forces represent large, tightly-organized power centers of their own, semi-autonomous and with their own rules and their own leaders), there is also the big university, the big hospital, the big labor union, and many others.

Business was only the first sphere in American society in which the large organization appeared—which explains in part why we tend to think of "business" whenever we say "bigness." American society, as indeed every modern industrial society, has become a *Pluralist Society* of big organizations, each serving one—but only one—of the purposes and needs of society.

The decisive interactions in American society today—and increasingly in American politics—are therefore interactions between highly organized, large, powerful, and professionalized institutions, each concerned with its own specific task.

iv. Traditional federalism sees relationships of co-existence and competition between the Federal government and the various states. But in the *New Federalism* other political units in addition to the states (especially the metropolitan areas) are directly in relation with the Federal government and work directly with it. More important, perhaps, institutions that are not "government" but "private" increasingly become the agents of government in the fulfillment of public functions and even in the formulation of public policy—the universities, the big corporations, the large teaching hospitals.

v. There is an emergence of new power centers in our society, rivalling if not already over-shadowing the traditional power centers of American politics, such as the traditional economic interests. These new power centers are: *The Military, Education,* and *Big Science.* True, education, while rapidly becoming the largest single employer in this country and the largest single investor of capital, is not yet organized as a power center. Yet surely the emphasis on the diploma as a condition of employment represents a tremendous social victory for the educator and puts him in a position of social control such as this country never before granted to any single group.

Military strength and educational strength are now seen as the twin pillars of national strength in the modern world, and as the two attributes of great power status.

These two power centers, the military and education, come together in the commitment of government to the promotion of *Scientific and Technological Thrust* as a major new national responsibility and a major new national purpose.

New Domestic Issues

i. In domestic politics we have already *shifted from economically-centered issues to issues that are basically political: constitutional, moral, and aesthetic.* The outstanding example is of course civil rights. Indeed civil rights is a major issue only because it became apparent that economics alone cannot provide citizenship to the American Negro.

The "War on Poverty," too, though it uses economic terminology, is a shift away from the economic and towards the political. It was imposed by an affluent society on itself by its own bad conscience—and, in large measure, by an aesthetic concern with the squalor and ugliness in which so many live in an economy of abundance.

The educated professional employee, on the other hand, is altogether

- prone to alienation rather than to poverty;
- beset by the fear of futility rather than by lack of income.

What he lacks is not a job but the satisfaction of achievement and a sense of function. The creation of such satisfaction will be a basic purpose of American politics.

ii. *Congress* and its function may well become an issue by itself. The developments of the last two decades have largely pushed Congress out of being a partner in political decisions. It is being reduced, instead, in a good many areas, to being a critic and commentator. The complex arrangements of the New Federalism are largely beyond the power of Congress, if not altogether beyond its purview.

Issues in International Politics

The central reality which is likely to generate, or at least to shape, the issues in American international politics is the fading away of the two axioms on which American foreign policy has been based since World War II: the axiom that the international economy was dependent upon the U.S. economy, rather than that there was interdependence; and the much more important axiom that "Communism" and "Russia" were synonymous, and both words for "the enemy."

As the result of the erosion of these axioms, it is no longer possible to assume that any action taken by the United States in its capacity of leader of the Free World community is automatically in the interest of the United States as a nation, and vice versa. The national-interest approach might, for instance, give us a "soft" policy in respect to China where the world-leadership approach might lead to a very "hard" one, i.e., containing Chinese aggression anywhere and everywhere.

Bi-partisanship in foreign affairs cannot last. "Pragmatism" has had its day; we now need policy again.

POLITICAL ALIGNMENTS

The most important decisions of the last fifteen years in American politics were made essentially outside of the political process proper. They could have hardly been made within it—they concerned issues on which no decision is possible within the traditional alignments.

The two crucial decisions in domestic politics during the last decade or so were probably School Segregation and Reapportionment. Both were reached—without any political discussion to speak of—by the Supreme Court, that is by an organ outside of party politics.

Similarly in foreign affairs: the most important decision was surely the one that committed us to a major war in Vietnam. This decision was reached without any "decision" whatever, and certainly without any public debate. I happen to believe the Vietnam choice to have been the right one. Still, what is amazing is not that there has been criticism of our involvement in Vietnam but that there has been so little discussion and so little dissent.

Indeed, the most important among the traditional alignments of American policy are in the process of disappearing altogether.

The South Loses Its Casting Vote

During the last few years, one of the two main bases of the traditional alignments, the "Compromise of 1876," has in effect been repealed.

The history books tell us little of this Compromise other than that it seated a Republican presidential candidate (Rutherford Hayes) who had actually been outpolled by his Democratic opponent, in exchange for which the Federal government withdrew the troops that had kept the "carpet-bagger" administrations in power in the states of the former Confederacy. But implicit in this deal—as was clearly understood by all concerned—was a far-reaching compact between North and South. It guaranteed the South non-interference in its "domestic institution," that is, the unchallenged maintenance of white supremacy. In exchange the South promised tacitly to accept and not to challenge the leadership of the North in all areas excepting only race relations. This was expressed in the common saying that no Southerner could become president.

The compromise gave the South power in American politics, and especially in Congress, way beyond its population strength, way beyond even the quality of Southern leadership. One reason for this was the control by the Southerners of the chairmanship of important congressional committees as a combined result of the congressional seniority system and the unchallenged one-party structure of the South.

More important, perhaps, though much less visible, was the function of the South as the *bridge* between the major parties and major factions; this guaranteed almost every president a workable majority in Congress, but also made the South indispensable. It was obviously to the interest of the South not to have any one party predominate in Congress: the Southerners in Congress, therefore, always tended to make common cause with the minority—except in times of great emergency, such as the outbreak of war or the first hundred days of Roosevelt's New Deal.

For ninety years, practically every Administration has faced a coalition in Congress in which the South, though the junior partner, essentially dictated the terms.

The proximate cause for the "repeal" of the Compromise of 1876 was the northward migration of the Negro which began after World War I. With the Negro in the North having formal political equality, deprivation of the same rights in the South could no longer be considered a "domestic affair." As soon as —following the Supreme Court school decision of 1954—the Federal government attacked white supremacy in the South, the Southerners ceased, therefore, to honor their part of the bargain. This in large part explains the frustration of President Kennedy's domestic policies.

But the ultimate cause of the sharp change in the position of the South in American politics is the shift in the white population and its distribution. Because the Old South has tended to stay heavily rural and small-town, it no longer has the numbers to support a bridge-role and to cast the deciding vote. Or, rather, a South that stays rural and small-town cannot have enough population to matter —while a South that becomes metropolitan ceases to be the "Solid South," as Atlanta and Miami have demonstrated.

That both Mr. Truman and Mr. Johnson were not supported by the South amounted to a renunciation of the traditional alliance. But that both could be elected without the votes of the South was much more important: it proved that the South no longer held the balance of power. Even Mr. Kennedy would still have been elected, despite the hair-line margin in his popular vote, if most of the states of the Old Confederacy had given their electoral votes to a States Right Southerner. That, as a by-product, a Southerner has been shown to be capable of winning both nomination and election to the presidency is a rather meager consolation.

The price in civil rights that the nation paid for the bridge-role of the South was, of course, exorbitant. But in terms of contemporary American politics, during these ninety years, the peculiar role of the South has on the whole been healthy and productive.

There is a belief abroad that the Southerners in Congress tended to be "reactionaries." But this holds true only for their position on race relations, which did not become an issue in American politics until the Depression and perhaps not until World War II. Otherwise, the Southerner in Congress was more often than not a populist radical. But above all, to preserve the power position of the South, the Southerner in Congress had no choice but to seek a consensus. National policy did not shift to the left or to the right because the South shifted: the South shifted because the national center shifted first. In effect, the Southerners always had to make it possible for "liberals" and "conservatives" to agree at least sufficiently to permit the business of government to go on.

The long-serving committee chairmen, while often autocratic and immovable, also usually did their homework and thoroughly knew their area. They endowed Congress with a solid backbone of expertise such as no other parliamentary body in the world possesses. One would be hard-pressed to find men who worked harder or who knew their area better than the two men from Georgia, Senator Russell and Congressman Vinson, who for so many years headed the Armed Services Committees in their branches of Congress. It is this expert knowledge that makes Congress still capable of dealing with the Federal bureaucracy and gives us a degree of political and policy control over the Civil Service such as is unknown in any other modern nation.

In foreign affairs, the absence of major manufacturing and labor union interests in the South enabled the Southerner often to regard the national interest, and to take a much larger view than the Midwesterner or New Englander, swayed as he so often has been by the immediate, short-sighted interests of this or that company or industry.

Finally, "that no Southerner could become President" meant that the senior Southerners in Congress had no further ambition, and knew that they had to make their mark in history through their performance as legislators.

For better or worse this position of the South is gone.

It is no accident that for the first time in the history of the Senate a civil-rights filibuster could be broken so decisively (in the fight over President Kennedy's Civil Rights bill) that, two years later, the South did not even try to filibuster against Mr. Johnson's much more sweeping bill of 1965. It is no accident, either, that, for the first time since the present system of committee chairmen was introduced around the turn of the century, committee members have successfully revolted against their chairman (against Representative Smith of Virginia, the Chairman of the House Rules Committee, and Representative Patman of Texas of the House Banking Committee).

I am by no means convinced that the South will abandon the one-party system. It is conceivable that, for many years to come, the pressures toward conformity, and for resistance to an alien and critical outside world, may enforce strict voting discipline—to the point where opposition candidates have no chance at all in large areas.

But even if nothing changes in the South, it would not matter greatly one way or another. For almost a century, the arrival of a two-party system in the South has been looked forward to by "liberals," inside and outside the South, as the hour of deliverance, if not as the panacea for all the ills of the South. It is ironic that, just when the two-party system has a real chance to establish itself in the South, it has also become quite unimportant. In national affairs the South must increasingly cease to be something separate, indeed something unique. Whatever is left of the "Old South" is rapidly becoming just another sparsely settled and relatively poor section of the country—and, as such, a fairly unimportant one.

The Erosion of the Economic Blocs

The second major shift in the structure of alignments in American politics is the steady erosion of the traditional economic blocs. These blocs—whether "labor" or "farmer" or "business"—*can no longer be carriers of policies.* They can only, increasingly, become *obstacles* to any policy whatever—for any change is, in effect, a threat to them.

The three agencies of the Federal government which reached cabinet status between the Civil War and World War II were Agriculture, Commerce, and Labor. Each was created to represent a major economic estate of the realm, and to make sure that its interests were protected. The particular interest group which any one of these bureaucracies represented had a virtual veto power over the appointment of the Secretary. Indeed, the secretaries often behaved like ambassadors of a powerful foreign sovereign rather than as members of the President's Cabinet.

By sharp contrast, the two new Cabinet posts created since World War II (leaving out Defense as a special case in which formerly separate agencies of Cabinet rank were consolidated) were Health, Education and Welfare, and Housing and Urban Affairs—both established not to represent economic interests but *to remove major areas of policy from the control of, and domination by, economic interests.* And the proposal to make Transportation a Cabinet department serves the same purpose.

Of all the traditional groups, only one has an opportunity to remain influential and a carrier of policy: the "managers." For managing is a function that is essential in all the new big organizations; indeed, managing is the specific function of big complex organizations—whether business or armed service, university or government agency or hospital. But, of course, the only reason why this group might survive as a distinct and organized power-center is that the "capitalist" of yesterday had been replaced by the "professional manager" of today who is not confined to one economic interest but pervades the entire society and who is not exclusively economically oriented. The extent to which managers have succeeded in the much-publicized attempt to make themselves "trustees" for all the interests in the organization—employees, investors, customers and so on—is a moot point. That they are trying is the important point. This explains why President Johnson has been wooing them—they are a bridge between yesterday's alignments and tomorrow's alignments and, as such, essential to Mr. Johnson's "consensus."

"Labor," by contrast, has not even begun such a transformation. Except in the event of a major economic crisis, it seems rather unlikely that a sufficiently large part of the "employed professional middle class" will unionize itself, not only to restore "labor's" vitality and growth potential, but also to change the characteristics of "labor" even more drastically than the change from "capitalist" to "manager" has transformed the characteristics of the "business" interest. The aims of a unionized professional middle class are, in any case, likely to be social rather than economic. And insofar as they are economic, they are likely to be in direct conflict with the economic aims of the rank-and-file blue-collar worker of the traditional unions.

The traditional economic blocs no longer represent the dynamics of American society, if only because the big tasks and the big problems are not economic but political, social, moral, or aesthetic. This does not mean that the economic blocs will become unimportant or powerless. The farmer, for instance, has long ceased to have the key position he had up until World War I; but the farm lobby is losing its importance only very slowly.

What does, however, happen is that such groups become purely negative. Any change is a threat to them. The aims of policy are not their aims. They therefore become increasingly "vested interests," concerned with the maintenance of a privileged status. Extortion, rather than policy, becomes their business.

The Changing Role of Ethnic Blocs

The most confusing area is that of ethnic and religious blocs, such as the Irish Catholics, the Jews, the Italians, and so on.

In different parts of the metropolis, their importance will change in different directions.

In the core city, the old "downtown"—the five boroughs of New York, for instance—such blocs should become much more important. The Negro clearly is just now emerging as an organized and powerful ethnic bloc in the core city. His tendency to act as a bloc in city politics must increase; for the individual Negro can achieve advancement and access to opportunities only through organized use of his political power, that is, as a bloc and through "patronage." The same applies to the Puerto Rican and to the Mexican-American.

This, in turn, is likely to force other groups in the core city to organize themselves and act as blocs. The way in which Irish Catholics in Boston, for instance, have again coalesced as a bloc to beat off a Negro attack on the "neighborhood school" is only an example. And the same holds true of other ethnic groups largely composed of industrial workers or lower-grade service employees, such as the Czechs in Chicago, the Poles in Cleveland, and the Hungarians in Pittsburgh.

Outside the core city, however, in the suburban areas of the metropolis, ethnic blocs are likely to become very much less important. Regardless of his origin (unless he should be a Negro), the suburbanite sees himself characterized by his education—which tends to be advanced—and by his cultural level, rather than by his origin. In fact, he is likely to resent too blatant an appeal to his origin, as questioning his status in the American community.

Ethnic or religious blocs are, therefore, likely to become complicated—with both appeal to them and non-appeal equally unpredictable. Inside the core city, the blocs can be expected to become far more important—and with this advent would come the strong "boss" and the appeal to "solidarity" instead of issues, ideas, or men. Outside the core city, ethnic origin is likely to mean less and less —though religious affiliation may still play an important role in a number of areas.

Core City and Suburb

The different appeal of ethnic and religious blocs in core city and suburb respectively is only one of the differences that are likely to characterize these two elements of the metropolis and that eventually might divide them sharply in national politics.

Altogether, *the core city is increasingly likely to present yesterday's politics, yesterday's issues, and yesterday's alignment.* The very fact that bloc voting is likely to be such a factor will make the core city look to the past rather than to the future—plus the fact, of course, that the core city is likely to be the least affluent part of the "affluent society." The suburbs, representing the young people and therefore the more highly educated and more prosperous citizens, are likely to be looking, increasingly, towards tomorrow's problems, especially towards the problems of the metropolitan area.

Also, the core city will increasingly have to bear the burden of the metropolitan services while having fewer and fewer tax resources. These latter will be in the suburbs—indeed, it is conceivable that deterioration of the core city will bring a mass exodus of business headquarters to the suburbs. Some of the biggest companies have already moved out. This will create increasing demands on the part of the core city that the suburbs become part of its tax domain—and increasing resistance to the core city on the part of the suburbanites.

But more important than these tangible factors are probably the intangible ones. Increasingly, these two parts of the metropolis will represent two facets of metropolitan culture. It is not only the man from Iowa who says, "New York is a nice place to visit but I wouldn't want to live there." The man from Westchester County feels this even more strongly.

It is, therefore, conceivable that the geographic alignments in this country— between North and South; between country and town; between agrarian and industrial society—may be gradually replaced by *a split between the core city and the suburbs throughout all regions and all areas of the country.* It is conceivable that tomorrow the job of building a national party will, in effect, mean bringing together enough groups from those two constituent parts of the metropolis behind one program and one candidate. It is also conceivable that tomorrow's political parties will primarily be characterized by having a "core city" or a "suburban" temperament.

The Impact on the Parties

The change in alignments which is already in full swing is likely to present serious problems to both parties.

The Struggle for a Republican Future In terms of its traditional vote base, the Republican Party has become *the permanent minority party*—and becoming the majority in the Old South would not in any way change this; it would rather accentuate the isolation of the Republican Party. The reason for this is that the Republican Party today is "White Protestant" by temperament, no matter how many Jews, Catholics, or Negroes vote the Republican ticket. And the "White Protestant" is no longer the political majority.

Statistically, of course, white Protestants do constitute two-thirds of the population. Culturally, also, this is, and will remain, a white Protestant country (despite the prevalence of Jewish jokes and Italian pizza). But, politically, a "White Protestant" party is no longer capable of organizing majority support. Almost half of the white Protestants in the country are rural and small-town, and as such are not an adequate foundation for national power any more. In the metropolis, the white Protestant group is just about half or less, but does not see itself as a coherent group and does not vote as such—precisely because it does not see itself as the minority. And minorities, that is, groups that otherwise would have little influence and little voice, are the ones that see the need for organizing themselves for the fight for power.

What the strategies are that are available to the permanent minority party we know. For this was the position of the Democrats for sixty long years, from the Civil War until Franklin D. Roosevelt's election in 1932. In fact, there are only two strategies available—and the Party is likely to be torn internally by the fight between the adherents of either.

There is, first, the *"moderate"* strategy—the strategy of those who essentially say "me too." They expect to come to power precisely because it is not easy to tell them apart from the majority party—except that they are "out" and therefore not responsible for a catastrophe, a scandal, or whatever accident befalls the majority party in power. In such a situation, the "moderates" hope to be able to attract enough protest votes from the majority party to get into power and to start working on making themselves in turn the permanent majority.

The second strategy is the *radical* one which aims to recreate a new party "dedicated to principles." In tune with the ancestor-worship that characterizes the rhetoric of American politics, this strategy is likely to present itself as aiming at the restoration of the ideals of the past. William Jennings Bryan was a "Fundamentalist" and Goldwater a "Conservative." Actually, the strategy aims at creating a major crisis and hopes to capitalize on it.

Both strategies have rather stringent prerequisites—none of which is likely to be satisfied for the Republicans in the present situation. The moderates can only operate if they control some important power centers—such as the Democrats' control of the Solid South and of the big cities of the North in the long years of their exile after the Civil War. Specifically, the Republican moderates would have to gain control of major metropolitan areas. This would probably require the consolidation of core city and suburbs into one political unit. The voting strength of the Republicans in the suburbs, however, rests squarely on their promise not to let the core city "gobble up" the suburbs.

For the radical strategy to work—short of a catastrophe such as this country has so far been spared—requires a candidate who has shown ability for political leadership and enough maturity not to frighten off potential recruits from the moderate ranks of his own party as well as from the opposition. If all he does is to attract the radicals of the other party (as Bryan and Goldwater did), he almost insures defeat through distrust on the part of the great majority which fears (and rightly) political adventurers.

This, however, only means that the *Republican Party is unlikely to make up its mind for either strategy*—just as Democrats did not decide, before the New Deal. This would guarantee long years of internal turmoil for the Republican Party, in the course of which the first aim of each Republican politician is likely to be to prevent the victory of another Republican rather than to defeat a Democrat. As John Lindsay's campaign in New York City showed, the only way for a Republican to win in such a situation is to be as little of a Republican as possible and to try to be accepted as a genuine "Independent."

The Republicans will, therefore, be forced to look for issues that can unite them and to shun issues that must divide them. Because of the shift in alignments within the country, domestic issues are almost certain to divide the Republicans—save only in the event of international catastrophe, serious depression, or truly sensational scandal. The Republicans may, therefore, attempt to make foreign policy into the platform that unites them; and it is possible that, for the first time since the very early days of the Republic, a major party will organize itself on a foreign affairs platform rather than on a domestic platform.

The Dilemma of the Democrats The Democratic Party, too, will be seriously affected by the shifting alignments. It has to gain the allegiance of the "new majority," the educated employed middle class. But it must at the same time hold the allegiance of the old power groups, the economic blocs and the ethnic blocs. The attempt to hold the one is likely to alienate the other. It may alienate both—as did the Democratic strategy in the 1965 New York City elections, in which the patent attempt to have the "right" old-fashioned ticket—one Jew, one Irish Catholic, one Italian and so on—only made the younger and better-educated members of these groups cross over and go Republican in large numbers.

In this dilemma, the Democratic Party will try to focus on the issues likely to unify these two groups—and these are the *urban issues:* the metropolis, health care, and—above all—education. By the same token it is likely to play down what will divide these two groups: the old-style economic issues, and foreign affairs.

Creating a New Majority Victory, in the long run, will not go to the party that does the best job glueing together the shards of yesterday. Victory will go to whoever creates a new national alignment and a new power base, resting not on economic interests but on the "new majority" of the educated professional middle class, and capable of crystallizing the issues that are meaningful to them. (The last time a similar job was done in American politics was after the election of 1896, when Marc Hanna used the economic blocs to erect the structure that is still housing American politics, even though the tenant has changed.) Today one can barely even speculate what these alignments might be and on what they might rest.

There is, thus, great opportunity for creative party politics—and great need for it. Politicians are needed who can establish the new alignments—politicians who can dramatize the new issues and mobilize the new power centers.

POLITICS FOR A NEW GENERATION

So far I have given an inventory rather than an analysis. Even if correct in every detail, it would still not enable us to anticipate American politics in the years ahead. What matters in politics is far less the specific problems and the answers found to them, than the pattern, the configuration. It is not what issues are debated, but what emphasis is given to issues in relation to each other and in a scale of political values. It is not so much what laws are being written as what kind of personality can exercise leadership. Measures and policy matter less than the mood and the basic assumptions.

The most important fact with respect to this configuration of tomorrow may well be that the United States—indeed the whole world—is in the midst of a major generational shift.

The outward sign of this is, of course, that so many of the world's political leaders—from President Johnson to Chairman Mao—are so clearly the last of their line, by age alone. Their formative years were the 'twenties and 'thirties—but even the post-war era of the 'forties and 'fifties is rapidly becoming history.

In terms of age structure of the population, the United States is not a particularly young country today—compared with the underdeveloped Latin America, India, or China, for instance, where the "population explosion," propelled by drastic cuts in infant mortality, is pushing the average age of population down to 15 or so. But compared to its own history and recent experience, *the United States is becoming a very young country indeed*, with half the population already less than 26 years old—and most of them highly educated and with experiences and expectations that differ markedly from those that still underlie our social, political, and economic policies. The middle generation (ages 30 to 50), by contrast, is very thin in this country today and bound to get thinner for another decade—the result, of course, of the lean birth years of the 'thirties. By 1972, more than half of all Americans old enough to vote will be under 32 (a fact which, however, no politician, except Senator Robert Kennedy, seems to have found out).

Power and position are therefore likely to pass fast from people whose working life began before or during the Great Depression to people to whom the depression is, at the very best, a dim childhood memory—if not to people to whom even World War II is something they heard about in their high school courses. President Johnson's young men—his Assistants in their early thirties—are only the advance guard of the generation that must get to the top in all important areas of American life very soon—in business and in government, in the universities and in the Armed Services, and perhaps even in the labor unions.

But this, even more than a shift in chronological age, is a shift in outlook, perception, and formative experience. The world this new generation of Americans considers as "normal" is one of long years of advanced education, of very high job security, of affluence, a world dominated by science and technology. It is also a world of international turmoil and dangers such as would have been unimaginable to their parents at the same age.

Even greater perhaps is the jump in perception. What the new generation takes for granted, the older one has not really learned to see. For the new generation takes for granted

• the "global village": that is, the integration of the entire earth through communications into one locus of immediate experience;

- "man in space": that is, the reaching out beyond what were considered the human limits of existence;
- technology, both in respect to doing physical tasks and in respect to making economic problems amenable to systematic, organized, and essentially technical solutions.

This new perception may not at all have the results most people envisage. But it will have very significant results.

The perception of the "global village" may not make us more "internationalist." Indeed, it may considerably discourage the old American missionary impulse to do things *for* others without necessarily increasing the desire—also an old American tradition—to do things *with* others. The perception of the "global village" is, however, likely to make us stop seeing the outside world through European glasses (whether that of the German *savant* or the English Fabian), which is the way the American "liberal" has always seen the world.

There are even strong indications that the new generation will turn away from the "secularism" of their parents—not to organized religion but to a new "inner-directedness" with stress on personal values and personal commitment. Most of the "crazy mixed-up kids" on the campuses today will, of course, grow up into depressingly sane adult conformists—and they are a tiny minority, in any case. But they might signal a shift ahead in values and concerns; a shift towards moral and aesthetic values and towards a concern with the person.

This is, however, mere speculation. What one can say with a good deal of assurance is that the generation shift ahead is likely to be also a political shift—a shift in the climate, the mood, the values, the alignments and issues of American politics.

Such a shift is bound to be disorderly. It implies a *time of transition* likely to be characterized by vocal dissent, by sudden sharp landslides burying long-familiar landmarks, by partisanship, and by political passion. It is not likely to be a time of "consensus"; it is exceedingly unlikely to be a time of political apathy; and foreign affairs is likely to be one of the political storm centers.

The election of 1964 clearly marked a watershed in American politics. We now face a period rather similar to that after 1896, if not after 1822—periods that ended an "Era of Good Feeling" and brought lasting realignment to American politics.

CHAPTER TWO

POLITICAL PARTIES

3

The Political Party

Frank J. Sorauf

As there are many roads to Rome and many ways to skin a cat, there are also many ways to look at a political party. One can see in the party a burning contemporary issue or an ideological way of life, a bustling corps of political militants, a casual alliance of indifferent or even cynical voters, or a compelling and charismatic leader. For political parties as complex and multi-faceted as the major American parties, what they appear to be may depend on the general political context of the moment, on the particular part or activity of the party one views, or on the eye of the beholder. Amid this variety and diversity the greatest problem is that of perceiving the political party in its entirety.

Indeed, the inclination is great to let the political party slip out of focus entirely. It easily gets lost in the colorful and anecdotal milieu of American politics. So intently may we follow the progress of Presidential campaigns in the United States, so fascinated may we be by the clash of great personalities, by campaign charges and counter-charges, that we lose sight of the role the parties play in the nomination and election of Presidential candidates. Even if we do not, we have seen only some parts of the American parties engaged in only one aspect of one of their functions—the contesting of elections.

From *Political Parties in the American System* by Frank J. Sorauf, pp. 1–15. Copyright © 1964, by Little, Brown and Company (Inc.). Reprinted by permission of the publisher.

A full-length portrait of the political party demands full assessment of the various organizations and personnel within the political party, as well as a complete picture of the functions the party performs in the political system. And so greatly do the political parties differ in structure and function that the generic concept of a "political party" may include the competitive electoral parties of Great Britain and the United States, the class-based parties of Latin American ruling elites, and the mass movements for independence in the new nations of Asia and Africa. Even within the United States "party" embraces the vital, electoral, major parties and esoteric splinter movements devoted to abolishing the income tax or alcoholic beverages.

PARTY AS FUNCTION AND ROLE

Unquestionably the most common function among the parties of the world's democracies—and the one that separates them most efficiently from other political organizations—is the mobilization of voters behind candidates for election. The major American parties, far more than most other parties, are dominated by the electing function. They are, indeed, great and overt conspiracies for the capture of public office. Yet within the entire American party system parties differ in the vigor and seriousness with which they pursue the electing function. For the major parties it is virtually the alpha and the omega. The cycle and seasons of their activity depend almost completely on the calendar of elections. But for the minor parties the election is little more than a convenient occasion for the achievement of some other political purpose. Not in their moments of wildest optimism can the Socialist Workers or Prohibitionists hope to capture the American Presidency or any of the governorships for which they contend. The ballot is for them a priceless, and low-priced, vehicle for publicizing and proselytizing their views.

Second only to the electing function is the party's role as a teacher—its function as a propagandist for political attitudes, ideas, and programs. Generally, the American parties have avoided the burden of promoting the vast world view that ideological parties such as the European Socialists assume. Their ambitions are more modest: a diffuse identification with the interests of labor or business or agriculture, for instance, or a platform with indistinct and often ambiguous policy stands. At a given time the American party may even adopt no more than a broad posture as the party of peace or prosperity.

The American parties—as all others—also perform the even more general educational role of political socialization. For its loyalists the party arranges the confusion of the political world. It teaches them how to view the political universe and its options. Its symbols offer them a point of reference in judging officeholders or in finding the "right" side in an issue or controversy. At the simplest level the parties help their clienteles to divide the political world into the statesmen and the scoundrels. For the more sophisticated follower the party relates a value or set of values—conservatism, racial equality, or national pride—to the policy or candidate alternatives he faces. Even though the American political parties share this function of organizing and directing political perceptions with the mass media and interest groups, they remain nonetheless a potent focus for organizing knowledge about American politics.

The parties of the democracies, third, assume in varying degrees the function of organizing the policy-making machinery of government. In the United States

Congress and in state legislatures the basic unit of organization is the party caucus; from it flows the appointment of powerful presiding officers, committee chairmen, floor leaders, and steering committees. Performance of this function, of course, depends on the party's success as an electoral organization. The American party unable to win more than a handful of legislative seats and only an occasional executive post plays little or no part in organizing legislative and executive branches. Even though small bodies of voters may enable parties in multi-party systems to garner a share of parliamentary and cabinet power, policy-making power within the American political system depends on majorities.

The failure of the American parties to seize and use the policy-making power they so frantically pursue in their electing function has occasioned a fifteen-year debate within American political science. The academic advocates of "party responsibility" castigate the parties for failing to elect men who are loyal to an articulated program and who will enact the program into public policy once elected. More of that controversy later. It suffices to point out here that the failure of the American parties to assume this party function has become a subject of prickly controversy. Indeed, the major share of the history of the major American parties has been marked by an inversion of the usual party policy-making roles within government. Within the parliamentary systems of the Western democracies the parties have organized legislative majorities and blocs, at the same time as inviolable traditions of professional administrative services have kept them isolated from much of executive and administrative control. In the United States, though, the major parties have traditionally organized legislative chambers without using the party power for party-originated and party-identified policies. But they have, thanks to a long and largely honorable tradition of patronage, often been able to control the selection and operation of administrative services. Even as they yield the bulk of the patronage to merit-system appointees, they continue to control more top-level administrative appointments than do, say, the British political parties.

Finally, the political parties seem to be involved in a series of "non-political" functions. European parties, more frequently than the American, sponsor boy scout troops, social clubs for senior citizens, adult-education classes, and benevolent societies that offer group health and life insurance programs. In its fabled heyday the urban machine in America offered the new arrivals to the cities a range of services that made it, in contemporary terms, a combination of employment agency, legal aid society, social worker, domestic relations counselor, and community social center. And in the new style, urban "club" parties in the American cities and suburbs, the parties cater to the social and intellectual needs of a mobile, educated, ideological, often isolated upper middle class. The style may have changed from "beer all around" at the local tavern to martinis at the cocktail hour, but the parties continue to concern themselves with more than just campaigns and elections.

To refer to these functions as "non-political" is, of course, somewhat misleading. Although they may not seem to promise an immediate political payoff, the party hopes that in the long run they will create loyalties, obligations, and ties that will facilitate the successful performance of the other, more directly political tasks. The political party, in fact, exists solely for political purposes and performs only political functions. The other forms of political organization—the Church, the ethnic group, the informal community elite, the voluntary interest group such as a trade union or medical association—move freely from the non-political to the political function and quickly back again. Not so the political party. Its exclusively political character sets it apart from the other political organizations.

The emphasis a party places on one or two of these functions, and the style with which it carries them out, distinguishes it from its competitors and from the parties of the other political systems. The balance of these functions that any party achieves, however, is not only a matter of making scarce energies and resources go around. Within many political systems the performance of one may be incompatible with the successful performance of another. In this regard American parties have long argued that they would compromise their success as electoral organizations were they to stress the development of programs and ideologies. They devote themselves entirely to the electing function and pay comparatively little attention to the business of promoting ideologies or organizing the powers of government. That electoral preoccupation distinguishes them not only from the minor parties in the United States but from the competitive parties of the other mature democracies as well.

The fact that political parties are exclusively political in function is no assurance that they monopolize the functions of contesting elections, proclaiming political programs and values, and organizing the machinery of government. The American parties, in fact, share the function of selecting and electing candidates with informal community elites in many localities. They also share with interest groups the maintenance of a system of responsibility in the American legislature. And in the function of spelling out political programs and alternatives they operate in uneasy competition with the mass media, educational institutions, and voluntary associations. The classic urban machine in the United States came close to monopolizing these functions, but its palmier days are past. That the parties can no longer monopolize them suggests a changing role for them within the American political system.

THE PARTY AS STRUCTURE

The political party, though, is more than the sum of its fervid electoral campaigns, its advocacy of issues and programs, and its attempts to discipline officeholders. It is a stable organization, and it is a number of individuals and groups of individuals held together in a reasonably stable pattern of relationships by a multitude of purposes, incentives, and traditions.

There is an old and hoary image that pictures the political party as a series of concentric circles, like the ever-widening pattern of waves and ripples created by the pebble thrown into the pond. At the party's center of impact are the most active and most deeply committed partisans—the party cadre, the officialdom that maintains and leads the party organization. Then, in circular waves of decreasing vigor and impulse are arranged the party regulars and workers, the rank and file of party members, and finally the party's voters and identifiers.

The image is a simple and orderly one, although too precise for the reality of any political party, least of all the loosely organized American parties. Its shortcomings, however, suggest the problems in viewing any political party purely as an organization. For one thing, the metaphor of concentric circles suggests a regular, stable pattern of authority and activity within the party. Though some American parties may contain a series of groups differentiated by their activity and degree of involvement, others do not. It is a significant fact for countless local party organizations that their "active cadre" consists of no more than a county chairman and a few spiritless hangers-on. The lines of authority and the degrees of activity also may shift in time. The circles shrink, contract, and even collapse in the slack periods between elections.

Indeed, the image of the concentric circles assumes a party organization with a clear division of labor among its parts, a continuous pattern of activity through the year, and a clearly defined body of members and activists. The American political party matches none of these assumptions. None of the concentric circles within the American parties are clearly marked out. Because in many communities the American precinct committeeman is elected at an open primary, he may be either hostile to party leadership or largely uninterested in party operations. Informal leadership groups, coopted by a powerful party chairman or a party elite, frequently supplant the formal party organization. Nor is it easy to separate the party cadre and party workers from the personal followings of officeholders and candidates. Most local American parties are, especially around election time, an irrational and confusing amalgam of formal party officeholders, informal party leadership groups, and the personal followings of candidates. And since in the United States card-carrying party membership is not widespread—and is, indeed, even faintly suspect—the circle of formal membership does not even exist in many American parties.

The most vexing problem with the analysis of the concentric-circle model concerns the question of whether or not, in searching for the party as an organization, we follow the circles to infinity. The party officials, the party actives, and even the party members, we may call the party "organization." Popular usage in the United States does. Beyond the "organization" are the party's voters, its supporters, and its "identifiers." Their ties of loyalty and activity are often most tenuous. These identifiers, the passive "fellow travellers" of the party, may share the party goals or ally themselves loosely with its prospects and fortunes. In those Western countries systematically furrowed by the opinion pollers, they are the men and women who respond to questions such as: "Do you think it will make a good deal of difference to the country whether the Democrats or the Republicans win the elections this November, or that it won't make much difference which side wins?" or "In politics, do you consider yourself a Democrat or a Republican or a member of some other party?" With the identifiers on the outer peripheries of the party are the partisans who vote (with some regularity) for the candidates of the party. The identifiers and the voters overlap considerably. But even though their support is crucial to the party's success, they hardly share the stable relationships and authority of the party structure. In this sense the "party-in-the-electorate" is less an organization than a reaction to a symbol and a tradition.

The political party as an organization consists, however, of much more than a series of concentric circles or superimposed layers of organization. It is a hierarchy of parties, from local unit to national party, through which the parties achieve a geographical division of effort. In federal systems such as that in the United States the parties' decentralized internal relations parallel and reflect the decentralization of the political system. The multitude of delicate relationships between and among the party units suggest another important aspect of party organization. So do the decision-making processes by which the party selects leaders and candidates, makes and enforces policy decisions, and allocates effort and responsibility within the party. Furthermore, the political party may be approached organizationally as a system of incentives and goals that bind the partisans together and spur them to action.

Viewed as systems of power and authority, the political parties exhibit sharply contrasting organizational features. They run from the centralized, militant, and disciplined structures of the European Socialist and Communist parties to the decentralized, virtually autonomous, cadre organizations of the American major parties. Even within American local party organizations the range extends from the tough, almost hyperactive urban machine to the immobile, chaotic, disorganized parties of many rural areas, from the traditional party of the exclusive circle of workers to the new, membership, club types of parties. Often, indeed, the variations in party organization from time to time and place to place within one party are more interesting and instructive than the differences among a number of parties.

PARTY IN THE DEMOCRATIC SYSTEM

When we talked earlier of the functions the parties perform, we referred only to their immediate ones: the manifest functions. These are the tasks party leadership sets out consciously to perform and on the performance of which the party's immediate success or failure depends. In performing them the parties also perform remoter, indirect, "latent" functions. It is as if, by performing immediate functions A, B, and C, the party fortuitously performs also the useful functions X, Y, and Z. For example, as the party goes about the immediate tasks of nominating and electing candidates for office, it is at the same time recruiting political leadership. Indeed, as it selects candidates from its own cadre of active workers, it may also be functioning as a training school for political leaders. To put the matter in another way, the party performs certain tasks (the manifest ones) that ensure its own successful functioning, at the same time performing others (the latent ones) that contribute to the functioning of the entire political system.

Only in the party's latent functions is the relationship between it and the political system clear. The chief manifest functions the parties perform—the nomination and election of candidates, the support of issues and ideology, and the organization of government power—can be and are performed by the parties of totalitarian political systems as well as by the democratic parties. But the ways in which the parties choose, and are permitted, to perform them determine the sharply different latent consequences. When one begins to list the latent functions of the American and British parties it soon becomes clear that he is talking of parties operating in and forming an integral part of democratic political systems. And a comparison of those of the British and American parties with those of the parties of the new nations of Asia and Africa soon indicates the different party contributions to differing varieties of democracy. The dominant, single parties of some of the new nations clearly function within a Rousseauist democracy of solidarity and national purpose rather than in the pluralist, competitive democracy of the United States.

The parties of the democracies, both by supporting candidates for office and by representing interests and issues, simplify the choices confronting the voters. By reducing the contestants for public office and the options of public policy to two, three, or even a handful, the party simplifies—doubtless oversimplifies—the political choices into terms the average citizen can grasp. The stability and continuity of the party symbols, heroes, and slogans gives him fixed points of political reference, thus maintaining the simplicity of choices over the years. In the various ways in which the parties nominate and elect they play a crucial role in the recruitment of political leadership. Especially in those vigorous American party organizations in which the office-seeker must work his way tortuously up the party hierarchy, the party is the gateway through which the ambitious must pass and be passed. Finally, by organizing individuals, interests, and groups into broader political aggregates, the parties mediate and compromise the clash of political interests and ideologies.

In all of these ways the tie between the political party and the democratic regime is clear. The parties facilitate the popular participation, the representation of interests, and the presentation of alternatives on which the processes of democracy depend. They augment the representational processes of the democratic system by providing an organizational link between political man and the institutions of government beyond the one provided by the formal election machinery. They organize the loyal opposition and the democratic dialogue of the "ins" and "outs." So closely are our concepts of party tied, not only to democracy, but also to Western democracy, that they have limited relevance to the parties of national independence and development in the newer nations. Most Americans find it difficult to think of the single, dominant parties of these nations as "genuine" political parties. Much less than the parties of the older democracies do they propose alternative candidates and programs, but to a far greater extent, they do carry out the more general functions of political education, socialization, and communication.

The relationship between the party and the democratic regime, though, is neither fixed nor beyond challenge. Much of the scholarly criticism of the parties of the United States grows out of the deep-seated suspicion that the American parties fail to carry their share of the democratic burdens. The American parties, their critics charge, fail in their obligation to augment—and give meaning to—the democratic system of representation and policy making. The difficulty lies in the haphazard and sporadic way in which they perform the manifest functions of contesting elections, stating programs, and organizing the machinery of government. Their critics would have the parties pursue the three functions more vigorously and systematically so that they might provide the information, the choices, and the promise of action the citizen needs for his democratic decisions to be meaningful. In this sense the dispute over "party responsibility" is in reality a dispute over the kind of democracy we are to have. Those who argue for it maintain simply that the democracy of a direct individual-to-government relationship depends for success on the intermediate organizing services of a political party.

The American political party also acts in another sense on behalf of majoritarian democracy. It has increasingly become the instrument through which massive, popular majorities exert their influence within the political system. By organizing sheer numbers it offsets the advantages of wealth, expertise, status, and access that minorities may enjoy. As William Chambers has put it:

> . . . parties may serve as democratic counterforces to advantages in power. Only through time can they affect the economic and social conditions of "the poor and middling class." They can exert a more immediate impact on other factors of power potential, however, if certain minimal conditions ob-

tain in the populace, such as awareness of interests, some propensity for political participation or initiative, and receptivity to association or organization. Parties may offer leaders and leadership; and through their structure they may diffuse knowledge and skill in political tasks, stir the sense of political consciousness and efficacy, promote cohesion in their followings, and develop tools of association or organization. They may also counteract the weakness of "divisions" among the "common people," in Melancthon Smith's words, by drawing them together into popular partisan combinations. Thus they may call forth and mobilize the latent strength of numbers.[1]

Especially in this century the political party, joined increasingly with strong and vigorous executive leadership, has helped create a truly popular, mass democracy.

The relationship between the democratic political system and its political parties is a complex one, full of reciprocal influences. The party is to a great extent an essential instrument, a necessary condition or ingredient of democracy as we know it. But though it may be in this sense a prerequisite of democracy, it also is democracy's child. The rise of the political party in the Western democracies parallels the rise of demands for greater popular participation in public affairs. The first enduring party in the United States, the Jeffersonian Republicans, extended its support to the grass roots to meet the growing democracy there. Its early competitor, the Federalist party, failed at least in part because its elitist, antidemocratic values prevented it from building the loyalties and following it increasingly needed. It could neither serve nor survive as a party of notables committed to notions of a closed, governing elite. Later the mass, presidential politics of the Jacksonians built largely on a rapidly expanding electorate and an expanding democratic participation. Even the early urban machine of the late 19th century must be understood in part as an attempt on the part of the newcomers to the cities to wrest their governance from old elites and aristocratic families.

In England during the 19th century the Tories and Whigs, at that time not much more than legislative caucuses, were forced by the expansion of the electorate to send out organizers to set up constituency political parties in order to maintain their strength in Parliament. The origin of the modern parties in Britain dates directly to the expansion of the suffrage in the great Reform Acts of 1832 and 1867. Later expansions in the European electorates to include the new industrial workers found expression in the new, mass-membership workers' parties. The expansion of the democratic suffrage not only created the need for the party to aid in the organization of democratic consensus; it also meant that no man or group could any longer maintain itself in political power apart from great aggregates of popular approval and support.

TOWARD A DEFINITION OF PARTY

Of all our major political institutions the political parties have most developed in a spirit of improvisation and jerry-building. The American constitution mentions them not at all, nor has the Congress tried to define their structure or activities. They have been left to develop in response both to diverse local political styles

[1] William Chambers, *Political Parties in A New Nation* (New York: Oxford University Press, 1963), p. 111.

and needs and to varying state legislation. To a large extent party is as party does. The resulting diversity complicates the problem of defining the political party broadly enough to encompass all the American parties. That problem reaches staggering proportions when one broadens the task to include the parties of all the democracies.

Popular usage often confuses the partisan with the political. All party activity is political, but not all political activity is partisan. The concept of politics suggests that complex of individual and group attempts to exert influence on the selection of public officials and on the making of public policy. The debate over what is and is not political—and over where the boundaries of politics run—is probably the oldest unsettled and unsettling issue in political science, but this is hardly the place to measure again the terrain of that battlefield. There is, however, a consensus that it is in this political process that the parties perform their tasks. They may dominate it, but they never completely monopolize it. In fact, they may yield the major role to other political organizations in some sectors of the political process. One often finds interest groups playing roles of greater influence than the parties in the passage of bills in the United States Congress.

The chief definitional problem, then, rests in distinguishing the political party from other organizations, organizers, and intermediaries in the political process. It has been common to belabor the differences between the party and the interest group, or "pressure group," if one prefers a less neutral term. But the party must also be distinguished from the informal elites of the community, the personal clique, the fluid and restless faction, and the basically non-political group—a corporation or a church, for instance—engaged in sometime political activity. They too, with the political party, perform organizing and coalescing functions in the political process.

With these considerations in mind, the political party may be defined as an agency for the organization of political power characterized by exclusively political functions, by a stable structure and inclusive membership, and by the ability to dominate the contesting of elections.

In function the political party limits itself to the political. Other political organizations—the interest group, the community elite, the newspaper, for instance—have non-political lives and functions. The American Medical Association devotes only part of its energies to protecting its interests through political action. Not so the political party. It arises and exists solely as a response to the problems of organizing the political process. One of its greatest continuing problems, indeed, is that of minimizing the political roles and influence of its non-party competitors.

Among those political functions the one the parties come the closest to monopolizing is the electing function. So successful have the parties been here, aided by state laws that define the parties solely according to their electing roles, that the temptation is great to define them in that way. The parties, however, execute the electing functions in many ways and with many degrees of seriousness and success. Though that may be their distinguishing function, it need not be their chief one. A definition of party resting on the elective role risks that confusion. It may also overlook the fact that non-party organizations increasingly—especially in the non-partisan elections of the United States—recruit and support candidates for office. But, making all allowances for these reservations, the party remains the electoral organizer par excellence in the democracies.

A stable and inclusive organization also marks the political party. It is *stable* in that it persists beyond the single cause or the single election. It acquires traditions, clienteles, and ideologies that live on beyond the fleeting policy issue or mortal man. Given this stability it may become a symbol, a focus of loyalty, and a point of orientation for its public. The party is *inclusive* in the sense that it appeals for and welcomes new adherents to its goals, its candidates, and its symbols. The party expands willingly, seeking constantly to broaden and solidify its base of support. And, as easy as it is to overlook it, the political party is an organization, with the ordered internal relationships and the division of labor that the word "organization" implies.

By these criteria the political party is more purely political than the voluntary organization or elite turned to politics for a passing issue. Its range of political activities extends more regularly to the elective role than do those of interest groups. Furthermore, it develops a public life and existence of greater duration and impersonality than does the faction, the *ad hoc* political organization, or the political clique. And it develops more stable and more elaborately differentiated organizations than those of any of its competitors.

This definition of a political party is nothing if it is not modest. It merely describes the parties, especially those of the United States, as they are, not as they "ought to be." It is intended to meet what is probably the greatest test of a definition of political party—the two major American parties. They are so atypical of the democratic parties in so many ways that one generalizes from their experience only at the greatest peril. Only the broadest definitional categories will embrace them along with the parties of the Western democracies and the developing nations.

4
Political Parties in Western Democracies: Some Skeptical Reflections

Anthony King

. . . Do parties play as large a role in Western democracies as is usually assumed? How crucial are parties to the performance of certain important political functions?

PARTIES IN ACTION AND PARTY FUNCTIONS

Two ways of dealing with these questions suggest themselves, one highly impressionistic but perhaps suggestive, the other more systematic. The first is to select a number of important episodes in the recent history of Western democracies and to ask what role political parties played in them. If parties are as important as political scientists are inclined to suppose, then they ought, either as groups or as sets of patterned actions, to have featured prominently in the cases chosen—and in most of the other cases that might have been chosen. Three examples come to mind, one chosen from each of three major Western countries: the Negro revolution in the United States; the efforts of two British governments to gain entry to the European Economic Community; and the upheaval in France in the summer of 1968. Each of these developments was at least potentially critical for the coun-

From *Polity*, II, no. 2 (Winter 1969), 116–118, 120–141. Reprinted by permission of author and publisher.

try concerned. Two of the three—the Negro revolution and the May riots in France—directly involved large numbers of people. All three raised questions, central to the putative functions of political parties, concerning the relationship in a democracy between governors and governed. The main facts concerning the three are reasonably well known, and there is no need to go into detail here.

What seems fairly obvious is that neither the political parties of the three countries nor (except very indirectly) their party systems played a central role in any of these developments. Historical accounts of them could be produced, and indeed have been, in which political parties figure hardly at all.[1] Moreover, few political scientists analyzing these events as case studies in the workings of particular political systems would single out parties as having been critical actors. If parties were made the focus of scholarly attention, it would probably be with a view to showing that the parties and party systems of all three countries had in one way or another failed to perform the functions that are conventionally attributed to them.[2] Any amount of evidence can be drawn on to reinforce these points. Many of the leading figures in all three episodes—Martin Luther King, Sir Eric Roll, Daniel Cohn-Bendit, not least General de Gaulle himself—were recruited outside the party system. To the extent that political integration and mobilization took place, they occurred in structures largely set apart from the parties: civil rights organizations in America, the Campaign for Europe and other less formal groupings in Britain, trade unions and student organizations in France. In no case did a political party, as a party, formulate policy in any strict sense; nor, except briefly in Britain (1963–1965), did the political parties structure the choices available to either the mass publics or the governments concerned. The aggregation of interests proceeded to a greater or less degree in all three countries, but political parties were seldom the chief agencies involved.

But, it may be objected, to proceed in this way, episode by episode, is to miss a large part of the point. Individual parties may or may not be critical actors in particular situations; but parties and party systems play a large part in creating and maintaining the political culture and political structures which characterize political systems as a whole and in the context of which particular situations develop. To take the British case, the Conservative and Labour Parties as such may not have had much to do with the efforts to enter Europe; but the British party system produced the governments which took the decisions, recruited the chief political decision-makers, and (at least in 1964) created the circumstances in which the electorate could choose between a party committed to entering Europe and one not so committed. In other words, even though parties and party systems may in large part be the products of their political environment, nonetheless they perform, it is claimed, certain critical functions in all Western democratic systems.

This line of reasoning has to be treated with respect, and it brings us to the second, more systematic way of assessing the importance of parties. This is to analyze in turn each of the alleged functions of party. Fortunately, lists of such

---

[1] See, e.g., Miriam Camps, *Britain and the European Community 1955–1963* (London: Oxford University Press, 1963), and Anthony Lewis *et al.*, *Portrait of a Decade* (New York: Random House, 1966).
[2] Cf. Scarrow's comments in Howard A. Scarrow, "The Function of Political Parties: A Critique of the Literature and the Approach, *Journal of Politics*, 29 (November 1967), p. 790, n.56.

functions are ready to hand; at least one list is to be found in almost every book on political parties, usually toward the beginning. No definitive compilation exists, and the functions generally cited are often interrelated and overlapping. Even so, there is a broad consensus about what the main functions are, and some of the differences between the lists are largely verbal. The aim in what follows is not to produce a new, more coherent catalog of functions but to examine the catalog already in general use.

Two further points should be made before proceeding. The first is that the term "function" is used both here and in most of the literature in a fairly loose way. A few writers, adopting a self-consciously functionalist approach, wish to assert that the performance of certain functions is critical to the maintenance of some particular system or class of systems, the relevant characteristics of which are specified. But most writers, at least most writers on parties, although they may allude to the fact that the performance of this or that function helps to maintain this or that political system, are really using "function" to mean "productive of consequences." As Nagel puts it, "the word 'function' is frequently employed . . . to designate a more or less inclusive set of consequences that a given thing or activity has either for 'the system as a whole' to which the thing or activity supposedly belongs, or for various other things belonging to the system."[3] Thus, the phrase "parties perform the leadership recruitment function" can be translated to read "the activities of parties have as one of their consequences [intended or unintended] the recruitment of leaders." It does not matter much which language is used so long as the principles of translation are borne in mind. The language of functions perhaps has the advantage of drawing attention to the fact that, if there are needs that for one reason or another have to be met and if one entity or process is not meeting them, then some other entity or process must be.

The second point concerns the infrequency with which the standard catalog of party functions is examined empirically. As Lowi has remarked, "The more traditional students of politics . . . tend so strongly to assume the importance of their institutions that they move directly into descriptions of how they are organized and what they do."[4] Thus, most writers on parties note what they take the functions of party to be, but they do not go on to ask whether parties actually perform these functions and, if so, to what extent and under what conditions.[5]

To quote Lowi again:

> . . . textbooks and studies of political parties usually present an inventory of "the functions of party" as though these were as regularly a part of the political process as stages in the passage of a bill or what the judicial system does . . . At the present time, political scientists cannot state with any degree of confidence the conditions under which any political structure will

---

[3] Ernest Nagel, *The Structure of Science* (New York: Harcourt, Brace, 1961), p. 525.
[4] Theodore J. Lowi, "Toward Functionalism in Political Science: The Case of Innovation in Party Systems," *American Political Science Review*, 57 (September 1963), 582. Traditional political scientists in Lowi's sense may use the most up-to-date methods.
[5] A notable exception is Sorauf; see *Political Parties in the American System* (Boston: Little, Brown, 1964) and *Party Politics in America* (Boston: Little, Brown, 1968) both *passim*. Sorauf does not produce a theory of party functioning, but is consistently sceptical about whether parties in fact monopolize the functions claimed for them. See also Leon D. Epstein, *Political Parties in Western Democracies* (New York: Praeger, 1968), esp. pp. 7–8.

function in a particular way, and yet we continue to talk about [party] functions as though the whole issue was settled.[6]

Lowi is surely right in urging in the same passage that the alleged functions of party "should be guides for inquiry rather than items in an inventory."

What, then, are the alleged functions of party, and what can be said about them? It probably does relatively little violence to the complexity of the subject to discuss six, and only six, of the most general functions: (1) the structuring of the vote; (2) the integration and mobilization of the mass public; (3) the recruitment of political leaders; (4) the organization of government; (5) the formation of public policy; and (6) the aggregation of interests. Other functions will be touched on in passing, but these seem to be the main ones referred to in the literature.

STRUCTURING THE VOTE

"Structuring the vote," in Epstein's words, "is the minimum function of a political party in a modern democracy." [7] A group or organization that did not attempt to structure the vote in its own favor would not normally be called a party; a group that did would generally be regarded as a party even if, like the typical French rally, it tried to claim it was not one. Efforts to structure the vote can range from the simple allocation of party labels to candidates to the conduct of large-scale educational and propaganda campaigns. Indeed, vote-structuring is often bound up with the educational, persuasive, and representational functions to which many writers refer.[8] Whether in a particular political system the parties are in fact performing a vote-structuring function depends ultimately on whether the voters respond (at a single election or over a longer period) to the labels the parties present. On the one hand, parties might make heroic efforts, yet find that the voters responded much more to considerations of class or race or personality. On the other hand, the parties might (say, in a particular election) make few efforts to appeal to voters, yet discover when the behavior of voters was analyzed that party had been the main structuring factor. In the latter case one would probably want to say, not simply that party had structured the vote, but rather that the vote had been structured along party lines as a consequence of past or present party activity, or as a consequence of the past or present workings of the party system.

The political scientist is thus presented with two broad questions: What entities seek to structure the vote? What entities, as the result of their activities or even of their mere existence, have the effect of structuring the vote? And of course political scientists are right in asserting that the best single answer to both questions is "political parties." Formally-organized political parties in all Western democracies attempt to structure the vote more assiduously, more continuously, and more single-mindedly than any other kind of agency. As regards how the

[6] Lowi, "Toward Functionalism," p. 571.
[7] Epstein, *Political Parties*, p. 77.
[8] See, e.g., Sorauf, *Parties in the American System*, pp. 2–3; Roy C. Macridis, "Introduction," in Macridis (ed.), *Political Parties: Contemporary Trends and Ideas* (New York: Harper Torchbooks, 1967), p. 18. Sigmund Neumann (ed.), *Modern Political Parties: Approaches to Comparative Politics* (Chicago: University of Chicago Press, 1956), p. 396.

vote is actually structured, it is clear from an abundance of studies that in most countries at most times the major electoral alignments are in large part party alignments.[9] The scholar who wishes to study vote-structuring will inevitably find himself studying parties—although not only parties, since parties in all Western systems share this function with a wide variety of other agencies: candidates, who may not wish (especially in the United States) to associate themselves too closely with the party label, elements in the media of communications, interest groups and broader social movements, and other kinds of citizen groups. And in exceptional circumstances vote-structuring may take place without parties at all, as in the numerous American jurisdictions with nonpartisan elections.[10]

But there is another point to which attention ought to be drawn. The term "structuring" and others like it—Bryce referred to parties' "bring[ing] order out of chaos"[11]—may be used in rather different senses. They may refer simply to parties' efforts to persuade voters to respond to particular party labels, and to voters' responses to those labels. Or they may refer to parties' efforts to persuade citizens to adopt particular opinions, and to the consequences of party activity and the configuration of the party system for the structure of political opinion in a community. Epstein is clearly using the term in its minimal sense when he writes:

> All that is meant by the awkward word "structuring" is the imposition of an order or pattern enabling voters to choose candidates according to their labels. . . . The structure may be little more than that provided by the label itself and the voters' acquaintance with it. . . .[12]

But Neumann, although using similar terminology, evidently had something more elaborate in mind when he said of parties:

> They are brokers of ideas, constantly clarifying, systematizing, and expounding the party's doctrine. . . . They maximize the voters' education in the competitive scheme of at least a two-party system and sharpen his free choice.[13]

Vote-structuring, in short, is related to opinion-structuring.

To some extent the point is obvious. Political scientists have long been aware, for instance, that political parties are programmatic in widely varying degrees, the communist and social democratic parties of Western Europe contrasting with the mainly nondoctrinal parties of the United States and Canada. They have long been aware, too, that even doctrinal parties often fail to communicate their doctrines to the mass of voters or even to their own supporters. But there is another more profound point at issue. Irrespective of whether the parties in a system seek to structure opinion in any elaborate way, there may come to exist, for one reason or another, a radical discontinuity between the structure of alternatives presented to the electorate by the parties and the attitudes and demands of the electorate or

---

[9] Although true, this point may on occasion be fairly jejune. If, for example, the party division within a particular country is in some way a consequence of a pre-existing class division, it will not be adding very much to say that the resulting alignment is a "party" alignment. Scarrow makes a similar point in a different context; see "The Function of Political Parties," pp. 783–785.
[10] See Epstein, *Political Parties*, pp. 93–97.
[11] Quoted in Neumann, *Modern Political Parties*, p. 396.
[12] Epstein, *Political Parties*, p. 77.
[13] Neumann, *Modern Political Parties*, p. 396.

46 Political Parties

of important sections of it. There may, in other words, cease to be a high degree of "fit" between the pattern of party opinion and the pattern of mass opinion.[14]

That this is not a remote possibility is suggested by the recent history of a number of Western countries. The last half-decade has witnessed the increasing violence of the Negro revolution in the United States and the mounting evidence of Negro alienation from conventional political life, the rapid growth in Britain of Scottish and Welsh nationalist movements intent on breaking up the United Kingdom, the momentary descent of France into chaos in 1968, the student unrest in West Germany following on the creation of the grand coalition, and the growth in Canada of French Canadian separatism. The list could be extended further.[15]

It is not yet possible to explain these phenomena fully. In particular, it is not clear to what extent the explanation for them lies in the "malfunctioning" (however that term is used) of the party system in the countries in question; indeed it may be that the nature and workings of the various party systems have been such as to reduce levels of conflict that might have been even higher under other circumstances. Even so, the altered temper of a good deal of Western politics in the late 1960s raises serious questions: To what extent are parties performing an opinion-structuring function? Is it necessary that this function be performed? If so, is it necessary that it be performed by parties? If not by parties, then by what other agencies? If by other agencies, then what are the consequences for parties and party systems and for the other functions of party? Whatever the answers to such questions, it is evident that when political scientists speak of the representational or linkage or communication functions of parties they are speaking of functions that parties may perform completely, incompletely, or not at all. And the extent to which they are performing such functions is to be determined by empirical inquiry, not by fiat.

At this point discussion has shifted from the structuring of the vote to another alleged function of party: the integration and mobilization of the political community.

INTEGRATION AND MOBILIZATION

This function, like most of the others, has been described in a variety of ways. LaPalombara and Weiner note that somehow "the party must articulate to its followers the concept and meaning of the broader community. . . ."[16] Kirchheimer similarly observes that parties have functioned "as channels for integrating individuals and groups into the existing political order. . . ."[17] Neumann went rather further and maintained that parties transformed the private citizen himself:

---

[14] Needless to say, one should not take it for granted that mass opinion is highly structured, as regards either individuals or aggregations of individuals; see Philip E. Converse, "The Nature of Belief Systems in Mass Publics," in David E. Apter (ed.), *Ideology and Discontent* (New York: Free Press, 1964).

[15] See the brief discussion in the editors' Introduction to Seymour M. Lipset and Stein Rokkan (eds), *Party Systems and Voter Alignments* (New York: Free Press, 1967), pp. 54–56.

[16] Joseph LaPalombara and Myron Weiner (eds.), *Political Parties and Political Development* (Princeton, N.J.: Princeton University Press, 1966), p. 3.

[17] Otto Kirchheimer, "The Transformation of the Western European Party Systems" in LaPalombara and Weiner, pp. 188–189.

They make him a *zoon politikon;* they integrate him into the group. Every party has to present to the individual voter and to his powerful special-interest groups a picture of the community as an entity.[18]

Such ideas are clearly part of what is normally understood by the concept of political socialization. However the ideas are phrased, those who use them are referring to the processes whereby individuals acquire psychological and social attachments to political parties and, through them, to the wider political order. (It goes without saying that some parties seek to do the reverse, to engender hostility to the established order; but in a discussion as brief as this such parties will have to be ignored even though they raise serious conceptual problems in connection with almost any kind of functional analysis.)

The problems that confront the political scientist are to ascertain whether political integration and mobilization are taking place at all and, if so, to what extent and with respect to whom; and also, if integration is taking place, to discover which agencies or processes are responsible for it. In this connection it is worth noting that students of politics, especially students of Western politics, have tended to assume, sometimes in a rather Panglossian way, that a satisfactory degree of integration is in fact taking place. They have assumed, in other words, that the mass publics of Western democracies (at any rate the assertive elements in them) accept the existing political order or at least accept the existing rules for changing it. Events in the past two decades in the United States, France, Canada and elsewhere should give one pause before this assumption is made too readily —quite apart from the political turmoil that has characterized the history of many European countries since at least the beginning of this century.

But, insofar as integration is taking place, is it taking place as a consequence of the presence and activities of parties? A full answer to this question would have to be very complex, since parties could in principle perform an integrative function in various ways. Individuals and groups in mass publics could be integrated into the political system by party because they developed favorable attitudes toward parties and party systems as such; or because they came to have favorable attitudes toward particular parties (which were not themselves hostile to the system); or because, in addition to developing favorable attitudes, they came into personal contact with parties either as citizens whose votes were being solicited or as party members or activists.

Comparatively little empirical work has been done on any of these processes; some of them, indeed, would be extraordinarily hard to study, certainly within the confines of any one country. But what few findings are available cast doubt on the centrality of party's role. Dennis investigated support for the American party system amongst a section of the American public and found "mixed and not highly supportive feelings about the institution of party." He concluded:

> In our system, as no doubt in many others—where leaders from Mobutu to de Gaulle have been calling for an end to partisan politics—anti-party norms and images are present as a living part of the political culture.[19]

Parties can hardly be said to be performing a positive integrative function if there exists widespread antipathy or even indifference toward them; rather the reverse.

---
[18] Neumann, *Modern Political Parties*, p. 397.
[19] Jack Dennis, "Support for the Party System by the Mass Public," *American Political Science Review*, 60 (September 1966), 613, 615.

As Dennis points out, lack of enthusiasm for parties could at a time of great environmental stress deprive a political system of an important potential source of support.[20]

Equally problematical is the strength of the psychological bond connecting citizens to individual parties and thence to political systems as a whole. Most American research testifies to the widespread incidence and strength of partisan identifications in the United States, and it seems reasonable to suppose that in America favorable dispositions toward a particular party as one main element in the citizen's political universe are associated with, and even reinforce, favorable views of much else in his universe. Certainly the stronger the individual's sense of attachment to one of the parties, the greater his psychological involvement in politics generally, although the nature of the causal nexus here is far from clear.[21] Moreover, when the pattern of party identification is fairly stable, as it is in the United States, an important stabilizing factor is thereby introduced into the political system as a whole.

It seems, however, that what is true for America—and probably most of the other Anglo-Saxon democracies—is not true for some of the continental countries in Europe, notably France. Kirchheimer noted that, "In the single-load job of integrating the *couches populaires* into the French polity the performance of the political party remained unimpressive." [22] He was referring to the Third Republic, but recent French history suggests that French parties and the French party system have not performed an integrative function any more effectively since the war than before. This conclusion is buttressed by the well-known finding of Converse and Dupeux that the incidence of party identification is much lower in France than in the United States.[23] If parties are playing a part in integrating successfully the political communities of West Germany and Italy, it would seem that they have been doing so only fairly recently, given the frequent changes of both regime and party system in both those countries.[24]

Political integration may take a purely psychological form; it may in addition involve the mobilization of men and women into active political work. Political activists may, as a by-product of their activities, more fully integrate their less active fellows into the political system; persons not active in politics may become more completely members of the political community as the result of having their votes solicited on the doorstep or of attending a party picnic or bazaar. At the same time, the political activists may themselves become more fully integrated into the system as a consequence of their efforts.

Leaving aside the question of how important political mobilization is for the achievement of political integration (assuming that the two are not defined as the same thing), we can question the effectiveness of the activities of those active in political parties as distinct from other agencies. We can also ask how important parties are generally in promoting political activity.

---

[20] Dennis, p. 614. The whole passage is of great interest.
[21] Angus Campbell *et al.*, *The American Voter* (New York: Wiley, 1960), p. 143.
[22] Kirchheimer in LaPalombara and Weiner, p. 180.
[23] Philip E. Converse and George Dupeux, "Politicization of the Electorate in France and the United States" reprinted in Angus Campbell *et al.*, *Elections and the Political Order* (New York: Wiley, 1966), pp. 269–291.
[24] On the role of German parties, see Lewis J. Edinger, *Politics in Germany* (Boston: Little, Brown, 1968), pp. 276–290.

There exist several studies dealing with the impact of party activity on the mass public. Their findings are broadly similar, and it is probably fair to take Eldersveld's study of Wayne County as representative (although how far the data gathered in one American city are useful for comparative purposes is of course open to question).[25] Exposure to party activity, Eldersveld found in Detroit, did have an impact on individuals' political dispositions. For example, an analysis of the relationship between exposure to party activity and indices of political optimism and pessimism led Eldersveld to conclude: "Party contact appears . . . to fortify and accentuate public confidence by making the citizen feel that he has some importance in our complex political system."[26] Yet at the same time, even though the Wayne County study was conducted in a densely-populated urban area with a highly-articulated party system, fully 44 percent of the sample had not been exposed to party activity at all. The writer notes that as a result "party impact is severely restricted."[27] Moreover, when Eldersveld tried to assess the relative roles of television and party in fostering support for the political system, television seemed at least as powerful an agency as party.[28] And there are many other agencies at work: family, friends, work associates, formal associations, the press, contact with government officials. Some of these agencies mediate the influence of party, but others do not, at least not in any direct way.

It remains to consider, not the impact of political activity, but the activists themselves, whether their participation takes place via party or through other channels. Active political participation often leads to consensus and integration. The acts of participation—voting, soliciting votes, collecting campaign contributions, speaking at meetings, leading delegations, and so on—may themselves contribute to the functioning of political systems; and active participants in politics usually have, if anything, a more favorable attitude toward existing political procedures than do mass publics. One may recall the famous dictum that two deputies, one of whom is a revolutionary, have more in common than two revolutionaries, one of whom is a deputy. But of course participation may on occasion be linked to profound disagreements and may lead to dissensus and even disintegration.

Whatever its impact on integration, to what extent in modern democracies does political activity take the form of party activity?[29] Although hard data are

[25] In addition to Samuel J. Eldersveld, *Political Parties: A Behavioral Analysis* (Chicago: Rand McNally, 1964), p. 1, see, e.g., Daniel Katz and Samuel J. Eldersveld, "The Impact of Local Party Activity upon the Electorate," *Public Opinion Quarterly*, 25 (Spring 1961), 1–24; and Phillips Cutright and Peter Rossi, "Grassroots Politicians and the Vote," *American Sociological Review*, 23 (1958), 171–179. A brief summary of the available findings is provided by Fred I. Greenstein, *The American Party System and the American People* (Englewood Cliffs, N.J.: Prentice-Hall, Inc.), pp. 46–47. Detroit's usefulness for comparative purposes is limited by the fact that its municipal elections are conducted on a nonpartisan basis. However, Greenstein reports (p. 46) that even in non-southern cities of over 100,000 population the proportion of voters reached by the parties in the presidential campaign of 1956 was only about 20 per cent.
[26] Eldersveld, *Political Parties*, p. 500.
[27] Eldersveld, *Political Parties*, pp. 442, 526.
[28] Eldersveld, *Political Parties*, pp. 519–522.
[29] What is being discussed here is, in effect, the ratio of party activity to all political activity. The suggestion being made is that party activity has declined in amount. But of course we cannot be sure whether the ratio has declined unless we know, which we do not, whether the total level of political activity has changed over time.

not easy to come by, the incidence of specifically partisan activity has almost certainly declined in most Western countries, perhaps partly as a result of the growing professionalization of party politics. Other kinds of politically-engaged groupings, however, appear to flourish. In the United States in recent years an increasing proportion of political activity has been channelled through civil rights and student organizations, citizens' political clubs, protest movements (of right as well as left), and the followings of individual candidates for office. All seek to influence party structures; but many combine outside the existing party system, some against it. As Sorauf has noted:

> . . . men and women continue to participate in the political process and perform the traditional political services. But they no longer work exclusively or largely within the political party. . . . the political party in the United States finds it progressively harder to monopolize its traditional political activities.[30]

And of course a significant proportion of current political activity in America (as elsewhere) is not "traditional" in any usual sense.

In most European countries political parties still play a more dominant role. A larger proportion of political participation has long been organized via the party, and the more militant parties continue to perform an expressive function not undertaken by the parties of the United States.[31] Even so, there have been manifestations of anti-party activism in France, Germany, the Netherlands and Denmark, and Britain is frequently reported, possibly accurately, to be going through a phase of disillusionment with traditional party politics. More to the point, Epstein has thoroughly documented the secular decline in the mass-membership basis of many of Europe's major parties. In France, to take the extreme case, the membership of the Communist Party declined from more than 900,000 just after the war to about 500,000 in the late 1950s; the Socialists' membership fell from a peak of 354,000 to about 50,000, the MRP's from 400,000 to roughly 40,000.[32] In Europe as in America, party is likely to remain one important factor in political integration and mobilization: in Europe as in America it has never been the only one and it seems possible that its importance is declining.

So far we have considered two functions having to do with mass politics. The next has to do with political leadership and with the relationship between political leaders and led.

LEADERSHIP RECRUITMENT

The recruitment function can be dealt with somewhat more straightforwardly, partly because the concept of recruitment is itself tolerably precise, and partly because the role of party in recruitment is relatively—though only relatively—easy to delimit. All those who have catalogued party functions refer to leadership recruitment. It is seldom defined in detail as a function, but presumably it has to do with the processes by which men and women are selected out of the broader so-

---

[30] Sorauf, *Parties in the American System*, p. 55; cf. p. 56.
[31] See Giovanni Sartori, "European Political Parties: The Case of Polarized Pluralism," in LaPalombara and Weiner.
[32] Epstein, *Political Parties*, pp. 253–254; see generally pp. 164–165, 251–255.

ciety to fill political positions or to play more or less full-time political roles.[33] A full discussion of recruitment would have to deal with, among other things, the motives which lead individuals to seek or accept political roles or inhibit them from doing so; the "catchment pools" from which the political classes are drawn, whether social strata, parties or other groupings; the criteria by which they are selected; and the characteristics and aims of those selecting them.

That recruitment does take place in Western democracies—that the recruitment function is being performed—is beyond question. Whether it is performed well or badly in particular systems is not immediately relevant; what we are interested in is how important a part political parties play in the recruitment process. Certainly the claims made on behalf of party in this connection are sometimes extreme. Seligman, while not sharing this view fully himself, notes that, "for some, the functions of nominating and electing candidates for political elective office are attributed exclusively to political parties."[34] He observes at another point that "in selection of leadership, political parties play a special and sometimes exclusive function."[35]

There is one sense in which the central role of parties cannot be doubted. Insofar as political leaders are popularly elected, and insofar as parties play a large part in elections, parties are undoubtedly deeply implicated in the performance of the recruitment function. To assess the overall role of parties, however, requires asking, among other things, the extent to which political leaders are in fact popularly elected. Much depends on how broadly or narrowly the notion of political position or role is defined. It is often defined—by Seligman in his work and Schlesinger in his—in such a way that parties are bound to loom large.[36] Schlesinger, for example, confines himself (perfectly appropriately, given his interests) to senators and governors, and notes that others have analyzed the backgrounds and careers of presidents, cabinet members, Supreme Court justices, congressmen, and state legislators.[37] Epstein (again appropriately, given his concerns) deals exclusively with the selection of candidates for elective office.[38]

Yet to narrow the definition of political position in this way is to introduce distortion, since by any of the usual criteria the chief political decision-makers in developed political systems include not only elective office-holders but also appointed executive officials, senior civil servants, military officers, judges appointed rather than elected, and the leading figures in interest groups and social movements. Occupants of some of these positions may be appointed by elected

[33] This is a narrower definition than the one suggested by Almond; see Gabriel A. Almond and James S. Coleman (eds), *The Politics of the Developing Areas* (Princeton, N.J.: Princeton University Press, 1960), p. 31.
[34] Lester G. Seligman, "Political Parties and the Recruitment of Political Leadership," in Lewis J. Edinger (ed.), *Political Leadership in Industrialized Societies* (New York: Wiley, 1967), p. 295.
[35] Seligman, "Political Parties," p. 315.
[36] Seligman, on p. 307 of "Political Parties," writes: "The full leadership recruitment tasks of parties include the following: (1) the nomination of candidates for public office . . . ; (2) the selection of officials for executive positions; and (3) the selection of party organization officials. Throughout this chapter, we shall refer only to the selection of parliamentary candidates." See Joseph A. Schlesinger, *Ambition and Politics: Political Careers in the United States* (Chicago: Rand McNally, 1966).
[37] Schlesinger, *Ambition and Politics*, p. 12.
[38] Epstein, *Political Parties*, pp. 167, 201.

officials who have themselves been recruited via the party system, but the role that party plays is no more than indirect. It may be that Europeans are more sensitive than Americans to this fact, given Europe's long history of a strong, nonpartisan civil service and the relatively recent appearance in some countries of party government. Daalder has suggested that:

> Perhaps the best measure to distinguish the relative hold of party elites on a political system as against that of other elites is to ask how far positions of political influence can be obtained through, as compared to outside, party channels.[39]

By this measure, Daalder implies, European countries would vary considerably. And even in the United States it would seem that the hold of party on political recruitment is weaker than some writers suggest. American cabinet officers, not to mention senior career bureaucrats, military officers and interest group leaders, are often selected irrespective of party affiliation and by procedures which have little or nothing to do with party.

Even in connection with recruitment to elective offices, the role of party is at least problematical. Seligman and Sorauf have testified to the importance of "self-recruitment" in leading individuals to seek candidatures in the United States, and there is reason to believe that in all countries the motives that lead men to seek elective office may arise independently of party.[40] In most jurisdictions in the United States it is hard for candidates to be elected who do not bear a party label; they are thus recruited by party in the sense that the law provides mechanisms for attaching labels to candidates and voters respond almost exclusively to label-bearing candidates. In this sense the successful candidates are recruited to political office via the party system. At the same time, however, the role of party, conceived of as group or organization, may be quite limited. The institution of the direct primary makes it possible for men to seek nominations (especially at state and substate level) who have little or no connection with organized party; the primary electorate in turn is likely to consist of voters few of whom are party "members" in any more than a psychological sense (and perhaps not even in that); primary electors may consciously cast their ballots for candidates they believe to be independent of organized party. "The fact is," in the words of Epstein, "that there are large areas of American politics in which candidate selection is not controlled by any regular party process."[41] Parties, indeed, monopolize the candidate-selection aspect of recruitment more successfully in Europe than in America.

Thus, although parties are everywhere deeply implicated in the leadership recruitment process, the importance of the role they play varies and it may on occasion be little more than tautologous to say that parties perform the recruitment function. The same point can be made in connection with the next alleged function of party, which has to do with one of the roles of party in government.

---

[39] Hans Daalder, "Parties, Elites and Political Developments in Western Europe," in LaPalombara and Weiner, p. 75.
[40] See, e.g., Lester G. Seligman, "Political Recruitment and Party Structure: A Case Study," *American Political Science Review*, 55 (March 1961), 77–86; Frank J. Sorauf, *Party and Representation* (New York: Atherton, 1963), pp. 107–120.
[41] Epstein, *Political Parties*, p. 205; cf. Sorauf, *Parties in the American System*, pp. 113–115.

ORGANIZATION OF GOVERNMENT

In dealing with recruitment, we touched on what might be called the "reach" of political parties; i.e., the range of decision-making positions—legislative, executive, judicial, etc.—which are filled by men chosen by or from the parties or somehow via the party system.[42] The reach of party may extend into the judiciary and the upper echelons of the administration as in the United States, or it may be restricted to legislature and cabinet as in Britain. When we come to deal with the organization function, we are concerned with the "grasp" of parties: how far they are able as organized entities to extend their authority over the various elements of government, or alternatively how far the conduct of government bears the imprint of the presence of parties, their nature and their activities. It is apparent that parties in one system may recruit for a wide range of decision-making offices yet have little subsequent impact on the decision-makers. Equally, in another system the parties may recruit to few offices but have an impact on many. The Anglo-American contrast comes to mind once again.

The organization function is referred to in almost all writings on parties but, like the recruitment function, is seldom defined precisely. In some contexts words like "control" and "integration" are as appropriate as "organization." What is meant is the arrangements under which, or the processes whereby, persons in government or the various elements of government come to act in concert. Unlike the recruitment function, the organization function is one that need be performed not at all, or at least only to a limited degree. Men in government and the various elements of government may not act in concert; on the contrary, governments are at least as likely to be at the mercy of centrifugal as of centripetal forces, with colleague divided from colleague, department from department, judiciary from executive, executive from legislature.

To the extent that organization in this sense takes place, it may be achieved constitutionally, extra-constitutionally, formally or informally. There is likely to be not one organizing agency but many: administrators and their allies in the legislature, friendship networks, groups that come together *ad hoc* on the basis of shared interests. But such agencies are unlikely to have the effect of organizing more than fragments of government. If more general integration is to occur, it will almost certainly have to be as the result of the presence and activities of more highly articulated, probably more formal structures. Governments have from time to time been organized by military juntas, religious sects, powerful industrial combines, and even (if certain nineteenth-century writers are to be believed) by the Freemasons. But in modern democracies it seems fairly clear that the only entity through which governments can be organized—if they can be organized at all—is the political party.

How far is party an organizing agency in governments in the West? The question is not a simple one, partly because this is clearly a point at which it is essential to make overt the distinction between party conceived of as a cluster of individual human beings and party conceived of as a patterned set of actions or behaviors. If party is thought of as a group of human beings, then the question "Did party have influence?" will usually refer to a party or coalition of parties

---

[42] The term "reach" is being used in a more precise sense here than in Daalder; cf. Daalder in LaPalombara and Weiner, pp. 58–67.

and will be resolvable into questions of the form, "Did the party leader, or the legislative party, or the party activists, have influence?" Similarly, questions about party policy resolve themselves into questions about the authoritative procedures for making policy within the party (if any) and about the decisions taken by particular individuals or groups in the context of those procedures. If, however, party is conceived of not as an actor or actors but as a set of patterned activities, then the question "Did party have influence?" resolves into a number of questions, possibly quite a large number, about men's recruitment and socialization into parties, their psychological ties to them, their associations within them, their ambitions, the place of party in their attitude structures, and so on. Conceived of in this way, party may have influence without any party leader or group attempting to wield influence and possibly without any individual's being aware that his attitudes or behavior are in fact party-influenced. Greenstein and Jackson have shown that the answers to the question "Did party have influence?" may be very different indeed depending on which concept of party is being used.[43] The disadvantage of the group concept, as we have already remarked, is that it may be unnecessarily restrictive. The disadvantage of the patterned-behaviors concept is that it may be extremely difficult to use operationally: it may be very hard to separate "party" influence from other kinds of influence.[44]

Whichever concept is used, it remains to be determined empirically how firm the grasp of party is in a particular government and into how many elements of government it extends. This is a point on which a certain amount of evidence exists, at least as regards the United States, because of course the whole question of party-in-government got caught up some twenty years ago in the (by now rather tiresome) debate over whether or not the American parties should become more "responsible." The proponents of the idea of responsible party government agreed on using a group concept of party—as they were bound to do given their reformist aims—and both they and their critics agreed that party grasp of government in the United States was in fact quite limited. Grodzins went so far as to describe American parties as "anti-parties," since they dispersed segments of power instead of gathering them together and wielding them as one.[45] Looking abroad, both sides in the debate also agreed on the existence of a sharp contrast between the United States and most countries in Europe. In America political parties, for good or ill, did not govern; in Europe, for good or ill, they did. The matter is too complex to be gone into in detail here, but this contrast almost certainly was—and is—overdrawn. Britain provided the model to which most advocates of responsible party government looked, yet in a recent paper Rose concludes that Britain has "a political system in which administrative government is much more nearly the case than party government."[46] Daalder has similarly noted that:

> Partly as a consequence of historical factors European parties have differed greatly in the extent to which they have permeated and enveloped other

---

[43] Fred I. Greenstein and Elton F. Jackson, "A Second Look at the Validity of Roll-Call Analysis," *Midwest Journal of Political Science*, 7 (May 1963), pp. 160–164.
[44] See Scarrow, "The Function of Political Parties," pp. 783–785.
[45] Morton Grodzins, "Party and Government in the United States," in Robert A. Goldwin (ed.), *Political Parties, U.S.A.* (Chicago: Rand McNally, 1964), pp. 132–133.
[46] Richard Rose, "Party Government vs. Administrative Government: A Theoretical and Empirical Critique," paper delivered to the Political Studies Association of the United Kingdom, York, April 1969, p. 13.

political elites. In some countries the role of parties has become all-pervasive; in others the parties have penetrated far less successfully to the mainsprings of political power.[47]

Certainly party cohesion is greater in the parliaments of Europe than in American legislatures, but of course it does not follow from this that European parties have also been able to extend their grasp over the executive and administration and, for example, publicly-owned industries.

Moreover, a party's or coalition's grasp of government, even if it were firm and extensive, and even if it achieved concerted action, might not serve ends which were distinctively its own. The policies of the authoritative decision-makers, although acquiesced in or even enforced by the party or coalition, might not have emanated from party sources and indeed might run counter to the declared aims of the party or parties in government. We must turn therefore to a consideration of the fifth alleged function of party: the formation of public policy.

POLICY FORMATION

When scholars maintain that parties perform a policy-making function, they are clearly using party in its group or association sense. The activities of parties and the operations of the party system might, of course, have an impact on public policy formation in a particular system without any particular party's policy becoming public policy and even without the parties in the system deliberately seeking to make policy. But in these circumstances one would not normally say that parties had formed policy; and most of those who have discussed parties as policy-formers have been concerned with the policy stances of particular parties, the content and quality of the debate amongst particular parties, and the power of parties to impose their policies upon governments. Like the organization-of-government function, the policy function conceived of in these terms has lain for a long time at the heart of the controversy over party government and, because of the controversy, American students of parties refer to the policy function less consistently than to the others. When they do refer to it, it is in a somewhat diffident manner.

The policy-making role of party can be discussed from two different points of view: in terms of the relationship between party and electorate (Schattschneider and the party reformers, for instance, wanted parties to formulate policy so that they could perform their representational function more effectively); and in terms of the relationship between party and government. Parties in government may implement party policy for electoral reasons; they may implement it for all sorts of other reasons ranging from conscientious ideological belief to pressure from (say) the party militants; or they may not implement it at all. The electoral aspect of the policy function has been discussed fully elsewhere, notably by Epstein.[48] It is worth saying a word here about the governmental aspect.

The question is: How far in Western democracies are parties as associations or organizations influential in the making of public policy? Of course, if a particular government is organized by party, there is a wholly trivial sense in which it can

---

[47] Daalder in LaPalombara and Weiner, p. 58; this essay as a whole is full of interest.
[48] See Epstein, *Political Parties*, ch. X.

always be said that the government's policies are *ipso facto* party policies.[49] But there are probably only three strict ways in which political parties can influence public policy apart from the role they play in the selection of political leaders: by influencing the content of political thought and discussion; by adopting specific policies or programs which the party's leaders, once elected, feel constrained (for whatever reason) to implement; or by successfully bringing pressure to bear on government, as when a governing party's followers in the legislature or in the country use the processes of the party to force the government to adopt particular policies.

Simply to list these three possibilities is to be reminded that organized parties in the United States do not play a central role in forming public policy and probably never have. American parties are not major forums for policy discussion; party platforms in the United States are more significant as indices of the strength of party factions than as statements of what future administrations are likely to do; American party organizations seldom wield much influence in government, certainly not at the federal level and in most of the larger states. So much is generally agreed. What is less widely recognized is that the policy role of party is also sharply restricted outside the United States. With the general decline of parties as bearers of ideology has gone a reduction in the role that parties play as vehicles for policy innovation, and also in the importance that even socialist parties attach to detailed programs and platforms. To take a simple example, the British Labour Party manifesto of 1945 consisted of a detailed catalog of pledges which both electors and party members could regard as authoritative; the same party's manifesto in 1966 had about the same uncertain status as an American presidential platform. The same tendencies have been manifested widely in Europe and the white Commonwealth, although perhaps rather less in Italy than elsewhere. Epstein has concluded:

> The plain fact of the matter is that a cohesive party, assuming an organizational responsibility for governing in the style of a British parliamentary party, is only somewhat more of a policymaker than a loose American party. It may enact policies as a party in a way that an American party cannot regularly manage, but the policies may be the product of particularized interest groups rather than of any programmatic commitments backed by majority support.[50]

The policies may, as Epstein says, be the product of interest groups. They may also be the product of individual politicians, civil servants, departments and interdepartmental committees, academics, television and the newspapers. They may also, as often as not, be the product largely of force of circumstances.

Nor have party organizations outside the United States been particularly successful in imposing their will when their own leaders have either formed the government or participated in a governing coalition. The past decade or so in Europe provides several examples of new governments, mainly radical ones, pursuing much the same policies as the governments they replaced, and of existing govern-

[49] Labour prime ministers in Britain are sometimes sophistical in this way, when they reply to the criticism that they are deviating from party policy by claiming that whatever is the policy of a Labour government is automatically also the policy of the Labour Party. See the pertinent remarks of Scarrow, "The Function of Political Parties," pp. 783–785.
[50] Epstein, *Political Parties*, p. 282; see in general pp. 272–288.

ments executing abrupt policy shifts without prior warrant from the party organizations of their supporters and sometimes in the face of strong party opposition. To refer to Britain again, the Labour administration elected in 1964 has applied to join the Common Market despite the Labour Party's hostility to joining, expressed both before and after the 1964 and 1966 elections; and the government persisted in supporting United States policy in Vietnam despite the passage at successive Labour Party conferences of resolutions calling on the Labour government to dissociate itself from America.[51] Similarly, when the socialist parties of Germany and Italy joined coalition governments in those countries, the policy changes that followed were at the margin only. The role of party in policy-making in France has been negligible at least since 1958. Organized party generally remains one of the forces with which Western governments must contend in the formation of public policy; but it has never been the only one, and there is reason to suppose that in many countries in the late 1960s it is not even a major one.

It may be contended, however, that although the policy role of parties is circumscribed they nevertheless perform a related, perhaps more important function, one that may indeed subsume the policy-making function: the function of interest aggregation. This is the sixth and last of the functions in our catalog.

INTEREST AGGREGATION

The aggregation of interests is the newest functional concept to be associated with party (at least the phrase is new), and it deserves separate treatment even though it overlaps all of the functions discussed already. As it happens, however, the concept is not an easy one to work with. Etymologically the verb "to aggregate" means simply to gather together, to unite; the noun "aggregation" has two distinct meanings, referring either to the act of aggregating, or to the whole or mass formed as the result of acts of aggregation. In political analysis, by contrast, the concept has not been defined precisely. Almond in one of the original formulations wrote:

> Every political system has some way of aggregating the interests, claims, and demands which have been articulated by the interest groups of the polity. Aggregation may be accomplished by means of the formulation of general policies in which interests are combined, accommodated, or otherwise taken account of, or by means of the recruitment of political personnel, more or less committed to a particular pattern of policy.[52]

Almond and Powell say simply that, "The function of converting demands into general policy alternatives is called interest aggregation." [53]

It is fairly clear from these definitions that their authors do not wish to assert that the interest-aggregation function is being performed simply by virtue of the existence of certain aggregations of interest (broadly-based political parties or peak interest associations). Nor (somewhat surprisingly) do the authors seem to want to refer to the bringing into being of such aggregations of interests (as in

---

[51] For a more general discussion see Richard Rose, "Party Government vs. Administrative Government."
[52] Almond and Colemen, *Politics of Developing Areas*, p. 39.
[53] Gabriel A. Almond and G. Bingham Powell, Jr., *Comparative Politics: A Developmental Approach* (Boston: Little, Brown, 1966), p. 98; cf. p. 29.

the formation by a number of interest groups of a peak association). Rather, the definitions clearly refer to the actions of groups or associations that are already in existence. The actions referred to cover a wide range, from simply "taking account" of interests through "accommodating" them to "converting them into general policy alternatives." It is evident that these may be very different actions; a group or association could take account of various demands placed before it without accommodating them, just as it could accommodate them without necessarily converting them into a general policy alternative. It is equally evident that the results of an empirical assessment of whether the interest-aggregation function were being performed and, if it were, of whether it were being performed by political parties, would depend on whether the concept of interest aggregation was being used in (say) its accommodation-of-interests sense or in its general-policy-alternatives sense. Moreover, as those who use the concept recognize, it is exceedingly difficult to separate acts of interest aggregation conceptually from acts of interest articulation and rule-making, and also to distinguish between acts of aggregation that are more and less inclusive.[54]

In a diffuse way interest aggregation of one sort or another undoubtedly takes place in all political systems just as it takes place in all societies, associations, interest groups, trade unions, bowling clubs, and families. It is a matter of contingent fact whether interest aggregation in the sense of accommodation takes place in any given system in such a way as to contribute to the system's capacity to maintain and adapt itself. Almond and Powell suggest that the "political party may be considered the specialized aggregation structure of modern societies," yet they also note that "party may or may not be a major interest aggregator in a given system."[55] Given that interest aggregation occurs everywhere to some extent, whether or not successfully in the system-maintenance sense, the question arises: Are parties in fact the major interest aggregators in the West?

The answer, irrespective of whether aggregation is used in its accommodation-of-interests sense or in its general-policy-alternatives sense, would seem to be "no"—that the interest aggregation function, like most of the others discussed here, is performed by a variety of structures of which the political party is only one and not necessarily the most important. As regards the reaching of accommodations and compromises, the workings of party systems in some countries do appear to contribute to the creation of a political climate conducive to accommodation and compromise (although of course it is usually hard to say whether a particular kind of party system engenders a particular kind of political culture, or vice versa). But the role of the parties themselves is often rather peripheral.[56] One can think of trade union demands in France, which are increasingly dealt with at the centre by face-to-face confrontations between unions and government; or of the claims of the North and the Mezzogiorno in Italy, which are accommodated, if at all, by the civil service, semi-autonomous public bodies, and loose alliances of individual politicians, hardly at all by the parties; or of the claims of different sections of the farming community in the United States, which are typically adjusted by the Department of Agriculture and by Congress and its committees;

[54] Almond and Powell, *Comparative Politics*, p. 99.
[55] Almond and Powell, *Comparative Politics*, p. 102.
[56] It is fairly clear that when Almond and Powell and others discuss parties in this connection they are thinking of parties as groups or organizations; see, e.g., the examples in *Comparative Politics*, pp. 98, 104.

or of the competing demands of rival linguistic and religious groups in Belgium and the Netherlands, which tend to be compromised, if at all, as much in the national legislatures and bureaucracies as by political parties; or of the competing claims of European co-operation and an independent aircraft industry in Britain, which have hardly even been discussed, much less compromised, in any party arena.[57]

As regards the conversion of demands into broad policy alternatives, here too the role of organized parties is often not central. Instead alternatives are typically formulated by individual political leaders, as when de Gaulle offered the French people the choice between regional devolution and continuing centralization; by cabinets, as with the British government's 1969 proposals for the reform of trade union law; by civil servants, as witness the determining part played by the Department of Health, Education and Welfare in structuring the Medicare debate in the United States; by individual politicians, publicists and intellectuals, as in the American debate over Vietnam. The most that parties seem generally able to do is to present electorates with highly generalized platforms and with alternative candidates committed to very general policy standpoints. Probably on major issues, given their desire to mobilize the maximum number of votes, most parties in the West could do little else. But they thereby leave the function of interest aggregation largely to others.

CONCLUSIONS

This brings us to the end of our discussion of the six major functions which, it is claimed, political parties perform in Western systems. In the opening part of the paper we examined briefly a number of different concepts of party and considered the implications of the various usages. Throughout the subsequent discussion a good deal of attention was paid to the importance, whether in analyzing parties or party functions or both, of conceptual clarity. The discussion has been brief, and almost every point that has been made is open to some sort of qualification and elaboration. Nevertheless, on the basis of the discussion it would seem that we are entitled, at the very least, to a certain scepticism concerning the standard catalog of party functions, and also concerning the great importance attached to parties in large segments of the political science literature. What conclusions should we draw?

There is one conclusion that we should not draw: namely, that parties are unimportant and therefore undeserving of study. It has been suggested that political parties are, after all, "organizations whose purpose it is to affect a process which would continue with or without them." [58] This is undoubtedly true as stated, and indeed there exist in most countries small jurisdictions in which parties are scarcely active and have hardly any impact. But the experience of all Western societies suggests that, where there is any degree of freedom and where power is both worth having and hard to get, men and women will combine to form political parties. The parties they form are certain to play a large part in almost every process of democratic politics, the electoral, the legislative, the administrative,

---

[57] See the brief discussion in Scarrow, "The Function of Political Parties," p. 782.
[58] Joseph A. Schlesinger, "Political Party Organization," in James G. March (ed.), *Handbook of Organizations* (Chicago: Rand McNally, 1965), p. 774.

even the judicial. If the study of political parties did not exist, it would clearly have to be invented.

The conclusions suggested by the argument of this paper have to do, not at all with abandoning the study of parties, but rather with the way in which parties should be studied. In the first place, if the role played by party in the performance of this or that political function is to be assessed, it is crucial that the function in question be defined precisely and in detail. Too many discussions of party function are bogged down by conceptual muddle, although the authors of them often seem unaware of it (indeed this paper may well not have escaped entirely). In the second place, if a party function is to be studied, the focus should almost certainly be on the function and not on the party, since otherwise the importance attached to party is likely to be exaggerated simply as the result of the approach employed. It may be that in future the most significant findings about political parties will emerge from studies that, in conception at least, have not focused on party at all. In the third place, as Lowi has pointed out, what is needed above all else are attempts to specify the conditions under which political parties and other political structures will or will not perform the various political functions.[59] Many of the statements in this paper may well be shown to be false by future research. Even if they all turn out to be true, they will not constitute in themselves the kind of comparative empirical theory required.

Once the theory exists—and constructing it, although a difficult task, ought not to be an impossible one—what will be its general import? My hunch is that it will show, in the words of Kirchheimer, that "the political party's role in Western industrial society today is more limited than would appear from its position of formal preeminence." [60] But that is only a hunch, and hunches are no substitute for disciplined inquiry.

[59] Lowi, "Toward Functionalism," p. 571.
[60] Kirchheimer in LaPalombara and Weiner, p. 200.

5
The End of American Party Politics
Walter Dean Burnham

American politics has clearly been falling apart in the past decade. We don't have to look hard for the evidence. Mr. Nixon is having as much difficulty controlling his fellow party members in Congress as any of his Democratic predecessors had in controlling theirs. John V. Lindsay, a year after he helped make Spiro Agnew a household word, had to run for mayor as a Liberal and an Independent with the aid of nationally prominent Democrats. Chicago in July of 1968 showed that for large numbers of its activists a major political party can become not just a disappointment, but positively repellent. Ticket-splitting has become widespread as never before, especially among the young; and George C. Wallace, whose third-party movement is the largest in recent American history, continues to demonstrate an unusually stable measure of support.

Vietnam and racial polarization have played large roles in this breakdown, to be sure; but the ultimate causes are rooted much deeper in our history. For some time we have been saying that we live in a "pluralist democracy." And no text on American politics would be complete without a few key code words such as "consensus," "incrementalism," "bargaining" and "process." Behind it all is a rather

From *TRANS-action* (December 1969), pp. 12–22. Copyright © 1969 by *TRANS-action*. Reprinted by permission of the publisher.

benign view of our politics, one that assumes that the complex diversity of the American social structure is filtered through the two major parties and buttressed by a consensus of middle-class values which produces an electoral politics of low intensity and gradual change. The interplay of interest groups and public officials determines policy in detail. The voter has some leverage on policy, but only in a most diffuse way; and, anyway, he tends to be a pretty apolitical animal, dominated either by familial or local tradition, on one hand, or by the charisma of attractive candidates on the other. All of this is a good thing, of course, since in an affluent time the politics of consensus rules out violence and polarization. It pulls together and supports the existing order of things.

There is no doubt that this description fits "politics as usual," in the United States, but to assume that it fits the whole of American electoral politics is a radical oversimplification. Yet even after these past years of turmoil, new efforts have been made to appraise the peculiar rhythms of American politics in a more realistic way. This article is an attempt to do so by focusing upon two very important and little celebrated aspects of the dynamics of our politics: the phenomena of critical realignments of the electorate and of decomposition of the party in our electoral politics.

As a whole and across time, the reality of American politics appears quite different from a simple vision of pluralist democracy. It is shot through with escalating tensions, periodic electoral convulsions and repeated redefinitions of the rules and general outcomes of the political game. It has also been marked repeatedly by redefinitions—by no means always broadening ones—of those who are permitted to play. And one other very basic characteristic of American party politics that emerges from an historical overview is the profound incapacity of established political leadership to adapt itself to the political demands produced by the losers in America's stormy socioeconomic life. As is well known, American political parties are not instruments of collective purpose, but of electoral success. One major implication of this is that, as organizations, parties are interested in control of offices but not of government in any larger sense. It follows that once successful routines are established or reestablished for office-winning, very little motivation exists among party leaders to disturb the routines of the game. These routines are periodically upset, to be sure, but not by adaptive change within the party system. They are upset by overwhelming external force.

It has been recognized, at least since the publication of V. O. Key's "A Theory of Critical Elections" in 1955, that some elections in our history have been far more important than most in their long-range consequences for the political system. Such elections seem to "decide" clusters of substantive issues in a more clear-cut way than do most of the ordinary varieties. There is even a consensus among historians as to when these turning points in electoral politics took place. The first came in 1800 when Thomas Jefferson overthrew the Federalist hegemony established by Washington, Adams and Hamilton. The second came in 1828 and in the years afterward, with the election of Andrew Jackson and the democratization of the presidency. The third, of course, was the election of Abraham Lincoln in 1860, an election that culminated a catastrophic polarization of the society as a whole and resulted in civil war. The fourth critical election was that of William McKinley in 1896; this brought to a close the "Civil War" party system and inaugurated a political alignment congenial to the dominance of industrial capitalism over the American political economy. Created in the crucible of one massive depression, this "System of 1896" endured until the collapse of the economy in a second. The election of Franklin D. Roosevelt in 1932 came last in this series, and brought a major realignment of electoral politics and policy-making structures into the now familiar "welfare-pluralist" mode.

Now that the country appears to have entered another period of political upheaval, it seems particularly important not only to identify the phenomena of periodic critical realignments in our electoral politics, but to integrate them into a larger—if still very modest—theory of stasis and movement in American politics. For the realignments focus attention on the dark side of our politics, those moments of tremendous stress and abrupt transformation that remind us that "politics as usual" in the United States is not politics as always, and that American political institutions and leadership, once defined or redefined in a "normal phase" seem *themselves* to contribute to the building of conditions that threaten their overthrow.

To underscore the relevance of critical elections to our own day, one has only to recall that in the past, fundamental realignments in voting behavior have always been signalled by the rise of significant third parties: the Anti-Masons in the 1820s, the Free Soilers in the 1840s and 1850s, the Populists in the 1890s and the LaFollette Progressives in the 1920s. We cannot know whether George Wallace's American Independent Party of 1968 fits into this series, but it is certain—as we shall see below—that the very foundations of American electoral politics have become quite suddenly fluid in the past few years, and that the mass base of our politics has become volatile to a degree unknown in the experience of all but the very oldest living Americans. The Wallace uprising is a major sign of this recent fluidity; but it hardly stands alone.

Third-party protests, perhaps by contrast with major-party bolts, point up the interplay in American politics between the inertia of "normal" established political routines and the pressures arising from the rapidity, unevenness and uncontrolled character of change in the country's dynamic socioeconomic system. All of the third parties prior to and including the 1968 Wallace movement constituted attacks by outsiders, who felt they were outsiders, against an elite frequently viewed in conspiratorial terms. The attacks were made under the banner of high moralistic universals against an established political structure seen as corrupt, undemocratic and manipulated by insiders for their own benefit and that of their supporters. All these parties were perceived by their activists as "movements" that would not only purify the corruption of the current political regime, but replace some of its most important parts. Moreover, they all telegraphed the basic clusters of issues that would dominate politics in the next electoral era: the completion of political democratization in the 1830s, slavery and sectionalism in the late 1840s and 1850s, the struggle between the industrialized and the colonial regions in the 1890s, and welfare liberalism vs. laissez-faire in the 1920s and 1930s. One may well view the American Independent Party in such a context.

The periodic recurrence of third-party forerunners of realignment—and realignments themselves, for that matter—are significantly related to dominant peculiarities of polity and society in the United States. They point to an electorate especially vulnerable to breaking apart, and to a political system in which the sense of common nationhood may be much more nearly skin-deep than is usually appreciated. If there is any evolutionary scale of political modernization at all, the persistence of deep fault lines in our electoral politics suggests pretty strongly that the United States remains a "new nation" to this day in some important political respects. The periodic recurrence of these tensions may also imply that—as dynamically developed as our economic system is—no convincing evidence of *political* development in the United States can be found after the 1860s.

Nationwide critical realignments can only take place around clusters of issues of the most fundamental importance. The most profound of these issues have been cast up in the course of the transition of our Lockeian-liberal commonwealth from an agrarian to an industrial state. The last two major realignments—those of 1893–1896 and 1928–1936—involved the two great transitional crises of American industrial capitalism, the economic collapses of 1893 and 1929. The second of these modern realignments produced, of course, the broad coalition on which the New Deal's welfarist-pluralist policy was ultimately based. But the first is of immediate concern to us here. For the 1896 adaptation of electoral politics to the imperatives of industrial-capitalism involved a set of developments that stand in the sharpest possible contrast to those occurring elsewhere in the Western world at about the same time. Moreover, they set in motion new patterns of behavior in electoral politics that were never entirely overcome even during the New Deal period, and which, as we shall see, have resumed their forward march during the past decade.

As a case in point, let me briefly sketch the political evolution of Pennsylvania —one of the most industrially developed areas on earth—during the 1890–1932 period. There was in this state a preexisting, indeed, preindustrial, pattern of two-party competition, one that had been forged in the Jacksonian era and decisively amended, though not abolished, during the Civil War. Then came the realignment of the 1890s, which, like those of earlier times, was an abrupt process. In the five annual elections from 1888 through November 1892, the Democrats' mean percentage of the total two-party vote was 46.7 percent, while for the five elections beginning in February 1894 it dropped to a mean of 37.8 percent. Moreover, the greatest and most permanent Republican gains during this depression decade occurred where they counted most, numerically: in the metropolitan areas of Philadelphia and Pittsburgh.

The cumulative effect of this realignment and its aftermath was to convert Pennsylvania into a thoroughly one-party state, in which conflict over the basic political issues were duly transferred to the Republican primary after it was established in 1908. By the 1920s this peculiar process had been completed and the Democratic party had become so weakened that, as often as not, the party's nominees for major office were selected by the Republican leadership. But whether so selected or not, their general-election prospects were dismal: of the 80 statewide contests held from 1894 through 1931, a candidate running with Democratic party endorsement won just one. Moreover, with the highly ephemeral exception of Theodore Roosevelt's bolt from the Republican party in 1912, no third parties emerged as general-election substitutes for the ruined Democrats.

The political simplicity which had thus emerged in this industrial heartland of the Northeast by the 1920s was the more extraordinary in that it occurred in an area whose socioeconomic division of labor was as complex and its level of development as high as any in the world. In most other regions of advanced industrialization the emergence of corporate capitalism was associated with the development of mass political parties with high structural cohesion and explicit collective purposes with respect to the control of policy and government. These parties expressed deep conflicts over the direction of public policy, but they also brought about the democratic revolution of Europe, for electoral participation tended to rise along with them. Precisely the opposite occurred in Pennsylvania and, with marginal and short-lived exceptions, the nation. It is no exaggeration to say that the political response to the collectivizing thrust of industrialism in this American state was the elimination of organized partisan combat, an extremely severe decline in electoral participation, the emergence of a Republican "coalition of the whole" and—by no means coincidentally—a highly efficient insulation of the controlling industrial-financial elite from effective or sustained countervailing pressures.

IRRELEVANT RADICALISM

The reasons for the increasing solidity of this "System of 1896" in Pennsylvania are no doubt complex. Clearly, for example, the introduction of the direct primary as an alternative to the general election, which was thereby emptied of any but ritualistic significance, helped to undermine the minority Democrats more and more decisively by destroying their monopoly of opposition. But nationally as well the Democratic party in and after the 1890s was virtually invisible to Pennsylvania voters as a usable opposition. For with the ascendancy of the agrarian Populist William Jennings Bryan, the Democratic party was transformed into a vehicle for colonial, periphery-oriented dissent against the industrial-metropolitan center, leaving the Republicans as sole spokesmen for the latter.

This is a paradox that pervades American political history, but it was sharpest in the years around the turn of this century. The United States was so vast that it had little need of economic colonies abroad; in fact it had two major colonial regions within its own borders, the postbellum South and the West. The only kinds of attacks that could be made effective on a *nationwide* basis against the emergent industrialist hegemony—the only attacks that, given the ethnic heterogeneity and extremely rudimentary political socialization of much of the country's industrial working class, could come within striking distance of achieving a popular majority—came out of these colonial areas. Thus "radical" protest in major-party terms came to be associated with the neo-Jacksonian demands of agrarian smallholders and small-town society already confronted by obsolescence. The Democratic party from 1896 to 1932, and in many respects much later, was the national vehicle for these struggles.

The net effect of this was to produce a condition in which—especially, but not entirely on the presidential level—the more economically advanced a state was, the more heavy were its normal Republican majorities likely to be. The nostalgic agrarian-individualist appeals of the national Democratic leadership tended to present the voters of this industrial state with a choice that was not a choice: between an essentially backward-looking provincial party articulating interests in opposition to those of the industrial North and East as a whole, and a "modernizing" party whose doctrines included enthusiastic acceptance of and co-operation with the dominant economic interests of region and nation. Not only did this partitioning of the political universe entail normal and often huge Republican majorities in an economically advanced state like Pennsylvania; the survival of national two-party competition on such a basis helped to ensure that no local reorganization of electoral politics along class lines could effectively occur even within such a state. Such a voting universe had a tendency toward both enormous inbuilt stability and increasing entrenchment in the decades after its creation. Probably no force less overwhelming than the post-1929 collapse of the national economic system would have sufficed to dislodge it. Without such a shock, who can say how, or indeed whether, the "System of 1896" would have come to an end in Pennsylvania and the nation? To ask such a question is to raise yet another. For there is no doubt that in Pennsylvania, as elsewhere, the combination of trauma in 1929–1933 and Roosevelt's creative leadership provided the means of overthrowing the old order and for reversing dramatically the depoliticization of electoral politics which had come close to perfection under it. Yet might it not be the case that the dominant pattern of political adaptation to industrialism in the United States has worked to eliminate, by one means or another, the links provided by political parties between voters and rulers? In other words, was the post-1929 reversal permanent or only a transitory phase in our political evolution? And if transitory, what bearing would this fact have on the possible recurrence of critical realignments in the future?

WITHERING AWAY OF THE PARTIES

The question requires us to turn our attention to the second major dynamic of American electoral politics during this century: the phenomenon of electoral disaggregation, of the breakdown of party loyalty, which in many respects must be seen as the permanent legacy of the fourth-party system of 1896–1932. One of the most conspicuous developments of this era, most notably during the 1900–1920 period, was a whole network of changes in the rules of the political game. This is not the place for a thorough treatment and documentation of these peculiarities. One can only mention here some major changes in the rules of the game, and note that one would have no difficulty in arguing that their primary latent function was to ease the transition from a preindustrial universe of competitive, highly organized mass politics to a depoliticized world marked by drastic shrinkage in participation or political leverage by the lower orders of the population. The major changes surely include the following:

• The introduction of the Australian ballot, which was designed to purify elections but also eliminated a significant function of the older political machines, the printing and distribution of ballots, and eased a transition from party voting to candidate voting.
• The introduction of the direct primary, which at once stripped the minority party of its monopoly of opposition and weakened the control of party leaders over nominating processes, and again hastened preoccupation of the electorate with candidates rather than parties.
• The movement toward nonpartisan local elections, often accompanied by a drive to eliminate local bases of representation such as wards in favor of at-large elections, which produced—as Samuel Hays points out—a shift of political power from the grass roots to citywide cosmopolitan elites.
• The expulsion of almost all blacks, and a very large part of the poor-white population as well, from the southern electorate by a series of legal and extralegal measures such as the poll tax.
• The introduction of personal registration requirements the burden of which, in faithful compliance with dominant middle-class values, was placed on the individ-

ual rather than on public authority, but which effectively disenfranchised large numbers of the poor.

BREAKDOWN OF PARTY LOYALTY

Associated with these and other changes in the roles of the game was a profound transformation in voting behavior. There was an impressive growth in the numbers of political independents and ticket-splitters, a growth accompanied by a sea-change among party elites from what Richard Jensen has termed the "militarist" (or ward boss) campaign style to the "mercantilist" (or advertising-packaging) style. Aside from noting that the transition was largely completed as early as 1916, and hence that the practice of "the selling of the president" goes back far earlier than we usually think, these changes too must be left for fuller exposition elsewhere.

Critical realignments, as we have argued, are an indispensable part of a stability-disruption dialectic which has the deepest roots in American political history. Realigning sequences are associated with all sorts of aberrations from the normal workings of American party politics, both in the events leading up to nominations, the nature and style of election campaigning and the final outcome at the polls. This is not surprising, since they arise out of the collision of profound transitional crisis in the socioeconomic system with the immobility of a nondeveloped political system.

At the same time, it seems clear that for realignment to fulfill some of its most essential tension-management functions, for it to be a forum by which the electorate can participate in durable "constitution making," it is essential that political parties not fall below a certain level of coherence and appeal in the electorate. It is obvious that the greater the electoral disaggregation the less effective will be "normal" party politics as an instrument of countervailing influence in an industrial order. Thus, a number of indices of disaggregation significantly declined during the 1930s as the Democratic party remobilized parts of American society under the stimulus of the New Deal. In view of the fact that political parties during the 1930s and 1940s were once again called upon to assist in a redrawing of the map of American politics and policy-making, this regeneration of partisan voting in the 1932–1952 era is hardly surprising. More than that, regeneration was necessary if even the limited collective purposes of the new majority coalition were to be realized.

Even so, the New Deal realignment was far more diffuse, protracted and incomplete than any of its predecessors, a fact of which the more advanced New Dealers were only too keenly aware. It is hard to avoid the impression that one contributing element in this peculiarity of our last realignment was the much higher level of electoral disaggregation in the 1930s and 1940s than had existed at any time prior to the realignment of the 1890s. If one assumes that the end result of a long-term trend toward electoral disaggregation is the complete elimination of political parties as foci that shape voting behavior, then the possibility of critical realignment would, by definition, be eliminated as well. Every election would be dominated by TV packaging, candidate charisma, real or manufactured, and short-term, ad hoc influences. Every election, therefore, would have become deviating or realigning by definition, and American national politics would come to resemble the formless gubernatorial primaries that V. O. Key described in his classic *Southern Politics*.

The New Deal clearly arrested and reversed, to a degree, the march toward electoral disaggregation. But it did so only for the period in which the issues generated by economic scarcity remained central, and the generation traumatized by the collapse of 1929 remained numerically preponderant in the electorate. Since 1952, electoral disaggregation has resumed, in many measurable dimensions, and with redoubled force. The data on this point are overwhelming. Let us examine a few of them.

A primary aspect of electoral disaggregation, of course, is the "pulling apart" over time of the percentages for the same party but at different levels of election: this is the phenomenon of split-ticket voting. Recombining and reorganizing the data found in two tables of Milton Cummings' excellent study *Congressmen and the Electorate*, and extending the series back and forward in time, we may examine the relationship between presidential and congressional elections during this century.

Such as array captures both the initial upward thrust of disaggregation in the second decade of this century, the peaking in the middle to late 1920s, the recession beginning in 1932, and especially the post-1952 resumption of the upward trend.

Other evidence points precisely in the same direction. It has generally been accepted in survey-research work that generalized partisan identification shows far more stability over time than does actual voting behavior, since the latter is subject to short-term factors associated with each election. What is not so widely understood is that this glacial measure of party identification has suddenly become quite volatile during the 1960s, and particularly during the last half of the decade. In the first place, as both Gallup and Survey Research Center data confirm, the proportion of independents underwent a sudden shift upwards around 1966: while from 1940 to 1965 independents constituted about 20 percent to 22 percent of the electorate, they increased to 29 percent in 1966. At the present time, they outnumber Republicans by 30 percent to 28 percent.

Second, there is a clear unbroken progression in the share that independents have of the total vote along age lines. The younger the age group, the larger the number of independents in it, so that among the 21–29 year olds, according to the most recent Gallup findings this year, 42 percent are independents—an increase of about 10 percent over the first half of the decade, and representing greater numbers of people than identify with either major party. When one reviews the June 1969 Gallup survey of college students, the share is larger still—44 percent. Associated with this quantitative increase in independents seems to be a major qualitative change as well. Examining the data for the 1950s, the authors of *The American Voter* could well argue that independents tended to have lower political awareness and political involvement in general than did identifiers (particularly strong identifiers) of either major party. But the current concentration of independents in the population suggests that his may no longer be the case. They are clearly and disproportionately found not only among the young, and especially among the college young, but also among men, those adults with a college background, people in the professional-managerial strata and, of course, among those with higher incomes. Such groups tend to include those people whose sense of political involvement and efficacy is far higher than that of the population as a whole. Even in the case of the two most conspicuous exceptions to this—the pile-up of independent identifiers in the youngest age group and in the South—it can be persuasively argued that this distribution does not reflect low political awareness and involvement but the reverse: a sudden, in some instances almost violent, increase in both awareness and involvement among southerners and young adults, with the former being associated both with the heavy increase in southern turnout in 1968 and the large Wallace vote polled there.

Third, one can turn to two sets of evidence found in the Survey Research Center's election studies. If the proportion of *strong* party identifiers over time is examined, the same pattern of long-term inertial stability and recent abrupt change can be seen. From 1952 through 1964, the proportion of strong Democratic and Republican party identifiers fluctuated in a narrow range between 36 percent and 40 percent, with a steep downward trend in strong Republican identifiers between 1960 and 1964 being matched by a moderate increase in strong Democratic identifiers. Then in 1966 the proportion of strong identifiers abruptly declines to 28 percent, with the defectors overwhelmingly concentrated among former Democrats. This is almost certainly connected, as is the increase of independent identifiers, with the Vietnam fiasco. While we do not as yet have the 1968 SRC data, the distribution of identifications reported by Gallup suggests the strong probability that this abrupt decline in party loyalty has not been reversed very much since. It is enough here to observe that while the ratio between strong identifiers and independents prior to 1966 was pretty stably fixed at between 1.6 to 1 and 2 to 1 in favor of the former, it is now evidently less than 1 to 1. Both Chicago and Wallace last year were the acting out of these changes in the arena of "popular theater."

Finally, both survey and election data reveal a decline in two other major indices of the relevance of party to voting behavior: split-ticket voting and the choice of the same party's candidates for President across time.

It is evident that the 1960s have been an era of increasingly rapid liquidation of preexisting party commitments by individual voters. There is no evidence anywhere to support Kevin Phillips' hypothesis regarding an emergent Republican majority—assuming that such a majority would involve increases in voter identification with the party. More than that, one might well ask whether, if this process of liquidation is indeed a preliminary to realignment, the latter may not take the form of a third-party movement of truly massive and durable proportions.

The evidence lends some credence to the view that American electoral politics is undergoing a long-term transition into routines designed only to fill offices and symbolically affirm "the American way." There also seem to be tendencies for our political parties gradually to evaporate as broad and active intermediaries between the people and their rulers, even as they may well continue to maintain enough organizational strength to screen out the unacceptable or the radical at the nominating stage. It is certain that the significance of party as link between government and the governed has now come once again into serious question. Bathed in the warm glow of diffused affluence, vexed in spirit but enriched economically by our imperial military and space commitments, confronted by the gradually unfolding consequences of social change as vast as it is unplanned, what need have Americans of political parties? More precisely, why do they need parties whose structures, processes and leadership cadres seem to grow more remote and irrelevant to each new crisis?

FUTURE POLITICS

It seems evident enough that if this long-term trend toward a politics without parties continues, the policy consequences must be profound. One can put the matter with the utmost simplicity: political parties, with all their well-known human and structural shortcomings, are the only devices thus far invented by the wit of Western man that can, with some effectiveness, generate countervailing collective power on behalf of the many individually powerless against the relatively few who are individually or organizationally powerful. Their disappearance as active intermediaries, if not as preliminary screening devices, would only entail the unchallenged ascendancy of the already powerful, unless new structures of collective power were somehow developed to replace them, and unless conditions in America's social structure and political culture came to be such that they could be effectively used. Yet *neither* of these contingencies, despite recent publicity for the term "participatory democracy," is likely to occur under immediately conceivable circumstances in the United States. It is much more probable that the next chapter of our political history will resemble the metapolitical world of the 1920s.

But, it may be asked, may not a future realignment serve to recrystallize and revitalize political parties in the American system?

The present condition of America contains a number of what Marxists call "internal contradictions," some of which might provide the leverage for a future critical realignment if sufficiently sharp dislocations in everyday life should occur. One of the most important of these, surely, is the conversion—largely through technological change—of the American social stratification system from the older capitalist mixture of upper or "owning" classes, dependent white-collar middle classes and proletarians into a mixture described recently by David Apter: the technologically competent, the technologically obsolescent and the technologically superfluous. It is arguable, in fact, that the history of the Kennedy-Johnson Administrations on the domestic front could be written in terms of a coalition of the top and bottom of this Apter-ite mix against the middle, and the 1968 election as the first stage of a "counter-revolution" of these middle strata against the pressures from both of the other two. Yet the inchoate results of 1968 raise some doubts, to say the least, that it can yet be described as part of a realigning sequence: there was great volatility in this election, but also a remarkable and unexpectedly large element of continuity and voter stability.

It is not hard to find evidence of cumulative social disaster in our metropolitan areas. We went to war with Japan in 1941 over a destruction inflicted on us far less devastating in scope and intensity than that endured by any large American city today. But the destruction came suddenly, as a sharp blow, from a foreign power; while the urban destruction of today has matured as a result of our own internal social and political processes, and it has been unfolding gradually for decades. We have consequently learned somehow to adapt to it piecemeal, as best we can, without changing our lives or our values very greatly. Critical realignments, however, also seem to require sharp, sudden blows as a precondition for their emergence. If we think of realignment as arising from the spreading internal disarray in this country, we should also probably attempt to imagine what kinds of events could produce a sudden, sharp and general escalation in social tensions and threatened deprivations of property, status or values.

Conceivably, ghetto and student upheavals could prove enough in an age of mass communications to create a true critical realignment, but one may doubt it. Student and ghetto rebellions appear to be too narrowly defined socially to have a *direct* impact on the daily lives of the "vast middle," and thus produce transformations in voting behavior that would be both sweeping and permanent. For what happens in times of critical realignment is nothing less than an intense, if temporary, quasi revolutionizing of the vast middle class, a class normally content to be traditionalists or passive-participants in electoral politics.

Yet, even if students and ghetto blacks could do the trick, if they could even begin, with the aid of elements of the technological elite, a process of electoral realignment leftward, what would be the likely consequences? What would the quasi revolutionizing of an insecure, largely urban middle class caught in a brutal squeeze from the top and the bottom of the social system look like? There are already premonitory evidences: the Wallace vote in both southern and nonsouthern areas, as well as an unexpected durability in his *postelection* appeal; the mayoral elections in Los Angeles and Minneapolis this year, and not least, Lindsay's narrow squeak into a second term as mayor of New York City. To the extent that the "great middle" becomes politically mobilized and self-conscious, it moves toward what has been called "urban populism," a stance of organized hostility to blacks, student radicals and cosmopolitan liberal elites. The "great middle" remains, after all, the chief defender of the old-time Lockeian faith; both its material and cultural interests are bound up in this defense. If it should become at all mobilized as a major and cohesive political force in today's conditions, it would do so in the name of a restoration of the ancient truths by force if necessary. A realignment that directly involved this kind of mobilization—as it surely would, should it occur—would very likely have sinister overtones unprecedented in our political history.

Are we left, then, with a choice between the stagnation implicit in the disaggregative trends we have outlined here and convulsive disruption? Is there something basic to the American political system, and extending to its electoral politics, which rules out a middle ground between drift and mastery?

The fact that these questions were raised by Walter Lippmann more than half a century ago—and have indeed been raised in one form or other in every era of major transitional crisis over the past century—is alone enough to suggest an affirmative answer. The phenomena we have described here provide evidence of a partly quantitative sort which seems to point in the same direction. For electoral disaggregation is the negation of party. Further, it is—or rather, reflects—the negation of structural and behavioral conditions in politics under which linkages between the bottom, the middle and the top can exist and produce the effective carrying out of collective power. Critical realignments are evidence not of the presence of such linkages or conditions in the normal state of American electoral politics, but precisely of their absence. Correspondingly, they are not manifestations of democratic accountability, but infrequent and hazardous substitutes for it.

Taken together, both of these phenomena generate support for the inference that American politics in its normal state is the negation of the public order itself, as that term is understood in politically developed nations. We do not have government in our domestic affairs so much as "nonrule." We do not have political parties in the contemporary sense of that term as understood elsewhere in the

Western world; we have antiparties instead. Power centrifuges rather than power concentrators, they have been immensely important not as vehicles of social transformation but for its prevention through political means.

The entire setting of the critical realignment phenomenon bears witness to a deep-seated dialectic within the American political system. From the beginning, the American socioeconomic system has developed and transformed itself with an energy and thrust that has no parallel in modern history. The political system, from parties to policy structures, has seen no such development. Indeed, it has shown astonishingly little substantive transformation over time in its methods of operation. In essence, the political system of this "fragment society" remains based today on the same Lockeian formulation that, as Louis Hartz points out, has dominated its entire history. It is predicated upon the maintenance of a high wall of separation between politics and government on one side and the socioeconomic system on the other. It depends for its effective working on the failure of anything approximating internal sovereignty in the European sense to emerge here.

The Lockeian cultural monolith, however, is based upon a social assumption that has come repeatedly into collision with reality. The assumption, of course, is not only that the autonomy of socioeconomic life from political direction is the prescribed fundamental law for the United States, but that this autonomous development will proceed with enough smoothness, uniformity and generally distributed benefits that it will be entirely compatible with the usual functioning of our antique political structures. Yet the high (though far from impermeable) wall of separation between politics and society is periodically threatened with inundations. As the socioeconomic system develops in the context of unchanging institutions of electoral politics and policy formation, dysfunctions become more and more visible. Whole classes, regions or other major sectors of the population are injured or faced with an imminent threat of injury. Finally the triggering event occurs, critical realignments follow, the universe of policy and of electoral coalitions is broadly redefined, and the tensions generated by the crisis receive some resolution. Thus it can be argued that critical realignment as a periodically recurring phenomenon is as centrally related to the workings of such a system as is the archaic and increasingly rudimentary structure of the major parties themselves.

PARTY VS. SURVIVAL

One is finally left with the sense that the twentieth-century decomposition of partisan links in our electoral system also corresponds closely with the contemporary survival needs of what Samuel P. Huntington has called the American "Tudor polity." Electoral disaggregation and the concentration of certain forms of power in the hands of economic, technological and administrative elites are functional for the short-term survival of nonrule in the United States. They may even somehow be related to the gradual emergence of internal sovereignty in this country —though to be sure under not very promising auspices for participatory democracy of any kind. Were such a development to occur, it would not necessarily entail the disappearance or complete suppression of subgroup tensions or violence in American social life, or of group bargaining and pluralism in the policy process. It might even be associated with increases in both. But it would, after all, reflect the ultimate sociopolitical consequences of the persistence of Lockeian individualism into an era of Big Organization: oligarchy at the top, inertia and spasms of self-defense in the middle, and fragmentation at the base. One may well doubt whether political parties or critical realignments need have much place in such a political universe.

CHAPTER THREE

PRESSURE GROUPS

6
American Hybrid

Robert A. Dahl

If majorities in a democracy nearly always govern in the broad meaning of the term, they rarely rule in Madison's terms: for as we have seen, specific policies tend to be products of "minorities rule." In the sense in which Madison was concerned with the problem then, majority rule is mostly a myth. This leads to our fourth proposition: If majority rule is mostly a myth, then majority tyranny is mostly a myth too. For if the majority cannot rule, surely it cannot be tyrannical.

The real world issue has not turned out to be whether a majority, much less "the" majority, will act in a tyrannical way through democratic procedures to impose its will on a (or the) minority. Instead, the more relevant question is the extent to which various minorities in a society will frustrate the ambitions of one another with the passive acquiescence or indifference of a majority of adults or voters.

That some minorities will frustrate and in that sense tyrannize over others is inherent in a society where people disagree, that is, in human society. But if frustration is inherent in human society, dictatorship is not. However, if there is anything to be said for the processes that actually distinguish democracy (or polyarchy) from dictatorship, it is not discoverable in the clear-cut distinction between government by a majority and government by a minority. The distinction comes much closer to being one between government by a minority and government by *minorities*. As compared with the political processes of a dictatorship, the charac-

From Robert A. Dahl, *A Preface to Democratic Theory*. Chapter 5, Part IV, pp. 133–134, and Parts VIII and IX, pp. 145–151.© 1956 by *The University of Chicago*. *All rights reserved*. Reprinted by permission of the University of Chicago Press and the author.

teristics of polyarchy greatly extend the number, size, and diversity of the minorities whose preferences will influence the outcome of governmental decisions. Furthermore, these characteristics evidently have a reciprocal influence on a number of key aspects of politics: the kinds of leaders recruited, the legitimate and illegitimate types of political activity, the range and kinds of policies open to leaders, social processes for information and communication—indeed upon the whole ethos of the society. It is in these and other effects more than in the sovereignty of the majority that we find the values of a democratic process. . . .

I defined the "normal" American political process as one in which there is a high probability that an active and legitimate group in the population can make itself heard effectively at some crucial stage in the process of decision. To be "heard" covers a wide range of activities, and I do not intend to define the word rigorously. Clearly, it does not mean that every group has equal control over the outcome.

In American politics, as in all other societies, control over decisions is unevenly distributed; neither individuals nor groups are political equals. When I say that a group is heard "effectively" I mean more than the simple fact that it makes a noise; I mean that one or more officials are not only ready to listen to the noise, but expect to suffer in some significant way if they do not placate the group, its leaders, or its most vociferous members. To satisfy the group may require one or more of a great variety of actions by the responsive leader: pressure for substantive policies, appointments, graft, respect, expression of the appropriate emotions, or the right combination of reciprocal noises.

Thus the making of governmental decisions is not a majestic march of great majorities united upon certain matters of basic policy. It is the steady appeasement of relatively small groups. Even when these groups add up to a numerical majority at election time it is usually not useful to construe that majority as more than an arithmetic expression. For to an extent that would have pleased Madison enormously, the numerical majority is incapable of undertaking any co-ordinated action; it is the various components of the numerical majority that have the means for action.

As this is familiar ground, let me summarize briefly and dogmatically some well-known aspects of the constitutional rules: the groups they benefit, those they handicap, and the net result. When we examine Congress we find that certain groups are overrepresented, in the sense that they have more representatives (or more representatives at key places) and therefore more control over the outcome of Congressional decisions than they would have if the rules were designed to maximize formal political equality.[1] Equal representation in the Senate has led to overrepresentation of the less densely populated states. In practice this means that farmers and certain other groups—metal mining interests, for example—are overrepresented. State legislatures overrepresent agricultural and small-town areas and hence do not redistrict House seats in accordance with population changes; even the House significantly underrepresents urban populations. The operation of the seniority principle and the power of the committee chairman has led the voters in one-party or modified one-party states to be significantly overrepresented. Accord-

[1] "Formal" because whether rules designed to maximize formal political equality would actually maximize political equality more than the present rules is a tough empirical question I wish to avoid.

ing to one recent estimate, there are twenty-two such states.[2] Geographically these include the solid South, the border states, upper New England, four midwestern states, Oregon, and Pennsylvania. Of these only Pennsylvania is highly urban and industrial. Because of the operation of the single-member district system in the House, on the average, a net shift of 1 per cent of the electorate from one party to the other will result in a net gain of about 2.5 per cent of the House seats for the benefited party; and because of the operation of the two-member

FIGURE 1

Popular Votes and Congressional Seats Won: Democrats in the House of Representatives, 1928–1954.

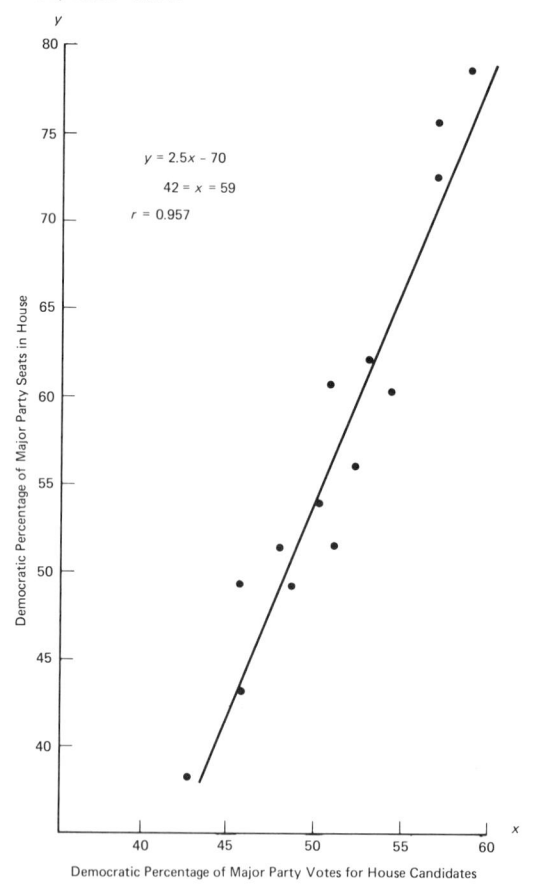

$y = 2.5x - 70$
$42 = x = 59$
$r = 0.957$

Democratic Percentage of Major Party Seats in House

Democratic Percentage of Major Party Votes for House Candidates

district in the Senate, a shift of 1 per cent will result in a net gain for the benefited party of about 3 per cent of the Senate seats. Hence when large heterogeneous groups, like the farmers, shift their party support the legislative effects are likely to be considerably exaggerated. (Cf. Figs. 1 and 2.)

All those politicians and officials concerned with the election or re-election of a

[2] Austin Ranney and Willmoore Kendall, "The American Party Systems," *American Political Science Review*, 48 (June 1954), 477.

President, and hence with the vagaries of the electoral college, must necessarily be responsive to a somewhat different set of groups. Again, the general picture is so well known that I need only enumerate a few points. In general the presidential politicians must be responsive to populous states with large electoral votes; to states that are marginal between the parties, i.e., to the two-party states; to the "key" states, i.e., those both marginal and populous; to key groups in the key states—ethnic, religious, occupational; to relatively large nationwide groups; and

FIGURE 2

Popular Votes and Congressional Seats Won: Democrats in the Senate, 1928–1952.

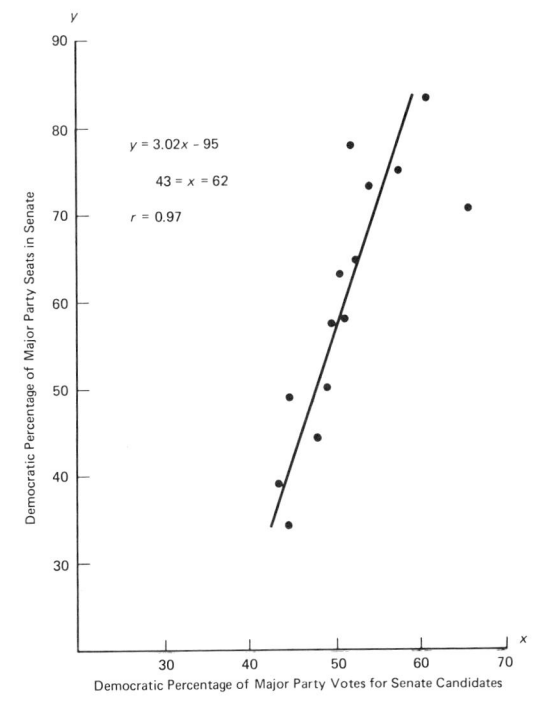

$y = 3.02x - 95$

$43 = x = 62$

$r = 0.97$

Y-axis: Democratic Percentage of Major Party Seats in Senate

X-axis: Democratic Percentage of Major Party Votes for Senate Candidates

to heavily populated urban and industrial areas. A careful examination of these will show, I think, that they are different from, and often have goals that run counter to, the groups that predominate in Congress.

The bureaucracies are much more complex. In varying degrees they must be responsive to both presidential and Congressional politicians. But the presidential and Congressional politicians to whom they must respond are themselves rather a narrow and specialized group. In Congress, typically, it is the chairmen of the House and Senate Appropriations Committees, of the relevant subcommittees, and of the relevant substantive committees. Among presidential politicians, administrators must usually be responsive to the Budget Bureau, to the departmental secretary, and, of course, to the President himself. They must also be responsive to their own specialized clienteles. The most effective clientele obviously is one like the farmers, that is also well represented in Congress and even in the executive branch; sometimes bureaucracy and clientele become so intertwined that one cannot easily determine who is responsive to whom. . . .

This is the normal system. I have not attempted to determine in these pages whether it is a desirable system of government nor shall I try to do so now. For appraisal of its merits and defects would require a subtle and extended discussion lying beyond the bounds of these essays.

This much may be said of the system. If it is not the very pinnacle of human achievement, a model for the rest of the world to copy or to modify at its peril, as our nationalistic and politically illiterate glorifiers so tiresomely insist, neither, I think, is it so obviously a defective system as some of its critics suggest.

To be sure, reformers with a tidy sense of order dislike it. Foreign observers, even sympathetic ones, are often astonished and confounded by it. Many Americans are frequently dismayed by its paradoxes; indeed, few Americans who look upon our political process attentively can fail, at times, to feel deep frustration and angry resentment with a system that on the surface has so little order and so much chaos.

For it is a markedly decentralized system. Decisions are made by endless bargaining; perhaps in no other national political system in the world is bargaining so basic a component of the political process. In an age when the efficiencies of hierarchy have been re-emphasized on every continent, no doubt the normal American political system is something of an anomaly, if not, indeed, at times an anachronism. For as a means to highly integrated, consistent decisions in some important areas—foreign policy, for example—it often appears to operate in a creaking fashion verging on total collapse.

Yet we should not be too quick in our appraisal, for where its vices stand out, its virtues are concealed to the hasty eye. Luckily the normal system has the virtues of its vices. With all its defects, it does nonetheless provide a high probability that any active and legitimate group will make itself heard effectively at some stage in the process of decision. This is no mean thing in a political system.

It is not a static system. The normal American system has evolved, and by evolving it has survived. It has evolved and survived from aristocracy to mass democracy, through slavery, civil war, the tentative uneasy reconciliation of North and South, the repression of Negroes and their halting liberation; through two great wars of world-wide scope, mobilization, far-flung military enterprise, and return to hazardous peace; through numerous periods of economic instability and one prolonged depression with mass unemployment, farm "holidays," veterans' marches, tear gas, and even bullets; through two periods of postwar cynicism, demagogic excesses, invasions of traditional liberties, and the groping, awkward, often savage, attempt to cope with problems of subversion, fear, and civil tension.

Probably this strange hybrid, the normal American political system, is not for export to others. But so long as the social prerequisites of democracy are substantially intact in this country, it appears to be a relatively efficient system for reinforcing agreement, encouraging moderation, and maintaining social peace in a restless and immoderate people operating a gigantic, powerful, diversified, and incredibly complex society.

This is no negligible contribution, then, that Americans have made to the arts of government—and to that branch, which of all the arts of politics is the most difficult, the art of democratic government.

7
Tolerance

Robert Paul Wolff

Democratic pluralism and its attendant principle of tolerance are considerably more defensible than either of the traditions out of which they grow; nevertheless, they are open to a number of serious criticisms which are, in my opinion, ultimately fatal to pluralism as a defensible idea of social policy. The weaknesses of pluralism lie not so much in its theoretical formulation as in the covert ideological consequences of its application to the reality of contemporary America. The sense of "ideological" which I intend is that adopted by Karl Mannheim in his classic study *Ideology and Utopia*. Mannheim defines ideology as follows:

> The concept "ideology" reflects the one discovery which emerged from political conflict, namely, that ruling groups can in their thinking become so intensively interest-bound to a situation that they are simply no longer able to see certain facts which would undermine their sense of domination. There is implicit in the word "ideology" the insight that in certain situations the collective unconscious of certain groups obscures the real condition of society both to itself and to others and thereby stabilizes it.

From *The Poverty of Liberalism* by Robert Paul Wolff, pp. 150–161. Reprinted by permission of the Beacon Press and the author. Copyright © 1968 by Robert Paul Wolff.

Ideology is thus systematically self-serving thought, in two senses. First, and most simply, it is the refusal to recognize unpleasant facts which might require a less flattering evaluation of a policy or institution or which might undermine one's claim to a right of domination. For example, slaveowners in the antebellum South refused to acknowledge that the slaves themselves were unhappy. The implication was that if they were, then slavery would be harder to justify. Secondly, ideological thinking is a denial of unsettling or revolutionary factors in society on the principle of the self-confirming prophecy that the more stable everyone believes the situation to be, the more stable it actually becomes.

One might think that whatever faults the theory of pluralism possessed, at least it would be free of the dangers of ideological distortion. Does it not accord a legitimate place to all groups in society? How then can it be used to justify or preserve the dominance of one group over another? In fact, I shall try to show that the application of pluralist theory to American society involves ideological distortion in at least three different ways. The first stems from the "vector-sum" or "balance-of-power" interpretation of pluralism; the second arises from the application of the "referee" version of the theory; and the third is inherent in the abstract theory itself.

According to the vector-sum theory of pluralism, the major groups in society compete through the electoral process for control over the actions of the government. Politicians are forced to accommodate themselves to a number of opposed interests and in so doing achieve a rough distributive justice. What are the major groups which, according to pluralism, comprise American society today? First, there are the hereditary groups which are summarized by that catch-phrase of tolerance, "without regard to race, creed, color, or national origin." In addition there are the major economic interest groups among which—so the theory goes, a healthy balance is maintained: labor, business, agriculture, and—a residual category, this—the consumer. Finally, there are a number of voluntary associations whose size, permanence, and influence entitle them to a place in any group-analysis of America, groups such as the veterans' organizations and the American Medical Association.

At one time, this may have been an accurate account of American society. But once constructed, the picture becomes frozen, and when changes take place in the patterns of social or economic grouping, they tend not to be acknowledged because they deviate from that picture. So the application of the theory of pluralism always favors the groups in existence against those in process of formation. For example, at any given time the major religious, racial, and ethnic groups are viewed as permanent and exhaustive categories into which every American can conveniently be pigeonholed. Individuals who fall outside any major social group —the nonreligious, say—are treated as exceptions and relegated in practice to a second-class status. Thus agnostic conscientious objectors are required to serve in the armed forces, while those who claim even the most bizarre religious basis for their refusal are treated with ritual tolerance and excused by the courts. Similarly, orphanages in America are so completely dominated by the three major faiths that a nonreligious or religiously mixed couple simply cannot adopt a child in many states. The net effect is to preserve the official three-great-religions image of American society long after it has ceased to correspond to social reality and to discourage individuals from officially breaking their religious ties. A revealing example of the mechanism of tolerance is the ubiquitous joke about "the priest, the minister, and the rabbi." A world of insight into the psychology of tolerance can be had simply from observing the mixture of emotions with which an audience greets such a joke, as told by George Jessel or some other apostle of "interfaith understanding." One senses embarrassment, nervousness, and finally an explosion of self-congratulatory laughter as though everyone were relieved at a difficult moment got through without incident. The gentle ribbing nicely distributed in the story among the three men of the cloth gives each member of the audience a chance to express his hostility safely and acceptably, and in the end to reaffirm the principle of tolerance by joining in the applause. Only a bigot, one feels, could refuse to crack a smile!

Rather more serious in its conservative falsifying of social reality is the established image of the major economic groups of American society. The emergence of a rough parity between big industry and organized labor has been paralleled by the rise of a philosophy of moderation and cooperation between them, based on mutual understanding and respect, which is precisely similar to the achievement of interfaith and ethnic tolerance. What has been overlooked or suppressed is the fact that there are tens of millions of Americans—businessmen and workers alike—whose interests are completely ignored by this genial give-and-take. Nonunionized workers are worse off after each price-wage increase, as are the thousands of small businessmen who cannot survive in the competition against great nationwide firms. The theory of pluralism does not espouse the interests of the unionized against the nonunionized, or of large against small business; but by presenting a picture of the American economy in which those disadvantaged elements do not appear, it tends to perpetuate the inequality by ignoring rather than justifying it.

The case here is the same as with much ideological thinking. Once pluralists acknowledge the existence of groups whose interests are not weighed in the labor-business balance, then their own theory requires them to call for an alteration of the system. If migrant workers, or white-collar workers, or small businessmen are genuine *groups,* then they have a legitimate place in the system of group-adjustments. Thus, pluralism is not explicitly a philosophy of privilege or injustice—it is a philosophy of equality and justice whose *concrete application* supports inequality by ignoring the existence of certain legitimate social groups.

This ideological function of pluralism helps to explain one of the peculiarities of American politics. There is a very sharp distinction in the public domain between legitimate interests and those which are absolutely beyond the pale. If a group or interest is within the framework of acceptability, then it can be sure of winning some measure of what it seeks, for the process of national politics is distributive and compromising. On the other hand, if an interest falls *outside* the circle of the acceptable, it receives no attention whatsoever and its proponents are treated as crackpots, extremists, or foreign agents. With bewildering speed, an interest can move from "outside" to "inside" and its partisans, who have been scorned by the solid and established in the community, become presidential advisers and newspaper columnists.

A vivid example from recent political history is the sudden legitimation of the problem of poverty in America. In the postwar years, tens of millions of poor Americans were left behind by the sustained growth of the economy. The facts were known and discussed for years by fringe critics whose attempts to call attention to these forgotten Americans were greeted with either silence or contempt.

Suddenly, poverty was "discovered" by Presidents Kennedy and Johnson, and articles were published in *Look* and *Time* which a year earlier would have been more at home in the radical journals which inhabit political limbo in America. A social group whose very existence had long been denied was now the object of a national crusade.

A similar elevation from obscurity to relative prominence was experience by the peace movement, a "group" of a rather different nature. For years, the partisans of disarmament labored to gain a hearing for their view that nuclear war could not be a reasonable instrument of national policy. Sober politicians and serious columnists treated such ideas as the naive fantasies of bearded peaceniks, communist sympathizers, and well-meaning but hopelessly muddled clerics. Then suddenly the Soviet Union achieved the nuclear parity which had been long forecast, the prospect of which had convinced disarmers of the insanity of nuclear war. Sober reevaluations appeared in the columns of Walter Lippmann, and some even found their way into the speeches of President Kennedy—what had been unthinkable, absurd, naive, dangerous, even subversive, six months before, was now plausible, sound, thoughtful, and—within another six months—official American policy.

The explanation for these rapid shifts in the political winds lies, I suggest, in the logic of pluralism. According to pluralist theory, every genuine social group has a right to a voice in the making of policy and a share in the benefits. Any policy urged by a group in the system must be given respectful attention, no matter how bizarre. By the same token, a policy or principle which lacks legitimate representation has no place in the society, no matter how reasonable or right it may be. Consequently, the line between acceptable and unacceptable alternatives is very sharp, so that the territory of American politics is like a plateau with steep cliffs on all sides rather than like a pyramid. On the plateau are all the interest groups which are recognized as legitimate; in the deep valley all around lie the outsiders, the fringe groups which are scorned as "extremist." The most important battle waged by any group in American politics is the struggle to climb onto the plateau. Once there, it can count on some measure of what it seeks. No group ever gets all of what it wants, and no *legitimate* group is completely frustrated in its efforts.

Thus, the "vector-sum" version of pluralist theory functions ideologically by tending to deny new groups or interests access to the political plateau. It does this by ignoring their existence in practice, not by denying their claim in theory. The result is that pluralism has a braking effect on social change; it slows down transformation in the system of group adjustments but does not set up an absolute barrier to change. For this reason, as well as because of its origins as a fusion of two conflicting social philosophies, it deserves the title "conservative liberalism."

According to the second, or "referee," version of pluralism, the role of the government is to oversee and regulate the competition among interest groups in the society. Out of the applications of this theory have grown not only countless laws, such as the antitrust bills, pure food and drug acts, and Taft-Hartley Law, but also the complex system of quasi-judicial regulatory agencies in the executive branch of government. Henry Kariel, in a powerful and convincing book entitled *The Decline of American Pluralism*, has shown that this referee function of government, as it actually works out in practice, systematically favors the interests of the stronger against the weaker party in interest-group conflicts and tends to solidify the power of those who already hold it. The government, therefore, plays a conservative, rather than a neutral, role in the society.

Kariel details the ways in which this discriminatory influence is exercised. In the field of regulation of labor unions, for example, the federal agencies deal with the established leadership of the unions. In such matters as the overseeing of union elections, the settlement of jurisdictional disputes, or the setting up of mediation boards, it is the interests of those leaders rather than the competing interests of rank-and-file dissidents which are favored. In the regulation of agriculture, again, the locally most influential farmers or leaders of farmers' organizations draw up the guidelines for control which are then adopted by the federal inspectors. In each case, ironically, the unwillingness of the government to impose its own standards or rules results not in a free play of competing groups, but in the enforcement of the preferences of the existing predominant interests.

In a sense, these unhappy consequences of government regulation stem from a confusion between a theory of interest-conflict and a theory of power-conflict. The government quite successfully referees the conflict among competing *powers*—any group which has already managed to accumulate a significant quantum of power will find its claims attended to by the federal agencies. But legitimate *interests* which have been ignored, suppressed, defeated, or which have not yet succeeded in organizing themselves for effective action, will find their disadvantageous position perpetuated through the decisions of the government. It is as though an umpire were to come upon a baseball game in progress between big boys and little boys, in which the big boys cheated, broke the rules, claimed hits that were outs, and made the little boys accept the injustice by brute force. If the umpire undertakes to "regulate" the game by simply enforcing the "rules" actually being practiced, he does not thereby make the game a fair one. Indeed, he may actually make matters worse, because if the little boys get up their courage, band together, and decide to fight it out, the umpire will accuse them of breaking the rules and throw his weight against them! Precisely the same sort of thing happens in pluralist politics. For example, the American Medical Association exercises a stranglehold over American medicine through its influence over the government's licensing regulations. Doctors who are opposed to the AMA's political positions, or even to its medical policies, do not merely have to buck the entrenched authority of the organization's leaders. They must also risk the loss of hospital affiliations, speciality accreditation, and so forth, all of which powers have been placed in the hands of the medical establishment by state and federal laws. Those laws are written by the government in cooperation with the very same AMA leaders; not surprisingly, the interests of dissenting doctors do not receive favorable attention.

The net effect of government action is thus to weaken, rather than strengthen, the play of conflicting interests in the society. The theory of pluralism here has a crippling effect upon the government, for it warns against positive federal intervention in the name of independent principles of justice, equality, or fairness. The theory says justice will emerge from the free interplay of opposed groups; the practice tends to destroy that interplay.

Finally, the theory of pluralism in all its forms has the effect in American thought and politics of discriminating not only against certain social groups or interests, but also against certain sorts of proposals for the solution of social problems. According to pluralist theory, politics is a contest among social groups for control of the power and decision of the government. Each group is motivated by some interest or cluster of interests and seeks to sway the government toward action in its favor. The typical social problem according to pluralism is therefore some instance of distributive injustice. One group is getting too much, another too little, of the available resources. In accord with its modification of traditional liberalism, pluralism's goal is a rough parity among competing groups rather than among competing individuals. Characteristically, new proposals originate with a group which feels that its legitimate interests have been slighted, and the legislative outcome is a measure which corrects the social imbalance to a degree commensurate with the size and political power of the initiating group.

But there are some social ills in America whose causes do not lie in a maldistribution of wealth, and which cannot be cured therefore by the techniques of pluralist politics. For example, America is growing uglier, more dangerous, and less pleasant to live in, as its citizens grow richer. The reason is that natural beauty, public order, the cultivation of the arts, are not the special interest of any identifiable social group. Consequently, evils and inadequacies in those areas cannot be remedied by shifting the distribution of wealth and power among existing social groups. To be sure, crime and urban slums hurt the poor more than the rich, the Negro more than the white—but fundamentally they are problems of the society as a whole, not of any particular group. That is to say, they concern the general good, not merely the aggregate of private goods. To deal with such problems, there must be some way of constituting the whole society a genuine group with a group purpose and a conception of the common good. Pluralism rules this out in theory by portraying society as an aggregate of human communities rather than as itself a human community; and it equally rules out a concern for the general good in practice by encouraging a politics of interest-group pressures in which there is no mechanism for the discovery and expression of the common good.

The theory and practice of pluralism first came to dominate American politics during the depression, when the Democratic party put together an electoral majority of minority groups. It is not at all surprising that the same period saw the demise of an active socialist movement, for socialism, both in its diagnosis of the ills of industrial capitalism and in its proposed remedies, focuses on the structure of the economy and society as a whole and advances programs in the name of the general good. Pluralism, both as theory and as practice, simply does not acknowledge the possibility of wholesale reorganization of the society. By insisting on the group nature of society, it denies the existence of society-wide interests —save the purely procedural interest in preserving the system of group pressures —and the possibility of communal action in pursuit of the general good.

A proof of this charge can be found in the commissions, committees, institutes, and conferences which are convened from time to time to ponder the "national interest." The membership of these assemblies always includes an enlightened business executive, a labor leader, an educator, several clergymen of various faiths, a woman, a literate general or admiral, and a few public figures of unquestioned sobriety and predictable views. The whole is a microcosm of the interest groups and hereditary groups which, according to pluralism, constitute American society. Any vision of the national interest which emerges from such a group will inevitably be a standard pluralist picture of a harmonious, cooperative, distributively just, *tolerant* America. One could hardly expect a committee of group representatives to decide that the pluralist system of social groups is an obstacle to the general good!

Pluralist democracy, with its virtue, tolerance, constitutes the highest stage in the political development of industrial capitalism. It transcends the crude "limitations" of early individualistic liberalism and makes a place for the communitarian features of social life, as well as for the interest-group politics which emerged as a domesticated version of the class struggle. Pluralism is humane, benevolent, accommodating, and far more responsive to the evils of social injustice than either the egoistic liberalism or the traditionalistic conservatism from which it grew. But pluralism is fatally blind to the evils which afflict the entire body politic, and as a theory of society it obstructs consideration of precisely the sorts of thoroughgoing social revisions which may be needed to remedy those evils. Like all great social theories, pluralism answered a genuine social need during a significant period of history. Now, however, new problems confront America, problems not of distributive injustice but of the common good. We must give up the image of society as a battleground of competing groups and formulate an ideal of society more exalted than the mere acceptance of opposed interests and diverse customs. There is need for a new philosophy of community.

8
Statement of Ralph Nader, Attorney, Washington, D.C., April 4, 1966

Mr. NADER. Thank you.

Mr. Chairman, distinguished members of the Senate Commerce Committee, I am grateful for the opportunity to present comments on that section of S. 3005, the proposed Traffic Safety Act of 1966, over which this committee has jurisdiction.

S. 3005 represents, of course, the administration's proposal to Congress as to how the executive branch would like to have its mission defined in the area of motor vehicle safety. A superficial reading of S. 3005 might lead some to conclude that at last the Federal Government is facing up to the fundamental democratic issue of giving a meaningful and continuous voice to the public in deciding how much safety the motorist is to receive when he purchases an automobile.

A closer reading of the bill, however, indicates that such an objective is in no way required by the bill whose form beguiles its substance. The fact that most of the language of S. 3005 rests on the shifting sands of discretionary authority by the Congress diminishes much the significance of the bill's sometimes encouraging prose.

U.S., Congress, Senate, Commitee on Commerce, *Traffic Safety: Hearing on S. 3005*, 89th Cong., 2d sess., 16, 17, 29, 30 March, 4, 5, 6 April 1966, ser. no. 89–49.

There is entirely too much self-contained authority and determination inherent in administering any large programs, such as those described in the bill, without beginning with the absence of any explicit grant of authority, adequate legislative guidelines and review in the enabling legislation itself. Clearly, the function of the Congress must be more specific, more embracing, and more enduring than a proposed law which can be summed up as saying to the executive branch: "There seems to be a problem here; here is some money to do something about it if you think it is necessary at some time in the future."

Such a casual allocation of discretionary authority, or standby authority, is inconsistent with the urgency of the traffic tragedy which consumes 50,000 lives a year and injures over 4 million people. This year, fatalities have risen by 5 percent in January and February over the comparable 2-month period in 1965—then an alltime high.

In our theory of government, the initiative for legislation rests with the Congress. But as is well known, the complexities of modern life, together with other factors, are leading to a large share of this initiative coming from the executive branch. But the content of such initiative does not, by that reason, have to proceed to finality without challenge. It is with the hope that the Congress will undertake a close analysis of the proposed bill that I submit these remarks.

In the interests of time, I wish to be permitted to supply later for the record some of the more procedural recommendations by way of analysis and amendment which I believe will improve the administration of the law and its effectiveness.

Senator HARTKE. Are these lengthy?

Mr. NADER. No, Senator. Refinements of existing language, perhaps with the addition of a few sentences here or there.

Senator HARTKE. Without objection from the committee, this will be permitted.

Mr. NADER. The following suggestions are offered for your consideration:

1. The legislative history of this act should clearly indicate that the definition of "motor vehicle safety" in section 101(a) includes the protection of pedestrians from hazardous external design of automobiles, and covers those accidents during the nonoperating usage of vehicles such as those occurring in repairing or servicing the vehicle or in the very common "hand caught in the door" situations. Proper vehicle design can prevent many such occurrences or minimize their severity.

The General Services Administration (GSA) experience cautions us to specify the above protections. Although pedestrian protection was interpreted by GSA's General Counsel in 1964 as being within the intent of Public Law 88–515 (the Roberts law), that agency has not written any standards for pedestrian protection —notwithstanding the ease of proscribing protruding ornaments, for example, as some European countries have done.

Incidentally, nearly 500,000 pedestrians are struck by motor vehicles every year, and the overwhelming majority survive, but their injuries are frequently needlessly aggravated by external hazards on the automobile.

2. Section 101(b) should be written to define "motor vehicle safety standard" so as to include (1) publication of the technical reasoning employed for its promulgation, and (2) a statement of the conditions of usage for which it is designed to be effective. The first requirement discloses the evidential process leading to

the accepted safety level and limits the extreme impacts of special interests desiring abolition or weakening of the standard.

GSA does not do this and the constant insistence last year of Ford Motor Co. that the standards be weakened—right up to the 11th hour—scored greater success than would have been the case if the discipline of technical reasoning held sway. I can't explain why Ford is so far ahead of the other manufacturers in trying to present its viewpoint in these areas. I don't think it can be shrugged off with the latest cliche that because they are second they have to try harder.

The second requirement would pierce the customary abstruse manner of writing standards, employed by the Society of Automotive Engineers and others, and allow the reader to know at what speed and for what range of human weight and height the standard was applicable—to name two conditions. Mr. William Stieglitz last week illustrated before this committee how standards could be written by GSA in such a way as not to disclose such severe limitations to the conditions of usage covered by the standards, such as the height of the seat to protect cervical injury.

3. The judgment that there is a prompt need for comprehensive motor vehicle safety standards is one which Congress should make specifically in the legislation. The Secretary of Transportation—or the Secretary of Commerce—should be required to establish within 1 year of date of enactment such standards to be effective on automobiles produced a year later. Such standards should be upgraded regularly through a critical review by the Department. Other functions, now couched in discretionary terms, such as research, testing, and facilities thereof—should be made mandatory.

The accommodation of safety values, long ignored or suppressed by the auto industry, will not come about by voluntary means. Neither the lessons of history nor any of the available means of prediction point to the contrary. To expect that the process of innovation and its utilization for motor vehicle safety will be basically and lastingly quickened voluntarily by an industry mired in technological stagnation is an exercise in self-deception.

The encouragement of a private industry government over vehicle safety, envisioned by S. 3005, is contrary to our democratic values which militate against the corporate state that blurs the distinction between industry and government. This committee, as other congressional committees in the past, will probably be treated by industry to proposals whose thrust will be in just that direction; that is, to obtain a preferential role by the manufacturers in any governmental decisionmaking body. The development and operation to date of the Vehicle Equipment Safety Commission exemplifies this trend.

The safety advertising emphasis of two foreign car manufacturers in recent months is a refreshing reminder of the potential metabolism in the private sector for safety given an upsurge in the quality of competition. Wherever competiton fails to advance the safety level in one framework or another, it is the function of government to fill the gap directly—not by exhorting the auto companies to develop a united front of policy that conforms with the conscious parallelism of a highly concentrated industry. Too much of this latter practice has already been undertaken by the auto industry in the 15-year foot dragging over auto exhaust control systems, an episode presently under investigation by the Antitrust Division of the Justice Department.

Since the domestic auto industry wishes to speak with one voice on this subject, the diversity of viewpoints by the auto companies cannot be presented to the committee. It might be quite informative consequently to have the Congress hear such foreign manufacturers as Rover, Mercedes, and Volvo express their experience, performance, and attitudes on vehicle safety.

4. Section 102(b) which provides for preemption by any Federal motor vehicle safety standard when it conflicts with State or local standards has sound merit in avoiding a tangle of varying State standards. However, care should be taken in more rigorously defining the limits of the preemption so as to avoid uncertainty and lengthy judicial determinations of conflicts in this area. Furthermore, on the principle of keeping open multiple sources of initiative, the States should be contributing to Federal policymaking in the standards developed and in the provision of new ideas and necessities.

While the past performance of the States toward the motor vehicle has left much to be desired, recent activity in New York State, Iowa, and Massachusetts show the value of keeping the doors open wherever possible. States can help generate that residual consumer alertness and vigilance so necessary for the quality of government in consumer protection.

5. In section 103—judicial review of orders—there is no definition of "adversely affected party." Left as is, it is likely to be interpreted so as not to include consumers and other interested groups but only those, such as the automakers, who have a differentiated economic interest. Clearly, insurance companies, automobile clubs, consumer organizations and consumers have a legitimate interest in such standards.

The question of who has "standing" to challenge agency determinations is not an easy one. It is also a legal concept undergoing both theoretical and judicial evolution in the direction of a more liberal, less restrictive, definition permitting greater access to users and consumers. Last month, for example, a decision by the U.S. Court of Appeals for the District of Columbia allowed members of the public at large to challenge renewals of broadcasting licenses by the Federal Communications Commission. As part of the amendments which I shall submit, there will be some suggested guidelines for determining who has "standing" as an adversely affected party.

6. There should be explicit provision in the law for the design, construction, and testing of prototype safety cars suitable for mass production. Comprehensive innovation in automotive technology comes through no more clearly than when embodied in operational automobiles. Prototype safety cars can have many beneficial consequences. They can raise the public's vision of the possible in safety technology and help sharpen buyer demands through the marketplace. They can facilitate the development of an aggregate velocity standard for crash-worthiness, whereby the entire automobile is crashed according to a series of tests and required to meet minimum passenger compartment integrity levels and "g" loads. They can produce the data and comparative measures for judging the relative safety of commercially produced automobiles.

By providing opportunities for feedback through Government and the marketplace, prototype car projects diminish the control over automobile design—"design" is used in the engineering sense and is not to be confused with "style"—by the manufacturers.

Because the industry does not like to share its power over design, it is not surprising, however disappointing, that Karl Richards, representing the Automobile Manufacturers Association at an Iowa auto safety hearing in January, contemptuously described the pioneering New York safety car project as a "silly political move."

7. The automobile manufacturers should be required to shoulder the responsibility of filing with the administering Department the technical performance data showing just how safe their cars are each year. The auto companies will tell the car buyer what the rated horsepower or the acceleration capability of this automobile is, but they will not tell him such important facts as the vehicle's brake stopping ability, glare level, seat strength, dash panel and windshield cushioning ability, door latch and door hinge strength, roof collapse strength, tire blowout and skid resistance, tire cornering performance, vehicle side crash resistance, the flammability or melting threshold of upholstery and carpets—there are about 400,000 auto fires yearly according to the National Fire Protection Association—and the rearward displacement of the steering column under forward crash conditions.

These values can all be given in quite precise terms against clearly expressed criteria. Since the auto companies boast about all the testing they do, they should have the answers to these and other questions for the motoring public. Since about 1 of every 2 automobiles will be involved in an injury-producing accident sometime during usage, such information is vital. The motorist who demands it cannot get it. Nor is the Government in possession of such information, unlike in the aviation field, for instance. What is known, however, is that no auto company has dared put one of its test drivers in a vehicle and crash-test it at 15 miles per hour into a fixed barrier, much less at higher speeds. One can sympathize with their reluctance.

Industry wants safety standards to be technically justified and quite rightly so. But they decline to tell the car buyers about the road-worthiness and crash-worthiness features of their automobiles.

Divulging safety performance information publicly is highly important. If, for example, 20 years ago, the public knew that the so-called safety windshield in their cars could be penetrated at an impact as low as 12 miles per hour (this was the case through the 1965 models), it might not have taken two decades for improvements to be made. Similarly, if the carmakers had to justify the safety of their vehicles, the motoring public might have been spared the visual distortion of the wraparound windshield, the useless cosmetic bumper, the reduction in tire size, the dagger pointed fins and ornaments, or the lethal dash panels, to name a few design hazards arising out of the present system whereby people use their bodies to test involuntarily the risks of the automakers' stylistic creations.

In addition to filing such data about the operational safety and crash-worthiness of their vehicles, the auto companies should clearly indicate in an annual report to the agency just how much progress or deterioration has occurred as a result of an annual model change. Roy Haeusler, Chrysler's chief vehicle safety engineer, acting as a citizen-member of Governor Romney's special commission on traffic safety in 1964, recommended that there be such public reports detailing such improvements or regressions.

8. The enforcement provisions in S. 3005 merit more precise definition, particularly with respect to the extent of having more enforcement responsibilities within the administering department. The brake fluid law (76 Stat. 437, 15 U.S.C., secs. 1301–1303) and the seat belt law (77 Stat. 15 U.S.C., secs.

1321–1323) do not provide the basis for adequate enforcement and such deficiency should not be repeated in this bill. As long as drivers can be fined and imprisoned for negligent driving, corporate entities and personnel should be subjected to similar legal controls and penalties. Again, I shall submit my recommendations in an amendment for your consideration.

9. Congress should specifically require the filing with the administering department of all communications (including service bulletins, confidential releases and information orally communicated) between manufacturers and dealers pertaining to defects and deficiencies of motor vehicles. This suggestion has been made by other witnesses testifying before this committee. I would like to offer a few concrete examples of why such a public filing should be made obligatory.

New cars come into dealer showrooms routinely with defects. Some are minor and others are of a more serious nature. The practice of correcting these defects after the automobiles are sold is entirely too casual, too dilatory and, horrifyingly enough, frequently nonexistent.

Undoubtedly, as a result of the congressional concern over auto safety design, Chevrolet Division has finally launched a campaign to recall all 1964 and 1965 Chevelles and all 1965 Chevrolets with Powerglide automatic transmissions —some 1,500,000 cars in all. The objective is to install a splash guard over the throttle linkage near the transmission housing to prevent the accelerator from sticking after the driver lifts his foot off it. This uncomfortable situation has occurred with these models, as in other models, such as a number of 1958 Mercury automobiles.

Under our primitive form of accident investigation, people can be killed in such accidents and the diagnosis will go no further than a label of reckless driving. People have complained often of stuck accelerator problems in their vehicles but there is no public authority with a clear mission to listen and investigate and remedy.

Elsewhere I have spoken of the necessity to recall all remaining 1960–1963 Corvairs to their dealers for installation of simple components which will substantially improve the stability of these vehicles at a labor and materials cost to General Motors under $20 per vehicle.

Recently, J. P. Connor, an insurance broker in Philadelphia, described an experience that is altogether too frequent:

> In April of 1960 I took delivery of a new Corvair coupe. Just a few days later the front brakes suddenly failed, which caused me to lose about 80 percent of the braking effect. I was able to avoid a serious accident—but only by a narrow margin. I returned the car to the dealer, who "just happened" to have a factory modification kit on hand. When questioned he denied knowing of any other Corvair with brake trouble, but he still couldn't quite explain the fact that modification kits had been made available to all dealers. I wonder how many 1960 Corvairs were involved in accidents because of a momentary failure of the front-wheel brakes? I also wonder why these cars weren't called in for modification? This brake failure was the type which would have been untraceable after an accident. It was caused by an inadequate seal on the drum lip.

To whom could Mr. Connor or John Smith bring his difficulties? We need a governmental process to safeguard the public by uncovering such hidden factors in auto deaths for which drivers now take the rap.

It should be remembered that design or construction defects in a mass production industry are multiplied over thousands of vehicles. The case of the 1961 Pontiac Tempest is instructive. Apart from the poor handling qualities of that vehicle model, many thousands of Tempests that year came with a front cross member design without a skidplate and with low road clearance. This configuration exposed the vehicle to hanging up on elevations in road surfaces such as railroad grade crossings. Dozens of claims by injured people whose Tempest stopped in this manner while occupants kept going against windshield, dash panel, or steering assembly were paid by General Motors, who admitted responsibility for such mishaps.

These "accidents" were mostly at railroad grade crossings where some investigation is made of the vehicle's role. Others killed or injured on streets or highways in such "accidents" were left without investigation as is routinely the practice. Perhaps General Motors should be asked to explain its long-delayed and inadequate attempt to call back these Tempests so as to incorporate incomplete corrections while Pontiac Division was trying to curtail spread of the news.

How many of these Tempests remain entirely uncorrected and their owners uninformed as to the hazard? What led to such a design defect? Costcutting or incompetence? How frequently do such things occur for the various companies? Perhaps a filing of all such defect notices for the past 10 years would yield the kind of detailed historical perspective for Government policymaking as well as provide unsuspecting owners of existing vehicles with some overdue warning.

It is significant to note that some insurance companies have handled these Tempest claims and turned to General Motors for indemnification. These underwriters have not however seen fit to even warn their policymakers. Such is the disease of protective anonymity which has left the motorist without protection even by those in the private sector whose natural thrust would seem to be disclosure. Such is not the case in the insurance industry, however, which continues to behave as the noncountervailing power to the auto industry.

Against such a background, how tragic indeed would it be for section 307 of the present bill, which provides for the withholding of publicly funded accident investigation reports from use in civil or criminal cases arising out of the injuries in such accidents, to be passed as written. A person might go to jail or be denied compensation for his injuries because the fact that a defectively designed stuck accelerator caused the accident was kept secret in a report which his taxes helped fund.

I would like to conclude my statement by stressing the important function of congressional review of administration which must be performed if the law is to be administered and enforced adequately. As a start, Congress should require that the administering department submit to it an annual report which goes beyond the routine nature of such periodicals. It should summarize for Congress its research and development findings, reveal what is going on to continually reduce the gap between the production of knowledge and its application, describe the extent to which performance standards are observed and revised to reflect technological progress, point out the efforts being made to make publicly available the research, fact-finding and experience of the agency for the education of both specialists and the general public, assess the manner in which it is encouraging the flow of inventive ideas from the public and processing them for their utility, and provide a thorough statistical compilation of the accident-injury situation. At present, unlike any other field of mortality and morbidity statistics, the statistical task is left up to a private agency, the National Safety Council—an agency with its own distinct view of the public interest and industry preferences.

A major purpose of congressional review is to give visibility to activities that too often get hidden behind administrative doors where regulator and regulatee soon find a modus vivendi that translates into the comforting tradition of industry groups governing themselves. Examples are abundant in the motor vehicle area, notwithstanding the limited involvement of the Government in this field.

What is holding up, for example, month after month the Interstate Commerce Commission's tire accident study, when its release was expected in the spring of 1965? When will the President's Committee for Traffic Safety be reorganized, as intimated in the recent transportation message by the President, to eliminate the ungainly spectacle of private business interests operating an executive agency which for over a decade has purported to speak for and has exploited the office of the President?

To what extent have tire companies misrepresented their certifications of quality and safety to the General Services Administration as a basis for selling tires to the Government? What accounts for the endemic lethargy and lack of leadership over automobile safety in the Department of Health, Education, and Welfare as well as its obstinate stance toward sound urgings that the method of funding research be reconsidered to take into account the mission-oriented nature of the vehicle safety quest and the action mandate of HEW's Division of Accident Prevention?

Can the research grants philosophy be allowed to hold sway over endeavors crying for the application of directed research policies? Why hasn't the Division of Accident Prevention spoken out, for example, against the growing practice of deluding motorists to pay more in order to see less by opting for tinted windshields?

Why hasn't the Division explained why a $900,000, 5-year grant to the Harvard Medical School in 1959 to investigate fatal accidents was terminated prematurely? The Division has a responsibility to do this to other researchers, at least, who wish to know whether the published information from this study is accurate and reliable. And since the committee has shown an interest in this problem in previous hearings, let me add the following:

I think Congress should look into the entire problem of grants research policy, holding sway in the funding of highway safety research. Let me specify.

The Division of Accident Prevention has patterned its research grants procedures entirely after those used in the basic medical research area by HEW, but the situations are not comparable. Within this grants framework, research is not directed by the Division—not directed by the Division. Indeed, according to an official of the Division of Accident Prevention:

> The definition of the research problem, the delineation of the research design, and the ultimate conduct of the research are the responsibility of the grantee institution [such as Cornell] and the investigator in whose name the award is made. Accordingly, the research proposal is initiated and generated by the investigator at his institution.

Even the proportion of the annual budgeting for research grants that goes to any one field within accident prevention is determined by the uncoordinated interests of the applicants, not by the social demands of the task.

According to Dr. Leon Goldstein of the Division of Accident Prevention, this "proportion is not the result of any deliberate decision of the Public Health Service nor of the reviewers but simply reflects an interest of those who have applied for grants."

I ask, how can the action mandate under which the Division of Accident Prevention is supposed to operate, be carried out under such a casual hit-or-miss policy which leans over backward not to give priorities and apply criteria of utilization and effectiveness of the research supported in order to quicken the framing of effective accident-injury prevention measures. This is hardly the way to speed the flow from knowledge to policy.

Ultimately it is the successful implementation of research findings that provides the public support for increased basic and applied research.

If research works, the public is more willing to support more research. The fact that the Division of Accident Prevention funded studies have been piling up with little interpretation and less integration into policy formation, both for research and action programs, is one reason why the level of support and pay-off of such traffic safety research has been so minumum.

The grants-research policy of the Division of Accident Prevention permits such private organizations as the Cornell Aeronautical Laboratory to exercise—and this is important—to exercise full control over the utilization of its case histories, which is misleadingly labeled "raw data," and the when and the how far to compile its case histories in reports at the same time that the laboratory is receiving supplementary funds for its project from the auto industry. Fundamentally, I think such work as engaged in by Cornell's crash injury research is so controversial and involves such strong commercial interests in the outcome that it should be carried out directly by a public agency.

In addition, no one would think of granting funds in such a laissez-faire framework to a private organization to gather facts about a typhoid epidemic, or an airline crash, or a ship disaster. Similarly, this practice should not prevail in such a survey of the highway epidemic.

Other questions will arise after the bill's passage. Nagging questions such as the possible use by the auto industry of the safety issue to unjustifiably raise car prices or to enter into industrywide agreements that might raise serious antitrust problems. Congress must remain alert to prevent a degeneration of the law's purpose.

There is an old Roman adage which says: "Whatever touches all should be decided by all." The automobile touches all in the most ultimate manner. The refinement of democratic participation in the control of the harmful effects of technology, in the motor vehicle as well as other areas, requires the continuing review by the legislative branch of Government as befits the branch that is closest to the people.

Thank you.

TOWARD ISSUE-ORIENTED POLITICS

In an influential book on American political thought, Louis Hartz contends that nonfeudal America has lacked the extremes of both a "genuine revolutionary tradition" and "a tradition of reaction." [1] The events of recent years, however, have led other political scientists to conclude that the consensus Hartz ascribes to American politics has given way to intense ideological conflict or, at the very least, a greater concern with controversial political issues. On the one hand, some affluent middle-class Americans, concerned with liberal issues and principles, have joined together in "Reform" clubs and challenged what they perceive as the nonideological, overly pragmatic politics of the Democratic party. Other liberal Democrats and Republicans have coalesced at election time to support the candidacies of such issue-oriented candidates as Eugene McCarthy and Paul O'Dwyer. The children of liberal Democrats, primarily youth in college, have turned to more radical movements of the left in order to air their dissatisfaction with what they view as the moral bankruptcy of American life. Through widespread campus disruptions and demonstrations (sometimes violent) against governmental authority on all levels, particularly with regard to the war in Vietnam, student protesters have become a vocal force on the American political scene.

Like their counterparts on the left, conservative Americans have sought to alter the centrist character of the major parties through intraparty activities (such as the nomination for President of Barry Goldwater in 1964) and through nonparty movements (including the John Birch Society and the Minutemen). These ideological pressures may prove to have a significant impact on political parties and, as a result, on the American system of government.

Some of those who have become disenchanted with the degree of speed and access they have encountered in using customary political channels have sought to utilize other vehicles for political influence, including third parties. Traditionally, third parties in the United States have been short-lived, although many of the principles they have advocated ultimately have achieved recognition and legitimacy through co-optation by the major parties. Third parties have usually been built on strong ideological appeals, regionally based support, and charismatic leadership. In recent years, third parties of the left and right have appeared on the American scene, with varying degrees of success. One must ask: Does the significant electoral showing of George Wallace in the 1968 presidential election auger the decline of the two party system or is it simply a customary third party challenge which lacks the broad-based support with which to sustain itself? [2] Will radicals—white and black—of the left be able to transform the Dem-

---

[1] Louis Hartz, *The Liberal Tradition in America* (New York: Harcourt, 1955), p. 5.
[2] A Gallup poll of March 2, 1970 had indicated that Wallace retains support equal to that he received in the election of 1968—approximately 12 percent—thus apparently defying the usual fate of defeated third-party candidates. *New York Times,* March 22, 1970.

ocratic party into their own image or will they seek an independent base of power without the "constraints" of major party politics?

In Chapter Four, Seymour Lipset contends that, because of the difficulty of building durable third parties in the United States, radical mass movements that rely on extremist tactics have often been substituted as mechanisms of political change. Arnold Kaufman analyzes the prospects for a third party of the left, while Earl Raab and Seymour Lipset assess the future of the Wallace party on the right.

In Chapter Five, Jerome Skolnick provides an historical overview of the "Student Left" in the 1960s, while Kenneth Keniston suggests that student rebellion has been the outgrowth of the success—not the failure—of both democratic egalitarianism and postindustrial society. Irving Howe, a member in good standing of the "Old Left," presents a critique of the activities of the "New Student Left."

Chapter Six examines the "Right." Sheilah Koeppen outlines a brief political history of the right, indicating a high correlation between rightist activity and Republican party membership, as well as a recent tendency for members of the "Radical Right" to focus on "real" problems in American society. Ira Rohter presents a somewhat different view of the typical "rightist," indicating that he is likely to be an alienated, distrustful individual with a "paranoid view of society," who is apt to be undergoing a status crisis. Eugene Schneider attempts to place the "Radical Right" in the broad context of American society.

CHAPTER FOUR

THE THIRD-PARTY SOLUTION

9
On the Politics of Conscience and Extreme Commitment

Seymour Martin Lipset

The frequently expressed idea that the United States is a conservative nation characterised by consensus politics has been sharply challenged by recent events. The emergence of aggressive Civil Rights and Black Power movements and the considerable success of the struggle against the Viet Nam War suggest to some that the United States is on the verge of a new era of sharp civil strife. In fact, a consideration of American political history points up the conclusion that moralistic militant mass movements dedicated to attaining their ends through demonstrations and even illegal tactics of civil disobedience have occurred on many past occasions. The politics of conscience which leads men to ignore the accepted means of democracy to secure their objectives has motivated Americans towards a willingness to accept the risk of social opprobrium, economic loss, and even prison.

The long-term successful struggle for social reform, often involving the use of extreme tactics, clearly belies the view that the United States has been among the most conservative countries from a political standpoint. The conservative image, of course, has been bolstered by the fact that all efforts to create radical "third" parties, whether of the left or right, have failed miserably. The United

From *Encounter* (August 1968), pp. 66–71. Reprinted by permission of publisher and author.

States remains one of the few democratic countries without any socialist representation in its legislative bodies. The Democratic Party rightly claims to be the oldest party in the world with continuous existence. Although its opposition has changed format, one can trace a line of continuity among the more élitist-based Federalist, Whig, and Republican parties.

But the fact of partisan continuity in two electoral coalitions has not prevented the enactment of major changes. The clue to the flexibility of the American two-party polity in policy terms has been the relative ease with which a variety of "social movements" dedicated to major reforms have arisen. These include the Abolitionist movement, the large Nativist and anti-Catholic organisations of the nineteenth century, the Prohibition movement, the various radical Agrarian movements of the second half of the nineteenth century, the women's Suffragettes and the Progressive movements of early twentieth century, the multi-million-member Ku Klux Klan of the 1920s, the profascist mass-based movements of Father Coughlin and others of the 1930s, the various socialist and other liberal-left organisations of the first four decades of this century, the McCarthyite movement of the 1950s, the assorted white segregationist groups of the post World War II era fighting a losing battle with the rising Civil Rights and Black Nationalist movements, and finally, the campus-based movement against the Viet Nam War.

Thus, it may be noted that while it has been difficult to build a new *party* in the United States, largely because of the electoral system which presses electors to choose between two major candidates for the Presidency and Governorship, it has been relatively easy to create new *movements*. The politics of social movements as distinct from that of parties creates a sharply divergent image of the degree of stability and instability, and of the ability of dissident groups to foster change. If we contrast the American polity with that of a number of affluent European nations (e.g., Great Britain and Scandinavia) with respect to the frequency and importance of major mass movements, the U.S. is clearly less stable, i.e., gives rise to more movements. In a sense, the pressure for movements is linked to the difficulty in building new parties.

The implications of this distinction between Movement and Party may be pointed up by a comparative look at Canada and the United States. Since World War I, Canadian politics has witnessed the growth of many "third parties." These include the Progressives in the 1920s, who became the second largest party for a brief period, and controlled the government of a number of provinces; New Democracy, the Cooperative Commonwealth Federation (CCF), now renamed the New Democratic Party (NPD), and Social Credit formed during the 1930s; and a host of French Canadian parties which have had transient but significant electoral success in Quebec. The proverbial man from Mars, if given a statistical table reporting on Canadian and American federal and provincial and state election results since 1920, could conclude that Canadians have been among the world's most unstable and tension-ridden people, while the United States electorate is relatively quite conservative and unmovable, except in terms of switching between the two major parties. The only major American third party vote in the same period was that cast for Senator Robert Lafollette in the Progressive campaign in 1924. But such a conclusion could only derive from an evaluation of political stability and conservatism in terms of the rise and fall of ideological parties to the right and left of the two major moderate ones; and it would clearly, in my view, be in error. What limits the potential for new parties in America (as compared to Canada and much of Europe) has been disparate electoral systems. A parliamentary system with single-member districts in which electors do not vote for a central executive, but solely for a local representative permits new movements with ecologically distinct sources of strength (i.e., in occupations, ethnic, religious, or regional groupings) to focus on electing members to parliament, while systems of proportional representation are even more encouraging to efforts to convert new movements or interest groups into parties.

The equivalent of new minor parties in the American context has been extra-parliamentary social movements. Not being part of the normal partisan political game, they are all the more likely to be extremist in their tactics. Untamed by the need to win the support of moderate voters—and seeking to force the leaders of the electoral coalitions to respond to their demands—such movements have often appealed to racial and religious tensions. Frequently they sought to label their opponents as agents of foreign-based conspiracies; or (like the Abolitionists, the Ku Klux Klan, the Southern segregationists, or the current anti-war movement) they have engaged in civil disobedience, employing tactics which violate what they have held to be "immoral law," even if democratically enacted. Some movements, whether extremist or not in tactics, have been radical in their objectives, e.g., seeking to upset existing concepts of property rights.

There can, I think, be little doubt that reliance on extremist methods has played a major role in effecting change through much of American history. By now it is a truism to point out that the United States is "a violent country." What is not so clearly recognised is the extent to which many of the major changes in American society have been a product of violence, a result of the willingness of those who feel that they have a morally righteous cause to take the law into their own hands to advance it. By its extreme actions, the moralistic radical minority has often secured the support (or the acquiescence) of the moderate elements of the community, who come to accept the fact that change is necessary in order to gain a measure of peace and stability.

Thus, the Abolitionists were willing to violate Congressional law and Supreme Court decisions to help Negro slaves escape to Canada. They were ready to fight with arms in order to guarantee that the Western territories would remain free of chattel slavery. John Brown's armed raid on Harpers Ferry played a major role in convincing both Southerners and Northerners that the slavery debate had to be ended, either by secession or by some form of manumission. The women's suffrage movement, as it gained strength, also manifested the depth of its commitment by various forms of civil disobedience: in particular through efforts to disrupt the orderly operation of government by illegal demonstrations (women chaining themselves to buildings, etc.). Prohibitionists also showed the intensity of their feelings against "demon rum" by their efforts to ridicule those patronising saloons, and even by violent attempts to prevent them from doing business. The violence of the first Klan after the Civil War helped convince the North to desist in its efforts to prevent white domination of the South. The violence of the second Klan following on World War I intimidated opposition to nativism and Protestant fundamentalism, and helped pass legislation against non-Protestant immigration. During the 1930s, Agrarian movements brought about moratoriums on mortgage-debt collection (and changes in the banking laws) by their armed actions designed to prevent sales of farms for non-payment of debt. In the cities, the Industrial Labour movement won its right to collective bargaining by illegal "sit-ins" in factories in Akron and Detroit. Authority found itself helpless to remove workers from factories, and anti-union employers were forced to accept unions in their plants.

Ironically, the two major protest movements which upset French politics in 1936 and 1968 both involved the diffusion of tactics which originated in America to Europe. The first factory sit-ins of the 1930s occurred in the rubber factories of Akron in 1934, and spread to Europe. The student use of the sit-in directed against the University itself took hold in Berkeley in 1964, and also diffused to Europe, initially to Germany, but from there to other countries.

Since the Supreme Court desegregation decision in 1954, the issue of Negro rights in the South has stimulated both sides to engage in civil disobedience to attain their opposing moral ends. The Southern white upholders of segregation initiated such tactics when organisations like the White Citizen's Councils and the Klan, and various elected officials (including Governors, police chiefs, and judges) deliberately disregarded the law of the land as enunciated by the Supreme Court and Congress. Supporters of Negro rights—both Negroes and white students alike—often resorted to civil disobedience to counter the illegal actions of their opponents. The tactics of "sit-ins" spread to the North, first in the context of Civil-Rights activities, and later in the protest movement against the Viet Nam War. The current resort to armed violence by some extreme Negro groups parallels, in a sense, earlier efforts by Klansmen and other segregationists.

Most recently, the advocates of civil rights have shown a greater degree of commitment, of willingness to take extreme actions to further moral objectives, than their opponents. To some extent, this reflects a change in the sentiments of the black and white populations. Blacks express more bitterness about their depressed situation than in the past, while white prejudice against them has declined considerably. Even the more bigoted sections of the white population have come to accept the proposition that Negroes are entitled to various legal and economic rights. This shift in the attitudes of the racial groups has brought about a change in "who is more likely" to resort to violence. Racial violence in American cities from World War I down to World War II largely involved actions by Whites against Negroes. Essentially, the political system upheld the position of the white bigots. Currently, the Negroes are on the offensive (although Negroes rather than Whites continue to predominate among those killed), and the political structure is adapting itself to the Negro demands. Negro violence, though condemned by all political leaders, is generally followed by administrative, community, and legislative action to improve the condition of Negroes. Consequently, as in the past, the movement which feels most deeply about its goals, and which is most willing to act extremely to gain them, seems to win its objectives.

The anti-war movement is another case in point. The opponents of the Viet Nam War clearly have shown a greater dedication to their cause than have the supporters. The former have been willing to violate accepted democratic political procedures to gain their objectives. The greater tolerance for anti-war activities shown by pro-war groups which has characterised this war—as compared with the Korean War (the period of McCarthyism), or the two World Wars—reflects, in my judgment, a greater degree of self-doubt about the objectives of the war rather than a greater commitment to the political rights of dissenters. Thus, the committed anti-war minority appears to be gaining its objectives.

Any realistic appraisal of the process of political change in America must recognise that violence, extremism, and the resort to extra-legal and extra-parliamentary tactics, are a major part of the story. Reliance on extremist tactics may be related to two aspects of American culture: the emphasis on the attainment of ends, on one hand, and the strong hold of religious moralism, on the other.

The strong emphasis on an "open society," on achievement, on "getting ahead," has been linked by many analysts of American society (especially the sociologist Robert Merton) with making it an "ends-oriented" culture as distinct from a "means-oriented" one. In the former type winning is what counts, not how one wins. Conversely, social systems with a more rigid status-system, with a greater emphasis on the norms of aristocracy or élitism, are more likely to be concerned with appropriate means; the norms place greater stress on conforming to the proper code of behaviour. The comment by the famed Ameican baseball manager, Leo Durocher, that "nice guys finish last," may be counter-posed against the old Olympic motto that "it matters not who wins the game, it matters how you play." The latter, of course, is the aristocratic code of a ruling class which "won" some generations back, and which, in effect, is seeking to prevent the "outs" from pressing too hard to replace it. The differences between an achievement- and "ends-oriented" society and an élitist- and "means-oriented" one are subtle, and hard to demonstrate in any rigorous fashion, but they are real and determine, in my view, many aspects of life, including the crime rate and general willingness to rely on militant political tactics. American extremism may be seen as another example of the propensity to seek to attain ends by any means, whether legitimate or not.

Moralism is also a source of extremism. Americans tend to be a moralistic people, an orientation which they inherit from their Protestant sectarian past. This is the one country in the world dominated by the religious traditions of Protestant "dissent," Methodists, Baptists, and the other numerous sects. The teachings of these denominations have called on men to follow their conscience, in ways that the denominations that have evolved from state churches (Catholic, Lutheran, Anglican, and Orthodox Christian) have not. The American Protestant religious ethos is basically Arminian. It assumes, in practice, if not in theology, the perfectibility of man, his obligation to avoid sin; while the churches accept the inherent weakness of man, his inability to escape sinning and error, the need for the church to be forgiving and protecting.

The American, therefore, as political and religious man, has been a utopian moralist who presses hard to attain and institutionalise virtue, or to destroy evil men and wicked institutions and practices. Almost from the beginning of the Republic, one finds a plethora of "do-good" reform organisations seeking to foster Peace, protect the Sabbath, reduce or eliminate the use of alcoholic beverages, wipe out the corrupt irreligious institution of Free Masonry, destroy the influence of the Papists, and Slavery, eliminate Corruption, extend the blessings of Education, etc., etc.

The strength of such moralistic pressures can be best seen in the widespread opposition to almost every war in which the United States has participated, with the possible exception of World War II. Conscientious objection to participation in "unjust wars" has been more common in the United States than in any other country in the world. Large numbers of people refused to go along with the War of 1812, with the Mexican War, with the Civil War, with World War I, and with the Korean War. They took it as self-evident that they must obey their conscience rather than the dictates of their country's rulers. And the same moralistic element which has fostered resistance to each war has led some Americans to press hard for those political changes which are in line with their conscience. Such extreme behaviour by moralistic reformers has made the task of running this country extremely difficult. Those in authority have often found themselves in the position of President Johnson, denounced as wicked men who sponsor evil and corrupt policies. Consensus politics has never been an effective answer to moralistic politics. As a result, the moralistic reformers have often obtained their objectives, by winning the agreement of the moderate majority. Outraged by their tactics, the moderates have often given in either because they came to feel that the activists are "basically in the right," or in order to keep the peace, to reduce divisiveness and restore the broken consensus.

Extremism in act, if not in objective, is (to paraphrase Rap Brown) "as American as cherry pie." The contemporary reliance on civil disobedience tactics by elements in the Civil Rights and anti-war movements clearly places a severe strain on the operation of a democratic system, but the American system has survived such efforts in the past. There is, in my view, little reason to fear or hope that the current unrest will topple the established order.

It is important to recognise, moreover, that those who have engaged in civil disobedience and confrontation tactics have not always achieved their objectives. By resorting to such tactics, they run the risk of turning many moderates against them, of creating a "backlash" which strengthens their opponents, and not only defeats them, but helps to reverse social trends which they favour. Inherently, civil disobedience weakens the respect for the rule of law which guarantees the rights of all minorities, of all whose opinions or traits are considered obnoxious by the majority. Hence, the use of civil disobedience as a political tactic is only justified as an extreme last-ditch measure, to be employed when there are no other means available to realise certain moral values. Indiscriminate use of confrontationist tactics can only result in the undermining of the rule of law and the encouragement to all groups (including the military) to take the law and general power into their hands whenever they feel frustrated politically.

10
Strategies for a New Politics: New Party or New Democratic Coalition

Arnold S. Kaufman

Two strategies for radical change compete for the favor of those on the Left who are not willing to abandon electoral activity as the principal focus of their political efforts. Some favor building a new party. Others believe the main attempt must be made within the Democratic party. Both groups think of electoral politics as the key part—but *only* a part—of a more general strategy that includes community action and political education. For example, efforts to mobilize support for the grape boycott, to develop informed opposition to the continuation of the arms race, to build grassroots organizations that serve the needs of poor people—all are generally accepted by both groups.

I favor working within the Democratic party by helping to build the New Democratic Coalition. In this essay I have two aims: to defend this preference, and to describe a larger design by means of which those who share this preference can, over time, transform *The System* by working within it. I direct my argument toward those now involved in the New party led by Marcus Raskin, but of course the argument applies to other such efforts as well.

From *Dissent* (January–February 1969). Reprinted by permission of publisher and author.

I

Modest optimism about the prospects for transforming the Democratic party into an instrument of radical change seems justified. But that is *not* what I have to show. It will be enough to establish that, however difficult traveling the Democratic party route may be, *it is more likely to succeed than building a new party*. In political life, when support for a lesser evil is based on reason and morality, it is also support for the best available alternative.

Those who want a New party seem to suppose that they need only to show that enormous obstacles must be surmounted by others who favor reconstituting the Democratic party. But their answer as to why they think the New-party road has fewer pitfalls is left clouded in mystery. Their faith seems often based on the following syllogism:

> Those who work within a corrupt Democratic party, the Party of Daley, Johnson, and Eastland, are themselves bound to be or become corrupt. But corrupt people cannot effect morally urgent radical change.
> Therefore, only those committed to building a New party have any prospect of achieving success.

The syllogism is, alas, unsound. Those of us committed to working in the Democratic party find the major premise understandably self-righteous. But we also find it difficult to understand how working within a new party will immunize one against such mortal political sins as co-optation and opportunism. For even if people who originally join the New party possess a moral fervor making them impregnably virtuous, the first glimpse of success will bring many others, less endowed with iron moral constitutions, flocking to the new center of power. After all, the gloriously new Labor party of Keir Hardie and Beatrice Webb soon became the party of Ramsay McDonald and later Harold Wilson. And take a sharp, objective look at what is happening within SDS. It appears that something more than original virtue is needed to build an organization that is proof against acquired vice.

Marcus Raskin and others began their efforts to build a New party some months before the Democrats convened in Chicago. New party supporters hoped to induce Senator McCarthy to lead their national ticket once his inability to capture the Democratic nomination became clear. Since then the New party has developed to the point, according to Raskin, where it has new groups in 39 states. Raskin does not say how successful these state organizations have been, or how large they are. The impact they had on the November elections was almost nil. If the Senate race in California can be taken as an indication, then Paul Jacobs' one per cent of the vote cannot be considered an optimistic omen.

The political effort made within the Democratic party, in the primaries and in national, state, and local conventions, has meanwhile achieved some significant results. Lyndon Johnson was forced to commit self-regicide. A politically organized electoral pressure has constrained further escalation of the war. Hundreds of delegates at the Democratic national convention forced meaningful concessions and gave the nation a sense of liberal ferment. But the main goal, nomination of a suitable Presidential candidate, was lost.

During this fight a wedge of insurgency was driven deep into established party power in well over half the states. Young, intelligent, morally committed leaders emerged from the struggle: Julian Bond, Channing Phillips, Al Lowenstein, Don

Peterson, Dave Hoeh, John Cashin, Paul Schrade, Jack Gore, Rudy Ortiz, and Adam Walinsky, to mention only a few. Some have achieved national stature.

These men are all members of the National Steering Committee of the New Democratic Coalition—a coalition of forces founded during the waning hours of the Chicago debacle. In Minneapolis in October, about 250 leaders of the Democratic insurgency from more than 40 states met and chose a temporary steering committee—almost half of whose members are from the minority and youth communities. State organizations now exist in 19 states; and another 8 or 9 are being formed. In many states groups loosely affiliated with NDC have made substantial inroads into established Party power.

I mention a few admittedly modest successes to indicate that NDC is past the drawing-board stage. It is a growing, partially-organized segment of that national constituency to which the Democratic party must appeal if it is again to win electoral victories in major states and at the national level.

Against this background of accomplishment, consider the obstacles the New party must surmount before it can build a base of power in order to have a hope of carrying out its program of radical change. A New party that lacks the preponderant support of black Americans is politically absurd. And there is no evidence that this organization can induce the enormous majority of black citizens to identify with it. It is true that outside those areas in which registration has sharply risen in recent years, the black vote fell far below what it had been in 1964. This certainly indicates some lack of enthusiasm for the Democratic party. Yet those who did go to the polls voted for Humphrey by huge majorities. Few ballots were cast for Dick Gregory and Eldridge Cleaver. Almost every important black leader endorsed, even if often with reluctance, the Democratic Presidential candidate. The evidence that black Americans, despite their distrust, still identify with the Democratic party is overwhelming. It seems clear that, like it or not, black Americans voted and will continue to vote for "lesser evils" nominated by the Democratic party.

In defending his idea of a New party, Raskin makes much of the fact that there has been a vast increase in the number of political independents. This is true. More than 50 million qualified voters failed to go to the polls in November. Most of these Americans, and millions of others as well, are indifferent to politics or turned off by the major parties. But Raskin deludes himself when he claims that they are ripe for involvement in the New party. Most of the independents are not radical. Most are likely to be satisfied by rejuvenated Republican or Democratic parties. Under Nixon, the Republican party is almost certain to tend a bit leftward. And Democratic insurgents have already provided the Democratic party with a more exciting image than it had during the Johnson Administration. This last may not mean much in policy terms. It certainly will not mean much if genuine radicals disdain Democratic party activity. But the point I am making—that Raskin and his friends delude themselves if they think the presence of large numbers of independent voters makes their New party effort viable—is not affected even if the new Democratic insurgency fails to have a significant impact on Democratic party programs.

Moreover, the NDC is better able than the New party to attract those independents who are potentially militant. Why? Principally because it will use, without self-consciousness, the moral rhetoric of liberalism—a rhetoric that still evokes an affirmative response among most of those to whom an appeal must be made.

For the NDC views itself as a custodian of authentic liberal values. By contrast, a large part of the New party's claim to newness is based precisely on its rejection of the language and tradition of American liberalism. Whether this judgment is morally right or wrong, it does have adverse political effects.

I want, however, to emphasize that, taken seriously, liberal ideals can have an explosive impact on policy. Just suppose due process of law, democracy, fundamental human rights, and more generally the conditions of a dignified human existence were seriously instituted within American industry. The result must be to transform property relationships, forms of industrial control, and basic conditions of work. The pursuit of private profit could not remain the controlling consideration which, despite all public-relations chatter to the contrary, it continues to be within American industrial life—as Michael Harrington, a member of the National Steering Committee of the NDC, skilfully explains in *Toward a Democratic Left*.

The New party is not now able to point to any significant national leaders, with the exception of Dr. Benjamin Spock. By contrast, in addition to those already mentioned, the NDC has a host of young, vital, nationally prominent leaders, as well as many well-known within constituent state and national groups. Besides Phillips, Bond, and Cashin, Congressman John Conyers and Tom Bradley of Los Angeles have accepted invitations to join the National Steering Committee. Albert Pena of Texas and Bert Corona of California are among its Spanish-speaking representatives. Sam Brown, leader of McCarthy's youth cadres, and David Borden, a co-leader of the Kennedy youth movement, are aboard. State leaders like Zolton Ferency of Michigan, Daniel Gaby of New Jersey, George Brown and Donald Edwards of California, and George Williams of Colorado identify with the NDC. Senators McCarthy, McGovern, and Kennedy are friendly.

But it is important to emphasize that the NDC is no man's political property. Its commitments are to values and issues; and it will actively work only for those who firmly support core commitments. The NDC means to be done with the kind of politics that makes loyalty to a candidate or a party take precedence over loyalty to moral commitments.

A salient fact in this discussion is that in those states where a deep wedge has already been driven into the base of established party power, Democratic insurgents will simply refuse a call to a New party. In California, Michigan, Wisconsin, New Mexico, New Hampshire, Washington, and Alabama, radical insurgents will not willingly squander what they have gained in recent months and years. Nor should they abandon gains agonizingly wrung from prevailing centers of power unless there is an absolutely decisive case in favor of doing so. Here we come to what many within the New party regard precisely their decisive claim. They argue that the Democratic party can never become sufficiently radical to cope with society's urgent needs. This is so because great concentrations of corporate power absolutely bar the way to radical change; and it is impossible to transform the existing system, within which the Democratic party is an integral component, in ways essential to mounting an effective assault on those centers of corporate power. New party advocates believe that those who think otherwise delude themselves.

While not clearly identified with the New party, Christopher Lasch has expressed an essential part of this analysis when he proclaimed that "as a social philosophy, liberalism is dead." He derives this remarkable conclusion from his assumption that liberalism's core values are "self-reliance, sexual self-discipline, ambition, acquisition, and accomplishment," which, he believes, "have come to be embodied in a social order resting on imperialism, elitism, racism, and inhuman acts of technological destruction." Having thus defined liberalism in terms of a certain kind of bourgeois culture, Lasch has little difficulty showing that liberalism, *so defined*, is incompetent to provide a philosophical basis for reconstructing that society. But his criticism succeeds only by ignoring what those who identify themselves as radical liberals are saying and doing.

Part of the explanation for this is the tendency of New party supporters to identify American liberalism with the Old Coalition that kept the Democratic party in power for some 35 years. Now Lasch, Raskin, and others are absolutely right when they claim that an Old Politics based on the Old Coalition has no chance of assaulting basic corporate power effectively. And they are also correct in claiming that unless corporate power is successfully challenged, radical change cannot be fashioned. So, if the choice between a New party and the Old Politics exhausts the possibilities, then those who are unwilling to lapse into political quiescence would have no choice but to try to build a New party whatever the odds.

But this argument begs the very point at issue; whether there is a viable, intermediate alternative. For from the legitimate claim that the Old Politics cannot succeed, it does not follow that a New Politics requires a New Party.

Quite the reverse. Consider the issue concretely. In order to make radical institutional change we shall have to master corporate behemoths like General Motors, AT&T, Boeing, the U.S. armed forces, and so on. Now how is one to bring these vast concentrations of corporate power under some kind of humane control? Sloganizing about revolution, guerrilla assaults, participatory democracy, or even "autonomous enclaves of socialism in the ghettos and elsewhere" (Lasch) will not do it. There is a need to gain control of the only concentration of corporate power that is greater and more legitimate than the ones inimical to liberal values: the federal government.

And if one acknowledges, as both Lasch and Raskin do, that revolutionary effort must fail; that to propose it now is a fraud or delusion, then there exists only one route to federal power: electoral activity.[1] Now I hope I have shown that in comparison with the NDC, the New party suffers enormous electoral disabilities. There is then little reason for going the New party route. It is not that New party people are too radical; they are not radical enough. Or more precisely, they abandon a *radicalism of aims* for the sake of a *radicalism of militancy* —a self-indulgence that those suffering the chronic evils of American life can ill afford. An authentic radicalism does not dismiss unpleasant institutional facts by wishing them away.

---

[1] There are those who, like Stokely Carmichael and John Gerassi, wait for the oppressed in the Third World to throw off the shackles of economic imperialism, thereby plunging the American economy into collapse. The resulting disorder, they reason, will make it possible to mount an effective revolutionary movement. Quite independently of the morality of such a strategy, it is based on wish, not fact. In this connection Michael Harrington again offers a devastating critique. See chapters VII and VIII of his *Toward a Democratic Left*.

II

Let me remind the reader of what I emphasized at the beginning. Working within the Democratic party is the principal part, but *only* a part, of a total strategy for radical change. Keeping this in mind, what is the New Coalition's optimal course?

The first and most important task is to build an organized, new coalition of forces within the Democratic party. The Old Coalition failed, and must fail, because it is unresponsive to emerging interests and concerns, and because the more powerful segments of the Old Coalition (especially the unions) have traditionally tended to use the electoral power of black Americans, Spanish-speaking Americans, poor whites, and other politically disabled groups rather than involving them as full partners and promoting their claims for justice.

The principle of participation based on balanced involvement in leadership must therefore be guaranteed. At the Minneapolis NDC meeting a plan of organization was accepted that gave minority caucuses the right to designate representatives of their own choice, and in what they acknowledged were adequate numbers, to the National Steering Committee. Again, a balance was struck among those who supported different candidates in the various primary campaigns, and who represent various constituency components of the New Coalition. At the first meeting of the Steering Committee, this approach was underlined by a resolution to guarantee that additional members will be designated from state organizations as they develop in a balanced way, and from national constituency groups like students, farmers, poor whites, and so on. These representatives are to be chosen, whenever feasible, by the groups themselves.

The Coalition must be organized at every relevant political level: municipal, state, and national. It is vital that any national effort be based solidly on grass-roots work in towns, cities, counties, Congressional districts, and states. For reasons I will develop in a moment, it would be unfortunate if NDC were to become a federation of principalities. It needs to be a truly *national* organization. But its prospects depend on its remaining in touch with, servicing, and helping to organize at grass-root levels. Basic as local organization is, the country needs urgently a potent national group dedicated to radical institutional change.

A national organization will provide the appropriate frame of organization for national constituency groups that have traditionally been denied effective power and participation in the Democratic party. These groups have interests that transcend geographic divisions. They range from liberal academicians who are sick of the ways in which our cultural and moral life are corrupted, to American Indians who eke out livings on reservations. They include Spanish-speaking Americans, members of the peace movement, clergymen who think that religion has more than a passing moral interest in chronic social ills, women who refuse to send their boys to fight in unjust wars, and so on. But two groups are particularly important components of the New Coalition: black Americans and college students.

Black Americans make up the largest oppressed segment of American society. Suffering the consequences *now* of a fantastically unjust distribution of resources, they cannot afford a politics of pure conscience and futuristic goals. Only the affluent can think and act exclusively in such terms. That is why black Americans voted by overwhelming majorities for Humphrey, despite profound reservations and distrust. That is why there is little reasonable basis for expecting them to act otherwise in the future.

By contrast student militants are often the materially secure offspring of prosperous parents. They know in their gut the spiritual impoverishment that certain forms of affluence breed. They seek to live an authentic life; lacking inhibiting investment in family and career, they are prepared to act on behalf of great moral issues without the barrier of prudent self-interest. Students, more than any others, can save us all from unwarranted accommodation for the sake of comfort and career. They constantly remind us how often material prosperity and social success can contaminate man's powers of critical thought.

There is a tension between the demands typically made, the vision typically expressed by black people and by militant students. It is a healthy tension, one that is essential for the New Coalition. The one reminds us that there is suffering here and now, that every sacrifice made for the sake of millennial aspirations is a sacrifice of *somebody*. The other reminds us that there exists a future moral prospect whose achievement depends on assaulting basic institutional structures, that if we focus too completely on the here and now we may squander the chances for a qualitatively better tomorrow. No social movement that fails to grapple with the tension embodied in these two forces can hope to retain both integrity and effectiveness.

Beyond the concern for involving militant students is the fact that 55 percent of all high school graduates are going to college now. According to Lou Harris, this year the college educated account for 28 percent of the electorate. In 1972 they will come to over 35 percent, and by 1976 they will make up over 40 percent of all voters. Basing his assessment on polling data, Harris claims,

> The mark of this affluent group is that it is committed to change. These dominantly white people are in favor of open housing, in favor of accommodation with the Communist nations and for compromise in Vietnam, and are highly tolerant of student, hippie, and antiwar demonstrators, as well as boys with long hair and girls with short skirts.

In brief, a conscience constituency based on the college educated will soon become a numerically potent segment of the voting public. Hence, college students must become an essential component of the NDC, not only because their relative degree of moral freedom is needed to keep us all honest, but also for the political reasons that they are large in numbers, energy, and potential resources.

To expand its national constituency, the New Coalition must maintain openings to Right and Left. And it must work vigorously to develop relations of trust and commitment among those who are only loosely, and suspiciously, tied to its organization and program. There are two intermeshing ways by which best to accomplish this task: community organization and political education.

One way of winning the trusting allegiance of the poor, the alienated, the racial minorities is by supporting and engaging in meaningful community action. A wildcat strike sparked by inhuman conditions of work, a grape boycott, or a Poor Peoples' campaign are all actions that result quite naturally from conditions of oppression. This means for the NDC not only programs and lobbying, not only electoral activity for candidates who care, but also direct action on picket lines, sit-ins, and mass demonstrations. We must be with those who compose our coalition in body as well as spirit. This is a lesson militant students have been learning. We should learn from them. Only if one is perceived as *caring* will he be trusted. And only if he actually *cares*, will he be perceived as caring. And only if one *acts* at some cost or risk to self when there is tactical justification for doing so, can one be sure that he really cares.

Political education should be an important part of everything we do. The National Steering Committee has established a National Priorities Committee charged with developing program, priorities, and research necessary to develop our case with reason and effectiveness. Potentially it has a vast human resource at its disposal: intellectuals and writers, but also the resources of sympathetic peace, civil liberties, and civil rights groups.

Of very great importance is the NDC's relationship to the trade union movement. Too many radicals are prepared to write the unions off as bastions of conservatism and reaction. No judgment could be less discriminating. One of NDC's co-chairmen, Paul Schrade, is an elected regional director for the UAW. He as well as hundreds of other trade-union leaders sympathize with our cause. For one thing, many unions were shaken by the amount of Wallace support within their membership. Though the tide was reversed, in large part because of unstinting trade-union efforts, they recognize that there is a vast third of the nation who are not poor yet have legitimate grievances that too few seem to care about. If the NDC can articulate the discontents of the "affluent poor," can develop programs of amelioration, can convince them that they are not the forgotten men of American political life, it can earn the support of many union members.

Finally, let me review the relationship between the NDC and the New party. Just as it is quite predictable that most people will not go the New party route, so it is certain that many will. Those who choose that road are generally good and dedicated people. A New party as a minor element in a broad strategy for change can serve positive functions. It would help keep many who will otherwise drop out relevant to the political process. It will provide an additional and salutary pressure from the Left. In some cases, as recently in my own community of Ann Arbor, it can put someone on the ballot when the major parties utterly fail to provide a reasonable choice of candidates. And it can, merely by existing and functioning, provide a fall-back position should the NDC's effort to work within The System fail.

From this perspective, the NDC should regard a relatively small New party—one that does not constitute an undue drain on potential membership and resources—as a potential ally when matters of common concern arise. The danger, and I really do not regard it as a significant one, is that a New party will drain away so many good and resourceful people that its prediction that the NDC must fail will be self-fulfilling. And if that happens, the darker forces of American life, not the New party, are bound to be the chief beneficiaries.

Can the New Democratic Coalition succeed? New party supporters do well to remind those of us committed to the other alternative that the effort will not be easy, and will not be completed in a day or a year. It will take many years, probably generations, of hard and diligent work. But we must not permit knowledge of the difficulties to breed despair that cuts the nerve of our effort. For the will to believe we can succeed is itself one of the important conditions of success.

11
The Wallace Whitelash

Seymour Martin Lipset
Earl Raab

The American Independent Party of George C. Wallace brought together in 1968 almost every right-wing extremist group in the country, and undoubtedly recruited many new activists for the rightist cause. Today many of the state parties organized under his aegis have formal legal status and have announced that they intend to nominate candidates for state and local office during the next few years in an effort to build the party. George Wallace himself has sent out a clear signal that he has plans for the future. He has begun to mail the *George Wallace Newsletter* monthly to a mailing list of over one million names which had been assembled during the election. The old address for Wallace activities was Box 1968, Montgomery, Alabama. It is now Box 1972.

The effort to maintain and build the party, however, faces the perennial problem of ideological extremist movements—splits among its supporters. Even during the 1968 campaign, sharp public divisions over local vs. national control occurred in a number of states, usually because complete control over the finances and

From *TRANS-action* (December 1969), pp. 23–25. Copyright © 1969 by *TRANS-action*. Reprinted by permission of publisher and authors. This article is excerpted from Lipset and Raab, *The Politics of Unreason: Right-Wing Extremism in America 1790–1970* (New York: Harper & Row, 1970).

conduct of the party's work was kept in the hands of coordinators directly appointed by Wallace and responsible to the national headquarters in Montgomery. In some states, two separate organizations existed, both of which endorsed the Wallace candidacy but attacked each other as too radical. Since the 1968 election, two competing national organizations have been created, and again each is attacking the other as extremist.

The group directly linked to Wallace has had two national conventions. The first, held in Dallas in early February, attracted 250 delegates from 44 states and set up a group known as The Association of George C. Wallace Voters. The Dallas meeting was attended by a number of top Wallace aides, including Robert Walter, who represents Wallace in California; Tom Turnipseed, a major figure in the Wallace presidential effort since it started; Dan Smoot, the right-wing radio commentator; and Kent Courtney, the editor of the *Conservative Journal*. The same group met again on May 3 and 4 in Cincinnati, and formally established a new national party to be called The American Party. A Virginian, T. Coleman Andrews, long active on the ultraconservative front, was chosen as chairman. Wallace gave his personal blessing to the new party and its officers. One of his Montgomery aides, Taylor Hardin, who maintains a national office with 20 employees in Montgomery, indicated that the party would have a considerable degree of "central control."

The competing national group met in Louisville on February 22, 1969, and established a new national conservative party to be composed largely of autonomous state parties. As if to emphasize the extent to which it fostered local control, this organization called itself "The National Committee of the Autonomous State Parties, known as the American Independent Party, American Party, Independent Party, Conservative Party, Constitutional Party." This group, or constellation of groups, was united in its opposition to domination by Wallace and his Montgomery aides. Although the former candidate received compliments at the convention, the delegates were much more concerned with building a movement that was not limited to his supporters in 1968. The national chairman of the new group, William K. Shearer of California, editor of the *California Statesman*, had already broken with Wallace during the campaign on the issue of local autonomy. At the Louisville convention, Shearer said:

> Governor Wallace has not shown any interest in a national party apart from a personal party. A candidate properly springs from the party and not the party from the candidate. The party should not be candidate-directed. While we have great respect for Mr. Wallace, we do not think there should be a candidate-directed situation. We want our party to survive regardless of what Mr. Wallace does.

The Shearer group also appears to be more conservative on economic issues than the Wallace-dominated one. During the convention, Wallace was criticized for being "too liberal" for his advocacy during the campaign of extended social security and farm parity prices.

The leaders of each faction claim that the other includes extremists. Robert Walters attacked Shearer's group as composed of "radicals and opportunists" and as having "a pretty high nut content." Shearer, on the other hand, has said that he finds many in the Wallace-dominated party "not too savory."

The publications of the competing groups indicate that each is supported by

114   The Third-Party Solution

viable segments of the 1968 party. The Shearer National Committee, however, is clearly much weaker financially, since the Wallace national group retained a considerable sum from the 1968 campaign for future activities. It is also unlikely that they can attract many Wallace voters against the opposition of the candidate. The competition for support, however, does give each group an immediate function; and both national organizations appear to be busy holding state and local conventions designed to win over those who were involved in the presidential campaign.

It is difficult to tell how much support the American Party retains. Early in 1969 the party ran a candidate in a special election for Congress in Tennessee's Eighth District. Wallace ran first in this district in the presidential race, but the AIP congressional candidate, William Davis, ran a bad second to the Democrat. The AIP secured 16,319 votes (25 percent) in the congressional race, compared to 32,666 for the Democrat and 15,064 for the Republican. Wallace himself took an active part in the campaign, making speeches for Davis, but he was clearly unable to transfer his presidential support to his follower.

While Davis's showing in Tennessee was fairly respectable, another AIP by-election candidate, Victor Cherven, who ran for the state senate in Contra Costa County in California in late March, secured only 329 out of the 146,409 votes cast. Cherven even ran behind two other minor party nominees. In mid-June, in a by-election for a seat in the California assembly from Monterey, an AIP candidate, Alton F. Osborn, also secured an insignificant vote, 188 out of 46,602. The first effort to contest a congressional seat outside the South failed abysmally, when an American Party candidate in a Montana by-election received half of 1 percent of the vote, 509 out of 88,867 ballots on June 25. Election day, November 4, 1969, produced the best evidence of the inability of the Wallace followers to develop viable local parties. In Virginia, a state in which Wallace had secured 322,203 votes or 23.6 percent in 1968, both rightist parties ran candidates for governor. Dr. William Pennington, the gubernatorial nominee of the Andrews-Wallace American Independent Party, obtained 7059 votes, or .8 percent of the total; and Beverly McDowell, who ran on the Conservative Party ticket of the Shearer segment of the movement, did slightly better, with 9821 votes, or 1.1 percent of the electorate. Pennington's and McDowell's combined total in 1969 only equalled 5 percent of Wallace's vote in Virginia.

But if Wallace's strength cannot be transferred to local and state candidates, most of it still remains with him on the level of national politics. The Gallup Poll, which chronicled George Wallace's rise in popularity through 1967 and 1968, has continued to examine his possible strength in a future presidential contest. In three national surveys in April, July, and September, samples of the electorate were asked how they would now vote in a contest between Nixon, Edward Kennedy, and Wallace. Nixon appeared to have gained from both parties, as compared with the 43 percent he received in the 1968 election. His support remained consistently high, 52 percent in April, 52 in July, and 53 in September. Kennedy's backing fluctuated more, 33, 36, 31, as contrasted with the 43 percent that Humphrey had secured. Wallace also dropped, securing 10, 9, and 10 percent in the same three polls. Thus, he lost about a quarter of his support during 1969, but still retains a respectable following for a new campaign. Wallace's social base remains comparable to that which backed him in the election, and he remains a major force in the South, where he pulls 25 percent of the choices as compared with 5 percent in the rest of the country.

Who *did* support George Wallace in 1968? A detailed answer to that question will perhaps tell us more than anything else about his chances for the future, as well as about the potentiality of right-wing extremism in America.

ELECTION RESULTS

Election Day results confirmed the basic predictions of the preelection opinion polls. George Wallace secured almost ten million votes, or about 13.5 percent of the total voting electorate. He captured five states with 45 electoral votes, all of them in the Deep South: Mississippi, Georgia, Alabama, Louisiana, and Arkansas. With the exception of Arkansas, which had gone to Johnson in 1964, these were the same states Barry Goldwater won in that year. But Wallace lost two states carried by Goldwater—South Carolina, the home state of Nixon's southern leader, the 1948 Dixiecrat candidate Strom Thurmond, and Arizona, Goldwater's home state.

Since the support for Wallace seemingly declined considerably between early October and Election Day, falling from about 21 percent to 13 percent, an analysis of his actual polling strength is obviously important. Fortunately, the Gallup Poll conducted a national survey immediately after the election in which it inquired both how respondents voted, and whether they had supported another candidate earlier in the campaign. The data of this survey were made available by the Gallup Poll for our analysis. They are particularly useful since it would appear that most voters who had supported Wallace, but shifted to another candidate, did report this fact to Gallup interviewers. Thirteen percent indicated they had voted for Wallace, while another 9 percent stated that they had been for him at an earlier stage in the campaign.

From the national results among whites, it is clear that the data are heavily influenced by the pattern of support in the South. Wallace's voters were most likely to be persons who did not vote in 1964, or who backed Goldwater rather than Johnson. The pattern of an extremist party recruiting heavily from the ranks of nonvoters coincides with the evidence from previous extremist movements both in this country and abroad. Wallace also clearly appealed to those in smaller communities, and his strength was greatest among those with the least education. With respect to income, his backers were more likely to come from the poorer strata than the more well-to-do, although he was slightly weaker among the lowest-income class—under $3000—than among the next highest. He was strongest among those in "service" jobs, a conglomerate which includes police, domestic servants, and the military. Of the regular urban occupational classes, his support was highest among the unskilled, followed by the skilled, white-collar workers, those in business and managerial pursuits, and professionals, in that order. The number of farmers voting for Wallace was relatively low, a phenomenon stemming from differences between farmers in the South and in the rest of the country. Among manual workers, Wallace was much weaker with union members than nonunionists.

VOTING PATTERNS

The vote behavior with respect to other factors also corresponds in general to preelection predictions. Wallace was backed more heavily by men than by women, a pattern characteristically associated with radical movements, whether of the left or right. Surprisingly, young voters were more likely to prefer him than middle-aged and older ones, with the partial exception that voters in the 25- to 29-year-old category were a bit more likely to prefer Wallace than the 21- to 24-year-old age group. Religion also served to differentiate: Wallace received a higher proportion of the votes of Protestants than Catholics, a product of his strength in the predominantly Protestant South.

Viewed nationally, however, the pattern of support for Wallace is a bit deceiving since so much of his support was in the South. He carried five southern states and received a substantial vote in all the others, plus the border states. To a considerable extent, his movement in the South took on the character of a "preservatist" defense of southern institutions against the threat from the federal government. In most southern states, it was a major party candidacy. In the rest of the country, however, the Wallace movement was a small radical third party, organized around various extreme right-wing groups. While it obviously gave expression to racial concerns, it also included a number of other varieties of the disaffected. One would expect, therefore, differences in the types of voters to whom he appealed in the different sections. . . .

The variations between the sections are apparent along a number of dimensions. Northern Wallace voters were more likely to come from the ranks of identified and committed Republicans than were those from the South. Thus in the South, a much larger proportion of people who were identified as Democrats (37 percent) than as Republicans (10 percent) voted for him. Conversely in the North, a slightly larger segment of the Republicans voted for him than did Democrats. This emphasis is reversed, however, with respect to the 1964 vote. In both sections, larger proportions of Goldwater voters opted for Wallace than did Johnson supporters. Relatively, however, he did better among the southern Goldwater voters. The seeming contradiction may be explained by the fact that Wallace did best among "independents," and that there were proportionately many more independents in the South than in the North. Southern independents presumably are people who have opted out of the Democratic party toward the right, many of whom voted for Goldwater in 1964 and Wallace in 1968. His greatest support, both North and South, of course, came from the ranks of those who did not vote in 1964. Almost half of the southern nonvoters in the 1964 election who voted in 1968 chose Wallace.

The effect of the social stratification variables were relatively similar in both parts of the country. In general, the better educated, the more well-to-do, and those in middle-class occupations were less likely to vote for Wallace than voters in the lower echelons.

As far as religion is concerned, nationally Wallace appeared to secure more support among Protestants than Catholics, but a sectional breakdown points up the fact that this was an artifact of the relatively small Catholic population in the South. Outside of the South, Wallace secured more support from Catholics than from Protestants. The pattern appears to be reversed in the South, but the number of Catholics in the sample is too small to sustain a reliable estimate. What is perhaps more significant than the Catholic-Protestant variation is the difference among the Protestant denominations. Wallace's greatest backing, North and South, came from Baptists, followed by "other," presumably mainly fundamentalist sects which have a history of disproportionately backing right-wing groups.

Wallace, after all, became the protector of the "southern way of life" and the status of those who bear it, not only for southerners, but for southern migrants to the North. This, apart from education, is one significance of the disproportionate support of Wallace by northern Baptists.

As noted earlier, perhaps the most surprising finding of the polls was the consistent report by Gallup, Harris, and the Michigan Survey Research Center that youth, whether defined as 21 to 24 or 21 to 29 years old, were more favorable to the third-party candidate than those in older age groups. Two special surveys of youth opinion also pointed in this direction. One was commissioned by *Fortune* and carried out by the Daniel Yankelovich organization among 718 young people aged 18 to 24 in October 1968. It revealed that among employed youth 25 percent were for Wallace, as compared to 23 for Humphrey, 31 for Nixon, and 15 without a choice. Among college students, Wallace received 7 percent of the vote. A secondary analysis of this survey indicated that class and education level differentiated this youth group as well. Thus 31 percent of young manual workers who were the sons of manual workers were for Wallace, as contrasted with but 6 percent among nonmanuals whose fathers were on the same side of the dividing line. A preelection survey by the Purdue Opinion Poll among a national sample of high school students, reported that Wallace had considerable strength among them as well: 22 percent, backing which came heavily from members of southern, and economically less affluent families.

This "shift to the right" among youth had first been detected among young southerners. Although various surveys had found a pattern of greater youth support for integration in the South during the forties and fifties, by the 1960s this finding had been inverted, according to two NORC polls reported by Paul Sheatsley and Herbert Hyman. They suggested that southern youth who grew up amid the tensions produced by the school integration battles reacted more negatively than the preceding generations who had not been exposed to such conflicts during their formative political years. And as the issue of government-enforced integration in the schools and neighborhoods spread to the North, white opinion in central city areas, which are usually inhabited by workers, also took on an increased racist character.

What has happened is that increasing numbers of white young people in the South and in many working-class districts of the North have been exposed in recent years to repeated discussions of the supposed threats to their schools and communities posed by integration. They have been reared in homes and neighborhoods where anti-Negro sentiments became increasingly common. Hence, while the upper-middle-class scions of liberal parents were being radicalized to the left by civil rights and Vietnam war issues, a sizeable segment of southern and northern working-class youth were being radicalized to the right. The consequence of such polarization can be seen in the very different behavior of the two groups in the 1968 election campaign.

The indications that the Wallace movement drew heavily among youth are congruent with the evidence from various studies of youth and student politics that suggests young people are disposed to support the more extreme or idealistic version of the politics dominant within their social strata. In Europe, extremist movements both of the right and left have been more likely to secure the support of the young than the democratic parties of the center. Being less committed to existing institutions and parties than older people, and being less inured to the need to compromise in order to attain political objectives, youth are disproportionately attracted to leaders and movements which promise to resolve basic problems quickly and in absolute fashion.

So much for those who actually voted for Wallace. Equally significant are those who supported Wallace in the campaign but didn't vote for him. Presumably many who shifted from Wallace did so because they thought he could not win, not because they would not have liked to see him as president. This is the uneasiness of the "lost vote." There is also the "expressive" factor, the votes in polls which do not count. Casting a straw vote for Wallace was clearly one method of striking a generalized note of dissatisfaction in certain directions. But since total considerations take over in the voting booth, the nature of the defections becomes one way to measure these dissatisfactions in various quarters. On another level, there is the factor of the social reinforcements that may or may not exist in the voter's milieu and are important for the ability of a third-party candidate to hold his base of support under attack.

THE DEFECTORS

In general, Wallace lost most heavily among groups and in areas where he was weak to begin with. Individuals in these groups would find less support for their opinions among their acquaintances, and also would be more likely to feel that a Wallace vote was wasted. In the South, however, almost four-fifths of all those who ever considered voting for Wallace did in fact vote for him. In the North, he lost over half of his initial support: only 43 percent of his original supporters cast a ballot for him. Similarly, Baptists and the small "other" Protestant sects were more likely to remain in the Wallace camp than less pro-Wallace religious groups.

There were certain significant differences in the pattern of defections with respect to social stratification. In the South, middle-class supporters of Wallace were much more likely to move away from him as the campaign progressed. He wound up with 90 percent of his preelection support among southern manual workers, and 61 percent among those in nonmanual occupations. In the North, however, Wallace retained a larger porportion of his middle-class backers (52 percent) than of his working-class followers (42 percent).

The data from the Gallup survey suggest, then, that the very extensive campaign of trade union leaders to reduce Wallace support among their membership actually had an effect in the North. Almost two-thirds (64 percent) of northern trade union members who had backed Wallace initially *did not* vote for him, while over half of those southern unionist workers (52 percent) who had been for him earlier voted for him on Election Day. A similar pattern occurred with respect to the two other measures of stratification, education and income. Wallace retained more backing among the better educated and more affluent of his northern supporters, while in the South these groups were much more likely to have defected by Election Day than the less educated and less privileged.

The variations in the class background of the defectors in the different sections of the country may be a function of varying exposures to reinforcing and cross-pressure stimuli in their respective environments. On the whole we would guess that middle-class Wallace supporters in the North came disproportionately from persons previously committed to extreme rightist ideology and affiliations. Wallace's support among the northern middle class corresponds in size to that given to the John Birch Society in opinion polls. If we assume that most people who were pro-Birch were pro-Wallace, then presumably Wallace did not break out of this relatively small group. And this group, which was heavily involved in a reinforcing environment, could have been expected to stick with him. In the South, on the other hand, he began with considerable middle-class support gained from people who had been behind the effort to create a conservative Republican party in that section. The majority of them had backed Barry Goldwater in 1964. This large group of affluent southern Wallace-ites encompassed many who had not been involved in extremist activities. And it would seem that the efforts of the southern conservative Republicans (headed by Strom Thurmond) to convince them that a vote for Wallace would help Humphrey were effective. Conversely, among northern manual workers, an inclination to vote for Wallace placed men outside the dominant pattern within their class.

BACK TO THE HOME PARTY

Which of the other two candidates the Wallace defectors voted for clearly depended on background. Three-fifths of those who shifted away from Wallace during the campaign ended up voting for Nixon. But those Wallace backers who decided to vote for one of the major party candidates almost invariably reverted to their traditional party affiliation. The pattern is even clearer when southern Democrats are eliminated. Among the 29 northern Democrats in our sample who defected from Wallace, 90 percent voted for Hubert Humphrey. Humphrey recruited from among the less educated and poorer Wallace voters, Nixon from the more affluent and better educated.

The pattern of shifting among the Wallace voters points up our assumption that Wallace appealed to two very different groups: economic conservatives concerned with repudiating the welfare state, and less affluent supporters of the welfare state who were affected by issues of racial integration and "law and order." As some individuals in each of these groups felt motivated to change their vote, they opted for the candidate who presumably stood closer to their basic economic concerns. The data also point up the difficulty of building a new movement encompassing people with highly disparate sentiments and interests.

After specifying what kinds of groups voted for whom, the most interesting question still remains, especially with respect to deviant and extremist political movements such as Wallace's: What creates the differentials within each of these groups? Why, in other words, do some members of a group vote for a particular candidate, but not others? Quite clearly, members of the same heuristic group or class may vary greatly in their perception of the world, and will therefore differ as to political choice. Since candidates do differ in their ideology and position on particular issues, we should expect that the values of the electorate should help determine which segments of a particular strata end up voting one way or another.

Data collected by the Louis Harris Poll permit us to analyze the connection between political attitudes and voter choice in 1968. The Harris data are derived from a special reanalysis of the results of a number of surveys conducted during the campaign that were prepared by the Harris organization for the American Jewish Committee. Based on 16,915 interviews, it points up consistent variations. The question that best indicated differing political attitudes among those voting for a given candidate was one in the Harris survey that asked, "Which groups are responsible for trouble in the country?" Choices ranged from the federal government to Communists, students, professors, Jews, and others. . . .

The findings of the Harris organization clearly differentiate the supporters of the different candidates in 1968 and 1964. On most items, the rank order of opinions goes consistently from right to left, from Wallace to Goldwater to Nixon to Johnson to Humphrey. That is, the Wallace supporters show the most right-wing opinions, while the Humphrey ones are most left. As a group those who voted for Goldwater in 1964 are somewhat more "preservatist" than the Nixon supporters in 1968. There is, of course, a considerable overlap. Since none of these items bear on attitudes toward the welfare state, what they attest to is the disdain which rightists feel toward groups identified with social changes they dislike.

The Wallace supporters differ most from the population as a whole with respect to their feelings toward the federal government, Negroes, the Ku Klux Klan, and most surprisingly, "ministers and priests." Although Wallace himself did not devote much attention to attacking the liberal clergy, his followers were seemingly more bothered by their activities than by those of professors. Although the electorate as a whole was inclined to see "students" as a major source of trouble, Wallace backers hardly differed from the supporters of the two other candidates in their feelings. As far as we can judge from these results, they confirm the impression that Wallace appealed strongly to people who identified their distress with changes in race relations, with federal interference, and with changes in religious morality. It is of interest that the Wallace supporters in the South and those in the non-South project essentially the same pattern. The southern differential is very slight with respect to blaming Negroes, still slight but higher in blaming clergymen, and higher yet in blaming the federal government.

Fears that Wallace would convert his following into an extraparliamentary influence on the government and terrorize opponents by taking to the streets—fears based on statements that Wallace himself made during the campaign—have thus far proved unwarranted. Wallace seems largely concerned with maintaining his electoral base for a possible presidential campaign in 1972. The effort to continue control of the party from Montgomery seems to be dedicated to this end.

THE MOVEMENT IN '72

The existence of local electoral parties, even those willing to follow Wallace's lead completely, clearly poses a great problem for him. Wallace's electoral following is evidently much greater than can be mobilized behind the local unknown candidates of the American Party. To maintain the party organizations, they must nominate men for various offices. Yet should such people continue to secure tiny votes, as is likely in most parts of the country, Wallace may find his image as a mass leader severely injured. He seems to recognize this, and though concerned with keeping control over the party organization, he has also stressed the difference between the "movement" and the "party," describing the two as "separate entities" which agree on "purposes and aims." Wallace is emphatic about this: "The *movement* will be here in 1972. The *movement* is solvent and it will be active." Speaking at the Virginia convention of the American Party in mid-July of 1969, he said, "A new party ought to go very slow. It ought to crawl before it walks. It ought to nominate a candidate only if he has a chance to be elected." In

Tulsa he again warned his followers to move slowly, if at all, in nominating congressional and local candidates. He argued that if he were elected president in the future he "wouldn't have any trouble getting support from Congress, because most of its [major party] members were for the things he's for."

One aspect of the nonparty "movement" may be the reported expansion of the Citizens Councils of America, whose national headquarters is in Jackson, Mississippi. Its administrator, William J. Simmons, helped direct Wallace's presidential campaign in Mississippi, where he received 65 percent of the vote. In June 1969, Simmons said: "There has been no erosion in Wallace strength. Wallace articulates the hopes and views of over 99 percent of our members. This state is not enchanted with Nixon, and Wallace sentiment is very strong indeed." He also reported that the Council, mainly concerned with the maintenance of segregation in the schools, had expanded "as a result of backlash generated by campus riots and better grassroots organizational work." The impetus of the Wallace campaign also had obviously helped. The Citizens Councils remain one reservoir of future organizational strength for Wallace.

Moreover, Wallace has attempted to maintain his ties to other groups whose members had backed him in 1968. The Birch Society's principal campaign during 1969 has been against sex education and pornography; Wallace has devoted a considerable part of his talks during the year to the subject. In addition he publicly embraced for the first time the ultraconservative "Christian Crusade" of Billy James Hargis by attending its annual convention.

In his speeches and *Newsletter* Wallace has retained the same combination of "preservatist" moralism and populist economic issues that characterized his presidential campaign. On the one hand, he continues to emphasize the issues of "law and order," "campus radicalism," "military failures in Vietnam," and "the need for local control of schools." On the other hand, speaking in Tulsa, one of the principal centers of the oil industry, he called for tax reform that would benefit the little man, adding that "the 27½ percent oil depletion allowance ought to be looked into." He argued that we must "shift the [tax] burden to the upper-class millionaires, billionaires, and tax-exempt foundations." Since this kind of rhetoric flies in the face of the deep-dyed economic conservatives among his supporters, such as the Birchers, it is clear that Wallace's cafeteria of appeals still suffers from the same sort of contradictions that characterized it in 1968, contradictions, it might be added, which have characterized most other right-wing extremist movements in American history.

RIGHTEOUS RIGHTISTS

Another problem that Wallace faces comes from supporters who want to build an extremist movement, rather than an electoral organization for one man's candidacy. This can be seen in the activities of an autonomous youth organization, the National Youth Alliance, formed by those active in Youth for Wallace. As of September 1969, the NYA claimed 3000 dues-paying members recruited from the 15,000-person mailing list of the Youth for Wallace student organizations. The group has a more absolutist and militant character than either adult party, and it is much more unashamedly racist. Members wear an "inequality button" emblazoned with the mathematical symbol of inequality. Among other things, the Alliance advocates "white studies" curricula in colleges and universities. According to its national organizer, Louis T. Byers, "The purpose of these will be to demonstrate the nature of mankind. The equality myth will be exploded forever." In an article describing its objectives the then-national vice-president, Dennis C. McMahon, stated that NYA "is an organization with the determination to liquidate the enemies of the American people on the campus and in the community." The tone of this pro-Wallace youth group sounds closer to that of classic fascism than any statements previously made by Wallace's associates. As McMahon wrote,

> The National Youth Alliance is an organization that intends to bury the red front once and for all. . . . The NYA is made up of dedicated self-sacrificing young people who are ready to fight, and die if necessary, for the sacred cause.
> . . . Now is the time for the Right Front terror to descend on the wretched liberals. In short, the terror of the Left will be met with the greater terror of the Right. . . .
> Tar and feathers will be our answer to the pot pusher and these animals will no longer be allowed to prowl and hunt for the minds of American students.
> . . . A bright future full of conquest lies ahead of us . . . Soon the NYA will become a household word and the Left will be forced to cower in the sewers underground as they hear the marching steps of the NYA above them.

The racism of NYA leaders includes approval, if not advocacy, of virulent anti-Semitism. Its national headquarters in Washington distributes literature by Francis Parker Yockey, including his book *Imperium*, which defines Jews, Negroes, Indians, and other minorities as "parasites" on the Western world. The five members of its adult advisory board have all been involved in anti-Semitic activities. Two of them, Revilo P. Oliver and Richard B. Cotten, were forced out of the Birch Society because of their overt racist and anti-Semitic views. A third, retired Rear Admiral John Crommelein, ran for president on the anti-Semitic National States Rights Party ticket in 1960; while a fourth, retired Marine Lieutenant General Pedro A. Del Valle, is an officer of the Christian Educational Association, which publishes the overtly anti-Semitic paper *Common Sense*. The fifth member of the board, Austin J. App, former English professor at LaSalle College, is a contributing editor to the anti-Semitic magazine *American Mercury*.

Perhaps most interesting of all the problems that Wallace will have to deal with is the fact that the national chairman of his American Party, T. Coleman Andrews, has publicly advocated the Birch Society's version of that hoary international conspiracy, the historic plot of the Illuminati. The Illuminati, which was an organization of Enlightenment intellectuals formed in Bavaria in 1776, and dissolved according to historical record in 1785, has figured in the conspiratorial theories of assorted American right-wing movements as the insiders behind every effort for religious liberalism, economic, and social reform since the 1790s. In recent times, both Father Coughlin, the foremost right-wing extremist of the 1930s, and Robert Welch, the head of the Birch Society, have explained various threats to "the American way" from the French Revolution to the Communist movement, as well as the behavior of most key officials of the government, as reflecting the power of this secret cabal of satanically clever plotters. In a newspaper interview following the establishment of the American Party in May, Andrews bluntly announced:

> I believe in the conspiratorial theory of History. . . . [The Birch Society has been] responsible, respectable. . . . [R]ecently, the Birch Society has begun to prosper. People are beginning to see that its original theories were right. . . . There is an international conspiracy.

Though George Wallace himself has never publicly stated a belief in the conspiracy of the Illuminati (he prefers to talk about the role of Communists, pseudo-intellectuals, and the Council on Foreign Relations), the formal organization of his personally controlled national party is headed by a man who has no such hesitation. On May 26, 1969, Wallace formally sanctioned the American Party as the political arm of the movement and said that if he ran for president again it would be under the American Party's banners.

However, while the pulls toward conspiracy theory and toward ideological racism are evident in the background, the logic of the Wallace-ite movement and its future as a mass movement obviously rest on other foundations. S. M. Miller points out that many had been shocked by "the attraction of George Wallace as a presidential candidate to a large number of union members . . . racism appeared to be rampant in the working class." When the vote came, however, racism seemed to have receded before economic concerns. Their disaffection remains nevertheless. As Miller writes, "About half of American families are above the poverty line but below the adequacy level. This group, neither poor nor affluent, composed not only of blue-collar workers but also of many white-collar workers, is hurting and neglected." It is the members of this group that the Wallace-ite movement must grow on if it is to grow, not out of their ideological racism as much as out of their general sense of neglected decline.

TEMPERED EXTREMISM

Whether the Wallace movement itself will have returned to full or fuller electoral vigor by 1972 depends on a number of factors which emerge from an examination of America's right-wing extremist past. Determinative—not just for the Wallace movement but for any extremist movement—will be the larger historical circumstances. The disaffection of the white working class and lower middle class has been noted; if that disaffection grows, and *at the same time* the pressures of an increasingly disaffected black population increase, the soil will of course be fertile for a George Wallace kind of movement. It is the pressure of the emergent black population that provides an essentially preservatist thrust to the social and economic strains of the vulnerable whites. Whether the major political parties can absorb these concomitant pressures in some pragmatic fashion as they have in the past is another conditional factor, which is also partly dependent on historical development.

Wallace, however, is clearly preparing to use another issue in 1972, the responsibility for American defeat in Vietnam. Like others on the right, he has repeatedly argued that if the U.S. government really wanted to win the war, it could do so easily, given America's enormous superiority in resources and weapons technology. Consequently, the only reason we have not won is political: those who have controlled our strategy consciously do not want to win. But, he argued recently, if it "should be that Washington has committed itself to a policy of American withdrawal, irrespective of reciprocal action on the part of the enemy, in effect acknowledging defeat for our forces, which is inconceivable, we feel that such withdrawal should be swiftly accomplished so that casualty losses may be held to a minimum." And he left on October 30 for a three-week tour of Vietnam and Southeast Asia, announcing that he would run in 1972 if Vietnam were turned over to the Communists "in effect or in substance." Clearly Wallace hopes to run in 1972 on the issue that American boys have died needlessly, that they were stabbed in the back by Lyndon Johnson and Richard Nixon.

In order to do so, however, Wallace must keep his movement alive. As he well recognizes, it is subject to the traditional organizational hazards of such a movement, notably fragmentation, and the ascendancy of overt extremist tendencies that will alienate the more respectable leadership and support. During the year following the election, Wallace has performed as though he understood these hazards well. He has avoided expressions of overt extremism. He has attempted to keep his organization formally separated from the fringe groups and more rabid extremists, even those who were in open support of him. In a letter sent to key Wallace lieutenants around the country, asking about the local leadership that might be involved in the next Wallace campaign, James T. Hardin, administrative assistant to Wallace, carefully emphasized that "perhaps of greatest importance, we would like your opinion as to those who demonstrated neither ability nor capability to work with others and who were, in fact, a detriment to the campaign. . . ."

Whether Wallace can succeed in avoiding the organizational hazards of which he seems aware, and whether historical circumstances will be favorable, is of course problematical. But whether his particular movement survives or not, George Wallace has put together and further revealed the nature of those basic elements which must comprise an effective right-wing extremist movement in America.

CHAPTER FIVE

THE POLITICS OF THE LEFT

12

Student Protest

Jerome Skolnick

The Berkeley student rebellion of 1964 sent shock waves through the academic community and puzzled the nation. Today, campuses throughout the country have been rocked by student protest, and the major campus that has not experienced a certain amount of turmoil and disruption is the exception. According to the National Student Association, during the first half of the 1967–1968 academic year there were 71 separate demonstrations on 62 campuses—counting only those demonstrations involving 35 or more students. By the second half of the year, the number had risen to 221 demonstrations at 101 schools.[1] On several campuses, massive student demonstrations have become a familiar and almost banal occurrence. Moreover, there has been a discernible escalation of the intensity of campus conflict, in terms of both student tactics and the response of authorities. Indeed, the early months of 1969 were characterized by a hardening of official response

From *The Politics of Protest*. A Report submitted by Jerome Skolnick, Director, Task Force on Violent Aspects of Protest and Confrontation of the National Commission on the Causes and Prevention of Violence (Washington, D.C.: Government Printing Office, 1969).

[1] Data supplied by Legal Rights Desk, U.S. National Student Association; also, see Richard E. Peterson, *The Scope of Organized Student Protest in 1967–68* (Princeton: Educational Testing Service, 1968).

to student protest on many campuses, as evidenced by the presence of bayonet-wielding National Guard troops at the University of Wisconsin and the declaration of a "state of extreme emergency" at Berkeley.[2]

Further, student protest now involves a wider *range* of campuses and a wider range of students. The past few months have seen the rise of intense protest by black and other Third World students, on both "elite" and "commuter" campuses.

The scope and range of contemporary student protest make certain kinds of explanation grossly inadequate. To explain away student protest as the activity of an insignificant and unrepresentative minority of maladjusted students is inaccurate on two counts. First, as a recent *Fortune* magazine survey suggests, roughly two fifths of the current college-student population express support for some "activist" values.[3] Second, fact-finding commissions from Berkeley to Columbia tend to present a rather favorable group portrait of student activists. In the words of the Cox Commission report on the Columbia disturbances:

> The present generation of young people in our universities is the best informed, the most intelligent, and the most idealistic this country has ever known. This is the experience of teachers everywhere.
>
> It is also the most sensitive to public issues and the most sophisticated in political tactics. Perhaps because they enjoy the affluence to support their ideals, today's undergraduate and graduate students exhibit, as a group, a higher level of social conscience than preceding generations.
>
> The ability, social consciousness and conscience, political sensitivity, and honest realism of today's students are a prime cause of student disturbances. As one student observed during our investigation, today's students take seriously the ideals taught in schools and churches, and often at home, and then they see a system that denies its ideals in its actual life. Racial injustice and the war in Vietnam stand out as prime illustrations of our society's deviation from its professed ideals and of the slowness with which the system reforms itself. That they seemingly can do so little to correct the wrongs through conventional political discourse tends to produce in the most idealistic and energetic students a strong sense of frustration.[4]

Empirical research into the personalities and social backgrounds of student activists tends to confirm this portrait. These studies recurrently find student activists to have high or at least average grades, to come from politically liberal families whose values can be described as "humanist," and to be better informed about political and social events than nonactivists.[5]

---

[2] See the discussion in *Newsweek,* February 24, 1969, pp. 22–23.
[3] *Fortune,* January 1969, p. 68.
[4] *Crisis at Columbia: Report of the Fact-Finding Commission Appointed to Investigate the Disturbances at Columbia University in April and May 1968* (New York: Vintage Books, 1968), p. 4.
[5] Relevant studies of the personality and background of student activists include the following: Richard Flacks, "The Liberated Generation," *J. Social Issues,* 23 (1967), 52–75; J. Katz, *The Student Activist* (United States Office of Education, 1967); P. Heist, "Intellect and Commitment; The Faces of Discontent" (Berkeley, Center for the Study of Higher Education, 1965); K. Mock, "The Potential Activist and His Perception of the University" (Berkeley, Center for the Study of Higher Education, 1968); D. Westly and R. G. Braungart, "Class and Politics in the Family Backgrounds of Student Political Activists," *American Sociological Review,* 31 (1966), 690–692; C. Weissberg, "Students against the Rank" (unpublished M.A. essay, Department of Sociology, University of Chicago, 1968); W. A. Watts and David Whittaker, "Free Speech Advocates at Berke-

The dimensions of student protest must be understood as part of a worldwide phenomenon. At the same time, the American student movement developed in the context of American institutions in general and of the American university in particular. Accordingly, in the first section of this chapter, we examine American student activism in international perspective. Next, we trace the development of student activism in America in the 1960s, giving special attention to the rise of the Students for a Democratic Society; and briefly, to black and Third World student protest. We then consider the organization of colleges and universities in the United States in relation to campus conflict. Finally, we consider some implications of our analysis for administrative response.

AMERICAN STUDENT PROTEST IN INTERNATIONAL PERSPECTIVE [6]

Our understanding of the current American student movement can perhaps be advanced by analyzing some of the ways in which it resembles or differs from student movements in other nations.

To the casual observer it is clear that student protest is now a worldwide phenomenon. In 1968 alone, student demonstrations and strikes paralyzed universities in nations as far apart, geographically and culturally, as Japan, France, Mexico, West Germany, Czechoslovakia, Italy, and Brazil. Indeed, a recent study commissioned by the United Nations estimated that those in the 12–25 age group now number 750 million and will total a billion by 1980. At that time, the study predicted, "Youth of the world will begin to predominate in world affairs.

"World opinion is going to become increasingly the opinion of the world's youth and the generational conflict will assume proportions not previously imagined.

ley," *Journal of Applied Behavioral Science*, 2 (January–March 1966); S. Lubell, "That Generation Gap," *The Public Interest* (Fall 1968), 52–61; C. Derber and R. Flacks, "Values of Student Activists and Their Parents" (University of Chicago, 1967), mimeo; R. Flacks, "Student Activists—Result, Not Revolt," *Psychology Today* (October 1967); N. Haan *et al.*, "The Moral Reasoning of Young Adults" (Berkeley: Institute for Human Development, 1967); Lamar E. Thomas, unpublished dissertation research (Committee on Human Development, University of Chicago, 1968).
[6] The following sources provide a theoretical and empirical foundation for our discussion of the "classical" student movement in "transitional societies": S. Eisenstadt, *From Generation to Generation* (New York: Free Press, 1966); P. Altbach, "Students and Politics," in S. M. Lipset (ed.), *Student Politics* (New York: Basic Books, 1967), pp. 74–93; J. Ben-David and R. Collins, "A Comparative Study of Academic Freedom and Student Politics," ibid., pp. 148–195; S. M. Lipset, "University Students and Politics in Underdeveloped Countries," ibid., pp. 3–53; D. Matza, "Position and Behavior Patterns of Youth," in R. Faris (ed.), *Handbook of Modern Sociology* (Chicago: Rand McNally, 1964), pp. 191–215; E. Shils, "The Intellectuals in the Political Development of New States," *World Politics* (April 1960), 329–368; A. Yarmolinsky, *Road to Revolution* (New York: Collier, 1962); R. Lifton, "Youth and History: Individual Change in Postwar Japan," *Daedalus* (November 1962), 172–191; J. P. Worms, "The French Student Movement," in Lipset, *Student Politics*, pp. 267–279; Walter Lacqueur, *Young Germany* (New York: Basic Books, 1962); Frank Pinner, "Tradition and Transgression: Western European Students in the Postwar World," *Daedalus* (Winter 1968), 137–155. The discussion of current student rebellion in Latin America, France, West Germany, and Czechoslovakia has been greatly aided by conversations with Mario Machado, Martin Verlet, Wolfgang Neitsch, and Tomas Kohut—all active participants in the student movements of their respective countries.

"Young people in all walks of life," they add, "are prepared to march, to demonstrate and to riot if necessary in support of views which may not be those of the electorate, nor of the majority; nor yet of the government." [7]

Conventional wisdom is much given to the view that youth is "naturally" rebellious. We are not surprised when young persons experiment with adult ways and criticize those who enforce constraints, because we know that youth is "impatient." Nor are we unduly shocked when young persons protest the failure of adults to live up to their professed values, since we know that youth is "idealistic." Such views, whatever their ultimate truth, have the virtue of providing comfort for adults and, no doubt, for many young people. Such views assume that young people will outgrow their impatience and will experience the difficulties of actualizing ideals. Moreover, adults who hold these views need feel no special responsibility or guilt over the rebelliousness of youth, since it is "inevitable." And, equally inevitably, it will pass away. As S. M. Lipset has pointed out, nearly every country has a version of the saying: "He who is not a radical at twenty does not have a heart; he who still is one at forty does not have a head." [8]

Unfortunately, conventional wisdom neglects the salient fact that widespread student movements, such as we are witnessing in the United States today, do not occur at all times and places, nor do they exhibit the same characteristics and orientations everywhere.

First, student idealism has not always been revolutionary. Students were very active in the right-wing movements that led the rise of fascism in Western Europe in the 1930s. Far from demanding basic social change, they were concerned with the defense of tradition and order against the threats and insecurities of change.

Second, even where they are oriented toward progress and change, student movements do not always express an autonomous rebellion against the larger society. A good example is the contemporary Czechoslovakian student movement, which is more directly linked to liberalizing movements in Czechoslovakian society as a whole than to any distinct student radicalism.

Third, historically the phenomenon of revolutionary student movements has been primarily a feature of transitional societies—that is, societies in which traditional, agrarian-based cultures were breaking down and modern values congenial to industrialization were becoming influential. Thus, student revolutionary activity was a constant feature of Russian life during the nineteenth century; it played a major role in the revolutions of 1848 in Central Europe; the Communist movements in China and Vietnam grew out of militant student movements in those countries; and, in Latin America, student movements have been politically crucial since the early part of this century.

Such societies tend to promote the formation of autonomous student movements for several reasons. First, traditional values, transmitted by the family, are increasingly irrelevant to participation in the emergent industrial occupational structure. Students are acutely aware of this irrelevance in the relatively cosmopolitan atmosphere of the university and in their training for occupations which represent the emerging social order. Second, although students are ostensibly being trained to constitute the future, more modern elite, it is usually true that

---

[7] Quoted in the *New York Times*, February 16, 1968.
[8] S. M. Lipset, "Student Activism," *Current Affairs Bulletin*, 42, no. 4 (July 15, 1968), 58.

established elites continue to represent traditional culture, resist modernizing reform, and refuse to redistribute power. Paradoxically, established elites typically sponsor the formation of the university system to promote technical progress while simultaneously resisting the political, social, and cultural transformations such progress requires. In this situation, students almost inevitably come into conflict with established institutions.

If any generalization can be made, it would be that student movements arise in periods of transition, when, for example, the values inculcated in children are sharply incompatible with the values they later need for effective participation in the larger society, or when values which are prevalent in universities are not supported by established political elites in the larger society. As S. M. Lipset writes:

> Historically . . . one would learn to expect a sharp increase in student activism in a society where, for a variety of reasons, accepted political and social values are being questioned, in times particularly where events are testing the viability of a regime and where policy failures seem to question the legitimacy of social and economic arrangements and institutions. And more observation shows that in societies where rapid change, instability, or weak legitimacy of political institutions is endemic, there is what looks like almost constant turmoil among students.[9]

In other words, the formation of student movements *in general* may be a reflection of technological, cultural, and economic changes that require new forms and mechanisms for distribution of political power. Political expressions of discontent arise if political authorities are identified as the agents of the status quo. Intellectuals and students are most likely to criticize established authorities because they, more than any other stratum of society, are concerned with the problem of creating and articulating new values. When an existing political order loses its legitimacy, the young intellectuals search for alternative forms of authority, new grounds for legitimacy, and ideological rationales for their attack on the established order. Characteristically (and both the "classical" and "new" student movements are similar in this respect), the emergent ideology of the student movement is populist, egalitarian, and romantic. That is, it justifies its attack on established authority by asserting that the true repository of value in the society is the people rather than the elites; it seeks to undermine deferential attitudes toward authority by asserting anti-hierarchical and democratic principles; it defends the rejection of conventional values by celebrating the idea of free expression and individualism; and it provides inspiration to its participants by emphasizing that the conflict of generations must be won by the young, since the old must die.

This analysis might lead one to expect that advanced industrial societies of the West would be the least likely places for radical student movements to emerge. In these societies, it is said, the move to modernity has been made, and sharp value conflicts are absent; Western nations are not ordinarily seen as "developing" or "in transition." Yet such movements have appeared with increasing frequency in Western societies during the past decade. How can we understand this? The American situation differs from classical ones in that it does not arise from the standard problems of modernization. But the existence of a student movement in America and other advanced industrial societies forces on us the conjecture that these societies, too, are "transitional"—not in the same terms as developing coun-

---

[9] Lipset, "Student Activism," pp. 52–53.

tries, and perhaps more subtly, but just as meaningfully. While educated youth in developing countries experience the irrelevance of traditional, religious, prescientific, authoritarian values for modernization, industrialization, and national identity, educated youth in the advanced countries perceive the irrelevance of commercial, acquisitive, materialistic, and nationalistic values in a world that stresses human rights and social equality and requires collective planning. Politicized young people in the developing countries were usually absorbed by socialist, communist, or other working-class movements, since these appeared to be offering opposition to the old society and culture and to be addressing the problems of modern society. But in advanced industrial societies, the organized left has moved toward integration into the established political system and abandoned its radical vision. In the United States the labor movement became similarly integrated, purged itself of radical influence, and organized radicalism slid into obscurity. Thus it has devolved upon students in the West to reconstitute radical political action and ideology. In so doing, they adopt the populist, egalitarian, romantic, and generational rhetoric and style which characterized the classical student movements in the early stages of their development. But they also reject the ideological orientations and modes of action that were characteristic of the revolutionary left in earlier phases of industrialization and modernization.

Of all the new student movements, that among white American students shows the least resemblance in its origins to the classical model. The French student movement, although it probably has some of the same roots as the American, resembles the classical case in some respects: it is in part a call for modernization, and a rebellion against traditional culture and the archaic forms of authoritarianism that still pervade French society and the organization of its universities.

West Germany's student movement has similar characteristics. On the one hand, West Germany, like the United States, is dominated by giant corporate bureaucracies, by increasing centralization of political life, by an absence of organized and effective political opposition to corporate capitalism, and by militarization; on the other hand, it is also marked by a greater persistence of traditional cultural and political values. Like its American counterpart, the German student movement appeals to an idealized conception of democracy in modern society; it differs in its emphasis on the rejection of the archaic forms of authority and status distinctions Europe has inherited from its feudal past. It is aware that many of the cultural and political factors that contributed to Hitlerism have not been eradicated, while it is itself imbued with a profound hatred of the legacy of Nazism.

Thus the current wave of student protest throughout the world is, in part, the result of coincidence: on the one hand, the student movements in Latin America and Asia continue to function as part of a relatively long tradition of student activism; on the other hand, new student movements in the West have emerged in response to rather different problems and issues. Despite the differences among student movements in developed and underdeveloped countries, however, it is clear that a process of mutual influence is at work among them. For example, the white student movement in America received inspiration in its early stages from dramatic student uprisings in Japan, Turkey, and South Korea. More recently, American activists have been influenced by street tactics learned from Japanese students and by ideological expressions emanating from France and West Germany. The French students were certainly inspired by the West Germans, and the Italians by the French. The symbols of "alienated" youth culture, originating in Britain and the United States, have been adopted throughout Eastern and Western Europe. The spread of ideology, symbols, and tactics of protest is, of course, powerfully aided by television and other mass media and also by the increased opportunities for international travel and study abroad available to European and American students. The increasing cross-fertilization and mutual inspiration which are certainly occurring among student movements are, then, the outcome of mass communication and informal contact. Whatever similarity exists among student movements around the world is thus neither completely spontaneous nor centrally coordinated.

AMERICAN STUDENT ACTIVISM IN THE 1960s

Those who believe that disorder and conflict are unique to the campuses of the 1960s are unacquainted with the history of American colleges. Dormitory life in nineteenth-century America was marked by violence, rough and undisciplined actions, and outbreaks of protest against the rules and regulations through which faculties and administrations attempted to govern students.[10] Although collegiate life became more peaceful after the turn of the century, protest, activism, and collective action continued to be part of college life. The depression of the 1930s and the pre-World War II period of the 1940s were marked by protest, often of a political character. An examination of college and university disruption even during the 1950s provides a notable record of activity.

Student activism during the 1960s appears, however, to have unprecedented qualities. Compared to earlier activism, that of the 1960s involves more students and engages them more continuously, is more widely distributed on campuses throughout the country, is more militant, is more hostile to established authority and institutions (including radical political organizations), and has been more sustained. Such activism seems better considered as part of a student *movement,* something largely unknown before in the United States, rather than as a collection of similar but unconnected events. And although it involves issues of special interest to students, the movement has usually integrated student concerns with political issues of wider currency.

The emergence of such a movement in the 1960s is particularly striking. The ten previous years—despite outbreaks of campus disruption—were notable mainly as a period of political indifference or privatized alienation among students.[11] Campus observers at that time remarked on student conformity to conventional values and private goals. Social scientists hardly anticipated that large numbers of students would become engaged in substantial social action. . . .

The two general phases of the movement—before and after 1965—may be viewed as follows: In phase one, the student movement embodied concern, dissent, and protest about various social issues, but it generally accepted the legitimacy of the American political community in general and especially of the university. In those years, many students believed that the legitimacy of the existing

---

[10] The standard history of American higher education is Frederick Rudolph, *The American College and University* (New York: Vintage, 1965).
[11] See, for example, Kenneth Keniston, *The Uncommitted: Alienated Youth in American Society* (New York: Harcourt, Brace, 1965).

political structure was compromised by the undue influence of corporate interests and the military. They made far-reaching criticisms of the university and of other social institutions, but their criticisms were usually directed at the failure of the American political system and of American institutions to live up to officially proclaimed values. Thus, despite their commitment to reform and to support for civil disobedience and direct action, the student activists in the first half of this decade generally accepted the basic values and norms of the American political community. And despite their discontent with the university, they usually operated within the confines of academic tradition and felt considerable allegiance to the values of the academic community.

In phase two of the student movement, a considerable number of young people, particularly the activist core, experienced a progressive deterioration in their acceptance of national and university authority. The ideology of this phase of the movement was recently stated by Mark Rudd, leader of the local SDS during the Columbia crisis:

> Many have called us a "student power" movement, implying that our goal is student control over the "educational process," taking decision-making power away from the administrators and putting it in the hands of "democratic" student groups. . . . Student power used to be the goal of S.D.S., but as our understanding of the society has developed, our understanding of the university's role in it has also changed.
>
> We see the university as a factory whose goal is to produce: (1) trained personnel for corporations, government and more universities, and (2) knowledge of the uses of business and government to perpetuate the present system. Government studies at Columbia, for example, attempt to explain our society through concepts of pluralism and conflicting group interest, while the reality of the situation is quite different.
>
> In our strike, we united with many of the people who have been affected by the university's policies—the tenants in Columbia-owned buildings, the Harlem community, the university employees. Many other people throughout the world saw us confront a symbol of those who control the decisions that are made in this country.
>
> In France, the workers and students united to fight a common enemy. The same potential exists here in the United States. We are attempting to connect our fight with the fight of the black people for their freedom, with the fight of the Mexican-Americans for their land in New Mexico, with the fight of the Vietnamese people, and with all people who believe that men and women should be free to live as they choose, in a society where the government is responsive to the needs of all the people, and not the needs of the few whose enormous wealth gives them the political power. We intend to make a revolution.[12]

The process of "delegitimation" and "radicalization" was gradual, and it may be useful to suggest key events and experiences contributing to it.

1. *The Nonviolent Southern Civil Rights Movement* The treatment of civil rights workers and Negroes seeking to exercise constitutional rights by Southern police officials and racist groups was seen as brutal by civil rights organizers and their student allies, and as never adequately responded to by federal authorities. Instead, the latter were thought to be primarily interested in "cooling off" the

---

[12] Quoted in *The Saturday Evening Post* (September 21, 1968).

movement rather than in achieving full implementation of political rights. These events marked the beginning of the sharp split between the student left and established liberal leadership and organization, and disillusionment with the idea that the federal government could be a major agency for protection of rights and promotion of equality and welfare. This disillusionment increased with the failure of the Democratic Convention to grant recognition to the Mississippi Freedom Democrats, and the associated unwillingness by prominent liberal Democrats to wage a floor fight in their behalf.

2. *The "War on Poverty"* Young people saw the rhetoric of public officials as overstated and unfulfilled. Young poverty workers alleged that political machines and other established agencies used federal funds to preserve existing power relationships, saw the erosion of the promise of "maximum feasible participation by the poor" as a basic element of the new programs, regarded public bureaucracies as callous toward the poor, and saw local police being used to attack legitimate protest activity by indigenous organizations of the poor. SDS and other student groups that had embarked on anti-poverty activities had hoped that the new federal programs signified the beginning of significant reform efforts, and that the new programs would facilitate the political organization of deprived groups. The failure of these expectations was a severe disillusionment.

3. *The Events at Berkeley* These marked a change in the perception of university administrators by campus activists. Administrators came to be seen as actively interested in preventing students from effectively organizing for off-campus protest, as more responsive to political pressure from conservative interests than to student concerns or traditional principles of civil liberties, and as devious and untrustworthy in negotiating situations. Moreover, President Clark Kerr, in his book *The Uses of the University*, supplied ideologically oriented activists with an image of the university as fundamentally hostile to humane values, to undergraduate education as such, to internal democratic functioning—and as necessarily involved in servicing the needs of powerful interest groups. The combination of actual experience with university authority at Berkeley with exposure to administrators' self-proclaimed values helped to change students' perception of the university from an essentially congenial institution—needing reform—to an institution whose primary functions were directly opposed to the needs, interests, and values of activist and intellectual students.

4. *The Escalation of the War in Vietnam* Escalation occurred despite campaign promises of President Johnson. Peaceful protest activity had no discernible impact on policy, which continued to harden while students became increasingly aware of the diverse moral, legal, and practical arguments for disengagement from Vietnam. Administration officials often refused to participate in campus debates on the war; when spokesmen for the President's policy were present, their arguments were often based on historical and political grounds which many students and professors regarded as questionable. Particularly damaging were the frequent instances of deceitfulness on the part of Administration spokesmen—the mass media providing much documentation for the view that the Administration was misrepresenting the facts about the war and the diplomatic situation. Many students were as deeply affected by the "credibility gap" as they were by the war itself.

5. *Cooperation by Academic Institutions with the War Effort and with Military Agencies Generally* An early revelation was the fact that faculty members

at Michigan State University had worked with U.S. intelligence agencies in South Vietnam to bolster the regime of Ngo Dinh Diem. Shortly thereafter, an extensive research operation concerning biological warfare was publicized at the University of Pennsylvania. Finally, there were widely publicized revelations of the covert sponsorship of research by the Central Intelligence Agency, operating through a variety of bona fide and "paper" foundations, and the concomitant subsidy by the CIA of various student, labor, religious, and educational organizations in their overseas operations. These revelations, plus the obvious fact that major universities depended on Defense Department funds for large portions of their budgets, raised deep questions in the academic community about the intellectual independence of universities and of the scholarly enterprise in general. For student activists, they provided further evidence of the untrustworthiness and bias of the universities, and provided easy targets for politically effective protest against university authority. The involvement of the universities and the scientific and scholarly disciplines in the war effort and with the defense establishment, while continuing to proclaim their "nonpartisanship," "neutrality," and insistence on academic values, has been a severe and continuing reason for the erosion of university authority for many studnts and academics.

6. *The Draft* Student immunity from the draft began to weaken in 1966, with General Hershey's announcement of restrictions on student deferments. This announcement focused students' attention on the possibility that they themselves would have to participate in the war; it also made them aware of the fact that young men were in competition to avoid the draft, and that their student status had provided them with a special privilege—one that was not available to lower-income, noncollege youth. Many students entertained doubts about a system of compulsory service in a society that celebrated individualistic and voluntaristic values: many had doubts about the use of conscription for a war that had not been declared and for which no general mobilization had been undertaken. Of course, many had strong moral objections to participation in or support for the war in Vietnam in particular, or to war in general; the Selective Service law's narrow definitions of conscientious objection, however, prevented most pacifists and other moral objectors from achieving exemption for their claims of conscience. Moreover, the legitimacy of the draft was weakened by the frank admission by Selective Service, in a widely circulated document, that the threat of the draft was useful in "channeling" young men into "socially useful" careers, that avoiding the draft by legitimate means involved a considerable amount of self-deception as well as deception of others, that in fact the very course of one's youth and young adulthood was shaped and distorted by either the fear of the draft or officially encouraged calculation to avoid it. At the same time, many middle-class students deeply resented the interruption of career and the frustration of plans and aspirations which the draft represented, especially if they felt that no adequate justification for this interruption had been provided. Considerable cynicism about the operations of the system prevailed as a result of widely disseminated folklore about techniques for evading the draft through the faking of disabilities. Finally, many young people resented the imposition of the draft by a political system in which they had no voice or representation and which seemed entirely unresponsive to their opinions regarding the war. Further resentment was encouraged by the use of the draft to punish anti-war dissenters.

7. *Race, Poverty, and Urban Decline* The failure of the political system to

deal effectively with these problems has been a continuing source of student disaffection. Students in large numbers saw the war as a major barrier to effective action on domestic problems; in addition, they saw considerable hypocrisy in the efforts of the government to "preserve freedom" in and "pacify" a remote country when these goals could not be achieved in America's cities. For white activists, whose original interest in social action had been sparked by the civil rights movement, the increasing militance of black youth created new problems, especially when ghetto rebellions were met with massive police repression. For many white activists, the moral and political choices had narrowed to that of siding with black revolutionaries or remaining identified with white authority, which was increasingly defined as "colonial" in nature. Black militants constantly, and understandably, challenged the commitment and seriousness of whites who claimed to be their allies; in this context, tactics of aggressive resistance seemed the only morally commensurate response for white radical students. Thus, for example, at Columbia, the SDS-led protest turned into a serious effort to seize control of university buildings only after black students openly expressed doubt that the white students were prepared to take serious action. Similar events occurred on many campuses.

8. *Police on Campus* Unquestionably, a major source of disaffection—perhaps especially for moderate or previously uncommitted students—has been the nature of campus encounters with the police. Even commentators who are unsympathetic to the goals of the Columbia SDS have agreed that police violence contributed greatly to the radicalization of the Columbia student body during the 1968 crisis. Daniel Bell, for example, describes this process as follows:

> In all, about a hundred students were hurt. But it was not the violence itself that was so horrible—despite the many pictures in the papers of bleeding sudents, not one required hospitalization. It was the capriciousness of that final action. The police simply ran wild. Those who tried to say they were innocent bystanders or faculty were given the same flailing treatment as the students. For most of the students, it was their first encounter with brutality and blood, and they responded in fear and anger. The next day, almost the entire campus responded to a call for a student strike. In a few hours, thanks to the New York City Police Department, a large part of the Columbia campus had become radicalized.[13]

Thus, however one may criticize the strategic and tactical responses of the student radicals, their ranks are characteristically enlarged by a sense of moral outrage at what students take to be the ineffectiveness, insincerity, and finally tactics of harsh repression on the part of the authorities. Therefore, a "politics of confrontation" has become the most effective strategic weapon of student radicals, thrusting such groups as SDS into positions of campus leadership when they can develop a sense of outrage in students and faculty, and isolating them, in numerous instances, when they cannot.

THE POLITICS OF CONFRONTATION

During the past three years, "resistance" and "confrontation" have come to occupy an increasingly prominent position in the strategy and tactics of the student

---

[13] "Columbia and the New Left," *The Public Interest* (Fall 1968), 81.

movement. "Resistance" and "confrontation" refer to such forms of direct action as deliberate disruption of or interference with normal, routine operations of persons or institutions by large masses of persons; deliberate violation of authoritative orders to disperse; forceful retaliation against police use of clubs, chemicals, or other force; the use of barricades or "mobile tactics" to prevent or delay policy efforts to disperse a crowd; the use of ridicule, rudeness, obscenity, and other uncivil forms of speech and behavior to shock, embarrass, or defy authorities; refusal to comply with orders or to accept authoritative commands or requests as legitimate.

Even so, confrontations arranged by students have been usually more "symbolic" than "disruptive" or "destructive." Much rhetoric flows in university circles, and elsewhere, about "interference with institutional functioning." Whatever the intent of radicals, however, they have usually not been successful in disrupting the routines of most university members—until massive police formations were called to campus.

Doubtless some student radicals hope for physical confrontations with the police. But there is little evidence that such a hope is widespread. Further, there is little evidence that many students are willing (much less able) to disrupt functioning, attack persons, or destroy property in the university. But they are willing to engage in symbolic protest—to symbolically "throw their bodies on the machine." This leads to showdowns with the police, and then to violence from the police—and retaliation by some students.

Many observers who have tried to understand the student movement and who express sympathy for many of its objectives find the turn toward confrontation, disruption, and incivility highly irrational and self-destructive. Increasingly, SDS and the "new left" are criticized for the style of their actions and rhetoric. Although many such critics can understand the frustration which contributes to extreme militancy, they argue that the strategy of confrontation serves only to defeat the aims of the movement, and that student radicals ought to exercise self-restraint if they sincerely wish to achieve their political and social ends. For example, it is frequently argued that confrontation tactics accomplish little more than the arousal of popular hostility, thus fueling the fires of right-wing demagoguery and increasing the likelihood of government repression. Confrontation tactics in the university, the critics argue, do not promote reform; they mainly achieve the weakening of the university's ability to withstand political pressure from outside, and consequently they threaten to undermine the one institution in society that offers dissenters full freedom of expression. Some critics conclude their arguments by assuming that since in their view the main effect of new left activity is to create disorder, intensify polarization, increase the strength of the far right, and weaken civil liberties, then these must be the results actually desired by the student radicals.

We have interviewed new left activists in an effort to understand the basis for their actions from their point of view. The following is an attempt to present the case for confrontation tactics as the militants themselves might make it.[14]

[14] On the rationale for resistance and confrontation tactics: informal interviews and conversations were conducted with the following new left leaders: Thomas Hayden, Rennard Davis, Todd Gitlin, Carl Davidson, Paul Potter, Clark Kissinger, Michael Rossman, Steve Halliwell, Frank Bardacke; public speeches by Mark Rudd, Michael Klonsky; conversations with Staughton Lynd and David Dellinger; a systematic monitoring of the

1. *Confrontation and militancy are methods of arousing moderates to action.* The creation of turmoil and disorder can stimulate otherwise quiescent groups to take more forceful action in their own ways. Liberals may come to support radical demands while opposing their tactics; extreme tactics may shock moderates into self-reexamination. Student radicals can claim credit for prompting Senator McCarthy's Presidential campaign, for increased senatorial opposition to the Vietnam War, and for the greater urgency for reform expressed by such moderate bodies as the Kerner Commission.

2. *Confrontation and militancy can educate the public.* Direct action is not intended to win particular reforms or to influence decision-makers, but rather to bring out a repressive response from authorities—a response rarely seen by most white Americans. When confrontation brings violent official response, uncommitted elements of the public can see for themselves the true nature of the "system." Confrontation, therefore, is a means of political education.

3. *Confrontation, militancy and resistance are ways to prepare young radicals for the possibility of greater repression.* If the movement really seriously threatens the power of political authorities, efforts to repress the movement through police state measures are inevitable. The development of resistant attitudes and action toward the police at the present time is a necessary preparation for more serious resistance in the future. Fascism is a real possibility in America; and we don't intend to be either "Jews" or "good Germans."

4. *Combative behavior with respect to the police and other authorities, although possibly alienating "respectable" adults, has the opposite effect on the movement's relationships with nonstudent youth.* Educated, middle-class, nonviolent styles of protest are poorly understood by working-class youth, black youth, and other "dropouts." Contact with these other sectors of the youth population is essential and depends upon the adoption of a tough and aggressive stance to win respect from such youth. Militant street actions attract a heterogeneous group of nonstudent youth participants who have their own sources of alienation from middle-class society and its institutions.

following "new left" periodicals: *New Left Notes, The Movement, San Francisco Express Times, The Guardian, The Rat, Village Voice, Liberation.* Particularly helpful writing on the issues raised in our discussion frequently appears in these publications, especially in articles by the following persons: Julius Lester, Robert Allen, Jack Smith, Carl Davidson, Greg Calvert (*The Guardian*); Marvin Garson (*Express Times*); Michael Klonsky, Les Coleman (*New Left Notes*); interviews with Tom Hayden and Jerry Rubin (*The Movement*, October, November 1968).

We have participated in and observed numerous meetings and informal group discussions among students.

On the growing "alienation," pessimism and radicalism of students on the campus, a recent study of campus opinion at Columbia: A. Barton, "The Columbia Crisis: Campus, Vietnam and the Ghetto" (Bureau of Applied Social Research, Columbia University, July 1968). A pilot study just completed by Richard Flacks, of student attitudes toward the "movement" at the University of Chicago, shows a similar pattern of disillusionment with the political system, but also a strong pattern of hostility toward SDS because of its "revolutionary" posture.

On the spontaneity of major campus confrontations: Berkeley—Max Heirich, *The Free Speech Movement at Berkeley* (New York: Columbia University Press, forthcoming); Columbia—Cox; Brooklyn College—Interview with Professor Norman Weissberg, Department of Psychology, Brooklyn College.

On the police as a provocative force: Cox, "Tactics for Handling Campus Disturbances," *College and University Business* (August 1968), 54–58.

5. *The experience of resistance and combat may have a liberating effect on young middle-class radicals.* Most middle-class students are shocked by aggressive or violent behavior. This cultural fear of violence is psychologically damaging and may be politically inhibiting. To be a serious revolutionary, one must reject middle-class values, particularly deference toward authority. Militant confrontation gives resisters the experience of physically opposing institutional power, and it may force students to choose between "respectable" intellectual radicalism and serious commitment to revolution, violent or otherwise.

6. *The political potency of "backlash" is usually exaggerated.* Those who point to the possibility of repression as a reaction to confrontation tactics wish to compromise demands and principles and dilute radicalism. Repression will come in any case, and to diminish one's efforts in anticipation is to give up the game before it starts.

Some movement spokesmen would add that the possibilities of polarization, repression, and reaction do require more careful attention by the movement if it wishes to win support and sympathy among middle-class adults. They would argue that such support can be obtained, even as militant action is pursued, by concerted efforts at interpretation to and education of such adult groups. The Chicago convention demonstrations are cited as an instance in which adult moderate and liberal sympathy was *enhanced* by militant action, because some care was taken to maintain good relations with these groups, and because the actual events in the street were directly observable by the general public.

We have no way of knowing how many participants in such actions share these perspectives; many rank and file participants may engage in militant or violent action for more simple and direct reasons: they have been provoked to anger, or they feel moral outrage. The rationale we have tried to depict is at least partly the result of student outbursts rather than the cause—after an event (e.g., Columbia), movement strategists try to assimilate and rationalize what occurred. Nevertheless, when movement participants maintain that confrontation and resistance are politically necessary, the arguments described above are those most frequently used.

To a large extent, acceptance of the moral or practical validity of these arguments depends on one's view of the nature of American society and of the university as an institution. Radical activists base their commitment to a politics of confrontation on a kind of negative faith in the repressive and illiberal character of American institutions, including the university. These perceptions have been augmented by an increasing sense that the American university is deeply implicated in the perpetuation of racial injustice. The increasing protest of nonwhite students has brought the issue to the foreground of campus conflict in recent months. . . .

COLLEGES AND UNIVERSITIES IN CRISIS

Student protest has turned many American campuses into arenas of political conflict. To many people both in and out of the universities, the very idea of the politicization of the campus is abhorrent, for it conflicts sharply with a cherished image of the university as a forum for free inquiry, academic values, and "civility": in short, an institution whose fundamental concerns transcend politics. The conception of the university as a *community,* sharing common values and culture and standing apart from both internal political conflict and external political influence, is embedded in academic tradition and, not infrequently, in law. Tradition has conferred a kind of sanctity on the special character of the university as an institution. To many people concerned with the university, the character of student protest in the 1960s marks an unwarranted and inappropriate assault on this sanctity; an injection of profane concerns into what is felt to be a sacred institution.

Indeed, an insistence on the profane character of the university characterizes contemporary student activism and . . . is basic to the radical tactics of the late 1960s. The radical image of the university is that of an institution which functions as an integral part of the "system," providing that system with the skilled personnel and technical assistance required for the furthering of its political objectives.

In fact, most universities and colleges can best be seen as falling somewhere between these two conceptions. The university has long since ceased to be—if indeed it ever was—purely a community of shared values; on the other hand, it has become deeply involved in the larger political community without conscious direction and occasionally without intent, and without careful consideration of the problematic character of its enlarged commitments. This is the context of its current crisis.

The Changing Role of Higher Education

In 1900, approximately 1 percent of the college-age population attended academic institutions; by 1939 this had grown to 15 percent. It nevertheless remained true that both private and public institutions of higher learning largely served upper-income groups in the United States. The plenitude of denominational colleges in the United States is evidence of the ways in which colleges served specific ethnic or religious populations. Public universities were hardly different: state schools largely served the agricultural and business needs of local and state groups.

In recent years the American university has become a national institution; its students are likely to be drawn into occupational groups and communities outside the local confines of its formally designated clientele. Denominational colleges have lost a great deal of their special cultural character. Research has become diverse as the populations served have extended through many institutional areas of society and as federal needs have become a major competitor with state and local demands. The University of California at Berkeley currently lists 101 departments in 15 colleges and schools and has 89 separate research institutes, centers, and laboratories. Private universities draw significant proportions of their funds from federal and private foundation research monies, and large state universities depend heavily on the same sources.

Behind these nationalizing and homogenizing trends lies the central role which education and research have come to play in the American economy. The development of new products, new procedures, and new programs is a major dynamic in an economic structure geared to scientific advancement. In addition, welfare and human relations programs have created an intense demand for training and research in social sciences. These technological trends are reinforced by the capacity of an affluent economy for distributing more and more education as a consumer good. By 1970, it is expected that approximately 50 percent of college-age persons will be attending institutions of higher learning. The present college and university population of 6,500,000 includes representatives of most social levels in the population, although it is still true that children of laborers and nonwhites are underrepresented. Whether they wish it or not, American universities, both public and private, are deeply embedded in the social institutions of American life and have become greatly affected by public policy and public interests.

Most universities, indeed, have developed an ethos of service to community and nation. The provision of technical services and trained personnel by centers of higher learning is indispensable in an advanced society at a high level of technological development. So too is the extension of higher education to wider and wider segments of the community. These services, however, necessarily and substantially increase the university's involvement in matters of political significance. The model of the university as a "neutral" institution probably described its pretensions more closely than its uses, even in the past. In our time, at any rate, it is clear that the university is not and cannot be "neutral" if this means, as some seem to think, not at the service of any social interests. Nor, clearly, is the university, as presently constituted, "neutral" in the sense of being equally at the service of all legitimate social interests. In our time, the university is an important cultural and economic resource; it is also much more fully in the service of some social interests than others. The provision of defense research, for example, necessarily aligns the university with the course of national foreign policy and military strategy. In thus entering the service of the political order, the scientific and technological functions of the university become politicized. Given these circumstances, it is understandable that the university has become the scene of conflict and protest focused on control over the nature and direction of the services it provides, or fails to provide, to actual and potential publics.

Moreover, the extension of higher education to lower-income and minority groups usually means the attempt to extend norms and values of privileged classes and cultures. Lower-income and minority groups may find it difficult to assimilate the cultural artifacts of the privileged, at least on a competitive basis. Moreover, the established culture may conflict with the claims of minority groups for cultural autonomy. Under these conditions, the accepted values of the university—including its norms defining the nature of competence and academic qualification—become contested political issues.

In thus extending their sphere of interest, influence, and involvement, American universities have gained neither clarity of purpose nor direction. They are not necessarily willing or able to assess the relative importance and value of their greatly extended interests, or the problematic character of certain of their own value premises and standards. Few would deny that the basic "service" the university offers to society is understanding and criticism. Yet the university's independence from outside agencies, political powers, and interest groups may be seriously compromised by the high cost of both education and research, which requires the university to seek financial support from the very groups which its scholars are obliged to study and criticize. As a recent study of university governance suggests:

> We have imperceptibly slumped into a posture in which the demands of external interests—strongly reinforced by economic lures, rewards of prestige and status, and other powerful resources which only those with power

can marshall and wield—have increasingly dominated the ethos of the university and shaped the direction of its educational activities.[15]

The Fragmentation of University Interests

These basic problems in the relation of the university to the society at large are compounded by the development of different bases of interest and influence among the various segments of the university community. Put simply, the university barely resembles a community at all, if by community is meant a group sharing common interests and values. Given this fragmentation of interests, the university is unable to deal effectively with conflict, whether internal or external; it has been unable to develop new modes of governance in line with its increased and disparate commitments. Whether it *can* develop effective modes of governance while retaining its present commitments is a matter of considerable doubt. It is certain that it cannot do so without substantial alteration of its structure of power. This is evident from an analysis of the nature of the internal divisions within the university.

Trustees

The governing boards of colleges and universities vary greatly in composition, attitudes, and interests, depending on the type and quality of the institution. Nevertheless, a recent survey by the Educational Testing Service of over 5000 college and university trustees sheds some light on the characteristics of trustees as a group. From these data, a troubling picture emerges; the trustees tend to be strikingly indifferent to academic values and uninformed about issues and problems in contemporary higher education, and very much convinced of the inappropriateness of student and faculty decision-making power on crucial academic issues.[16]

The average trustee is in his fifties; over 98 percent are white; over half have yearly incomes exceeding $30,000; over 35 percent are business executives. The majority regard themselves as politically "moderate." Their attitudes toward certain issues involving academic freedom reflect their frequent distance from campus concerns.

Over two thirds of the trustees surveyed, for example, advocate a screening process for campus speakers. Thirty-eight percent agreed that it is reasonable to require loyalty oaths from faculty. Twenty-seven percent *disagreed* with the statement that "faculty members have a right to free expression of opinions." Many trustees—especially those with business connections—agreed that running a university is "basically like running a business."

The attitudes of trustees concerning the location of university decision-making tend to be strongly at variance with those of many students and faculty. Trustees tend to feel that student decision-making, to the extent that it should exist at all,

---

[15] *The Culture of the University: Governance and Education*, Report of the Study Commission on University Governance (University of California, Berkeley, January 15, 1968), p. 9.
[16] The following material is adapted from Rodney T. Hartnett, *College and University Trustees: Their Backgrounds, Roles, and Educational Attitudes* (Princeton, New Jersey: Educational Testing Service, 1969).

should concern only "traditional" student concerns such as fraternities and sororities, student housing regulations, and student cheating. Seventy percent of the trustees surveyed believed that students and faculty should not have major authority in choosing a university president; 64 percent felt that students and faculty should not have major authority on tenure decisions; 64 percent felt students and faculty should not have major authority in appointing an academic dean.

It should be stressed again that these attitudes vary considerably depending on the type of university represented. Still, the overall picture is inconsistent with a conception of the university as an integrated academic community. Distant in values and interests from most faculty and students, the average trustee has little conception of the problematic nature of campus issues. For that matter, as the ETS data make clear, most trustees rarely bother to remain well-informed about trends and problems in higher education; the vast majority have not read many major books on higher education, and are unfamiliar with most of the relevant periodicals.

Faculty and Administration

In using the term "multiversity," Clark Kerr indicates the fragmented character of the contemporary American institution of higher learning, its separation into specialized units united in nothing save connection to a central administration.[17] One important cause of this fragmentation is the development of professors and graduate students from generalists into specialists.[18] This process, made necessary by a veritable explosion of information in all fields of study, has resulted in a trend toward professionalism—that is, identifying oneself more with one's colleagues everywhere and less with one's local community. Increasingly, it is according to the demands of his field of study, not those of the local campus community, that a scholar's values, success, and acceptance are determined. Only a few universities, such as Harvard and Chicago, have traditions of sufficient prestige to assure the loyalty of their faculties. Then, too, the members of these faculties come from all over the world. In general, the prestige of any institution comes from the eminence of its individual scholars rather than from the mystique of the institution itself.[19]

This derivation of prestige from the faculty makes for an academic seller's market, with sellers whose interests are professional and national, if not international, and buyers whose interest are largely organizational and local. Such disparity of interests is a major source of conflict, in which the faculty opposition is more effective today than it has been in the past.[20] Whatever their sources, mistrust and animosity between faculties and administrations are very much in evidence at many American universities, and this hostility is very little assuaged by a sense of common commitment to the university as a repository of unique values and traditions.

[17] Kerr, *The Uses of the University* (New York: Harper & Row, 1963).
[18] For a description of this change see Christopher Jencks and David Riesman, *The Academic Revolution* (Garden City, N.Y.: Doubleday, 1968), chap. 1.
[19] Seymour Lipset and Philip Altbach, "Student Politics and Higher Education in the United States," *Comparative Education Review*, 10 (June 1966), 326–329.
[20] For an influential study of local faculty contrasted to cosmopolitan professors see Alvin W. Gouldner, "Cosmopolitans and Locals: Toward an Analysis of Latent Social Roles," *Administrative Science Q.*, 2 (1957–1958), 281–306, 444–480.

Studies of student activists indicate that they have close ties to faculty; activists are not unknown and anonymous faces in the classroom.[21] But outside the classroom, faculty have little effect on rules governing student conduct. At Columbia there was no senate or single body in which the undergraduate faculty met regularly to consider policy of any kind. The distance of the faculty from decisions related to student life—especially the final say in disciplinary proceedings—has led to mistrust and resentment of administration by both students and segments of the faculty.

In most student confrontations and protest actions on campus, the administration is singled out as the target. Students tend to accept the premise that these officials can, at will, develop and carry out policies in major areas of political concern. For example, "new left" critiques of universities imply that research policy and use of government funds is largely a matter of administrative decision rather than of faculty desire. Yet the administration's capacity for controlling the content of faculty research is greatly limited by the universities' need for capable research personnel. At major institutions, significant portions of the faculty adopt a research-oriented perspective that stresses the requirements of their particular discipline. Appointments and promotions typically stress ability within the discipline, rather than teaching or university service. The result is that faculty tend to follow the reward structure, which they themselves have created.

University policy is usually arrived at by a series of compromises, committees, and balancings of interests. University officials are severely limited in both power and authority by faculty values and interests.

Faculty interests fail to generate bonds with the university as an institution. There is no definition of what the university "stands for" around which to rally the university "community" when crises occur. There are few shared criteria of university operation to which appeals can be made.

The lack of power or authority of administrators within their faculties makes the faculties in turn seem capricious and irresponsible while the administration seems intransigent and unresponsive. When officials do speak, it is difficult to know whether they represent faculty or students, trustees, or other interested parties. The "double-talk" and evasion about which students so often complain is a standard defense against clear commitments in situations where great constraints exist.

Students

The existence of powerful student movements has meant a significant increase in the power and influence of students on American campuses. Such power is not entirely new. Throughout the history of higher education in the United States, students have wielded some influence. At times they have developed activities which, while extracurricular, served as important sources of new educational content. Student culture, whether congruent or not with faculty or administrative goals, has influenced curriculum, university regulations, and policy through informal pressures.[22] But this influence has rarely amounted to genuine and formal

[21] James Trent and Judith Craise, "Commitment and Conformity in the American Culture," *Journal of Social Issues*, 23 (July 1967), 34–51.
[22] Frederick Rudolph, "Changing Patterns of Authority and Influence," in Owen Knorr and W. John Minter (eds.), *Order and Freedom on the Campus* (Boulder, Col.: Western Interstate Commission for Higher Education, 1965), pp. 1–10.

participation in university governance. That students are beginning to be heard and considered in university policies is largely a result of the political activity and organization of students in recent years. Out of the agitation and activism of nonacademic issues, student power within academic and campus affairs has grown.

The activism of students may be seen as one response to situations in which student opinion and influence have been ignored in the administration of colleges and universities. Lacking effective representation for the expression and alleviation of grievances, students have resorted to more militant measures. In this sense, the character of contemporary student protest can be seen as one consequence of the lack of genuine political mechanisms within the university. As is the case with any social institution, where "normal channels" for participation and influence are underdeveloped, political action tends to take place outside those channels. In the process, hostility and conflict over the *style* of protest and response tends to displace substantive issues as the focus of concern.

It is particularly at this critical point that the fragmentation of interests within the university becomes most significant. A distant governing board, uncommitted to academic values, may invoke simplistic calls for order on the campus, perhaps backed by threats of punitive action. A managerial administration, under pressure and fearful of conservative community reaction, may respond to protest with force and bureaucratic intransigence. A faculty concerned with professionalism may retreat from serious involvement in the issues. Under these conditions, the university drifts further and further away from the possibility of constructive change.

13
You Have to Grow Up in Scarsdale to Know How Bad Things Really Are

Kenneth Keniston

The recent events at Harvard are the culmination of a long year of unprecedented student unrest in the advanced nations of the world. We have learned to expect students in underdeveloped countries to lead unruly demonstrations against the status quo, but what is new, unexpected and upsetting to many is that an apparently similar mood is sweeping across America, France, Germany, Italy and even Eastern European nations like Czechoslovakia and Poland. Furthermore, the revolts occur, not at the most backward universities, but at the most distinguished, liberal and enlightened—Berkeley, the Sorbonne, Tokyo, Columbia, the Free University of Berlin, Rome and now Harvard.

This development has taken almost everyone by surprise. The American public is clearly puzzled, frightened and often outraged by the behavior of its most privileged youth. The scholarly world, including many who have devoted their lives to the study of student protest, has been caught off guard as well. For many years, American analysts of student movements have been busy demonstrating that "it can't happen here." Student political activity abroad has been seen as a reaction to modernization, industrialization and the demise of traditional or tribal

From the *New York Times*, April 27, 1969. © 1969 by the New York Times Company. Reprinted by permission of publisher and author.

societies. In an already modern, industrialized, detribalized and "stable" nation like America, it was argued, student protests are naturally absent.

Another explanation has tied student protests abroad to bad living conditions in some universities and to the unemployability of their graduates. Student revolts, it was argued, spring partly from the misery of student life in countries like India and Indonesia. Students who must live in penury and squalor naturally turn against their universities and societies. And if, as in many developing nations, hundreds of thousands of university graduates can find no work commensurate with their skills, the chances for student militancy are further increased.

These arguments helped explain the "silent generation" of the nineteen-fifties and the absence of protest, during that period, in American universities, where students are often "indulged" with good living conditions, close student-faculty contact and considerable freedom of speech. And they helped explain why "superemployable" American college graduates, especially the much-sought-after ones from colleges like Columbia and Harvard, seemed so contented with their lot.

But such arguments do not help us understand today's noisy, angry and militant students in the advanced countries. Nor do they explain why students who enjoy the greatest advantages—those at the leading universities—are often found in the revolts. As a result, several new interpretations of student protest are currently being put forward, interpretations that ultimately form part of what Richard Poirier has termed "the war against the young."

Many reactions to student unrest, of course, spring primarily from fear, anger, confusion or envy, rather than from theoretical analysis. Governor Wallace's attacks on student "anarchists" and other "pin-headed intellectuals," for example, were hardly coherent explanations of protest. Many of the bills aimed at punishing student protesters being proposed in Congress and state legislatures reflect similar feelings of anger and outrage. Similarly, the presumption that student unrest *must* be part of an international conspiracy is based on emotion rather than fact. Even George F. Kennan's recent discussion of the American student left is essentially a moral condemnation of "revolting students," rather than an effort to explain their behavior.

If we turn to more thoughtful analyses of the current student mood we find two general theories gaining widespread acceptance. The first, articulately expressed by Lewis S. Feuer in his recent book on student movements, "The Conflict of Generations," might be termed the "Oedipal Rebellion" interpretation. The second, cogently stated by Zbigniew Brzezinski and Daniel Bell, can be called the theory of "Historical Irrelevance."

The explanation of Oedipal Rebellion sees the underlying force in all student revolts as blind, unconscious Oedipal hatred of fathers and the older generation. Feuer, for example, finds in all student movements an inevitable tendency toward violence and a combination of "regicide, parricide and suicide." A decline in respect for the authority of the older generation is needed to trigger a student movement, but the force behind it comes from "obscure" and "unconscious" forces in the child's early life, including both intense death wishes against his father and the enormous guilt and self-hatred that such wishes inspire in the child.

The idealism of student movements is thus, in many respects, only a "front" for the latent unconscious destructiveness and self-destructiveness of underlying motivations. Even the expressed desire of these movements to help the poor and exploited is explained psychoanalytically by Feuer: Empathy for the disadvantaged is traced to "traumatic" encounters with parental bigotry in the students' childhoods, when their parents forbade them to play with children of other races or lower social classes. The identification of today's new left with blacks is thus interpreted as an unconscious effort to "abreact and undo this original trauma."

There are two basic problems with the Oedipal Rebellion theory, however. First, although it uses psychoanalytic terms, it is bad psychoanalysis. The real psychoanalytic account insists that the Oedipus complex is universal in all normally developing children. To point to this complex in explaining student rebellion is, therefore, like pointing to the fact that all children learn to walk. Since both characteristics are said to be universal, neither helps us understand why, at some historical moments, students are restive and rebellious, while at others they are not. Second, the theory does not help us explain why some students (especially those from middle-class, affluent and idealistic families) are most inclined to rebel, while others (especially those from working-class and deprived families) are less so.

In order really to explain anything, the Oedipal Rebellion hypothesis would have to be modified to point to an unusually *severe* Oedipus complex, involving especially *intense* and unresolved unconscious feelings of father-hatred in student rebels. But much is now known about the lives and backgrounds of these rebels —at least those in the United States—and this evidence does not support even the modified theory. On the contrary, it indicates that most student protesters are relatively *close* to their parents, that the values they profess are usually the ones they learned at the family dinner table, and that their parents tend to be highly educated, liberal or left-wing and politically active.

Furthermore, psychological studies of student radicals indicate that they are no more neurotic, suicidal, enraged or disturbed than are nonradicals. Indeed, most studies find them to be rather more integrated, self-accepting and "advanced," in a psychological sense, than their politically inactive contemporaries. In general, research on American student rebels supports a "Generational Solidarity" (or chip-off-the-old-block) theory, rather than one of Oedipal Rebellion.

The second theory of student revolts now being advanced asserts that they are a reaction against "historical irrelevance." Rebellion springs from the unconscious awareness of some students that society has left them and their values behind. According to this view, the ultimate causes of student dissent are sociological rather than psychological. They lie in fundamental changes in the nature of the advanced societies—especially, in the change from industrial to postindustrial society. The student revolution is seen not as a true revolution, but as a counterrevolution—what Daniel Bell has called "the guttering last gasp of a romanticism soured by rancor and impotence."

This theory assumes that we are moving rapidly into a new age in which technology will dominate, an age whose real rulers will be men like computer experts, systems analysts and technobureaucrats. Students who are attached to outmoded and obsolescent values like humanism and romanticism unconsciously feel they have no place in this postindustrial world. When they rebel they are like the Luddites of the past—workers who smashed machines to protest the inevitable industrial revolution. Today's student revolt reflects what Brzezinski terms "an unconscious realization that they [the rebels] are themselves becoming historically obsolete"; it is nothing but the "death rattle of the historical irrelevants."

This theory is also inadequate. It assumes that the shape of the future is already technologically determined, and that protesting students unconsciously "know" that it will offer them no real reward, honor or power. But the idea that the future can be accurately predicted is open to fundamental objection. Every past attempt at prophecy has turned out to be grievously incorrect. Extrapolations from the past, while sometimes useful in the short run, are usually fundamentally wrong in the long run, especially when they attempt to predict the quality of human life, the nature of political and social organization, international relations or the shape of future culture.

The future is, of course, made by men. Technology is not an inevitable master of man and history, but merely provides the possibility of applying scientific knowledge to specific problems. Men may identify with it or refuse to, use it or be used by it for good or evil, apply it humanely or destructively. Thus, there is no real evidence that student protest will emerge as the "death rattle of the historical irrelevants." It could equally well be the "first spark of a new historical era." No one today can be sure of the outcome, and people who feel certain that the future will bring the obsolescence and death of those whom they dislike are often merely expressing their fond hope.

The fact that today's students invoke "old" humanistic and romantic ideas in no way proves that student protests are a "last gasp" of a dying order. Quite the contrary: *All* revolutions draw upon older values and visions. Many of the ideals of the French Revolution, for example, originated in Periclean Athens. Revolutions do not occur because new ideas suddenly develop, but because a new generation begins to take *old* ideas seriously—not merely as interesting theoretical views, but as the basis for political action and social change. Until recently, the humanistic vision of human fulfillment and the romantic vision of an expressive, imaginative and passionate life were taken seriously only by small aristocratic or Bohemian groups. The fact that they are today taken as real goals by millions of students in many nations does not mean that these students are "counterrevolutionaries," but merely that their ideas follow the pattern of every major revolution.

Indeed, today's student rebels are rarely opposed to technology *per se*. On the contrary, they take the high technology of their societies completely for granted, and concern themselves with it very little. What they *are* opposed to is, in essence, the worship of Technology, the tendency to treat people as "inputs" or "outputs" of a technological system, the subordination of human needs to technological programs. The essential conflict between the minority of students who make up the student revolt and the existing order is a conflict over the future direction of technological society, not a counterrevolutionary protest against technology.

In short, both the Oedipal Rebellion and the Historical Irrelevance theories are what students would call "put-downs." If we accept either, we are encouraged not to listen to protests, or to explain them away or reject them as either the "acting out" of destructive Oedipal feelings or the blind reaction of an obsolescent group to the awareness of its obsolescence. But if, as I have argued, neither of these theories is adequate to explain the current "wave" of student protest here and abroad, how can we understand it?

One factor often cited to explain student unrest is the large number of people in the world under 30—today the critical dividing line between generations. But this explanation alone, like the theories just discussed, is not adequate, for in all historical eras the vast portion of the population has always been under 30. Indeed, in primitive societies most people die before they reach that age. If chronological youth alone was enough to insure rebellion, the advanced societies—where a greater proportion of the population reaches old age than ever before in history—should be the *least* revolutionary, and primitive societies the *most*. This is not the case.

More relevant factors are the relationship of those under 30 to the established institutions of society (that is, whether they are engaged in them or not); and the opportunities that society provides for their continuing intellectual, ethical and emotional development. In both cases the present situation in the advanced nations is without precedent.

Philippe Aries, in his remarkable book, "Centuries of Childhood," points out that, until the end of the Middle Ages, no separate stage of childhood was recognized in Western societies. Infancy ended at approximately 6 or 7, whereupon most children were integrated into adult life, treated as small men and women and expected to work as junior partners of the adult world. Only later was childhood recognized as a separate stage of life, and our own century is the first to "guarantee" it by requiring universal primary education.

The recognition of adolescence as a stage of life is of even more recent origin, the product of the 19th and 20th centuries. Only as industrial societies became prosperous enough to defer adult work until after puberty could they create institutions—like widespread secondary-school education—that would extend adolescence to virtually all young people. Recognition of adolescence also rose from the vocational and psychological requirements of these societies, which needed much higher levels of training and psychological development than could be guaranteed through primary education alone. There is, in general, an intimate relationship between the way a society defines the stages of life and its economic, political and social characteristics.

Today, in more developed nations, we are beginning to witness the recognition of still another stage of life. Like childhood and adolescence, it was initially granted only to a small minority, but is now being rapidly extended to an ever-larger group. I will call this the stage of "youth," and by that I mean both a further phase of disengagement from society and the period of psychological development that intervenes between adolescence and adulthood. This stage, which continues into the 20s and sometimes into the 30s, provides opportunities for intellectual, emotional and moral development that were never afforded to any other large group in history. In the student revolts we are seeing one result of this advance.

I call the extension of youth an advance advisedly. Attendance at a college or university is a major part of this extension, and there is growing evidence that this is, other things being equal, a good thing for the student. Put in an oversimplified phrase, it tends to free him—to free him from swallowing unexamined the assumptions of the past, to free him from the superstitions of his childhood, to free him to express his feelings more openly and to free him from irrational bondage to authority.

I do not mean to suggest, of course, that all college graduates are free and liberated spirits, unencumbered by irrationality, superstition, authoritarianism or blind adherence to tradition. But these findings do indicate that our colleges, far from cranking out only machinelike robots who will provide skilled manpower for the economy, are also producing an increasing number of highly critical citizens —young men and women who have the opportunity, the leisure, the affluence and the educational resources to continue their development beyond the point where most people in the past were required to stop it.

So, one part of what we are seeing on campuses throughout the world is not a reflection of how bad higher education is, but rather of its extraordinary accomplishments. Even the moral righteousness of the student rebels, a quality both endearing and infuriating to their elders, must be judged at least partially a consequence of the privilege of an extended youth; for a prolonged development, we know, encourages the individual to elaborate a more personal, less purely conventional sense of ethics.

What the advanced nations have done is to create their own critics on a mass basis—that is, to create an ever-larger group of young people who take the highest values of their societies as their own, who internalize these values and identify them with their own best selves, and who are willing to struggle to implement them. At the same time, the extension of youth has lessened the personal risks of dissent: These young people have been freed from the requirements of work, gainful employment and even marriage, which permits them to criticize their society from a protected position of disengagement.

But the mere prolongation of development need not automatically lead to unrest. To be sure, we have granted to millions the opportunity to examine their societies, to compare them with their values and to come to a reasoned judgment of the existing order. But why should their judgment today be so unenthusiastic?

What protesting students throughout the world share is a mood more than an ideology or a program, a mood that says the existing system—the power structure —is hypocritical, unworthy of respect, outmoded and in urgent need of reform. In addition, students everywhere speak of repression, manipulation and authoritarianism. (This is paradoxical, considering the apparently great freedoms given them in many nations. In America, for example, those who complain most loudly about being suffocated by the subtle tyranny of the Establishment usually attend the institutions where student freedom is greatest.) Around this general mood, specific complaints arrange themselves as symptoms of what students often call the "exhaustion of the existing society."

To understand this phenomenon we must recognize that, since the Second World War, some societies have indeed begun to move past the industrial era into a new world that is postindustrial, technological, postmodern, posthistoric or, in Brzezinski's term, "technectronic." In Western Europe, the United States, Canada and Japan, the first contours of this new society are already apparent. And, in many other less-developed countries, middle-class professionals (whose children become activists) often live in postindustrial enclaves within preindustrial societies. Whatever we call the postindustrial world, it has demonstrated that, for the first time, man can produce more than enough to meet his material needs.

This accomplishment is admittedly blemished by enormous problems of economic distribution in the advanced nations, and it is in terrifying contrast to the overwhelming poverty of the Third World. Nevertheless, it is clear that what might be called "the problem of production" *can*, in principle, be solved. If all members of American society, for example, do not have enough material goods, it is because the system of distribution is flawed. The same is true, or will soon be true, in many other nations that are approaching advanced states of industrialization. Characteristically, these nations, along with the most technological, are those where student unrest has recently been most prominent.

The transition from industrial to postindustrial society brings with it a major shift in social emphases and values. Industrializing and industrial societies tend to be oriented toward solving the problem of production. An industrial ethic—sometimes Protestant, sometimes Socialist, sometimes Communist—tends to emphasize psychological qualities like self-discipline, delay of gratification, achievement-orientation and a strong emphasis on economic success and productivity. The social, political and economic institutions of these societies tend to be organized in a way that is consistent with the goal of increasing production. And industrial societies tend to apply relatively uniform standards, to reward achievement rather than status acquired by birth, to emphasize emotional neutrality ("coolness") and rationality in work and public life.

The emergence of postindustrial societies, however, means that growing numbers of the young are brought up in family environments where abundance, relative economic security, political freedom and affluence are simply facts of life, not goals to be striven for. To such people the psychological imperatives, social institutions and cultural values of the industrial ethic seem largely outdated and irrelevant to their own lives.

Once it has been demonstrated that a society *can* produce enough for all of its members, at least some of the young turn to other goals: for example, trying to make sure that society *does* produce enough and distributes it fairly, or searching for ways to live meaningfully with the goods and the leisure they *already* have. The problem is that our society has, in some realms, exceeded its earlier targets. Lacking new ones, it has become exhausted by its success.

When the values of industrial society become devitalized, the élite sectors of youth—the most affluent, intelligent, privileged and so on—come to feel that they live in institutions whose demands lack moral authority or, in the current jargon, "credibility." Today, the moral imperative and urgency behind production, acquisition, materialism and abundance has been lost.

Furthermore, with the lack of moral legitimacy felt in "the System," the least request for loyalty, restraint or conformity by its representatives—for example, by college presidents and deans—can easily be seen as a moral outrage, an authoritarian repression, a manipulative effort to "co-opt" students into joining the Establishment and an exercise in "illegitimate authority" that must be resisted. From this conception springs at least part of the students' vague sense of oppression.

And, indeed, perhaps their peculiar feeling of suffocation arises ultimately from living in societies without vital ethical claims.

Given such a situation, it does not take a clear-cut issue to trigger a major protest. I doubt, for example, that college and university administrators are in fact *more* hypocritical and dishonest than they were in the past. American intervention in Vietnam, while many of us find it unjust and cruel, is not inherently *more* outrageous than other similar imperialistic interventions by America and other nations within the last century. And the position of blacks in this country, although disastrously and unjustifiably disadvantaged, is, in some economic and legal respects, better than ever before. Similarly, the conditions for students in America have never been as good, especially, as I have noted, at those élite colleges where student protests are most common.

But this is *precisely* the point: It is *because* so many of the *other* problems of American society seem to have been resolved, or to be resolvable in principle, that students now react with new indignation to old problems, turn to new goals and propose radical reforms.

So far I have emphasized the moral exhaustion of the old order and the fact that, for the children of postindustrial affluence, the once-revolutionary claims of the industrial society have lost much of their validity. I now want to argue that we are witnessing on the campuses of the world a fusion of *two revolutions* with distinct historical origins. One is a continuation of the old and familiar revolution of the industrial society, the liberal-democratic-egalitarian revolution that started in America and France at the turn of the 18th century and spread to virtually every nation in the world. (Not completed in any of them, its contemporary American form is, above all, to be found in the increased militancy of blacks.) The other is the new revolution, the postindustrial one, which seeks to define new goals relevant to the 20th and 21st centuries.

In its social and political aspects, the first revolution has been one of universalization, to use the sociologist's awkward term. It has involved the progressive extension to more and more people of economic, political and social rights, privileges and opportunities originally available only to the aristocracy, then to the middle class, and now in America to the relatively affluent white working class. It is, in many respects, a *quantitative* revolution. That is, it concerns itself less with the quality of life than with the amount of political freedom, the quantity and distribution of goods or the amount and level of injustice.

As the United States approaches the targets of the first revolution, on which this society was built, to be poor shifts from being an unfortunate fact of life to being an outrage. And, for the many who have never experienced poverty, discrimination, exploitation or oppression, even to *witness* the existence of these evils in the lives of others suddenly becomes intolerable. In our own time the impatience to complete the first revolution has grown apace, and we find less willingness to compromise, wait and forgive among the young, especially among those who now take the values of the old revolution for granted—seeing them not as goals, but as *rights*.

A subtle change has thus occurred. What used to be utopian ideals—like equality, abundance and freedom from discrimination—have now become demands, inalienable rights upon which one can insist without brooking any compromise. It is noteworthy that, in today's student confrontations, no one requests anything. Students present their "demands."

So, on the one hand, we see a growing impatience to complete the first revolution. But, on the other, there is a newer revolution concerned with newer issues, a revolution that is less social, economic or political than psychological, historical and cultural. It is less concerned with the quantities of things than with their qualities, and it judges the virtually complete liberal revolution and finds it still wanting.

"You have to have grown up in Scarsdale to know how bad things really are," said one radical student. This comment would probably sound arrogant, heartless and insensitive to a poor black, much less to a citizen of the Third World. But he meant something important by it. He meant that *even* in the Scarsdales of America, with their affluence, their upper-middle-class security and abundance, their well-fed, well-heeled children and their excellent schools, something is wrong. Economic affluence does not guarantee a feeling of personal fulfillment; political freedom does not always yield an inner sense of liberation and cultural freedom; social justice and equality may leave one with a feeling that something else is missing in life. "No to the consumer society!" shouted the bourgeois students of the Sorbonne during May and June of 1968—a cry that understandably alienated French workers, for whom affluence and the consumer society are still central goals.

What, then, are the targets of the new revolution? As is often noted, students themselves don't know. They speak vaguely of "a society that has never existed," of "new values," of a "more humane world," of "liberation" in some psychological, cultural and historical sense. Their rhetoric is largely negative; they are stronger in opposition than in proposals for reform; their diagnoses often seem accurate, but their prescriptions are vague; and they are far more articulate in urging the immediate completion of the first revolution than in defining the goals of the second. Thus, we can only indirectly discern trends that point to the still-undefined targets of the new revolution.

What are these trends and targets?

First, there is a revulsion against the notion of quantity, particularly economic quantity and materialism, and a turn toward concepts of quality. One of the most delightful slogans of the French student revolt was, "Long live the passionate revolution of creative intelligence!" In a sense, the achievement of abundance may allow millions of contemporary men and women to examine, as only a few artists and madmen have examined in the past, the quality, joyfulness and zestfulness of experience. The "expansion of consciousness"; the stress on the expressive, the aesthetic and the creative; the emphasis on imagination, direct perception and fantasy—all are part of the effort to enhance the quality of this experience.

Another goal of the new revolution involves a revolt against uniformity, equalization, standardization and homogenization—not against technology itself, but against the "technologization of man." At times, this revolt approaches anarchic quaintness, but it has a positive core as well—the demand that individuals be appreciated, not because of their similarities or despite their differences, but because they *are* different, diverse, unique and noninterchangeable. This attitude is evident in many areas: for example, the insistence upon a cultivation of personal idiosyncrasy, mannerism and unique aptitude. Intellectually, it is expressed in the rejection of the melting-pot and consensus-politics view of American life in favor of a posthomogeneous America in which cultural diversity and conflict are underlined rather than denied.

The new revolution also involves a continuing struggle against psychological or institutional closure or rigidity in any form, even the rigidity of a definite adult role. Positively, it extols the virtues of openness, motion and continuing human development. What Robert J. Lifton has termed the protean style is clearly in evidence. There is emerging a concept of a lifetime of personal change, of an adulthood of continuing self-transformation, of an adaptability and an openness to the revolutionary modern world that will enable the individual to remain "with it"—psychologically youthful and on top of the present.

Another characteristic is the revolt against centralized power and the complementary demand for participation. What is demanded is not merely the consent of the governed, but the involvement of the governed. "Participatory democracy" summarizes this aspiration, but it extends far beyond the phrase and the rudimentary social forms that have sprung up around it. It extends to the demand for relevance in education—that is, for a chance for the student to participate in his own educational experience in a way that involves all of his faculties, emotional and moral as well as intellectual. The demand for "student power" (or, in Europe, "co-determination") is an aspect of the same theme: At Nanterre, Columbia, Frankfurt and Harvard, students increasingly seek to participate in making the policies of their universities.

This demand for participation is also embodied in the new ethic of "meaningful human relationships," in which individuals confront each other without masks, pretenses and games. They "relate" to each other as unique and irreplaceable human beings, and develop new forms of relationships from which all participants will grow.

In distinguishing between the old and the new revolutions, and in attempting to define the targets of the new, I am, of course, making distinctions that students themselves rarely make. In any one situation the two revolutions are joined and fused, if not confused. For example, the Harvard students' demand for "restructuring the university" is essentially the second revolution's demand for participation; but their demand for an end to university "exploitation" of the surrounding community is tied to the more traditional goals of the first revolution. In most radical groups there is a range of opinion that starts with the issues of the first (racism, imperialism, exploitation, war) and runs to the concerns of the second (experiential education, new life styles, meaningful participation, consciousness-expansion, relatedness, encounter and community). The first revolution is personified by Maoist-oriented Progressive Labor party factions within the student left, while the second is represented by hippies, the "acid left," and the Yippies. In any individual, and in all student movements, these revolutions coexist in uneasy and often abrasive tension.

Furthermore, one of the central problems for student movements today is the absence of any theory of society that does justice to the new world in which we of the most industrialized nations live. In their search for rational critiques of present societies, students turn to theories like Marxism that are intricately bound up with the old revolution.

Such theories make the ending of economic exploitation, the achievement of social justice, the abolition of racial discrimination and the development of political participation and freedom central, but they rarely deal adequately with the issues of the second revolution. Students inevitably try to adapt the rhetoric of the first to the problems of the second, using concepts that are often blatantly inadequate to today's world.

Even the concept of "revolution" itself is so heavily laden with images of political, economic and social upheaval that it hardly seems to characterize the equally radical but more social-psychological and cultural transformations involved in the new revolution. One student, recognizing this, called the changes occurring in his California student group, "too radical to be called a revolution." Students are thus often misled by their borrowed vocabulary, but most adults are even more confused, and many are quickly led to the mistaken conclusion that today's student revolt is nothing more than a repetition of Communism's in the past.

Failure to distinguish between the old and new revolutions also makes it impossible to consider the critical question of how compatible they are with each other. Does it make sense—or is it morally right—for today's affluent American students to seek imagination, self-actualization, individuality, openness and relevance when most of the world and many in America live in deprivation, oppression and misery?

The fact that the first revolution is "completed" in Scarsdale does not mean that it is (or soon will be) in Harlem or Appalachia—to say nothing of Bogotá or Calcutta. For many children of the second revolution, the meaning of life may be found in completing the first—that is, in extending to others the "rights" they have always taken for granted.

For others the second revolution will not wait; the question, "What lies beyond affluence?" demands an answer now. Thus, although we may deem it self-indulgent to pursue the goals of the new revolution in a world where so much misery exists, the fact is that in the advanced nations it is upon us, and we must at least learn to recognize it.

Finally, beneath my analysis lies an assumption I had best make explicit. Many student critics argue that their societies have failed miserably. My argument, a more historical one perhaps, suggests that our problem is not only that industrial societies have failed to keep all their promises, but that they have succeeded in some ways beyond all expectations. Abundance was once a distant dream, to be postponed to a hereafter of milk and honey; today, most Americans are affluent. Universal mass education was once a utopian goal; today in America almost the entire population completes high school, and almost half enters colleges and universities.

The notion that individuals might be free, en masse, to continue their psychological, intellectual, moral and cognitive development through their teens and into their 20s would have been laughed out of court in any century other than our own; today, that opportunity is open to millions of young Americans. Student unrest is a reflection not only of the failures, but of the extraordinary successes of the liberal-industrial revolution. It therefore occurs in the nations and in the colleges where, according to traditional standards, conditions are best.

But for many of today's students who have never experienced anything but affluence, political freedom and social equality, the old vision is dead or dying. It may inspire bitterness and outrage when it is not achieved, but it no longer animates or guides. In place of it, students (and many who are not students) are searching for a new vision, a new set of values, a new set of targets appropriate to the postindustrial era—a myth, an ideology or a set of goals that will concern itself with the quality of life and answer the question, "Beyond freedom and affluence, what?"

What characterizes student unrest in the developed nations is this peculiar mixture of the old and the new, the urgent need to fulfill the promises of the past and, at the same time, to define the possibilities of the future.

14
The Agony of the Campus

Irving Howe

This is a good time to remember what we owe the students. Owe, not to one or another group and certainly not to the "actions" of last year, but to the fresh and undogmatic young people who in 1963–1964 began to assault the injustices of American society.

There were striking moments: busloads of youth heading South to help voter-registration drives, the early teach-ins stirring opposition to the war, the later involvement, at once practical and idealistic, in the McCarthy campaign. At such moments—they seem painfully distant right now—we could glimpse the potential of an aroused generation. The students cast off the cheap tokens of careerism; they shook their teachers out of apathy and made them pay attention to the dangers of a militarized university; they even led their parents to hope that the aborted dreams of *their* youth might yet be realized.

By now, it's mostly gone bad. Though only a part, and far from the best part, of the campus turmoil, the New Left has grown stronger; but it has also become entangled with musty authoritarian dogmas and a nasty cult of violence.

Is there an iron law that makes this decline from idealism to sectarianism inevitable? Must history, especially "our" history, repeat itself?

From *Dissent* (September–October 1969). Reprinted by permission of publisher and author.

Seen from an international perspective, it does look as if the changes between 1963 and 1969 had an internal momentum of their own; as if throughout the world there were some fatal tropism to repeat the disasters, the foolishness, the corruptions of the recent past. Yet there are also reasons for the decline that seem special to the U.S.

It is American liberalism, and with it the labor movement, that must bear some of the responsibility for what has happened. Not all the responsibility, but some. If liberalism had been aggressive and independent in the sixties, even to the extent it had been in the thirties, we would not be facing now the shambles on the campus that we do. You need only compare the electrifying impact of a John L. Lewis with the stupefying impact of a George Meany to understand why no segment of American students finds its moral yearnings and political needs satisfied by the unions.

I will be told that conditions have changed, things cannot be as in the thirties —and that is true. But for a liberal leadership both insurgent and sensitive, the challenge of the sixties could have yielded enormous opportunities. For a labor movement warmly responsive to the poor and the blacks, ready to assert an independent course against militarism and the war, there would have been major possibilities for gaining the friendship of the young. And let no one delude himself: that friendship is worth something, both politically and morally.

Today, when some liberal and labor leaders point, accurately enough, to the destructiveness of recent campus events, one feels impelled to reply:

> Yes, of course, but look also to yourselves. Look to the role you played at the Bay of Pigs, look to the monotone of AFL-CIO support for the war, look to the shamefulness of the Chicago Democratic convention and the way Hubert Humphrey was chosen. If the kids have turned to the false prophets of left authoritarianism, it is partly because you abandoned them. You gave them no vision of militant idealism as a way of fighting the evils they correctly rebelled against. And if you want to know what might have been, you need only imagine the support the students gave McCarthy multiplied a hundred times and set into motion behind a united and vigorous left-liberalism. Imagine what that might have done for this country!

II

The present campus turmoil is far more extensive than anything we have ever known in this country. Earlier notions that it was the work of a tiny minority skillful at publicity and provocation should simply be dropped. More important than SDS (which nevertheless is larger and reaches into more schools than all the student groups of the thirties) is the fact that major segments of student bodies can be activated for such desirable ends as abolishing ROTC, protesting university involvement with military research, and demonstrating against the Vietnam war. The ideology of one or another student group may be of interest only to the sequestered ranks of the American left; but the political mood of the students as a generation is a fact of major political importance.

III

The SDS has split. Whether the breakup will carry over into local campuses we do not yet know; but what seems clear, and depressing, is that a once-promising student movement has sealed its eventual doom at the moment of its greatest strength. Again, seemingly, the fatal rhythm of American radicalism: a fresh idealistic start, rapid growth, and abandonment to factional convolutions and absurdities, and then a surrender to authoritarian ideology.

Greg Calvert, former SDS National Secretary, writes in a recent *Liberation* that he has not been able to attend an SDS meeting for the past year, so revolted has he been by what he himself calls "the Stalinization of the Left." Staughton Lynd, polemicizing against SDS, writes: "I am ashamed of a movement which calls policemen pigs. I don't want to belong to it. Similarly, I feel deeply troubled by the attitude that, since we are right, we can take away civil liberties from others which we insist on for ourselves."

By all accounts the SDS convention in Chicago this summer was a bizarre event, putting to shame even the early Communist sects in the twenties. Two organized factions—one Maoist and the other vaguely Castroite—shout mass slogans at each other, or merely the name of patron saints: Mao Mao Mao and Ho Ho Ho. Overwhelmed by this mutual illumination, they proceed to split, each group denouncing the other as "counter-revolutionary" and "racist." Where did they learn these charming methods?

I remember a meeting arranged in the early sixties between the then leaders of SDS and some DISSENT editors. We had read the Port Huron statement and been impressed; but alas, the hoped-for link between radical generations did not occur. Whose fault? Perhaps both. We weren't flexible enough in responding to their rhetoric, they not interested in our experiences that made us uneasy before signs of infatuation with charismatic dictators. Some of the SDS people struck us as admirable; others, like Tom Hayden, the most gifted of the group, already had the bearing of the *apparatchik* about them, speaking of "participatory democracy" but inducing doubt as to how long they'd remain attached to the more commonplace versions of democracy. Still, the differences then were not a fraction of what they have since become.

With its Chicago split, SDS has taken a giant step down the path of earlier American radicalism: the politics of cannibalism, with one split preparing another. The National Office or anti-Maoist group is held together mainly by common antipathy to the PL Maoists; now that the latter are out of the way, the former may discover the range of its internal differences.[1]

On many campuses, however, SDS—or two groups calling themselves SDS—remains a significant force. In some places the two factions will consume themselves through bitter disputation; in others, they will compete in proving who can be more "revolutionary"; in still others, the local SDS chapter will continue pretty much as in the past, without much concern for the national organization. But anyone who thinks the split removes the political-social phenomenon dramatized by SDS is deluding himself. The alienation of the young runs deep, and much of it is justified. There will not soon be peace on campus.

---

[1] This very process, the summer interval notwithstanding, seems already to have begun. The *Guardian*, the Guevarist weekly sympathetic to SDS, reports in its July issues a series of further factional battles, including a fairly serious physical one in New York between PL and National Office groups. The University of Wisconsin SDS has voted not to support either tendency, and according to the *Guardian* there are other such "rank-and-file" rumblings.

IV

A major criterion for evaluating campus activities must be their off-campus consequences. Right now student militancy has become a significant force, or symbol, in American politics; every cheap-jack politician of the right sees in campus disturbance an opportunity to gain advantage among the voters. Absolute proof may be hard to come by, but it seems reasonable to suggest that confrontation politics on the campus contributed notably to the victories of backlash candidates in Los Angeles and Minneapolis, perhaps also in the New York primaries.

This is a fact which seems unable to penetrate the mind of Dr. Benjamin Spock. He writes letters to newspapers gleefully noting that confrontation tactics lead to academic reforms, arguing, it should be noted, in terms of effective tactics, not intractable conscience. His judgment suffers from at least one delusion and two errors:

Delusion: that there is an automatic rightness in every demand raised by students, so that if a proposal, say, for a segregated black studies program is called a reform, then it is indeed a reform.

Errors: that if certain demands of militant students are granted, this constitutes a political victory—without regard to the possibility that thereby we may have created on the campus conditions that later will be damaging to freedom;

that if certain demands of militant students are granted, there are not going to follow off-campus repercussions that outweigh in disaster the supposed gains made on the campus.

Politics is, among other things, the art of anticipating consequences, and even trying to anticipate unfamiliar consequences. If the recent events at San Francisco State and Berkeley have strengthened the hand of Ronald Reagan (and the polls show his popularity in California to be at an all-time high), then might it not be argued that this is too high a price to pay for campus "victories"? The black studies program at San Francisco State, such as it is, may have been purchased at the cost of subjecting the poor blacks of Watts to four more years of Reagan: does that strike Dr. Spock as a fair exchange?

V

Socialists—others too—have no choice, I think, but to work for *a liberal course* for the U.S. in the coming period. That signifies:

• the premise that we are not and will not soon be in a "revolutionary situation"
• the subpremise that if "revolutionary activity" in the next few years comes to more than loud talk, it will have an elitist, desperado and adventurist character
• the belief that it is in our interest to preserve and improve the present agencies of democratic politics, marred as they may be, requiring changes as they do, and even liable to sudden collapse as they are
• the prognosis that the necessary social and economic reforms can be achieved only through a reactivated coalition of left-liberal-labor forces, though one that would be different in political stress and internal composition from the coalition we have just seen distintegrating

I take these statements to be self-evident, and what is more important, I would claim that many of those who attack Dissent from the "left" actually wok from not very different premises. That the realization of this political perspective would not bring socialism and that it is therefore necessary to keep asserting the idea of socialism, is self-evident; but socialism is not, alas, an immediate possibility or issue in American politics. Major social reforms, however, are on the immediate agenda.

Behind these remarks lies the assumption that in the U.S. today liberal values and institutions are in some jeopardy, both from left authoritarians on the campus and, from the far more powerful forces of the right, on and off campus. It is troubling that some of the militant students either take for granted the survival of democratic institutions, or have little sense of how inherently fragile they are, or worst of all, don't believe that in their present form they are worth preserving.

They are wrong, utterly and profoundly wrong. The backlash that has developed thus far is relatively "moderate" and conceived by its spokesmen and supporters as "defensive"; but it has the potential for becoming something far uglier. Democratic institutions need to be defended; their preservation is the absolute condition for the major reforms the country needs.

In campus situations where, in the name of real or alleged reforms, liberal procedures are threatened, either by quasi-insurrectionary methods or a "plebiscitary democracy," we must continue to insist—whether or not it makes us popular—that democracy is impossible without agreed-upon rules (including rules for changing the rules) and that the destruction of such procedures is likely to come at too great a price. If this be called "legalism," then I simply shrug my shoulders and reflect upon the persistence of foolishness in human affairs.

VI

To which we must add some qualifications:

In speaking about democracy on the campus, it is sometimes said that universities are not "really" democratic. Almost always such remarks point to failures to realize proclaimed democratic values, or to areas in which democratic procedures have not been sufficiently extended, or to areas in which there can be legitimate uncertainty, even disagreement, as to the relevance or applicability of democratic procedures. A few discriminations:

• If by democracy on the campus we mean the right of students and professors to express and organize in behalf of their political views, then without doubt the American university provides the most liberal and tolerant arena in the whole of our society.

• If by democracy on the campus we mean the right of teachers and students to share in university governance, then the situation is very uneven, rather good in some schools and very bad in others. Here reforms are in order, though there may be honest disagreement among radical and liberal professors and students as to which reforms make sense and which do not. In principle, for example, it is desirable to question the powers of boards of trustees. In practice, because of financial and other pressures, it may be necessary to put up with such institutions, while trying to steadily whittle down their powers. But surely on issues of this kind it ought to be possible to make significant changes without either confrontation politics or the ricochet of backlash. Nevertheless, it ought in fairness to be said that student agitation has done a good deal to rouse faculties that had not shown much interest in the rights that ought to be theirs.

• If by democracy on the campus we mean the right of students to have equal powers in making tenure decisions and curriculum determination, as well as in deciding the procedures and subject-matter of particular classes, then once more men of good will and democratic inclination can have serious disagreements. Without getting into nettlesome details, I would say that insofar as students are members of a community (the university), they should have rights of consultation and should share in the making of decisions—though obviously the university is not a place where one man, one vote is a relevant standard. But insofar as students are learners or apprentices, they submit themselves to the guidance and supervision of those who have mastered the discipline.

To say this is not at all to imply that even as learners and apprentices they have no rights of free speech, etc.; for they surely do. It is to suggest, however, that in the learning situation, majority votes are not, as a rule, decisive. Among other things, teaching means that men who know transmit, pass on, communicate their knowledge to those who do not. This signifies that teachers thereby have a measure of authority, which is of course sharply different from unchecked power. The exercise of legitimate (which must always mean, limited) authority is not necessarily authoritarian. Some students believe that it is; and here, I would guess, we will come to a clash in the university that in a decade or two will be more fundamental than those now taking place.

VII

Barring a sudden end to the war *and* major domestic reforms, student unrest seems likely to grow. The positive aspect of this will be that thousands of young people will enter American society determined to put an end to poverty, discrimination, injustice. With a proper joining of circumstances, this could lead to tremendous social gains. The negative aspect is the likelihood, meanwhile, that the kamikaze-style politics of the desperado-totalitarian left will also flourish. In Germany a new student group, the APO, with several thousand members, openly preaches arson, violence, individual harassment, and terror: its declarations sound as if composed by Peter Verhovensky in the pages of *The Possessed*. Is it not possible, or even likely, that some elements in SDS will be driven by a mixture of success and desperation toward similar views? (It is the dilemma of SDS politics that its kind of success must often lead to desperation.) Once social movements achieve some momentum, they must, so to say, act out their destiny. And one factor likely to speed this development is the readiness of black student groups to use violence, thereby prompting white radical students to escalate their methods of struggle as a way of establishing their "revolutionary credentials."

The politics of Bakunin and Nechaev sprang up in the most backward country of nineteenth-century Europe; they may now be fulfilled in the most advanced country of the twentieth century.

VIII

It would be foolish, at this point, to pretend that we have a unified explanation for the character and magnitude of student revolt. The two greatest mistakes are, taking at face value everything the students say about themselves and refusing to accept anything the students say about themselves. The familiar "sympathetic" explanations contain some truth: revolt against bureaucratism, revulsion against the Vietnam war, guilt over draft exemption, concern with poverty, etc. So do the "hostile" explanations: boredom among middle-class youth, purposelessness among those in "soft" disciplines like sociology and literature, delusions as to charismatic dictators in the Third World, abandonment of liberal norms, etc. But when you have so many explanations, then in truth you are still in a preliminary stage of analysis and are still sorting out the relative weights to assign to the various explanations.

Yet there is one aspect of student unrest that ought to be grasped more clearly than it has been by people outside the university. Together with the idealism and despair, there is a growing current of irrationalism and anti-intellectualism. There seems to be some line of continuity between the antihistoricism of the mindlessly contented students of the fifties and the antihistoricism of the passionately discontented students of the sixties. Since the phenomenon is worldwide (see, for a brilliant quasi-satirical portrait, Godard's *La Chinoise*), distinctively American factors of explanation cannot be sufficient. I think we are experiencing a worldwide cultural revolt against the modernist tradition, with its stress on complexity, irony, ambivalence and the problematical, to which is linked a worldwide revulsion not merely against the industrial-bureaucratic state but the idea of technique itself. The signs of a romantic primitivism are everywhere on the campus, and even those who cannot accept the deeper implications of this trend must admit that some of its external tokens are attractive. I think we are also witnessing, in some strange and inverted way, a quasi-religious impulse which through secular nihilism and alienated idealism seeks to break into a condition of religious transcendence. My own view is that the desire to achieve religious states of being through nonreligious, and especially political, agencies is full of serious dangers, both to religion and society; but let that rest for another occasion.

One immediate consequence on campus of this melange of styles and impulses is sometimes a revolt against knowledge as such. A few months ago I spoke at a university in California before an audience of graduate students, and for two hours I found myself arguing with them—graduate students, mind you—as to whether scholarship had a place in the university! Nor is this an atypical experience. That is why people outside the university ought to be a little cautious in rushing to support everything that a fraction of students or teachers (among whom, by the way, anti-intellectualism is also spreading) declares to be an "academic reform." One of the leading philosophy departments in the country recently voted to drop the foreign language requirement for its Ph.D. candidates. Is this move a "reform" or an act of panicky submission to current student moods? It will be said, of course, that traditional foreign language requirements for the Ph.D. have been mainly ritualistic and thereby in need of change; which may well be true, but should hardly lead serious academics to conclude that a Ph.D. candidate *in philosophy* need not be required to know one foreign language.

IX

We face extremely grave, perhaps insoluble, difficulties on the campus, and for those of us who believe both in social change and democratic values these difficulties will be especially severe:

• Much recent behavior of insurgent students goes against the grain. Destroying computers, burning buildings, breaking up meetings, shouting down teachers in classrooms, carrying guns—this has nothing to do with the socialist, or radical, tradition. It is a strange mixture of Guevarist fantasia, residual Stalinism, anarchist braggadocio, and homemade tough-guy methods. This is not the path for serious radicals.

• Nor are our objections merely tactical. The kind of "revolution" envisaged by both SDS factions has nothing to do with the large-scale social transformation this country needs. Who, with a reasonable impulse to self-preservation, would care to test out the dispensation of a Tom Hayden or Mark Rudd? Worthy fellows, no doubt; but better powerless.

• Our major campus perspective should be to help, whenever we can, the more "moderate" (which these days means liberal-left and radical) students to establish themselves as an independent force. People like ourselves must therefore try to help—not "lead"—like-minded students. Such students are there, and in rather large numbers; what they lack is self-confidence and organizational coherence.

• In many universities, faculties have become politicized—at Harvard there now exists the equivalent of a two-party system within the faculty. If by no means an unmixed blessing, this is an undeniable fact; and in any case, for some time ahead we may have no choice. This means the creation of loosely-knit liberal-left blocs of teachers who simultaneously push for genuine reforms (removal of ROTC, no "classified research" on campus, consultative and participatory rights for students) while firmly resisting violence, disruption, and terrorism.

X

Do we want the university to survive? the university as it is, with all its faults and contaminations?

My own answer is, yes, we want it to survive. Improved, transformed, cleansed—but a university and neither a prep school for militarism nor a training center for guerrilla warfare; a university that serves as a haven for free thought and disinterested (which doesn't mean unimpassioned) scholarship.

A formula: The ideal university would not be subservient to the surrounding society, it would exist solely for the life of the mind and the transmission of knowledge. No university fully satisfies this ideal. None can, either in this or any other society, and perhaps none will in any foreseeable society. The pressures of the containing world cannot, under the best of circumstances, be avoided entirely; but they can be sharply minimized.

The university may be *like* the surrounding society, and one can—indeed, should—legitimately complain that it is too much *like* the surrounding society. But insofar as it is a university at all, it is not *the same as* the surrounding society in its nature, its quality, its ends. If some of our students who have seen the Marxist light were to read basic Marxist texts, they would learn about the autonomy—incomplete but significant—that some institutions can achieve within "the superstructure" of a class society. That autonomy—incomplete but significant—has not been gained easily; it is inherently fragile and open to destruction; and we propose to defend it both against those administrators and faculties who would tie the university to the war machine and those students and professors who would like to transform it into an agency of their political will.

About this matter students have often been confused, and sometimes disingenuous. (So too have those administrators and professors who see nothing wrong with military research or other contaminating involvements but who, when confronted by student protest, suddenly start mumbling about the autonomy of the campus. If professors really cared strongly enough about university autonomy to promote it on their own, a great part of the energies that now go into campus "confrontation" would be disarmed in advance. As it is, the cry of autonomy is too often used as a shield for indifference.) Students must decide: toward which idea of the university do they wish to move? You cannot behave on the campus as if it were merely a carbon-copy of the external society and then claim the idea of a disinterested and autonomous university as your defense against retaliation. You cannot bring guns onto campus and then grow sincerely indignant when the police are called in. Only insofar as protesters live up to the standards of the university as sanctuary and enclave, can they legitimately and persuasively demand that the other side do likewise. Once you violate those standards fundamentally, you are either engaged in a form of civil disobedience—which, seriously undertaken and warranting serious respect, implies nonviolence and a readiness to accept legal penalties—or in a version of insurrection—which means that you must expect your experiment in force to be met with the crushing reply of force.

Here we must face a frequent student rebuttal: "The university is not really autonomous, you only talk as if it were, that is mere ideological decoration; the campus is caught up with the war machine, it serves imperialism, etc. etc." This view breaks down into at least two versions: (a) that because we live in a capitalist society, the university *cannot* be significantly autonomous, and (b) that universities have been allowed by sleepy professors and calloused administrators to drift far from their original or proclaimed purposes and are now seriously contaminated.

The first of these views seems to me not worth taking seriously: it is *quatsch*-Marxism, an insult to Marx, and of a piece with the argument that democracy isn't real either, because we live under capitalism. The second deserves much more serious consideration, particularly in certain universities. And here I think we must ask our students, and ourselves, whether the American universities are so badly distorted that they no longer serve any educational uses of a significant kind, whether in consequence these universities are worth teaching and studying in, and whether they can be seriously improved short of changing the entire society. (I leave aside the fact that many of those who now speak about changing the entire society have no idea of the university that is worthy of respect and often defend uncritically societies such as Cuba and China where universities are far less autonomous and open to critical thought than the worst of the American ones.)

I believe that the university as we know it remains valuable, first as a repository of learning available to rebels as well as conformists, and probably more useful to rebels than conformists; second, as an agency which increasingly enables plebeian youth to transform its social and cultural condition; third, as a relatively or partially autonomous institution which reflects decades of struggle, both by disinterested teachers within and insurgent movements without, to make education available to all classes. That struggle is far from won, but it would be wanton to dismiss what has been achieved.

XI

When the issue arises of whether to call the police onto campus, it clearly signifies that an earlier political battle has been lost. It is important to say this; but not enough. Politically, tactically, humanely, universities should hold off as long as they can, and then a bit longer, before calling the police; the experience of most schools where the police have been called indicates that doing so was a mistake. In the coming period we may even have to accustom ourselves to a kind of "dual power" on campus, with a building or two "taken over" by SDS and the remainder of the university going about its business. At times, that may be preferable to handing the SDS the kind of confrontation on which it thrives. But we must also have the courage to declare that once student protest enters the stage of disruption and violence, once it flouts the rights of other students and teachers, we cannot say that under no conditions would we favor calling the police. It is not a happy choice. Sit-ins and even certain kinds of occupations are better than "busts," especially if the university is not totally disrupted and no effort is made forcibly to prevent others from performing their usual academic duties; yet to forgo in advance the resort to authority is to give a free hand to those who would impose the will of a minority through violence and intimidation.

XII

The solution to campus problems rests mainly outside the campus. Most students one encounters—greatly troubled, sympathetic with some protest demands, strongly inclined to close ranks against punitive adult authority—remain vaguely committed to liberal values and radical reforms. Valuable energy lies unused here, and all that is needed is an adult movement the young can respect.

That movement, however, isn't likely to appear in the next year or two, and those of us on campus will have to bear the consequences. It will be a test of integrity and fortitude: to succumb neither to fellow-traveling with "the young" nor backlash, but to persist in our devotion to rational discourse, democratic procedures, and radical change.

CHAPTER SIX

THE POLITICS OF THE RIGHT

15

The Republican Radical Right

Sheilah Koeppen

Protest movements which view contemporary social and economic policies as evidence of a conspiracy have been a recurring phenomenon of American politics. To the supporters of these movements, the detested policies are being foisted off on the people by Americans in league with a foreign power or infected by a foreign ideology. The charge of conspiracy has been made both by spokesmen for right-wing movements, such as the Native American party, the Know-Nothings, the American Protective Association, and the Ku Klux Klan of the 1920s, and by such left-wing spokesmen as Populist leaders and the publicists of the Nye Committee's investigation of the munitions industry. Since World War I, most believers in a conspiracy theory of American politics have been supporters of right-wing movements, and the conspirators against whom they inveigh have been American Communists and Communist sympathizers, who are supposedly determined to convert the United States into a Communist country by means of "socialistic" economic and social policies. During the decade 1954–1963 anti-Communist groups acquired a large following, a great deal of notoriety, and a

From *The Annals of the American Academy of Political and Social Science* (March 1969), pp. 131–144. Reprinted by permission of publisher and author.

label, the "radical right." [1] Each year since the 1964 presidential election has seen a decrease in the publicity given the Radical Right, and in the rhetoric of some radical-right leaders. "Crime in the streets" has been conjoined with, although not substituted for, "Communists in the State Department." Many of the old radical-right organizations remain active, however, and, if their leaders can be believed, have increased in membership. This "New Right" shares with its predecessor movement a hatred for "socialistic" government programs and a belief that America is threatened from within; it differs from the Radical Right of the post-McCarthy era by placing emphasis on the mysterious Communist conspiracy as well as on objective phenomena of the present day. The "New Right" is still too new for empirical studies to reveal whether the change in style reflects a change in membership and appeal.

This essay will explore the ideology and strategy of the Radical Right. Various conjectures as to the motivations of radical-right supporters will be described and criticized. The trait of the Radical Right for which evidence does exist—their loyalty to the Republican party—will be examined, and conclusions will be drawn as to the impact of the extreme Right on Republican politics.

THE RADICAL RIGHT'S IDEOLOGY AND STRATEGY

The Radical Right's ideology rests on the premise that a minority of Americans are conspiring to capture control of the nation's political and social institutions in order to turn the nation into a Communist satellite. Spokesmen of the Radical Right have described the conspirators as comprising a small group of "card-carrying" Communist agents aided and abetted by a larger group of American socialists, "naïve" liberals, and government officials anxious to advance their careers and economic interests.[2] To the rightists, American Communists and their allies and dupes employ tactics so subtle and insidious that most well-meaning, loyal Americans are likely to be unaware of the danger. Thus, loyal citizens are led unsuspectingly, and often willingly (when they are taken in by promises of benefits from the government), into accepting communism.

---

[1] The John Birch Society became the best known radical-right organization. Other radical-right organizations include: The Christian Anti-Communism Crusade, the Christian Crusade, Veritas Foundation, Freedom in Action, Responsible Enterprise Association, Americans for Constitutional Action, the Minutemen, the Minutewomen, the National Committee for Economic Freedom, Discussion Unlimited, the National Indignation Convention, and Texans for America. Most of these organizations have published newsletters to establish contact with their supporters and solicit contributions. A few radical-right leaders have maintained newsletters but no organization, notably Clarence Manion (*Manion Forum*) and Dan Smoot (*The Dan Smoot Report*). The latter also had a television program of fairly wide distribution, sponsored by Dr. Ross's pet foods. The National Education Program, an Arkansas-based organization, became the best-known producer of anti-Communist pamphlets, books, and films. It produced *Communism on the Map*, the film which is perhaps the one most frequently shown at radical-right meetings.

[2] For example, see James Burnham, *The Web of Subversion* (New York: John Day, 1954); Frederick C. Schwarz, *You Can Trust the Communists (to be Communists)* (Englewood Cliffs, N.J.: Prentice-Hall, 1960); Robert Welch, *The Blue Book of the John Birch Society* (Belmont, Mass.: Author, 1961). The theme can be found in nearly every edition of the newsletters printed by the organizations mentioned in footnote 1 of this article.

This ideology of conspiracy permits easy opposition to most governmental programs. The less the government does, the less machinery it needs to regulate the nation, and the smaller is the danger that the machinery will be taken over by the Communists. The Radical Right has vehemently opposed foreign aid, civil-rights legislation, and the war on poverty. Robert Welch, founder and president of the John Birch Society, has claimed that American Communists promoted American involvement in Vietnam, to distract public attention from their subversive activities. Conversely, leaders of the Radical Right have maintained that policies they favor have been defeated by the machinations of domestic Communists. For example, Welch has argued that Communists engineered the defeat of the Bricker Amendment, the "loss" of China, and Robert A. Taft's failure to win the Republican nomination for president in 1952.[3]

The Radical Right, however, has never restricted its discovery of Communist influence to governmental programs. At one time or another, its leaders have labeled as Communist, or conducive to communism, such disparate features of the American scene as college teachers, the National Council of Churches, the fluoridation of water, and the novels of Vladimir Nabokov and J. D. Salinger.

The first step in the program advocated by the Radical Right for fighting the "Communist conspiracy" is recognition of the conspiracy's existence. Americans are urged to learn about the danger from Communist subversion. Radical-right organizations have staged "schools" of anticommunism and have distributed books, kits for organizing home courses on communism, tapes of lectures, and films. Once apprised of the danger from communism, the follower is urged to study Communist tactics and strategy. The final step is to use these tactics, when participating in civic and political activities, in order to defeat Communist programs and purge Communists and their allies from government, the public schools, and colleges and universities.[4]

Considering the source of their training manual, it is not surprising that some methods by which some rightists have participated in politics and civic affairs are unacceptable: threatening telephone calls to opposition-party candidates and voters; disrespectful treatment of opponents, such as the jeers greeting Rockefeller at the 1964 Republican Convention and the jostling of Adlai Stevenson in 1963; and the paramilitary training programs of the Minutemen. However, these extreme tactics were not used by many supporters of the Radical Right, and, what is probably more important, those rightists who did undertake them did not refrain from also engaging in conventional political activities.

MOTIVATIONS ATTRIBUTED TO SUPPORTERS OF THE RADICAL RIGHT

From 1955 through 1964, the era of postmortems on McCarthyism and of the Radical Right's greatest activity, journalists, social scientists, and historians contributed many analyses of the appeal, the sources of support, and the political im-

---

[3] Robert Welch, *The New Americanism and Other Speeches and Essays* (Boston: Western Islands, 1966), pp. 20–23.
[4] For example, see Schwarz, *You Can Trust the Communists;* J. Allen Broyles, *The John Birch Society* (Boston: Beacon Press, 1964), p. 72.

pact of the Radical Right.[5] Most of the observers, perhaps fascinated by the banner that the Radical Right carried into political battles, focused on its rhetoric of conspiracy. As a result, supporters of the Radical Right were pictured as disturbed people who subscribed to warnings of Communist subversion in order to rationalize grievances and secure a scapegoat for their discontent. A sizable number of conjectures were made concerning what motivated people to accept a conspiracy theory and to use it as a guide in assessing public policies, but these various conjectures can be boiled down to five major psychosociological theses.

Authoritarianism

A classic study of personality and politics has suggested that persons with extremely conservative political preferences (and not specifically the Radical Right) also have authoritarian social and personal standards of conduct.[6] An authoritarian person is obsessed by the need to conform to rigid, conventional codes of behavior, and to comply with the orders of leaders, and is resentful of people whose behavior deviates from these codes. Authoritarian persons oppose changes in existing social norms and in the social structure. The Radical Right's attack on contemporary socioeconomic trends was said to appeal to the authoritarian's inherent opposition to social change.

Alienation

The suggestion that supporters of the Radical Right are alienated has been advanced in recent analyses.[7] People who are alienated feel that they have no stake in society, that they are the helpless victims of forces beyond their control. The politically alienated believe that they are neglected by the government, and that they can do little or nothing to influence governmental policies. Such people were considered likely to be attracted to the Radical Right because the contention that Communists dominate the government would provide them with a rationalization of the government's neglect of their interests.

---

[5] The essays collected by Daniel Bell (ed.), in *The Radical Right* (Garden City, N.Y.: Doubleday, 1963), provide a wide range of comments on and analyses of radical-right phenomena. Most of the issue of the *Journal of Social Issues*, 19 (April 1963), devoted to extremism, concentrated on the Radical Right. A selection of popular writings on the movement includes: Fred J. Cook, "The Ultras: Aims, Affiliations and Finances of the Radical Right," *The Nation*, 194 (June 30, 1962), 1–68; R. Dudman, *Men of the Far Right* (New York: Pyramid Books, 1962); Benjamin R. Epstein and Arnold Foster, *The Radical Right: Report on the John Birch Society and Its Allies* (New York: Random House, 1967); Philip Horton, "Revivalism on the Far Right," *The Reporter*, 25 (July 20, 1961), 25–29; David Jansen and Bernard Eismann, *The Far Right* (New York: McGraw-Hill, 1963); Harry and Bonaro Overstreet, *The Strange Tactics of Extremism* (New York: W. W. Norton, 1964); Mark Sherwin, *The Extremists* (New York: St. Martin's Press, 1963).
[6] Theodore Adorno et al., *The Authoritarian Personality* (New York: Harper & Row, 1950).
[7] Edward Shils, *The Torment of Secrecy* (New York: Free Press, 1956), p. 231; Gilbert Abcarian and Sherman M. Stanage, "Alienation and the Radical Right," *Journal of Politics*, 27 (November 1965), 776–796.

Fundamentalism

The Fundamentalist movement of the 1920s is generally considered a right-wing manifestation.[8] Richard Hofstadter and Daniel Bell suggested that the radical-right organizations of the 1960s have attracted people with Fundamentalist religious values who are disturbed because these values are no longer dominant in America.[9] Fundamentalists have been considered likely recruits to the Radical Right because the movement's ideology offers an explanation of the decline of Christian values in America: because Communists are "Godless," the fact that Fundamentalist values no longer prevail is a result of Communist subversion.[10]

Concern about Social Status

The most popular descriptions of supporters of radical-right organizations have been based on the "status-frustration hypothesis."[11] According to one version of this hypothesis, people have joined the Radical Right to protest social changes and governmental policies which have deprived them of the position in society to which they feel entitled by virtue of their education or the social standing of their parents.[12] Supporters of the Radical Right have been described as feeling not only that they have been cut down from their former high social position, but that change has conferred "their" position upon Americans with newer skills and values.[13] Alternatively, supporters of the Radical Right have been described as a sort of *nouveau riche*, uneasy in a status higher than that of their parents. A third variation of the hypothesis identifies, as likely supporters of the Radical Right, first- and second-generation Americans descended from ethnic groups native to southern and eastern Europe, who are more sensitive about their status than are descendants of earlier northern European immigrants. These newer ethnic groups are said to be attracted to a movement whose avowed purpose is to protect the United States from subversives because they believe that their support will prove them good Americans.[14]

---

[8] See Norman F. Furniss, *The Fundamentalist Controversy, 1918–1931* (New Haven, Conn.: Yale University Press, 1954), *passim*.

[9] Richard Hofstadter, *The Paranoid Style in American Politics and Other Essays* (New York: Alfred A. Knopf, 1965), p. 81; Daniel Bell, "The Dispossessed (1962)," in Bell (ed.), *The Radical Right*, pp. 19–21.

[10] Hofstadter, *The Paranoid Style*, pp. 80–81.

[11] Hofstadter introduced this hypothesis in *The Age of Reform* (New York: Alfred A. Knopf, 1955). In his 1955 essay, "The Pseudo-Conservative Revolt," Hofstadter uses the notion of status-frustration to describe the supporters of right-wing movements.—Bell (ed.), *The Radical Right*, pp. 63–80. While confessing to "mixed feelings" about the validity of the concept as applied to the radical right, Hofstadter continues to employ it. See *The Paranoid Style in American Politics and Other Essays*, pp. 75–86. Seymour M. Lipset uses the concept in his analysis of "Three Decades of the Radical Right: Coughlinites, McCarthyites, and Birchers (1962)," in Bell (ed.), *The Radical Right*, pp. 313–377.

[12] David Riesman and Nathan Glazer, "The Intellectuals and the Discontented Classes (1955)," in Bell (ed.), *The Radical Right*, pp. 89–90.

[13] Bell, "The Dispossessed (1962)," p. 17.

[14] Hofstadter, "The Pseudo-Conservative Revolt (1955)," p. 74; Lipset, "Three Decades," p. 334.

Anxiety over Urbanization

It is unquestionable that a sizable number of Americans are resentful of the nation's rapid change from a rural to an urban society. Some analyses of the Radical Right have suggested that such people joined the movement to protest the decline in importance of the interests and values of the farm and the small town.[15] The attack by the Radical Right on economic regulation and welfare was seen as providing these people with a convenient means of asserting opposition to claims associated with urban interest groups. A more sophisticated version of this "unhappy farmer" theme has predicted strong support for the Radical Right from residents of areas of the country which are experiencing rapid growth. The enormous changes in economic, political, and cultural institutions in such areas, it has been suggested, have produced feelings of confusion and insecurity in the long-time residents, and the large number of newcomers will arrive, and remain, insecure. Seymour M. Lipset has suggested this as the reason for the Radical Right's success in southern California;[16] Daniel Bell applied the hypothesis to the new urban centers of the Southwest.[17]

PARTY IDENTIFICATION OF SUPPORTERS OF THE RADICAL RIGHT

Despite the considerable attention given to the Radical Right, little data has been collected to establish these speculations about its supporters. Such data as exist suggest that the supporters may be more accurately discerned by their political loyalties than by their conjectured social and psychological traits.

In an empirical study of support for Senator Joseph McCarthy, Nelson Polsby has found that McCarthy's political power was based more on the increasing Republican power in the United States than on support from particular social or economic groups.[18] Daniel Bell has suggested that the radical-right movement is also much more likely to attract Republicans than Democrats or Independents,[19] and three empirical studies support this hypothesis. Seymour M. Lipset found that Californians who consider themselves Republicans were more likely to be sympathetic to the John Birch Society than were Democrats or Independents.[20] Survey research on the clientele of two "schools" of anticommunism held by Dr. Fred Schwarz' Christian Anti-Communism Crusade in the San Francisco Bay Area in 1962 revealed that two-thirds of these "Crusaders" were Republicans. Of the remaining third, Independents outnumbered Democrats two to one, and many of the Independents indicated that they voted for Republican candidates.[21] If sup-

---

[15] Bell, "The Dispossessed," pp. 19–24; Talcott Parsons, "Social Strains in America: A Postscript, 1962," in Bell (ed.), *The Radical Right*, p. 197.
[16] Lipset, "Three Decades," pp. 362–363.
[17] Bell, "The Dispossessed," p. 19.
[18] Nelson W. Polsby, "Toward an Explanation of McCarthyism," *Political Studies*, 8 (October 1960), 250–271.
[19] Bell, "The Dispossessed," p. 3.
[20] Lipset, "Three Decades," pp. 353–357.
[21] Raymond E. Wolfinger, Barbara Kaye Wolfinger, Kenneth Prewitt, and Sheilah Rosenhack, "America's Radical Right: Politics and Ideology," in David Apter (ed.), *Ideology and Discontent* (New York: Free Press, 1964), pp. 267–269; Sheilah R. Koeppen,

port for a referendum measure which was drafted to inhibit the activities of American Communists is an indirect indicator of sympathy for the Radical Right, the foregoing studies are buttressed by the results of a survey of voters in one southern California assembly district. The survey found a greater number of Republicans than of Democrats or Independents to be in favor of the measure.[22]

The two studies of the Crusaders reveal not only the fact of their Republicanism, but its depth as well. Crusaders are far more active than the average in party politics, and the most dedicated Crusaders are also the most active in politics.[23] Although Crusaders perceive Communist influence in a wide variety of American political and social institutions, few of them think that Communists have penetrated the Republican party, which is considered by them to be about as trustworthy as the Federal Bureau of Investigation. In contrast, 60 percent of the Crusaders surveyed at the second Crusade school think that Communists "have a lot of influence in" the Democratic party.[24]

These findings, indicating an association between Republicanism and support for the Radical Right, are in sharp contrast to the absence of findings confirming most psychosociological descriptions of radical-right supporters.[25]

The Radical Right's attraction for authoritarian persons has not been proved. Neither the Crusade studies nor a study of a group of graduate students which included persons of all political persuasions found any evidence of an association between rightist views and authoritarian attitudes.[26]

Alienated people tend to be apathetic about politics or to engage solely in protest activities. But, as indicated by the Crusade studies, supporters of the Radical Right are active in partisan politics as well as in organizations formed specifically to promote their preferences. While the Radical Right is distressed about American politics, it does not feel incapable of effective political action.

The proposal that Fundamentalists are attracted to the Radical Right has a certain surface validity. A few radical-right organizations, most notably, Billy Hargis' Christian Crusade, are affiliated with a Fundamentalist church, and radical-right leaders like Dan Smoot and Dr. Schwarz make no secret of their membership in a Fundamentalist denomination. However, only a small Fundamentalist group was isolated in the first Crusade survey, and none at all was found at the second Crusade school. On the whole, Crusaders were affiliated with non-Fundamentalist, high-status Protestant churches and did not attend church more often

---

"Dissensus and Discontent: The Clientele of the Christian Anti-Communism Crusade" (Ph.D. diss., Stanford University, 1967), pp. 28–30.

[22] Thirty percent of the people who consider themselves Democrats, 32 percent of those who consider themselves Independents, and 52 percent of those who consider themselves Republicans were in favor of the "Francis Amendment" in 1962.—Jenniellen W. Ferguson and Paul J. Hoffman, "Voting Behavior: The Vote on the Francis Amendment in the 1962 California Election," *Western Political Quarterly*, 17 (December 1964), 771–772.

[23] Wolfinger et al., in Apter (ed.), *Ideology and Discontent*, p. 277; Koeppen, "Dissensus and Discontent," pp. 33–34.

[24] Koeppen, "Dissensus and Discontent," p. 101.

[25] Wolfinger and associates delineated most of these psychosociological propositions; their persistence in the literature provided an impetus for empirical study of a radical-right group.—Wolfinger et al., in Apter (ed.), *Ideology and Discontent*.

[26] Koeppen, "Dissensus and Discontent," pp. 61–65; Edwin N. Barker, "Authoritarianism of the Political Right, Center and Left," *Journal of Social Issues*, 19 (April 1963), 63–74.

than white Northern Protestants.[27] It appears doubtful that the defense of Fundamentalist religious values can serve to explain the support for the Radical Right on a nationwide basis.

The conjectures about the status-frustration of the Radical Right are also of dubious validity. The Crusade schools did not attract people with traits denoting status-anxiety. Crusaders, on the average, possess high status by virtue of their education and occupations; their parents enjoyed a similar high status. Crusaders are no more mobile than the Bay-area population, and are native-born, of northern European stock.[28] Other studies of the general population have found that social mobility is not linked with a preference for rightist positions,[29] and have discerned no consistent association between uncertainty about social status and right-wing extremism.[30]

At the psychological level, the hypothesis that anxiety over urbanization motivates the supporters of the Radical Right is also not established. A recent study of the population of San José and San Diego in California, both of which are areas experiencing explosive urban growth, indicates that only in San Diego does the populace show a preference for ultraconservative politics.[31] However, support for the Radical Right does display some regional associations. While radical-right groups have been active throughout the nation, western and southwestern communities have been most vulnerable to the appeal of the Radical Right and have provided radical-right meetings with the largest audiences.[32] It is perhaps noteworthy that the West and Southwest are the areas of the United States which are experiencing the most rapid population growth, and therefore, presumably, more rapid urbanization. Yet, the affinity of these areas for the Radical Right need not be explained on the basis of the urban-anxiety thesis. A form of regionalism has been a factor in earlier radical movements. Populism was strongest in midwestern and central states, whose people resented eastern financial institutions; in the

[27] Wolfinger et al., in Apter (ed.), *Ideology and Discontent*, pp. 268, 281–283; Koeppen, "Dissensus and Discontent," pp. 27–28, 49, 131.
[28] Wolfinger et al., in Apter (ed.), *Ideology and Discontent*, pp. 278–280; Koeppen, "Dissensus and Discontent," pp. 50–56.
[29] James Alden Barber, Jr., "Social Mobility and Political Behavior" (Ph.D. diss., Stanford University, 1965), pp. 326–329; Robert W. Hodge and Donald J. Trieman, "Occupational Mobility and Attitudes Toward Negroes," *American Sociological Review*, 31 (February 1966), 93–102.
[30] See Donald J. Trieman, "Status Discrepancy and Prejudice," *American Journal of Sociology*, 71 (May 1966), 651–664. One survey of a general population did find that people with a low level of education who held white-collar jobs expressed some preference for rightest attitudes. But the author admits that the small number of people so classified in his sample makes the finding tentative, and he found an even slighter preference for rightist attitudes among people with the reverse inconsistent social status, a high level of education and a blue-collar job.—Gary Rush, "Status Consistency and Right-Wing Extremism," *American Sociological Review*, 32 (February 1967), 86–92.
[31] Raymond E. Wolfinger and Fred I. Greenstein, "The Political Cultures of California," in press, pp. 8–9.
[32] There is evidence in support of this statement if a preference for Goldwater is considered to indicate support for the Radical Right. An intensive analysis of Gallup polls on preference for Goldwater as the Republican presidential candidate in 1964 found a preference for Goldwater to be associated more closely with region—greatest in the West and South—than with any social or economic trait. A preference for the Republican party is the next most significant indicator of a preference for Goldwater.—Irving Crespi, "The Structural Basis for Right-Wing Conservatism: The Goldwater Case," *Public Opinion Quarterly*, 29 (Winter 1965–1966), 523–543.

McCarthy era, denunciations of those federal officials born or educated on the East Coast were common. The rightist activity in the West and Southwest today may reflect, in part, a protest against the continuing dominance of eastern economic and political institutions, despite the enormous growth of the West.

By questioning these conjectures concerning sources of support for the Radical Right, I do not mean to imply that no common psychosociological factors can be found among the members of radical-right organizations. There is simply no proof of what these factors are. There is proof of the loyal Republicanism of the Radical Right.

THE RADICAL RIGHT, THE NEW RIGHT, AND PARTY POLITICS

The loyalty of the Radical Right to the Republican party, and its willingness to undertake political-party activity, have been discussed. To the extent that the supporters of the Christian Anti-Communism Crusade provide a fair measure of the Radical Right, this loyalty is founded upon trust in the Republican party. The Radical Right is obsessed by a fear of Communist subversion, and the Republican party is the only entity of government—state, local, or national—which the majority believes to be free of the Communist taint.

This allegiance of the Radical Right has been a dubious blessing to the Republican party. Many, if not most, Republicans consider the ideology of the Radical Right ridiculous, its policy proposals outmoded, and the more extreme of its political tactics outrageous. Yet, the support of the Radical Right is valuable to a political party, less in the numbers of rightists than in the time and money which they are willing to devote to Republican activities.[33] The result has been an uneasy alliance between the Radical Right and the Republican party. Republican party leaders have denounced political extremism in general terms, but have usually refrained from singling out for attack a particular radical-right organization.[34] At its 1965 meeting, the Republican Co-ordinating Committee endorsed a "compromise" statement on accepting support from rightists; Republicans were urged not to join extremist movements, but no radical-right organization was named as extremist.[35] The Radical Right appears to be able to live with this qualified rejection, as witnessed by its acceptance by John Rousselot, public relations director of the John Birch Society,[36] and the determination to remain active within the Republican party expressed by radical-right leaders at a 1965 Congress of Conservatives organized by Kent Courtney.[37]

[33] The Radical Right is not only a source of campaign funds for the Republican party but a potential drain on regular Republican contributions. Reporters have noted that, in their heyday, the radical-right organizations were getting financial support from some sources that previously donated funds to the Party.—"Bidding for the Right-Wing Dollar," *The Nation*, 194 (January 20, 1962), 42–43; Richard Rovere, "Letter from Washington: Factional Conflict," *New Yorker*, 38 (February 14, 1962), 122.
[34] For example, see Richard Nixon's statement, *San Francisco Chronicle*, January 10, 1962, p. 9.
[35] *San Francisco Chronicle*, December 14, 1965, p. 14.
[36] *San Francisco Chronicle*, December 14, 1965, p. 14.
[37] One delegate to the congress was quoted as representing the sentiment of many supporters of the Radical Right. " 'Only through the Republican Party would we have a chance. If we split into two parties it would produce a Democratic-Socialist landslide that would open the way to complete one party rule and to dictatorship.' "—Raymond R. Coffey, "The Patrioteers Convene," *The Nation*, 200 (May 17, 1965), 520.

In some areas, the Radical Right has had considerable success in controlling or influencing the Republican party. Since 1962, radical rightists and conservative allies have gained control of much of the Republican party machinery in California. No extremists have been elected to state-wide office, but an avowed member of the John Birch Society sits in the state Senate; Senator George Murphy and Governor Ronald Reagan are more conservative than most Republican officeholders since World War II; and the conservative Max Rafferty has defeated the liberal Thomas Kuchel for the Republican nomination for the second Senate seat. Criticism of the Radical Right by local Republican leaders is minimal, and only one successful effort has been made to oust the rightists and conservatives from their party posts.[38] It has been observed that (then) Governor Brown's attack on Reagan for his affiliations with the Radical Right apparently won Brown little voter support.[39]

But this uneasy alliance might be subjected to new strains. While concern is still voiced by radical-right leaders over the Communist menace, the focus of the "New Right" is on specific problems: the increase in crime, the use of drugs, the ghetto riots, student rebellions and demonstrations, and the Supreme Court decisions which are seen as protecting these "lawless" activities. The more the attention of the rightists swings from a vague and mysterious Communist conspiracy to focus on the patent problems of today, the more difficult it might be for the Republican party to satisfy the extremists by what they will consider half-measures. Nearly all Republicans, if not nearly all Americans, were in favor of removing Communists from the State Department ten years ago (although many found the methods used objectionable). There is no comparable unanimity within the Republican party on the proper method of handling ghetto riots and student demonstrations. The Republican party cannot move far to the right without sacrificing the major part of its support. In the area of real problems, and despite the notable party loyalty of the extremists, it is questionable that the Party can edge far enough to the right to satisfy the New Right, but not so far as to alienate its moderate members.

On the other hand, it is likely that the "alliance" between extremists of the Right and the Republican party will continue, at least for the next few years. The material and symbolic rewards that the party in power can distribute are an inducement to unity among its factions. In addition, the rightists view a Republican administration with a confidence born of the belief that the Party's officials are not subject to Communist influence. Their inclination to trust the current administration will constrain rightist agitation.

---

[38] From 1964 to date, the officers of two of the three major state party organizations—the California Republican Assembly and the United Republicans of California—have been hostile to moderate and liberal candidates and their proposals.—Totten J. Anderson and Eugene C. Lee, "The 1964 Election in California," *Western Political Quarterly*, 18 (June 1965), 455–460. See also the same authors' "The 1966 Election in California," *Western Political Quarterly*, 20 (June 1967), 538–539, 512–543. From 1964 until February 1968, when they lost the control of the organization required to elect its president in a bitter convention fight, a right-wing faction dominated the California Young Republicans.

[39] Anderson and Lee, "The 1966 Election," pp. 539, 543.

16
The Righteous Rightist
Ira S. Rohter

- The Watts riots have been traced directly to plans laid down by Lenin in Moscow. (The Los Angeles Communists, who organized the riots, cleverly blew up their own headquarters in order to appear as innocent martyrs.)
- Progressive education (a term including most modern educational methods) was inaugurated by a Columbia University professor on his return from Moscow; it is a deliberate design to expedite the Red take-over by turning our children into un-Christian, un-American, mindless, and will-less robots. For proof of success, we have only to look at Berkeley.

The two stories above—much more heavily elaborated and "documented"—are typical of the items that appear in radical right publications. They illustrate well the characteristic that distinguishes radical rightists from other Americans.[1]

From *TRANS-action* (May 1967), pp. 27–35. Copyright © 1967 by *TRANS-action*. Reprinted by permission of publisher and author. A more complete presentation of this study appeared in "Social and Psychological Determinants of Radical Rightism," in Robert Schoenberger (ed.), *The American Right Wing* (Holt, Rinehart and Winston, 1969).

[1] Radical rightists generally keep their membership lists secret. Therefore, for the purposes of this study they were defined in terms of their characteristic activities and beliefs.

Radical rightists were defined as those people who believed, to a large degree, in the existence of an internal Communist conspiracy infiltrating all levels of government and

Radical rightists are not merely conservatives or even arch-conservatives. What occupies them full time, what gives them their unique voltage and drive, is not their reverence for old-fashioned fiscal policies and morals, but what Richard Hofstadter calls their "paranoid style"—the overriding and galvanizing belief in a gigantic, insidious Communist conspiracy that has infiltrated and infected all levels of American government and most of its social institutions. The calm conservative who would merely like to see a balanced budget and less welfare is not really a rightist, and they both know it.

Another distinct characteristic by which the rightist (I shall call him that for brevity) may be known is his dedication to *action*. When the enemy is already within the gates attacking all that we hold dear, the true patriot does not sit idly by discussing the income tax or civil rights—he mounts the counterattack.

For the purposes of this study, therefore (and because membership lists and other identifications are often secret), I have used these two characteristics—belief in Communist conspiracy and in direct action—to define and describe rightists, and I have drawn my samples accordingly.

WHO'S RIGHT?

How do people get to be rightists? A major thesis of this article is that rightists are the victims of *status frustration*. That is, for some reason they are dissatisfied or insecure about their places in society and feel that others do not esteem them sufficiently; further, they express their frustration, and compensate for it, by political and social acts which give them emotional identity and support as well as real influence.

Many psychologists regard the striving for self-regard as an essential social and psychological need. To a large extent self-regard must depend on how others regard us. Nobody can really tolerate feeling downgraded or ignored; he must make some defense. The rightist chooses the path of radical right ideology and action, which pinpoints and personifies his enemy as a horrendous evil (and the rightist, therefore, as a kind of St. George) and gives him a means to combat it—not merely for himself but as a champion for all decent mankind.

The rightist becomes loudly superpatriotic—which makes anyone disagreeing suspect of un-Americanism. Those who are higher or richer than he (as the Communist-infiltrated world sees them) or who possess different values can be pulled down to their true levels—below the rightist on the scale of virtue—by being exposed as "Communist."

---

most social institutions in the United States and who were deeply involved in action to counter this Communist threat.

The sample was selected from lists of people who, through such activity and through their expressions, had made their rightist orientations matters of public record. Specifically, names were taken from a newspaper article listing members of the John Birch Society and the Liberty Amendment Committee in a Northwestern city; others were found through published "letters to the editor." Fifty-six came from a list of contributors and subscribers to a radical right organization and publication. Similarly, the sample of non-rightists was selected through content analysis of other "letters to the editor" and from referenda petitions. The final sample from which the analysis was made contained 169 rightists and 167 non-rightists.

DUEL WITH THE DEVIL

Of course, such an orientation—and such action—depend heavily on a highly charged emotionalism and a closed system of paranoid-like logic that is impervious to objective facts that happen to differ. For instance, Communism cannot be considered primarily a political, social, and economic movement and system of thought capable of objective study. Such an idea horrifies the rightist. Communism is Satan personified; it can be faced only in a fight to the death, and only by those properly armed and inoculated.

People who undergo status frustration generally fall into three categories: the *decliners*, the *new arrivals*, and the *value keepers*.

The Decliners

These are the people in our modern, changing society who are going down in the social scale—undeservedly, as they see it.

Modern technology and modern organizations increasingly require new skills, new orientations, more education. Those trained under different and outmoded disciplines (small farmers, for instance) and those with insufficient or outdated educations must feel their positions becoming more and more insecure.

Also threatened are the old professional and entrepreneur classes, especially from the smaller communities: the small-town general practitioner in medicine, the small home builder, gas station owner, neighborhood grocer—in fact most independent operators trying to survive in the shadows of the great corporations, large labor unions, and big government agencies. The well-educated professionals and corporate executives are taking over the small businessman's role in the community. He is being shoved aside; the hard work and independence on which he had built his self-esteem and his concept of the good and righteous life become increasingly worthless and irrelevant. He begins to ask *why*? Who is doing this to me?

A similar process affects workers, both white and blue collar, displaced by new methods and machinery. They find themselves useless, and their self-regard wavers. The elderly without funds are in an even worse situation—our society no longer respects age, especially when it pulls no economic weight.

As these groups decline, their consciousness of rejection is made even more acute by the rise of those formerly considered low-class or rejected. An Irish Catholic, grandson of an immigrant, is elected President; a Negro "agitator" receives many honors and confers frequently at the White House. Jews are everywhere in prominent places. Again the decliner—often of old white stock—asks *why*?

The New Arrivals

Status frustration occurs not only on the way down, but on the way up. There is almost always a lag between the time the gauche new arrival achieves success and the time those who got there first accept him as an equal. Like the decliner he can easily feel that he has come into a closed and unfriendly society that will not recognize virtue. He is especially upset since he earned it himself in the good old American way instead of being handed prestige on a silver platter.

To the newly arrived, radical rightism can be a potent weapon to destroy their mighty enemies—those who had the opportunity to be better educated, better mannered, more cosmopolitan, and, obviously, more prone to liberal ideas and "bohemian" behavior and immoralities. The charge of "Communism" is a great leveler, and the newly rich can often be counted upon to be twice as narrowly patriotic as anybody.

The Value Keepers

Those moving up or down the ladder of success are bound to find themselves, temporarily at least, among aliens who know not the Lord, but so should those who merely stand still long enough in a society that changes as fast as ours.

A person of any conviction or integrity has social and moral values and beliefs that help determine his behavior, his self-definition, and his place in the community. But let the community begin to re-examine those values critically or displace them with others, and the foundation of his whole universe begins to turn to sand.

For the great majority of us, many of the traditional rural or small-town ways or virtues are no longer useful or true. Modern society needs education and expertise more than hard work and self-denial; an expanding economy rather than thrift; organized community welfare programs rather than primary reliance on savings, personal charity, relatives, and contemplation of the sufferings of Job.

Moreover, the preponderance of political and economic power, for good or ill, has definitely shifted from the country with its white settlers to the metropolis with its combinations of minority populations. Those whose beliefs and behavior were shaped by older traditions—who, as they see it, settled and built this country—now find themselves, in effect, increasingly disinherited.

Even more important than the objective loss of power and prestige are the *subjective* feelings of loss, of being displaced and discredited. God and the devil, good and evil, are absolutes and do not change; therefore, the change that discredits and displaces the old morality must be evil triumphing over good. Only by such rationalization can true believers retain their orientation and self-regard.

The values defended include hard work, saving, prudent investment, and self-discipline—the Protestant ethic. As the name implies, these values are not only economic but moral, with deep psychological meaning. They are supposed to result in independence and individualism, as the rightist sees them. An apparent attack on them—such as increased government control or taxes—becomes not only an economic change but an immorality and must be answered.

Therefore, as experience demonstrates daily, those most closely identified with older traditional values reduce and discuss almost all social problems to moralistic terms: If the wayward society or individual would only cease transgression and return to the old tried-and-true paths of religion, decency, and family virtue, all would in time be well.

This accounts for much of the intense and emotional opposition to social change by rightists—the counterattack, often blind, to government controls, integration, religious secularism, welfare, the United Nations, foreign aid, Supreme Court decisions, modern education, and even such apparently non-controversial scientific and health advances as fluoridation and mental health programs.

Fundamentalism is an important source of rightist fervor. In fact, from their titles and rhetoric, it is hard to distinguish between a rightist political rally and an evangelistic campaign—note the Rev. Carl McIntire's "Twentieth Century Reformation" and Dr. Fred Schwarz's "Christian Anti-Communist Crusade." Communism, a twentieth-century abomination, becomes the catch-all for everything that seems evil and unacceptable in the easygoing, affluent, sophisticated, urban twentieth century.

These then are the theses advanced about the rightist which I tested in this study:

• Rightists are people undergoing status frustration. They feel they do not have the prestige and power they should have if the world were just—and their enemies have too much. They are on the move as far as status is concerned—either they are going down in a changing world (which should be true of most of them), they are standing still as the world passes them by, or they are rising more rapidly in economic position than in social recognition.
• They identify themselves with the older, traditional (Protestant ethic) values of work, religion, and morality, so that their fight for status recognition also becomes a crusade for truth, justice, decency, God, and America.
• They believe that their troubles—and therefore also the attack against Christianity and America—are caused by an all-pervasive conspiracy, wholly evil and implacable, called Communism.
• They relieve their anxieties and feelings of resentment and inadequacy by radical right belief and activity. This gives them an effective explanation and compensation for their difficulties, a means of bringing their enemies down, and a method of gaining power, prestige, and mutual support.

Do these hypotheses survive empirical examination?

To start with objective findings first: Are the rightists of our sample actually undergoing status mobility and frustration?

The data show that there are only 10 percent of rightists in the highest occupations, such as executives and professionals, compared to 24 percent of non-rightists; and that rightists are over-represented among the lower-middle class (such as clerical and salesworkers)—15 to 4 percent.

Further, nearly twice as many rightists as others are retired—removed, for most practical purposes, from economic importance to society altogether. Rightists also tend to be older (median age 54 compared to 45) and are more often self-employed (although at lower levels)—if businessmen, they tend to run smaller businesses; if professionals, their standing is lower.

In profile, therefore, the radical rightist is older, less secure financially, and less often an important part of a major modern industrial enterprise; he more often has a low prestige white-collar job or is thrown on his own resources—retired or operator of a marginal "independent" business. Such a picture is quite consistent with the status frustration hypothesis; such a person, especially if he identifies with an older tradition that was once dominant, could hardly help feeling frustrated.

Occupation alone, however, is not enough to measure social standing. What of education? In our increasingly sophisticated society, education is not only a necessity but a mark of prestige, especially in the middle and upper classes. But even in these occupational strata the rightists have less education than their non-rightist equivalents. In the highest levels (high executives, proprietors, major professionals, etc.) almost twice as many non-rightists as rightists have graduate degrees (64 percent to 33 percent), while three times as many rightists (12 percent to 4 percent) never went beyond high school. In the middle levels over twice as many non-rightists got college degrees (27 percent to 12 percent) while over twice as many rightists (54 percent to 24) never went beyond high school.

DOWN AND TO THE RIGHT

What about mobility? Comparing a male rightist's (or a female rightist's husband's) occupation and education with those of his father (this is called "intergenerational status mobility"), we found, as hypothesized, that the rightist did undergo much more status mobility than non-rightists, most often downward.

In the *lowest* occupations (typically, unskilled blue-collar) the rightists had fallen farther and more consistently than non-rightists had done anywhere. Thirty-eight percent of rightist men compared to 6 percent non-rightist had declined sharply. Rightist laborers were quite apt to have had middle-class or farm-owning fathers.

In the *middle* groups (white-collar, small business) rightists were more mobile, both up and down, than non-rightists. Relatively few had stayed at the same occupational and educational level as their fathers (14 to 29 percent). There tended to be a few more losers than winners.

In the *highest status*, however, rightists on the way up surpass not only those on the way down but even the relatively static non-rightists. This fits in very well with the thesis that the "newly arrived" undergo status frustration.

As predicted, therefore, the rightists had significantly greater mobility, especially downward, and less education where it counted most.

Another way to measure mobility should be by length of residence in a neighborhood. The old fundamentalist morality is closely associated with a rural and small-town past; many people from that background, who cling to the old standards, have moved to a faceless Babylon of a city where they have few skills they can use. Those on the way down—or in from the farm—must move into poorer neighborhoods; those on the way up, though they take their values and their accents with them, are most likely, as soon as possible, to move to higher-status suburbs or neighborhoods. Those who stay the shortest time should therefore be the most mobile.

Studying length of residence of people under 50, we found two basic groups of rightists. One seems to be primarily composed of people new to the community who seem unable to accept or be accepted by that community; also, they are declining in status more rapidly than a similar group of equally mobile non-rightists.

The other rightist cluster is composed of old-timers who have lived in their communities most of their adult lives; they are considerably older than their neighbors, and many more turn up in the 50 and 60 age brackets. Their neighborhoods have gone down, and they have declined in status with them. Here too, therefore, there seems a clear association between decline (whether in new or old residency) and radical rightism.

THAT OLD-TIME RELIGION

Are rightists to any significant extent fundamentalists? Belief in traditional values, along with many rightist attitudes, was earlier related to religious fundamentalism. Empirically, this is true. Rightists very much subscribe to fundamentalist tenets and belong to these churches; nearly half the rightists (44 percent compared to 17 percent of the non-rightists) are affiliated with fundamentalist denominations. Rightists were also more often raised in rural areas or small towns, environments most likely to produce traditionalism and hostility toward modernity.

So much for objective factors. How do the people themselves view their plights?

Fewer rightists than non-rightists actually belong to the upper class; but more of them *rated themselves* "upper class." When asked, "How hard do you think it is for people today to move upward from one social class to another?" their answers revealed a view of society as essentially closed, dominated by personalities, controlled by the wrong kinds of people:

> Not much opportunity anymore; it's getting harder; depends on having money, knowing the right people.

The views of the non-rightists were much more objective and impersonal:

> Depends on education; must work hard and have abilities to get it; special skills; hard to change direction of early life. . . .

We asked, "Do you think that people . . . influential in this community are, in *general,* friendly . . . or cliquish?" Rightists answered "cliquish and unfriendly" more often than non-rightists. When those answering "cliquish" were asked to give reasons, rightists more often indicated belief in a closed structure run by a small group:

> Old residents tend to look on new people as outsiders; certain families run things here; segregated groups want their own way; all have common political views.

The rightist, then, more often sees himself as the outsider, discriminated against in a closed society run by an elite.

What about the predicted concern with the Protestant ethic? We asked, "Are there any differences between what you believe should be the American way of life, and the way things are done in the country nowadays?" "In what way are things different?" Typically, from the rightists:

> Morality and standards are going bad; the American way of life is deteriorating because of a suppression of morality; we need a moral and spiritual revival among our leaders; we need to follow the Ten Commandments more.

RUGGED INDIVIDUALISTS

What about individual initiative, self-reliance, respect for authority?

> I am worried about the drift of the country; the amount of crime and disrespect for authority shows things are going the other way; we must instill more emphasis on respect, integrity, and individual responsibility; parents aren't teaching their children the right things any more.

Traditional morality and values dominate many rightists' perception of everything. No matter what the topic—what things they worried about, what community concerns they had, what qualities they admired, what things Communists actually believed in, whatever—sooner or later they indicated that if we would only return to the old morality every problem would be solved.

Our findings are clear: The rightists are more dissatisfied with the values of contemporary American society; they adhere to the "old truths" and believe everyone else should "return" to them. They suffer severe frustration because of this, a frustration heavily reinforced by a religious righteousness expressed in absolute and positive terms.

"In your own case . . . do you think that *everyone* gives you as much respect as *you feel you* deserve?" This question was deliberately worded to emphasize extremes—yet rightists answered "no" more frequently than non-rightists. This is true both of rightists who are on the way up and those on the way down; but the decliners say "no" *twice* as often as those on the rise—emphasizing that it is the losers who are most impelled to seek radical rightism. (Presumably, once those on the rise secure recognition, they will cease attacking high-status people and changing times.)

Rightists felt more unaccepted than non-rightists, and rightists on the decline more unaccepted than anybody.

Does joining radical right organizations and causes help the rightist combat his anxieties successfully? By being more patriotic and anti-Communist than anybody else, the rightist seems to wrap himself in greatness and goodness, in importance, righteousness, and self-satisfaction. He is a savior carrying out a holy crusade. As the *John Birch Society Bulletin* (November 1964) points out, if you join their society ". . . you feel a tremendous satisfaction . . . to save for our children and their children the glorious country and humane civilization which we ourselves inherited."

We asked them to select "two great Americans" and describe what is admirable about them. Later, we asked them to describe "the typical member of an anti-Communist group"—that is, in effect, an idealized version of themselves. Their great people, they said, were "true" Americans and "very" patriotic; 75 percent found the same things true of themselves (compared to 22 percent of non-rightists, who tended to use less extravagant terms). Courage, strength, and "guts" were likewise qualities they shared with the great, as was deep Christian faith and high moral standards. And 50 percent further saw the great to be honest, truthful, and sincere—like themselves.

Non-rightists, however, viewed rightists very differently—"dishonest," "hypocrites," "no integrity," "use character assassination."

This tactic of rightists to acquire status and importance by associating themselves closely with the great and the good is perhaps best illustrated by their emphasis on "self-education." They are, in fact, less well-educated than the non-rightists. But the world of radical rightism is full of parades of quasi-experts, study groups, monographs, footnotes, and bibliographies—almost all with no standing among scholars. But the rightists study them avidly, mention intelligence and education highly among those things they admire in the great, and give themselves strong ratings as "intellectuals, very brilliant," "well informed," "people with sound judgment, good reasoning," and "lots of sense." Needless to add, non-rightists hold almost precisely the opposite view of them.

THE RIGHTIST PERSONALITY

The need to relieve status anxiety and to attack values that do not conform to their beliefs are not enough to explain why some people become radical rightists and others, in like circumstances, do not. The rightist tends also to have certain personality characteristics—to be, in effect, a particular kind of human being.

Simplism

Psychologists say that a basic need of man is his desire for meaning, to understand what is happening to him. In an important sense the rightist, a traditionalist in changing times, is adrift in frightening darkness—he needs landmarks, he needs simple guidelines, before he loses direction altogether. Radical rightism gives him this "understanding"—and this security. All becomes clear and very simple. It is all a conspiracy. Nothing is really changed—God is still in His heaven; but He needs help.

Extremely simple explanations have great attractions for the confused. They are a necessity for those personalities who have what psychologists call "simplistic cognitive structure"—who have a strong need for simple, firm, stereotyped views of people and events, with no place for ambivalence or ambiguity. Such persons reject unbelievers, need external authorities, and, for emotional reasons, hold their beliefs so rigidly that compromise is intolerable.

Testing for this rigidity of belief, using statements on Communism and Russia ("Communism is a total evil." "The Soviet Union is 'mellowing.' "), on intolerance of ambiguity ("There is usually only one right way to do anything."), on anti-compromise and closed-minded stances ("The compromise of principles leads to nothing but destruction." "A group which tolerates too much difference of opinion cannot exist for long."), we found the rightist to fit this description. He is intolerant of ambiguity, opposed to compromise, and closed-minded.

Extra-Punitiveness

It is difficult not to be struck by the strident negativism and combativeness of rightist writings, thought, and speech. Terrible things exist all about, the future is steeped in gloom; everything is in strong blacks and whites—the forces of light are locked in mortal combat with the forces of darkness. It is not only necessary, therefore, but moral and virtuous to be resentful, discontented, belligerent, and full of hate. While the rightist justifies his behavior in the name of Americanism and anti-Communism, the actual thrust of his attacks are against the political, social, and intellectual leaders of the community—those who have the respect and influence he does not.

This vehement scapegoating is characteristic of a psychological defense mechanism called "extra-punitiveness." The extra-punitive have a great deal of free-floating hate and aggression they project outward, blaming others or the world for their personal or social failures. Their view of the world is paranoid.

We tested for extra-punitiveness by asking what measures they would take against "Communists" and, in later questions, against other "safe" scapegoats (those with few defenders, such as delinquents, sex deviants, homosexuals, and "disrespectful persons"). Rightists were more in favor of strong measures against Communists (sample statement with high response: "Take them out and hang them"); but their *generalized* hostility showed up even more clearly in their attitudes toward nonpolitical deviants. (Sample statements: "There is hardly anything lower than a person who does not feel a great love, gratitude, and respect for his parents." "Homosexuals are hardly better than criminals and ought to be severely punished.")

Rightists not only condemn Communists but define them so differently that it is sometimes hard to believe they are talking about real people. There is a heavy emphasis on religion and black-or-white morality: To believe that we can live with Communism is to be a dupe or worse. Communism is the anti-Christ, it is evil incarnate. This allows for convenient projection of personal hatreds. Rightists often find the highly educated—including professors—to be Communists. "From what racial or religious groups are Communists most likely to come?" Rightists frequently mentioned "atheists," "Jews," "Methodists," "Unitarians," and "modernistic religious groups." (Non-rightists denied more frequently and more vigorously that race or religion was involved.)

Powerlessness

It is a basic tenet of rightism that individual freedom—as they define it—is being lost and that the ordinary citizen (meaning themselves) is being ignored. Is "the federal government . . . extending too much . . . power into . . . everyday life?" Nearly 70 percent of the rightists "agreed very much." "Are there any groups . . . that you think have too much power or influence?" "Yes," the rightists said, significantly more often than non-rightists, and listed labor (and its leaders), Communists, big government, and such groups as the ADA, ACLU, and Council on Foreign Relations. Who has *too little* power? They mentioned twice as many groups as the non-rightists, most often the two surrogates for themselves: the individual "common man" and "conservative" organizations.

Do rightists, as hypothesized, feel maligned and persecuted? They pointed out with considerable heat that their idealized "great men," with whom they identify, were mistreated: "Got a raw deal; treated badly by others, his country; a victim of injustice."

Alienation

We found our rightists to be significantly more alienated politically than the non-rightists, to feel that their elected public officials do not actually represent them, that local officials avoid or ignore them, responding only to special interests. On referenda on community issues—such as new bond issues or taxes—they more consistently than others vote "no."

Do they trust other people? (A person who feels lost, who has little sense of personal competence, often lives in a jungle of suspicion and distrust.) We found a significant association between radical rightism and low trust in others. Generally, the rightists in our sample were less often involved in social and community organizations.

Finally, the rightist *feels* that by joining other rightists he can overcome his own powerlessness and estrangement.

Extra-punitiveness, a paranoid view of society, a great deal of free-floating hostility and aggression, desire for direct action, a rigid devotion to absolutes in religion and morality and to black-or-white standards—all these characteristics describe particular kinds of closed-minded, insecure, authoritarian persons undergoing particular kinds of status crises. And that is who the radical rightists are.

17
The Radical Right
Eugene V. Schneider

In spite of optimistic predictions following the demise of McCarthyism, the voice of the right-wing radical is heard loud and clear in our land once more. Of course, it has never been completely silent, but of late it seems to have acquired new decibels. This seems to have come as a surprise to many, who assumed that right-wing radicalism had been all but eliminated, or at least relegated to the fringes of society. How can we account for its persistence, its constant resurgence?

Of one thing we can be sure: right-wing radicalism is endemic in industrial-capitalist society at a certain stage of development; there has been no advanced industrial-capitalist society free of it, though it has appeared in varying degrees of effectiveness, virulence and self-consciousness. This would suggest that it is indigenous to our milieu; that, whatever one may think of it, it arises out of the experience of living in modern society. At the same time, one must recognize that each right-wing radicalism—including our own brands—is a response to a particular concatenation of social forces, existing at a special time and undergoing its own process of development.

From *The Nation* (September 30, 1961), pp. 199–203. Reprinted by permission of publisher and author.

Whatever social forces are producing this radicalism at a given time, and whatever form it may take, there is a certain unity to its interpretation of the world and to the remedies it proposes for the world's ills. The essence of right-wing radicalism is a special kind of *ahistoricism*. Speaking generally, and no doubt too hastily, the ahistorical position is that history is without meaning or design; it is the accidental, meandering, aimless result of powerful wills, or chance, or an unchanging human nature. It is not social forces such as the development of economic relations, the progress of technology or science, the concentration of men in cities, the struggles of people for freedom, which are the prime movers of history; it is individual men who make history, and some of them, at any rate, can make it as they choose.

Now, whether one happens to agree or not with this position, it is an intellectually respectable one, and many people who are not right-wing radicals adhere to it, consciously or unconsciously, in one form or other—a point to which we will return. But the right-wing radical interprets this doctrine in a special way. For him it is not really essential to believe in a past course of history (though some doctrines are, no doubt, more compatible to him than others). It is around the present that his ahistoricism is concentrated. The point for the right-wing radical is that the present order of society, or some part of it—its economic institutions (except as they have been distorted and perverted), its property relationships, its class and race structure, or whatever else he cherishes—is the only natural, sane, morally correct, viable order. Whether this has come about as the result of chance, through the acts of great men, or as the result of historical evolution, hardly matters. We have arrived at the millennium, achieved God's Kingdom on Earth, out-utopia'd all Utopias. By the same token, deviation from this Garden of Eden is insane, unnatural and immoral.

But, alas, there are flies in the ointment, and others are buzzing around the bottle. The forces of social change—to alter the metaphor—beat continually on the ramparts, and here and there they have breached the walls; our cities continue to grow, technology and science develop apace, caries are controlled, new forms of art develop, the doctrines of religion alter, new forms of family life emerge, Negroes continue to demand. Change is everywhere, inexorable, enveloping, insidious. But if this society—never mind whether it exists or ever existed—is perfect, then change can only be the result of imperfect men, perverse men, subversive men. In fact, *all* social change (except that which might conceivably benefit the radical himself, and not even always then) is the outcome of chicanery, fraud, propaganda and plot. Instead of conflict between capital and labor, there is a plot of labor leaders or capitalists or Jews. Instead of an upsurge of Negro masses, there is a plot of Negro leaders. Underlying all attempts to find solutions for the intellectual problems of our times—whether it be a new system of education, a search for a new philosophy, or for a new style in art—is a cabal of eggheads and long-hairs. And yet, all of these separate plots are but aspects of a larger plot, world-encompassing, eternal, evil. This master plot—triumph of radical-right thinking—bears the name of Jew, Catholic, communism, the Devil.

This is how the world appears to the right-wing radical. What does he propose to do about it? Of course, the first item on his agenda is to uncover the plot, to expose it for all to see—whether by the Question, investigation by Congressional committee, or denunciation. The stridency of the right-wing radical's tone, the stringency of his measures, fully match, one can be sure, the enormity of the depravity. At any rate, once the Revelation has been made, the society will, presumably, return to its perfect, unchanging state.

Undoubtedly, many right-wing radicals never go beyond this point in their thinking or in their action. But not all of them are so naive. Recognizing that the forces of change cannot be halted merely by exposure and denunciation, these have evolved a plan, or at least an orientation, for the reconstruction of society, and in a way it is a radical plan. Its essence is the creation of a social order which bypasses or diverts or suppresses the social forces which lie at the basis of the social change that the right-wing radical fears and hates, yet without disturbing the institutions which he cherishes. Men of all classes and stations (except, of course, for the plotters) must somehow be united—in common loyalty to a set of ideas, to a leader. Or, perhaps they can be united in common hatred of someone or something. Conceivably the unity could be achieved on the basis of love, as the late Dr. Buchman wished. But since this item seems to be in scarce supply, the basis for unity is more likely to be sought in irrationality, fear, hatred, frustration, aggression, of which there seems to be no dearth. At any rate, in place of a society marked by those divisions and conflicts which breed change, there will be created a homogeneous, mass society, in which men's hopes, thoughts and loyalties will be severed from their social roots. If even this is not enough, then new institutions will be formed, or old ones exalted—a party?, the state?, a church?—which will unite men under a common rubric of loyalties and discipline. This "new institution" is doubly useful, for it can also serve as the instrument for the forcible suppression of historical evolution, even to the point, as Herr Himmler proposed, of breaking up the large cities—those notorious breeding places of social and intellectual ferment.

Now, there should be no mystery about which groups and individuals might find this doctrine congenial and meaningful. Every group which has suffered more psychological and material loss than gain from the social processes of our society is a potential recruit to right-wing radicalism. Every individual in whom the deprivations and defeats of life have not somehow been compensated for is a potential recruit. The real questions, for a sociologist, are where these groups and individuals are concentrated in society, why our society should produce so many of them, and what social forces predispose them to accept right-wing radical doctrines as an answer to their ills. The reader should note that there is no attempt here at psychological analysis of the individual recruit, whether he be follower, activist or leader.

At the outset, let us beware of the temptation to explain right-wing radicalism as the expression of an all-powerful "ruling class." The matter is more complicated. For one thing, it is not confined to the "ruling class"; it finds its supporters and breeding places among diverse classes, races, religious groups, ethnic groups and organizations. For another thing, it can be shown, I think, that the "ruling class" is divided in its reactions to right-wing radicalism. All the elites, status groups, molders of public opinion, heads of organizations, who make up the "ruling class," may share the right-wing radical's love for the present order of things. Many of them have been willing to use right-wing radicalism as a means to achieve certain ends. But it is also a fact that many of the present social forces in society operate to protect and further the interests of numerous elite groups. Nor would these groups—let us call them the "entrenched elites"—necessarily welcome any radical reordering of society. It is always a question of whether, in such a reordering, the entrenched elites can retain their preeminence, or even their positions, in society. Those who argue for a class interpretation of right-wing radicalism often point to the relationship between Hitler and the "ruling class" of Germany, but in that instance practically all the elites felt threatened by practically all of the social forces in society.

But there are also certain elites that are by no means so dedicated to the present establishment, either because they feel that certain social forces are inimical, or because they feel cut off from the real centers of power and prestige in the country. As Sweezy and Huberman have shown in their essay on the social backing of McCarthyism, one type of elite is made up of the new millionaires whose wealth is so recent that they have not yet been able to breach the central citadels of power. The Southern elites strive to protect their caste-ridden society against the Negro, and at the same time to carry out a program of industrialization without bother from organized labor. Certain elements of the Johnny-come-lately military elite feel that their roles in the present establishment could be improved, though here hostility to liberal institutions is historical and is based on the military orientation to a seamless society as a framework for its operations. Similarly-oriented elites can be found in other institutions—in churches, in government, in education—expressing either a sense of frustration or the institutional ideology. Then there are what may be called the "sub-elites"—the small manufacturer or businessman can serve as an example—who dislike their own relatively minor roles in society, or who feel threatened by the social forces within it. Every community has them. None of these elites and sub-elites are wedded to the present establishment; some of them fear the social forces within it, some would welcome a reordering along radical lines. It is from among these groups that the major backing for right-wing radicalism comes: the bulk of its financial support, its access to mass media, some of the social respectability it has thus far achieved.

But whence comes the social following, the mass support? The question poses difficulties, because at first glance it would seem that large numbers of people have been treated kindly by many of the social forces which have been operating since World War II. Prosperity, though uneven and spasmodic, has been general. It is not engaging in mythology or apologetics to say that incomes have risen for more people, that gains have been made in status and class position. Even the position of the Negro has improved. Why, then, should right-wing radicalism—supposedly the creation of a society in profound crisis—strike a responsive chord among so many people? Or is there some kind of hidden crisis in our society, not expressed in its general level of material well-being?

The answer lies, I think, in this paradoxical fact: while society as a whole is obviously not in a state of crisis, many groups and people within it are. This latter type of desperation has two separate, though interrelated, aspects. Following Durkheim, I might point out first that the process of social rising is also a process of disorientation; goals recede as fast as they are attained, ties to community are constantly broken, the familiar world is fragmented. People suffer from this as surely as they do from an economic depression; there is something of the same sense of loss, of alienation, of isolation, without even the unifying effects along class lines that a depression may have. Right-wing radicalism offers to such people an outlet for their ambivalence of feeling toward the society: a profound attachment to a social order from which they have benefited, mixed with a profound resentment toward it. It also offers to the most alienated the hope of a less complex, less frenetic state-of-things. Let it be noted that this type of alienation is not a class phenomenon; it involves all those, of whatever class, who have been caught up in the great American game of social (and geographical) mobility.

The second aspect to consider is the nature of social mobility in the United States today. The process is so vast and complex that it is extremely difficult to generalize about it, and virtually impossible to describe in any detail. But, using what evidence is at hand, it can be described more as social churning than social rising. It is not a matter of the appearance of new classes, or of the rise to power of old classes; industrial-capitalism has not changed *that* much. Rather, the situation today is one in which sections of the population, drawn from many different areas of society, have been set into motion of varying kinds and directions. Some groups are rising or falling absolutely; some are rising in reference to certain groups, but falling in relation to others. Even standing still may be the equivalent of rising or falling, relative to other groups. Underlying this churning process are economic, technological and social factors. The prosperity of an arms-oriented economy is not spread evenly over the entire population; in this respect capitalism is almost as anarchistic as it ever was. Automation has disrupted the traditional structure of the working class, and the shock is now spreading to the white-collar groups. Urbanization, suburbanization, the rise of the Negro, the continued depopulation of the countryside, the shifts of population from region to region—all these and other factors have contributed to the turbulence.

The result has been that there are numerous groups and individuals in this country who have reason to hate and fear certain social forces, or who are ambivalent in their feelings toward the society. There is the case of the newly-arrived, who fear that their hard-won status may be threatened by the same social forces through which they have risen. There are those who have experienced real defeat or deprivation either through a failure to rise, or a failure to rise fast enough. There are those who have skidded. This, I think, is the source of the feeling of personal crisis which haunts many Americans today. It is forces of this kind which find expression in the man who has increased his income and his status, but who hates the social forces which are threatening to give him a Negro or a Jew for a neighbor. It is these forces which lead to a blind hatred of change, to the conspiratorial view of the world, and so by direct or indirect paths to right-wing radicalism. And again, let it be noted that except at the very top and the very bottom of society, no section of society is immune to this malaise; it is not, primarily, a class phenomenon.

Now, at this point I have to offer, in a sense, a demurrer to the argument of this paper. The question is: can the present virulence, bellicosity and self-confidence of the right-wing radical movement be explained solely in terms of its roots in the social structure? Undoubtedly, the pressure from certain of the forces described above—automation, unemployment, the Negro upsurge—is increasing. It is possible that the tension from the social-churning process is becoming unbearable in certain sections of society. But for all that, right-wing radicalism remains a fringe movement; in numbers, in the quality of the people it attracts, in the exotic quality of its doctrines. Even those for whom it has a natural attraction continue, for the most part, to act within the structure and definitions of the present social order: for instance, in their voting behavior. The present strength of right-wing radicalism arises, I think, from another source: to wit, from its functional relations to the present establishment, not from its opposition to it.

First, right-wing radicalism served as a handy instrument for liquidating the New Deal, and the climate of opinion which that Establishment had generated. It functioned, and still does, as a means of prosecuting the Cold War and maintaining the armaments economy. It has been used, furthermore, to stifle opposition to these policies. It is true that in the process certain harm has been done to the morality and morale of the country, and this, I think, certain elites really deplore —but not quite to the extent of a willingness to lay aside so potent a bludgeon. What these elites—the entrenched ones—would really deplore would be any attempt of the radical right to implement their remedies. The rise and fall of Joseph McCarthy can serve as an object lesson—to the left as an example of what weapons can be used against them, and to the right as an example of what happens to a radical rightist who gets too big for his britches.

In this connection, it may be that one of the causes of the very latest outbreak is the removal of the restraining hand of Eisenhower. Both Eisenhower and Kennedy represent what is in essence—though not in every particular—about the same balance of forces in this country; that is, they are both of, by and for the present establishment. But Eisenhower had more control over the extreme right. In part this may have been because of his great prestige. But, in addition, Eisenhower divided the loyalties of the right radicals and confused their aims; he was in so many ways the exact mirror image of themselves, he personified so neatly the stability, the simplicity, the unity, they were seeking. With his (whatever liberals may think) uncanny ability to communicate with, and get the trust of, the American people, he must have restrained many who were teetering on the brink of right-wing radicalism. It is possible that the retirement of Eisenhower from public office has, in these senses, swelled the numbers and vociferousness of the extreme right recently.

Secondly, if right-wing radicalism is on the attack today it is because it is consonant with the entire climate of opinion generated by the existing establishment. It is not a matter merely of a common antipathy to communism, or a common dedication to the Cold War. It goes beyond that. It is a matter of the degree to which ahistoricism has entered into almost every aspect of modern thought, its literature, its science (notably its social science), its philosophy, even its art. Just as the New Deal establishment created the climate of opinion in which left radicalism could flourish, so this one creates the conditions which give a certain reasonableness even to extreme right thinking, and—even more important—eviscerates the defense against it.

Really to analyze the deeper-lying causes of this universal ahistoricism would be to write the history of this century: the disillusionment with what social development has brought us, the end-result of scientific progress, the devastating effects of Nazism on hope and trust in humanity, the bitter experience with the Soviet version of socialism. But, in addition, this ahistoricism is powerfully reinforced from within the establishment. As I have said, the ahistorical view of things has not triumphed domestically, where the potentialities of development have not by any means been exhausted. Nor does it spring from the prevailing view of other countries in which industrial-capitalism is strong. It arises, rather, from the attempt of today's establishment to interpret what is going on in many of the non-industrial or non-capitalistic nations.

In those countries, comprising an enormous population with great potentialities of wealth and power, social forces are operating which seem directly contrary to the interests and mentality of our establishment. Nor, try as we may, have we had much success in harnessing these forces to our ends, or turning them in a direction congenial to ourselves. The result has been the almost universal tendency in our society to interpret what is happening as the handiwork of evil or perverse men, the outcome of machination, plot and subversion. (Note how this is reversed for the Russians. For them, what is going on in Africa, Asia and Latin America is the result of inevitable historical forces; it is in Western Europe and Japan that they detect the plots of native and American capitalists.) Furthermore, like any right-wing radical, we detect the master plot behind all of these separate plots. Even the solutions offered are of the radical variety: suppression of the hated social forces by violence, or by diverting or bypassing them.

The ahistoricism which this establishment has generated has emboldened the right-wing radical, even lent him a certain respectability. But it has had an even more insidious effect on those who would normally have formed the core of the opposition to it; and here I am referring primarily to the liberals and the intellectuals, who have accepted some aspect of this ahistorical thinking. A full analysis of the bowdlerization of the liberal and intellectual must await another occasion. Here I should like to point out that by accepting ahistorical thought, the liberal-intellectual grants the premises of right-wing radical thought, weakens his own moral position, and lessens his powers of resistance. Energies that might have been used against the totalitarians of the right are diverted—into self-analysis, into escape, into disgust and despair with the world.

With every worsening of the Cold War, with the appearance of each new revolutionary movement abroad, with every increase of social tension at home, the ahistorical view of the world is strengthened, and by that much the voice of the extreme right radical will become bolder and louder. In this sense, right-wing radicalism is not so much the reflection of America today as it is a barometer of its spirit.

NEW SOCIAL FORCES: SOCIAL SCIENCE AND COMMUNICATIONS

It is apparent that the old-time campaign methods of political parties are increasingly under challenge from skilled practitioners in the arts of public relations, mass communications, and poll taking. The resources and talents of local party clubs, which for years have been the locus of party power in the United States, no longer appear relevant to many Americans. Some candidates avoid recourse to party organization and turn instead to the mass-audience appeal provided by the media and the "feedback" made possible through survey research. As for the voter, a 1964 study indicated that while 41.3 percent of the voters interviewed said they had received political information through television, only 26 percent said they had been contacted by a precinct worker. In the same survey, 56.5 percent of the respondents said they had received the most campaign exposure through television.[1]

However, though electoral victory can no longer be assured by "organization" support, in many areas—particularly in local elections—the party organization still remains the major structural form for the nomination of, and the mobilization of support for, particular candidates. It is not yet clear whether the party organization's role in the electoral process will be completely absorbed someday by other, less strictly "political," organizations, and what the implications of such a take-over would be.

Another factor that should be considered, when the role of the media and social science techniques in the political arena is being examined, is the manner in which the practitioners of "organization" politics have adapted and utilized the methodology of mass communications and modern technology. It is general knowledge that in the past decade the bulk of campaign expenditures have been allocated to media presentations by the candidates.[2] Joe McGinniss' *The Selling of the President, 1968* [3] is a testament to the strategic and effective use of television made by Richard Nixon in his second race for the presidency. It has also been widely recognized that the success of John Lindsay's campaign for reelection as Mayor of New York in 1969 was largely due to personal public opinion polls and well-planned television appearances.[4] Lawrence O'Brien, the National Chairman of the Democratic party, recently indicated that although he made his reputation as a precinct-by-precinct organizer, he now believes that media campaigning is at least as important as precinct organizing. Under Mr. O'Brien's aegis, the Democratic party intends to establish a communications department to develop methods of using the media, computers, and other modern technology. The Democrats will also, as the Republicans have already done, retain consultants in television, the graphic arts, and computers. Mr.

[1] Survey Research Center, University of Michigan; quoted by Frank Sorauf, *Party Politics in America* (Boston, Mass.: Little, Brown, 1968), p. 249.
[2] See Bernard Hennessy, *Public Opinion* (Belmont, Calif.: Wadsworth, 1965), p. 288.
[3] New York: Trident Press, 1969.
[4] *New York Times,* November 6, 1969.

O'Brien has commented: "I . . . have to emphasize one word—communicate, communicate, but the media revolution costs money and that's the trouble."[5]

Prior to the advent of television electioneering, successful campaigns could be conducted at considerably lower cost than they can today. In 1948 the presidential campaign included no expenditures for television, while in 1964 approximately $9 million was expended by Barry Goldwater and Lyndon Johnson for television time.[6] The 1968 presidential campaign expenditures for television and radio exceeded four times the amount spent in 1956.[7] The rapid escalation of campaign costs over the past two decades has led to a variety of problems. Primarily, although party organization may not be as important in the process of mobilizing votes as it was in the past, organization *is* necessary in order to raise the money to finance a campaign, unless exclusive reliance is placed on an individual candidate's personal fortune or the fortunes of a coterie of wealthy supporters (the most obvious implication of the latter situation is that politics could become a game whose players are limited to only the rich). Although traditional political organizations may be made obsolete by the media, probably some organizational form will still be essential if the two major parties lose their dominant roles. Organizational forms of more than a transient nature will be needed to raise the vast sums required for political campaigns in a technological society that relies so heavily on the mass media and other costly techniques.

In Part III, evidence is presented both for and against the view that the media (including radio, the press, and television) and applied social science have had a profound influence on the political behavior of Americans. In Chapter Seven, Marshall McLuhan examines the degree to which "technological innovations" will "inexorably reshape the society that created the technology," while social scientists William Glaser, Angus Campbell, and Kurt and Gladys Lang report on the effects of mass media on voting behavior, as measured by several studies. Robert Rosenstone examines the role of popular music as a means of keeping young people in touch with serious critiques of American life made by the intellectual community.

In Chapter Eight, the implications of applied social science for the political process are assessed. The Crossleys conclude that the predictive role of pollsters in the 1968 presidential election was remarkably accurate, while Allen Schick speculates on the future of politics in an age dominated by technology and computers.

[5] *New York Times,* March 29, 1970.
[6] Sorauf, *Party Politics in America,* p. 306.
[7] *New York Times,* November 9, 1969.

CHAPTER SEVEN

THE MEDIA AND POLITICS

18
Television: The Timid Giant

Marshall McLuhan

Perhaps the most familiar and pathetic effect of the TV image is the posture of children in the early grades. Since TV, children—regardless of eye condition—average about six and a half inches from the printed page. Our children are striving to carry over to the printed page the all-involving sensory mandate of the TV image. With perfect psycho-mimetic skill, they carry out the commands of the TV image. They pore, they probe, they slow down and involve themselves in depth. This is what they had learned to do in the cool iconography of the comic-book medium. TV carried the process much further. Suddenly they are transferred to the hot print medium with its uniform patterns and fast lineal movement. Pointlessly they strive to read print in depth. They bring to print all their senses, and print rejects them. Print asks for the isolated and stripped-down visual faculty, not for the unified sensorium.

The Mackworth head-camera, when worn by children watching TV, has revealed that their eyes follow, not the actions, but the reactions. The eyes scarcely deviate from the faces of the actors, even during scenes of violence. This head-camera shows by projection both the scene and the eye movement simultane-

From *Understanding Media: The Extensions of Man* by Marshall McLuhan. Copyright © 1964 by Marshall McLuhan. Used with permission of McGraw-Hill Book Company and Routledge & Kegan Paul Ltd.

ously. Such extraordinary behavior is another indication of the very cool and involving character of this medium.

On the Jack Paar show for March 8, 1963, Richard Nixon was Paared down and remade into a suitable TV image. It turns out that Mr. Nixon is both a pianist and a composer. With sure tact for the character of the TV medium, Jack Paar brought out this *pianoforte* side of Mr. Nixon, with excellent effect. Instead of the slick, glib, legal Nixon, we saw the doggedly creative and modest performer. A few timely touches like this would have quite altered the result of the Kennedy-Nixon campaign. TV is a medium that rejects the sharp personality and favors the presentation of processes rather than of products.

The adaptation of TV to processes, rather than to the neatly packaged products, explains the frustration many people experience with this medium in its political uses. An article by Edith Efron in *TV Guide* (May 18–24, 1963) labeled TV "The Timid Giant," because it is unsuited to hot issues and sharply defined controversal topics: "Despite official freedom from censorship, a self-imposed silence renders network documentaries almost mute on many great issues of the day." As a cool medium TV has, some feel, introduced a kind of *rigor mortis* into the body politic. It is the extraordinary degree of audience participation in the TV medium that explains its failure to tackle hot issues. Howard K. Smith observed: "The networks are delighted if you go into a controversy in a country 14,000 miles away. They don't want real controversy, real dissent, at home." For people conditioned to the hot newspaper medium, which is concerned with the clash of *views*, rather than involvement in *depth* in a situation, the TV behavior is inexplicable.

Such a hot news item that concerns TV directly was headlined "It finally happened—a British film with English subtitles to explain the dialects." The film in question is the British comedy "Sparrows Don't Sing." A glossary of Yorkshire, Cockney, and other slang phrases has been printed for the customers so that they can figure out just what the subtitles mean. Sub subtitles are as handy an indicator of the depth effects of TV as the new "rugged" styles in feminine attire. One of the most extraordinary developments since TV in England has been the upsurge of regional dialects. A regional brogue or "burr" is the vocal equivalent of gaiter stockings. Such brogues undergo continual erosion from literacy. Their sudden prominence in England in areas in which previously one had heard only standard English is one of the most significant cultural events of our time. Even in the classrooms of Oxford and Cambridge, the local dialects are heard again. The undergraduates of those universities no longer strive to achieve a uniform speech. Dialectal speech since TV has been found to provide a social bond in depth, not possible with the artificial "standard English" that began only a century ago.

An article on Perry Como bills him as "Low-pressure king of a high-pressure realm." The success of any TV performer depends on his achieving a low-pressure style of presentation, although getting his act on the air may require much high-pressure organization. Castro may be a case in point. According to Tad Szulc's story on "Cuban Television's One-man Show" (*The Eighth Art*), "in his seemingly improvised 'as-I-go-along' style he can evolve politics and govern his country— right on camera." Now, Tad Szulc is under the illusion that TV is a hot medium, and suggests that in the Congo "television might have helped Lumumba to incite the masses to even greater turmoil and bloodshed." But he is quite wrong. Radio is the medium for frenzy, and it has been the major means of hotting up the tribal blood of Africa, India, and China, alike. TV has cooled Cuba down, as it is cooling down America. What the Cubans are getting by TV is the experience of being directly engaged in the making of political decisions. Castro presents himself as a teacher, and as Szulc says, "manages to blend political guidance and education with propaganda so skillfully that it is often difficult to tell where one begins and the other ends." Exactly the same mix is used in entertainment in Europe and America alike. Seen outside the United States, any American movie looks like subtle political propaganda. Acceptable entertainment has to flatter and exploit the cultural and political assumptions of the land of its origin. These unspoken presuppositions also serve to blind people to the most obvious facts about a new medium like TV.

In a group of simulcasts of several media done in Toronto a few years back, TV did a strange flip. Four randomized groups of university students were given the same information at the same time about the structure of preliterate languages. One group received it via radio, one from TV, one by lecture, and one read it. For all but the reader group, the information was passed along in straight verbal flow by the same speaker without discussion or questions or use of blackboard. Each group had half an hour of exposure to the material. Each was asked to fill in the same quiz afterward. It was quite a surprise to the experimenters when the students performed better with TV-channeled information and with radio than they did with lecture and print—and the TV group stood *well* above the radio group. Since nothing had been done to give special stress to any of these four media, the experiment was repeated with other randomized groups. This time each medium was allowed full opportunity to do its stuff. For radio and TV, the material was dramatized with many auditory and visual features. The lecturer took full advantage of the blackboard and class discussion. The printed form was embellished with an imaginative use of typography and page layout to stress each point in the lecture. All of these media had been stepped up to high intensity for this repeat of the original performance. Television and radio once again showed results high above lecture and print. Unexpectedly to the testers, however, radio now stood significantly above television. It was a long time before the obvious reason declared itself, namely that TV is a cool, participant medium. When hotted up by dramatization and stingers, it performs less well because there is less opportunity for participation. Radio is a hot medium. When given additional intensity, it performs better. It doesn't invite the same degree of participation in its users. Radio will serve as background-sound or as noise-level control, as when the ingenious teenager employs it as a means of privacy. TV will not work as background. It engages you. You have to be *with* it. (The phrase has gained acceptance since TV.)

A great many things will not work since the arrival of TV. Not only the movies, but the national magazines as well, have been hit very hard by this new medium. Even the comic books have declined greatly. Before TV, there had been much concern about why Johnny couldn't read. Since TV, Johnny has acquired an entirely new set of perceptions. He is not at all the same. Otto Preminger, director of *Anatomy of a Murder* and other hits, dates a great change in movie making and viewing from the very first year of general TV programming. "In 1951," he wrote, "I started a fight to get the release in motion-picture theaters of

The Moon Is Blue after the production code approval was refused. It was a small fight and I won it." (*Toronto Daily Star,* October 19, 1963)

He went on to say, "The very fact that it was the word 'virgin' that was objected to in *The Moon Is Blue* is today laughable, almost incredible." Otto Preminger considers that American movies have advanced toward maturity owing to the influence of TV. The cool TV medium promotes depth structures in art and entertainment alike, and creates audience involvement in depth as well. Since nearly all our technologies and entertainment since Gutenberg have been not cool, but hot; and not deep, but fragmentary; not producer-oriented, but consumer-oriented, there is scarcely a single area of established relationships, from home and church to school and market, that has not been profoundly disturbed in its pattern and texture.

The psychic and social disturbance created by the TV image, and not the TV programming, occasions daily comment in the press. Raymond Burr, who plays Perry Mason, spoke to the National Association of Municipal Judges, reminding them that, "Without our laymen's understanding and acceptance, the laws which you apply and the courts in which you preside cannot continue to exist." What Mr. Burr omitted to observe was that the Perry Mason TV program, in which he plays the lead, is typical of that intensely participational kind of TV experience that has altered our relation to the laws and the courts.

The mode of the TV image has nothing in common with film or photo, except that it offers also a nonverbal *gestalt* or posture of forms. With TV, the viewer is the screen. He is bombarded with light impulses that James Joyce called the "Charge of the Light Brigade" that imbues his "soulskin with sobconscious inklings." The TV image is visually low in data. The TV image is not a *still* shot. It is not photo in any sense, but a ceaselessly forming contour of things limned by the scanning-finger. The resulting plastic contour appears by light *through,* not light *on,* and the image so formed has the quality of sculpture and icon, rather than of picture. The TV image offers some three million dots per second to the receiver. From these he accepts only a few dozen each instant, from which to make an image.

The film image offers many more millions of data per second, and the viewer does not have to make the same drastic reduction of items to form his impression. He tends instead to accept the full image as a package deal. In contrast, the viewer of the TV mosaic, with technical control of the image, unconsciously reconfigures the dots into an abstract work of art on the pattern of a Seurat or Rouault. If anybody were to ask whether all this would change if technology stepped up the character of the TV image to movie data level, one could only counter by inquiring, "Could we alter a cartoon by adding details of perspective and light and shade?" The answer is "Yes," only it would then no longer be a cartoon. Nor would "improved" TV be television. The TV image is *now* a mosaic mesh of light and dark spots which a movie shot never is, even when the quality of the movie image is very poor.

As in any other mosaic, the third dimension is alien to TV, but it can be superimposed. In TV the illusion of the third dimension is provided slightly by the stage sets in the studio; but the TV image itself is a flat two-dimensional mosaic. Most of the three-dimensional illusion is a carry-over of habitual viewing of film and photo. For the TV camera does not have a built-in angle of vision like the movie camera. Eastman Kodak now has a two-dimensional camera that can match the flat effects of the TV camera. Yet it is hard for literate people, with their habit of fixed points of view and three-dimensional vision, to understand the properties of two-dimensional vision. If it had been easy for them, they would have had no difficulties with abstract art, General Motors would not have made a mess of motorcar design, and the picture magazine would not be having difficulties now with the relationship between features and ads. The TV image requires each instant that we "close" the spaces in the mesh by a convulsive sensuous participation that is profoundly kinetic and tactile, because tactility is the interplay of the senses, rather than the isolated contact of skin and object.

To contrast it with the film shot, many directors refer to the TV image as one of "low definition," in the sense that it offers little detail and a low degree of information, much like the cartoon. A TV close-up provides only as much information as a small section of a long-shot on the movie screen. For lack of observing so central an aspect of the TV image, the critics of program "content" have talked nonsense about "TV violence." The spokesmen of censorious views are typical semiliterate book-oriented individuals who have no competence in the grammars of newspaper, or radio, or of film, but who look askew and askance at all nonbook media. The simplest question about any psychic aspect, even of the book medium, throws these people into a panic of uncertainty. Vehemence of projection of a single isolated attitude they mistake for moral vigilance. Once these censors became aware that in all cases "the medium is the message" or the basic source of effects, they would turn to suppression of media as such, instead of seeking "content" control. Their current assumption that content or programming is the factor that influences outlook and action is derived from the book medium, with its sharp cleavage between form and content.

Is it not strange that TV should have been as revolutionary a medium in America in the 1950s as radio in Europe in the 1930s? Radio, the medium that resuscitated the tribal and kinship webs of the European mind in the 1920s and 1930s, had no such effect in England or America. There, the erosion of tribal bonds by means of literacy and its industrial extensions had gone so far that our radio did not achieve any notable tribal reactions. Yet ten years of TV have Europeanized even the United States, as witness its changed feelings for space and personal relations. There is new sensitivity to the dance, plastic arts, and architecture, as well as the demand for the small car, the paperback, sculptural hairdos and molded dress effects—to say nothing of a new concern for complex effects in cuisine and in the use of wines. Notwithstanding, it would be misleading to say that TV will retribalize England and America. The action of radio on the world of resonant speech and memory was hysterical. But TV has certainly made England and America vulnerable to radio where previously they had immunity to a great degree. For good or ill, the TV image has exerted a unifying synesthetic force on the sense-life of these intensely literate populations, such as they have lacked for centuries. It is wise to withhold all value judgments when studying these media matters, since their effects are not capable of being isolated.

Synesthesia, or unified sense and imaginative life, had long seemed an unattainable dream to Western poets, painters, and artists in general. They had looked with sorrow and dismay on the fragmented and impoverished imaginative life of Western literate man in the eighteenth century and later. Such was the message of Blake and Pater, Yeats and D. H. Lawrence, and a host of other great figures.

They were not prepared to have their dreams realized in everyday life by the esthetic action of radio and television. Yet these massive extensions of our central nervous systems have enveloped Western man in a daily session of synesthesia. The Western way of life attained centuries since by the rigorous separation and specialization of the senses, with the visual sense atop the hierarchy, is not able to withstand the radio and TV waves that wash about the great visual structure of abstract Individual Man. Those who, from political motives, would now add their force to the anti-individual action of our electric technology are puny subliminal automatons aping the patterns of the prevailing electric pressures. A century ago they would, with equal somnambulism, have faced in the opposite direction. German Romantic poets and philosophers had been chanting in tribal chorus for a return to the dark unconscious for over a century before radio and Hitler made such a return difficult to avoid. What is to be thought of people who wish such a return to preliterate ways, when they have no inkling of how the civilized visual way was ever substituted for tribal auditory magic?

At this hour, when Americans are discovering new passions for skin-diving and the wraparound space of small cars, thanks to the indomitable tactile promptings of the TV image, the same image is inspiring many English people with race feelings of tribal exclusiveness. Whereas highly literate Westerners have always idealized the condition of integration of races, it has been their literate culture that made impossible real uniformity among races. Literate man naturally dreams of visual solutions to the problems of human differences. At the end of the nineteenth century, this kind of dream suggested similar dress and education for both men and women. The failure of the sex-integration programs has provided the theme of much of the literature and psychoanalysis of the twentieth century. Race integration, undertaken on the basis of visual uniformity, is an extension of the same cultural strategy of literate man, for whom differences always seem to need eradication, both in sex and in race, and in space and in time. Electronic man, by becoming ever more deeply involved in the actualities of the human condition, cannot accept the literate cultural strategy. The Negro will reject a plan of visual uniformity as definitely as women did earlier, and for the same reasons. Women found that they had been robbed of their distinctive roles and turned into fragmented citizens in "a man's world." The entire approach to these problems in terms of uniformity and social homogenization is a final pressure of the mechanical and industrial technology. Without moralizing, it can be said that the electric age, by involving all men deeply in one another, will come to reject such mechanical solutions. It is more difficult to provide uniqueness and diversity than it is to impose the uniform patterns of mass education; but it is such uniqueness and diversity that can be fostered under electric conditions as never before.

Temporarily, all preliterate groups in the world have begun to feel the explosive and aggressive energies that are released by the onset of the new literacy and mechanization. These explosions come just at a time when the new electric technology combines to make us share them on a global scale.

The effect of TV, as the most recent and spectacular electric extension of our central nervous system, is hard to grasp for various reasons. Since it has affected the totality of our lives, personal and social and political, it would be quite unrealistic to attempt a "systematic" or visual presentation of such influence. Instead, it is more feasible to "present" TV as a complex *gestalt* of data gathered almost at random.

The TV image is of low intensity or definition, and therefore, unlike film, it does not afford detailed information about objects. The difference is akin to that between the old manuscripts and the printed word. Print gave intensity and uniform precision, where before there had been a diffuse texture. Print brought in the taste for exact measurement and repeatability that we now associate with science and mathematics. . . .

Because the low definition of TV insures a high degree of audience involvement, the most effective programs are those that present situations which consist of some process to be completed. Thus, to use TV to teach poetry would permit the teacher to concentrate on the poetic process of actual *making*, as it pertained to a particular poem. The book form is quite unsuited to this type of involved presentation. The same salience of process of do-it-yourself-ness and depth involvement in the TV image extends to the art of the TV actor. Under TV conditions, he must be alert to improvise and to embellish every phrase and verbal resonance with details of gesture and posture, sustaining that intimacy with the viewer which is not possible on the massive movie screen or on the stage.

There is the alleged remark of the Nigerian who, after seeing a TV western, said delightedly, "I did not realize you valued human life so little in the West." Offsetting this remark is the behavior of our children in watching TV westerns. When equipped with the new experimental head-cameras that follow their eye movements while watching the image, children keep their eyes on the faces of the TV actors. Even during physical violence their eyes remain concentrated on the facial *reactions*, rather than on the eruptive *action*. Guns, knives, fists, all are ignored in preference for the facial expression. TV is not so much an action, as a re-action, medium. . . .

Just as TV, the mosaic mesh, does not foster perspective in art, it does not foster lineality in living. Since TV, the assembly line has disappeared from industry. Staff and line structures have dissolved in management. Gone are the stag line, the party line, the receiving line, and the pencil line from the backs of nylons.

With TV came the end of bloc voting in politics, a form of specialism and fragmentation that won't work since TV. Instead of the voting bloc, we have the icon, the inclusive image. Instead of a political viewpoint or platform, the inclusive political posture or stance. Instead of the product, the process. In periods of new and rapid growth there is a blurring of outlines. In the TV image we have the supremacy of the blurred outline, itself the maximal incentive to growth and new "closure" or completion, especially for a consumer culture long related to the sharp visual values that had become separated from the other senses. So great is the change in American lives, resulting from the loss of loyalty to the consumer package in entertainment and commerce, that every enterprise, from Madison Avenue and General Motors to Hollywood and General Foods, has been shaken thoroughly and forced to seek new strategies of action. What electric implosion or contraction has done inter-personally and inter-nationally, the TV image does intra-personally or intra-sensuously.

It is an especially touchy area that presents itself with the question: "What has been the effect of TV on our political life?" Here, at least, great traditions of critical awareness and vigilance testify to the safeguards we have posted against the dastardly uses of power.

When Theodore White's *The Making of the President: 1960* is opened at the section on "The Television Debates," the TV student will experience dismay. White offers statistics on the number of sets in American homes and the number of hours of daily use of these sets, but not one clue as to the nature of the TV image or its effects on candidates or viewers. White considers the "content" of the debates and the deportment of the debaters, but it never occurs to him to ask why TV would inevitably be a disaster for a sharp intense image like Nixon's, and a boon for the blurry, shaggy texture of Kennedy.

At the end of the debates, Philip Deane of the London *Observer* explained my idea of the coming TV impact on the election to the *Toronto Globe and Mail* under the headline of "The Sheriff and the Lawyer," October 15, 1960. It was that TV would prove so entirely in Kennedy's favor that he would win the election. Without TV, Nixon had it made. Deane, toward the end of his article, wrote:

> Now the press has tended to say that Mr. Nixon has been gaining in the last two debates and that he was bad in the first. Professor McLuhan thinks that Mr. Nixon has been sounding progressively more definite; regardless of the value of the Vice-President's views and principles, he has been defending them with too much flourish for the TV medium. Mr. Kennedy's rather sharp responses have been a mistake, but he still presents an image closer to the TV hero, Professor McLuhan says—something like the shy young Sheriff—while Mr. Nixon with his very dark eyes that tend to stare, with his slicker circumlocution, has resembled more the railway lawyer who signs leases that are not in the interests of the folks in the little town.
>
> In fact, by counterattacking and by claiming for himself, as he does in the TV debates, the same goals as the Democrats have, Mr. Nixon may be helping his opponent by blurring the Kennedy image, by confusing what exactly it is that Mr. Kennedy wants to change.
>
> Mr. Kennedy is thus not handicapped by clear-cut issues; he is visually a less well-defined image, and appears more nonchalant. He seems less anxious to sell himself than does Mr. Nixon. So far, then, Professor McLuhan gives Mr. Kennedy the lead without underestimating Mr. Nixon's formidable appeal to the vast conservative forces of the United States.

Another way of explaining the acceptable, as opposed to the unacceptable, TV personality is to say that anybody whose *appearance* strongly declares his role and status in life is wrong for TV. Anybody who looks as if he might be a teacher, a doctor, a businessman, or any of a dozen other things all at the same time is right for TV. When the person presented *looks* classifiable, as Nixon did, the TV viewer has nothing to fill in. He feels uncomfortable with his TV image. He says uneasily, "There's something about the guy that isn't right." The viewer feels exactly the same about an exceedingly pretty girl on TV, or about any of the intense "high definition" images and messages from the sponsors. It is not accidental that advertising has become a vast new source of comic effects since the advent of TV. Mr. Khrushchev is a very filled-in or completed image that appears on TV as a comic cartoon. In wirephoto and on TV, Mr. Khrushchev is a jovial comic, an entirely disarming presence. Likewise, precisely the formula that recommends anybody for a movie role disqualifies the same person for TV acceptance. For the hot movie medium needs people who look very definitely a *type* of some kind. The cool TV medium cannot abide the typical because it leaves the viewer frustrated of his job of "closure" or completion of image. President Kennedy did not look like a rich man or like a politician. He could have been anything from a grocer or a professor to a football coach. He was not too precise or too ready of speech in such a way as to spoil his pleasantly tweedy blur of countenance and outline. He went from palace to log cabin, from wealth to the White House, in a pattern of TV reversal and upset. . . .

WHY THE TV CHILD CANNOT SEE AHEAD

The plunge into depth experience via the TV image can only be explained in terms of the differences between visual and mosaic space. Ability to discriminate between these radically different forms is quite rare in our Western world. It has been pointed out that, in the country of the blind, the one-eyed man is not king. He is taken to be an hallucinated lunatic. In a highly visual culture, it is as difficult to communicate the nonvisual properties of spatial forms as to explain visuality to the blind. In *The ABC of Relativity* Bertrand Russell began by explaining that there is nothing difficult about Einstein's ideas, but that they do call for total reorganization of our imaginative lives. It is precisely this imaginative reorganization that has occurred via the TV image.

The ordinary inability to discriminate between the photographic and the TV image is not merely a crippling factor in the learning process today; it is symptomatic of an age-old failure in Western culture. The literate man, accustomed to an environment in which the visual sense is extended everywhere as a principle of organization, sometimes supposes that the mosaic world of primitive art, or even the world of Byzantine art, represents a mere difference in degree, a sort of failure to bring their visual portrayals up to the level of full visual effectiveness. Nothing could be further from the truth. This, in fact, is a misconception that has impaired understanding between East and West for many centuries. Today it impairs relations between colored and white societies.

Most technology produces an amplification that is quite explicit in its separation of the senses. Radio is an extension of the aural, high-fidelity photography of the visual. But TV is, above all, an extension of the sense of touch, which involves maximal interplay of all the senses. For Western man, however, the all-embracing extension had occurred by means of phonetic writing, which is a technology for extending the sense of sight. All non-phonetic forms of writing are, by contrast, artistic modes that retain much variety of sensuous orchestration. Phonetic writing, alone, has the power of separating and fragmenting the senses and of sloughing off the semantic complexities. The TV image reverses this literate process of analytic fragmentation of sensory life.

The visual stress on continuity, uniformity, and connectedness, as it derives from literacy, confronts us with the great technological means of implementing continuity and lineality by fragmented repetition. The ancient world found this means in the brick, whether for wall or road. The repetitive, uniform brick, indispensable agent of road and wall, of cities and empires, is an extension, via letters, of the visual sense. *The brick wall is not a mosaic form,* and neither is the mosaic form a visual structure. The mosaic can be *seen* as dancing can, but is not *structured* visually; nor is it an extension of the visual power. For the mosaic is not uniform, continuous, or repetitive. It is discontinuous, skew, and nonlineal, like the tactual TV image. To the sense of touch, all things are sudden, counter, original, spare, strange. The "Pied Beauty" of G. M. Hopkins is a catalogue of the notes of the sense of touch. The poem is a manifesto of the nonvisual, and like Cézanne or Seurat, or Rouault it provides an indispensable approach to understanding TV. The nonvisual mosaic structures of modern art, like those of modern physics and electric-information patterns, permit little detachment. The mosaic form of the TV image demands participation and involvement in depth of the whole being, as does the sense of touch. Literacy, in contrast, had, by extending the visual power to the uniform organization of time and space, psychically and socially, conferred the power of detachment and noninvolvement.

The visual sense when extended by phonetic literacy fosters the analytic habit of perceiving the single facet in the life of forms. The visual power enables us to isolate the single incident in time and space, as in representational art. In visual representation of a person or an object, a single phase or moment or aspect is separated from the multitude of known and felt phases, moments and aspects of the person or object. By contrast, iconographic art uses the eye as we use our hand in seeking to create an inclusive image, made up of many moments, phases, and aspects of the person or thing. Thus the iconic mode is not visual representation, nor the specialization of visual stress as defined by viewing from a single position. The tactual mode of perceiving is sudden but not specialist. It is total, synesthetic, involving all the senses. Pervaded by the mosaic TV image, the TV child encounters the world in a spirit antithetic to literacy.

The TV image, that is to say, even more than the icon, is an extension of the sense of touch. Where it encounters a literate culture, it necessarily thickens the sense-mix, transforming fragmented and specialist extensions into a seamless web of experience. Such transformation is, of course, a "disaster" for a literate, specialist culture. It blurs many cherished attitudes and procedures. It dims the efficacy of the basic pedagogic techniques, and the relevance of the curriculum. If for no other reason, it would be well to understand the dynamic life of these forms as they intrude upon us and upon one another. TV makes for myopia.

The young people who have experienced a decade of TV have naturally imbibed an urge toward involvement in depth that makes all the remote visualized goals of usual culture seem not only unreal but irrelevant, and not only irrelevant but anemic. It is the total involvement in all-inclusive *nowness* that occurs in young lives via TV's mosaic image. This change of attitude has nothing to do with programming in any way, and would be the same if the programs consisted entirely of the highest cultural content. The change in attitude by means of relating themselves to the mosaic TV image would occur in any event. It is, of course, our job not only to understand this change but to exploit it for its pedagogical richness. The TV child expects involvement and doesn't want a specialist *job* in the future. He does want a *role* and a deep commitment to his society. Unbridled and misunderstood, this richly human need can manifest itself in the distorted forms portrayed in *West Side Story*.

The TV child cannot see ahead because he wants involvement, and he cannot accept a fragmentary and merely visualized goal or destiny in learning or in life.

MURDER BY TELEVISION

Jack Ruby shot Lee Oswald while tightly surrounded by guards who were paralyzed by television cameras. The fascinating and involving power of television scarcely needed this additional proof of its peculiar operation upon human perceptions. The Kennedy assassination gave people an immediate sense of the television power to create depth involvement, on the one hand, and a numbing effect as deep as grief, itself, on the other hand. Most people were amazed at the depth of meaning which the event communicated to them. Many more were surprised by the coolness and calm of the mass reaction. The same event, handled by press or radio (in the absence of television), would have provided a totally different experience. The national "lid" would have "blown off." Excitement would have been enormously greater and depth participation in a common awareness very much less.

As explained earlier, Kennedy was an excellent TV image. He had used the medium with the same effectiveness that Roosevelt had learned to achieve by radio. With TV, Kennedy found it natural to involve the nation in the office of the Presidency, both as an operation and as an image. TV reaches out for the corporate attributes of office. Potentially, it can transform the Presidency into a monarchic dynasty. A merely elective Presidency scarcely affords the depth of dedication and commitment demanded by the TV form. Even teachers on TV seem to be endowed by the student audiences with a charismatic or mystic character that much exceeds the feelings developed in the classroom or lecture hall. In the course of many studies of audience reactions to TV teaching, there recurs this puzzling fact. The viewers feel that the teacher has a dimension almost of sacredness. This feeling does not have its basis in concepts or ideas, but seems to creep in uninvited and unexplained. It baffles both the students and the analysts of their reactions. Surely, there could be no more telling touch to tip us off to the character of TV. This is not so much a visual as a tactual-auditory medium that involves all of our senses in depth interplay. For people long accustomed to the merely visual experience of the typographic and photographic varieties, it would seem to be the *synesthesia*, or tactual depth of TV experience, that dislocates them from their usual attitudes of passivity and detachment.

The banal and ritual remark of the conventionally literate, that TV presents an experience for passive viewers, is wide of the mark. TV is above all a medium that demands a creatively participant response. The guards who failed to protect Lee Oswald were not passive. They were so involved by the mere sight of the TV cameras that they lost their sense of their merely practical and specialist task.

Perhaps it was the Kennedy funeral that most strongly impressed the audience with the power of TV to invest an occasion with the character of corporate participation. No national event except in sports has ever had such coverage or such an audience. It revealed the unrivaled power of TV to achieve the involvement of the audience in a complex *process*. The funeral as a corporate process caused even the image of sport to pale and dwindle into puny proportions. The Kennedy funeral, in short, manifested the power of TV to involve an entire population in a ritual process. By comparison, press, movie, and even radio are mere packaging devices for consumers.

Most of all, the Kennedy event provides an opportunity for noting a paradoxical feature of the "cool" TV medium. It involves us in moving depth, but it does not excite, agitate or arouse. Presumably, this is a feature of all depth experience.

19
Television and Voting Turnout
William A. Glaser

Whenever an innovation enters politics or any other area of social life, people speculate about its effects. The search for effects has been a central theme of mass media research for decades. And since television from the start seemed such a gripping instrument and so widely distributed, it was assumed that television "must" affect the political behavior of its audience. This paper will examine whether television use is associated with voting turnout, whether television's association with voting turnout differs from the effects of other mass media, and whether television affects some people more than others. The article is a secondary analysis of data from several nationwide sample surveys.

Some observers have guessed that television has important effects on voting turnout. They believe that television has direct effects by continually reminding

From *Public Opinion Quarterly* (Spring 1965), pp. 71–86. Reprinted by permission of publisher and author. Dr. Glaser acknowledges the following: Publication A-405 of the Bureau of Applied Social Research, Columbia University. For enabling me to use previously unpublished data, I am indebted to Messrs. Brendan Byrne of the American Heritage Foundation; Philip K. Hastings of the Roper Public Opinion Research Center; Irving Crespi of the American Institute of Public Opinion; and Maxwell Fox of the Advertising Council.

people to vote through exhortations in spot announcements and in speeches. They believe that television raises the level of political interest by graphic presentation of the news and by creating a closer contact between a candidate and viewer than can be provided by other media.[1] Like commercial advertisers seeking higher sales, civic organizations attempt to stimulate turnout by heavy investments of their budgets and efforts in television. These hypotheses appear plausible: research before the age of television suggested that communications media are increasingly persuasive over attitudes and actions as they come closer to personal influence [2]; and since television presents the viewer face-to-face with messengers and persuaders, one might think it peculiarly effective. Some early research provided apparent corroboration: as television watching rates increased among individuals, so did turnout.[3]

But one might approach the subject more hesitantly. Research about the other mass media has failed to reveal the clear-cut effects once predicted for them, and one might expect that television, too, would have only limited effects upon certain types of people under special circumstances.[4] Some research seems to corroborate this skeptical view. Herbert Simon's ecological data from Iowa showed that counties with widespread ownership of television sets had turnouts no higher than counties with low television density.[5] Comparing national turnout rates over the period since women's suffrage, Angus Campbell finds that they have risen because of other social factors—including the advent of radio several decades ago—but do not appear to have increased because of the introduction of television. Comparing successive interview surveys, Campbell finds that levels of interest and information—both correlates of political participation—have not risen since the advent of television.[6] Doubt about the special efficacy of television alone is consistent with several studies suggesting that the effects of television on candidate choice depend on many other personal predispositions, social stimuli, and media effects.[7]

---

[1] Robert Bendiner, "How Much Has Television Changed Campaigning?" *New York Times Magazine*, Nov. 2, 1952, pp. 13ff.
[2] Joseph T. Klapper, *The Effects of Mass Media* (New York: Bureau of Applied Social Research, 1949), Memorandum II; Carl I. Hovland, "Effects of the Mass Media of Communication," in Gardner Lindzey (ed.), *Handbook of Social Psychology* (Cambridge, Mass.: Addison-Wesley, 1954), pp. 1080–1084.
[3] Leo Bogart, *The Age of Television* (2d ed.; New York: Ungar, 1958), pp. 243–244; Morris Janowitz and Dwaine Marvick, *Competitive Pressure and Democratic Consent* (Ann Arbor: University of Michigan, Institute of Public Administration, 1956), pp. 66–68.
[4] Joseph T. Klapper, *The Effects of Mass Communication* (New York: Free Press, 1960); Bernard Berelson, "Communications and Public Opinion," in Wilbur Schramm (ed.), *Communications in Modern Society* (Urbana: University of Illinois Press, 1948), pp. 167–185.
[5] Herbert A. Simon and Frederick Stern, "The Effect of Television upon Voting Behavior in the 1952 Presidential Election," *American Political Science Review*, 49 (June 1955), 10–13.
[6] Angus Campbell, "Has Television Reshaped Politics?" *Columbia Journalism Review*, 1 (Fall 1962), 10–13.
[7] Kurt Lang, Gladys Lang, and Ithiel de Sola Pool, articles about the political effects of television and other mass media, in Eugene Burdick and Arthur J. Brodbeck (ed.), *American Voting Behavior* (New York: Free Press, 1959), chaps. 12 and 13.

RECALL OF REMINDERS TO VOTE

Television acquaints many people with political information that they might have missed or underemphasized in the newspapers and over radio. Several studies have documented the immense public exposure to politics that has resulted from television, an exposure far greater than that achieved by previous media, particularly during presidential elections.[8]

The widespread public use of television has led to heavy reliance upon it during the get-out-the vote campaigns sponsored by civic organizations, although the other media are not neglected. Conducted by the American Heritage Foundation, the Advertising Council, and other public service associations, these promotional campaigns consist of one-minute, thirty-second, and twenty-second films that remind people to register and vote. Kits including both films and literature are furnished without charge to all American television stations and networks. Similar recorded statements and literature are given to all radio stations, while mats for ads are sent without charge to newspapers and magazines. The television and radio stations are expected to donate time for such public service announcements as a condition for keeping their licenses from the Federal Communications Commission, but no statutory obligations control the newspapers.

TABLE 1

Percentages Recalling Reminders to Vote (N = 1645)

Media	Reminded	Could Describe
Television	69	22
Newspapers	57	8
Radio	40	3
By mail	28	2
Posters	22	2
Outdoor billboards	20	2
Magazines	17	1
Movies	6	*
None of these	17	64

* Less than 1 percent.
Questions: "Through which of these ways, if any, do you remember having been reminded to register or to vote?" Respondents were shown a card listing the various media in the table, in an order different from the one given here.
"Which of these appeals can you recall well enough to describe?"
Source: Gallup Survey 638 K, November 1960. Data in Tables 1 through 5 are reprinted by permission of the American Institute of Public Opinion (The Gallup Poll).

At first sight, the data seem to document the superiority of television. According to Table 1, more people recall reminders through television than through the other media, and they can describe the television reminders far more readily. The

---

[8] Elihu Katz and Jacob J. Feldman, "The Debates in the Light of Research: A Survey of Surveys," in Sidney Kraus (ed.), *The Great Debates* (Bloomington: Indiana University Press, 1962), pp. 190–191; Joseph C. Seibert *et al., The Influence of Television on the Election of 1962* (Oxford, Ohio: Oxford Research Associates, 1954), p. 35; Richard S. Salant, "The Television Debates: A Revolution That Deserves a Future," *Public Opinion Quarterly*, 26 (1962), 338 and sources cited.

salience of television is even more evident from Table 2. Television ranks at or near the top among all types of media user. Only the radio listeners and newspaper readers recall reminders more frequently from any other channels, and even they are able to *describe* the television reminders more easily or almost as easily. Among those who rely on both television and another medium for information, television is consistently listed as reminding more people. Among the apathetic, too, television is cited more often.

TABLE 2

Recalling Reminders to Vote, by Type of Media User

Principal Source of Information	Per Cent Reminded by			Per Cent Who Could Describe Reminders from			Number of Cases
	Television	Radio	Newspapers	Television	Radio	Newspapers	
Television	72	26	40	24	1	5	385
Print (magazines and newspapers)	68	43	68	20	4	12	588
Radio	38	47	36	9	10	6	87
Television and print	78	37	67	27	2	6	287
Television and radio	73	50	37	24	7	0	41
Print and radio	57	63	65	17	8	6	63
Television, print, and radio	75	52	65	22	3	7	143
None	42	29	39	13	3	6	31

Question for classifying type of media user: "Where do you get most of your information about what's going on in the world—from magazines, TV, radio or newspapers?"
Source: Gallup Survey 638 K, November 1960.

In part, the more frequent recall of reminders over television may be due to the greater impact of the medium itself. Some experimental studies have found that people remember information best—in the order of successful recall—over television, radio, and print.[9] On the other hand, television reminders may be recalled more often because they are encountered more often. Nielsen Ratings and other estimates suggest that the Register-and-Vote campaign conducted during 1960 by the Advertising Council and the American Heritage Foundation had the following results: 2.5 billion home impressions from commercial television networks and stations, where a "home impression" is one message heard once in one home; over 200 million home impressions from commercial radio networks and stations; 3,340 million lines of advertising in newspapers throughout the country; advertisements in magazines with circulation of over 25 million.[10]

[9] D. C. Williams et al., "Mass Media, Learning and Retention," *Canadian Journal of Psychology*, 11 (1957), 157–163; Bruce H. Westley and L. C. Barrow, *Exploring the News* (Madison: University of Wisconsin Television Laboratory, 1959). But mean differences among media are small and may diminish as recall is tested at successive times. The superiority of television has been challenged in other experimental tests of recall reported in *Sponsor*, July 16, 1962, p. 8, and Jan. 20, 1964, p. 42.
[10] These are the Advertising Council's estimates of its organized campaign. Voluntary and unrehearsed reminders by radio announcers (such as disk jockeys) and by newspa-

EFFECTIVENESS OF REMINDERS

If televised reminders are more salient and more frequently encountered, are they more effective in getting out the vote? Table 3 presents the voting rates among people who could recall and describe the messages from the various channels. Being reminded by any of the media—including television—may lead to higher voting rates than not receiving (or not remembering) such messages. But the special superiority of television now disappears. Reminders may be far more effective by mail and slightly more effective in the press. As other students of the mass media have pointed out,[11] the recall of messages is not the same thing as the stimulation to action.

TABLE 3
Turnout and the Recall of Reminders to Vote

Media	Percentages Who Voted — Among Those Reminded by Each of the Media	Percentages Who Voted — Among Those Who Could Describe Reminders	Number of Cases — Reminded	Number of Cases — Could Describe
Television	81	81	1112	348
Newspapers	83	88	930	125
Radio	81	72	642	54
By mail	91	91	453	33
Posters	83	86	358	37
Outdoor billboards	84	68	324	37
Magazines	83	(10 cases)	268	15
Movies	85	(3 cases)	88	4
None of these	65	76	273	1036

Source: Gallup Survey 638 K, November 1960.

Of course, Table 3 must be interpreted with the usual cautions about inferring effects from respondents' reports about experience and behavior. Nonvoters may not recall reminders from certain media, thus inflating the apparent statistical effectiveness of those media. Certain media may appear to rank high because they solicit persons with conscientious voting habits: for example, reminders may be sent by mail disproportionately to those affiliated with political and civic organizations, while newspapers are read and recalled disproportionately by the better educated and by those more interested in politics.

Recalling messages declines by social class, as does turnout itself. Are there any social groups for whom television reminders make a special difference? Table 4 compares turnout rates for persons of various educational backgrounds who did and did not recall reminders to vote. Reminders in general seem to make a difference for the grammar school group and for the dropouts from high school, but

pers may have diminished the numerical superiority of television. But televised messages were doubtless more often encountered, because of the more widespread use of available sets and because of the longer hours of use. There are many more radio than television stations—in late 1960 radio's 3,539 AM stations and 815 FM stations greatly outnumbered the 583 television stations—but the participation of the television networks in the Register-and-Vote campaign ensured an immense audience.

[11] For example, Harold Mendelsohn, "Measuring the Process of Communications Effects," *Public Opinion Quarterly*, 26 (1962), 411–416; Harry B. Watton, "Can Statistics Measure Ad Effectiveness?" *Industrial Marketing*, 41 (October 1956), 148–152.

TABLE 4

Education and Response to Reminders

	Per Cent Who Voted				Number of Cases			
Recall of Messages from Each Medium	Grammar School and Less	Did Not Complete High School	High School Graduate	College	Grammar School and Less	Did Not Complete High School	High School Graduate	College
Television								
Reminded	71	81	83	88	263	216	347	283
Not reminded	59	70	90	86	225	115	71	85
Newspapers								
Reminded	80	79	83	87	192	183	282	270
Not reminded	56	74	88	89	296	148	136	98
Radio								
Reminded	72	79	84	86	148	115	189	187
Not reminded	63	76	85	90	340	216	229	181

Source: Gallup Survey 638 K, November 1960.

less so for those with more education. Television does not have special effects: hearing reminders from all three channels is associated with turnout differences; although television appears "stronger" than radio, it may be "weaker" than newspapers. When other socio-economic variables are run according to the format of Table 4, the same results occur: the lowest social class appears sensitive to reminders while higher classes are not; reminders seem to have so little effect on the higher classes that often recall is inversely related to turnout; television appears "stronger" than radio and "weaker" than newspapers, a theme that will recur throughout this paper.

The usual *caveat* must govern the interpretation of data like those in Table 4. Statistical differences may reflect an increment in turnout due to additional stimuli. Or perhaps lower-class persons who report recalling messages over the mass media are simply more alert and articulate generally, and higher turnout habits

TABLE 5

Knowledge and Response to Reminders

	Per Cent Who Voted among Those Who Gave		Number of Cases	
Recall of Messages from Each Medium	Correct Answer	Incorrect or No Answer	Correct Answer	Incorrect or No Answer
Television				
Reminded	88	73	615	497
Not reminded	87	62	179	322
Newspapers				
Reminded	88	75	537	393
Not reminded	86	62	257	426
Radio				
Reminded	87	71	376	266
Not reminded	88	67	418	553

Question for ascertaining knowledge: "Do you happen to know what is meant by the term 'balancing the federal budget'?" (If yes): "What?"
Source: Gallup Survey 638 K, November 1960.

are part of their more active way of life. But the special sensitivity to stimuli by the less politically involved has been documented by me elsewhere, and it would be consistent to discover that otherwise comparable lower-class people are more likely than upper-class people to show large turnout differences when some are stimulated.[12]

A more direct test of the special susceptibility to reminders among the less involved politically appears in Table 5. The questionnaire surveys available to me contained various tests of political understanding. Table 5 classifies respondents by whether they understood the meaning of "balancing the budget." As the table shows, reminders make little difference to those with greater knowledge but are associated with turnout differences among those with less. As in the other findings of this paper, television appears "weaker" than newspapers but "stronger" than radio.

ASSOCIATION BETWEEN MEDIA USE AND TURNOUT

If the transmission of turnout reminders over television has uncertain effects upon turnout, what are the results of television use generally? Tables 6 through 8 tell how watching television, reading newspapers, and listening to radio are associated with turnout. The same results appear whether the variables are mere ownership of television and radio sets, length of time using the media, or getting political information from the media.

TABLE 6

A. Association between Media Use and Turnout

	Voted (N = 1147)	Did Not Vote (N = 343)	Total (N = 1490)	φ
Has TV in home	997	243	1240	+0.18
Reads newspaper regularly	1003	217	1220	+0.26
Has radio in home	1088	318	1406	+0.04

B. Joint and Partial Associations among Television Ownership, Newspaper Reading, and Turnout

Television	Newspaper	Per Cent Who Voted	Number of Cases
Own	Read	83	1073
Do not own	Read	73	147
Own	Do not read	61	167
Do not own	Do not read	41	103

Source: Gallup Survey 576 K, December 1956. By permission of the American Institute of Public Opinion (The Gallup Poll).

Whether it is television watching or newspaper reading, the break comes between those who do and those who don't. Television owners (and watchers) vote at higher rates than non-owners (and non-watchers). Newspaper readers vote at higher rates than those who do not read. But length of time watching and read-

[12] William McPhee et al., *Public Opinion and Congressional Elections* (New York: Free Press), chaps. 1 and 9.

ing does not add successively higher increments in turnout. Voting is relatively easy and socially expected—particularly in presidential years—and only low thresholds of motivation and social stimulation need be crossed. Only for more difficult acts are successive stimuli likely to affect a steadily increasing number of people. The relative ease of voting limits the sizes of the associations between media use and turnout: most of the non-users vote anyway, because voting is socially expected, because personal contact influences them, or because of other reasons.[13]

Perhaps uniquely powerful influences are expected from television's personal images, thorough absorption of viewers' attention, and long hours of viewing. But Tables 6 and 7 show that the association between television use and turnout is *lower* than the association between newspaper reading and turnout. For example, the phi coefficient in Table 6A is larger for newspapers than for television. And in Table 6B the partial associations suggest that newspaper reading "adds more" than television viewing: turnout rates are higher for the readers without sets than for the viewers without newspapers. Either newspapers are more "stimulating" than television programs, or newspaper reading and television tend to be parts of slightly different styles of life, with newspaper readers being more conscientious, informed, and interested in politics.

A remarkable and consistent pattern in these tables is the present weakness of radio listening, once a significant correlate of turnout. Whether the variable is set ownership or listening in general, radio use is independent of turnout. One might think that listening to campaign speeches and special events would strengthen the association, but the result according to the data in Table 8 is a weakening. Most people do not listen to speeches and special events on radio. These listening habits correlate with turnout so insignificantly as to be significant ($\phi = 0.002$). Past predictions about the decline of radio as a political vehicle in the television age have been borne out.[14]

Approximately the same relationship between media use and turnout holds true when the full sample is partitioned by background variables. Table 7 classifies people by sex, wealth, and education. The well-known turnout differences between social categories are evident: at each level of media use men vote more than women, the upper classes more than the lower, and, in general, the better educated more than the less educated. Within each social group, turnout jumps between those who do not and do watch television and read newspapers. Classifying people by background variables does not reduce these percentage differences, and therefore something else is at work besides the well-known relationships between media use, and—on the other hand—sex, education, and social class.[15] And something else is at work in highly publicized presidential elections

---

[13] One might think that media use should make more of a difference in the less fashionable and less discussed midterm elections. But the same moderate association with turnout appeared in midterm data summarized by me in McPhee et al., *Public Opinion and Congressional Elections*, chaps. 1, 9, and 11.

[14] Angus Campbell et al., "Television and the Election," *Scientific American*, 188 (May 1953), 47. On the transformation of radio listening and programming under the impact of television, see Fredric Stuart, "The Effects of Television on the Motion Picture and Radio Industries" (New York: Columbia University Library, 1960), unpublished doctoral dissertation.

[15] On the social correlates of turnout, see Robert E. Lane, *Political Life* (New York: Free Press, 1959), chaps. 4, 13–17. On the social correlates of media use, see Wilbur

besides the stimulating effects of the media alone: the basic answer seems to lie in general patterns of political involvement and political apathy, of which media use is a part.

SELECTIVE EFFECTIVENESS OF THE MEDIA

Let us assume that the turnout differences in Table 7 reflect the effects of the mass media. (The assumption, as I have said earlier, is debatable.) Are the media in general and is television in particular more stimulating for some population groups than for others? Are certain categories of the electorate likely to drop out if they are not presented with televised stimuli? Measuring effectiveness by percentage differences between users and non-users can be done in two ways: (1) by comparing rises in the aggregate turnout rates for each population group, as in the "per cent who voted" rows of the table; (2) by comparing the success of the media in bringing out those who might not have voted in the absence of the media, as in the "Relative increment in turnout" rows of the table.

By the first criterion, television and newspapers may succeed in raising the turnout rates of the less involved groups more than the rates of the more involved. Media use brings turnout differences slightly closer together between men and women, between the rich and poor, and between the better educated and the less educated. Thus, media stimuli might bring into the electorate a larger *number* of the politically less involved than of the population groups more interested in politics. There are hints that television may be slightly less effective in narrowing the gaps than newspaper reading. But the top rows of each background variable in Table 7 contain too many statistical fluctuations for firm conclusions.

If we define effectiveness as the capacity to bring to the polls people who otherwise might have stayed home and if we calculate it from rates, as in the "relative increment" rows of Table 7, the case for selective effectiveness weakens. If the media are effective in bringing out the apathetic, the relative increments in Table 7 should be consistently higher for women than for men, for the poor than for the rich, and for the less educated than for the better. But no such consistent pattern can be found for the media generally or for television alone. The less involved groups have more nonvoters in the absence of media use; therefore, even though the media may help bring more of them to the polls, many are left unaffected.

MEDIA EFFECTS ON THE EXECUTION OF INTENTIONS

A better way to infer effects is to study processes over time. Table 8 shows how pre-election turnout intentions are carried out, when persons are classified by their exposure to speeches and news during the intervening campaign.

Two common facts are evident in Table 8. As in much media research, media stimuli in real-life situations do not strike people randomly: those who intend to vote early in the campaign have the higher frequencies of subsequent media ex-

Schramm (ed.), *Mass Communications* (2d ed.; Urbana: University of Illinois Press, 1963), pp. 421–462; Bogart, *The Age of Television,* chap. 4; Campbell, "Television and the Election," as cited; Cornelius Du Bois, "What Is the Difference between a Reader and a Viewer?" *Mediascope,* 3 (September 1959), 53–58, and (October 1959), 46–51.

TABLE 7
Media Use and Turnout, by Sex, Rental Value of Home, and Education

Hours Spent on a Typical Weekday

	Watching Television					Reading Daily Paper(s)				Listening to Radio		
	0	1 or Less	1–3	3–4	4 or More	0	½ or Less	½–1	More Than 1	0	1 or Less	More Than 1
By sex												
Percent who voted												
Men	68	85	82	85	85	62	86	82	86	78	81	81
Women	55	75	81	81	75	45	78	81	83	72	77	72
Relative increment in turnout*												
Men	0	53	44	53	53	0	63	53	63	0	14	14
Women	0	44	58	58	44	0	60	65	69	0	18	0
Number of cases												
Men	151	123	188	108	145	125	192	225	173	188	325	192
Women	139	76	172	141	251	136	300	231	122	167	247	365
By rental value												
Percent who voted												
Lower	50	68	72	74	69	44	75	75	67	58	66	68
Middle	76	83	81	81	81	65	81	79	92	83	85	75
Upper	76	88	89	91	82	68	86	88	89	86	87	85
Relative increment in turnout												
Lower	0	36	44	48	38	0	55	55	41	0	19	24
Middle	0	29	21	21	21	0	46	40	77	0	12	−47
Upper	0	50	54	63	25	0	56	63	66	0	7	−7
Number of cases												
Lower	143	47	93	74	116	142	134	118	79	114	177	182
Middle	79	52	121	88	137	66	170	149	92	120	154	203
Upper	50	92	134	80	129	40	175	169	101	109	212	164

By education													
Percent who voted													
Grammar school or less	54	68	69	83	79	51	76	76	82	74	66	68
Some high school	56	80	81	68	71	46	72	76	81	65	77	70
High school graduate	74	82	88	91	81	68	90	84	82	82	89	82
College	83	88	89	86	87	63	84	93	93	80	89	89
Relative increment in turnout												
Grammar school or less	0	30	33	63	54	0	51	51	63	0	−31	−23
Some high school	0	55	57	27	34	0	48	56	65	0	34	14
High school graduate	0	30	54	65	27	0	69	50	44	0	39	0
College	0	29	35	18	24	0	57	81	81	0	45	45
Number of cases												
Grammar school or less	149	41	98	63	128	153	115	129	82	125	174	180
Some high school	52	30	86	53	99	46	105	102	67	71	124	125
High school graduate	39	56	94	85	113	41	148	126	72	94	135	158
College	42	66	74	36	47	19	104	85	57	56	119	90

* 0 stands for the base line from which relative increment is computed. "Relative increment" is the additional amount of turnout associated with each level of media use as a fraction of the maximum possible gain. "Maximum possible gain" is the difference between turnout associated with no media use and 100 percent. For example, the relative increment for one hour of television watching among men is (85 − 68)/(100 − 68) = 53. The relative increment for three to four hours of television watching among women is (81 − 55)/(100 − 55) = 58.
Source: Gallup Survey 576 K, December 1956. By permission of the American Institute of Public Opinion (The Gallup Poll).

TABLE 8
Media Use, Intention, and Turnout

Questions and Responses	Per Cent Who Expressed Intention to Vote in September and October (1)	Relative Trend between September–October and November* (2)	Total Per Cent Who Voted in November (3)	Per Cent Who Voted in November — Among Those Who Intended to Vote (4)	Per Cent Who Voted in November — Among Those Who Did Not Intend to Vote (5)	Number of Cases — Total (6)	Number of Cases — Intended to Vote (7)	Number of Cases — Did Not Intend to Vote (8)
"Did you watch any programs about the campaign on television?"								
No	63	−8	58	90	3	233	146	87
Yes, just one or two	86	−13	75	86	4	181	155	26
Yes, several	86	−3	83	95	18	509	436	73
Yes, good many	90	−6	85	93	12	832	752	80
"Did you read about the campaign in any newspaper?" (If yes): "How much did you read newspaper articles about the election?"								
No	64	−13	56	84	16	344	220	124
Yes, from time to time; once in a great while	81	−6	76	94	6	402	326	76
Yes, often	90	−2	89	93	7	210	190	20
Yes, regularly	95	−4	91	95	5	763	722	41
"Did you listen to any speeches or discussions about the campaign on the radio?"								
No	83	−4	79	94	10	1014	837	177
Yes, just one or two	87	−12	76	88	4	178	154	24
Yes, several	85	−4	82	94	11	303	259	44
Yes, good many	91	−9	83	89	18	255	233	22

* "Relative trend" shows the amount of change undergone by an aggregate group relative to the number of members who intended to vote at the time of the pre-election interview. It is computed by the following formula: (number who voted in November − number who intended to vote in September)/number who intended to vote in September.

Source: University of Michigan, Survey Research Center, Project 440, Pre- and Post-election Panel Interviews, 1960. Reprinted by permission.

posure. People are more likely to defect from an intention to vote than to reverse an intention not to vote; consequently, effectiveness increases as the negative trend approaches zero and as turnout rates increase among those intending to vote (i.e., the sorts of data appearing in columns 2 and 4 of Table 8).

The trends in the second column of Table 8 suggest that newspaper reading is more effective than television watching in regulating the carrying out of intentions. Readers' over-all voting behavior declines during the campaign less than nonreaders' rates; television viewers' rates do not decline consistently less than nonviewers' rates. The same difference appears in column 4 of Table 8: among those who intend to vote, newspaper reading produces a turnout increase over the absence of reading, while television viewing produces only ambiguous results.[16] As in previously mentioned relationships between radio and turnout, listening appears to lack any effects on the fulfillment of intentions. Last-minute exposure by television and radio thus does not seem to bring out the vote.

CONCLUSION

Television leaves a more lasting impression than newspapers and radio when conveying reminders to vote. But recollection of televised messages does not appear to have a potency lacking in any other mass medium: recollection of a reminder in any mass medium is associated with higher turnout than the absence of any recollection. Newspaper reading may be more effective than television watching in affecting turnout and in affecting the fulfillment of intentions to vote. Or, perhaps a more accurate statement is that newspaper reading and television watching are associated with partly different modes of life with different political patterns. When practiced jointly, newspaper reading and television watching are associated with very high rates of turnout, but television may "add" less to the combination than newspapers. The association between media use and turnout distinguishes only between users and non-users: extra hours do not steadily increase voting probabilities. Radio listening has become independent of turnout. Perhaps television is more effective in stimulating increases in the voting of less politically involved people, but the data are uneven and the same differential effect (if any) may be true of newspaper reading. All these generalizations are gross statistical associations based on national sample surveys; adequate verification and more specific conclusions would require more precisely designed samples and variables.

These statements are based on surveys in presidential elections, when there are abundant communications through many channels, and high turnouts; possibly, media effects differ in other situations. Possibly, television would have more specific influence in elections about which the public was more apathetic. Or, possibly, the advent of television has placed a higher floor under the public's interest in presidential elections, thus preventing repetitions of the low turnouts sometimes encountered in the past.

Although television reminders to vote appear to have only limited effects, perhaps they could be more influential if they were better adapted to the situation of

[16] Television—and even newspapers in a high-turnout year like 1960—may have weaker effects on the fulfillment of intention than many other personal motivations and social influences. Compare Table 8 with the more systematic and clear-cut results summarized in McPhee et al., *Public Opinion and Congressional Elections*, chap. 9.

the nonvoter. At present, the messages reach and are recalled disproportionately by the upper classes and better educated, who are likely to vote without reminders.[17] Also, these messages are phrased for all audiences together. Reminders might stimulate more voting if they were aimed more frequently at the lower classes and at other groups with lower turnouts, and if they were phrased specifically to appeal to these audiences. Also, turnout reminders should not merely exhort people to vote but should explain how to overcome barriers. Although most people find voting easy, many nonvoters are confused by legal prerequisites, by registration and absentee ballot procedures, by ignorance of the electoral system, etc.[18] Thus, turnout reminders over television must increase knowledge and skill as well as increase motivation. This implies varying turnout reminders in each community according to the situations confronted by the mobile, the sick, and the apathetic.[19]

A common generalization in media research today is that the effect of any medium depends on how the subject responds to all other media. Therefore, the effects of television on turnout (or on anything else) can best be identified by focused interviewing involving each subject's total communications experience. Television watching is closely connected with some newspaper reading and with some personal conversations within the family, and both these other variables—particularly family behavior—have higher correlations with turnout than has television alone. Thus, one future problem is to identify how television adds to or subtracts from the influence of the press and family; another problem is to identify how television affects the collective political behavior of the family.

Finally, another common generalization in contemporary media research is that users approach the media with a variety of needs and predispositions, and thus they acquire diverse satisfactions.[20] Thus, any precise identification of the effects of television watching on voting must identify the uses sought and made of television by the various types of viewer: the effects of television upon the viewer's political behavior will doubtless prove to be a subtle product of the total interaction between him and his set.[21]

---

[17] The correlation between social class and recall appears clearly in the data used to prepare Tables 1 through 5. One such correlation can be seen in the base figures of Table 4.

[18] Brendan Byrne, *Let's Modernize Our Horse-and-Buggy Election Laws!* (Washington, D.C.: Center for Information on America, 1961).

[19] Gerhart Wiebe correctly points out that neither television nor any other medium can improve citizenship practices unless the messages inform the public about the appropriate mechanisms for action. "Merchandising Commodities and Citizenship on Television," *Public Opinion Quarterly*, 15 (Winter 1951–1952), 679–691.

[20] Elihu Katz and David Foulkes, "On the Use of the Mass Media as 'Escape': Clarification of a Concept," *Public Opinion Quarterly*, 26 (1962), 377–388 and sources cited.

[21] Of course, the precise effectiveness of television would require a carefully designed study of people in their natural settings, along the lines of Irwin M. Towers *et al.*, "A Method of Measuring the Effect of Television through Controlled Field Experiments," *Studies in Public Communication*, no. 4 (Autumn 1962), 87–110. A problem in such a field experiment during a political campaign is control of all the televised stimuli, but some control of reminders to vote might be possible.

20
Has Television Reshaped Politics?

Angus Campbell

The advent of television in the late 1940s gave rise to the belief that a new era was opening in public communication. As Frank Stanton, president of the Columbia Broadcasting System, put it: "Not even the sky is the limit." One of the great contributions expected of television lay in its presumed capacity to inform and stimulate the political interests of the American electorate.

"Television, with its penetration, its wide geographic distribution and impact, provides a new, direct and sensitive link between Washington and the people," said Dr. Stanton. "The people have once more become the nation, as they have not been since the days when we were small enough each to know his elected representative. As we grew, we lost this feeling of direct contact—television has now restored it."

As time has passed, events have seemed to give substance to this expectation. The televising of important congressional hearings, the national nominating conventions, and most recently the Nixon-Kennedy and other debates have appeared to make a novel contribution to the political life of the nation. Large segments of the public have been given a new, immediate contact with political events. Television has appeared to be fulfilling its early promise.

From the *Columbia Journalism Review* (Fall 1962), pp. 10–13. Copyright © 1962 *Columbia Journalism Review*. Reprinted by permission of publisher and author.

Impressive as the audiences have been, however, it is not safe to assume that they reflect a basic change in the nature of political communication or in the force of its impact. Television has no doubt succeeded in making a sizable part of the electorate direct witnesses to episodes in recent political history, but the effect of this exposure remains a question. Has it raised the level of political interest in the American electorate? Has it broadened public information about political issues and events? Has it brought the ordinary citizen closer to the government he elects?

These are not questions to which we can hope to find simple answers. During the period of television's phenomenal growth other great changes were also taking place. The nation's economy moved to unprecedented levels. The trend toward urbanization was accelerated. The high schools and universities poured millions of graduates into the electorate to take the place of a much less educated older generation. To isolate and dissect the contribution that television made to public affairs during this restless period would require surgery of a delicacy we cannot at present perform. The evidence at hand does not have this kind of precision, but it is instructive.

The most commonly accepted indicator of public involvement in politics is the turnout in national elections. Presumably, if television has made political communication more effective a large portion of the electorate will make the effort to vote. In fact, there has been only a slight rise in the turnout figures during the last ten years. In the presidential elections of 1952, 1956, and 1960 the turnouts —that is, the proportions of adult citizens who voted—were considerably higher than in the elections of 1944 and 1948, but if we drop back to the period just before the war we find that the turnouts in 1936 and 1940 were almost as high as they have been in the most recent elections. There has been a small proportionate increase in the presidential vote during the television era, although it has fluctuated and at its lowest point in 1956 (60.4 percent) exceeded by only a percentage point the high of the pre-television period.

The off-year congressional elections do not show even this increase. The turnout in the off-year elections during the 1950s was never as high proportionately as it was in the off-year election of 1938.

We gain a perspective on recent figures if we make a similar comparison of turnout in the elections preceding and following the development of radio as a medium of mass communication. Radio broadcasts of campaign events were put on the air as early as 1924, but radio did not achieve full coverage of the electorate until after the 1932 election. Turnout in the early 1920s rose substantially when women received the vote and reached a new high point in 1928, a level that was maintained in 1932. Between the elections of 1932 and 1940, however, the turnout records jumped more than 8 percentage points; the off-year congressional vote increased even more markedly—from 31.7 percent in 1930 to 44.1 percent in 1938.

These increases in the national vote, as radio reached the less educated and less involved sections of the population, are impressive. This was a time of depression and political urgency, of course, but the turnout in 1932 when the depression was at its worst point was scarcely higher than it had been in 1928. It was not until 1936 that the presidential turnout moved up sharply, and we know that Roosevelt's great majority in that year was based not so much on defecting Republicans as on citizens who had not previously voted. Some factor not present in 1932 brought them to the polls four years later. It is hard to believe that radio, exploited with great artistry by Roosevelt, did not play a crucial role.

Election statistics are notoriously difficult to interpret, but one thing is apparent: The advent of radio was followed by a general and significant increase of turnout in national elections; the arrival of television was not. Whatever new ingredients television has brought into the political life of this country, it has not yet greatly affected the willingness of the average American to go to the polls.

The election statistics are not the only data at hand. Since 1952 the Survey Research Center has been conducting national surveys of the electorate immediately before and after each presidential election. In these surveys we have asked our respondents two questions intended to indicate the extent of their personal involvement in the campaigns. One of these questions asked whether the respondent "personally cared which party won the presidential election" and the other asked "how much interested" he had been in "following the election campaign." These questions were asked in an identical form of those we interviewed in 1952, 1956, and 1960.

The pattern of response to these questions varied over the three elections in very much the same way that the total turnout varied. The proportion who "cared" how the election turned out declined somewhat in 1956 from its 1952 level and then rose again in 1960 to its 1952 position. The proportion who described themselves as "interested" in the campaign also slid off in 1956 and then came back in 1960 to a level slightly higher than that of 1952. In other words, the degree of political involvement expressed in the three campaigns paralleled the actual turnout.

But while interest and involvement fluctuated, there was a tremendous increase in television coverage during these same years. If television had demonstrated a unique capacity to activate political interest among its viewers we should find a substantial increase in the number expressing high interest over the 1952 to 1960 period. This we do not find.

Neither do we find an increase in the extent of political information of our respondents. It is not easy by any means to assess the range of facts, beliefs, hearsay, and folklore that people have regarding politics. In our interviews we ask people to talk to us in a conversational way about the parties and the presidential candidates, and to tell us the good points and bad points of each. From their answers we can extract all the bits and pieces of content that make up their "image" of the two candidates and the two parties.

This image varies from one election year to the next. The Democratic Party, for example, was seen much more favorably in 1956 than it had been in 1952 when "the mess in Washington" was still fresh in the public mind. The image of Adlai E. Stevenson was considerably more favorable in his first campaign than it was in his second. But aside from these changes in the quality of the images of parties and candidates there are also changes in the total number of bits of information and belief that make up these images. The public has more on its mind about the candidates and parties in one election than it has in another; the images are more elaborated in some years than in others. We may assume that it is largely the mass media that provide this detail.

We find when we examine the evidence from our three surveys that the 1952 election brought out the greatest volume of comment about the candidates and parties. People were more voluble about what the parties stood for, what their strengths and weaknesses were, what groups they represented than in either of the succeeding elections. They also had a fuller picture of Eisenhower than they had of Nixon. On the other hand, they had a good deal more to say about Kennedy in 1960 than they had about Stevenson in either of his campaigns, a difference partly accounted for by negative reactions to Kennedy's religion. If we consider the total volume of comment in the three election years we find a pattern like that of the measures of involvement—highest in 1952, lowest in 1956, higher again in 1960.

These comparisons of the national elections during the era of television raise serious doubt as to whether this new medium, despite its tremendous audience, has greatly altered the basic relationship of the electorate to its national government. In its first decade, it seems neither to have elevated the general level of political interest nor to have broadened the total range of political information. It has greatly extended the purely visual dimension of political communication; the public no doubt finds it easier to form an image of its political leaders through television than it did through the older media. In individual cases this visual image may have a decisive influence on political choice, as it apparently did with an elderly respondent who told our interviewer she couldn't vote for Nixon because she "didn't like the look in his eyes, especially the left one."

There may also be occasions when public opinion as a whole may be moved one way or another by the uniquely visual quality of television communication. There is reason to believe the television debates in 1960 provide such an instance. But these reactions, either individual or collective, do not reflect any greater depth of commitment or understanding of political matters than existed before television.

Why has television not produced a lift in the political involvement of the electorate similar to the rise that followed the introduction of radio? The explanation lies in the answers to three fundamental questions: Was there a virgin area of the population not being reached by the mass media when television came on the scene? Was television as effectively different from existing media as radio had been a generation earlier? Was there an unsatisfied demand for political communication in the electorate when television appeared?

The first of these questions is perhaps the easiest to answer. There was in fact no remaining frontier for further penetration by the mass media when television appeared in the late 1940s. At that time 90 per cent of the population reported listening to radio and 80 percent read a daily newspaper. So far as simple availability of information was concerned it seems clear that all but the largely inaccessible population—the very old, the very dull, the very antisocial—was being reached. During the 1930s radio must have made contact with millions who were beyond the reach of printed media. But there was very little room for further expansion with television.

The question of what new element television introduced into the total flow of public communication is perplexing. Despite its capacity for immediate visual presentation, television has not proved as revolutionary a medium of political communication as many expected it would. Rather than adding an important new dimension to the total flow of information to the public it seems largely to have taken over the role of radio. Like radio, it can be attended to passively without the effort required by the printed media. This is not to say, of course, that television does not have unique qualities; it is because of these qualities that most people now prefer to watch political programs on television rather than listen to them on radio. But the impact does not seem to be much greater in one case than the other.

The essential problem of all political communication is the character of the public demand for it. No one can doubt that many persons make a special effort to watch public-affairs programs on television; they are seeking information. If they came from that part of the population that is out of contact with the other media and lacks information, television would certainly contribute to their political education and stimulation. But this is not the way things happen. If there is one dependable law in the world of mass communication, it is that those most likely to seek information are already the best informed. Thus we find that the people who follow the election campaigns most closely on television are precisely the same ones who read the most about them in the newspapers and magazines.

It is among those at the other end of the scale, the quarter or third of the population that is generally uninvolved and uninformed, that television might have hoped to have its greatest impact. This is where the potential gains were greatest. But this group, alas, is very incurious about politics; its demands for information are exceedingly modest. Its members can apparently be induced to watch an occasional "spectacular," like the conventions or the debates, but their detachment from political matters is undisturbed.

Radio succeeded in rolling back this barrier of apathy appreciably during the 1930s by making it possible for people to receive at least rudimentary political information without the effort of reading. But these gains do not seem to have been extended greatly during the 1950s. Television has shown a capacity to catch the public eye but it has yet to demonstrate a unique ability to engage the public mind.

21
The Late Vote: Summary of Findings and Their Implications

Kurt Lang
Gladys Engel Lang

The reporting of the 1964 national election made communications history. For the first time there was the chance that conclusive returns, including projections of the final outcome, would be available to many voters in Western states before they themselves had voted. While networks had used computers to "pick winners" as early as 1952, such machines, fascinating as they were to broadcasters and audiences alike, had remained a novelty or sensation not to be taken too seriously. By 1964 computer application in this area had reached a new stage of sophistication, and the networks and press associations decided to pool resources to provide the public with the fastest possible tally of results. The new technology combined with the collaborative effort held a clear prospect that the networks would be able to point to significant trends indicated by bellwether precincts within minutes—and certainly within the hour—after voting ended at 6:30 P.M. in several strategic Eastern states.

Citizens throughout the country, but especially in California, were forewarned of possible political effects in the event the networks announced a probable winner early on election night. Newspaper editors and columnists, radio and television commentators, and others voiced their active concern. Political managers and

Reprinted by permission of the publisher, from Kurt Lang and Gladys Lang, *Voting and Nonvoting* (Waltham, Mass.: Ginn and Company, 1968), Chapter 8.

their candidates took to the air and called press conferences urging those who might vote late not to be dissuaded by whatever they might hear.

Some of these warnings raised the specter of vote shifts as returns began coming in. There were allusions to bandwagon effects benefiting the man shown to be ahead, as well as talk of a large sympathy vote for the apparent underdog. These were not, however, the chief concern. The great expectation was that, were early returns to show Johnson with a decisive lead in the East, a drop in Western voter turnout could have a determinate influence on the outcome of the election. People who would otherwise have gone to the polls might be led to think that their votes no longer mattered, and in particular those who had already experienced some disinclination to vote might be discouraged from going to the polls. Finally, there was concern over the number who might put off voting until they could first check the returns. These persons would also be open to dissuasive influences.

Events on election day 1964 clearly corroborated the expectation of an early declaration of the winner from very incomplete returns, long before the polls in California had closed. In the precincts studied, three out of five registered voters who had not yet gone to the polls by 4:00 P.M. local time had heard something about how the race for president was going by the time they voted, or, in the case of nonvoters, before the polls had closed. Over half of these (or one out of three persons interviewed) were able to conclude from what they had heard that a Johnson victory was certain and that the race for president had, for all practical purposes, already been decided. Only six persons (less than 2 percent of the sample) had heard some returns that left them with the impression that Goldwater was making a comparatively strong showing.

The two broadcast media were, beyond doubt, the chief source of these previewing perceptions; they were mentioned as the primary source of information by 81 percent of those who had been exposed to election news by the time they voted. More people mentioned radio than television, probably because many tuned in as they drove home from work or to the polls. Yet television was clearly the more effective in apprising viewers of the outcome. This effectiveness does not appear to be so much an attribute of the medium as of media use. In contrast to radio listening, television viewing was more likely to occur after work, when the returns coming in were more definitive and viewers could give them more attention. The network coverage provided a fairly clear indication of the impending Johnson victory from the minute it went on the air: 71 percent of those who followed these returns from 4:00 P.M. on said that, as soon as they turned on their set, they knew "right away" that the race was more or less decided. This proportion increased to near 90 percent among persons who first tuned in at a later hour. The 15 percent who received what information they got before voting from other people were probably hearing secondhand what originally came over radio or television.

It must nevertheless be emphasized that not all the information with which California late voters went to the polls, nor the conclusion they drew, came from the early network election coverage, which had begun at 4:00 P.M. local time and had made full use of computer-based projections. Even in Cleveland, where these network broadcasts did not begin until after polls had closed, one out of seven late voters and nonvoters interviewed claimed that he had heard something of how the election was going while he could still make a vote decision, and a few said that they had become certain of the impending Johnson landslide. Consequently, one can assume that even if the network election coverage had been delayed until polls everywhere had closed, Californians voting late would still have had more information about election trends before they voted than late voters in the East. This is because polls in the East Bay area closed four and a half hours later than in Ohio, and news bulletins on local stations could carry reports of voting trends from other sections of the country.

Most people indicated that they drew their conclusions about the probable outcome *not* from computer predictions but from tallies of the popular vote and of the electoral vote shown by the networks. Yet the 16 percent who did base their conclusion on computer reports were more often certain that Johnson would win by the time they voted. These persons were better informed both about what computers could do and about politics. The latter characteristic, by itself, might account for why they were able to draw this conclusion earlier than others.

Interest in an early prediction appears to have been stronger among late voters in Ohio, where 25 percent chose this as one of their reasons for selecting a particular channel, than in California, where this reason was chosen by only 11 percent. Apparently Easterners wanted to know the outcome of an election without having to stay up most of the night, whereas Californians could count on hearing significant results by poll closing time. Yet sizeable minorities both in California (45 percent) and in Ohio (38 percent) agreed with the statement that "being told who the winner will be early in the evening before most votes have actually been counted takes the fun out of election-night broadcasts."

The conclusion a person drew from returns available did not depend solely on these reports, but also on what he had expected beforehand. It obviously took more information to invalidate an expectation that Goldwater would win than to confirm one about a Johnson landslide. Those who had anticipated a landslide became certain of the outcome prior to voting about twice as often as those who had given Goldwater a chance—in a close race or otherwise. Political preference, by contrast, made little difference: Goldwater supporters were as likely as Johnson supporters to accept the fact of a Johnson victory.

THE BROADCASTS AND VOTER TURNOUT

How much late-election-day slack can be traced to the special network broadcasts? Our interviews with 364 Californians, all of them registered, supplemented by an effort to account for 339 other nonvoters whose names appeared on precinct rosters, paid off in one single case of late-election-day slack in response to the broadcasts: an angry Goldwater supporter, who said he had never given Goldwater much chance but was so dismayed by the lopsided Johnson margin that he simply gave up and did not vote.

A single case hardly provides a sound basis for quantitative generalization. As a further check we therefore compared the nonvoting rate within our thirty-three California precincts with that in the nine comparable Ohio precincts, using for this purpose the official tabulations of the vote. Our investigation disclosed the dangers inherent in deducing effects from differences in rates between the two areas. Approximately two thirds of so-called nonvoting in the precincts in both these states was due to failure to remove from voting rosters the names of voters who had died or moved to another district; thus these official nonvoting rates reflect a good deal of residential mobility and mortality. After the appropriate corrections had been made, the actual amount of nonvoting among registered voters in California turned out to be a mere 4 percent instead of 13 percent. This figure of 4 percent represents the upper limit of the range within which broadcast-induced late-election-day slack could possibly have occurred. This is to say, if *every* registrant who did not vote had heard network returns before polls closed and had thereby been dissuaded from casting a vote, a maximum of 4 percent of the electorate could have been so affected.

The California nonvoting rate of 4 percent was actually lower than the rate in Ohio, where it amounted to 7 percent. Much of the verified nonvoting in both states was due either to illness, or to the unavoidable and unanticipated necessity to be out of town. Hence this logical—but obviously improbable—upper limit must be further reduced by at least the number who were physically unable to vote. Among those remaining—perhaps 2.5 percent of all registered voters—lack of political interest was clearly the most important reason for failure to appear at the polls.

When we focused specifically on the impact of network broadcasts, their subordinate importance as a cause of slack became still clearer. To begin with, a smaller proportion of nonvoters than late voters had been following returns before polls closed. Nonvoters as a group had clearly less interest and were less involved in the election campaign. Since both these characteristics—interest and involvement—would lead a person to follow network election returns before voting and stay with them until the early hours of the morning, long after all doubts about the outcome had been dispelled, the relatively lower exposure of nonvoters gains further credence.

As far as those who voted are concerned, the time a person went to the polls seems to have had more influence on the time he started following returns than vice versa. Though late voters who cast ballots during the last ninety minutes of voting more often had been following returns by that time, or heard at least something about election trends, than those voting earlier, we failed to locate a single person who had deliberately delayed his vote until he could first learn how things were going. Rather than seeking politically useful information, those who had watched before voting did so for the spectacle the returns normally offer or simply out of habit, absorbing whatever is on the air.

VOTE DECISIONS

We also investigated the alternative possibility, namely that the election broadcasts may have encouraged vote switching or helped crystallize the votes of persons who had serious doubts about whether they should vote and whom to vote for. Long before the interview turned to the broadcasts, we asked all late voters whether they had made any vote decision on election day itself.

Most decisions mentioned by respondents related to their votes on candidates for lower offices or for a proposition. An identical 2 percent in California and Ohio reported a decision affecting their vote for president. None of these decisions involved a switch. Rather they were crystallizations—i.e., decisions to vote by people who had thought about abstaining. The number of crystallizations in Ohio, obviously, cannot be attributed to the election broadcasts, but neither could we establish any cause-effect relationship between the returns and the decisions made by the California late voters. In fact, the crystallizers had less often heard returns before voting and were less likely to have become certain than those who merely followed through on decisions made before election day.

The process of vote crystallization can also be viewed in its temporal sequence. We asked each voter whether he had ever "seriously considered," at *any time* during the campaign or on election day itself, any one of these three alternatives: (1) not voting at all; (2) voting without casting a ballot for president; or (3) voting without casting a ballot for U.S. senator. We found that of the twenty-four voters who had played with the first alternative, every one ultimately voted. Indicative of the central role played by the presidential contest in getting out the vote is that only three of the thirty-seven persons who had considered not voting for president actually cast a ballot without pulling the lever for the highest office; among the persons who had entertained this alternative with regard to voting for United States senator, a much larger proportion (six out of twenty-one) actually abstained. Again the pattern was similar in California and Ohio, providing no indication that the returns played any significant part in this regard.

ATTITUDINAL REACTIONS

Analysis of reactions went beyond the impact of the broadcasts on votes to the more general issue of why people should continue to cast ballots for president after it had become evident that the outcome could not possibly be overturned. We had collected data meant to get at people's covert and attitudinal responses to what they heard and saw. From these reports about how they felt, one can gain some insight into how they might react under circumstances when these tendencies pass over the threshold from covert responses to overt behavior.

Asked whether election information had made them more eager or less eager to vote, the large majority (72 percent) of those who had heard returns while they could still make a vote decision said that it had made no difference at all. Among the others, the number who became more eager to vote outnumbers those who became less eager by a 3 to 2 ratio. The likelihood that there would be a change of attitude, and the direction it would take, depended in part on the perceptions of voters and on what these perceptions implied about the outcome of the race.

To begin with, the attitude changes follow a fairly persistent pattern: the larger the proportion within any category to report a change, the more "less eager" reactions there were relative to the number of "more eager" reactions. Thus, persons who had become certain of the outcome experienced more attitude change, and more of them felt less like voting, than persons who had not drawn such definite conclusions from the returns. In other words, as more complete returns began coming in, their unambiguous implications began to persuade a larger number of the futility of casting a vote. Yet there were many others who, this apparent futility notwithstanding, became even more determined to vote. Similarly, there were more changes among those whose expectations were invalidated by the information of the Johnson landslide, and again this was accompanied by a disproportionate increase in the number of "less eager" reactions. Indeed, the impact of "certainty" on feelings about voting depended in large measure on whether a person had become certain of a previously-held expectation or whether he had been definitely proved wrong. Finally, if certainty about the outcome involved at the same time an underdog perception, some demoralization occurred, but there were also a good many others all the more determined to have their ballots counted.

In the California Senate race, however, the very scattered and partial returns available to a few by the time they went to vote resulted in a much more definite increase in eagerness than did the conclusive presidential returns. The largest number of "more eager" reactions came from Salinger supporters who saw their man was trailing. Slight underdog perceptions, coming at a time when the outcome of that contest was still very much in doubt, appeared to have a definite mobilizing effect.

Some statements volunteered by late voters about their perceptions of the presidential race indicate that concern over the outcome of the senatorial contest may in fact have helped forestall any tendency toward slack. Salinger voters became distinctly "more eager" to vote after hearing that Johnson had definitely won than did those who were voting for Murphy. Especially prone to this reaction were Salinger voters who thought the Senate contest would be extremely close. By contrast, those confident their favorite would win were more inclined to react to news that the presidential contest was over, if they reacted at all, by becoming less eager to vote.

THE LAW OF MINIMAL CONSEQUENCES

Why was the effect of the returns on the behavior of voters so minimal? In explanation, we point to factors and conditions, some general and some specific to the 1964 election, that inhibited the potential of the election broadcasts to elicit behavior disjunctive with prior voting intentions. The fact that very few such specific consequences could be observed in the short run does not, of course, preclude the possibility of quantitatively and qualitatively more important effects in other elections or over the long run.

Attenuation of any impact returns could have had comes from (1) the smallness of the group potentially open to influences, (2) the neutralization of any impetus toward change by countervailing influences, and (3) the stability of attitudes that support voting and the different specific cognitions with which these attitudes are compatible.

The Susceptible Group

To be susceptible to any influence on election day, a person has to be registered in advance, defer voting until after significant returns have begun to come in, tune in on the election coverage or talk with someone who has, and then find the image on which his vote intention is based invalidated. Mere confirmation from returns heard before voting of what a person already believes in the offing is unlikely to cause him to deviate from prior intentions.

According to best estimates, some two thirds of all California citizens of voting age were registered in 1964. Between 25 and 30 percent on the lists from which the California sample was drawn had not voted by 4:00 P.M. local time. Some of these turned out to have moved or died. Fewer than half had been following network election returns prior to voting though about three fifths had heard at least some election news. The percentage of registrants thus susceptible to direct influence from broadcast news was certainly no higher than fifteen percent, and probably much lower. Among the exposed group, chances that returns would invalidate expectations were low; most respondents had never expected anything but a Johnson victory by at least a comfortable margin.

One is moreover led to expect, on theoretical grounds, that those persons most open to influence by broadcast returns are those least interested in the campaign and with the least partisan involvement. Yet many of these persons, because they do not register, are also beyond the range of possible influence from the returns. Nor was there any evidence that voters who showed up to vote during the last ninety minutes were an exceptionally volatile group, one that was disinterested in the election and pushed into voting only by a last-minute electioneering drive. On the contrary, this group of late-late voters included a rather larger number of politically sophisticated "independents," conflict-ridden as far as the 1964 election was concerned but not especially prone to rush on the bandwagon or cast a sympathy vote for the underdog. Since their concern extended to races other than that for the top office, casting a vote still made sense even after the presidential race appeared irrevocably decided.

The less politically interested, involved, and sophisticated a person, the smaller was the chance that he had heard something about the race or had been following network returns before he voted. These same characteristics were also associated with a person's ability to make an accurate assessment of Goldwater's chances before the election. Hence, a larger proportion of people whose expectations could have been invalidated were exposed to returns either only casually or not at all. That the election returns should have provided a shock for so few people implies that whatever bandwagon or underdog psychology was at work must already have had its effect on people prior to election day.

Countervailing Influences

The influence of returns reaching voters on election day might be offset by other communications to which they were being exposed. Among these were the urgings to Goldwaterites that they vote early to avoid the possibility of influence, and the warning Salinger issued to his followers not to be lulled into complacency by an apparent Democratic tide. At the same time, the nonpartisan saturation campaign to get out the vote continued right through election day and inundated voters from every side.

Many respondents reported that they themselves, on election day, had urged others to be sure to vote or had themselves been so urged by others. Reports of partisan attempts to switch votes by political argument were far fewer in number. Only twelve persons—all of whom voted—indicated either that they themselves had been the target of a suggestion that it no longer made much difference whether or not they voted, or that they had voiced their feeling to others. While all of these manifest dissuasion attempts were made with reference to election trends, it is at least highly probable that they nevertheless helped focalize attention on the election, contributed to the excitement, and emphasized that voting was the order of business for this day.

The Motivation to Vote

We identified three different orientations, all of which to some extent enter into the subjective significance of casting a ballot. The reactions of voters to returns will differ in accordance with which of these orientations is dominant. Thus, the common-sense expectation that news of a Johnson landslide would cause slack was predicated on an image of the voter as motivated primarily by the utility of his ballot, by whether it could influence the outcome. This type of voter would be dissuaded from casting a ballot once the election appeared decided and his ballot could no longer affect the outcome.

A voter's partisan involvement, the second of the orientations, contributes to the stability of reactions in the situation just described. Where the vote serves primarily as an ideological expression, as a declaration of solidarity, it is to that extent independent of practical political considerations; it has a strongly symbolic character. Moreover, when perceived within a context of partisan involvement, the belief that one's vote has utility can be maintained even after one or the other candidate appears clearly to have won. The partisan perspective helped some voters to assess the implications of the presidential returns for the outcome of other races and for future elections. Some became more eager to vote because of their concern over the possible effect of the news about the presidential race on the outcome of the Senate election in California. Still others wanted to hold down the Johnson margin, or to repudiate the Goldwater brand of Republicanism so unambiguously that it would cease being a political force to be reckoned with. In these various respects, a person's vote decision differs from a market decision. The partisan label, in giving consistency to a number of preferences, converts the vote into an expression of ideology.

Stability in electoral participation is further supported by a third orientation, one that neither takes account of the utility of the vote nor has anything to do with partisanship. The nonrational commitment to voting as an obligation of citizenship implies that the vote also serves as a testimonial of faith in democratic government. Not all who continued to cast ballots, especially those who became more eager to vote after hearing conclusive returns, were guided by a political logic. A confidence in the ballot as an effective instrument for influencing government policy gave their votes the character of a ratifying gesture. This type of commitment to voting, when widespread, is an indication of the legitimacy the electoral system enjoys among the electorate and, at the same time, is one of its main supports.

IMPLICATIONS

The findings just summarized document the degree to which the short-run effect traceable to the early broadcasting of returns in the 1964 election conformed to the law of minimal consequences. But this law, as we have pointed out, represents only a probability statement, one that applies to direct effects in the short run. Given the novelty, in 1964, of the early declaration of a presidential winner, the question naturally arises as to how much one can possibly generalize about future elections from a case study of a single election held in a unique historical context. Another question concerns the possible existence of other, more subtle effects operating over the long haul, namely such side effects as a result from attempts on the part of individuals and institutions to adapt themselves to similar contingencies in the future.

IMPACT IN OTHER ELECTIONS

The impact of early returns was shown to depend on four sets of factors: the content of *pre-voting perceptions* and how widely they are disseminated, *prior estimates* among the electorate as to the probable outcome, the *electoral choices* voters are being asked to make, and the characteristics of the *electorate*. The first of these is clearly the most variable, but any effect that these perceptions will have is mediated through the other three factors.

Returns that provide an unambiguous picture seem to have a greater impact on attitudes than returns whose significance is difficult to assay. Thus, late voters who had become certain of a Johnson victory were more likely than others to feel "more eager" or "less eager" to vote. That this should be so is, of course, highly plausible. The unambiguous character of the information reduces the opportunity to maintain by means of selective perception such beliefs as one prefers, or to preserve one's hopes by refusing to draw any conclusion at all. Characteristically, persons exposed to returns they judged to be inconclusive reported the least amount of attitude change in response to what they had heard. Ambiguity can, however, have two sources. The first is *the broadcasts themselves,* as when returns are just beginning to trickle in, when the projection shows the man with the fewer votes to be the likely winner, or when there is a contradiction in the predictions of two networks. Or, second, the ambiguity derives from a *race too close* for predictions to be made with any confidence. The analysis of the reactions of persons who drew different conclusions from these presidential returns does not, by itself, permit any inference about whether the two types of ambiguity will have the same or different effects.

In the California Senate race, we have an instance where the returns were, to be sure, altogether inconclusive, but where all the portents pointed to an unusually close race not likely to be decided early in the evening. These returns elicited an extremely high proportion of attitude changes from those exposed to them—almost all represented an increase in eagerness to vote.

It would seem, from our various findings, that returns that give an unambiguous indication of a close contest have the strongest mobilizing influence; a "decided" race apparently creates some tendency toward slack, though this was, as we have seen, partly inhibited by other factors. Returns that are confusing or open to a wide range of interpretations apparently have the least impact one way or the other. Consequently, the earlier a network can confidently predict the outcome from even a small proportion of the vote, and the more predictions of this sort find acceptance, the greater the potential demoralization of late voters as a result. On the other hand, the longer the drama of seesaw battle can be maintained, the more will the excitement so generated facilitate voting. In 1964, the effect of early presidential returns and of news of the Senate race worked in opposite directions.

The meaning of inconclusive returns was closely linked to what a respondent had been led to expect by pre-election forecasts. To a person counting on a Johnson landslide, returns that contained no indication of victory could only mean that more votes had still to be counted; to a person primed to expect a "cliffhanger" between Salinger and Murphy, even the first inconclusive returns were apt to serve as a reaffirmation. The point is that early returns have greater impact when they serve to invalidate what has been expected in advance.

Not only were there few instances of clear-cut invalidation in 1964, but the likelihood of an unusual number occurring in future elections is greatly reduced by the growing acceptance of pre-election forecasts based on scientific polls. Improvement in these techniques and the wider dissemination of the results contribute to a uniformity of expectations, based as they are on identical sources of information. The self-appointed expert with his ear close to the ground is disappearing, and the projective element in popular estimates is likewise on the wane.

Many respondents voiced their belief that pre-election polls had influenced the outcome in 1964. Whatever the validity of charges that the polls, by presenting Goldwater as the underdog, adversely affected his chances their influence on reactions to the election broadcasts cannot be denied. Because the forecasts of a completely one-sided race were so fully confirmed even by the earliest returns, they helped immunize voters against the possibility of an invalidation. Only if polls should undergo another fiasco, comparable to the one in 1948, will returns upset the expectations of many voters.

Finally, there is at least some suggestion that underdog perceptions have a stronger mobilizing effect than bandwagon perceptions. Even if the absolute magnitude of this effect is small, a combination of invalidation and underdog perceptions in what is proving to be a close race could have a definite influence on the outcome. Some partisans in particular would become more eager to vote. Under these circumstances, the mobilization of only a minuscule percentage of the electorate could overturn the result.

The likelihood of such an eventuality is very much reduced in an election where voter interest is widely dispersed among many electoral contests instead of being focused on a single race or referendum. Our data clearly indicate that slack can be inhibited by concurrent balloting for other offices, contests in which the outcome still hung very much in doubt even after the presidential race had been fully decided. Accordingly, all other things being equal, one predicts that the danger of slack is greatest in areas of one-party dominance (inasmuch as the outcome of other races is unlikely to be affected by any falling-off in the vote for president), in party primaries where the contest is only for a single office, in special by-elections, or in a referendum called to resolve some particular issue.

The above-mentioned types of contests have in common still another feature, namely a lower and generally more variable turnout rate. The efficacy of the last-minute effort to bring out the vote, as well as the possibility of slack, are increased to the extent that there are marginally-committed registered voters, who may decide to vote or not to vote in response to highly variable social-psychological influences. The electorate in a national election evidently does not have this character. Those who vote are strongly committed toward voting, and most non-voting, as we have seen, results from institutional and physical obstacles in the way of a 100-percent turnout. However, the easing of registration requirements or the institutionalization of some administrative procedure whereby registration would become "automatic" could swell the number of registered voters only marginally committed to voting in a national election, and so contribute to potential instability.

LONG-RANGE AND ANCILLARY EFFECTS

Any innovation in communications—the admission of the press to legislative debates, the broadcasting of political party conventions, the televising of presidential press conferences, etc.—has invariably evoked alarm. Some change always accompanies such innovation, but the potential danger to political institutions is, in retrospect, almost always found to have been exaggerated. The process by which individuals react and the ramifications of their reactions for the workings of institutions is always more complex, and hence the effects far more subtle, than the alarmists can anticipate. Indeed, the high-pitched sense of alarm may itself be one of the firmest guarantees against sudden disjunctive change.

Long-term adaptation to the fast count and computer-based predictions involves learning how to live with them. For the individual voter, this means learning to evaluate the meaning of any apparent trend or explicit prediction. Will repeated experience with computer-dominated election night reports increase, or decrease, any susceptibility to influence? The answer depends on many things, including whether trust in the returns (and their accuracy) grows or declines; the amount of critical reserve among the audience; the tendency to vote early or to avoid pre-voting exposure to returns.

To begin with, the accuracy of early electoral trends and predictions will have something to do with the credibility they will enjoy. Performance so far has been pretty mixed. It has already been mentioned that in 1960 one network first called the election for Richard Nixon, though this prediction was quickly modified as soon as sizeable returns began to come in. Again, in the June California primary preceding the 1964 election, an early prediction by pollster Lou Harris, vividly remembered by many voters there, nearly rebounded to the discredit of the network concerned. The narrow margin by which the prediction was vindicated in the final returns helped feed the subsequent controversy over broadcast-induced effects.

Past mistakes have evidently made broadcasters more cautious. They have become increasingly careful to explain the basis on which predictions are made and to hedge their predictions with semantic qualifications—"probable winners," "indicated winners," "declared winners," etc. In some state and local elections since 1964, first predictions had to be rescinded. Yet there was little embarrassment or public outcry. The broadcasters had made allowance for such possibilities from the start of their programs.

As broadcasters gain experience in living with computers, and viewers, too, become more experienced, trust in predictions appears to grow as well. The more experienced among the election night audience, we found, were not only more knowledgeable about how predictions are made long before all votes are in, but also had more faith in the accuracy of the predictions. Not everything about these predictions was new; elections have almost always been called before the official vote count was completed. It would seem likely that as more voters come to understand the distinction between the tally of the vote and the projection of trends from sample districts, more will also recognize that broadcasters are simply applying a new technology to improve their interpretations of trends in the returns.

If trust in the reliability of the fast returns is likely to increase with their increasing accuracy, there is still the question of whether voters will also increasingly act to avoid possible influence. There is by now an acute awareness among voters in Western states that they constitute special targets of influence. This awareness, bound to increase, coupled with the exercise of responsible caution by broadcasters, should minimize the amount of influence on voting behavior by exposure to incomplete returns. Beyond this, if broadcasts continue to begin before polls are closed, individuals and groups will act consciously or unconsciously to avoid influence, and will adapt to the speed-up in returns. People obviously can deliberately vote before returns become available; they can avoid hearing news; they can persuade themselves in advance of the importance of the margin of victory or of the other races.

Still, the general inference from this and other studies—that the net balance of changes in votes had no effect on the outcome of the election in 1964—does not mean that the broadcast of returns before polls closed had no effects upon voters or that there will not be effects in the future. While interviewees indicated that they had not changed their intention to vote (or not to vote) as a result of their exposure to news before voting, many did feel that casting a vote knowing the election was over amounted to a partial disenfranchisement. Their ballots seemed to count less.

Even when knowing the likely outcome before voting does not contribute to such feelings of alienation, it can make it more difficult to vote out of simple sense of obligation. It is altogether possible that in the future, in areas where early returns are available long before polls close, voters will learn to estimate the utility of their vote before voting. Imagine, for instance, a very close election where early returns indicate that California—or Oregon, or Hawaii, or Alaska—would supply the electoral votes necessary for victory. With the electoral votes in other states already accounted for, attention would turn to the West and what voters there would do. If the expectation of a close race had been widespread and if many people were undecided about whether to vote or for whom to vote, large numbers of people might delay going to the polls until they had first heard how the election was going. The fact that few voters waited around in 1964 does not mean that more might not do so in some future election.

Conceivably, having a good idea of how the race was going could, under some circumstances, alter the general tendency not to vote for a third party in presidential elections. The necessity, under a two-party system, for electoral coalitions presents a formidable barrier in the way of third-party protest. People who feel they are voting for the lesser of two evils are especially disinclined to defect to a minor party for fear of bringing the real evil to power. Early returns may give them a better knowledge of the odds. There is in this not so much the possibility that an election would be won or lost as a result, but that new considerations might enter the electoral choice. Instead of registering their preference between viable choices, voters would be encouraged to use what information they had from polls and returns to make their vote decisions in terms of a rational strategy.

Again, most outcry against the early returns centered on the disenfranchisement of the late Western voter. However, the time could come when those in states voting after returns were coming in are looked upon as unfairly advantaged. Any information that enables a person to see the consequence of his vote can be seen as giving him an advantage over others not so favorably situated. It is precisely to reduce disparities in access to knowledge that the press has insisted on unrestricted publicity.

In no sense, however, does this re-create the situation of a town meeting, where the roll is called and where everyone can see how the vote is about to go. Here persons can "pass" in order to cast their vote at a more crucial time; they can, for that matter, reverse their vote if, given the existing division, they come to find it advisable to do so. In a national election, by contrast, a ballot is irrevocably cast. Although the individual ballots are secret, those voting late have more opportunity to base their own vote on estimates of political trends. They may be the only ones to vote knowing that a decision has already been made. To carry this argument one step further: The canons of courtesy have generally enjoined a loser to concede—even long before the tally has been completed—as soon as the trend is unmistakable. Theoretically a candidate could concede even while balloting was still in progress. What would the voter do then?

Clearly all the above, though logically tenable, are not likely to occur in fact. In raising these possibilities we do mean to indicate that the way election returns are reported is an important part of political life in the United States. Alteration of the election night ritual is bound, over the long run, to have consequences for political behavior. To stay up on election night to learn who the new president will be has been, especially since the advent of radio, an opportunity to participate in a national event. Election night has been a unifying experience containing elements of the "sacred." To a query about whether the fun had gone out of election night, a near-majority of Californians responded by saying the experience was not the same. When, in addition, issues are raised about how many votes were changed or races determined as a consequence of the broadcasts, the returns become linked to the divisive controversies that any electoral campaign inevitably arouses.

Technological innovations, by their nature, call for new sets of rules to cope with their effects. Certainly the new technology for data processing and quick dissemination makes it possible to have more reliable forecasts within shorter spans of time. Predictions of winners are bound to come sooner and sooner after polls close. Many voters have a keen interest in learning the outcome of an election as soon as this information becomes available, and competition among the news media will make voluntary restraints difficult to enforce. Even were early returns to be banned all over the country until polls were closed, it would be difficult to keep information from private reports—campaign managers, partisans, etc.—from leaking out. The normal flow of news would not cease, but there would be less check on its reliability. Surely, a full coverage by a professionally competent and responsible staff is preferable to news leaks designed to advance partisan interests. Any measure that curtailed the right of news-gathering agencies to check up on returns, or to disseminate them to some areas, would indeed represent an interference with the right of the public to know.

The proposal, publicly proposed by Dr. Frank Stanton, for a uniform polling day with balloting all over the country ending at the same hour, would permit the fullest exploitation of the new technology. Results from all parts of the country would be available at about the same time, so all suspicion that early returns might affect the outcome of any given race would be eliminated. Indeed, there would be no "early returns". After all polls had closed, the quick answers provided could contribute to a feeling that people all over the country were sharing in a simultaneous experience. The fun and excitement of the long vigil into election night would be abbreviated, but it would no doubt be replaced by a new ritual of interpretation-in-depth of the returns (what groups and sections voted what way), and a new ritual of concession and victory statements. Perhaps more attention would be given to state and local contests.

The justification for new election regulations does not reside in the demonstration of direct effects: Actual changes in voting behavior were few in number though various types of voters felt either more eager or less eager to vote. But given the power inherent in the new communication technology, setting rules to maintain equality seems preferable to depending on self-immunization by individual voters, or to trusting that politicians will employ strategies to neutralize the advantage one or the other side might enjoy. It is the long-range and ancillary effects of broadcasting early returns before polls close with which social policy must be equally concerned.

22
The Times They Are A-Changin':
The Music of Protest

Robert A. Rosenstone

At the beginning of the 1960s, nobody took popular music very seriously. Adults only knew that rock n' roll, which had flooded the airwaves in the 1950s, had a strong beat and was terribly loud; it was generally believed that teen-agers alone had thick enough eardrums, or insensitive enough souls, to enjoy it. Certainly, no critics thought of a popular star like the writhing Elvis Presley as being in any way a serious artist. Such a teen-age idol was simply considered a manifestation of a subculture that the young happily and inevitably outgrew—and, any parent would have added, the sooner the better.

Today, the view of popular music has drastically changed. Some parents may still wonder about the "noise" that their children listen to, but important segments of American society have come to recognize popular musicians as real artists saying serious things.[1] An indication of this change can be seen in magazine

Reprinted, with minor revisions by the author, from *The Annals of American Academy of Political and Social Science* (March 1969), pp. 131–134. Reprinted by permission of publisher and author.

[1] The definition of "popular music" being used in this article is a broad one. It encompasses a multitude of style, including folk, folk-rock, acid-rock, hard-rock, and blues, to give just a few names being used in the musical world today. It does so because the old musical classifications have been totally smashed and the forms now overlap in a way

attitudes. In 1964, the *Saturday Evening Post* derided the Beatles—recognized giants of modern popular music—as "corny," and *Reporter* claimed: "They have debased Rock 'n Roll to its ultimate absurdity." Three years later the *Saturday Review* solemnly discussed a new Beatles record as a "highly ironic declaration of disaffection" with modern society, while in 1968 *Life* devoted a whole, laudatory section to "The New Rock," calling it music "that challenges the joys and ills of the . . . world." [2] Even in the intellectual community, popular music has found warm friends. Such sober journals as *The Listener, Columbia University Forum, New American Review,* and *Commentary* have sympathetically surveyed aspects of the "pop" scene, while in *The New York Review of Books*—a kind of house organ for American academia—composer Ned Rorem has declared that, at their best, the Beatles "compare with those composers from great eras of song: Monteverdi, Schumann, Poulenc." [3]

The reasons for such changes in attitude are not difficult to find: there is no doubt that popular music has become more complex, and at the same time more serious, than it ever was before. Musically, it has broken down some of the old forms in which it was for a long time straight-jacketed. With a wide-ranging eclecticism, popular music has adapted to itself a bewildering variety of musical traditions and instruments, from the classic Indian sitar to the most recent electronic synthesizers favored by composers of "serious" concert music.

As the music has been revolutionized, so has the subject matter of the songs. In preceding decades, popular music was almost exclusively about love, and, in the words of poet Thomas Gunn, "a very limited kind [of love], constituting a sort of fag-end of the Petrarchan tradition." [4] The stories told in song were largely about lovers yearning for one another in some vaguely unreal world where nobody ever seemed to work or get married. All this changed in the 1960s. Suddenly, popular music began to deal with civil rights demonstrations and drug experiences, with interracial dating and war and explicit sexual encounters, with, in short, the real world in which people live. For perhaps the first time, popular songs became relevant to the lives of the teen-age audience that largely constitutes the record-buying public. The success of some of these works prompted

that makes meaningful distinction between them impossible. Though not every group or song referred to will have been popular in the sense of selling a million records, all of them are part of a broad, variegated scene termed "pop." Some of the groups, like Buffalo Springfield, Strawberry Alarm Clock, or the Byrds, have sold millions of records. Others, like the Fugs or Mothers of Invention, have never had a real hit, though they are played on radio stations allied to the "underground." Still, such groups do sell respectable numbers of records and do perform regularly at teen-age concerts, and thus must be considered part of the "pop" scene.

[2] *Saturday Evening Post*, Vol. 237, March 21, 1964, p. 30; *Reporter*, Vol. 30, Feb. 27, 1964, p. 18; *Saturday Review*, Vol. 50, August 19, 1967, p. 18; *Life*, Vol. 64, June 28, 1968, p. 51.

[3] "The Music of the Beatles," *New York Review of Books*, Jan. 15, 1968, pp. 23–27. See also "The New Music," *The Listener*, Vol. 78, August 3, 1967, pp. 129–130; *Columbia University Forum* (Fall 1967), pp. 16–22; *New American Review*, Vol. 1 (April 1968), pp. 118–139; Ellen Willis, "The Sound of Bob Dylan," *Commentary*, Vol. 44 (November 1967), pp. 71–80. Many of these articles deal with English as well as American popular groups, and, in fact, the music of the two countries cannot, in any meaningful sense, be separated. This article will only survey American musical groups, though a look at English music would reveal the prevalence of most of the themes explored here.

[4] "The New Music," p. 129.

others to be written, and the second half of the decade saw a full efflorescence of such topical songs, written by young people for their peers. It is these works which should be grouped under the label of "protest" songs of the 1960s, for, taken together, they provide a wide-ranging critique of American life. Listening to them, one can get a full-blown picture of the antipathy that the young song writers have toward many American institutions.

Serious concerns entered popular music early in the 1960s, when a great revival of folk singing spread out from college campuses, engulfed the mass media, and created a wave of new "pop" stars, the best known of whom was Joan Baez. Yet, though the concerns of these folk songs were often serious, they were hardly contemporary. Popular were numbers about organizing unions, which might date from the 1930s or the late nineteenth century, or about the trials of escaping Negro slaves, or celebrating the cause of the defeated Republicans in the Spanish Civil War. Occasionally, there was something like "Talking A-Bomb Blues," but this was the rare exception rather than the rule.[5]

A change of focus came when performers began to write their own songs, rather than relying on the traditional folk repertoire. Chief among them, and destined to become the best known, was Bob Dylan. Consciously modeling himself on that wandering minstrel of the 1930s, Woody Guthrie, Dylan began by writing songs that often had little to do with the contemporary environment. Rather, his early ballads like "Masters of War" echoed the leftist concerns and rhetoric of an earlier era. Yet, simultaneously, Dylan was beginning to write songs like "Blowin' In the Wind," "A Hard Rain's A-Gonna Fall," and "The Times They Are A-Changin'," which dealt with civil rights, nuclear war, and the changing world of youth that parents and educators were not prepared to understand. Acclaimed as the best of protest-song-writers, Dylan in mid-decade shifted gears, and in the song "My Back Pages," he denounced his former moral fervor. In an ironic chorus claiming that he was much younger than he had been, Dylan specifically made social problems the worry of sober, serious, older men; presumably, youths had more important things than injustice to think about. After that, any social comment by Dylan came encapsulated in a series of surrealistic images; for the most part, he escaped into worlds of aestheticism, psychedelic drugs, and personal love relationships. Apparently attempting to come to grips in art with his own personality, Dylan was content to forget about the problems of other men.[6]

The development of Dylan is important not only because he is the leading song writer, but also because it parallels the concerns of popular music in the 1960s. Starting out with traditional liberal positions on war, discrimination, segregation, and exploitation, song writers of the decade turned increasingly to descriptions of the private worlds of drugs, sexual experience, and personal freedom. Though social concerns have never entirely faded, the private realm has been increasingly seen as the only one in which people can lead meaningful lives. Now, at the end of the decade, the realms of social protest and private indulgence exist side by side in the popular music, with the latter perceived as the only viable alternative to the world described in the former songs.[7]

[5] *Time*, Vol. 80, Nov. 23, 1962, pp. 54–60, gives a brief survey of the folk revival.
[6] Willis, "The Sound of Dylan," gives a good analysis of his work.
[7] It must be pointed out that, in spite of the large amount of social criticism, most songs today are still about love, even those by groups such as Country Joe and the Fish, best known for their social satire.

THE NEGRO IN SONG

In turning to the protest songs of the 1960s, one finds many of the traditional characters and concerns of such music missing. Gone are exploited, impoverished people, labor leaders, "finks," and company spies. This seems natural in the affluent 1960s, with youths from middle-class backgrounds writing songs. Of course, there has been one increasingly visible victim of exploitation in this decade, the Negro; and the songsters have not been blind to his plight. But, egalitarian as they are, the white musicians have not been able to describe the reality of the black man's situation.[8] Rather, they have chronicled Northern liberal attitudes towards the problem. Thus, composer-performer Phil Ochs penned works criticizing Southern attitudes towards Negroes, and containing stock portraits of corrupt politicians, law officials, and churchmen trembling before the Ku Klux Klan, while Paul Simon wrote a lament for a freedom rider killed by an angry Southern mob.[9] Similarly white-oriented was Janis Ian's very popular "Society's Child," concerned with the problem of interracial dating. Here a white girl capitulates to society's bigotry and breaks off a relationship with a Negro boy with the vague hope that someday "things may change." [10]

Increasingly central to white-Negro relationships have been the ghetto and urban riots, and a taste of this entered the popular music. Phil Ochs, always on top of current events, produced "In the Heat of the Summer" shortly after the first major riot in Harlem in 1964. Partially sympathetic to the ghetto-dwellers' actions, he still misjudged their attitudes by ascribing to them feelings of shame—rather than satisfaction—in the aftermath of the destruction.[11] A later attempt, by Country Joe and the Fish, to describe Harlem ironically as a colorful vacation spot, verged on patronizing blacks, even while it poked fun at white stereotypes. Still, it was followed by sounds of explosion that thrust home what indifference to the ghetto is doing to America.[12] The most successful song depicting the situation of the Negro was "Trouble Coming Everyday," written by Frank Zappa during the Watts uprising in 1965. Though the song does not go so far as to approve of rioting, it paints a brutal picture of exploitation by merchants, bad schooling, miserable housing, and police brutality—all of which affect ghetto-dwellers. Its most significant lines are Zappa's cry . . . [that lots of times he wishes he weren't white]. No song writer showed more empathy with the black struggle for liberation than that.[13]

---

[8] This article is concerned almost exclusively with music written and performed by white musicians. While popular music by Negroes does contain social criticism, the current forms—loosely termed "soul music"—make comments about oppression similar to those which Negroes have always made. The real change in content has come largely in white music in the 1960s.
[9] Phil Ochs, "Talking Birmingham Jam" and "Here's to the State of Mississippi," *I Ain't Marching Any More* (Elektra, 7237); Simon and Garfunkel, "He Was My Brother," *Wednesday Morning 3 A.M.* (Columbia, CS 9049). (Songs from records will be noted by performer, song title in quotation marks, and album title in italics, followed by record company and number in parentheses.)
[10] Dialogue Music, Inc.
[11] Ochs, *I Ain't Marching Any More*.
[12] "The Harlem Song," *Together* (Vanguard, VSD 79277).
[13] Mothers of Invention, *Freak Out* (Verve, 65005).

POLITICIANS

While the downtrodden are heroes of many traditional protest songs, the villains are often politicians. Yet, politics rarely enters the songs of the 1960s. Ochs, an unreconstructed voice from the 1930s, depicts vacillating politicians in some works, and Dylan mentions corrupt ones early in the decade. But the typical attitude is to ignore politics, or, perhaps, to describe it in passing as "A yardstick for lunatics. . . ."[14] It is true that the death of President Kennedy inspired more than one song, but these were tributes to a martyr, not a politician.[15] If Kennedy in death could inspire music, Lyndon Johnson in life has seemed incapable of inspiring anything, except perhaps contempt. In a portrait of him, Country Joe and the Fish pictured the, then, President as flying through the sky like an "insane" Superman. Then they fantasized a Western setting [with "Lyndon" outgunned and sent back to his Texas ranch].[16]

One traditional area, antiwar protest, does figure significantly in the music of the 1960s. With America's involvement in Vietnam and mounting draft-calls, this seems natural enough. Unlike many songs of this genre, however, the current ones rarely assess the causes of war, but dwell almost exclusively with the effect which war has on the individual. Thus, both Love and the Byrds sing about what nuclear war does to children, while the Peanut Butter Conspiracy pictures the effect of nuclear testing on everyone: a "firecracker sky" poisoned with radioactivity.[17] Most popular of the antiwar songs was P. F. Sloan's "Eve of Destruction," which, for a time in 1965, was the best-selling record in the country (and which was banned by some patriotic radio-station directors). The title obviously gives the author's view of the world situation; the content deals mostly with its relationship to young men like himself: . . . [as it asks why they tote guns if they don't believe in war].[18] There are alternatives to carrying a gun, and defiance of the draft enters some songs, subtly in Buffy St. Marie's "Universal Soldier" and stridently in Ochs' "I Ain't Marching Any More."[19] Perhaps more realistic in its reflection of youthful moods is the Byrds' "Draft Morning," a haunting portrait of a young man reluctantly leaving a warm bed to take up arms and kill "unknown faces." It ends with the poignant and unanswerable question, "Why should it happen?"[20]

If many songs criticize war in general, some have referred to Vietnam in particular. The Fugs give gory details of death and destruction being wreaked on the North by American bombers, which unleash napalm "rotisseries" upon the world.[21] In a similar song, Country Joe and the Fish describe children crying

---

[14] Strawberry Alarm Clock, "Incense and Peppermints," written by John Carter and Tim Gilbert, *Strawberry Alarm Clock* (Uni., 73014).
[15] Phil Ochs, "That Was the President," *I Ain't Marching Any More;* the Byrds, "He Was A Friend of Mine," *Turn! Turn!* (Columbia, CS 9254).
[16] "Superbird," *Electric Music for the Mind and Body* (Vanguard, 79244).
[17] Love, "Mushroom Clouds," *Love* (Elektra, EKL 4001); the Byrds, "I Come and Stand at Every Door," *Fifth Dimension* (Columbia, CS 9349); Peanut Butter Conspiracy, "Wonderment," written by John Merrill, *Great Conspiracy* (Columbia, CS 9590).
[18] Trousdale Music Publishers, Inc.
[19] Buffy St. Marie, "Universal Soldier," Southern Publishing, ASCAP; Ochs, *I Ain't Marching Any More.*
[20] *The Notorious Byrd Brothers* (Columbia, CS 9575).
[21] "War Song," *Tenderness Junction* (Reprise, S 6280).

helplessly beneath the bombs.[22] No doubt, it is difficult to make music out of the horrors of war, and a kind of black humor is a common response. In a rollicking number, the Fugs, with irony, worry that people may come to "love the Russians" and scream out a method often advocated for avoiding this: "Kill, kill, kill for peace." [23] And one of Country Joe's most popular numbers contains an attack on generals who think that peace will be won "when we blow 'em all to kingdom come." [24]

The injustice and absurdity of America's Asian ventures, perceived by the song writers, does not surprise them, for they feel that life at home is much the same. The songs of the 1960s show the United States as a repressive society where people who deviate from the norm are forced into conformity—sometimes at gunpoint; where those who do fit in lead empty, frustrated lives; and where meaningful human experience is ignored in a search for artificial pleasures. Such a picture is hardly attractive, and one might argue that it is not fair. But it is so pervasive in popular music that it must be examined at some length. Indeed, it is the most important part of the protest music of the decade. Here are criticisms, not of exploitation, but of the quality of life in an affluent society: not only of physical oppression, but also of the far more subtle mental oppression that a mass society can produce.

YOUTH AS VICTIM

Throughout the decade, young people have often been at odds with established authority, and, repeatedly, songs picture youth in the role of victim. Sometimes the victimization is mental, as when the Mothers of Invention complain of outworn thought patterns and say that children are "victims of lies" which their parents believe.[25] On a much simpler level, Sonny Bono voices his annoyance that older people laugh at the clothes he wears, and he wonders why they enjoy "makin' fun" of him.[26] Now, Bono could musically shrug off the laughs as the price of freedom, but other songs document occasions when Establishment disapproval turned into physical oppression. Thus, Canned Heat tells of being arrested in Denver because the police did not want any "long hairs around." [27] The Buffalo Springfield, in a hit record, describe gun-bearing police rounding up teenagers on the Sunset Strip. . . .[28] On the same theme, Dylan ironically shows that adults arbitrarily oppose just about all activities of youths, saying that they should "look out" no matter what they are doing.[29] More bitter is the Mothers' description of police killing large number of hippies, which is then justified on the grounds that because they looked "weird" it "served them right." [30] Though the incident is fictional, the Mothers clearly believe Americans capable of shooting down those who engage in deviant behavior.

[22] "An Untitled Protest," *Together*.
[23] "Kill for Peace," *The Fugs* (Esp. 1028).
[24] "I Feel Like I'm Fixin' to Die," *I Feel Like I'm Fixin' to Die* (Vanguard, 9266).
[25] *We're Only in It for the Money* (Verve, 65045).
[26] "Laugh at Me," *Five West Cotillion*, BMI.
[27] "My Crime," *Boogie* (Liberty, 7541).
[28] "For What It's Worth."
[29] "Subterranean Homesick Blues," *Bob Dylan's Greatest Hits* (Columbia, KCS 9463).
[30] *We're Only in It for the Money*.

Though the songs echo the oppression that youngsters have felt, they do not ignore the problems that all humans face in a mass society. Writer Tom Paxton knows that it is not easy to keep one's life from being forced into a predetermined mold. In "Mr. Blue" he has a Big-Brother-like narrator telling the title character, a kind of Everyman, that he is always under surveillance, and that he will never be able to indulge himself in his precious dreams of freedom from society. This is because society needs him to fill a slot, no matter that his personal desires. And Mr. Blue had better learn to love that slot, or "we'll break you." [31] Though no other writer made the message so explicit, a similar fear of being forced into an unwelcome slot underlies many songs of the period.

The society of slotted people is an empty one, partly described as "TV dinner by the pool. . . ." [32] It is one in which people have been robbed of their humanity, receiving in return the "transient treasures" of wealth and the useless gadgets of a technological age. One of these is television, referred to simply as "that rotten box," or, in a more sinister image, as an "electronic shrine." This image of men worshipping gadgets recurs. In the nightmare vision of a McLuhanesque world—where the medium is the message—Simon and Garfunkel sing of men so busy bowing and praying to a "neon god" that they cannot understand or touch one another. Indeed, here electronics seem to hinder the process of communication rather than facilitate it. People talk and hear but never understand, as the "sounds of silence" fill the world.[33] Such lack of communication contributes to the indifference with which men can view the life and death of a neighbor, as in Simon's "A Most Peculiar Man." [34] It also creates the climate of fear which causes people to kill a stranger for no reason other than his unknown origins in Strawberry Alarm Clock's "They Saw the Fat One Coming." [35]

Alienated from his fellows, fearful and alone, modern man has also despoiled the natural world in which he lives. With anguish in his voice, Jim Morrison of the Doors asks "What have they done to the earth?" and then angrily answers that his "fair sister" has been ravished and plundered.[36] In a lighter tone but with no less serious intent, the Lewis and Clark Expedition describe the way man has cut himself off from nature in the great outdoors, where chains and fences keep him from the flowers and trees. With a final ironic thrust, they add that there's no reason to touch the flowers because they are "plastic anyway." [37]

This brings up a fear that haunts a number of recent songs, the worry that the technological age has created so many artificial things that nothing natural remains. Concerned with authenticity, the songsters are afraid that man himself is becoming an artifact, or, in their favorite word, "plastic." Thus, the Jefferson Airplane sing about a "Plastic Fantastic Lover," while the Iron Butterfly warn a girl to stay away from people "made of plastic." [38] The image recurs most frequently in the works of the Mothers of Invention. In one song, they depict the country as being run by a plastic Congress and President.[39] Then, in "Plastic People," they

[31] "Mr. Blue," written by Tom Paxton, *Clear Light* (Elektra, 74011).
[32] Mothers of Invention, "Brown Shoes Don't Make It," *Absolutely Free* (Verve, 65013).
[33] "Sounds of Silence," *Sounds of Silence* (Columbia, CS 9269).
[34] *Sounds of Silence.*
[35] *Wake Up . . . It's Tomorrow* (Uni., 73025).
[36] "When the Music's Over," *Strange Days* (Elektra, 74014).
[37] "Chain Around the Flowers," *The Lewis and Clark Expedition* (Colgems, COS 105).
[38] *Surrealistic Pillow* (Victor, LSP 3766); "Stamped Ideas," *Heavy* (Atco, S 33-227).
[39] Unce Bernie's Farm," *Absolutely Free.*

start with complaints about a girlfriend who uses "plastic goo" on her face, go on to a picture of teen-agers on the Sunset Strip—who are probably their fans—as being "plastic," too, and finally turn on their listeners and . . . [advise them to check themselves].[40] Such a vision is frightening, for if the audience is plastic, perhaps the Mothers, themselves, are made of the same phony material. And if the whole world is plastic, who can be sure of his own authenticity?

LOVE RELATIONSHIPS

Toward the end of "Plastic People," the Mothers say . . . [that "true love" cannot be "a product of plasticity"].[41] This brings up the greatest horror, that in a "plastic" society like the United States, love relationships are impossible. For the young song writers, American love is viewed as warped and twisted. Nothing about Establishment society frightens them more than its attitudes towards sex. Tim Buckley is typical in singing that old Americans are "Afraid to trust in their bodies. . . ."[42] Others give graphic portraits of deviant behavior. The Fugs tell of a "Dirty Old Man" hanging around high school playgrounds; the Velvet Underground portray a masochist; and the Mothers depict a middle-aged man lusting after his own thirteen-year-old daughter.[43] The fullest indictment of modern love is made by the United States of America, who devote almost an entire album to the subject. Here, in a twisted portrait of "pleasure and pain," is a world of loveless marriages, homosexual relationships in men's rooms, venomous attractions, and overt sadism—all masked by a middle-class, suburban world in which people consider "morality" important. To show that natural relationships are possible elsewhere, the group sings one tender love lyric; interestingly, it is the lament of a Cuban girl for the dead Ché Guevara.[44]

The fact that bourgeois America has warped attitudes towards sex and love is bad enough; the songsters are more worried that such attitudes will infect their own generation. Thus, the Collectors decry the fact that man-woman relationships are too often seen as some kind of contest, with a victor and vanquished, and in which violence is more acceptable than tenderness.[45] Perhaps because most of the singers are men, criticisms of female sexual attitudes abound. The Mothers . . . [are disgusted with the American woman, who lies in bed gritting her teeth], while the Sopwith Camel object to the traditional kind of purity by singing . . . [that they don't want their women] "wrapped up in cellophane."[46] This is because such a woman . . . [talks endlessly "about sin"].[47] All the musicians would prefer the girl about whom Moby Grape sings who is "super-powered, deflowered," and over eighteen.[48]

Living in a "plastic" world where honest human relationships are impossible,

---

[40] "Plastic People," *Absolutely Free*.
[41] "Plastic People."
[42] "Goodbye and Hello," written by Tim Buckley, *Goodbye and Hello* (Elektra, 7318).
[43] *The Fugs;* "Venus in Furs," *The Velvet Underground and Nico* (Verve, V6-5008); "Brown Shoes Don't Make It," *Absolutely Free*.
[44] *The United States of America* (Columbia, CS 9614).
[45] "What Love," *The Collectors* (Warner Bros.-Seven Arts, WS 1746).
[46] *We're Only in It for the Money;* "Cellophane Woman," *The Sopwith Camel* (Kama Sutra, KLPS 8060).
[47] "Cellophane Woman."
[48] "Motorcycle Irene," *Wow* (Columbia, CS 9613).

the song writers might be expected to wrap themselves in a mood of musical despair. But they are young—and often making plenty of money—and such an attitude is foreign to them. Musically, they are hopeful because, as the title of the Dylan song indicates, "The Times They Are A-Changin'." Without describing the changes, Dylan clearly threatens the older generation, as he tells critics, parents, and presumably anyone over thirty, to start swimming or they will drown in the rising floodwaters of social change.[49]

In another work, Dylan exploits the same theme. Here is a portrait of a presumably normal, educated man, faced with a series of bizarre situations, who is made to feel like a freak because he does not understand what is going on. The chorus is the young generation's comment to all adults, as it mocks "Mr. Jones" for not understanding what is happening all around him.[50]

The changes going on are, not surprisingly, associated with the carefree, joyful experiences of youth. As Jefferson Airplane sings, "It's a wild time," one in which people are busy "changing faces."[51] The most full-blown description of the changing world is Tim Buckley's "Goodbye and Hello," a lengthy and explicit portrait of what the youth hope is happening. Throughout the song the author contrasts two kinds of people and their environments. On the one hand are the "antique people"—godless and sexless—of an industrial civilization, living in dark dungeons, working hard, worshipping technology and money, sacrificing their sons to placate "vaudeville" generals, and blinding themselves to the fact that their "masquerade towers" are "riddled by widening cracks." Opposed to them are the "new children," interested in flowers, streams, and the beauty of the sky, who wish to take off their clothes to dance and sing and love one another. What's more, the "antique people are fading away"; in fact, they are already wearing "death masks.". . .[52]

Buckley's vision of the new world that is coming is obviously that of a kind of idyllic Eden before the fall, a world in which men will be free to romp and play and indulge their natural desires for love. It is a pagan world, the antithesis of the Christian ideal that would postpone fulfillment to some afterlife. Elsewhere, Buckley explicitly condemns that part of Christianity which saves pleasure for an afterlife.[53] Similarly, the Doors' Jim Morrison wants to cancel his "subscription to the resurrection," and then shrieks for a whole generation: "We want the world and we want it now."[54] Here is the impatient demand of youth that all problems be swept aside and the world be made into paradise without delay.

HOW TO LIVE

Though the times may be changing, the songsters are well aware that—despite their brave words and demands—there is plenty of strength left in the old social order. Obviously, they can see the war continuing, Negro demands not being met, and the continuing hostility of society toward their long hair, music, sexual

[49] *Bob Dylan's Greatest Hits.*
[50] "Ballad of a Thin Man/Mr. Jones," *Highway 61 Revisited* (Columbia, CS 9189). Though this song has obvious homosexual overtones, it also stands as youth's criticism of the older generation.
[51] "Wild Tyme (H)," *After Bathing at Baxter's* (Victor, LSO-1511).
[52] "Goodbye and Hello," written by Tim Buckley, *Goodbye and Hello.*
[53] "Pleasant Street," written by Tim Buckley.
[54] "When the Music's Over," *Strange Days.*

behavior, and experimentation with drugs. Faced with these facts, the musicians must deal with the problem of how to live decently within the framework of the old society. Here they tend toward the world of private experience mentioned earlier in this article in connection with Dylan. Many of their songs are almost programs for youth's behavior in a world perceived as being unlivable.

The first element is to forget about the repressive society out there. As Sopwith Camel says, "Stamp out reality . . ." [before it stamps you out].[55] Then it is imperative to forget about trying to understand the outside world rationally. In a typical anti-intellectual stance, the Byrds describe such attempts as "scientific delirium madness."[56] Others combine a similar attitude with a strong measure of *carpe diem*. Spirit deride people who are "always asking" for "the reason" when they should be enjoying life, while H. P. Lovecraft admits that the bird is on the wing and states, "You need not know why."[57] What is important is that the moment be seized and life lived to the fullest. As Simon and Garfunkel say, one has to make the "moment last," and this is done best by those who open themselves fully to the pleasures of the world.[58]

The most frequent theme of the song writers is the call to freedom, the total freedom of the individual to "do his own thing." Peanut Butter Conspiracy carry this so far as to hope for a life that can be lived "free of time."[59] Circus Maximus and the Byrds—despite the fact that they are young men—long to recapture some lost freedom that they knew as children.[60] Such freedom can be almost solipsistic; Jimi Hendrix claims that even if the sun did not rise and the mountains fell into the sea, he would not care because he has his "own world to live through."[61] But for others, it can lead to brotherhood. . . . H. P. Lovecraft [asks all to] "Try and love one another right now."[62]

A desire for freedom is certainly nothing new. What is different in the songs of the 1960s is the conviction that this freedom should be used by the individual in an extensive exploration of his own internal world. Central to the vision of the song writers is the idea that the mind must be opened and expanded if the truths of life are to be perceived. Thus, the importance of external reality is subordinated to that of a psychological, even a metaphysical, realm. The most extensive treatment of this subject is by the Amboy Dukes, who devote half of a long-playing record to it. Their theme is stated quite simply: mankind would be happy if only people took the time "to journey to the center of the mind."[63] Like any mystical trip, what happens when one reaches the center of the mind is not easy to describe. Perhaps the best attempt is by the Iron Butterfly, who claim that an unconscious power will be released, flooding the individual with sensations and fusing him with a freedom of thought that will allow him to "see every thing." At

[55] "Saga of the Low Down Let Down," *The Sopwith Camel*.
[56] "Fifth Dimension," *Fifth Dimension*.
[57] "Topanga Window," *Spirit* (Ode, 212 44004); "Let's Get Together," *H. P. Lovecraft* (Phillips, 600-252).
[58] "Feeling Groovy," *Sounds of Silence*.
[59] "Time Is After You," *West Coast Love-In* (Vault, LP 113).
[60] "Lost Sea Shanty," *Circus Maximus* (Vanguard, 79260); "Going Back," *The Notorious Byrd Brothers*.
[61] "If 6 Was 9," *Axis* (Reprise, S 6281).
[62] H. P. Lovecraft, "Let's Get Together," written by Chester Powers, *H. P. Lovecraft*.
[63] "Journey to the Center of the Mind," *Journey to the Center of the Mind* (Mainstream, S 6112).

this point, man will be blessed with the almost supernatural power of knowing "all." [64]

Such a journey is, of course, difficult to make. But youth has discovered a short cut to the mind's center, through the use of hallucinogenic drugs. Indeed, such journeys are almost inconceivable without hallucinogens, and the so-called "head songs" about drug experiences are the most prevalent of works that can be classified as "protest." [65] In this area, the songs carefully distinguish between "mind-expanding," nonaddictive marijuana and LSD, and hard, addictive drugs which destroy the body. Thus, the Velvet Underground and Love both tell of the dangers of heroin, while Canned Heat warn of methedrine use and the Fugs describe the problems of cocaine.[66] But none of the groups hesitate to recommend "grass" and "acid" trips as a prime way of opening oneself to the pleasures and beauties of the universe. As the Byrds claim in a typical "head song," drugs can free the individual from the narrow boundaries of the mundane world, allowing him to open his heart to the quiet joy and eternal love which pervade the whole universe.[67] Others find the reality of the drug experience more real than the day-to-day world, and some even hope for the possibility of staying "high" permanently. More frequent is the claim that "trips" are of lasting benefit because they improve the quality of life of an individual even after he "comes down." [68] The Peanut Butter Conspiracy, claiming that "everyone has a bomb" in his mind, even dream of some day turning the whole world on with drugs, thus solving mankind's plaguing problems by making the earth a loving place.[69] An extreme desire, perhaps, but one that would find much support among other musicians.

A REPRESSIVE SOCIETY

This, then is the portrait of America that emerges in the popular songs of the 1960s which can be labelled as "protest." It is, in the eyes of the song writers, a society which makes war on peoples abroad and acts repressively towards helpless minorities like Negroes, youth, and hippies at home. It is a land of people whose lives are devoid of feeling, love, and sexual pleasure. It is a country whose institutions are crumbling away, one which can presumably only be saved by a sort of cultural and spiritual revolution which the young themselves will lead.

Whether one agrees wholly, partly, or not at all with such a picture of the United States, the major elements of such a critical portrait are familiar enough. It is only in realizing that all this is being said in popular music, on records that sometimes sell a million copies to teen-agers, in songs that youngsters often dance to, that one comes to feel that something strange is happening today. Indeed, if

---

[64] "Unconscious Power," *Heavy*.
[65] There are so many "head songs" that listing them would be an impossibly long task. Some of the most popular protest songs of the decade have been such works. They include Jefferson Airplane, "White Rabbit," *Surrealistic Pillow;* the Doors, "Light My Fire," *The Doors* (Elektra EKS 74007); Strawberry Alarm Clock, "Incense and Peppermints," *Incense and Peppermints;* and the Byrds, "Eight Miles High," *Fifth Dimension*.
[66] "Heroin," *Velvet Underground;* "Signed D. C.," *Love* (Elektra, 74001); "Amphetamine Annie," *Boogie;* "Coming Down," *The Fugs*.
[67] "Fifth Dimension," *Fifth Dimension*.
[68] See Country Joe and the Fish, "Bass Strings," *Electric Music for the Mind and Body;* or United States of America, "Coming Down," *United States of America*.
[69] "Living, Loving Life," *Great Conspiracy*.

parents fully understand what the youth are saying musically to one another, they must long for the simpler days of Elvis Presley and his blue suede shoes.

If the lyrics of the songs would disturb older people, the musical sound would do so even more. In fact, a good case could be made that the music itself expresses as much protest against the status quo as do the words. Performed in concert with electronic amplification on all instruments—or listened to at home at top volume—the music drowns the individual in waves of sound; sometimes it seems to be pulsating inside the listener. When coupled with a typical light show, where colors flash and swirl on huge screens, the music helps to provide an assault on the senses, creating an overwhelming personal experience of the kind that the songs advise people to seek. This sort of total experience is certainly a protest against the tepid, partial pleasures which other songs describe as the lot of bourgeois America.

Another aspect of the music which might be considered a kind of protest is the attempt of many groups to capture in sound the quality of a drug "trip," to try through melody, rhythm, and volume to—in the vernacular—"blow the mind" of the audience. Of course, youngsters often listen to such music while under the influence of hallucinogens. In such a state, the perceptive experience supposedly can have the quality of putting one in touch with regions of the mind and manifestations of the universe that can be felt in no other way. Such mysticism, such transcendental attitudes, are certainly a protest against a society in which reality is always pragmatic and truth instrumental.

To try to explain why the jingles and vapid love lyrics of popular music in the 1950s evolved into the social criticism and mystical vision of the 1960s is certainly not easy. Part of it is the fact that performers, who have always been young, started writing their own songs, out of their own life experiences, rather than accepting the commercial output of the older members of Tin Pan Alley. But this does not explain the popularity of the new songs. Here one must look to the youthful audience, which decided it preferred buying works of the newer kind. For it was the commercial success of some of the new groups which opened the doors of the record companies to the many that flourish today.

THE FUNCTION OF MUSIC

Though one cannot make definitive judgments about this record-buying audience, some things seem clear. Certainly, it is true that with increasingly rapid social change, parents—and adults in general—have less and less that they can tell their children about the ways of the world, for adult life experiences are not very relevant to current social conditions. Similarly, institutions like the school and the press suffer from a kind of cultural lag that makes their viewpoints valueless for youth. Into the place of these traditional sources of information have stepped the youth themselves, and through such things as the "underground" press and popular music they are telling each other exactly what is happening. In this way, the music has achieved popularity—at least in part—because it telegraphs important messages to young people and helps to define and codify the mores and standards of their own subculture. A youngster may personally feel that there is no difference between his parents' drinking and his use of marijuana. Certainly, it is comforting to him when his friends feel the same way, and when popular songs selling millions of copies deliver the same message, there are even stronger sanctions for his "turning on." Thus, the lyrics of the music serve a functional role in the world of youth.

It is interesting to note that the popular music also puts youth in touch with serious, intellectual critiques of American life. Perhaps it starts only as a gut reaction in the song writers, but they have put into music the ideas of many American social critics. Without reading Paul Goodman, David Riesman, C. Wright Mills, or Mary McCarthy, youngsters will know that life is a "rat race," that Americans are a "lonely crowd," that "white-collar" lives contain much frustration, and that the war in Vietnam is far from just. And they will have learned this from popular music, as well as from their own observation.

The other side of the coin from criticism of contemporary life is the search for personal experience, primarily of the "mind-expanding" sort. As is obvious by now, such expansion has nothing to do with the intellect, but is a spiritual phenomenon. Here a final critique is definitely implicit. Throughout the music—as in youth culture—there is the search for a kind of mystical unity, an ability to feel a oneness with the universe. This is what drugs are used for; this is what the total environment of the light and music shows is about; and this is what is sought in the sexual experience—often explicitly evident in the orgasmic grunts and moans of performers. Through the search for this unity, the music is implicitly condemning the fragmentation of the individual's life which is endemic in the modern world. The songsters are saying that it is wrong to compartmentalize work and play, wrong to cut men off from the natural rhythms of nature, wrong to stifle sex and love and play in favor of greater productivity, wrong to say man's spiritual needs can be filled by providing him with more material possessions.

This is obviously a criticism that can only be made by an affluent people, but these youth do represent the most affluent of all countries. And rather than wallow in their affluence, they have sensed and expressed much of the malaise that plagues our technological society. The charge may be made against them that they are really utopians, but the feeling increases today that we are in need of more utopian thinking and feeling. And while one might not wish to follow their prescriptions for the good life, they have caught something of the desire for freedom that all men feel. What could be more utopian and yet more inviting than the picture of the future painted by the Mothers of Invention, who see a time when loneliness will vanish and people will be free enough to take off their clothes and sing and dance and love.[70] If the youth have their way, perhaps the future is closer than we think.

[70] "Take Your Clothes Off When You Dance," *We're Only in It for the Money*.

CHAPTER EIGHT

THE USES OF SOCIAL SCIENCE

23
Polling in 1968

Archibald M. Crossley
Helen M. Crossley

If the polltakers are not merely reporting sentiment but rather are influencing and even creating it, then the whole idea of measuring public opinion becomes suspect.
—Tom Wicker, *New York Times*, November 5, 1968 (Election Day)

The entire campaign provided a useful corrective to the argument that the polls exert an inevitably tyrannical influence over the outcome. . . . There is no reason to believe that the polls were particularly inaccurate at any stage in recording the tremors of an exceedingly volatile voter sentiment.
—Editorial, *New York Times*, November 8, 1968

1968 PERFORMANCE OF POLLS AND NEWSMEDIA ESTIMATES

It is curious that those who oppose the polls which are taken by professional survey organizations do not extend their opposition to the relative standings which newspapers, magazines, and the broadcast media obtain from the estimates of local observers. The acceptance or rejection of either must be largely a question of method, of competence, and of integrity. As to method, it would seem logical

From *Public Opinion Quarterly* (March 1969), pp. 1–16. Reprinted by permission of publisher and authors.

TABLE 1

Electoral Vote Estimates and Election Results

Electoral Votes and Estimates	Nixon	Humphrey	Wallace	Undecided
Election Result	302	191	45	
Newsmedia Estimates:				
New York Times, Nov. 4	299	77	45	117
Washington Post, Nov. 3	295	67	53	123
Christian Science Monitor, Oct. 30	333	85	45	75
U. S. News & World Report, Nov. 4	348	46	53	91
Time Magazine, Oct. 30	278	46	53	161
Newsweek, Oct. 27	287	46	56	149
Congressional Quarterly, Oct. 25	317	32	53	136
CBS Television, Nov. 3	223	144	45	126
ABC Television, Oct. 31	287	79	39	133
Associated Press, Oct. 20	322	17	45	154

to expect a careful cross-sectioning of the people directly to be more accurate than estimates by others of what the people think. Either method, of course, might be handled better or more honestly than the other. If there is equality in these two respects, then opposition to the polls would seem to call for opposition to newsmedia estimates as well. The performance of both in 1968 merits acceptance.

The record of the newsmedia electoral vote estimates and national and state poll estimates of the popular vote are given in Tables 1, 2, and 3. It is clear from Tables 1 and 2 that the national polls were indicating a close election in what polltakers call a "tie range." It is also clear that the newsmedia estimates were indicating a leaning toward Nixon in electoral votes, with a large number of tossups (varying from 75 to 161 out of the total 538). The two information sources thus agreed that the election was likely to be close, and they also showed that Wallace was running at 14 percent to 15 percent of the popular vote and 39 to 56 electoral votes.

Both sources also indicated that the situation changed markedly in October, when the Humphrey appeal began to surge forward. On September 23 News-

TABLE 2

National Popular Vote Estimates and Election Results

Popular Vote and Estimates	Nixon	Humphrey	Wallace	Undecided
Election Result:[a]				
East	42.9%	50.2%	6.9%	
South	35.9	31.5	32.6	
Midwest	46.9	43.8	9.3	
West	49.0	43.9	7.1	
U. S.	43.5	42.9	13.6	
National Poll Estimates:				
Gallup, Nov. 3[b]	43	42	15	
Harris, Nov. 4[b]	41	45	14	
Gallup, Nov. 3	42	40	14	4
Harris, Nov. 3	42	40	12	6
Harris, Nov. 4	40	43	13	4
Sindlinger, Nov. 2	37	40	12	11

[a]Based on official final figures, as compiled by the Associated Press, Washington Post, December 13, 1968. Minor parties omitted.
[b]Undecideds allocated.

week gave Humphrey as low as 7 solid electoral votes and 47 leaning, well behind those for Wallace, while the national polls ran as low as 28 percent—a far cry from the 191 electoral votes that actually went for Humphrey and the near tie in popular vote, much of which was collected in the East.

TABLE 3

State Poll Estimates and Outcomes

State Poll Estimates	Poll Results[a]				Election Outcome		
	Nixon	Humphrey	Wallace	Undecided	Nixon	Humphrey	Wallace
California							
The State Poll, Nov. 4	43%	42%	4%	11%	48%	45%	7%
California Poll, Oct. 28	52	33	8	7			
Colorado							
Denver Post, Sept. 29	46	30	13	11	51	41	8
Illinois							
Chicago Sun-Times, Nov. 4	47	39	14		47	44	9
Indiana							
Indianapolis News, Oct. 27	46	25	17	12	50	38	12
Iowa							
Des Moines Register (Iowa Poll), Nov. 3	54	35	6	5	53	41	6
Massachusetts							
Boston Globe, Oct. 10	31	44	8	17	33	63	4
Michigan							
Detroit News, Nov. 4	38	47	11	4	42	48	10
Minnesota							
Minnesota Poll, Nov. 3	44	48	5	3	42	54	4
New York							
New York Daily News, Nov. 3	43	47	7	3	45	50	5
Ohio							
Cleveland Plain Dealer, Oct. 23	44	33	12	11	45	43	12
Oregon							
Portland Oregonian, Oct. 23	50	32	9	9	50	44	6
South Dakota							
South Dakota Poll, Oct. 16	49	21	18	12	53	42	5
Texas							
Texas Poll, Sept. 2	33	35	26	6	40	41	19
Utah							
Salt Lake Tribune, Nov. 1	54	28	13	5	57	37	6
Wyoming							
Denver Post, Oct. 13	50	26	15	9	56	35	9

[a] Based on data from media-sponsored published state polls, as available at press time. Excludes local polls and those sponsored by parties or candidates.

CREDIBILITY

Early in the campaign the hue and cry against the cross-section sampling polls, always simmering among some losers, had reached a boiling point. Legislators, calling for investigations and restrictive or regulatory laws, raised the specter of rigging. Public credulity ebbed seriously: "You can't believe the polls—look at 1948 and the *Literary Digest* in 1936." Mathematicians proclaimed the odds against a poll being "right," and even the polltakers themselves called for generous tolerance in the number of possible points of "error." It became popular for poll readers to think in terms of comparative spreads between the major candidates. Thus, when one polltaker reported Nixon at 44 percent and Humphrey at 29 percent, this was seen as a 15-point spread, not long after another poll had shown an 8-point spread. Over a period the Nixon figures were holding fairly steady, but the Humphrey percentage, first in one poll and then in another, showed considerable advances—too large, many thought, to be accurate.

PRINCIPLES LEARNED AND APPLIED

How good is "good" and how bad is "bad"? How accurate can a poll be, how accurate must a poll be, and what have we learned about making it accurate?

Beginning with the turning point in 1936 when polling methodology called for sampling all potential voters instead of the *Literary Digest*'s automobile owners and telephone subscribers, the polltakers have learned a great deal. Perhaps the lesson of 1948 was the most important of the thirty-two years. In that year reliance was placed on the theory that voting preferences changed very little in the later weeks of a campaign. One polltaker called Dewey the winner in September, two others predicted his election on the basis of final polls in mid-October. But the investigating committee of the Social Science Research Council reported that evidence at face value indicated one voter in seven deciding in the last two weeks, and three-quarters of them voting for Truman. An experimental reconstruction in that close election indicated a gain in voting intentions of 4.5 points for Truman and loss of 4.5 points for Dewey in the two-week period.

A close second in importance to the discovery of the principle that minds can change in a matter of weeks is the corollary principle that minds can change in two ways: (1) how to vote, and (2) whether to vote at all.[1] And this is a part of the wider discovery of the whole factor of apathy and indecision. People of voting age who are qualified to register are of three types so far as their voting interest is concerned—hard core, pivotal, and uninterested. Many of the uninterested, and some of the pivotals, are unlikely voters, whose preferences are of interest only so far as some situation could create actual voters out of them. It was established that a major difference existed between the preferences of a cross-section of all potential voters and the actions of those who would take the trouble to vote.

Thus it became necessary for the polltakers to take two steps: (1) To make it clearly understood that each poll report was not a prediction but applied only to the circumstances at the time of the interviews; and (2) to find a means of eliminating not only those who were not qualified to vote, but also those who for other reasons were unlikely to vote. Since poor interviewing procedure can be responsible for very large error, it was perhaps to be expected that the greatest improvement in polling methodology would occur in interviewing techniques. Improved questioning procedures and scales of various kinds were quite successful in sepa-

[1] The *Literary Digest* poll had been reasonably successful before 1936, but Roosevelt was promoting "the forgotten man" and the 1936 vote increased by six million over 1932, five million of them Democratic. Between 1940 and 1948 the percentage of persons of voting age who voted dropped from 59 to 51 percent; then in the 1952 election, with the help of the Ike Clubs, it jumped to nearly 63 percent, producing a gain of 12 million Republican votes compared to an increase of only 3 million for the Democrats.

rating likely voters from the others. For those who choose candidates, tests are used to determine the degree of apathy or enthusiasm which enters into such choices. Another considerable improvement in methodology has been the application of formulas to allocate the so-called undecideds proportionally in the later stages of a campaign.

In determining how good a poll must be, the polltaker must reckon not only with the public but with the medium through which the report is transmitted. Space restrictions usually prevent adequate presentation of the limitations of the findings. It is impractical for the poll story to carry a full explanation of the many factors that can affect an election outcome, and the polltakers themselves are probably somewhat to blame for accenting the sampling side. The only so-called "error" that can be calculated with any precision is that of sampling, but to give the general public the impression that all the figures against all hazards apply 95 percent of the time within three or four percentage points can be a disservice.

The fact is that sampling is only one of many possible types of errors in polling. If a polltaker wants to stay in business, he must do better than the total odds (not just sampling odds). Measurable or not, they are still odds, since we cannot foresee assassinations or the end of a war, or a last-minute campaign tactic. The challenge then is to plan an interview, and a sample, which will overcome as many hazards as possible. In a little over three decades the profession has unquestionably improved its sampling methods and learned how to operate more accurately and with smaller samples. And unless the statisticians can somehow produce a more practical probability device than currently known for dealing with the non-reachables, the sampling side of polling techniques would seem unlikely to improve very greatly in the future.

The criterion for a good poll is certainly not that of merely calling the winner. In 1936 two polltakers earned kudos for showing a Roosevelt lead, although they erred by some six points, and a few years later one was roundly criticized for being on the wrong side by one point. In the four presidential elections since 1952 Gallup's highest deviation on the winner was 2.7 in 1964; two of the others were less than one percentage point off, and one was off by 1.7. All four are better than the sampling odds alone. Since sampling tolerances tell only part of the story, they are almost meaningless as an exact measure of actual total odds. But the plus or minus three-point expectancy on the basis of experience under careful workmanship is not only a handy rule of thumb but a reasonable guide to good performance.

THE POLLING YEAR

Nineteen sixty-eight was a year of extensive use and intensive criticism of the polls. Almost on the eve of the first primary in New Hampshire, Governor Romney received the news from his private polltaker that his relative showing was likely to be very weak. His withdrawal set the stage for active consideration of entry by Governor Rockefeller, who had been giving support to Romney. Soundings by Rockefeller of potential delegate support were followed by his temporary withdrawal.

The New Hampshire primary pushed to the forefront the candidacy of Eugene McCarthy. Receiving 42 percent of the Democratic vote in that primary (almost as much as President Johnson's 48.5 percent), McCarthy galvanized the power of the young people and went on to win the primaries in Wisconsin, Massachusetts, and Oregon. Although rejected by the delegates at Chicago, his stand on Vietnam apparently triggered a turn in American public opinion toward the war. Polls had been showing a trend toward dissatisfaction with the handling of the war situation, but on January 30, about six weeks before the New Hampshire primary on March 12, the Vietcong sprang the Tet offensive and attacked the U.S. embassy in Saigon. The Gallup Poll showed the public aroused to a peak of hawkishness, and then changing suddenly. The hawks (by self-description) dropped 20 points —from 61 percent February 3–7, to 41 percent March 16–20.

On March 16 Robert Kennedy announced his candidacy and swelled the outcry against the war. The President's popularity declined sharply, and ultimately he withdrew from the race. In the contest for delegates Kennedy won the Indiana, Nebraska, and South Dakota primaries, and had just won the California primary when he was assassinated. Martin Luther King had been assassinated two months before, and the prevalence of riots, crime, war, and other domestic and foreign issues called, in Rockefeller's opinion, for a challenge to Nixon on the ability to provide needed leadership for the country. Nixon was clearly in the lead among Republican delegates selected both in the popular primaries and otherwise. But polls showed that Nixon's support among Independents and Democrats was thin enough to raise doubt about his ability to win the election.

Rockefeller began a very active campaign of promotion and public appearances, designed especially to attract non-Republicans and accenting ability to win the election with Democratic and Independent support. He challenged Nixon to join with him and with the Republican National Committee in financing a fifty-state poll. Arguing that Nixon's own performance against John F. Kennedy in 1960 had demonstrated that the strictly Republican approach could lose electoral votes because of the voting in cities and industrial areas, Rockefeller commissioned Political Surveys and Analyses to do his own poll of nine key states with a total of 226 electoral votes, the full report of which was released to the public. This poll showed Rockefeller at least three percentage points ahead of Humphrey for all 226 electoral votes. Nixon was shown ahead by at least three percentage points for 69 electoral votes, two points ahead to two points behind Humphrey for 112 votes, and more than three points behind Humphrey for 45 votes (Massachusetts, Maryland, and Michigan).

In the Gallup Poll, Humphrey had led Nixon since early May. On July 19 Eisenhower endorsed Nixon, and this was given tremendous publicity not only in the regular news stories on the air and on newspaper front pages but by heavy Nixon campaign advertising. The endorsement came on the eve of the Gallup interviewing July 20–23, and the poll results showed a five-point gain for Nixon and two-point loss for Humphrey from early July, putting Nixon ahead by just a two-point margin. The Nixon management capitalized heavily on this. About a week later, the Political Surveys and Analyses release showed Nixon one point below the Gallup figure, Humphrey two points below, and Wallace three points above.

THE GALLUP-HARRIS CONTROVERSY

Then a poll by Louis Harris, with interviewing July 26–29, showed Humphrey five points ahead of Nixon (Harris had shown Humphrey ahead by two points in

July 8–14 interviewing). With Gallup showing Nixon two points ahead of Humphrey at the time of the Eisenhower announcement publicity and Harris showing him five points behind not much more than a week later, the two nationally syndicated polls gave a contradictory impression just before the Republican convention, and newspapers headlined the "Incredible Polls."

Although not released to the newspapers with the Gallup report on July 20–23 interviewing, the Gallup figures by regions, which were published later, showed Nixon 12 points ahead of Humphrey in the West, 4 points ahead in the East, tied in the Midwest, and one point behind in the South. Thus, if the West were eliminated, Nixon's two-point popular lead could disappear. Wallace was leading in the South, and many Western states had few electoral votes. Therefore, in terms of electoral votes, the Nixon lead could seem precarious. The Political Surveys and Analyses results, which had been published, would appear to confirm this belief.

The Gallup figures for Rockefeller showed a tie with Humphrey nationally against a two-point lead for Nixon over Humphrey. In popular vote, therefore, as of late July and allowing for normal sampling and other fluctuations, the race seemed most likely to be close. If the electoral votes of large industrialized and urbanized close states were to be affected by Democratic turnout, Rockefeller, with his greater appeal to non-Republicans, would seem more likely than Nixon to benefit.

In a telephone conversation Harris pointed out to George Gallup Jr. that the public could be misunderstanding some of these things and not giving due allowance to fluctuation possibilities, therefore overemphasizing the Nixon lead over Humphrey, and perhaps the relative lead of one Republican candidate over the other. In the interest of better understanding of polling, Gallup and Harris jointly announced that "The race today would be extremely close." Unfortunately, they allowed themselves to assume sampling fluctuations and certain eventualities and that the two competing polls could be considered comparable in all respects except timing, and then stated that Rockefeller had "moved to an open lead"—a statement which at the very least should have been characterized as an opinion rather than a fact. While a statement in good faith and undoubtedly intended to be helpful, it not only created further confusion but even led to charges of collusion in some quarters.

THE NOMINATIONS

Both conventions chose to hold to party lines and picked candidates with lesser appeal outside of their parties. And both standard-bearers lacked popular enthusiasm. At the end of August Gallup pointed out that 29 million persons of voting age had still failed to register, and that these included a third of all those classifying themselves as Independents. By contrast, the popularity of Wallace had jumped in a matter of weeks from 9 percent to over 20 percent, and his request for petition signatures was so successful that ultimately he was accepted on the ballot in all fifty states.

The selections for Vice-President drew a mixed reception. Agnew was an unknown, and was subjected to very strong criticism. Muskie, on the other hand, appeared to establish good popular rapport quickly. Wallace held off for a considerable time his announcement of LeMay as running mate. And then LeMay took what seemed to be a belligerent attitude on the war and the use of nuclear weapons. The Democrats seized vigorously on the opportunity to promote Muskie and downgrade Agnew in full-page and very striking advertising.

POLL TRENDS

Shortly after the Republican convention both the Harris and Gallup polls showed Nixon well ahead of Humphrey, and the critics of sampling operations would do well to pay particular attention to the steadiness of the Nixon percentages from mid-August: Gallup, 45, 43, 43, 44, 43, 44, 42; Harris, 40, 39, 40, 40, 42, 40. With allowance for rounding tenths of a point and for expected sampling deviation, these figures showed remarkable stability.

Humphrey, on the other hand, showed a general decline in both polls from mid-June to the latter part of September. In the Harris Poll Wallace was at 21 percent in mid-September and dropped to 13 percent in the last published report, a decline of 8 percentage points compared with a gain of 12 percentage points in the same period for Humphrey, while Nixon remained practically constant at about 40 percent and Undecideds went down from 9 to 4. Gallup showed a rise for Humphrey also of 12 points in a similar period and a decline of 7 points for Wallace.

News events and poll trends would seem to have been telling the same story. Humphrey opened his campaign in New York in the first few days of September, but it was not until the end of the month that the first signs of progress began to appear. The candidate, who had been ill for a time and who had suffered from the effects of the Chicago situation at convention time, was considered by many too close in policies to President Johnson, whose popularity had dropped to a new low point. On September 10 Humphrey was reported to oppose a bombing halt, and had relatively small crowd turnouts. His speeches were drawing considerable heckling. On September 22 he was reported shunning a plea to counter Johnson's position on Vietnam. Also on that day one newspaper noted that there had been up to then very little campaign organization. The financial situation had become very serious. But at about this point television appeals for money began to show good results and an entirely new promotion campaign was mounted. Leading Democrats, such as Teddy Kennedy, heretofore inactive, gave their support.

In the meantime Senator Muskie went on the attack and was very well received. His comparative strength over both Agnew and Humphrey was so obvious that at one point the Humphrey campaign almost became one of competitive Vice-Presidential candidates. Full-page advertisements and television commercials were planned with such appeals as: "Agnew for Vice-President? This would be funny if it weren't so serious," and "Agnew—only a heartbeat away."

On September 30 in Salt Lake City Humphrey made a major policy speech pledging to stop the bombing of North Vietnam if Hanoi gave some favorable sign of response. This led to increased support from McCarthy backers and contrasted with the hawkish tone of General LeMay's acceptance remarks as Wallace's running mate on October 3. Then, a few days before the election, came the White House announcement of a bombing halt and the plan to start new negotiations the day after election.

Labor union members, according to recent reports, showed a dramatic swing away from Mr. Wallace to Mr. Humphrey in the last few days of the campaign, attributed in part to anti-Wallace activity by union leaders. A Gallup analysis shows that the Democratic ticket gained 15 percentage points with the labor union group between early October and the election, primarily at the expense of Wallace.

The events outlined above and others, plus aggressive campaigning in the great industrial states with large electoral votes, check reasonably well with the sharp rise in Humphrey popularity in the polls.

Although both polls showed the same general trends, as can be seen in Table 4 and Figure 1, the Nixon level showed a tendency to be a little higher in the Gallup figures and the Humphrey level a little lower; therefore the spread between Nixon and Humphrey tended to be somewhat larger for Gallup than for Harris. At Harris' widest spread Nixon was 8 points ahead of Humphrey, while Gallup's greatest spread was 15 points. But part of this may have been due to different interviewing dates, and possibly some part to differences in the handling of likely nonvoters. Thus, in the interim between interviewing midpoints of two Harris polls, Gallup had three interviewing midpoints with lower Humphrey percentages than at any other time during the campaign. The final Gallup poll, completed on Saturday, November 2, showed Nixon 42, Humphrey 40, Wallace 14, Undecided 4. The next-to-last Harris poll, with interviewing November 1 and 2, showed Nixon 42, Humphrey 40, Wallace 12, Undecided 6. Gallup made an allocation of the Undecideds and came very close to election results. Harris continued polling through Sunday and then showed Nixon 40, Humphrey 43, Wallace 13, Undecided 4; he allocated his final Undecideds to arrive at Nixon 41, Humphrey 45, Wallace 14. Sindlinger's final figures were Nixon 37, Humphrey 40, Wallace 12, Undecided 11.

CLOSE ELECTIONS

Nixon won by over 61 percent of the major party electoral vote, but by less than 50.5 percent of the major party popular vote. In 1960 Kennedy took 50.1 percent of the major party popular vote. In 1948 Truman took 52.3 percent. Because of the great cost of state-by-state polls, it is practical for the published polls to operate only on a national popular vote basis. This can be hazardous not only because of the occasional tenths-of-a-point national margins, but because of the complete inability to indicate how close the electoral margin is apt to be.

On a popular vote basis, a very few persons can determine whether we have a Republican or a Democratic administration, and these few can be influenced one way or the other on a given day by a fairly simple consideration—an event, an issue, an attitude, or lack of interest. The same thing can happen within a state, with a very few persons determining which way the electoral votes will go, but the balance of power in one state may be counterbalanced by that in another. Anyone taking a poll of a single state, therefore, has the problem of assessing the importance of some minority group which may have the power to swing the state in a close situation.

Some idea of the small margins by which states have swung may be obtained by the fact that in 1960 eleven states with a total of 156 electoral votes were within 2 percentage points of a tie, and in 1944 ten states representing 165 electoral votes were that close. Nixon in 1960 lost 103 electoral votes in five states by

TABLE 4
Trends in Candidate Standing as Shown in Gallup and Harris Polls

Nixon Gallup	Nixon Harris	Humphrey Gallup	Humphrey Harris	Wallace Gallup	Wallace Harris	Undecided Gallup	Undecided Harris	Dates[a]	Important Events
								FEB. 28	Romney withdraws from N. H. primary.
								MARCH 12	N. H. primary: McCarthy wins 20 of 24 Democratic delegates.
								16	Robert Kennedy announces candidacy.
								31	President Johnson withdraws.
34%		35%		12%		19%		APRIL 1–2	
								4	Martin Luther King, Jr. shot in Memphis; riots follow in many cities.
43%	36	34%	38	9%	13	14%	13	6–10	
								24–May 1	Humphrey formally enters race.
								27	Rockefeller announces candidacy. Mass. primary: Rockefeller defeats Nixon and Volpe on write-ins; McCarthy beats Kennedy and Humphrey.
								30	
39		36		14		11		May 4–8	
								7	Indiana primary: Kennedy beats McCarthy.
								14	Nebraska primary won by Kennedy.
36	37	42	41	14	14	8	8	16–18	
								25–29	
								28	Oregon primary: McCarthy wins over Kennedy.
								June 4	Kennedy wins S. D. and Calif. primaries; is assassinated in Los Angeles.
37	36	42	43	13	13	7	8	10–17	
35		40						15–16	
				14		7			
				16		9		29–July 3	

40	35		37		17		11	JULY 8–14	Eisenhower endorses Nixon.
								19
	36	38	41	16	16	6	7	20–23	Republican National Convention in Miami: Nixon and Agnew nominated.
								26–29
								AUG. 5–8
45	40	29	34	18	17	8	9	8–11	Democratic Convention in Chicago; violence between police and demonstrators.
								24	Humphrey opens campaign in New York.
								26–30
								SEPT. 3
43	39	31	31	19	21	7	9	3–7	AFL/CIO begins "education drive" to combat labor swing to Wallace.
								11–13
								17
43		28		21		8		20–22	Muskie bids hecklers share platform.
44		29		20		7		26	Humphrey holds strategy session to overcome adverse campaign problems.
								27–30
								29
								30	Humphrey makes foreign policy speech in Salt Lake City pledging Vietnam bombing halt if Hanoi shows sign of response. Wallace names LeMay as running mate.
								OCT. 4
43	40	31	35	20	18	6	7	3–12	Democrats emphasize anti-Agnew campaign.
								9–11
								10
44	40	36	37	15	16	5	7	17–21	Johnson halts bombing of North Vietnam, announces new talks.
								27–28
								31
42	42	40	40	14	12	4	6	31–Nov. 2	Nixon wins electoral majority with narrow popular plurality.
	40		43		13		4	NOV. 1–2
								3
								5

[a] Dates opposite poll results represent days of actual field interviewing.

266   The Uses of Social Science

these margins: Illinois 0.2; New Jersey 0.8; Michigan 1.1; Minnesota 1.4; Pennsylvania 2.4. In 1940 less than .002 (2 in 1,000) voters could have made Michigan Republican instead of Democratic. And in 1944 less than .006 could have made it Democratic instead of Republican.

In 1948 it was possible for just slightly over .001 of the voters in Ohio, .002 of the California voters, and .004 of the Illinois voters to prevent Dewey from taking over the presidency. These three states were in the uncertain column the morning after the 1968 election. And the electoral votes of one important state remained uncertain for several days because of absentee ballots.

Figure 1
Trends in Candidate Standing as Shown
in Gallup and Harris Polls,
April–November 1968

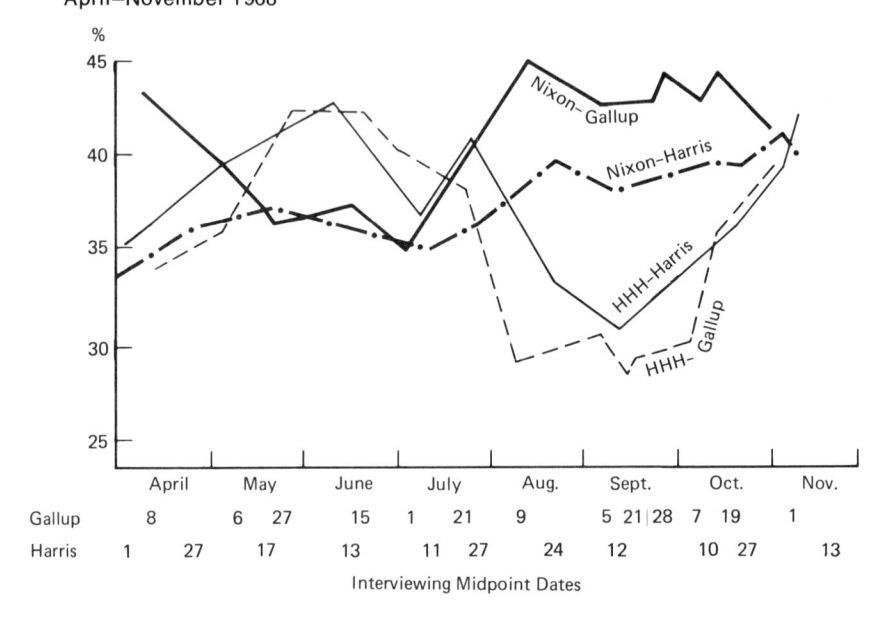

	April	May	June	July	Aug.	Sept.	Oct.	Nov.
Gallup	8	6 27	15	1 21	9	5 21 28	7 19	1
Harris	1	27	17	13	11 27	24	12	10 27	13

Interviewing Midpoint Dates

OTHER POLLING PROBLEMS

Polltakers have many other problems, one of the greatest of which is estimating the relative turnout of one party versus another, which can vary materially according to several different factors. The 1968 vote was overestimated at close to 75 million in spite of the lackluster major party presidential candidates. In actual fact the voting percentage was the lowest since that of 1956—less than 61 percent (73 million) compared with nearly 64 percent in the Nixon–Kennedy race in 1960. One fifth of the registered voters failed to vote in 1968, in spite of considerable gains in a number of Southern states.

While the polls stress that they report only current attitudes, there is a strong tendency on the part of readers to use them as a basis for estimating the future. One of the major questions for 1968 was whether the Wallace third party would follow the course of the Henry Wallace and Strom Thurmond efforts in 1948, which deteriorated during the campaigns. In September George Wallace appeared to be making strong inroads into the labor vote. If these had continued he might have taken a sizable electoral vote in the South and perhaps held the balance of power in some close Northern states. Instead, his meteoric rise went into reverse. The publicity attending the speculation on deadlocks may have played some part in influencing people to go back to their regular parties.

What would happen in Vietnam was a great imponderable. If Johnson ended the bombing and successful negotiations followed, the popularity of the Democratic candidate could rise precipitously. Sudden race riots could affect standings materially. Competitive promotion, unfortunate statements, the swing of leaders to a candidate—these and many other factors increased the polltaker's worries by threatening to make findings quickly out of date and at variance with later soundings by others.

THE RESPONSIBILITIES OF POLLING

Assuming that election polls and estimates of relative standing by the newsmedia are, in fact, reasonably accurate, what function do they serve? "If the accuracy of the polls is not in dispute," said the New York *Times* in "Score One for the Polls" on November 10, "their political effect is." The article went on to attribute to the polls a contribution to demoralization among Humphrey supporters and a drying up of financial contributions, plus a possibility of overconfidence on the Republican side. Like the problem of which came first, the chicken or the egg, it is conceivable that the low state of the Humphrey outlook in the first weeks after the convention may have stimulated major action by party managers, leading to a hairbreadth finish. There is considerable indication of this situation in the investigation of the 1948 polls. Polling in that year ended in mid-October at about the time of Truman's Cleveland speech calling on voters to "show up the polls," and at about the time of what were apparently several moves to bring out the Democratic vote.

Certainly it is again demonstrated that the polls do not have a bandwagon effect. If it were true that they have some influence toward making the vote participation closer for both parties, it remains to be proved whether this is a good or bad influence. Whichever it may be, the responsibility must be shared by both the published polls and the published reports of newsmedia correspondents.

In calling for an inquiry into the polls, resolutions by members of the California State Assembly implied (1) the need for safeguards against erroneous statements and figures "with the intent to diminish a candidate's chances" of election, and against attempts by political candidates to influence polltakers to produce favorable results; (2) that polls could influence a bandwagon vote; (3) possible collusion with ulterior motives; (4) that citizens have the right to know that polls meet certain standards of practice.

The National Council on Public Polls, recently formed by ten major regularly publishing polling firms, aims to develop and publicize such standards and to promote a better understanding of the meanings and limitations of polls. But the Council will not undertake to police the whole polling profession or provide penalties and enforcement of regulations against such fraudulent practices as might be found to exist in some quarters.

So far as private polls are concerned, and their leaks to the press or use to influence contributors, delegates, or others, the Council as of now will not enter this field, but will cooperate with efforts to achieve highest standards of practice. It is anticipated that its work in creating a better understanding of the limitations of individual polls, by the public and by newsmedia, will provide some safeguard against the misinterpretation of private polls that are leaked or improperly used. Private polling has developed greatly in recent years and provides candidates for office with needed information on public issues and attitudes.

The future of nationally published election polls may be affected by their cost of operation in relation to the revenue which newsmedia can provide. Already limited by cost to the popular vote and at best to sectional rather than state-by-state reporting, they may be further limited in frequency unless revenue can be derived from something other than candidate standing reports. In the racial situation, crime, education, transportation, health, welfare, cost of living, taxation, the war and many other domestic and foreign issues, there is much saleable polling material. It is not only saleable but of considerable usefulness. Popular interest in candidate standing can make reliable issue-type and other polls more saleable.

The horse-race function, alone, may entertain the reader but it is of doubtful value. If misunderstood, misused, or incompetently handled, it is hardly of major value to the polltaker. The future deserves much more than horse racing.

24
The Cybernetic State

Allen Schick

Visions of the cybernetic age always have been of two sorts. Some have foreseen a period of unparalleled freedom, with man possessing the autonomy and leisure he has sought for ages. The cybernetic state would care for many of man's needs but would not exact a loss of freedom and selfhood; freed from the bonds of necessity and collective action, man would attain new command over himself and the world. The other version sees man as inevitably enslaved by the state, surrendering to powerful and uncontrollable institutions the freedoms that mark his selfhood. He will be controlled by the seeing hand which dictates his actions and thoughts. Man will be programmed—genetically or through thought control. He will be free to obey.

One can make a plausible case for either version or for both. Certainly both potentials are latent in cybernetics, though the actualities of history lend scant encouragement to the hope that the potentials will be used only for good. The story has always been the same. Man discovers fire for warmth and sustenance, but he also uses it to burn and destroy. Prometheus unbound is not always beneficent.

The Constitution of the United States might not quite endure for the ages, but it has survived great transformations in the conduct of public affairs. In few sec-

From *TRANS-action* (February 1970), pp. 15–26. Copyright © 1970 by *TRANS-action*. Reprinted by permission of publisher and author.

tors have the changes been more pronounced or portentous than in the creation of the vast administrative structures that dominate the economy and the polity of the country today. The entire administrative staff of George Washington's government could be fitted comfortably into the offices of a medium-size bureau. As a government we have undergone several critical changes in the relationship between the administrative and the political. At the start the United States was designed as a political state; the growth of industry and public regulation in the nineteenth century led to the emergence of an administrative state; New Deal activism opened the door to the bureaucratic state; now, according to some expectations, we stand at the threshold of the cybernetic state.

Though it is possible to place each of these states into time zones, aspects of each appear in all periods of American history. The political, which was prominent in the earliest times, still carries over in the main representative theater—the Congress—as well as in other national institutions. The cybernetic, which appears to be the emergent form today, certainly was operative in Alexander Hamilton's day through some of the accounting controls maintained over financial transactions. What characterizes an age is the dominance of one form of political-administrative relation, not the total absence of the others. The computer may be the logo of the cybernetic age, but the dawn of this period was portrayed in various artistic and scholarly works long before the first computer was constructed. Moreover, long after a particular form has been replaced, certain of its characteristics continue to show vigor and growth. Even if bureaucratics is displaced by cybernetics, we can anticipate the further development of large-scale bureaucracies for particular functions.

The cybernetic state of 1984 is not a product of the constitutional decisions of 1787. The Framers were occupied with building a political state, that is, with creating representative institutions through which power would be exercised and controlled. They did not—and could not—look to administrative or bureaucratic structures for the power or the controls, nor could they deal with the myriad of administrative details pertaining to the operation of the new government. Thus, there is scarcely a hint in the Constitution of the great organizational machines that would be created in the nineteenth and twentieth centuries and which ultimately would recast the distribution of powers and rights into something other than was envisioned originally.

FROM THE POLITICAL TO THE ADMINISTRATIVE STATE

In designing the political state, therefore, the constitutional architects concentrated on rules of representation, qualifications for office, the scope and powers of the several branches, the allocations between national and state jurisdictions, and the establishment of limits on political action. These limits were aimed, for the most part, at the representative institutions, and primarily at the national legislature. "Congress shall make no law" was the First Amendment formula for protecting political rights; trial by jury, along with its associated procedures, was the formula for guarding judicial rights. No explicit protection was incorporated into the Bill of Rights against infringement by administrative fiat or proceeding. Of the basic rights, only the "search and seizure" prohibition was generalized to cover all public actions, though its actual intent was to curb police power.

The passage from the political to the administrative state was due largely to the growth of national industry, the creation of new regulatory instruments and agencies prompted by that growth, and the mobilization of administrative expertise to manage public activities. Whatever power Congress gave to administrators, it gave away voluntarily, and often with the blessing or the prodding of the president. The first national regulatory instrument, the Interstate Commerce Commission (ICC), was established in 1887, and three years later the Sherman antitrust controls were enacted. Resistance came from a different quarter, the judiciary, which insisted on applying the established constitutional standards to the new administrative structures.

One initial judicial response was to apply A.V. Dicey's "rule of law" doctrine to the administrative arena: ". . . no man is punishable or can be lawfully made to suffer in body or goods except for a distinct breach of law established in the ordinary courts of the land. In this sense the rule of law is contrasted with every system of government based on the exercise by persons in authority of wide, arbitrary, or discretionary powers of constraint." Applied strictly, this rule would have barred virtually all administrative adjudication, but it ultimately came to mean that the fundamental procedures of law (notice, hearing, examination, etc.) would have to be adhered to in administrative proceedings.

In striking out against the emergent administrative state, the courts relied on a parochial reading of the commerce clause and a stretched version of the 14th Amendment's due process clause. National power over the economy was curtailed in the Sugar Trust case (1895), the Child Labor cases (1918, 1922), and various New Deal cases. Much economic activity was deemed beyond the reach of the police powers of the states. For this view the courts found bountiful constitutional support by converting the 14th Amendment, which had been stripped of its Negro rights functions by the Slaughterhouse and Civil Rights cases (1873 and 1883), into a protection against state regulation of business activity.

But the emergence of the administrative state was to be determined in the legislative and executive arenas, and though the courts could harass and delay, they could not prevent the establishment of powerful regulatory instruments that were only feebly controlled by their creators. Following a spate of anti-New Deal decisions in the mid-1930s, the Supreme Court abruptly abandoned the review of economic legislation and began to concentrate on other areas of constitutional agitation. Since 1936 not a single piece of federal legislation has been invalidated as an unwarranted delegation of power to an administrative body.

Though it has some operating responsibilities of its own, the basic purpose of the administrative state is to regulate the new corporate concentrations of wealth and power. The administrative state, thus, continues to abide by the doctrines of the separation of public and private and of the basic soundness of the private market. Its task is not to impose a political solution, but to make use of specialized skills to correct for certain market defects or improprieties. To accomplish this requires a separation of the administrative from the political, a separation which was built into the major regulatory agencies and accepted as the cardinal precept by the intellectual fathers of the administrative state—Frank Goodnow, Woodrow Wilson, William F. Willoughby, and others. By means of this separation, administration is made superior to politics, and efficiency replaces representation as the key operational norm of public policy. The fundamental constitutional rules of representation continue to apply to the political sphere, but not to membership on regulatory agencies, advisory boards, and other appointive institutions. Regulatory agencies are made exempt from the sacred doctrine of separation of powers and are assigned substantial judicial, legislative, and executive powers. As larger and more diffuse grants of power are turned over to efficiency experts and new concentrations of functional expertise are established within the cabinet structure, executive departments, particularly their bureaus and subunits, gain a good deal of de facto independence for the political institutions. They are also liberated from the president, who is no longer capable of directing their regular affairs, and from Congress, which no longer can exercise close supervision of their actions.

FROM THE ADMINISTRATIVE TO THE BUREAUCRATIC STATE

The bureaucratic state began to displace the administrative state when the primary function of government changed from regulation to operation of business. Though the federal government had assumed a *doing* role in selected programs many years earlier, the New Deal era can be regarded as the great leap to bureaucratics. The bureaucratic state was designed to replace the market with public enterprises, not merely to correct for its deficiencies. It represented a refusal to accept the market's verdict that millions of elderly people must be poor, that rural communities must lack electric power lines, that the housing supply must be substandard and unable to meet demand, that farm incomes must sink below subsistence levels. The regulatory commissions that marked the administrative state have come to pale by every comparison with the operating bureaus of the federal government. Federal bureaucrats in the Bureau of Public Roads pass judgment on the location and design of federally aided but locally constructed highways and thereby exercise far greater sway over transportation policy than does the ICC; federal SST (supersonic transport) decisions probably will have greater air travel implications than will the combined regulatory actions of the Federal Aeronautics Administration and Civil Aeronautics board.

Federal jurisdictions sweep over state and local boundaries, for a bueaucracy must always be structured according to its functions rather than according to local tradition. This movement is fueled by massive grants-in-aid and by federal involvement in functions long reserved for local action, such as law enforcement, poor relief, and basic education.

In the bureaucratic state, the administrative and political are joined, united by interest-group brokers who traffic between the bureaucracies and the people and weave complex clientele—congressional bureau relationships for the purpose of channeling the public enterprises into the service of private interests. A new public market thus is created, resembling the private one in certain aspects, but lacking both the ultimate test of profit and the unremitting competition of adversaries. Interests bargain with one another at the public trough, but they also form coalitions and drive out competition when it suits their objectives. Politics and administration sometimes seem to be split again—in a divorce of convenience—as when advisory groups are comprised of functional specialists and community leaders in order to keep the program free of politics. But it all is for the sake of enhancing interest politics, and efficiency becomes the instrument of established group interests rather than a value in itself.

Interest groups form and begin to dominate the political-administrative process because in the bureaucratic state enormous interests are at stake, and the rewards for public success often far exceed what can be obtained in the private market. Moreover, all the political-administrative actors benefit in some way from the brokerage services provided by groups. Voters do not have an electoral mechanism for transacting their public business directly with the bureaucracy, nor do they often possess the skill or resources for doing so. Bureaucrats use the groups for stirring clientele support for their demands on the president and Congress and for protecting themselves from executive and legislative supervision. Congress looks to the groups for learning about what the public wants and for gaining electoral support. The president uses the groups for mobilizing the electorate and for communicating his policies to the masses. Each one must pay a fee for the brokerage services, and as a result, the interest groups govern the terms of the politics-administration process. Hence, the unification of politics and administration does not restore the constitutional representatives to their original political positions. As a matter of fact, each is further debilitated by the commanding role of the interest groups.

Of primary importance is the need to find constitutional support for the legitimacy of interest politics. Political writers rediscover Madison's *Federalist* No. 10 and elevate it to a status superior to the constitutional scriptures themselves. In providing an intellectual justification for group politics, this discovery establishes competition in the political arena as a desirable substitute for market competition. It enables social checks and balances to take the place of legal checks and balances. It provides a substitute for electoral representation. It satisfies the requirement for external control of administration. Congress doesn't do the job well any more, but the groups do. They distribute the benefits of public activity widely, at least among those within the ambit of group operations.

The courts lose interest in administrative regulation and become concerned with the nationalization of civil rights and the granting of constitutional status to the rights of association. Operating under the Frothingham rule, which bars taxpayer challenges to federal programs, the vast programmatic development of the New Deal through the Great Society period escaped judicial review. The courts nationalize the Bill of Rights and apply federal standards to a widening group of police and criminal actions. They nationalize racial policies in the schools and in other public programs. They nationalize representation and apply strict one-man, one-vote rules to state legislatures and municipal councils.

Interest groups gain constitutional status, but they thereby become affected with a public interest and become subject to public controls. In *Thornhill* v. *Alabama* (1940), the Supreme Court extends free speech protection to peaceful picketing in labor disputes. Almost two decades later, with the 1959 Labor-Management Reporting and Disclosure Act, Congress adopts a bill of rights for union members. The integrated bar (which means requiring membership in a state bar as a condition for eligibility to practice law) was upheld in *Lathrop* v. *Donohoe* (1961), and the courts frequently have upheld group-licensing requirements for particular professions. In a series of cases involving the NAACP, the Supreme Court affirmed the right of association. Certain interest group activities were brought under public control in the Federal Regulation of Lobbying Act of 1946 which was upheld in *United States* v. *Harriss* (1954).

Still another judicial response occurs when the bureaucratic state reaches its full form and the cybernetic age begins to dawn. Unlike previous eras in which the courts told governments what they must not do, the courts now begin to instruct governments as to what they must do. Thus, recent court decisions in the welfare field have required bureaucrats to provide welfare benefits to indigents who have not satisfied local residence requirements, to families which have a man in the house, and to pay benefits above ceilings enacted by the state legislature.

As the bureaucracy grows and creates the technological skills for its operation, certain critical transformations begin to occur in its character. The lines between public and private begin to break down, efforts are made to break away from the lockstep of functional bureaucracies, government regulation tends to become insular. These and many smaller and larger changes signal the beginning of the cybernetic state. And as the character of the state changes, so too does the focus of constitutional development, as it is expressed in the case law and in agitation for constitutional reform.

FROM BUREAUCRATICS TO CYBERNETICS

In the postindustrial cybernetic state, government functions as a servomechanism, concerting the polity and the economy to achieve public objectives. As a result, government changes from a *doer* of public activities to a distributor of public benefits, and the kinds of programs it operates reflect this change. For example, welfare has been one of the key programs of the bureaucratic state involving a large-scale welfare bureaucracy with thousands of governments and millions of people. As welfare becomes cybernated, it shifts to some form of guaranteed income, adjusted automatically as the income of the recipient rises or falls. (It doesn't matter for our purposes whether the guarantee is in the form of family allowances, negative tax, or other means, though of course each form carries a different set of costs and benefits.) Government action is triggered automatically by changes in the economic condition of the individual. Government writes the "program" (in the computer sense of the word), establishes sociostatic norms (such as the "poverty level"), monitors the system, and activates the money-disbursing machines. This is far different from the conventional welfare bureaucracy in which eligibility and benefits are determined by corps of case workers in accord with overall legislative and administrative rules.

Embryonic cybernetic-type programs have been established in health where Medicaid and Medicare now far exceed in cost the standard health programs such as local health clinics, public hospitals, Hill-Burton grants, publicly aided research, and so forth. But the new health programs are only imperfectly cybernated because government lacks the means of controlling medical costs or for monitoring the demands on the system made by its clients. We can anticipate that aspects of program cybernation will bloom in other functional areas—education, public transportation, and housing seem to be attractive possibilities.

In the public sector, perhaps the greatest advances have occurred in the macroeconomy where the refinement of national income accounts over the past 30 years has given federal authorities a substantial capability to guide the economy and to make quick adjustments as economic conditions change. But the macroeconomy is not yet fully cybernated. The accounts are not perfected to a reliability where governments can use servomechanistic controls; that is, it cannot fine-tune the economy and be sure that it will get the results it expects. Furthermore, Congress has not shown much enthusiasm for proposals to empower the executive to take nonlegislative corrective action. For example, it is not likely to adopt in the near future Herbert Stein's proposal for a permanent surtax that is adjusted upwards or downwards as rates of employment and other economic barometers fluctuate. Yet we should not underestimate the capabilities gained over the past generation, and it is possible that a cybernated macroeconomy is nearer than we think.

Cybernetic development lags behind in the microeconomy, partly because the accounts still are in a primitive condition, and partly because the resistances to cybernation are stronger here. Some first steps have been taken, as the recent publication of *Towards a Social Report* shows, but we will have to progress a long way before we have social indicators comparable in scope and reliability to the basic economic indicators. Cybernation cannot operate under uncertainty, for in this condition corrective action must always be tentative and discretionary. Moreover, there is little current evaluation of public programs and, hence, little feedback from results to decisions. The introduction of Program-Planning Budgeting (PPB) and related types of policy systems gives evidence of the directions in which reformers would like to move, but it is now four full years since PPB was launched in Washington, and its meager accomplishments demonstrate that the job is not easy. Furthermore, in the macroeconomy, adjustments could be made for the benefit of all, and though the relative shares might be altered as a consequence of public action (not everyone benefits equally from economic growth), almost everyone gains. In the microeconomy, however, adjustments mean taking from some to give to others. Government action has to be redistributive. Hence, it is likely that this will be one of the last policy functions surrendered by the representative institutions.

In the cybernetic state, the lines between public and private crumble. Government enters markets previously reserved for private entrepreneurs, but new private institutions enter arenas hitherto dominated by public bureaucracies. The penetration of government into private spheres is especially revolutionary in certain service areas such as doctor-patient and lawyer-client relationships. But as the lines between public and private erode, private institutions recapture some of the functions long regarded as public. Thus, in some instances, elementary education is turned over to private contractors, usually operating with public funds and always under public control. The market is rediscovered, but it is harnessed to public purposes, and its behavior little resembles that of the traditional form.

As public and private commingle, distinctions between them become meaningless. Private institutions acquire legal status as "public accommodations," as provided in the Civil Rights Act of 1964 and sustained by the Supreme Court in *Heart of Atlanta Motel Inc.* v. *United States* (1964). Some recent court rulings have brought private clubs, perhaps the last bastion of privatedom, within the orbit of public control. It is no longer possible to tell where the private ends and the public begins as public and private funds and workers flow and work side by side in SST development, job training, and countless other programs. In the basic social accounts, the public-private distinction no longer is significant; more and more, the accounts concentrate on the aggregate social input and output, regardless of its public or private character.

A similar amalgam occurs in the political and bureaucratic spheres. Administrative actions become politicized, and political actions become bureaucratized. Consider these two examples from the storehouse of current events. The supreme political act of determining legislative districts has been turned over to computer specialists, sometimes under court order, sometimes by legislative acquiescence. When this happens, legislative districting ceases being a political act, however great its political consequences are. Administrative actions have been politicized in the "maximum feasible participation" arenas as the floodgates of political activity, including formalized election procedures have been opened to policy decisions that previously were made bureaucratically.

The regulatory functions of government which loomed so large in the administrative state, turn inward as government develops self-regulatory devices essential for its servomechanistic role. Corps of federal regulators man the guidelines in the Departments of Housing and Urban Development, Health, Education and Welfare (HEW), Labor, and the Office of Economic Opportunity and regulate other public officials (mostly state and local) through a network of grant controls. Moreover, departments begin to use the computer to extend their program reporting, auditing and evaluating procedures to their own operations.

FROM EFFICIENCY TO EFFECTIVENESS

Yet even as government regulation turns inward, its policy perspectives turn outward. In the bureaucratic state, decision-making tends to be insular, concerned with the internal dynamics of the organization rather than with the effects on the citizenry. For preparation of his programs, the public official looks to his files and from there to the reports and accounts they contain, not to the hospital ward or the classroom. In drawing up his claim on public resources, he looks to last year's records and decides what to add and what to subtract. The cybernetic state, however, is goal-oriented. It is concerned with the income of families, the condition of the economy, the health of mothers, the intelligence of children. Efficiency norms which are relevant to the internal operation of organizations no longer hold the commanding positions they once had. Effectiveness criteria take their place as the guiding determinants of public policy.

To achieve this looking outward, the cybernetic state must be systemic rather than functional. In the development of the bureaucratic state, the functional arrangement was useful because it promoted efficiency, mobilized the use of specialists, and gave representation to professional interest. For a goal-directed cybernetic institution, the functional form is an encumbrance, for it allows the interests of the functionalists to get in the way of the results. To take a common case: An education bureaucrat in HEW cooperates with a contact in the National Education Association (NEA) and obtains agreement that 25,000 volumes is the appropriate minimum for a high school library. This standard is transmitted via the state functional bureaucracies to school boards and via NEA publications to school administrators. Soon the 25,000 minimum gets adopted by the accreditation agencies as one of the conditions for holding accreditation. While this numbers game is being played, it is hard to keep in mind how many books high schoolers read, what they read, what they learn from the books, and whether other forms of communications can substitute for books. In other words, the function gets in the way of the goal.

The cybernetic form of organization is based on systems such as model cities in which functional specialists may continue to operate, but not as the key policy makers. The system is guided by systems engineers, planners, and other generalists whose perspectives transcend the functional specialties.

In a full-blown cybernetic state, politics and bureaucracy would wither away, though their forms might remain. That is, there still might be contests for public office, but the process would not have its old importance. To the extent that sociostatic norms limit conflict, the scope of politics would be narrowed. Whether or not we ever reach the "political fiction" world of genetic or thought control, there will be less disagreement in the future than existed in the past. Already, in the macroeconomic sphere where the cybernetic condition is most advanced, differences between Democrats and Republicans now are minimal, despite the great stakes involved and the history of party controversy.

As government becomes self-regulative, with its actions guided by goal criteria, the bureaucracy also might begin to shrink in size and importance. Government will have nuclear "central guidance clusters," such as the Council of Economic Advisors, but it will not have the need for armies of bureaucratic doers. Thus, as welfare shifts from poor relief to income maintenance, the logic of maintaining thousands of social workers on the public payrolls decreases.

In similar fashion, the interest groupings which dominated the bureaucratic state no longer retain their central position. If it operates by means of cybernetic systems, government no longer requires the intermediation of these groups for communicating its goals, receiving policy preferences from the public, and controlling the actions of the bureaus and representative institutions. The president can use the mass communications media to reach the public more effectively than through group exertions. Mass, class, and individual identities become more important than group associations.

In the cybernetic state, there is both a massive collectivization of action, continuing the trends established in the earlier administrative period, as well as increasing privatization of life. Among the recent straws in the wind, we can point to the growing penetration of the hospital market by national corporations, the institutionalization of research, and the dominance of contemporary philanthropy by the foundations. At the same time, life is increasingly privatized; that is, individuals are more isolated from one another and have greater liberty in personal behavior. Individuals are freed from traditional social and communal bonds: the Pill enables them to engage in private sexual practice free of effective social sanction; a television in each room allows each member of the family to watch his program without obtaining approval from others; a multicar family can send the husband to his club and the wife to her group with both maintaining contact with one another via remote communications. The combination of collectivization and privatization is what gives the cybernetic state its Janus-like character, capable of elevating the individual to new levels of personal autonomy or of crushing him under the yoke of public oppression.

As the character of the state changes, so too do the methodologies for studying it. Political science is transformed into policy science, not merely a change in semantics, but in focus as well. For politics ceases to be the central concern; after all, if politics withers away, why study it? The policy sciences deal with the purposes of government and with the organization of intelligence for their attainment. They encompass both public and private spheres and concentrate on the content of policy rather than on the processes of choice. The analytic constructs also change—from processes and institutions to systems and communications nets.

At this point in the development, it is difficult to gauge how far we have moved from the bureaucratic to the cybernetic or to predict whether the cybernetic state will in fact be realized. The bureaucratic state has not yet reached its final development, and some of the current reform proposals are relevant to it rather than to the emergent cybernatic form. We do not know whether all the (good and bad) dreams of the future are technologically feasible or whether all that is feasible will be done. Perhaps there will be a Luddite uprising against cybernation and its systems. But our task here is not to foretell the future—there are enough year 2000 wizards on the market already—but to comment on the current state of affairs. Enough cybernetic tendencies have surfaced to have bestirred the minds and actions of reformers and to have created new kinds of constitutional issues.

CONSTITUTIONAL ISSUES IN A CYBERNETIC STATE

Examination of the potential character of the cybernetic state suggests the kinds of things that will stop being constitutionally active or will be less significant than they once were. Probably the greatest wane will be in the area of civil liberties, for as the political processes diminish in salience, there will be less incentive to try to stretch these rights through constitutional action. The traditional First Amendment rights, such as free speech, might be more important to individuals who are concerned about their personal lives than to those concerned about marshaling political resources to influence public action. Of what use will be the right to speak if the speaker has little ability to challenge the dominance of the experts and systems engineers and little ability to sway the course of public policy by his vote?

Yet it is possible to foresee agitation for two types of political rights in the cybernetic age. First might be the right *not* to engage in political activity, not to be part of the collective mass that is politicized in the service of the state. Though Supreme Court rulings stand in the way, the right to remain silent, the right not to speak or to answer, might once again become defensible on First Amendment grounds. Second, the concept of *speech plus* might be further stretched to provide constitutional protection for overt political actions above and beyond the protection conventionally afforded the expression of ideas. Search and seizure litigation will have a prominent place on court dockets as new cybernetic technologies are used for surveillance. But many of the hot criminal procedure issues of the 1960s probably will diminish in importance, and if this occurs, a chapter on the great constitutional battles of the bureaucratic period will be concluded.

In every age the list of constitutionally active issues consists of the things we want to gain and the things we want to avert. In the cybernetic age, four types of constitutional issues might move to the forefront: the protection of personal rights; control of the cybernetic system; forms of political participation; and the structure of government.

The Protection of Personal Rights

We have already noted that in a cybernetic state the distinction between public and private tends to dissolve and that, as institutions become more collective, the individual finds his life more privatized. For many future-gazers, the stereotype of the cybernetic tomorrow is of Big Brother watching over you, possessing the means to monitor every move and thought and constantly guiding your actions. Whether or not this fear is justified, constitutional guardians are already on the alert against moves that might bring us closer to 1984. The recent uproar over the questions to be asked in the 1970 census gives one indication of the sensitivity to governmental invasions of privacy. Still another indication was the opposition in Congress and elsewhere to proposals for a national data center. Despite all protestations of being misunderstood and despite the offering of assurances that privacy would be protected, the scientific and governmental proponents of the data bank were unable to sell their pet project to Congress.

Privacy already is a big issue in the courts, and it probably will get bigger. Until recent years the courts viewed the right of privacy as a derivative of protections against self-incrimination and unreasonable search. But in two landmark decisions, the Supreme Court established privacy as a fundamental constitutional right. In *Griswold* v. *Connecticut* (1965), a state law prohibiting the use of contraceptives was overturned. "We deal with a right of privacy older than the Bill of Rights—older than our political parties, older than our school system." The second decision, in *Stanley* v. *Georgia* (1969), voided a conviction for possession of obscene films. "If the First Amendment means anything, it means that a state has no business telling a man, sitting alone in his own house, what books he may read or what films he may watch." And in a clear reference to that awful cybernetic tomorrow, the Court declared: "Our whole constitutional heritage rebels at the thought of giving government the power to control men's minds."

It is unlikely that we have seen the end of privacy cases. Many new circumstances could bring the issue to the courts time and again: security checks, census questionnaires, rights of public employees, students or inmates protesting the use of TV monitors, the use of drugs in the home, the sexual conduct of consenting adults, invasion of privacy by private groups.

Privacy will perhaps be only one form of the coming constitutional issue: what is the state's and what is the individual's? As the lines between public and private become blurred and as the tensions between the state's thrust for collective action and the individual's quest for autonomous behavior increase, we can anticipate heightened uncertainty and controversy over the respective spheres of the state and the individual. For example, can the state compel an individual not to smoke? Can it require adults to work? Can it force mothers to send three-year-olds to school? None of these issues is distinctively new; but what is new is the ground on which they are being fought and will be decided. Prohibition was a moral issue, but smoking is already a scientific one.

Control of the Cybernetic Systems

Two types of visionaries want to control the cybernetic state; the first, to ensure the realization of its noble capabilities; the second, to avert its coming.

Inasmuch as the cybernetic system is fueled by the communications that course through its networks, carrying messages from command posts and feedback from monitors, control is often desired over the communications apparatus, both the network and the content of the messages. We have mentioned recent objections to census probes and central data systems. In addition to these attempts to withhold data from the state, control is exercised by opening up publicly held information to outsiders. If information gives power, its possession should not be monopolized by the state. This is the ethos of the Freedom of Information Act which became operative in 1967. The act enables an individual to sue a federal agency for access to information which has been denied to him. The initial experience under this act gives little encouragement to the hope that the government will eagerly open its books to public examination. It might be that only the confrontation tactics of "Nader's Raiders" and like groups can wrest the secrets from the state.

As the distinction between public and private narrows, the right to know also is applied to the private sector. The recent spate of truth-in-lending and truth-in-packaging legislation gives evidence of the ferment in this sector.

But the duality of rights sought in the cybernetic age reflects the dualism of visions of the future. The right of privacy is not always compatible with the right to know. The government that gives away information under the Freedom of Information statute might be taking away another man's privacy. Man can be manipulated by being kept in the dark or by being exhibited in the open. How these two rights are reconciled will be one of the critical constitutional tests of the cybernetic age.

A cybernetic state operates under sociostatic norms; employment rates, poverty levels, educational criteria. Traditionally, we have been willing to entrust the establishment of these standards to professional interests. Economists tell us what an acceptable rate of unemployment is; doctors tell us what the normal life expectancy is; school administrators decide norms of educational achievement. But as these norms come to be the servomechanistic trigger of public action, it is possible that the competence of professionals to set the standards will be challenged. Perhaps the Orshansky scale used by the Social Security Administration to define the level and incidence of poverty in the United States will be challenged in a "Brandeis" brief which demonstrates that it costs much more than $3400 a year for a family of four to subsist in New York City. Just as individuals quarrel over the setting of the thermostat in their homes, so they may begin to contest the official policy norms. The due process and equal protection clauses have the elasticity to do the job.

Many of the challenges are likely to come from those most affected by government action, especially recipients of public benefits and public employees. Welfare recipients have carried their case to the courts, the streets, and government offices, sometimes with conspicuous success. Groups of public employees such as FEDS (Federal Employees for a Democratic Society) have agitated for "the creation of a genuine 'participatory democracy' both within our Federal agencies and within our society-at-large."

The notion that those who benefit most from government control should have the greatest control over its policy seems to be a conflict of interest, but it is merely a new twist on the standard interest group ideology that those whose interests are most at stake legitimately have the largest voice in shaping the policy. Cross out welfare recipients and put in television stations, and the notion is neither revolutionary nor absurd.

Forms of Political Participation

The basic form of political participation was molded for the political state, a system of free elections for public representatives. This system has persisted through two centuries of change, but it no longer possesses the relevance it once had, at least not for those who are dissatisfied with the shape of things. As the character of the state changed, new forms of participation grew up, interest and functional representation in particular. The cybernetic state probably will continue the old rituals of participation, but it might add some new forms suited to the problem of controlling the cybernetic apparatus.

Judging from the activism of the New Left—and that might not be a reliable guide—we can expect both withdrawal from politics and political confrontation, with the same persons vacillating between the two patterns. "Woodstock," as one participant put it, "was just like government and politics and law just didn't exist."

The belief that what is important is not changing government but changing yourself might be one of the romances of youth, but it seems to enjoy wide currency today. Yet youth has also marched in the peace moratoriums, worked in the ghettos, blocked entrances, and challenged authority. Though they have no confidence in the efficacy of representative politics, the New Left does believe in direct political action. Yet the cry of "participatory democracy" so loud and clear at Port Huron seven years ago is muted these days. To participate is to offer oneself for co-optation, to join the establishment, and to surrender a commitment to radical change. Whether through withdrawal or confrontation, the challengers do not seek change through the Constitution.

The Structure of Government

The cybernetic age opens up two thrusts for change in government organization: new forms of community government and new structures for cybernetic guidance; the former to enhance the opportunities for participation, the latter to create a government that functions cybernetically.

Participation can be as part of a mass—faceless, remote, not able to relate to the central institutions. Or it can be in institutions that are cut down to man's size. Mass participation exists when man is politicized in the service of the state. Personal participation for most citizens, however, can only be within a community, the scope of which is immediate to their life wants. For the first time in many years, political scientists are concerned with the optimal size of cities, and government reformers want to reduce rather than expand the scale of local government. Maximum feasible participation, whatever its virtues or defects, can only occur in the neighborhood where one lives and transacts his personal life. Obstacles to community government exist at both the state and municipal levels. Dillon's rule has never been repealed: the state continues to enjoy constitutional preeminence over its subdivisions. Proposals for a constitutional structure that vests political status in the community have been voiced by several writers. Viewed from the perspective of the neighborhood, City Hall might be a bigger obstacle than the State House; indeed, enterprising community leaders now negotiate agreements with state officials to bypass the formal municipal structures. It is not likely that community recognition will come de jure; rather, through the operation of grant programs and government policy, neighborhood units might be able to gain a measure of political autonomy.

Community government is valued by minorities because it offers them some self-government apart from the larger majority. Blacks are approximately 10 percent of the national population, but their proportions and strength grow as the scale of government shrinks. Community control is a modern version of Calhoun's concurrent majority, and, accordingly, there are areas in the country where it can be made to work against the interests of blacks and others. But few among the minority—whether the blacks or the poor or the dissidents—take comfort in the minorities rule assurances of the pluralists; only members of the majority seem to benefit from that kind of minority rule Blacks see metropolitan consolidation—once the darling of the liberal set—as still another means of robbing them of the municipal power that their numerical status within the city entitles them to.

The second restructuring of the state is to provide for the conduct of its cybernetic functions. If government is to serve as the central guidance structure, it must be vested with that capability. While we would not rule out the possibility of constitutional overhaul to accomplish this, the more probable path to change will be through a buildup of the presidential capability to govern without undue dependence on the functional bureaucracies. We can expect a continued enlargement of presidential staff and perhaps a reorientation of the executive office to serve a policy development and evaluation role in the interdepartmental and intergovernmental arenas.

Thus, the two lines of development will be at the bottom and at the top, the community and the presidency. Whether these changes can be concordant—most reformers today believe that they are, that the president is more a friend of the ghetto than either the mayor or governor—we do not know. Much depends on which version of the cybernetic state triumphs.

The changes from the political state to the emergent cybernetic state have been linear, with few reversals or zig-zags. There has been a virtually continual closing of the gap between public and private and expansion of the scope of governmental jurisdiction.

But though the changes can be explained, they cannot always be predicted. In retrospect the cybernetic state might turn out to have been fantasy, compounded of fears and hopes. Much of the expectation of the coming cybernetic age is grounded on the capabilities of technology, not on the behavior of humans and organizations. Yet these latter, neglected factors might prove to be decisive. Citizens might resist the cybernetic penetration of their lives. Bureaucracies might refuse to wither away. Indeed, we have no precedent for such a dismantling to occur. President Nixon's new welfare scheme moved toward cybernation of benefits, but it also gave the welfare bureaucracy additional responsibilities for the determination of eligibility.

ETHNIC AND CLASS TENSIONS

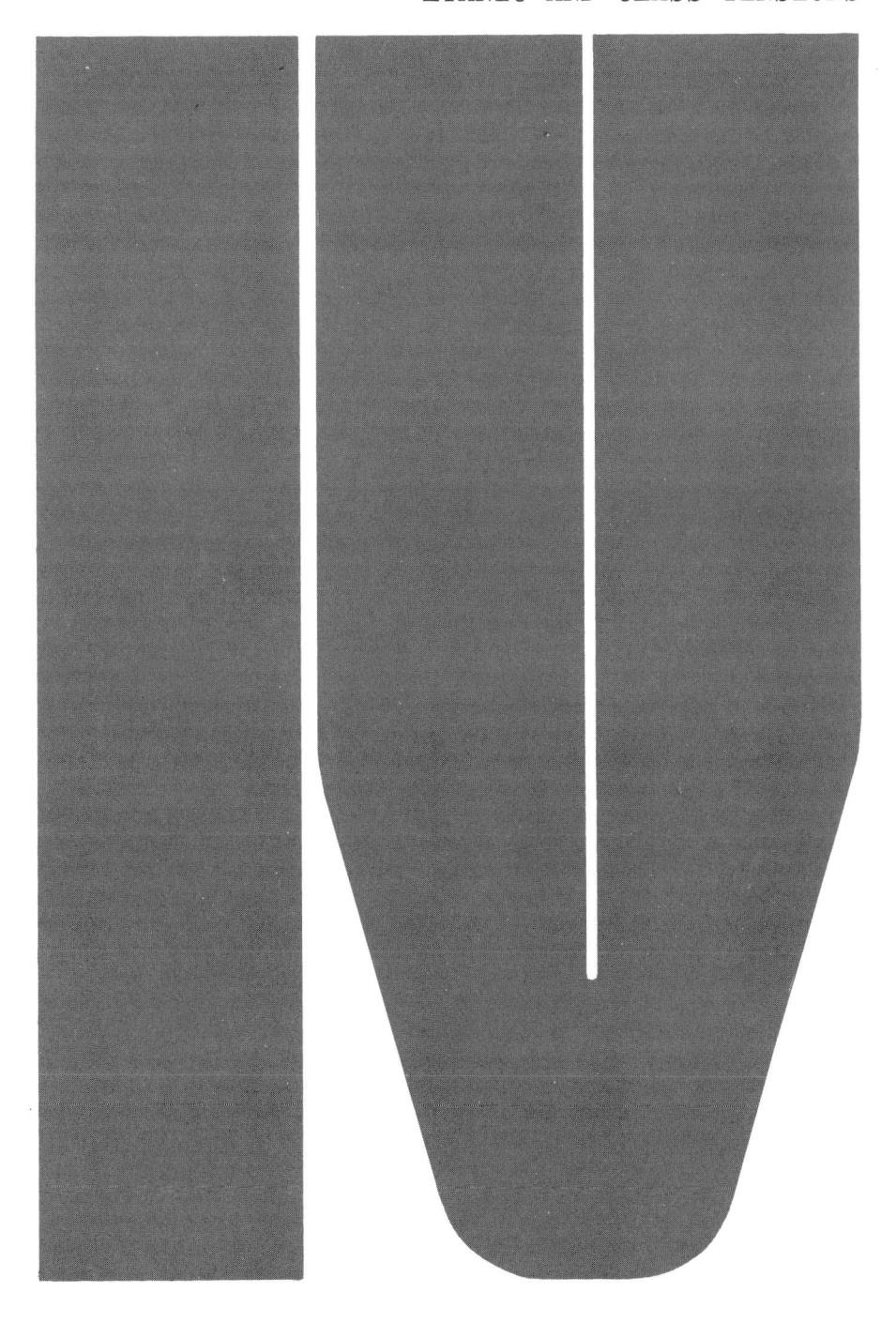

In recent years there has been a politicization of disadvantaged groups in the United States, who have attempted to gain entré into the political system in order to make claims for a fair share of society's resources. Primary among these groups have been the blacks, and it appears that the growing political militancy of black Americans has influenced other ethnic groups who have heretofore been ignored and underorganized. Thus the Mexican Americans, Indians, and Puerto Ricans are organizing now for political action. While James Q. Wilson has written that "American political institutions provide no way for the organized political pressure of a particular disadvantaged group to reshape in any fundamental sense social and economic conditions, since the issues at stake are economic and cultural, rather than political and legal," [1] many minority group members have sought to utilize the traditional political processes—following other ethnic group members who preceded them—in order to become active participants in the decision-making process. Other members of minority groups have sought to call attention to the urgent nature of their demands by utilizing extralegal and nonconventional techniques.

The increased participation of minority groups in the political system would significantly alter existing power relationships, and acquiescence to the demands presented by these groups would involve a major reorientation of traditional social and economic attitudes and priorities. Thus, reactions to minority group demands have frequently been hostile. While most white Americans no longer verbally express support of discriminatory practices, nevertheless there remains great resistance to rapid social change in race relations.[2] It is, of course, precisely such rapid change that blacks and other disadvantaged groups desire. Hence, in the 1970s, race remains an extremely divisive factor in American politics, and ethnic and racial tensions appear to be high.

Closely related to the rise of ethnic tensions in America is the role of class tensions. Spurred by the work of Marxist thinkers, numerous social scientists (among them C. Wright Mills and William Domhoff) have sought to document the political influence of the upper-class group which has been called the "ruling elite." Political scientists have increasingly focused on class-based attitudes and behavior among the lower and middle classes, as well.

Middle-class Americans apparently have utilized increased leisure time and economic security to become more actively involved in issue-oriented activities of both a "liberal" and "conservative" nature. As James Q. Wilson

---

[1] James Q. Wilson, "The Negro in Politics," in Lawrence Fuchs (ed.), *American Ethnic Politics* (New York: Harper & Row, 1968), p. 232.
[2] Jerome H. Skolnick, *The Politics of Protest* (New York: Ballantine Books, 1969), pp. 181–188.

and Harold Wilde have noted: "the 'new politics' of participation, direct personal contact, and right motives is no longer the province of the reformist or intellectual elite; it is the style of the middle class generally. . . . Because of this, the 'new politics' no longer leads inevitably to the support of very liberal candidates . . . this development is of crucial importance in understanding whatever conservative upsurge has taken place." [3]

Among working-class and lower-middle-class Americans, dissatisfaction with many trends in American life is becoming clear. Although labor union leaders succeeded in holding down the Wallace vote among unionized workers in 1968, many observers discern a "conservative" reaction among lower-class groups. The support that such "law and order" candidates as Roman Gribbs, Charles Stenvig, and Sam Yorty—running for Mayor in Detroit, Minneapolis, and Los Angeles, respectively—gained in 1969 among lower-class voters could provide evidence of increased group consciousness among such voters.

It appears that group consciousness, based on both economic and ethnic backgrounds, is at a high level in America today and that such consciousness has coincided with an increased interest in issue-oriented politics at all socioeconomic levels. What these developments may mean for the American political system is the subject of the readings in Part IV.

The selections in Chapter Nine, "The Dispossessed," analyze the attempts made by three ethnic groups—the Mexican Americans, Oklahoma Cherokees, and the blacks—to gain political and social mobility. In Chapter Ten, Peter Schrag seeks to explain why working-class Americans have become increasingly restive. Harry Scoble examines the role played by organized labor in American party politics, while J. David Greenstone contends that the American labor movement is more class-oriented (albeit in a unique fashion) than most Americans (and social scientists) believe. In Chapter Eleven, James Q. Wilson provides an account of both the development and the importance of "Reform" politics among middle-class Americans. Michael Rogin and Edward Schneier attempt to explain the vote for Wallace in 1964 and 1968 as manifestations of new middle-class consciousness.

[3] James Q. Wilson and Harold Wilde, "The Urban Mood," *Commentary,* 48 (October 1969), 55–56.

CHAPTER NINE

THE DISPOSSESSED

25
"La Raza": Mexican Americans in Rebellion

Joseph L. Love

In early June 1967 a group of Spanish-speaking Americans who call themselves the *Alianza Federal de Mercedes* (Federal Alliance of Land Grants) and claim that they are the legal and rightful owners of millions of acres of land in Central and Northern New Mexico, revolted against the governments of the United States of America, the State of New Mexico, and Rio Arriba (Up River) County, formally proclaiming the Republic of Rio Chama in that area.

On June 5 an armed band of forty or more *Aliancistas* attacked the Tierra Amarilla courthouse, released 11 of their members being held prisoner, and wounded a deputy sheriff and the jailer. They held the sheriff down on the floor with a rifle butt on his neck, searched for the District Attorney (who wasn't there), and for an hour and a half controlled the village (population 500). They took several hostages (later released when the getaway car stuck in the mud).

Despite some of the melodramatic and occasionally comic opera aspects of the affair, both the members of the *Alianza* and the local and state authorities take it very seriously. This is not the first time the Aliancistas have violated federal and state law, attempting to appropriate government property (in October 1966, for

From *TRANS-action* (February 1969), pp. 35–41. Copyright © 1969 by *TRANS-action*. Reprinted by permission of publisher and author.

instance, their militants tried to take over Kit Carson National Forest, and to expel the rangers found there as trespassers); nor is it the only time their activities have resulted in violence. In this case the state government reacted frantically, sending in armored tanks, 300 National Guardsmen and 200 state police. They rounded up dozens of Spanish-speaking persons, including many women and children, and held them in a detention camp, surrounded with guns and soldiers, for 48 hours. The raiders got away, but in several days all of them—including their fiery leader, former Pentecostal preacher Reies López Tijerina—were captured.

It has become common to associate these actions of the Alianza with other riots or revolts by poor, dark-skinned and disaffected Americans—with Watts, Newark and Detroit. Tijerina himself helps reinforce this impression by occasionally meeting with, and using the rhetoric of, some leaders of the black urban revolt. The fact is, however, that the Alianza movement is really a unique example in the United States of a "primitive revolt" as defined by Eric Hobsbawm, a kind almost always associated with developing nations, rather than advanced industrialized countries—and which includes such diverse phenomena as peasant anarchism, banditry, and millenarianism (the belief that divine justice and retribution is on the side of the rebels and that the millennium is at hand). The attack on the courthouse, in fact, had more in common with the millenarian Sioux Ghost Dance cult of 1889–1891 than with Watts.

As the Aliancistas see it, they are not violating any legitimate law. The territory around Rio Arriba belongs to them. They demand the return of lands—primarily common lands—taken from *Hispano* communities, most of which were founded in the Spanish colonial era. Their authority is the famous *Recopilación de leyes de los Reinos de Indias (Compilation of Laws of the Kingdoms of the Indies,* generally shortened to the *The Laws of the Indies*) by which the Crown of Castile governed its New World possessions. They claim that according to these laws common lands were inalienable—could not be taken away. Since most of such lands were in existence when the Treaty of Guadalupe Hidalgo was signed in 1848—and since in that treaty the United States government pledged itself to respect property rights established under Mexican rule—the Alianza insists that those land grants remain valid. The members speak primarily of common lands, rather than individual heirs, and define the towns in question as "closed corporations, with membership restricted to the descendants and heirs of the founding fathers and mothers"—that is, themselves.

The Alianza's interpretations of law and history are, of course, selective, and tend to ignore inconvenient facts and other interpretations. It claims that *The Laws of the Indies* were not abrogated when "Mexico invaded and occupied New Mexico," nor when the United States did the same in 1846. The Aliancistas are the early settlers, the legitimate heirs.

THE MAXIMUM LEADER

The Alianza and its actions cannot really be understood without knowledge of its background and its leader. First, the people from whom it draws its members and its strength—the Mexican-American minority in the U.S.—and specifically New Mexico; second, the rapid economic changes throughout the area since World War II that have so greatly affected their lives; and last but surely not least the dynamism, determination and charisma of Reies Tijerina, without whom the movement would probably never have risen.

In the 1960 census Mexican-Americans, though they made up only 2.3 percent of the population of the United States, constituted 12 percent of the population of Texas, New Mexico, Arizona, Colorado and California—almost three and a half million persons.

Generally they are a submerged minority that have only lately begun to articulate their demands. They formed "Viva Kennedy" committees in 1960; since then three Mexican-American Congressmen have gone to the House, and New Mexico's Joseph Montoya sits in the Senate. The end of the *bracero* program in 1964 opened the way to a successful unionization drive among agricultural workers; and the celebrated "Huelga" strike in Delano, California in 1965 was a symptom of and stimulus to the new awakening. The federal and state poverty programs, and the example of the Negro revolt, have also undoubtedly had their effects.

New Mexico is a distinctive area of Latin culture. It was the last state in the Southwest to be overwhelmed by Anglo-American civilization, and is the only one with two official languages. The Mexican-American population has been traditionally located along the Rio Grande and its tributaries, and extends into southern Colorado.

Until recent years, the Mexican-Americans of New Mexico have been isolated from other members of *la raza* (the Mexican-American "race"). Texas and California have more than 80 percent of the Mexican-American population of the Southwest, yet most of these crossed over from Mexico after 1900, or descended from persons who did. But, the New Mexican *Hispanos* (the local name) have resided there for many generations, and some strains go back to the seventeenth century (Santa Fe was founded in 1609). Moreover, large numbers of English-speaking Americans only began to compete seriously for rural property in the 1880s, and appropriation continued into the 1920s.

In the 1960 census New Mexico had a higher percentage of "native born of native parents" than any other Southwestern state (87.4 percent). The mobility of Hispano males between 1955 and 1960 (defined in terms of changing residence) was lower in New Mexico than elsewhere. In 1960 New Mexico had the highest percentage of rural non-farm inhabitants with Spanish surnames.

In absolute numbers New Mexico's Anglo population was for many years roughly in balance with the Hispano. It is now surging ahead as a result of the economic boom which began with the atomic testing program of World War II. In no other Southwestern state was the disparity between the growth of Anglo and Latin populations greater from 1950 to 1960 than in New Mexico, where the former increased by 59.1 percent and the latter by a mere 8.1 percent. Yet in spite of this, New Mexico in 1960 still had a greater proportion of Mexican-Americans than any other state: about two-sevenths of its inhabitants had Spanish surnames, compared to one-seventh of Texans, and one-eleventh of Californians.

The job situation for the Hispanos of New Mexico has also worsened more rapidly than in other states. In 1950 male Mexican-Americans had a greater percentage of jobless in California, Colorado, and Arizona than in New Mexico; but ten years later the Hispanos of New Mexico had the dubious distinction of leading the list.

As some observers have noted, in certain ways New Mexico resembles

Quebec: Both are centers of Latin culture founded in the seventeenth century, and both are subject to an increasing degree of Anglo domination. And like the Quebeckers, the New Mexicans have their fringe-group separatists—the *Alianza Federal de Mercedes*.

The Alianza was born in 1963, partly to combat the alienation and isolation of the Hispanos, but specifically to reclaim lands taken from the Spanish-speaking population since 1848. In colonial New Mexico (1598–1821), Spanish officials made land grants of indeterminate size to both individuals and to communities as commons, and the latter were respected through the era of Mexican rule (1821–1848). When Anglo-Americans began to enter New Mexico in significant numbers in the 1880s, they found it possible to wrest lands from the native inhabitants through the legal and financial devices of land taxes, mortgages, and litigation over disputed titles. By 1930, through legal and extralegal means, the Anglos had taken over most of the farming and ranching land in the state, and the state and federal governments appropriated much of the common lands that had previously belonged to the incorporated towns and villages. The Spanish-speaking population ultimately lost 1.7 million acres of community lands and two million acres in private holdings. The Hispanos sporadically reacted to this process by forming secret societies and vigilante groups; but at most this constituted harassment rather than effective resistance.

The Alianza now demands the return of these lands.

Yet in all probability, the Alianza would not exist but for the efforts of a single man, a leader who devotes his life to his cause, and inspires his followers to do likewise. Reies López Tijerina is a man of rare charisma who is most in his element when haranguing a large crowd. Of average height, he seems to have great physical strength as he grasps a microphone with one sinewy arm and gesticulates artfully and furiously with the other. He sometimes shouts violently as he asks rhetorical questions of his audience in Spanish—the language he uses by preference—and gets "Sí!" and "No!" bellowed back in appropriate cadences. The author witnessed a Tijerina performance last fall on the steps of the state capitol in Austin, Texas, where the Alianza leader told a group of Mexican-American Labor Day marchers he supported their demand for a state minimum wage of $1.25 an hour, but did so "with shame." Why should Mexican-Americans in Texas ask so little of the Anglos, whose government had repeatedly broken the Treaty of Guadalupe Hidalgo?

Reies Tijerina uses a demagogic style before a crowd, but he holds the tenets of his faith with unshakeable conviction: "It's something in me that must come out," Tijerina proclaims. His followers regard him with awe. He is "Caudillo" (leader) of the Alianza, but disclaims any desire to be dictator. He points out that a Supreme Council has ultimate control—though he, clearly, makes the decisions. It seems obvious that no one could step into his shoes, nor has anyone been groomed to do so. In any event Tijerina has no doubt that his followers require strong and able leadership. He justifies this by arguing that the Hispanos are a "young" race. They were "born," he explains, by virtue of a royal decree in 1514 allowing Spaniards to marry Indians; the term "Hispano" or "Spanish American" therefore can generally be equated with "mestizo." This young race is still learning, painfully, how to defend itself and requires strong direction. It is not an ancient and clever people like the Jews, he says.

Recognizing the diverse historical experiences of Texas, New Mexico, and California, the Caudillo realizes that his constituency for the foreseeable future will be limited to New Mexico. He does believe, however, that the land grants to Mexican-Americans in California can still be identified and claimed like those of New Mexico.

It is no coincidence that Tijerina's style and language recall Pentecostal protestantism. He has been a minister in the Assembly of God, and was an itinerant revival preacher for many years to Mexican-Americans throughout the Southwest.

But, unlike the vast majority of his followers, he was not born in New Mexico but in Texas ("A prophet is not without honor save in his own country"). One of seven children of a migrant farm family, once so desperate that they were reduced to eating field rats, he picked crops and preached in Illinois and Michigan as well as in Texas and Arizona. He did not settle in New Mexico until 1960; and, with his five brothers, formed the Alianza three years later.

The quasi-religious fervor of Tijerina has strongly shaped the aspirations and style of the Alianza. However, there is greater emphasis on Old Testament justice than New Testament love. *Justicia* is a word frequently on the Caudillo's lips.

The Alianza now claims to have 30,000 dues-paying members paying at least $2.00 per month. A scholar guesses that 10,000 may be closer to the true figure. It seems clear that Tijerina's computation includes sympathizers or at least persons who have only occasionally contributed funds.

As with some sectors of the American Negro movement, the Alianza's programs began with an emphasis on litigation; and when that failed, frustration and a disposition toward violence emerged.

In April 1966 the "President and Founder" of the Alianza journeyed to Spain in order to gather materials on the registration of New Mexican land grants in the colonial era; from such documents he hoped to generate a strong legal case to present in federal courts.

In July Tijerina presented a petition to the Governor of New Mexico, Jack Campbell, and stated, "We do not demand anything. We just want a full investigation of the issue." Yet Governor Campbell would do little more than receive Tijerina and hear him out.

In January 1967, the Caudillo, one of his brothers, and a self-styled legal expert in the Alianza named Gerry Noll made a trip to Washington, D.C., where they "limited" their claims to 500,000 acres in the Kit Carson National Forest and to an area around the city of Albuquerque. He only obtained a brief hearing with a State Department attorney and a sympathetic interview with New Mexico's Senator Montoya.

In 1966 the Alianza had already begun to give up hope of legal redress. The Supreme Council of the Alianza "passed a resolution of non-confidence in the Courts of the State of New Mexico and of the United States of America" because of "corruption" and "low standards of knowledge of law."

ALIANCISTAS PROCLAIM INDEPENDENT REPUBLIC

On October 22, 1966 the Aliancistas proclaimed the existence of the Republic of San Joaquín del Río de Chama (in Rio Arriba County) with Tijerina as "city attorney" (*procurador*) of the community; they simultaneously attempted to take over Kit Carson Forest, which covers most of the county. They arrested U.S. Forest Rangers for trespassing, decided to print hunting and fishing licenses, and commandeered government vehicles. The rebels were quickly dispersed by local authorities, and Tijerina and four lieutenants were charged on counts of assault, converting government property to private use, and conspiracy.

Demonstrations and protest meetings continued. On January 15, 1967 the Alianza declared it would seek redress in the United Nations if the U.S. Congress failed to act. On April 17 several hundred Aliancistas paraded before the State House in Santa Fe, and Reies Tijerina, out on bond, delivered an ominous message: "We will . . . issue to the public and the federal government and the world the last human legal notice exposing the truth. . . . The government is being warned and advised if anybody is found trespassing on these land grants they will be arrested and punished. . . ."

At the beginning of June the District Attorney of Santa Fe, Alfonso Sánchez, expressed concern about the "communist philosophy" of the Alianza and alleged that Aliancistas were amassing "machine guns, M-1 rifles, and 15,000 rounds" of ammunition. Eleven members of the Alianza were promptly arrested and jailed in Tierra Amarilla, an Alianza stronghold and the seat of Rio Arriba County.

The reaction was swift and violent: On June 5, as noted, the Aliancistas launched their revolt and attacked the Tierra Amarilla courthouse. This time, when caught, the Caudillo and his principal aides were charged with kidnapping, three counts of conspiracy to commit murder, and bombing a public building (the courthouse). Despite the gravity of the charges, Tijerina and some of his men were released on bond after six weeks in prison. The failure of the attack by no means dampened the spirits of the Aliancistas.

In the months following, Tijerina traveled throughout the Southwest to gain backing. He found it, both in radical organizations of Mexican-Americans and Negroes, and in the some Mexican-American associations with more traditional reformist leadership.

On October 15, Tijerina was in Los Angeles, linking his cause to the peace movement at an anti-war rally. Labeling the United States' involvement in Vietnam "the most criminal in the history of mankind," he contacted radical Negro and Mexican-American groups in the Los Angeles area. One week later, at a convention of the Alianza de Mercedes on October 21, Tijerina announced that a "Treaty of Peace, Harmony, and Mutual Assistance" had been contracted between his organization and SNCC, CORE, and the Black Panthers. The Caudillo also obtained statements of support from the Crusade for Justice, a Mexican-American organization of slumdwellers in Denver, and from MAPA, an important Mexican-American political action group in California.

While gathering support from non-Anglo groups outside New Mexico in the here and now, Tijerina and his deputies have not discouraged the movement's latent tendencies toward millenarianism and belief in special divine favor back home on the Upper Rio Grande. During the raid at Tierra Amarilla, several Aliancistas witnessed the appearance of a double rainbow, a sure sign of God's grace. According to others, the Caudillo is the prophet of Montezuma who will miraculously return in the imminent future to punish the Anglos for their appropriation of Hispano lands.

Another legend has it that a leader will come "from the east" and expel the foreigners who took the Mexican-Americans' lands. (Tijerina fits, since Texas is east of New Mexico.)

In the *"Corrido de Rio Arriba,"* which appeared shortly after the June raid,

the balladeer told his audience that when bullets started flying *"Las mujeres y los niños/iban corriendo y llorando,*
Y en este instante pensamos/Que el mundo se iba acabando."
("Women and children/Ran about in tears
And at that moment we thought/The world was coming to an end.")

Although the "free city-states" which Tijerina hopes to erect are of this world, they clearly represent a sort of secular paradise, a recaptured golden age, somewhat along the lines prescribed in *The Laws of the Indies*. The inhabitants will be able to do any work they please, explains the Caudillo; but most will be herdsmen using the common lands (*ejidos*) of the pueblos. Tijerina himself will simply become City Attorney of the Republic of Chama.

If "la raza" is specially favored and will come into its millennium, why is it suffering so now? This is explained as the result of a "fall from grace" which occurred after the Anglo-American invasion of New Mexico in 1846 and the collusion of certain Hispanos with the alien conquerors. An allegorical mural at Alianza headquarters tells the story: A sacred temple in the center of the mural represents paradise entwined by a serpent, which also clutches three figures symbolizing the oppressed races—the Negro, the Indian, and the Hispano. The snake personifies the "Santa Fe Ring"—the Anglo and upper-class Hispano politicians who appropriated the poor Hispanos' lands in the 1880s and later. Figures on the right side, representing the People, begin to emerge from the Darkness, and a reptile-devouring secretary bird, personifying Justice, arrives to attack the snake. At the top of the canvas is a rainbow (a symbol of God's blessing) and the phrase "Justicia." Just below this emblem is the City of Justice, which will once more be reconstituted on earth.

Yet there is a sinister element in the apocalypse which must precede the millennium: Anglos must be driven out. And Hispanos will be judged by whether they aided, stood aside from, or hindered the cause. Those who hindered will be treated harshly.

Gerry Noll, the Caudillo's lieutenant, has proclaimed as part of the Alianza creed:

> . . . KNOW YE that We have exclusive and supreme jurisdiction within [New Mexico] over all persons and property situated therein. . . .
> We cannot afford to permit the present status quo to be maintained without actually destroying Our independence and autonomy. Consequently, We must take measures calculated to curtail the activities of any aggressors with the utmost dispatch . . . We shall enter troops into these territories to restore Our authority . . . woe to him who obeys the orders of the aggressor, for he shall be punished without mercy. . . .
> THEREFORE KNOW YE that We shall commence to liberate Our kingdoms, realms, and dominions . . . We shall not take any prisoners of war, but shall take only war criminals and traitors and try [them] by a military tribunal and execute them.

At Tijerina's direction, the October 1967 convention of the Alianza unanimously set forth a weird dynastic claim: Gerry Noll was henceforth transformed into "Don Barne Quinto Cesar, King-Emperor of the Indies," the legitimate descendant of Ferdinand VII of Spain.

DYING IS PART OF A KING'S DAY'S WORK

In November Tijerina, "Don Barne," and several other Aliancistas stood trial for the charges stemming from the invasion of Kit Carson Forest in 1966. During the trial it was revealed that Noll's real name was Gerald Wayne Barnes, convicted of bank robbery in 1945, grand larceny in 1949, forgery in 1953, and third-degree assault in 1963. Found guilty, Noll and Tijerina were sentenced to three and two years respectively. At the trial Don Barne declared, "I am willing to die for my country and for my people. This is part of my job as king and all in a day's work." When sentenced in mid-December he retorted to the court, "It is I who make the laws—not the United States of America."

While waiting trial on the multiple charges of the June 1967 raid and appealing against the decision in the first case, Tijerina and his co-defendants were once more released on bond. On January 3, 1968, again in Tierra Amarilla, Deputy Sheriff Eulogio Salazar was kidnapped and beaten to death. Governor David Cargo, Campbell's successor, immediately revoked the bonds. Protests rapidly poured into the Governor's office from SNCC, MAPA, and other organizations, and a short time later Tijerina was out on bail again.

Since that time legal problems have necessarily absorbed most of Tijerina's energies, as he appealed the verdict of the first trial and prepared for the more serious set of charges (including kidnapping) stemming from the Tierra Amarilla affair. But the Caudillo found time to break into national headlines again in May and June when he led his followers at the Poor People's March on Washington. Alleging that the Negro leaders of the march refused to grant Mexican-Americans an adequate place in the sun, Tijerina cancelled Alianza participation in Resurrection City. Instead, he made use of his appearance in Washington to lecture State Department officials on the meaning of the Guadalupe Hidalgo Treaty—namely, the legitimacy of the Spanish land grants.

Tijerina had hoped to run for governor in the November 1968 elections, but the New Mexico Supreme Court disallowed his candidacy in October because of his conviction the previous year. Meanwhile the second (Tierra Amarilla) trial took place, during which Tijerina dramatically dismised his lawyers and conducted his own defense. In mid-December his self-confidence was justified by his acquittal of kidnapping and two lesser counts. Other charges against him and nine other defendants had yet to come before the courts at the end of 1968.

But the real historical and sociological meaning of the Alianza cannot be solely understood in terms of its current embroilments or recent history in New Mexico. Most of the literature on the movement, so far, has dealt with the spectacular, bizzare, or violent elements involved; but the roots of primitive revolt go far back.

Since the enclosure movement began in Europe in the twelfth century, there have been scores of peasant revolts. Many sought the restoration of common lands taken by nobles and gentry.

In medieval Spain, many villages owned herds and land in common, and a number of these arrangements survived as late as the Spanish Civil War. These towns had once enjoyed special legal sanctions called *fueros,* by which they could themselves decide whether or not to enforce royal decrees and pay taxes.

One historian has written that "The village communities spontaneously developed an extensive system of municipal services, to the point of their sometimes reaching an advanced stage of communism." A scheme was proposed in 1631 to "nationalize all pasturage and establish each peasant with sufficient head of sheep and cattle to support him." In 1633 the Crown tried to implement this project by regulating tenancy and fixing rents in perpetuity, making leases irrevocable and hereditary, and setting up regulation commissions. Though the plan failed, the demands of shepherds for adequate grazing land were part of the Hispanic tradition to which Tijerina appeals and went to Spain to study.

One student of Mexican-American culture, anthropologist Narcie González, writes that ". . . even now [1967] sheepherding remains an ideal way of life for the Hispano. . . . Virtually all contemporary accounts by social scientists comment upon the people's stated preference for this occupation. . . ." This preference explains why in Tijerina's Utopia the common lands are so highly valued. The Chama region, where the Tierra Amarilla revolt broke out, was principally a sheep-grazing area until after World War II.

What has occurred in New Mexico has been a breakdown of the traditional society, the ripping of the fabric of Hispano culture. In 1950, 41 percent of the Spanish-surname population in the state lived in urban areas; but by 1960, 61 percent did. Many of those moving to the cities (especially to Albuquerque) were ill prepared for their new way of life. In 1956 one investigator found that 834 out of 981 women in Albuquerque who received Aid to Dependent Children had Spanish surnames.

While the number of Anglo-Americans rapidly increased in New Mexico after World War II, the Mexican-American population was almost static, the high birth rate being offset by emigration to California. Consequently by 1960 the Anglo population in the state constituted almost two-thirds of the whole.

The legal structures of a modern capitalist society had by the late 1930s wrecked the traditional land-tenure patterns of the Upper Rio Grande. In 1940 Dr. George Sanchez reported that in Taos County "65 percent of the private lands represent land grants which have been subdivided or otherwise lost to the communities and families to which they were originally assigned. Of the original nine *mercedes* in Taos County, four were community grants and five were lands granted to individuals. . . . This cornerstone of Taos' economy has been destroyed by taxation and by uncontrolled exploitation." Furthermore, "Commercial livestock operators have acquired [the Hispano's] land grants and compete with him for grazing leases and permits on public lands. Exorbitant fees, taxes, and forced sales have crowded him out of his former grazing domain."

For a time the full impact of these changes was softened by the booming war and atomic energy economy in New Mexico, and by the fact that the National Forest Service seems to have acted as a surrogate patrón for the Hispano shepherd. Until drought in the 1960s forced a cutback, the Hispano could still obtain the use of federal lands for pasturing his livestock.

Rio Arriba County was one of the areas least affected by the state's economic growth. In 1960 it had the highest percentage of rural non-farm population of all New Mexico's counties (91.3 percent). It ranked high in native-born inhabitants, and low in the percentage of migrants. It had the third lowest median education and the fifth lowest median family income. In Rio Arriba and the other northern counties where the Spanish-speaking population predominates, the average per capita income in 1967 was less than $1,000, compared to the state average of $2,310 and the national average of $2,940. Furthermore, according to Governor

Cargo, "11,000 of 23,000 residents of Rio Arriba County are on welfare rolls." The 1960 census showed that county with the state's highest rate of unemployment—15.1 percent—almost three times the state average.

GOVERNMENT CONTROLS GRAZING LANDS

But it is not only unemployment that makes the residents of Rio Arriba dependent on federal and state largesse—72.1 percent of all land still available for grazing is owned by the U.S. government in Kit Carson Forest. And what the government grants, it can, and sometimes does, also refuse.

The disintegration of the traditional Hispano community seems well underway, and Tijerina articulates widely-shared feelings that his people do not want to assimilate into Anglo culture. He also rejects relief as demoralizing to its recipients, stating again and again, "We will no longer take powdered milk in exchange for justice." Recent increases in welfare assistance may actually have aggravated the situation by raising the Hispanos' hopes for greater improvement.

Reaction to social disintegration can take many forms, and the Hispanic religious tradition—plus Tijerina's own background as a Pentecostal preacher—have helped channel it into millenarianism. In the 1930s a religious group called the Allelujahs, an Hispano version of the Holy Rollers, became popular, and before it faded out as many as half the people of some northern New Mexico communities had joined, taking part in religious services in which "Passages from the Revelation of St. John are favorite texts [according to a 1937 report], and lead to frenzies of religious ecstasy." The Allelujah experience has helped prepare the ground. So perhaps have the *Penitentes,* a lay brotherhood of Hispano mystics and self-flagellants that traces its origins back to the colonial era.

When the Alianza failed to obtain redress through the courts, the hope for and belief in extralegal and supernatural means of relief—natural enough in the presence of the charismatic and fiery Tijerina—became exacerbated. When the National Forest Service recently cut back the use of grazing lands because of drought, the Hispanos were the hardest hit—and Tijerina was at hand to transform frustration into action. The frequency of millenarianism when belief in and identity with the dominant society are lost has been well documented in sociological literature. The Alianza constitutes an almost classic case.

Yet there is a "modern" dimension to the Alianza, and this is a direct outgrowth of its appearance in an industrial society with rapid transcontinental communications and ever-vigilant news media. The Alianza fits the requirements of a "primitive rebellion" or "revitalization movement," but its links with urban radical and reformist groups outside New Mexico show its potential for evolving into something more modern. Thus there are two distinct dimensions of the movement —the "primitive," rural, grassroots constituency on the tributaries of the upper Rio Grande; and the "modern," urban, nationally-connected leadership in Albuquerque. The "visible" media-oriented sector is modern, but the "invisible" millenarian sector is not.

Tijerina's primary concern is still regaining lost community lands, as his action at the Poor People's March showed. The hunger for community lands—the *ejidos* —remains the basis for the "real" movement, despite manifestos of solidarity with the Black Panthers and denunciations of the war in Vietnam.

The ignorance of government officials of the basic nature of the movement is almost monumental. They tend to explain the Alianza away by easy, modern clichés. Some find in the references to common lands the spore of modern communism.

At the November 1967 trial, the prosecuting attorney declared, "This is not a social problem we're trying. This is a criminal problem." Even some sympathetic observers have used singularly inappropriate terms. Tom Wicker of the *New York Times* and Congressman Joseph Resnick, chairman of the House Agriculture Subcommittee on Rural Development, have both referred to Rio Arriba County as a "rural Watts."

But Rio Arriba has little in common with Watts. The majority of Aliancistas, the rural grassroots, are not industrial proletarians but primitive rebels—peasants reacting and striking back in millenarian fashion against the modernization that is tearing their society apart.

26
Renaissance and Repression: The Oklahoma Cherokee

Albert L. Wahrhaftig
Robert K. Thomas

A week in eastern Oklahoma demonstrates to most outsiders that the Cherokee Indians are a populous and lively community: Indians *par excellence*. Still, whites in eastern Oklahoma unanimously declare the Cherokees to be a vanishing breed. Prominent whites say with pride, "we're all a little bit Indian here." They maintain that real Cherokees are about "bred out." Few Cherokees are left who can speak their native tongue, whites insist, and fewer still are learning their language. In twenty years, according to white myth, the Cherokee language and with it the separate and distinctive community that speaks it will fade into memory.

Astonishingly, this pervasive social fiction disguises the presence of one of the largest and most traditional tribes of American Indians. Six rural counties in northeastern Oklahoma contain more than fifty Cherokee settlements with a population of more than 9500. An additional 2000 Cherokees live in Indian enclaves in towns and small cities. Anthropologists visiting us in the field, men who thought their previous studies had taught them what a conservative tribe is like, were astonished by Cherokees. Seldom had they seen people who speak so little English, who are so unshakably traditional in outlook.

How can native whites overlook this very identifiable Indian community? The answers, we believe, will give us not only an intriguing insight into the nature of

From *TRANS-action* (February 1969), pp. 42–48. Copyright © 1969 by *TRANS-action*. Reprinted by permission of publisher and authors.

Oklahoma society, but also some general conclusions about the position of other ethnic groups in American society.

This myth of Cherokee assimilation gives sanction to the social system of which Cherokees are a part, and to the position Cherokees have within that system. This image of the vanishing Cherokee in some ways is reminiscent both of the conservative Southern mythology which asserts that "our colored folk are a contented and carefree lot," and of the liberal Northern mythology, which asserts that "Negroes are just like whites except for the color of their skins." The fiction serves to keep Cherokees in place as a docile and exploitable minority population; it gives an official rationale to an existing, historic social system; and it implies that when the Indian Territory, the last Indian refuge, was dissolved, no Indian was betrayed, but all were absorbed into the mainstream.

The roots of modern eastern Oklahoma are in the rural South. Cherokees, and whites, came from the South; Cherokees from Georgia and Tennessee; and whites from Tennessee, Kentucky, Arkansas and southern Illinois.

In the years immediately preceding 1840, Cherokees, forced out of their sacred homelands in Georgia and Tennessee, marched over an infamous "Trail of Tears," and relocated in a new Cherokee Nation in what is now the state of Oklahoma. They created an international wonder: an autonomous Cherokee Nation with its own national constitution, legislature, judiciary, school system, publishing house, international bilingual newspaper, and many other trappings of a prosperous Republic. The Cherokees, who as a people accomplished all this, along with their neighbors, the Creeks, Choctaws, Chicasaws and Seminoles, who followed similar paths, were called the five civilized tribes.

Promising as the Cherokee Nation's future might have seemed, it was plagued by internal controversy from birth. Bitterness between the traditional Ross Party and the Treaty Party was intense. The Ross Party resisted demands for relocating from the South until its followers were finally corralled by the Army; the Treaty Party believed cooperation with the United States Government was the more prudent course for all Cherokees.

The sons and daughters of the Ross Party kept their ancient villages together. They reestablished these in the hollows and rough "Ozark" country of the Indian territory. Hewing new log cabins and planting new garden spots, they hoped to live unmolested by their opponents. They are today's "full bloods," that is, traditional and Cherokee-speaking Cherokees. On the other hand, descendants of the Treaty Party, who concentrated in the flat bottomlands and prairies they preferred for farming, are now assimilated and functionally white Americans, though fiercely proud of their Cherokee blood.

The Ross Party was the core of the Cherokee tribes. It was an institution which emerged from the experience of people who lived communally in settlements of kinsmen. The Treaty Party was a composite of individuals splintered from the tribal body. There were of course great differences in life style among nineteenth-century Cherokee citizens. The Ross men, often well-educated, directed the Cherokee legislators from backwoods settlements. Treaty Party men were more often plantation owners, merchants, entrepreneurs, and professionals—conventional southern gentlemen. The overriding difference between the two factions, however, was between men who lived for their community and men who lived for themselves.

During the 1880s this difference came to be associated not with party but with blood. Geographically separated and ostracized by Ross men, members of the Treaty Party perforce married among the growing population of opportunistic whites who squatted on Indian land, defying U.S. and Cherokee law. The Treaty Party became known as the "mixed blood" faction of the tribe; the Ross Party as "full bloods." These terms imply that miscegenation caused a change of life style, a reversal of the historic events.

By 1907 when the Cherokee Nation was dissolved by Congressional fiat and the State of Oklahoma was created, the mixed bloods were already socially if not politically, part of the white population of the United States. The Ross Party settlements, now the whole of the functionally Cherokee population, are intact but surrounded by an assimilated population of mixed-blood Cherokees integrated with white immigrants.

From the 1890s and 1920s, development of this area was astonishingly rapid. A flood of whites arrived. Land was populated by subsistence farmers, small town trade boomed, commercial farming expanded, railroads were built, timber exhausted, petroleum exploited and token industrialization established.

Already shorn of their nation, full bloods were stunned and disadvantaged by the overnight expansion and growth. Change was rapid, the class system open. Future distinguished elders of small town society arrived as raggedy tots in the back of one-mule wagons. Not only was social mobility easy, few questions were asked about how the newly rich became rich. Incredible land swindles were commonplace. At the turn of the century, every square inch of eastern Oklahoma was allotted to Cherokees; by the 1930s little acreage remained in Indian possession.

The result of this explosive development was a remarkably stratified society, characterized by highly personal relationships, old time rural political machines, Protestant fundamentalism, reverence of free enterprise, and unscrupulous exploitation; in short, a system typical of the rural south.

Superficially, this society appears to be one with the most resourceful at the top, and the unworthy, who let opportunity slip by, at the bottom. In reality, however, the system consists of ranked ethnic groups, rather than classes. The successful old mixed-blood families, now functionally "white," whose self-identification as "Cherokee" is taken as a claim to the venerable status of "original settlers," dominate. Below them are the prosperous whites who "made something of themselves," and at the bottom, beneath the poor country whites, Cherokee "full bloods."

In primitive tribes, myth is a sacred explanation of the creation of the tribe and of its subsequent history. Myth specifies the holy design within which man was set to live. The fiction of Cherokee assimilation illustrates that modern man still uses myth, though differently. For in Oklahoma, the myth of Cherokee assimilation validates the social conditions men themselves have created, justifying the rightness and inevitability of what was done. As Oklahomans see it, the demise of the Cherokee as a people was tragic, albeit necessary. For only thus were individual Cherokees able to share in the American dream. The Oklahoman conceives of his society as an aggregate of individuals ranked by class, with unlimited opportunity for mobility regardless of individual ancestry. The high class position of the old Cherokee mixed bloods signifies to the Oklahoman that the job of building Oklahoma was well done. The "responsible" Indians made it. The Cherokees, as a single historic people, died without heirs, and rightfully all those who settled on their estate now share in the distribution of its assets. For the culturally Indian individuals remaining, Oklahoma can only hope that they will do better in the future.

Even as the mythology serves to sanctify their high rank position, it insulates whites from the recognition of the Cherokee as a viable but low ranked ethnic community with unique collective aims and interests. Where a real community exists, Oklahomans see only a residue of low status individuals. The myth, by altering perceptions, becomes self-perpetuating.

Paradoxically, the myth of Cherokee assimilation has also contributed to the survival of the Cherokee as a people. To the extent that Cherokees believed the myth, and many did, it was not only an explanation of how the tribe came into the present but a cohesive force. Since the end of a tribal movement led by Redbird Smith, a half century ago, in response to the final pressures for Oklahoma statehood, Cherokees have seemed inert, hardly a living people. Nevertheless, Cherokee communal life persisted, and is in a surprisingly healthy state. Cherokee settlements remain isolated, and if what goes on in them is not hidden, it is calculatedly inconspicuous. For the freedom from interference that it afforded, Cherokees willingly acceded to the notion that the Cherokees no longer exist.

In addition to sanctioning the form of Oklahoma society, the myth also gives credence to basic social and economic institutions. The economy of the area depends on Cherokees and country whites as an inexpensive and permanent labor market. Cherokees are expected to do low paying manual work without complaint. In 1963, Cherokee median per capita income, approximately $500, was less than half the per capita income of neighboring rural whites. In some areas, Cherokees live in virtual peonage; in others, straw bosses recruit Cherokee laborers for irregular work at low pay. Even though Cherokee communities are relatively hidden, Cherokee labor has become an indispensable part of the local economy. Apparently one would think that daily contact of white workers and bosses with these Cherokee laborers might expose the myth of the well-off assimilated Cherokee. On the contrary, the myth prevails because the humble occupations practiced by Cherokees are seen as evidence that Cherokee character is indeed that which the myth of assimilation predicts.

WHITE BLOOD MAKES GOOD INDIANS

Imbedded in the Oklahoma concept of assimilation is a glaring racism. Typical is the introductory page of a book published in 1938 entitled *A Political History of the Cherokee Nation*, written by Morris Wardell, a professor at the University of Oklahoma.

A selection: "Traders, soldiers, and treaty-makers came among the Cherokees to trade, compel and negotiate. Some of these visitors married Indian women and lived in the Indian villages the remainder of their days. Children born to such unions preferred the open and free life and here grew to manhood and womanhood, never going to the white settlements. This mixture of blood helped to produce strategy and cleverness which made formidable diplomats of many of the Indian leaders."

To white genes go the credit for Sequoyah's genius and John Ross's astuteness, whereas the remaining Cherokee genes contribute qualities that are endearing but less productive. Thus, in a history of the Cherokees published only six years ago, the author, an Oklahoman, says of modern "full bloods": "They supplement their small income from farms and subsidies from the government with wage work or seasonal jobs in nearby towns or on farms belonging to white men. . . . Paid fair wages, this type of worker usually spends his money as quickly as he makes it on whisky, and on cars, washing machines, and other items that, uncared for, soon fall into necessitous disuse."

Oklahomans divide the contemporary Cherokees into two categories: those who are progressive and those who are not. The page just quoted continues, "this progressive type of Indian will not long remain in the background of the growing and thriving, and comparatively new, State of Oklahoma." That a viable Indian tribe exists is apparently inconceivable. Either Cherokees are worthy, responsible and assimilating, or they are the dregs; irresponsible, deculturated and racially inferior.

Through mythology, the exploitation of Cherokee labor is redefined into benevolent paternalism. Some patrons have Cherokees deliver their welfare checks to them, deduct from these housing and groceries. Afterwards the remainder is handed over to Cherokee tenants. Unknown to the welfare department, these same Cherokees receive stingy wages for working land and orchards belonging to the patron or to his kin. Patrons consider that they are providing employment and a steady paternal hand for unfortunate people who they contend could never manage themselves. The same ethic enables whites in good conscience to direct vestigial Cherokee tribal affairs; including the disbursement of well over two million dollars in funds left from a tribal land claim settlement.

POLITICIANS ARE VICTIMS OF OLD FEARS

It might seem odd that no one seeking to improve his position in the local establishment has ever tried to weaken these relationships. Why has no political figure taken cognizance of those thousands of Cherokee votes, and championed their cause? Instead politicians rely on the inefficient machinery of county patronage to collect Cherokee ballots. Unfortunately no one has yet dared, because fear binds the system. Older whites remember living in fear of a blood bath. The proposal to create Oklahoma meant a new state to whites; to Cherokees it meant the end of their own national existence. Their resistance to statehood was most desperate. Cherokees were a force to be contended with. They were feared as an ominously silent, chillingly mysterious people, unpredictable and violent. And Cherokees did organize into secret societies, much akin to the committees of twenty-five delegated in days past to murder collaborators who signed treaties. The reward of public office, politicians feel, does not justify the risk of rekindling that flame. To the extent that Oklahomans are aware of the numbers of Cherokees and the force they might generate, the myth of the assimilated Cherokee is a form of wishful thinking.

Finally, the myth protects the specific relationships of rank and power which determine the stability of the present eastern Oklahoma social system. It does this in the following ways: By preventing recognition by whites and Indians alike of the Cherokees as a permanent community of people whose demands and aspirations must be taken seriously, it allows whites to direct the affairs of the region as they see fit.

By causing Cherokee aspirations to be discounted as romantic and irrelevant, it prevents the emergence of a competitive Cherokee leadership and discourages

Cherokees from taking action as a community. For example, by 1904 Cherokees were given what was thought of as an opportunity to develop individualism and responsibility. The U.S. Government divided their communally owned land and each Indian was given his own piece. Thus the efforts of the present day Cherokee Four Mothers Society to piece together individual land holdings, reestablish communal title, and develop cooperative productive enterprises, is smilingly dismissed as an atavistic retreat to "clannishness."

By fostering the notion that Cherokees are an aggregate of disoriented individuals, it allows whites to plan for Cherokees, to control Cherokee resources, and to reinforce their own power by directing programs devoted to Cherokee advancement.

By denying that there is a Cherokee community with which a Cherokee middle class could identify and to which a Cherokee middle class could be responsive, it draws off educated Cherokees into "white" society and leaves an educationally impoverished pool of Cherokees to perpetuate the image of Cherokee incompetence.

The myth prevents scholars, Indian interest organizations, and the like from becoming overly curious about the area. If Cherokees are assimilated and prosperous, as the myth implies, there is neither a problem nor a culture to study. For 40 years no social scientist has completed a major study of any of the five civilized tribes. For 40 years the spread of information which might cast doubt on the myth itself has been successfully impeded.

In all, the myth stabilizes and disguises the Oklahoma social system.

The stability of a local social system, such as that of eastern Oklahoma, is heavily influenced by events in the larger society. The past decade of civil rights activity shook Oklahoma. Gradually, Oklahomans are becoming aware that their society is not as virtuous, homogeneous, attractive, and open as they may have supposed. And Oklahomans will now have to deal with the old agrarian social system of Cherokees, hillbillies, mixed-blood Cherokees, and a new urban elite grafted onto the old.

Left behind in the rush of workers to industry and of power to industrialized areas, the Ozark east of Oklahoma is a shell, depopulated, and controlled by newly dominant cities, Tulsa and Oklahoma City. The area, quaint enough to attract tourists, is far too rustic for sophisticated Oklahoma urbanites to take seriously. Local politicians offer weak leadership. Beginning to suspect that the local establishment is no longer all powerful, Cherokees have begun to assert themselves as a tribal community. The Cherokees conceive of themselves as a civilized nation, waiting for the dark days of the foreigners' suppression and exploitation to end. Oklahomans regard Cherokees as an aggregate of disadvantaged people still in the background of an integrated state, a definition which Cherokees do not share. In fact, the Cherokees are flirting with political office and have entered the courts with a hunting rights case. In launching a "Five County Northeast Oklahoma Cherokee Organization," they are gaining recognition as a legitimate community with rights, aspirations, resources and competence.

Consequently, the reappearance of assimilated Cherokees threatens the newly emergent regional power structure. Cherokees and the local establishment have begun jousting on a field of honor extending from county welfare offices (where the welfare-sponsored jobs of suspect members of the "Five County Organizations" are in jeopardy) to annual conventions of the National Congress of American Indians. Besides threatening an already shaky white power structure, the militant Cherokee are challenging the self-esteem of the elderly and powerful "assimilated." Curiously, many white Oklahomans do not appear to be alarmed, but pleased, apparently, to relieve the tension that has developed between conflicting images of pretended assimilation and the reality of a workaday world.

The manner in which Oklahomans view their society is the manner in which American sociologists all too often view American society. Great emphasis is placed on class and on individual mobility. And, social description, in these terms, is seen very much as a product of the American ethos.

White Oklahomans consider themselves members of a class-stratified society in which any individual (Negroes excepted) has free access to any class. Descriptions of that system vary according to who is doing the describing. Generally, white Oklahomans conceive their society to be one in which the upper class is made up of prosperous whites and old Cherokee mixed-blood families, or their descendants; next in order is a layer of middle-class whites and assimilated Cherokees; then, a lower class of poor, country whites, full-blood Cherokees and Negroes. Young liberals see a two-class system: A middle class of "decent" whites and Cherokees and a socially unacceptable class of poor, country whites, Cherokees, and Negroes.

HOW MYTHICAL IS MOBILITY?

This latter classification suggests that younger people perceive a much more closed system than their elders. Everyone is viewed as part of the same *community*—a word Oklahomans are fond of using. Presumably all groups of people have an equal share in the life of the community. Nationality, the word Oklahomans use to denote ethnic origin, is a principal clue to class position. As evidence of how open their society is, eastern Oklahomans point to Cherokees and poor, country whites (although not yet to Negroes, to whom the system is closed) who occupy respected positions. These are store owners, bureaucrats, and entrepreneurs; Babbitts of the 1960s, though born of traditional Cherokee parents. Always, however, these have been individuals who followed the only approved channel of mobility by scrupulously conforming to standards of behavior defined by those in control of the system.

The classic sociological studies on class in America, such as those by W. Lloyd Warner and Robert Lynd, are essentially static descriptions of the rank position of aggregates of individuals similar to the native Oklahoman's conception of his society. These studies reflect a peculiarly American bias. First, they examine the system that has formed rather than study how the system was formed. Americans are phenomenologists, more concerned with the things they have created than with the lengthy processes whereby these things have developed, more interested in ends than concerned with means.

Secondly, Americans do not stress ethnic considerations. In the American dream all individuals can "make it," regardless of nationality. For sociologists, class is a phenomenon in which individuals have social rank; ethnicity is treated as no more than an important clue in determining that rank. Thus, to be Irish was to be an outcast in nineteenth-century Boston; not so today.

Thirdly, Americans, envisioning themselves as a nation of individualists, have assumed that social mobility for the most part rests on individual achievement.

Immigrant groups are seen as having migrated into lower class positions in a relatively fixed class system through which individual immigrants rapidly became mobile. By contrast, Oklahoma's rapid entry into the formative American industrial economy caused a class-like structure to form on top of pre-existing ethnic communities.

A more balanced view shows that in the parts of the United States which industrialized earlier and more gradually, whole immigrant communities were successively imported into and butted one another through a social system which was in the process of formation and closure. The ways in which entire ethnic communities achieve mobility are overlooked.

Now it is becoming obvious that this mobility has slowed, even for those ethnic communities (like Poles) already "in the system." For communities which were brought into the system late (like Puerto Ricans) or at its territorial fringe (like Mexican-Americans in the Southwest) the situation is different.

Cherokees maintained technical independence as an autonomous nation until 1907, and in fact held America at arm's length until the 1890s. They provide an example of incorporation of an ethnic group into the industrial system in an area where no earlier group has paved the way. Thus, Cherokees are a "case type" which illustrates the modern dynamics of our system in pure form. Cherokees are now caught in our "historically mature" system of rank ethnic groups—a system which, for some, is rigid and closed, with little chance for individual and less for communal mobility. The total rank-structure of eastern Oklahoma is cemented by the mythology Americans use to obscure and rationalize their privileged position in a closed system.

In their conception of class, American sociologists are often as wedded to myth as are Oklahomans, and the resulting large areas of American social science they have created obediently subscribe to official fictions within the American world view.

Now, successive summers of violence have exploded some of the folk and scientific mythology shrouding the structure of our nation. The *Report of the National Advisory Commission on Civil Disorders* declares: "What white Americans have never fully understood—but what the Negro can never forget—is that white society is deeply implicated in the ghetto. White institutions created it, white institutions maintain it, and white society condones it." Yet throughout this unusually clear report the phenomenon of white racism is barely alluded to, as though it were an "attitude" born by an uninformed populace and unrelated to the core of our national social system. That system, as we see it in operation in Oklahoma, beneath its mythology of assimilation, consists of a structure of ranked ethnic groups, euphemistically called "classes" by American sociologists; a structure which is growing more stable and more rigid. This kind of structure is general in America and, of course, implied in the above quote from the Kerner report. In Oklahoma such a system of relationships has enabled aggressive enterpreneurs to harness and utilize the resources of ethnic communities which are frozen into a low-ranked position by the dominant community's control over channels of mobility and by the insistence that the whole complex represents one single community differentiated only by personal capability. Thus, essentially "racist" perceptions and relationships are the "motor" driving the system and are embedded in the very day-to-day relationships of middle-class Oklahoma.

27
Blacks, Blocs and Ballots: The Relevance of Party Politics to the Negro

Joyce Gelb

The Report of the National Advisory Commission on Civil Disorders tacitly abandons the traditional party structure as a vehicle for Negro demands and advocates the creation of new institutions, such as the Urban Action Task Force, for "improved political representation" for the black community.[1] The commission's approach reflects a current view held by many political scientists, who believe that party politics, the organized attempt by a political group to recruit workers and candidates and mobilize votes in order to obtain the appointment and election of officials who can make politically relevant decisions for the community, is of little relevance to the black man in his quest for equality.

There appear to be four basic reasons for the disenchantment of political scientists with the political party as a vehicle for black advancement. The first, articulated by the Riot Commission, is that because of the demise of the urban political machine and the concomitant growth of "good government" concepts, the traditional party structure can no longer provide an "important link" between city government and low-income city dwellers.[2] As James Q. Wilson has said: "Ne-

From *Polity*, III, no. 1 (September 1970), pp. 44–69. Reprinted by permission of publisher and author.

[1] *Report of the National Advisory Commission on Civil Disorders* (New York: Bantam Books, 1968), pp. 283–299. (Henceforth called *Riot Report*.)
[2] *Riot Report*, p. 287.

groes are expected to climb a political ladder which, as a result of several decades of successful reform efforts, is now missing most of its rungs." [3] Second, both the Riot Commission and James Q. Wilson suggest that because of the transformation of economic issues into racial ones, the development of political alliances between blacks and whites, for shared objectives, has been made almost impossible.[4] Third, studies of Negro voting in the South have indicated that the Negro vote is far more potent in bringing about "legal justice" than in fostering meaningful "social justice," and that means other than traditional politics have brought about important changes for blacks.[5] And, finally, an important group of political scientists believes that the compromise-oriented "style" of party politics is unsuited to the radical nature of black political demands.[6]

This study of black politics in New York City from 1958 to 1968, based in part upon 100 interviews of black party politicians, community activists, and white party politicians in four boroughs of New York City (excluding Staten Island) during 1967–1968,[7] examines these assertions in an attempt to reach some conclusions about the relevance of party politics to the black man.

New York City is a particularly good setting in which to examine Negro politics because of the national implications of its politics. Moreover, since various studies of Negro politics have assumed that there is greater liberalism in New York City—primarily due to the presence of a large Jewish, professional, "good government"-oriented group, and that this liberalism has led to a climate in which Negro political aspirations will more readily be satisfied [8]—the efficacy of party politics can best be tested in New York. In addition, the diversity of political organization in New York City provides a good opportunity for analysis of black participation in different types of party structures. New York City politics is widely recognized as "borough politics" since there is no one city-wide political organization, and state law provides for county independence.[9] Black political activity is found in the concentrated areas of Negro settlement in each of the four boroughs (counties) under consideration here: South Jamaica in Queens, the Southeast Bronx, Bedford-Stuyvesant in Brooklyn, and Harlem in Manhattan.[10]

[3] James Q. Wilson, "The Negro in Politics," in Lawrence Fuchs (ed.), *American Ethnic Politics* (New York: Harper & Row, 1968), p. 238 (henceforth called Wilson, "The Negro in Politics"). See also Elmer E. Cornwell, Jr., "Bosses, Machines and Ethnic Groups," in Fuchs, *American Ethnic Politics*, pp. 209–216, for a similar view.
[4] *Riot Report*, p. 287; Wilson, "The Negro in Politics," pp. 234–239.
[5] See, for example, Donald Matthews and James Prothro, *Negroes and the New Southern Politics* (New York: Harcourt Brace Jovanovich, 1966), p. 481, and William Keech, *The Impact of Negro Voting* (Chicago: Rand McNally, 1968), esp. pp. 95–107.
[6] See especially Wilson, "The Negro in Politics," p. 242.
[7] 47 Black Democrats, 31 black Republicans, 6 black Liberals, and 16 black community leaders and white politicians were interviewed. Interviews were semistructured and open-ended.
[8] Nathan Glazer and Daniel Moynihan, *Beyond the Melting Pot* (Cambridge, Mass.: M.I.T. Press, 1963), p. 70; James Q. Wilson, *Negro Politics: The Search for Leadership* (New York: Free Press, 1960), p. 46.
[9] Wallace Sayre and Herbert Kaufman, *Governing New York City* (New York: Russell Sage Foundation, 1960), p. 17, and Hugh Bone, "Political Parties in New York City," *American Political Science Review*, 40 (April 1946), 272.
[10] Glazer and Moynihan, *Beyond the Melting Pot*, p. 54. (Each area shades off into a mixed area which becomes increasingly Negro.) Staten Island, the fifth borough, was excluded because of lack of discernible black activity there.

Although black political activity centers around the Democratic party,[11] Negroes are also active in the Republican party and in the Liberal party, a NewYork State third party. The structure and "style" of party organization varies from county to county. Democratic party politics in Manhattan (and increasingly in the Bronx as well) is distinguished by loose factionalism and substantial "Reform" influence. The Brooklyn Democratic structure and most Republican county organizations have retained a more "machinelike" organization. The Liberal party is characterized by a high degree of centralization with less emphasis on local clubs.

THE NEGRO IN NEW YORK PARTY POLITICS, 1958–1968

Initially, Negro political influence was limited by the small number of black men living in New York City—in the 1890s Negroes formed only 2 percent of the population.[12] As the Negro population increased, the participation of Negroes in party politics also increased, though never in direct proportion to population. Today Negroes hold numerous district leaderships in local party organizations, city and state legislative positions, judgeships, and supervisory posts in public agencies. However, although blacks now comprise approximately 20 percent of the total New York City population, they hold only about 5 percent of the elective positions in New York, as Table 1 (page 308) indicates.

Negroes have failed to gain influence through party politics for two reasons. First, the unresponsiveness of white party leaders to Negro demands for increased representation and policy-making power. Second, intragroup rivalry and disunity among Negro politicians themselves.

[11] Party Enrollment in Selected Black Assembly Districts, 1966

Assembly District	Republican (%)	Democrat (%)	Liberal (%)
Manhattan			
70	10.97	87.59	1.44
71	14.38	83.48	2.14
72	12.05	86.17	1.78
74	12.82	85.58	1.59
68	12.68	85.96	1.35
Kings			
55	13.86	84.34	1.80
56	16.12	82.18	1.70
37	14.14	84.08	1.78
Queens			
26	14.99	82.48	2.53
Bronx			
78	9.53	88.67	1.80

Source: New York City, Board of Elections, *1966 Survey*, pp. 26–27.

[12] Gilbert Osofsky, *Harlem: The Making of a Ghetto* (New York: Harper & Row, 1966), p. 160.

TABLE 1

Public Positions Held by Ethnic Groups in New York City—1968

	Number of Positions	Percent Jewish (32% of NYC pop)	Percent Italian (11% of NYC pop)	Percent Irish (4% of NYC pop)	Percent Negro (14% of NYC pop)[a]	Percent Puerto Rican (8% of pop)[a]
Civil Court	95	47	28	9	5	1
Criminal Court	77	45	17	11	6	1
Surrogate's Court	6	33	33	33	0	0
Supreme Court (Appellate Div.)	17	47	11	11	5	0
Supreme Court (5 counties)	91	48	16	13	3	1
Court of Appeals	7	28	14	0	0	0
State Assembly	150	38	25	5	5	3
City Council	38	32	13	8	5	2
Congress	19	36	16	32	5	0

[a] The latest figures available on ethnic distribution in the New York City population derive from the 1960 census. The population percentages for each ethnic group cited here are therefore based on 1960 statistics. In 1964, the estimated city population was as follows: 72% white, 18% Negro, 9% Puerto Rican. *Population Characteristics* (New York, New York: New York City Department of Health, April 1966), p. 2, Chart 1. Because of the drop in white population and rise in nonwhite and Puerto Rican group totals, the tendencies shown in this table are even more pronounced.

Source: Data based on Chuck Stone, *Black Political Power in America* (Indianapolis. Bobbs Merrill, 1968), pp. 105–148, 155; *The City of New York Official Directory*, 1968; and Nathan Glazer and Daniel Moynihan, *Beyond the Melting Pot* (Cambridge, Mass.: M.I.T. Press, 1963), Table 2, p. 318.

Unresponsiveness of White Party Leaders

Although most black politicians maintain a strong ideological tie to the party of their choice [13] almost all say they are disenchanted with what their party has accomplished, both for the Negro community and for them personally. Thus, Republicans tend to agree that their party does not really want the Negro vote and has done little to advance the careers of Negro Republicans. Democrats indicate that their party is doing little to actually promote social change. Liberals contend

TABLE 2
Black Perceptions of the "White Power Structure"

	Single Power Structure Based on			
Conspiracy	Economic Contacts	Vested Interests	"Just There"	Power Groupings
2%	44%	24%	13%	17%

that their party has failed to provide the financial resources which would enable them to challenge whites in the major parties. While black nationalist groupings have charged that a monolithic "white power structure" systematically excludes and oppresses Negroes, black politicians tend to disagree among themselves as to the existence and form of such a structure, but to agree, regardless of party, that they have been prevented from exercising a major policy-making role because of their color. Their attitudes may be placed along a continuum, ranging from those who perceive a single political structure, based upon interlocking economic ties, from which Negroes are excluded because of background (similar to the "power elite" of C. Wright Mills); to the view that the "power structure" is based upon the traditional reluctance of those who have power to share it; to the belief that there are several key power groupings (among whom Negroes are not included) who make policy on important issues (similar to the "minorities rule" set forth by Robert Dahl).[14] In this sample, the distribution of attitudes was as is illustrated in Table 2. Thus, although most Negro politicians reject the idea of a conspiratorial "white power structure," all view some aspects of the political structure as having racist overtones. Commonly held views are that "after the job was stripped of its power [the Manhattan Borough presidency, the New York County Leadership] we got it"; that "no Negro leader responsive to the black community gets a good press"; and that attacks on Negro politicians (from former Manhattan Borough President Hulan Jack to Congressman Adam Powell) were racially motivated.

Black politicians feel that they have not been admitted to a full decision-making role within their party. They attribute their inferior status to the hostility and indifference of white party leaders and the increasingly tendency of party and government leaders to circumvent the regular party structure in making appointments and nominations of Negroes to political office.

Negroes seeking political power have met with resistance from whites through

---

[13] Most Negro Democrats view their party as representative of the "little man" and the party most favorable to social change, while Republicans applaud what they see as their party's belief in individualism, private enterprise, and self-reliance.
[14] In *A Preface to Democratic Theory* (Chicago: University of Chicago Press, 1956), p. 45, Dahl speaks of the participation of "active and legitimate" minority groups in the decision-making process.

residential segregation, gerrymandering, district splitting, and the forced formation of "parallel" or segregated clubs. These methods, used historically to nullify Negro political influence even where blacks are a majority of voters, are still effective today. By gerrymandering districts, the 1966 New York State reapportionment cut Negro legislative representation from nine to eight assemblymen and from four to three state senators. Until 1968 Brooklyn's Bedford-Stuyvesant was parcelled out to five congressional districts and denied meaningful representation; only court-ordered reapportionment gave the largest black community in New York a congressional representative.[15] In Queens, predominantly black Corona-East Elmhurst has been divided between white districts, and gerrymandering has prevented the election of a black state senator, city councilman, or congressman. In the Queens Democratic County organization, the 300,000 Negroes who live in Queens are represented by one district leader—whose control has been limited to one-half of a predominantly black Assembly district. And, as recently as the 1960s, several white Democratic clubs in Queens have encouraged the formation of "parallel" clubs, while both Democrats and Republicans in that borough have discouraged Negro membership within the regular clubs.

In each party and borough, Negroes complain of lack of consideration when patronage is allocated and lack of consultation when policies regarding their communities are decided upon. But, in each party, over the past decade Negroes have slowly moved into positions of at least symbolic influence.[16] Most notable of all was the selection of J. Raymond Jones as New York County Democratic leader in 1964. Ironically, although Mayor Wagner's selection of J. Raymond Jones as county leader in 1964 was hailed by observers as a dramatic Negro victory [17] it was (except in a purely symbolic sense) a personal and not a "Negro victory." Jones, a frequent target of criticism within the Harlem community, was chosen as county leader as the "mayor's man"; one Harlem district leader voted for Jones only because of coercion from the mayor. Jones's lack of a strong personal base in Harlem was painfully clear and his position was never secure; he himself agreed that he would "be the first man to go" if his candidate to succeed Wagner as mayor lost.[18] When, in March 1967, Jones left his post, he indicated his lack of grass roots support by citing opposition from Robert Kennedy (the party's dominant white leader) and the ouster of Adam Powell from Congress as the major reasons for his resignation.[19]

---

[15] Almost 500,000 blacks in 1965. Lois Schwartz, *A Capsule History of Bedford-Stuyvesant* (Center for Urban Education, mimeographed).
[16] For example, Edward Dudley has been chairman of the New York County Democratic Committee as has Mark Southall; Ivan Warner has occupied the same role in the Bronx County Committee; Harold Burton is vice-chairman of the New York County Republican Committee; Benjamin McLaurin has been a vice-chairman of the Liberal party in New York State, while Simeon Golar and James Farmer serve at high levels in the party hierarchy. Both Golar and Dudley were nominated by their parties (1962 and 1966, respectively) as candidates for the state attorney generalship. It should be added, however, that even so, while Negroes comprise about 21 percent of the population, they hold only about 5 percent of the political jobs in New York City. See Table 1.
[17] See especially Theodore White, "The Harlem Fox," *Saturday Review*, 43 (May 1960), 4–5, for an earlier point of view along these lines; and Kenneth Clark, *Dark Ghetto* (New York: Harper & Row, 1965), p. 162.
[18] *New York Times*, September 12, 1965.
[19] *New York Times*, March 11, 1967. It is a tribute to Jones's political astuteness that he did retain enough skill and influence to block Senator Kennedy's choice for lieuten-

Increasingly, what "gains" have been made through the party have been offset by the tendency of party and government officials to circumvent the organized political structure in making appointment and nominations, thereby nullifying the influence Negroes have gained there over the past decade. White politicians have turned to blacks outside the party structure who they hope will "legitimize" their administrations and draw in black electoral support.

Republican party leaders, notably Governor Rockefeller, have made appointments by "tapping from above." Governor Rockefeller's policy of superimposing leadership on the black community dates back to 1960, when he appointed his son Rodman to head a "Harlem Planning Committee" intended to provide a liaison between the Negro community and the governor's office, and designated Rodman to head the Negro and Puerto Rican division of the New York State Republican campaign organization. More recently, Rockefeller has selected "name" Negroes, like former baseball player Jackie Robinson and Wyatt T. Walker (formerly an aide to Martin Luther King) as his "special assistants" for Negro affairs. The selection of men without community roots to "represent" the Negro community has been greatly resented by black party leaders. The 1968 nomination of James Farmer (former national CORE Director and another "name" Negro) as the Republican candidate for the new congressional seat to represent Bedford-Stuyvesant is a further example of this "paternalistic" approach to blacks. Imposed on the reluctant local Republican organization by the interference of Rockefeller, Lindsay, and Javits, Farmer was badly defeated by his Democratic opponent.[20]

Ad hoc appointments and nominations of individual Negroes who relate only marginally to the Negro Republican community or to any organized Negro community at all reveal the lack of political power among all Negroes and serve to perpetuate the dependence of Negroes on whites. The Negro politician who, as the elected representative of his community, can maintain constant channels of communication to both a broad-based and relatively stable group of constituents, continues to be overlooked by white political leaders, who apparently prefer to deal with unrepresentative elites and transient community groups. This trend has recently been exacerbated by the increased willingness of government officials to reach out to black "militants" in order to create a liaison with potential "troublemakers" in the hope of preventing riots. As A. W. Singham has written: "One of the clearest indications of the Negroes [sic] continued exclusion from the political system is that the duly elected political leaders are not treated by the power structure as the genuine leaders of the community. This was not the case with the ethnic or other important interest groups who have achieved political power in America."[21]

In contrast to the instances discussed above, the support of Adam Clayton Powell rests upon the black masses. Alone among New York's black politicians, Powell consistently articulated controversial community demands and proposals

---

ant governor at the Party State Convention in 1966 (after Wagner was no longer Mayor).
[20] Running on both the Republican and Liberal lines, Farmer polled 13,615 votes out of a total of 52,933 cast. *New York Times*, November 8, 1968.
[21] A. W. Singham, "The Political Socialization of Marginal Groups" (unpublished paper prepared for the Annual Meeting of the American Political Science Association, September 6–10, 1966), p. 14.

long before other public figures—white or black—did so. Powell's talent has lain not in leading mass trends, but in gauging and giving voice to them.[22] Powell's great strength among the black masses has meant that he has always been sure of continued community support, and because he had that support, opposition from other black politicians has been minimal. Even today, those who say Powell's power is waning refuse to be identified publicly by name.[23] It is worth noting that Powell's recent difficulties came not in New York City, where attempts to denigrate him have been persistent but unsuccessful, and where he was able to influence the content of party and city politics, but in Congress, which bears no relationship to his power base in New York City. Because he retained community support, despite the action of the House of Representatives, Adam Powell remained Harlem's congressman until 1970.

Intragroup Disunity

The second major reason for the failure of party politics to produce meaningful political and social gains has been disunity and rivalry among black politicians themselves. The inability of black politicians to work together in the interests of the community is best seen in the relationship between Adam Clayton Powell, the charismatic spokesman for the black masses, and J. Raymond Jones, the astute party politician. The interests of the black community should have cemented their political alliance, but because of the desire of each man to dominate the same territory, the promise of the United Democratic Leadership Team—which they founded in 1959 to gain greater patronage and increased political influence—was never fulfilled. The failure of Powell and Jones, who had complementary political "styles," to create an enduring relationship is symptomatic of the factional strife which Negro politics in New York embodies. Each year, in New York's black communities, former allies oppose one another. Thus, Harlem district leader George Miller, once a close associate of Manhattan Borough President Percy Sutton, now opposes his former ally. Hostility between J. Raymond Jones and Earl Brown, once a protege of Jones, became so intense that it prevented Manhattan Borough President Edward Dudley from resigning his office for fear of the bitter fight his departure would set off among the rivals.[24] Most attempts by insurgent Negro Republicans in Harlem and by various Democratic insurgent groups elsewhere in the city to oust archaic and ineffective leadership have failed because each splinter group wishes to retain power for itself.

Disunity has been manifest in the inability of black politicians to agree on a unified position on most issues, including the all-important question of party nominations, even nominations of Negroes. Unity is achieved only when a black politician is attacked with what is perceived as racial intent. Thus, when Hulan Jack,

[22] He protested urban renewal which destroyed Negro homes as early as 1958, and called for a Civilian Review Board in 1964, asking also that police play down the use of ammunition in civil disturbances and that investigations of misuse of police authority in such disturbances be held. *New York Times*, March 30, 1958, and July 23, 1964. Powell also often struck out at the New York County leader, the Democratic state chairman, and the mayor when they did not meet his demands for the appointment and nomination of more black men.
[23] *New York Times*, June 19, 1968. Evidently it is still politically risky to openly attack Adam Powell in his home territory.
[24] All three are black, *New York Times*, October 11, 1963.

Manhattan's first black borough president, was ousted from his office because of a bribery charge Harlem district leaders (who had all opposed him in a recent primary) issued a statement declaring "complete confidence in his integrity." [25] In 1966, when J. Raymond Jones and Senator Robert Kennedy feuded over a Surrogate Court nomination, all of New York City's Negro politicians (save just one), many of whom had been frequent critics of Jones, rallied behind the black politician, contending that Kennedy's opposition was "aimed solely at J. Raymond Jones because he is a Negro." [26] The same process was operative when Adam Clayton Powell was ousted from Congress in 1967. Cohesion has, however, been a defensive, negative phenomenon lacking programmatic content and therefore having little impact on the basic content of party policy. While it may be argued that other ethnic groups have been similarly divided in the political process and remain so today, failure to project even the image of cohesiveness cannot fail to be harmful, in view of the small number of black politicians who today participate in party politics.

"Disagreement on ends" [27] is not the source of disunity among Negro leaders. In this study, there appeared to be little ideological conflict between politicians. Thus, virtually all politicians interviewed are NAACP members, but many are critical of the organization's lack of responsiveness to grass roots pressure for greater militancy. On the other hand, few politicians maintain any kind of relationship with black nationalist organizations (four serve on the Advisory Council of CORE and one on the Board of SCLC). While black politicians say they support current community demands for "quality" facilities in the ghetto, to precede eventual integration, none advocate any form of violent revolution, a separatist society, or rediscovery of the African heritage. What the black politician means by his use of the term "Black Power" is the kind of ethnic organization utilized by other groups in our political system. Negro politicians are torn by their desire to identify with a movement that seems to have found some support among the Negro masses and recognition from white society, and their resentment at their own displacement in the public image. Thus, the value of the militants as spokesmen for community demands, racial pride, and ethnic power is applauded by black politicians, while the same politicians criticize the militants as men seeking riches and glory who have little enduring influence on the Negro masses. Although there is a significant feeling among politicians that nationalists provide the publicity and threats, while the politician then follows through with specific programs—seemingly an effective division of labor—most politicians contend that the na-

[25] *Pittsburgh Courier*, New York Edition, December 29, 1959.
[26] *New York Times*, June 10, 1966.
[27] Wilson, *Negro Politics*, p. 169. Wilson, Ladd, and others have sought to differentiate between "styles" of political leadership by classifying black leaders, on the basis of their rhetoric, means, and ends, largely along "militant" and "moderate" lines. However, the attitudes of Negro politicians in New York today toward major "race" issues and goals cannot be placed in the "militant-moderate" classification used by Wilson and Ladd in their studies of black political leadership because such a typology does not accurately reflect present political configurations within the Negro political community.

It should be noted that while other studies of Negro leaders have dealt with different types of Negro leaders, i.e., civic, protest, and party leaders, this study deals only with the party politician, who has traditionally been viewed as a "moderate" because of his vested interest in the survival of the political system and his awareness of the necessity for compromise. See Wilson, *Negro Politics*, p. 301, and Everett Carll Ladd, *Negro Leadership in the South* (Ithaca: Cornell University Press, 1966), pp. 311–318.

tionalists fail because they lack the skills essential to implementation of their demands. Those politicians who call for "Black Power" are often quickest to suggest that, as elected officials, they represent all citizens, not just black men. Similarly, while most politicians say riots have been useful in awakening the society and government to how bad things really are for the Negro, for giving vent to bottled up feelings of frustration and hostility, and for producing some concrete gains, the same men also lament the widespread destruction of Negro property and lives. In addition, these politicians are deeply concerned that communication with whites will henceforth be greatly strained, making eventual change more difficult to bring about, and also that the ultimate result of riots and revolutionary appeals may be repression and fascism. Thus, it appears that most black politicians would agree with Manhattan's Negro Borough President, Percy Sutton, when he advocates "evolution, not revolution" but adds that "the Negro will have to go out and get his equality, it won't come to him."[28] Ideological disagreement, therefore, does not appear to be a major problem among black politicians, although it is likely that the inability of black politicians to decide on precisely what methods and goals are desirable for their communities has lessened the effectiveness of these politicians within party organization and the political process.

Disunity appears to be a function of other factors. The "style" of Negro politics is dependent, at least in part, on the nature of white politics. Thus, the decline of the machine in most areas of New York City has given rise to a fluid and factional political system which has in turn influenced the Negro subsystem.[29] V. O. Key has pointed to the factional effects accompanying dominant one party systems, similar to those in black areas in New York.[30] However, these explanations alone do not account for black political rivalry. Part of the explanation lies in the fact that so many paths have been closed to Negroes. Because of the absence of an entrepreneurial class which would attract ambitious blacks, politics has been a major means for upward mobility. Especially in the Democratic party, which seems to promise the greatest rewards, the number of politically ambitious individuals far exceeds the number of political positions available at one time. Frustration occurs when success appears elusive—aspiring politicians want a "piece of the action" immediately. Because there is no one institutional channel to power (even machine-oriented Brooklyn is run more loosely than Mayor Daley's Chicago), aspirants will take their chances when support is offered by a dissident faction or pressure group.

The difficulty of obtaining financial incentives with which to sustain local support—party patronage in the form of jobs and financial assistance has been scarce in recent years—has also played a role in fragmenting the Negro political community. Conflicts over poverty programs which now provide a major source of political jobs and funding have exacerbated those already present. Because of the great financial burdens (most often borne by the black politician personally)[31] as well as the vast amount of time expended in local political activity, black politicians feel they are particularly entitled to rewards. The onerous aspects of local

[28] *New York Times,* September 30, 1966.
[29] Edward Banfield and James Q. Wilson, *City Politics* (New York: Vintage Books, 1966), p. 304.
[30] V. O. Key, *Southern Politics* (New York: Vintage Books, 1950), pp. 298–310.
[31] Due to the decline of party patronage, the poverty of the black community, and the traditional reluctance of the small black middle class to get involved in politics.

poltical leadership have led to an unwillingness to defer personal political gratification in the name of unspecified community goals.

NEW DEVELOPMENTS IN BLACK POLITICS

Because of the very real failure of black party politics in the past, the importance of parties in the future may well be questioned.

However, at least two relatively recent developments within the black political community appear to hold out some hope for a strengthened political leadership which could enable the Negro to make more effective use of parties.

The New Breed

In recent years, a "new breed" of black politicians has appeared to challenge the "old-timers." Needless to say, these "artificially polarized ideal types" [32] do not find completely accurate reflection in "real life"; they do, however, bear close resemblance to politicians in the black community.

The difference between the "new breeder" and the "old-timer" is a function of age, background, and involvement with the community.[33] While at least some "new breeders" have, under the influence of black nationalism, sought to create a closer relationship with the Negro masses (sometimes even at the risk of antagonizing important party leaders), the "old-timers" have continued to maintain political organizations for a select few and have disdained association with the larger black community.

The "old-timer" is likely to be a poorly educated businessman who perceives the benefits of politics largely in terms of personal rewards. "Old-timers" have been loyal party men, fearing that independence would cost them whatever small patronage they have. Thus in 1967, for example, the eleven black delegates to the New York State Constitutional Convention all supported the proposed State Constitution although it contained a provision to eliminate the state ban on aid to parochial schools—a measure opposed by virtually all liberal and civil rights organizations.[34] "Old-timers," at least in public, reject black nationalism, as one "old-timer" Negro legislator indicated: "I have tried not to be a Negro Assemblyman but an Assemblyman who happened to be Negro. I oppose all separate ethnic organizations—no other group has done it."

The "new breeder," on the other hand, has attempted to defend vigorously the interests of his community, particularly its lower-class members, believing that ultimate political success will rest on mass support.

This new group, composed largely of lawyers (see Table 3) first called for a "New Negro" in politics in the early 1960s, attacking the older politicians as "selfish, timid, and irresponsible," and "too quick to make deals that benefit themselves." They called for "better jobs, better schools, and better housing." [35] Today, many in this group have gained political office and influence.[36]

"New breeders"—who are not limited to one party or county—have frequently

[32] Wilson, *Negro Politics*, p. 214.
[33] Needless to say, all factors do not weigh equally for all involved.
[34] *New York Times*, October 16 and 22, 1967.
[35] *New York Times*, June 6, 1960.
[36] Including Percy Sutton, Basil Paterson, Charles Rangel, Shirley Chisholm.

been leaders of civic groups active in the civil rights movement (especially the NAACP) and the "Reform" movement in their party, as Table 3 indicates.

Because the thrust of such activity has been on improvements for the entire community, "new breeders," verbally at least, deemphasize material and personal rewards. As a result, the "new breeder" politician brings to his party activity a greater awareness of community problems and more interest in maintaining close ties with the community than does the "old-timer." "New breed" clubs are run as "open" institutions, with both diverse membership and vocal criticism encouraged, in contrast to the "old-timer" clubs, where membership is limited to a small loyal group and discipline strictly maintained.

TABLE 3

"New Breeders" and "Old-Timers"

Age	Percent Lawyers	Percent Businessmen	Percent Associated with "Reform"	Percent Leaders of NAACP and Urban League
Over 45	19	37	2	9
Under 45	48	9	21	25

Most "new breeders" appear to place less faith in strict adherence to the "party line"; rather, they stress the value of two party competition. This includes both Democrats and Republicans, although only the latter would obtain the most immediate and obvious advantages. In addition to the desire, as one city official put it, "to get a divorce from the Democratic party," some "new breeders" have demonstrated independence of their party on key policy decisions. In Brooklyn's Bedford-Stuyvesant, "new breeders" have successfully "bucked" the machine by running their own primary candidates. In Manhattan, Borough President Sutton and State Senator Paterson spoke out openly against the 1967 State Constitution, placing themselves in opposition to party leaders (and most of their fellow Negro politicians). Sutton stated that this was "clearly not a party issue, but a question of conscience and judgment." [37]

Political independence has been manifested in other ways as well. "New breeders" have publicly espoused a moderate form of "Black Power." Thus, a black Queens Republican asserted that "Stokely Carmichael and other advocates of black power have been good for the country because they have made Negroes start talking about themselves and flushed out white backlash," [38] while two Harlem candidates based a recent campaign on the slogan "blackness is greatness." "New breeders" have also attempted to demonstrate solidarity with the masses by speaking out on controversial issues of interest to the community: "new breed" legislators from Harlem led a fight to prevent Columbia University from building a gymnasium in Harlem's Morningside Park and sponsored a bill in the State Legislature requesting that Harlem be made into a separate school district. Manhattan Borough President Percy Sutton publicly criticized his colleagues on the Board of Estimate after he had failed to persuade them to rescind bills closing a Harlem hospital, leasing Morningside Park to Columbia University, and building

---

[37] *New York Times*, October 26, 1967. Shirley Chisholm and William Thompson also said they opposed the Constitution when questioned.
[38] *New York Times*, November 3, 1967.

a sewage plant in West Harlem, stating: "these are the indignities that make people feel they are not equal. As the only black representative on the Board, I am trying to communicate these feelings to you. I am hurt, deeply hurt that you do not understand what you are doing to Harlem." [39] In all of these instances, "new breed" politicians are attempting to emulate and perhaps surpass the master politician, Adam Clayton Powell, in gauging community trends and articulating them so as to build a mass base of support from which to seek political power.

The "new breed" sense of power and independence is also manifest in attempts by Negro politicians to exert unified pressure within the party structure. Black politicians—who have often been insecure and fragmented in the political process and have therefore failed to use even the limited resources available to them—say they will demand power rather than depend on "good will." The most significant result of this new attitude was the effort in late 1965 by Negro Democrats to organize a pressure group within the Democratic party. A "White Paper" was issued by Negro legislators and district leaders which declared: "We no longer want some tokens which will take us on a subway ride; we want some bread, some meat and a slice of pie; the same as any other group receives in our political system." [40] The group announced the formation of the Council of Elected Negro Democrats which promised to "advance candidates, establish policies and initiate programs," and assailed the party for having "blacked out" Negroes from important policy-making positions.[41] Several immediate gains were achieved by the group—for the first time a Negro was appointed as legislative leader in the State Assembly, and Negroes were appointed to key committees which had never had Negro membership before.[42] Since then, the council has voted as a bloc in Albany, however unsuccessfully, against bills considered racist (such as a $300 million State cut in Medicaid funds), and collective stands have been taken on such issues as a proposed Harlem sewage plant and a planned Queens expressway which would uproot many Negroes.

The establishment of the council has institutionalized the concept of bloc coordination on issues and created a base from which to present collective demands to the Democratic Party. As yet the council has encountered few successes and many defeats, largely because the number of black officeholders is sufficiently small that (except in unusual circumstances) black politicians may be overlooked with impunity. Ultimately, however, the council may enable the Negro politician to become part of the "power structure" within the party, rather than simply influencing those in power, as is now still the case.

[39] *New York Times*, May 3, 1968.
[40] *Amsterdam News*, December 18, 1965. It should be noted that following the Goldwater nomination in 1964, Negro Republicans formed the National Negro Republican Assembly to gain a larger state and national policy-making role. The New York regional grouping quickly became the most prominent. But although Negro Republicans agreed on the principle of bloc pressure within the party, the idea was never implemented, because of a power struggle within the group. Today, the NNRA remains the ineffective, paper organization it has always been.
[41] *New York Courier*, December 25, 1965.
[42] Bertram Baker, the senior Negro in the Assembly (and the only Negro nonmember of the Council), was appointed Majority Whip; Percy Sutton was placed on the Banks and Rules Committees; Bertram Baker on Rules and Ways and Means, the latter together with Mark Southall. Subsequently, Negroes came to head the Senate and Assembly Education Committees.

Black Nationalism and Party Politics

The growing importance of nationalism in the black community is not inconsistent with party organization and may, in fact, serve to make party politics effective for the black man.[43] Increased ethnic consciousness could create bloc solidarity which, in turn, could overcome the two major reasons for the past failure of parties to provide access to power for the black man: the hostility and unresponsiveness of white party leaders to black demands, and the petty competition of black political life.

Bloc solidarity may enable the black politician to present white party leaders with a strengthened "power base," controlling sufficient votes within both the electorate and the party to challenge past indifference to the needs of the black community. A meaningful threat to withhold support if black demands are not met will achieve more gains for the black man than reliance on the "good will" of white party officials. By emphasizing group gains rather than personal concerns, bloc solidarity may also prevent some of the disunity and personal rivalry which has characterized black politics in New York City. In order to be relevant, the black politician will have to emerge as a community leader, responsive to the demands of the black community.[44]

The concept of ethnic solidarity has already begun to create an effective "division of labor" between what James Q. Wilson has called "diverging" civic and political elites.[45] Although Wilson has argued that "cooperation (and sometimes even coexistence) seem impossible" among such groups, because of the difficulty of agreeing on goals, the differing interests, temperaments, and social backgrounds of the groups, and competition for scarce resources,[46] this view is not necessarily correct. For although community groups have been successful in politicizing a sizable number of black people (particularly young people) by drawing them into action organizations which stress issues and programs, no civic or protest group in New York has yet demonstrated either strength at the ballot box or enduring influence in the policy-making process. Thus, a new pattern could emerge in black politics, one in which protest groups articulate and publicize community demands and the politician utilizes his position within party and governmental structures in order to bargain for the implementation of these demands. The interview data gathered in this study indicate that such a "division of labor" may already exist, in an inchoate manner. And, the attempts of black politicians to "follow through" on controversial demands first articulated by protest groups (e.g., the Columbia Gym, a separate Harlem school district, and, most recently,

---

[43] Nationalism in this context implies solidarity. This term was suggested by Charles Hamilton in comments delivered on September 5, 1968 (Annual Meeting of the American Political Science Association, Washington, D.C.). Hamilton classified "black power" as having five basic meanings: black capitalism, solidarity, take-over through warfare, pluralism, separatism.

[44] As Richard Young suggests in a perceptive article on black politics in San Francisco: "Negro politicians have become responsive not only to the demands of the city as a whole, but also to the demands of the Negro masses as articulated by the Negro protest groups." In "The Impact of Protest Leadership on Negro Politicians in San Francisco," *Western Political Quarterly*, 22 (March 1969), 110.

[45] Wilson, *Negro Politics*, p. 333.

[46] James Q. Wilson, "The Strategy of Protest: Problems of Negro Civic Action," reprinted in Harry A. Bailey, Jr. (ed.), *Negro Politics in America* (Columbus, Ohio: Charles E. Merrill, 1967), p. 65.

the abandonment of plans to construct a State Office building in Harlem) provide additional evidence that a new relationship is developing between the two groups of leaders. In his discussion of Negro leadership, Jack Walker has suggested the efficacy of "unanticipated cooperation and sharing of functions" between protest and moderate leaders.[47] While community protest groups have gained a new place in black political life, they have not obviated the need for and function of political party organization.

THE RELEVANCE OF PARTY POLITICS TO THE BLACK MAN

As the black population of New York City increases (within the total population of the city and within each of the counties) [48] and becomes increasingly nationalistic, it appears that the "new breed" will be able to make better use of party politics. Party organization has several advantages over other types of political activity for the Negro although the relevance of party politics for black people has often been either ignored or denigrated by political scientists.

James Q. Wilson, perhaps the foremost analyst of trends both within Negro and urban politics, asserts that "Negro politics will accomplish only limited objectives" since the issues at stake are "economic and cultural, not political and legal." [49] To Wilson, American political institutions can provide no way for the organized pressure of a particular disadvantaged group to fundamentally reshape social and economic conditions.

Wilson overlooks the fact that political parties can be used to "facilitate the translation of popular interests and needs into authoritative legislative and administrative enactment," and can offset other types of political influence such as those based on wealth and influence.[50] The distinction made by Wilson between "political" and "economic" issues is untenable because probably the most important task of government is the allocation of economic resources to competing groups, or, put another way, "Who gets what, when, and why." That economic change can

---

[47] Jack Walker, "A Case Study of Negro Leadership in Atlanta, Georgia," in Bailey (ed.), *Negro Politics in America*, p. 132.

[48] The Negro population of New York City, estimated at 14 percent in 1960, is now estimated at 21 percent. Harlem, which contained two-thirds of the New York Negro population in 1940, has little more than a third today. From 1950 to 1960, the Negro population in the four boroughs changed as follows:

	Percent in 1950	Percent in 1960
Bronx	6.9	11.5
Manhattan	20.6	28.4
Brooklyn	7.8	14.1
Queens	3.5	8.1

Source: U.S. Bureau of the Census, *County and City Data Book, 1967*, Table 4. See also Report, Commission on Intergroup Relations, City of New York, 1961, cited in Glazer and Moynihan, *Beyond the Melting Pot*, p. 56.

[49] Wilson, "The Negro in Politics," pp. 232, 246.
[50] Allan P. Sindler, *Political Parties in the United States* (New York: St. Martin's Press, 1966), p. 11.

be brought about through politics is clearly illustrated by the successful political struggle mounted by organized labor several decades ago. While the problems faced by Negroes cannot be equated with those faced by labor, nevertheless the alliance between labor and the Democratic party is evidence of the importance of effective political organization.

Party politicians are able to gain for themselves and those they represent what Sorauf has called "preferments"—special treatment by government.[51] The Riot Commission Report notes that the middle-class city dweller can move "the system" to his benefit by calling on the assistance of elected representatives and friends in government.[52] Today, such important contacts are still largely limited to white groups.

At the very least, party politics provides a route of mobility for New York Negroes, permitting them entry to the middle class; the politicians, in turn, provide increased employment opportunities for other Negroes in government. In the absence of the political party, many political jobs would be closed to the Negro because he lacks "proper qualifications."

Finally, even if Wilson is correct in believing that "Negro politics may accomplish only limited objectives," this is not an argument against the effective use of party politics. Although absolute goals can rarely be realized through politics, because politics involves compromise, some goals can be achieved through effective organization.

Wilson, preferring interest group politics to party politics as a vehicle for black political aspirations, rejects what he calls the "grand alliance concept" and calls instead for "many different and conflicting alliances which would take into account the different kinds of support available for different kinds of issues." [53] However, as Carmichael and Hamilton have suggested in *Black Power*, short-term alliances on relatively minor issues "seldom come to terms with the root of institutional racism." [54] Such short-term coalitions may actually retard the resolution of more meaningful and conflicting issues. A meaningful alliance is not just agreement on a given issue; it should provide a mechanism for bargaining and compromise, when each group must be forced to give up something in order to gain the other's support. The political party provides an institutional mechanism through which distinct political interests may come together, work out disagreements, and agree on joint policies of mutual benefit. If it is acknowledged that the support of other groups is necessary for Negro political progress, as Wilson and the Riot Commission Report agree, and the black leaders vigorously assert,[55] the political framework for coalition politics may be found in the party.

[51] Frank Sorauf, *Political Parties in the American System* (Boston: Little, Brown, 1964), p. 82.
[52] *Riot Report*, p. 285.
[53] Wilson, "The Negro in Politics," p. 234.
[54] Stokely Carmichael and Charles Hamilton, *Black Power* (New York: Vintage Books, 1967), p. 79. According to Hamilton and Carmichael, such coalitions tend to convince both whites and blacks that either there are no difficult problems to solve, or that minor problems are the only ones capable of solution.
[55] Wilson, "The Negro in Politics," p. 234; *Riot Report*, p. 287; see also, Martin Luther King, *Where Do We Go From Here* (Boston: Beacon Press, 1968), pp. 150–151; Bayard Rustin, "From Protest to Politics," in Irving Howe (ed.), *The Radical Papers* (New York: Doubleday & Company, 1966), pp. 347–361; and Carmichael and Hamilton, *Black Power*, pp. 77–84, on the need for allies among liberals, religious groups, labor, and "poor whites."

Wilson, however, attacks parties for this very reason. He contends that parties constrain their members: "the city-wide political apparatus" makes of its participants "politicians first and Negroes second." [56] Wilson turns to indigenous, nonpartisan community organizations, which are free of "constraints"—or external limits on their effectiveness,[57] finding them better suited to black needs.

It should be noted that constraints in themselves lack importance. What is important is the result which any group can achieve. Thus, a Harlem street-corner speaker orating on 125th Street may be remarkably free of external constraints, but his influence on public policy is minimal. Moreover, the internal "constraints" on exclusively ideological community groups may be at least as restrictive for these groups as party membership is for the politician.[58] Community groups are often ideologically "overcommitted," so that they are not adaptable to the process of compromise required on any coalition grouping. In any event, community groups will have to turn to traditional politics if they wish to consolidate limited gains, and they, too, will be subject to the "constraints" of political office, often with little concomitant responsibility to any organized group of constituents.

Moreover, the indigenous nonpartisan groups cited by Wilson are ill-suited to the creation of a lasting power base. Competing community groups can only serve to deter the black political unity which virtually all black leaders see as essential to political progress.[59] The existence of many community groups and their leaders serves to diffuse political activity by fostering competition for scarce financial resources. In addition, the presence of many transient ad hoc political groupings may confuse whites as to which Negroes should be dealt with and, conversely, may allow for greater manipulation by whites, in either instance preventing the creation of a durable political alliance.

A final major objection to the utility of party politics for the Negro has also been suggested by James Q. Wilson. He has said that Negroes will be unable to take advantage of party politics because the black vote is tied to the Democratic party. As a result of this one-way relationship, the Republicans have abandoned all efforts to obtain Negro support, and the Democrats take the black vote for granted. Because of this, a black "balance of power" vote has never materialized in New York, and the Negro community, it is said, has suffered politically.[60] While this may be a serious problem, it should be noted that both the Jews and organized labor have been able to exercise considerable pressure and influence through association with only one party. In addition, many black politicians today are increasingly conscious of this one-way relationship, and some black Democrats, stressing their independence of party, have gone so far as to encourage the

[56] Wilson, "The Negro in Politics," p. 242; and Banfield and Wilson, *City Politics*, p. 293.
[57] Wilson, "The Negro in Politics," p. 242.
[58] Wilson himself has recognized this on other occasions. See James Q. Wilson, *The Amateur Democrat* (Chicago: University of Chicago Press, 1962), pp. 340–370. See also Michael Lipsky, "Protest as a Political Resource," *American Political Science Review*, 62 (December 1968), 1118–1151.
[59] Rustin "From Protest to Politics," p. 257; King, *Where Do We Go From Here*, pp. 148–150; Carmichael and Hamilton, *Black Power*, pp. 79–81; and Eldridge Cleaver, *Soul on Ice* (New York: Dell Publishing Co., 1968), pp. 125–126.
[60] Wilson, "The Negro in Politics," p. 241. See also Chuck Stone, *Black Political Power in America* (Indianapolis: Bobbs-Merrill, 1968), p. 57, and Henry Lee Moon, *Balance of Power: The Negro Vote* (Garden City, N.Y.: Doubleday & Company, 1948), for presentations of this view.

formation of new Republican clubs in their areas to frighten the Democratic party into action.

The political party provides enduring, clearly identifiable organization, which maintains stability of support and continuous access to government and other political groupings,[61] and which rests on indigenous leadership. Of the alternative forms of political activity which have been suggested for the black community, only the party meets these criteria.[62] Alternative forms include the Urban Action Task Force recommended by the National Advisory Commission on Civil Disorders, the poverty program, and ad hoc appointments of blacks to political office.

Programs like the Urban Action Task Force, which would bring together community people and city agency heads for discussions of grievances and formulation of programs, do represent a serious attempt to reach out to the ghetto. However, the Riot Commission's selection of the Task Force as the means of achieving "effective communication" between ghetto residents and local government misses the point.[63] Electing Negroes to public office can provide a means of communication: there appears to be little reason to create a new institution simply to further this goal. The aim should be greater participation by blacks in the decision-making process, rather than the "communication" of problems to white decision makers. Hence, the Task Force is not a meaningful alternative to the "indigenous leadership," whose importance the commission has recognized but has ignored in its recommendations.[64] Actually the goal of the Task Force is not the development of leadership at all, but rather that of providing temporary responses to community demands to forestall riots. The city officials who are the liaison men between the community and the city in the Task Force are selected by the mayor, and these officials in turn select the community people with whom they will work; the program is doubly removed from local determination. The commission itself recognizes that the Task Force would depend on the "continuing commitment of the Administration to (its) success." [65] For these reasons the Task Force does not provide a meaningful alternative to locally organized and directed political activity.

The commission's recommendation urging that "Negro representation and participation . . . can be furthered by a concerted effort to appoint Negroes to sig-

---

[61] William Chambers, *Political Parties in a New Nation* (New York: Oxford University Press, 1963), pp. 45–49. See also Robert Lewis Bowman, "Negro Politics in Four Southern Counties" (unpublished Ph.D. dissertation, University of North Carolina, Chapel Hill, 1964), for conclusions similar to mine on the superiority of a single broadly representative group to either unrepresentative elites or ad hoc community groups.

[62] A third all-black political party is not necessarily inconsistent with the concept of party utilized here, if—and only if—such a party could supply unity to the black community by providing a focus for political action while maintaining access to established party and government groupings. Such a party could, like the Liberal party in New York City politics, be a significant force in city politics by providing the margin of victory for one of the major parties, thereby influencing major party nominations and policies. Such a party would have to play the political game with consummate skill, harnessing the power of black nationalism in order to gain greater benefits in coalition with other, and necessarily white, allies.

[63] *Riot Report*, p. 228.
[64] *Riot Report*, p. 228.
[65] *Riot Report*, p. 291.

nificant policy positions" is subject to similar reservations.[66] Appointments, as they are most often made, serve to perpetuate the existing system in which whites select Negro leaders and confer the mantle of power upon them. "Experts" who lack a community base are entirely dependent upon the good graces of their employers and, because of the absence of institutionalized channels to the community, are often unresponsive to the needs of the black masses.

It should be noted that the "community action" program of the "War on Poverty," while providing opportunity for the development of various leadership skills, is not an alternative to party organization. Poverty programs combine the problems of the Urban Action Task Force, ad hoc appointments, and nonpartisan community groups. For one thing, because the source of poverty funding is outside the local community, the source of power does not rest with local people. Most observers agree also that the use of government resources in antipoverty programs greatly constrains the articulation of community demands, particularly when powerful established interests are threatened.[67] And, in addition, the competition among local groups—each claiming mass support—makes it difficult to allocate poverty funds and fosters rivalry and hostility, rather than unity, among blacks.[68]

Numerous political scientists, however, have pointed to the erosion of party influence on the election process, patronage, and appointments, while professional organizations and organized bureaucracies have increased their influence.[69] It is said that the widespread acceptance of "good government" principles has produced an increased emphasis on "expertise" and a preference for "nonclub types" in government. Thus it is contended that the traditional party structure would appear to be a dead end: "a ladder missing most of its rungs." [70]

It cannot be denied that there are stresses in the urban political system which were not present for earlier ethnic groups trying to make their way in politics. However, parties are not yet dead. Although the decline of job patronage has removed the major material incentive to party organization, it is well to remember that patronage does not consist only of political jobs. Business and legal contacts provide substantial benefits to party activists today.[71]

And, equally important, it is clear that material incentives are by no means the

[66] *Riot Report*, p. 296.
[67] See Daniel Moynihan, *Maximum Feasible Misunderstanding* (New York: Free Press, 1969), especially pp. 153–161, and Sar A. Levitan, *The Great Society's Poor Law* (Baltimore: Johns Hopkins Press, 1969), p. 111.
[68] Moynihan, *Maximum Feasible Misunderstanding*, pp. 125–126. It is possible, however, that although the Poverty program does not provide an alternative to the party, the Neighborhood Board Organization, which comprises part of the "community action" program and includes block-by-block representation (similar to precinct organization in the old-time clubs), could form the nuclei for new political clubs, to merge with the prevailing party organization when they are strong enough to maintain independent support.
[69] Sayre and Kaufman, *Governing New York City*, p. 219; Sorauf, *Political Parties in the American System*, p. 108; Banfield and Wilson, *City Politics*, p. 334; Theodore Lowi, *At the Pleasure of the Mayor* (New York: Free Press, 1964), pp. 199, 221; and James Q. Wilson, "The Changing Political Position of the Negro," in Arnold Rose (ed.), *Assuring Freedom to the Free* (Detroit: Wayne State University Press, 1964), p. 169.
[70] Wilson, "The Negro in Politics," p. 238.
[71] See *New York Times*, June 17, 1968, on the increase in lucrative patronage in New York State.

only ones which motivate people to join political organizations. What Wilson and Clark have called "purposive" incentives are also operative.[72] These incentives, which emphasize achievement of intangible goals rather than concrete political rewards, may well be ideally suited to the ideological mood of the black community today. It is important to note that among New York's Negro politicians, Adam Clayton Powell, who never maintained a traditional club organization and who was by far the black politician most oriented to articulation of black ideological demands, was able to gain the greatest popularity and also the greatest power and influence. Powell's success indicates that the effective use of ideological incentives can provide a route to political power and a continuing source of power once in office.

CONCLUSION

The National Advisory Commission on Civil Disorders and numerous political scientists believe that the traditional party system is irrelevant to the black community and that other forms of political organization are better suited to the Negro's quest for social change. However, although in the past political parties have played a clearly marginal role in the black struggle for equality, it is likely that in the future more effective use will be made of party politics by the black community. Increasing militancy and ethnic consciousness may well cause the Negro to turn away from the short-run, limited policy-making alternatives offered by other political institutions and toward the political party.

[72] James Q. Wilson and Peter B. Clark, "Incentive Systems: A Theory of Organizations," *Administrative Science Quarterly*, 6 (September 1961), 129–166.

28
Subcommunity Leadership in a Black Ghetto: A Study of Newark, New Jersey

Marian Lief Palley
Robert Russo
Edward Scott

PROFILE OF THE CITY

Newark, New Jersey, is a city with a population of just over 400,000. Its population has not increased significantly since 1960—perhaps 5000 or 6000 people—but the city's racial composition has shifted. In 1960, 34 percent of Newark's population were black. In 1967, 52 percent of Newark's population were black. In 1969, 54 percent of the city's people were black, and 10 percent were Puerto Rican. A large portion of the white population is of Italian ancestry. This increasingly nonwhite city is located in the New York Metropolitan area less than ten miles from New York City. In addition to being located in the New York City suburban ring, Newark is a central city in its own right. It has significant business and commercial enterprises, with several large insurance companies situated in the area.

Most of the residential sections of Newark are racially and ethnically defined, with the vast majority of blacks living in the oldest sections of the city. The age distributions vary from black to white areas in Newark. Forty-three percent of Newark's black population are under sixteen years of age, and only 8 percent are over fifty-four years of age. In the Central Ward, the section in which the 1967

From *Urban Affairs Quarterly* (March 1970). Reprinted by permission of publisher and authors.

civil disorders erupted, over one-half of the people are under sixteen years of age. In the white sections of the city, 22 percent of the people are under sixteen years of age and 27 percent are over fifty-four. Thus the black population in Newark is much younger than the white population.[1]

There has been substantial, overt, racial unrest since August 1967. In both black and white neighborhoods, local vigilante groups have developed to protect the local residents; often this has led to even greater intensification of fear and hatred between the races.

POLITICAL LEADERSHIP STUDY

After the serious civil disorders Newark experienced during the summer of 1967, it became evident that the political leadership in the black community was no longer drawn primarily from the traditional church and business elites which historically are associated with leadership in America's black ghettos. It was important, therefore, in order to understand the political process within the black subcommunity and the political process between the black subcommunity and the larger multiethnic Newark community, to determine whom the black population perceives as its leaders since the church and business elites have lost much of their political influence within the ghetto. It was also significant to comprehend the sociopolitical orientations of the current leaders since their views and actions may affect the nature of political activity and social order both for the largest racial group in the city and for the larger community of Newark.

In order to gain a better understanding of the future of politics in Newark's black ghetto and in the city of Newark as well, it was also useful to learn about the backgrounds of the community leadership. It was the contention of the authors at the outset of this study that various types of background variables might influence a person's orientation. Thus, each respondent's age, income, education, occupation, and place of residency was examined in order to determine relationships between sociopolitical orientation and background. Specifically the relationship between age and group preference was considered because of the well-publicized strains between youth and adults in the United States today. If world youth in general is more militant than their parents, it was assumed that black youth would be more militant than their parents. This possibility was interesting to examine in Newark because of the reports of arrests which were published after the August 1967 conflagration. During these disorders, 75 percent of all those black people arrested were less than thirty-two years old, and 50 percent of all blacks arrested were less than twenty-four (see Governor's Select Commission on Civil Disorders, 1968: 130).[2]

It was assumed that a growing number of Newark's black leaders, as they are perceived by the black community itself, were not reacting to society within the context of America's liberal democratic tradition (see Hartz, 1955: 270) because they did not perceive the institutions of traditional American society as relevant to individual and group success experience in the black ghetto (see Cleaver, 1968: 58). (We call these individual "radicals.") It was also assumed that there has been an increasing sense of urgency among black leaders leading to more mil-

[1] The statistics cited were drawn from the Institute of Management and Labor Relations (1967).
[2] References are listed at end of this selection.

itancy since the summer of 1967. In addition, it was believed that those individuals most likely to accept the traditional, liberal approaches to social, economic, and political change would be more successful members of the black community in terms of social, economic, and political achievement. Thus if a continuum were constructed with all of the respondents in this study placed along it, those individuals seeking to alter the fundamental underpinnings of society would be placed at the left of the continuum and would be labeled "radicals." People who advocated rapid change, but were generally satisfied with the basic political processes of American society, would be placed at the center of the continuum and would be labeled "militants." Those leaders who were reasonably well satisfied with the current methods and modes of change would be placed at the right of the continuum and would be labeled "traditionals."

The Study Approach

This is a report of a study of Newark's black leadership based upon a survey of twenty-five black leaders active in community affairs. This is not intended to be a statement of the findings and methods of other social scientists, or a compendium of alternative approaches to the study of subcommunity leadership.

In January and February 1968, the respondents were asked questions (in individual personal interviews) concerning their attitudes on the social, political, and economic status of the black community in Newark, and on government and politics generally. Opinions were also sought on matters of particular importance to the city's black community, such as the building of a university medical school with the concurrent relocation of black residents out of the area, the civil disorder of 1967, and the possibility of electing black city officials. This paper will report on the clustering of rights-group affiliations as an indicator of the degree of radicalism prevalent among Newark's black leaders, and on preferred modes of participation to enhance change—group action as opposed to individual action. The responses to those questions concerned with rights-group affiliation and preferred methods of participation to enhance change has permitted the relative placing of the leaders questioned on the "radical-militant-traditional" continuum, and thus the clustering of individuals into these three categories for the purpose of analysis.

In addition, information on each respondent's age, income, education, occupation, place of birth, and current residency was made available to the interviewers by each of the participating respondents. These specific background variables were chosen for inclusion in this study for very specific reasons. Since the original assumption was that an individual's socioeconomic status would be the best indicator of one's position on the radical-militant-traditional continuum, income, occupation, education, and place of residence were included as components of socioeconomic status. Age was included as an additional test variable because of reports on the 1967 disorders in Newark which noted that most of the arrested rioters were youths. Using these five background variables, a background profile was developed for each of the individual leaders and then for each of the different types of leaders—radical, militant, traditional.

All of Newark's black leaders were probably not contacted, but certainly a good cross-section of this subcommunity's leadership was interviewed. Only the problem of determining who are the leaders made a complete and exhaustive study impossible. "Leadership," of course, can be defined variously. Consequently, most of the people interviewed had differing opinions as to who were the "real leaders" in the city's black community. Furthermore, many of the people contacted discounted themselves as leaders. (These comments were "brushed aside" as expressions of modesty.) The leadership sample for this study was derived by using a reputational approach. That is, initially the highest ranking black person in the Board of Education, the director of the Newark community services, the leader of a large civil rights organization, and a black minister were contacted and interviewed. Each of these individuals was asked to name five black leaders who they thought were important in Newark. If a person's name was mentioned two or more times, he was contacted and asked to participate in the study. When these people were interviewed, they were asked also to name five black leaders who they thought were important in Newark. Again, if a person's name was mentioned two or more times he was contacted and asked to participate in this study. This process of contacting individuals for inclusion in the sample continued until twenty-five black leaders had been interviewed. Therefore, the individuals interviewed were the leaders of the black community as perceived by the black community, and not by a white-controlled business community, a white press, or a white political organization. Another consequence of using this approach was the inclusion in the sample of people who are active in the "grass roots" programs being carried on in the ghetto.

Grass-roots projects (some funded by the Office of Economic Opportunity), the local area planning boards, and the Welfare Rights Organization served as sources for contacting noncitywide, subcommunity leaders. Hence, due to the definition of leadership utilized in this study, the fact that contacts were largely active black leaders themselves, and the desire to obtain general black viewpoints, more black-perceived "real leaders" were interviewed. The formal chairmen of organizations were interviewed as well as some of the "activists" within those organizations. Men and women involved at the grass-roots level were reached as were those individuals who are heard at city hall by virtue of their names and positions. While concentrated on leaders least "removed" from the ghetto population, this study utilizes a fairly broad cross-section of the opinions and viewpoints of Newark's black leadership; it is not exhaustive, however.

The Methods

In framing a questionnaire for this study, there was an attempt to determine the specific attitudes and opinions of the individual respondents; there was also a need to gather background information for inclusion as dependent variables for later analysis.

The background information which was collected was related to age, employment, residence, education, family status, and income. Before the analysis of the data commenced, each of these six variables was categorized in the manner shown on the facing page.

In analyzing responses to the attitude and opinion questions, responses were also categorized on a 1–2–3 continuum. Number 1 represented the general category of radical; number 2 signified a response which was militant, that is, moderate; and number 3 represented the most moderate response possible, that is, traditional. The scores given to responses by the leadership sample were determined

Age	Employment	Residence
1. 20–30	1. Community action, poverty program, and civil rights group work	1. Born in South, live in Newark presently
2. 30–40	2. "Private" employment	2. Lifelong Newark resident
3. 40–50	3. Government work (that is, direct government employment)	3. Lived in Newark previously; now reside outside

Education	Family Status	Income
1. Elementary	1. Single	1. $4000–6000
2. High school	2. Married; 1–4 children	2. $6000–10,000
3. College	3. Married; 4 or more children	3. $10,000 and above

by a panel of three judges working independently of each other. The three judges included two of the authors of this study and a black school teacher from Newark. An average score from the scores submitted by the three judges was tabulated for all of the answers, and these scores were than used as response scores for each of the items. It is important to note that the third category of leaders being referred to in this study is traditional, and not conservative in the usual sense of the word.

By looking at the array of a respondent's answers, it was possible to derive an overall picture of an individual black leader; thus each respondent can be categorized by averaging his numerical responses. Needless to say, there were few ideal types—straight 1s, 2s or 3s—since few leaders were totally consistent in their responses. The individual leaders, as the overall sample itself, represent a mixture of attitudes and opinions. The numerical ratings of the black leaders ranged from 1.2 (most radical) to 2.6 (most traditional), with clear majority of the leaders with a score less than 2 (i.e., to the left of center on the scale). The average score, 1.6, which is clearly between militant and radical, reflects the overall militant attitude of the black leaders in the sample. The prevalence of scores less than 2 also reflects the general "unity" of the leadership on most of the issues raised in the interviews.

In order to facilitate the analysis of data (all of which is nominal data), contingency tables and graphs were constructed to show relationships between the independent variables (attitudes and opinions) and the dependent variables (backgrounds factors). And, as is noted above, a militancy score was tabulated for each of the respondents on the basis of answers to the questions posed to him at the interview. The score for each of the leaders was then placed on a continuum to determine the distribution of the respondents on the radical-militant-traditional continuum.

THE FINDINGS OF THE STUDY

Civil Rights Group Orientation

The results of the first area of questioning were significant and central to the overall findings of this study, for it is in large part the identification with certain civil rights groups which indicates a leader's "degree of militancy."

The individuals in the leadership sample were asked about membership in, and preference for, local civil rights organizations. The responses, as indicated by Table 1, were largely positive ratings for the more militant groups and generally negative opinions for the more traditional organizations.

TABLE 1

Civil Rights Group Preferences

Organization	Approximate Percentage	Number
Traditional		
Urban League	3	1
National Association for the Advancement of Colored People (NAACP)	17	4
Militant		
Congress of Racial Equality (CORE)	48	12
Radical		
Student Nonviolent Coordinating Committee (SNCC)	12	3
United Afro-American Association	12	3
Revolutionary Action Movement (RAM)	8	2

Out of the sample of twenty-five leaders, 48 percent indicated a preference for CORE's local Newark-Essex chapter. Some 12 percent indicated a preference for SNCC, 12 percent for the more recently formed Afro-American Association (a Black Nationalist organization), and about 8 percent for RAM (a black revolutionary group). Hence, nearly 80 percent of the black leadership interviewed favored militant to radical civil rights organizations, with CORE (termed by some as "militant and yet responsible") receiving the strongest overall support. The strictly radical groups received a combined favorable rating of about 30 percent—relatively large by most standards.

Indeed, the radical groups received a higher rating for the members of this sample than did the traditional organizations—the Urban League and the NAACP—which received a combined total of only 20 percent support. With the Urban League barely mentioned, it is the NAACP which makes up the bulk of this 20 percent traditional support. More significant than the small positive rating it received from Newark's black leaders, however, is the large number of those interviewed who expressed openly negative and hostile opinions of the local NAACP. A clear majority of those questioned—approximately 60 percent—rejected the NAACP locally, calling it "part of the establishment," "City Hall owned," "out of touch," or even "dead" in Newark. This negative black reaction stems partly from the inability or unwillingness of traditional organizations to push actively for social change or to maintain contact with the grass-roots community. Moreover, many black leaders contend that the NAACP is particularly "ineffective," inept, and lacking in leadership. Indeed, the "old line" leaders of the NAACP are claimed to have sold out to the "white power structure," and are tainted by their long association with Mayor Hugh Addonizio's political machine which controls city hall in Newark.

But if the traditional organizations like the NAACP have not provided much of the needed leadership, the vacuum they have left is apparently being filled by the local chapter of CORE. This militant organization is most often praised for being just what NAACP is not: active, "in touch" with the local community, and independent of City Hall domination. This generally favorable response to the more militant groups may indicate an overall shift in orientation among the city's black leadership from a relatively moderate and traditional to a more militant and even radical position.

It is significant to note that, although there is a general rejection of traditional organizations, there is a more or less open-minded attitude towards the newer radical and revolutionary groups, some of which preach the use of violence as the only effective instrument to foster change. Though many of the leaders voiced disagreement with some of the positions and tactics of these radical groups, they refrain from condemning them (as they might have been inclined to do in the past), and even acknowledge that they are an increasingly important force in the ghetto and have a definite role to play in the black community.

The main criticism of the radical groups like SNCC and RAM was that they have not been effective in getting action on major problems; they address themselves to small, less significant matters and emotional issues which are often not of prime importance to ghetto residents. Their goals were said to be short range, and their programs were viewed as lacking overall planning. Despite these faults, however, the radical groups are credited with a greater voice and following in the black community, and their growing significance is reflected in the findings of this study on rights group preferences.

Background Factors and Their Effects on Civil Rights Group Preference

Next consider the several background factors which would seem to contribute to shaping the viewpoints of members of the leadership sample. Age appears to be particularly significant in determining civil rights groups preference. Almost invariably, the younger leaders indicated greater favor for the more militant and radical organizations, and almost all leaders below the age of forty rejected traditional organizations—particularly the NAACP—for being out of touch with the black community. In contrast to this situation, the older leaders—those over the age of forty—showed a greater preference for the traditional organizations, though few of the older leaders rejected the radicals and their organizations completely.

Examined in greater detail, Table 2 indicates that of the eight respondents who voiced a preference for radical, or group 1, civil rights organizations, all eight (or 100 percent) were from age group one, between ages twenty and thirty. Thus, only the youngest leaders in the sample displayed radical civil rights group preferences.

Of the twelve individuals who indicated preference for militant, or group 2, civil rights organizations—i.e., CORE—42 percent were also from age group one, though by additional analysis these appeared to be "older" leaders of that age group, in either their late twenties or thirty years old. One-half of those favoring militant organizations were from age group two, between thirty and forty years old, while only one leader over forty showed a preference for CORE. Thus, the majority of CORE's support clearly comes from leaders in age group two.

TABLE 2

Age versus Civil Rights Group Preference[a]

Organizational Preference TOTAL	TOTAL 25 100%	1 (Radical) 8 100%	2 (Militant) 12 100%	3 (Traditional) 5 100%
Age Group				
20–30 1	13 52%	8 100%	5 42%	
30–40 2	7 28%		6 50%	1 20%
40–50 3	5 20%		1 8%	4 80%

[a] The data in all of the tables included in this study have been percentaged for columns and not for rows. The totals (n) have been computed for both columns and rows.

Of the five individuals who showed a preference for traditional civil rights organizations—i.e., group 3—a full 80 percent came from age group three, those leaders between forty and fifty years and above. Only one thirty-five-year-old individual indicated a preference for the NAACP. Clearly, the bulk of support for the NAACP and Urban League comes from the older leaders, those in the group above forty years old.

Thus, on the basis of the data collected, age appears to be directly related to civil rights group preference, with the age and civil rights group numbers on the preceding table generally matching each other (i.e., leaders in age group one prefer civil rights group 1, leaders in age group two prefer civil rights group 2, and so on).

Some traditional leaders noted the importance of the age factor themselves. As a forty-six-year-old member of the city's school system put it: "SNCC is for the younger people who have more time and energy to devote to civil rights and community action projects." Some leaders explained that their membership in traditional organizations was due primarily to their positions, or because they had first joined them long ago and never broke their ties. As one fifty-year-old member of the city administration put it: "I'm an NAACP member by tradition, and a moderate by position."

The younger black leaders, having developed a "civil rights consciousness" more recently and exhibiting an understandable impatience for rapid and meaningful change, reject overwhelmingly the "gradual" approach represented by the traditional organizations, an approach which they feel has gotten nowhere on the really basic issues and problems of the ghetto. It is, therefore, the very "irrelevance" of the activities of the traditional organizations in Newark which perhaps causes the younger leaders to turn to other, more militant groups.[3]

[3] Indeed, some observers have noted rejection by the ghetto population of the whole civil rights movement on grounds that drives for integration, legal rights, and equal opportunity are unrealistic, insignificant, and even irrelevant to the problems which afflict the poor blacks living in the ghetto.

When civil rights group preference is correlated with employment, it appears—as Table 3 indicates—that type of work seems to have a clear effect on identity with a civil rights organization. Those black leaders working in poverty or community action programs, even if government-related, tend to prefer the more militant and radical civil rights organizations. Of the sixteen people doing what can be termed grass-roots work, only one preferred the traditional organizations, ten favored CORE, and five indicated a preference for some radical group.

TABLE 3

Employment versus Civil Rights Group Preference

Organizational Preference	TOTAL	1 (Radical)	2 (Militant)	3 (Traditional)
TOTAL	25 100%	8 100%	12 100%	5 100%
Employment				
Community 1	16 64%	5 63%	10 83%	1 20%
Private 2	6 24%	3 37%	2 17%	1 20%
Government 3	3 12%			3 60%

Of those leaders privately employed, that is, having their own businesses or working for a company or some other employer, only one favored the traditional organizations, two favored CORE, and three (or half) preferred one of the radical groups.

Of those few leaders whose jobs are directly related to, or dependent upon, the local government, all favor the traditional civil rights organizations. Hence, it can be concluded from the data that the more closely a black leader's work brings him into contact with the community and its problems, the more militant his civil rights group preference is likely to be. And the more closely his employment is related to local government, the more traditional his preferences among rights groups is likely to be.

The effects of education on civil rights group preferences are not clear-cut, as is indicated by Table 4. Of those leaders who preferred traditional organizations,

TABLE 4

Education versus Civil Rights Group Preference

Organizational Preference	TOTAL	1 (Radical)	2 (Militant)	3 (Traditional)
TOTAL	25 100%	8 100%	12 100%	5 100%
Education				
Elementary 1	2 8%		1 8%	1 20%
High school 2	11 44%	5 63%	5 42%	1 20%
College 3	12 48%	3 37%	6 50%	3 60%

the majority are college-educated. But of the twelve college-level leaders interviewed, the clear majority preferred militant and even radical civil right groups.

Of those black leaders in education category two (i.e., those with high school educations) all but one prefer militant and radical civil rights organizations. And of the small number of leaders with only elementary school education, the tendency seems to be a preference for less militant groups (at least the data indicate that neither of these individuals favors a radical organization).

Based on the data, education appears to have the following general effect: the higher the level of education, the greater the militancy; the lower the level of education, the less militant a black leader is likely to be. But this pattern is challenged by the fact that the bulk of traditional leaders in the sample are clearly better educated men. Furthermore, attitudes may be related to the overlapping age and employment factors, and not education exclusively.

An interesting and perhaps significant finding based on the data is that income level is not a clear determinant of civil rights group preference among the black leadership sample. There were some leaders with low incomes who exhibited a traditional, moderate preference, while some very-high-income people were quite militant. The sample included six leaders making over $10,000 a year who favored militant and even black nationalist organizations. Also interviewed were two leaders who favored traditional organizations like the NAACP, though their incomes were below $7000 a year.

TABLE 5

Income versus Civil Rights Group Preference

Organizational Preference		TOTAL	1 (Radical)	2 (Militant)	3 (Traditional)
TOTAL		25 100%	8 100%	12 100%	5 100%
Income					
$4000–6000	1	1 4%	1 12%		
$6000–10,000	2	15 60%	7 88%	6 50%	2 40%
$10,000 and above	3	9 36%		6 50%	3 60%

Despite these "unusual" attitudes, the traditional tendency for the higher-income leaders (i.e., the more economically secure) to be less militant and the lower-income leaders to be more militant is still generally valid. As Table 5 indicates, there were no "poor" group one individuals favoring traditional groups, while the "upper-income" leaders made up the majority of those preferring traditional organizations. And the bulk of those black leaders favoring radical organizations came from the middle- to lower-income groups. Moreover, it should be noted that the leader with the very lowest income favored a radical organization, while the highest-income leader in the sample preferred the NAACP. The tendency becomes more obvious if the one leader in income category one is excluded from the considerations, and if income group two is used as the lower-income level, and group three as the higher-income level.

Table 6 on residence indicates that among those leaders who now live outside of the city, militant and traditional civil rights organizations are favored. The suburbanites do not favor radical groups. A clear majority of those leaders in group two, that is respondents who have lived in Newark all their lives, indicated a preference for militant civil rights organizations, though leaders in this residency are also found in each preference category. Of those black leaders who originally came from the South and now live in Newark, there was almost an even preference for radical and militant civil rights organizations, with none of these people favoring the traditional groups.

TABLE 6

Residence versus Civil Rights Group Preference

Organizational Preference	TOTAL	1 (Radical)	2 (Militant)	3 (Traditional)
TOTAL	25 / 100%	8 / 100%	12 / 100%	5 / 100%
Residence				
1 Born in South; lived in Newark at time of interview	9 / 36%	5 / 63%	4 / 33%	
2 Born in Newark; lived in Newark at time of interview	11 / 44%	3 / 37%	6 / 50%	2 / 40%
3 Previously lived in Newark; presently live in a suburb	5 / 20%		2 / 17%	3 / 60%

Thus it appears from the data collected that those black leaders with Southern backgrounds tend to be most radical and militant, while those who now reside outside the city, in the suburbs, tend to be militant and traditional in their preference for civil rights organizations.

On the basis of the above data, one can conclude that there are some seemingly positive relationships between a leader's background and his choice of an organization. Clearly, age appears to be the best indicator of radicalism or militancy among black leaders in Newark. In addition, the nature of one's employment, place of birth, and current residence also seem to have a direct relationship to one's position on the radical-militant-traditional continuum. One interesting finding was that education and income did not seem to have any clear-cut relationship to degree of radicalism and militancy. This is interesting since conventional wisdom suggests that the best educated and more affluent members of society (white or black) will be most satisfied with the status quo, and therefore more likely to accept traditional organizations, such as the Urban League and the NAACP. However, it might be noted that leadership for radical and militant groups will often come from a small segment of the higher socioeconomic group. As Gary T. Marx (1967: 68) noted:

> There are . . . concrete reasons why militancy should vary directly with social privileges. These involve the energy, resources, morale, and self-confidence needed to challenge an oppressive and powerful system. The mental and physical energy of severely deprived people is occupied in simply stay-

ing alive. A concern with somewhat abstract principles of racial justice is a luxury of the more privileged, who need not worry where their next meal is coming from. They are freer in both a mental and physical sense to challenge the status quo. In addition, their relatively well-to-do financial situation and the possession of occupational skills make them less vulnerable for civil rights activities. Further, they are more likely to have the intellectual and organizational skills and the savoir-faire that activism requires. Because they are less awed and overwhelmed by the power of society's institutions, and freer from concern for economic survival, they can more easily question and act.

Modes of Political Participation: Group versus Individual Action

The treatment received by Newark's black leaders from public officials certainly helps determine the way in which they attempt to influence local officials and affect city policies, and thus react to radical, militant and/or traditional modes of political behavior.

To discover the method of action most favored by the black leadership, the respondents were asked if they would try to do something about a problem or issue of concern to them or their community through a civil rights or community action organization or on their own. Though almost all of the leaders interviewed identified with, and were active in some civil rights organization (as is evident from the previous discussion of civil rights group preferences), a relatively large number, almost 30 percent, as indicated by Table 7, said they preferred individual to group action.

TABLE 7

Modes of Participation
(i.e., Type of Action)

	Percentage	Number
Individual action	28	7
Group action	72	18

Although not excluding action through an organization, many of these leaders pointed out that their positions and personal contacts within the city government made it both easier and possibly more effective for them to act on their own. Furthermore, some of the respondents noted that bureaucratic entanglements prevent an organization from reaching the real source of responsibility and obtaining meaningful results. A few of the leaders observed that it was difficult to mobilize a group behind an issue, while others noted that group protest and pressure carried little weight at city hall.[4]

Nevertheless, it is significant that over two-thirds of those leaders interviewed said they preferred to act through an organization rather than on their own, perhaps reflecting a belief that group action would be more effective in obtaining results from the city government than individual efforts.

[4] This corresponds to the opinion expressed by many of the respondents that public protest elicits little substantive response from city officials.

The general preference for group action seems to indicate a recognition among black leaders of the political realities in the city, a realization that the only way to become effective is to organize and act in unity. On the other hand, the substantial number of those leaders who expressed an initial preference for individual action—the generally more traditional leaders—are also recognizing another political fact of life: it is very often "who you know" at city hall that determines whether or not results can be obtained.

TABLE 8

Age versus Type of Action

Type of Action	TOTAL	1 (Group)	2 (Both)	3 (Individual)
TOTAL	25 100%	15 100%	6 100%	4 100%
Age				
20–30 1	13 52%	10 67%	2 33%	1 25%
30–40 2	7 28%	3 20%	3 50%	1 25%
40–50 3	5 20%	2 13%	1 17%	2 50%

Group action is preferred most often by the younger leaders who tend to identify with the more militant and active civil rights organizations. Their call for "black power" is essentially a desire for united black efforts on specific issues, reflecting a recognition that there is strength in numbers. (See Table 8.)

The older, more established leaders tend to prefer individual action, and many feel that their associations with certain officials can be more useful than group action, at least in the initial stages of an issue.[5] Moreover, individual action may be more satisfying to the older leaders, in the sense that they take pride in their ability to influence officials on their own.

These attitudes, of course, are partly a result of the fact that, over time, the older leaders may have developed personal contacts within the city government, whereas the younger leaders have perhaps not had the opportunity or time to do so. This, however, is probably more a consequence of position or employment than age.

As indicated by Table 9, most of those black leaders in government-related employment say they would rather act individually, at least in the initial stages of a developing issue, because their positions and contacts in city government make it easier and more effective for them to act on their own.

The majority of those leaders in private employment or community activities prefer group action. Most of those leaders in private employment have little personal contact with government officials, while many leaders in the poverty and community action programs who come into frequent contact with city officials, by virtue of their activities and backgrounds are often "prejudged" as "troublemakers," and find their individual petitions ignored.

---

[5] This reliance on self-action by older leaders fits in well with the emphasis of the traditional civil rights organizations on individual rights and responsibilities.

TABLE 9
Employment versus Type of Action

Type of Action TOTAL		TOTAL 25 100%	1 (Group) 15 100%	2 (Both) 6 100% (101%)[a]	3 (Individual) 4 100%
Employment					
Community	1	16 64%	11 73%	4 67%	1 25%
Private	2	6 24%	4 27%	1 17%	1 25%
Government	3	3 12%		1 17%	2 50%

[a] Contains error due to rounding.

As Table 10 indicates, those black leaders who presently live outside of the city tended to favor individual action, while those residing in Newark all their lives, and particularly those leaders who originally came from the South, tended to prefer group action.

It should be noted once again that these factors cannot be examined in a vacuum. Those leaders who live outside Newark also tend to be of higher income and work in government-related jobs; and these additional factors may have far greater effect in shaping their viewpoints than residency alone.

TABLE 10
Residence versus Type of Action

Type of Action TOTAL		TOTAL 25 100%	1 (Group) 15 100%	2 (Both) 6 100%	3 (Individual) 4 100%
Residence					
Born in South; lived in Newark at time of interview	1	9 36%	8 53%	1 17%	
Born in Newark; lived in Newark at time of interview	2	11 44%	6 40%	3 50%	2 50%
Born in Newark; lived in suburbs at time of interview	3	5 20%	1 7%	2 33%	2 50%

As Table 11 relating education to type of action indicates, those leaders with less schooling clearly favor group action, while those with college education have mixed preferences. Note should be made, however, that of those favoring individual action, most are from the higher education category.

TABLE 11
Education versus Type of Action

Type of Action		TOTAL	1 (Group)	2 (Both)	3 (Individual)
TOTAL		25	15	6	4
		100%	100%	100% (101%)[a]	100%
Education					
Elementary	1	2	1	1	
		8%	7%	17%	
High school	2	11	9	1	1
		44%	60%	17%	25%
College	3	12	5	4	3
		48%	33%	67%	75%

[a] Contains error due to rounding.

The effect of income on means of action preferred is fairly clear: those leaders favoring individual action tend to have higher incomes, while those favoring group action are almost all from the lower-income groups. (See Table 12.)

TABLE 12
Income versus Type of Action

Type of Action		TOTAL	1 (Group)	2 (Both)	3 (Individual)
TOTAL		25	15	6	4
		100%	100%	100%	100%
Income					
$4000–6000	1	1	1		
		4%	7%		
$6000–10,000	2	15	12	2	1
		60%	80%	33%	25%
$10,000 and over	3	9	2	4	3
		36%	13%	67%	75%

Thus, in conclusion, one can say that based on the data, it appears to be the older, upper-income leader, with better education, living outside of the city, whose work puts him in close contact with government officials, who prefers individual action; younger leaders, with lower income and education, working outside the city government and living in Newark, tend to favor group action as the most effective means of influencing government policies. Seemingly, group action, especially in light of collective efforts made by white and black students and the black ghetto population in the past five years, is a more radical method than individual action in trying to achieve one's goals insofar as the politics of confrontation always looms in the background in these collective maneuvers.

CONCLUSIONS

Despite differences in the backgrounds of the members of the leadership sample, it is evident that there is a growing sense of urgency and militancy among Newark's black leadership in relationship to the methods they condone for change, as well as in the changes in society they are willing to accept in order to see improvement for ghetto populations (as is seen by the rights groups with which these individuals associate). Thus it was noted that 32 percent of the black leaders interviewed in Newark supported radical groups, and 48 percent of the black leaders interviewed for this study preferred a militant group. The results of a survey conducted by Angus Campbell and Howard Schuman (1968: 21) on racial attitudes in fifteen American cities, including Newark, indicated that a somewhat similar orientation to the one found in Newark may exist for a large number of blacks living in urban areas. The question asked was: "Now I want to read to you a list of people active in civil rights. For each one, please tell me whether you approve or disapprove of what the person stands for, or don't know enough about him to say." The responses to the question follow.

In Percentages

	Carmichael	Dr. King	Wilkins	H. Rap Brown
Approve	14	72	50	14
Partly approve, partly disapprove	21	19	12	13
Disapprove	35	5	3	45
Don't know	30	4	35	28

Campbell and Schuman have made the observation that:

> In our survey, as in all previous studies we know of, their (black nationalist leaders) support is much less than that for the NAACP or for the late Martin Luther King. . . . Nevertheless, the at least partial support they have is not small, particularly when one considers that the militant figures . . . were hardly known at all several years ago. Stokely Carmichael's "stand" is approved or partly approved by 35 percent of the sample.

This move toward militancy and a sense of urgency for change seems to reflect a national mood prevalent in the nation's black ghettos. The National Advisory Commission on Civil Disorders (1968: 204–205) noted that:

> A climate that tends toward the approval and encouragement of violence as a form of protest has been created. . . . The frustrations of powerlessness have led some to the conviction that there is no effective alternative to violence as a means of expression. . . . More generally, the result is alienation and hostility toward the institutions of law and government and the white society that controls them. This is reflected in the reach toward racial solidarity and consciousness reflected in the slogan "Black Power."

One additional finding of this study, which in light of the recent student demonstrations is not surprising (as it was when the data were first analyzed), is that age, and not economic status or occupational and educational achievement, will be the most clear indicator of radicalism or militancy [6] among black leaders in

[6] Popular commentators have also made this type of observation. For example, *Newsweek* (1969: 21) noted:

> They are an angry new breed, come of age in the Northern ghettos, during a decade of revolt, and they stand across a wide generation gap from the rest of black America. Their elders may answer to "Negro," but Northerners under 30 prefer "black," thank you, and they wear the name and the color with a kind of

Newark. However, as noted earlier, age may be a factor reflecting socioeconomic position in Newark. James Q. Wilson (1969: 359–360) writes:

> When young people grow up and discover that their elders are also rebellious, there is perhaps an urge for even more extreme actions. Just as the sons and daughters of New Deal liberals regard their parents as "square" for confining their demands for change to the rules imposed by the existing political system, so also the sons and daughters of Negroes who have demanded integration and equal opportunity may feel that such demands are not enough because they are based on an acceptance of the distribution of power within the existing social order.

REFERENCES

Campbell, A., and H. Schuman (1968). "Racial attitudes in fifteen American cities," in Supplemental Studies for the National Advisory Commission on Civil Disorders (Washington, D.C.: Government Printing Office).

Cleaver, E. (1968). Soul on Ice (New York: McGraw-Hill).

Governor's Select Commission on Civil Disorders (1968). Report for Action, 1968 (Trenton, N.J.).

Hartz, L. (1955). The Liberal Tradition in America (New York: Harcourt Brace Jovanovich).

Institute of Management and Labor Relations (1967). Newark, New Jersey Population and Labor Force Characteristics, Spring 1967 (New Brunswick: Rutgers University).

Marx, G. T. (1967). Protest and Prejudice (New York: Harper & Row).

Newsweek (1969). "The tough new breed: ghetto blacks under 30." June 30.

Wilson, J. Q. (1969). "Why we are having a wave of violence," in A. Shank (ed.) Political Power and the Urban Crisis (Boston: Holbrook Press).

> chip on the shoulder pride . . . their faith in nonviolence has diminished and their trust in the white man's intentions curdled to a point where roughly half look on the riots of five summers past as justified acts of rebellion—and very nearly a third feel that the time has come . . . to take up arms.

CHAPTER TEN

THE WORKING CLASS

29
The Forgotten American

Peter Schrag

There is hardly a language to describe him, or even a set of social statistics. Just names: racist-bigot-redneck-ethnic-Irish-Italian-Pole-Hunkie-Yahoo. The lower middle class. A blank. The man under whose hat lies the great American desert. Who watches the tube, plays the horses, and keeps the niggers out of his union and his neighborhood. Who might vote for Wallace (but didn't). Who cheers when the cops beat up on demonstrators. Who is free, white, and twenty-one, has a job, a home, a family, and is up to his eyeballs in credit. In the guise of the working class—or the American yeoman or John Smith—he was once the hero of the civics book, the man that Andrew Jackson called "the bone and sinew of the country." Now he is "the forgotten man," perhaps the most alienated person in America.

Nothing quite fits, except perhaps omission and semi-invisibility. America is supposed to be divided between affluence and poverty, between slums and suburbs. John Kenneth Galbraith begins the foreword to *The Affluent Society* with the phrase, "Since I sailed for Switzerland in the early summer of 1955 to begin

Copyright © 1969, by Harper's Magazine, Inc. Reprinted from the August 1969 issue of *Harper's Magazine* by permission of the author.

work on this book . . ." But *between* slums and suburbs, between Scarsdale and Harlem, between Wellesley and Roxbury, between Shaker Heights and Hough, there are some eighty million people (depending on how you count them) who didn't sail for Switzerland in the summer of 1955, or at any other time, and who never expect to. Between slums and suburbs: South Boston and South San Francisco, Bell and Parma, Astoria and Bay Ridge, Newark, Cicero, Downey, Daly City, Charlestown, Flatbush. Union halls, American Legion posts, neighborhood bars and bowling leagues, the Ukrainian Club and the Holy Name. Main Street. To try to describe all this is like trying to describe America itself. If you look for it, you find it everywhere: the rows of frame houses overlooking the belching steel mills in Bethlehem, Pennsylvania, two-family brick houses in Canarsie (where the most common slogan, even in the middle of a political campaign, is "curb your dog"); the Fords and Chevies with a decal American flag on the rear window (usually a cut-out from the *Reader's Digest,* and displayed in counter-protest against peaceniks and "those bastards who carry Vietcong flags in demonstrations"); the bunting on the porch rail with the inscription, "Welcome Home, Pete." The gold star in the window.

When he was Under Secretary of Housing and Urban Development, Robert C. Wood tried a definition. It is not good, but it's the best we have:

> He is a white employed male . . . earning between $5000 and $10,000. He works regularly, steadily, dependably, wearing a blue collar or white collar. Yet the frontiers of his career expectations have been fixed since he reached the age of thirty-five, when he found that he had too many obligations, too much family, and too few skills to match opportunities with aspirations.
>
> This definition of the "working American" involves almost 23-million American families.
>
> The working American lives in the gray area fringes of a central city or in a close-in or very far-out cheaper suburban subdivision of a large metropolitan area. He is likely to own a home and a car, especially as his income begins to rise. Of those earning between $6000 and $7500, 70 percent own their own homes and 94 percent drive their own cars.
>
> 94 percent have no education beyond high school and 43 percent have only completed the eighth grade.

He does all the right things, obeys the law, goes to church and insists—usually —that his kids get a better education than he had. But the right things don't seem to be paying off. While he is making more than he ever made—perhaps more than he'd ever dreamed—he's still struggling while a lot of others—"them" (on welfare, in demonstrations, in the ghettos) are getting most of the attention. "I'm working my ass off," a guy tells you on a stoop in South Boston. "My kids don't have a place to swim, my parks are full of glass, and I'm supposed to bleed for a bunch of people on relief." In New York a man who drives a Post Office trailer truck at night (4:00 P.M. to midnight) and a cab during the day (7:00 A.M. to 2:00 P.M.), and who hustles radios for his Post Office buddies on the side, is ready, as he says, to "knock somebody's ass." "The colored guys work when they feel like it. Sometimes they show up and sometimes they don't. One guy tore up all the time cards. I'd like to see a white guy do that and get away with it."

WHAT COUNTS

Nobody knows how many people in America moonlight (half of the eighteen million families in the $5000 to $10,000 bracket have two or more wage earners) or how many have to hustle on the side. "I don't think anybody has a single job anymore," said Nicholas Kisburg, the research director for a Teamsters Union Council in New York. "All the cops are moonlighting, and the teachers; and there's a million guys who are hustling, guys with phony social-security numbers who are hiding part of what they make so they don't get kicked out of a housing project, or guys who work as guards at sports events and get free meals that they don't want to pay taxes on. Every one of them is cheating. They are underground people—*Untermenschen*. . . . We really have no systematic data on any of this. We have no ideas of the attitudes of the white worker. (We've been too busy studying the black worker.) And yet he's the source of most of the reaction in this country."

The reaction is directed at almost every visible target: at integration and welfare, taxes and sex education, at the rich and the poor, the foundations and students, at the "smart people in the suburbs." In New York State the legislature cuts the welfare budget; in Los Angeles, the voters reelect Yorty after a whispered racial campaign against the Negro favorite. In Minneapolis a police detective named Charles Stenvig, promising "to take the handcuffs off the police," wins by a margin stunning even to his supporters: in Massachusetts the voters mail tea bags to their representatives in protest against new taxes, and in state after state legislatures are passing bills to punish student demonstrators. ("We keep talking about permissiveness in training kids," said a Los Angeles labor official, "but we forget that these are our kids.")

And yet all these things are side manifestations of a malaise that lacks a language. Whatever law and order means, for example, to a man who feels his wife is unsafe on the street after dark or in the park at any time, or whose kids get shaken down in the school yard, it also means something like normality—the demand that everybody play it by the book, that cultural and social standards be somehow restored to their civics-book simplicity, that things shouldn't be as they are but as they were supposed to be. If there is a revolution in this country—a revolt in manners, standards of dress and obscenity, and, more importantly, in our official sense of what America is—there is also a counter-revolt. Sometimes it is inarticulate, and sometimes (perhaps most of the time) people are either too confused or apathetic—or simply too polite and too decent—to declare themselves. In Astoria, Queens, a white working-class district of New York, people who make $7000 or $8000 a year (sometimes in two jobs) call themselves affluent, even though the Bureau of Labor Statistics regards an income of less than $9500 in New York inadequate to a moderate standard of living. And in a similar neighborhood in Brooklyn a truck driver who earns $151 a week tells you he's doing well, living in a two-story frame house separated by a narrow driveway from similar houses, thousands of them in block after block. This year, for the first time, he will go on a cruise—he and his wife and two other couples—two weeks in the Caribbean. He went to work after World War II ($57 a week) and he has lived in the same house for twenty years, accumulating two television sets, wall-to-wall carpeting in a small living room, and a basement that he recently remodeled into a recreation room with the help of two moonlighting firemen. "We get fairly good salaries, and this is a good neighborhood, one of the few good ones left. We have no smoked Irishmen around."

Stability is what counts, stability in job and home and neighborhood, stability in the church and in friends. At night you watch television and sometimes on a weekend you go to a nice place—maybe a downtown hotel—for dinner with another couple. (Or maybe your sister, or maybe bowling, or maybe, if you're defeated, a night at the track.) The wife has the necessary appliances, often still being paid off, and the money you save goes for your daughter's orthodontist, and later for her wedding. The smoked Irishmen—the colored (no one says black; few even say Negro)—represent change and instability, kids who cause trouble in school, who get treatment that your kids never got, that you never got. ("Those fucking kids," they tell you in South Boston, "raising hell, and not one of 'em paying his own way. Their fucking mothers are all on welfare.") The black kids mean a change in the rules, a double standard in grades and discipline, and—vaguely—a challenge to all you believed right. Law and order is the stability and predictability of established ways. Law and order is equal treatment—in school, in jobs, in the courts—even if you're cheating a little yourself. The Forgotten Man is Jackson's man. He is the vestigial American democrat of 1840: "They all know that their success depends upon their own industry and economy and that they must not expect to become suddenly rich by the fruits of their toil." He is also Franklin Roosevelt's man—the man whose vote (or whose father's vote) sustained the New Deal.

There are other considerations, other styles, other problems. A postman in a Charlestown (Boston) housing project: eight children and a ninth on the way. Last year by working overtime, his income went over $7000. This year, because he reported it, the Housing Authority is raising his rent from $78 to $106 a month, a catastrophe for a family that pays $2.20 a day for milk, has never had a vacation, and for which an excursion is "going out for ice cream." "You try and save for something better; we hope to get out of here to someplace where the kids can play, where there's no broken glass, and then something always comes along that knocks you right back. It's like being at the bottom of the well waiting for a guy to throw you a rope." The description becomes almost Chaplinesque. Life is humble but not simple; the terrors of insolent bureaucracies and contemptuous officials produce a demonology that loses little of its horror for being partly misunderstood. You want to get a sink fixed but don't want to offend the manager; want to get an eye operation that may (or may not) have been necessitated by a military injury five years earlier, "but the Veterans Administration says I signed away my benefits"; want to complain to someone about the teen-agers who run around breaking windows and harassing women but get no response either from the management or the police. "You're afraid to complain because if they don't get you during the day they'll get you at night." Automobiles, windows, children, all become hostages to the vague terrors of everyday life; everything is vulnerable. Liabilities that began long ago cannot possibly be liquidated: "I never learned anything in that school except how to fight. I got tired of being caned by the teachers so at sixteen I quit and joined the Marines. I still don't know anything."

AT THE BOTTOM OF THE WELL

American culture? Wealth is visible, and so, now, is poverty. Both have become intimidating clichés. But the rest? A vast, complex, and disregarded world that was once—in belief, and in fact—the American middle: Greyhound and Trailways bus terminals in little cities at midnight, each of them with its neon lights and its cardboard hamburgers; acres of tar-paper beach bungalows in places like Revere and Rockaway; the hair curlers in the supermarket on Saturday, and the little girls in the communion dresses the next morning; pinball machines and the *Daily News*, the *Reader's Digest* and Ed Sullivan; houses with tiny front lawns (or even large ones) adorned with statues of the Virgin or of Sambo welcomin' de folks home; Clint Eastwood or Julie Andrews at the Palace; the trotting tracks and the dog tracks—Aurora Downs, Connaught Park, Roosevelt, Yonkers, Rockingham, and forty others—where gray men come not for sport and beauty, but to read numbers, to study and dope. (If you win you have figured something, have in a small way controlled your world, have surmounted your impotence. If you lose, bad luck, shit. "I'll break his goddamned head.") Baseball is not the national pastime; racing is. For every man who goes to a major-league baseball game there are four who go to the track and probably four more who go to the candy store or the barbershop to make their bets. (Total track attendance in 1965: 62 million plus another 10 million who went to the dogs.)

There are places, and styles, and attitudes. If there are neighborhoods of aspiration, suburban enclaves for the mobile young executive and the aspiring worker, there are also places of limited expectation and dead-end districts where mobility is finished. But even there you can often find, however vestigial, a sense of place, the roots of old ethnic loyalties, and a passionate, if often futile, battle against intrusion and change. "Everybody around here," you are told, "pays his own way." In this world the problems are not the ABM or air pollution (have they heard of Biafra?) or the international population crisis; the problem is to get your street cleaned, your garbage collected, to get your husband home from Vietnam alive; to negotiate installment payments and to keep the schools orderly. Ask anyone in Scarsdale or Winnetka about the schools and they'll tell you about new programs, or about how many are getting into Harvard, or about the teachers; ask in Oakland or the North Side of Chicago, and they'll tell you that they have (or haven't) had trouble. Somewhere in his gut the man in those communities knows that mobility and choice in this society are limited. He cannot imagine any major change for the better; but he can imagine change for the worse. And yet for a decade he is the one who has been asked to carry the burden of social reform, to integrate his schools and his neighborhood, has been asked by comfortable people to pay the social debts due to the poor and the black. In Boston, in San Francisco, in Chicago (not to mention Newark or Oakland) he has been telling the reformers to go to hell. The Jewish schoolteachers of New York and the Irish parents of Dorchester have asked the same question: "What the hell did Lindsay (or the Beacon Hill Establishment) ever do for us?"

The ambiguities and changes in American life that occupy discussions in university seminars and policy debates in Washington, and that form the backbone of contemporary popular sociology, become increasingly the conditions of trauma and frustration in the middle. Although the New Frontier and Great Society contained some programs for those not already on the rolls of social pathology—

federal aid for higher education, for example—the public priorities and the rhetoric contained little. The emphasis, properly, was on the poor, on the inner cities (e.g., Negroes) and the unemployed. But in Chicago a widow with three children who earns $7000 a year can't get them college loans because she makes too much; the money is reserved for people on relief. New schools are built in the ghetto but not in the white working-class neighborhoods where they are just as dilapidated. In Newark the head of a white vigilante group (now a city councilman) runs, among other things, on a platform opposing pro-Negro discrimination. "When pools are being built in the Central Ward—don't they think white kids have got frustration? The white can't get a job; we have to hire Negroes first." The middle class, said Congressman Roman Pucinski of Illinois, who represents a lot of it, "is in revolt. Everyone has been generous in supporting anti-poverty. Now the middle-class American is disqualified from most of the programs."

"SOMEBODY HAS TO SAY NO . . ."

The frustrated middle. The liberal wisdom about welfare, ghettos, student revolt, and Vietnam has only a marginal place, if any, for the values and life of the working man. It flies in the face of most of what he was taught to cherish and respect: hard work, order, authority, self-reliance. He fought, either alone or through labor organizations, to establish the precincts he now considers his own. Union seniority, the civil-service bureaucracy, and the petty professionalism established by the merit system in the public schools become sinecures of particular ethnic groups or of those who have learned to negotiate and master the system. A man who worked all his life to accumulate the points and grades and paraphernalia to become an assistant school principal (no matter how silly the requirements) is not likely to relinquish his position with equanimity. Nor is a dock worker whose only estate is his longshoreman's card. The job, the points, the credits become property:

> Some men leave their sons money [wrote a union member to the *New York Times*], some large investments, some business connections, and some a profession. I have only one worthwhile thing to give: my trade. I hope to follow a centuries-old tradition and sponsor my sons for an apprenticeship. For this simple father's wish it is said that I discriminate against Negroes. Don't all of us discriminate? Which of us . . . will not choose a son over all others?

Suddenly the rules are changing—all the rules. If you protect your job for your own you may be called a bigot. At the same time it's perfectly acceptable to shout black power and to endorse it. What does it take to be a good American? *Give the black man a position because he is black, not because he necessarily works harder or does the job better.* What does it take to be a good American? Dress nicely, hold a job, be clean-cut, don't judge a man by the color of his skin or the country of his origin. What about the demands of Negroes, the long hair of the students, the dirty movies, the people who burn draft cards and American flags? Do you have to go out in the street with picket signs, do you have to burn the place down to get what you want? What does it take to be a good American? *This is a sick society, a racist society, we are fighting an immoral war.* ("I'm against the Vietnam war, too," says the truck driver in Brooklyn. "I see a good kid come home with half an arm and a leg in a brace up to here, and what's it all for? I was glad to see *my kid* flunk the Army physical. Still, somebody has to say no to these demonstrators and enforce the law.") What does it take to be a good American?

The conditions of trauma and frustration in the middle. What does it take to be a good American? Suddenly there are demands for Italian power and Polish power and Ukrainian power. In Cleveland the Poles demand a seat on the school board, and get it, and in Pittsburgh John Pankuch, the seventy-three-year-old president of the National Slovak Society, demands "action, plenty of it to make up for lost time." Black power is supposed to be nothing but emulation of the ways in which other ethnic groups made it. But have they made it? In Reardon's Bar on East Eighth Street in South Boston, where the workmen come for their fish-chowder lunch and for their rye and ginger, they still identify themselves as Galway men and Kilkenny men; in the newsstand in Astoria you can buy *Il Progresso, El Tiempo,* the *Staats-Zeitung,* the *Irish World,* plus papers in Greek, Hungarian, and Polish. At the parish of Our Lady of Mount Carmel the priests hear confession in English, Italian, and Spanish and, nearby, the biggest attraction is not the stickball game, but the *bocce* court. Some of the poorest people in America are white, native, and have lived all of their lives in the same place as their fathers and grandfathers. The problems that were presumably solved in some distant past, in that prehistoric era before the textbooks were written—problems of assimilation, of upward mobility—now turn out to be very much unsolved. The melting pot and all: millions made it, millions moved to the affluent suburbs; several million—no one knows how many—did not. The median income in Irish South Boston is $5100 a year but the community-action workers have a hard time convincing the local citizens that any white man who is not stupid or irresponsible can be poor. Pride still keeps them from applying for income supplements or Medicaid, but it does not keep them from resenting those who do. In Pittsburgh, where the members of Polish-American organizations earn an estimated $5000 to $6000 (and some fall below the poverty line), the Poverty Programs are nonetheless directed primarily to Negroes, and almost everywhere the thing called urban backlash associates itself in some fashion with ethnic groups whose members have themselves only a precarious hold on the security of affluence. Almost everywhere in the old cities, tribal neighborhoods and their styles are under assault by masscult. The Italian grocery gives way to the supermarket, the ma-and-pa store and the walk-up are attacked by urban renewal. And almost everywhere, that assault tends to depersonalize and to alienate. It has always been this way, but with time the brave new world that replaces the old patterns becomes increasingly bureaucratized, distant, and hard to control.

Yet beyond the problems of ethnic identity, beyond the problems of Poles and Irishmen left behind, there are others more pervasive and more dangerous. For every Greek or Hungarian there are a dozen American-Americans who are past ethnic consciousness and who are as alienated, as confused, and as angry as the rest. The obvious manifestations are the same everywhere—race, taxes, welfare, students—but the threat seems invariably more cultural and psychological than economic or social. What upset the police at the Chicago convention most was not so much the politics of the demonstrators as their manners and their hair. (The barbershops in their neighborhoods don't advertise Beatle Cuts but the Flat Top and the Chicago Box.) The affront comes from middle-class people—and their children—who had been cast in the role of social exemplars (and from those cast as unfortunates worthy of public charity) who offend all the things on which working class identity is built: "hippies [said a San Francisco longshoreman] who fart around the streets and don't work"; welfare recipients who strike and march for better treatment; "all those [said a California labor official] who challenge the precepts that these people live on." If ethnic groups are beginning to organize to get theirs, so are others: police and firemen ("The cop is the new nigger"); schoolteachers; lower-middle-class housewives fighting sex education and bussing; small property owners who have no ethnic communion but a passionate interest in lower taxes, more policemen, and stiffer penalties for criminals. In San Francisco the Teamsters, who had never been known for such interests before, recently demonstrated in support of the police and law enforcement and, on another occasion, joined a group called Mothers Support Neighborhood Schools at a school-board meeting to oppose—with their presence and later, apparently, with their fists—a proposal to integrate the schools through bussing. ("These people," someone said at the meeting, "do not look like mothers.")

Which is not to say that all is frustration and anger, that anybody is ready "to burn the country down." They are not even ready to elect standard model demagogues. "A lot of labor people who thought of voting for Wallace were ashamed of themselves when they realized what they were about to do," said Morris Iushewitz, an officer of New York's Central Labor Council. Because of a massive last-minute union campaign, and perhaps for other reasons, the blue-collar vote for Wallace fell far below the figures predicted by the early polls last fall. Any number of people, moreover, who are not doing well by any set of official statistics, who are earning well below the national mean ($8000 a year), or who hold two jobs to stay above it, think of themselves as affluent, and often use that word. It is almost as if not to be affluent is to be un-American. People who can't use the word tend to be angry; people who come too close to those who can't become frightened. The definition of affluence is generally pinned to what comes in, not to the quality of life as it's lived. The $8000 son of a man who never earned more than $4500 may, for that reason alone, believe that he's "doing all right." If life is not all right, if he can't get his curbs fixed, or his streets patrolled, if the highways are crowded and the beaches polluted, if the schools are ineffectual he is still able to call himself affluent, feels, perhaps, a social compulsion to do so. His anger, if he is angry, is not that of the wage earner resenting management—and certainly not that of the socialist ideologue asking for redistribution of wealth— but that of the consumer, the taxpayer, and the family man. (Inflation and taxes are wiping out most of the wage gains made in labor contracts signed during the past three years.) Thus he will vote for a Louise Day Hicks in Boston who promises to hold the color line in the schools or for a Charles Stenvig calling for law enforcement in Minneapolis but reject a George Wallace who seems to threaten his pocketbook. The danger is that he will identify with the politics of the Birchers and other middle-class reactionaries (who often pretend to speak for him) even though his income and style of life are far removed from theirs; that taxes, for example, will be identified with welfare rather than war, and that he will blame his limited means on the small slice of the poor rather than the fat slice of the rich.

If you sit and talk to people like Marjorie Lemlow, who heads Mothers Support Neighborhood Schools in San Francisco, or Joe Owens, a house painter who is president of a community-action organization in Boston, you quickly discover that the roots of reaction and the roots of reform are often identical, and that the response to particular situations is more often contingent on the politics of the politicians and leaders who appear to care than on the conditions of life or the ideology of the victims. Mrs. Lemlow wants to return the schools to some virtuous past; she worries about disintegration of the family and she speaks vaguely about something that she can't bring herself to call a conspiracy against Americanism. She has been accused of leading a bunch of Birchers, and she sometimes talks Birch language. But whatever the form, her sense of things comes from a small-town vision of national virtues, and her unhappiness from the assaults of urban sophistication. It just so happens that a lot of reactionaries now sing that tune, and that the liberals are indifferent.

Joe Owens—probably because of his experience as a Head Start parent, and because of his association with an effective community-action program—talks a different language. He knows, somehow, that no simple past can be restored. In his world the villains are not conspirators but bureaucrats and politicians, and he is beginning to discover that in a struggle with officials the black man in the ghetto and the working man (black or white) have the same problems. "Every time you ask for something from the politicians they treat you like a beggar, like you ought to be grateful for what you have. They try to make you feel ashamed."

WHEN HOPE BECOMES A THREAT

The imponderables are youth and tradition and change. The civics book and the institution it celebrates—however passé—still hold the world together. The revolt is in their name, not against them. And there is simple decency, the language and practice of the folksy cliché, the small town, the Boy Scout virtues, the neighborhood charity, the obligation to support the church, the rhetoric of open opportunity: "They can keep Wallace and they can keep Alabama. We didn't fight a dictator for four years so we could elect one over here." What happens when all that becomes Mickey Mouse? Is there an urban ethic to replace the values of the small town? Is there a coherent public philosophy, a consistent set of beliefs to replace family, home, and hard work? What happens when the hang-ups of upper-middle-class kids are in fashion and those of blue-collar kids are not? What happens when Doing Your Own Thing becomes not the slogan of the solitary deviant but the norm? Is it possible that as the institutions and beliefs of tradition are fashionably denigrated a blue-collar generation gap will open to the Right as well as to the Left? (There is statistical evidence, for example, that Wallace's greatest support within the unions came from people who are between twenty-one and twenty-nine, those, that is, who have the most tenuous association with the liberalism of labor.) Most are politically silent; although SDS has been trying to organize blue-collar high-school students, there are no Mario Savios or Mark Rudds—either of the Right or the Left—among them. At the same time the union leaders, some of them old hands from the Thirties, aren't sure that the kids are following them either. Who speaks for the son of the longshoreman or the Detroit auto worker? What happens if he doesn't get to college? What, indeed, happens when he does?

Vaguely but unmistakably the hopes that a youth-worshiping nation historically invested in its young are becoming threats. We have never been unequivocal about the symbolic patricide of Americanization and upward mobility, but if at one time mobility meant rejection of older (or European) styles it was, at least, done in the name of America. Now the labels are blurred and the objectives indistinct. Just at the moment when a tradition-bound Italian father is persuaded that he should send his sons to college—that education is the only future—the college blows up. At the moment when a parsimonious taxpayer begins to shell out for what he considers an extravagant state university system the students go on strike. Marijuana, sexual liberation, dress styles, draft resistance, even the rhetoric of change becomes monsters and demons in a world that appears to turn old virtues upside down. The paranoia that fastened on Communism twenty years ago (and sometimes still does) is increasingly directed to vague conspiracies undermining the schools, the family, order and discipline. "They're feeding the kids this generation-gap business," says a Chicago housewife who grinds out a campaign against sex education on a duplicating machine in her living room. "The kids are told to make their own decisions. They're all mixed up by situation ethics and open-ended questions. They're alienating children from their own parents." They? The churches, the schools, even the YMCA and the Girl Scouts, are implicated. But a major share of the villainy is now also attributed to "the social science centers," to the apostles of sensitivity training, and to what one California lady, with some embarrassment, called "nude therapy." "People with sane minds are being altered by psychological methods." The current major campaign of the John Birch Society is not directed against Communists in government or the Supreme Court, but against sex education.

(There is, of course, also sympathy with the young, especially in poorer areas where kids have no place to play. "Everybody's got to have a hobby," a South Boston adolescent told a youth worker. "Ours is throwing rocks." If people will join reactionary organizations to protect their children, they will also support others: community-action agencies which help kids get jobs; Head Start parent groups, Boys Clubs. "Getting this place cleaned up" sometimes refers to a fear of young hoods; sometimes it points to the day when there is a park or a playground or when the existing park can be used. "I want to see them grow up to have a little fun.")

CAN THE COMMON MAN COME BACK?

Beneath it all there is a more fundamental ambivalence, not only about the young, but about institutions—the schools, the churches, the Establishment—and about the future itself. In the major cities of the East (though perhaps not in the West) there is a sense that time is against you, that one is living "in one of the few decent neighborhoods left," that "if I can get $125 a week upstate (or downstate) I'll move." The institutions that were supposed to mediate social change and which, more than ever, are becoming priesthoods of information and conglomerates of social engineers, are increasingly suspect. To attack the Ford Foundation (as Wright Patman has done) is not only to fan the embers of historic populism against concentrations of wealth and power, but also to arouse those who feel that they are trapped by an alliance of upper-class Wasps and lower-class Negroes. If the foundations have done anything for the blue-collar worker he doesn't seem to be aware of it. At the same time the distrust of professional educators that characterizes the black militants is becoming increasingly prevalent among the minority of lower-middle-class whites who are beginning to discover that the schools aren't working for them either. ("Are all those new programs just a cover-up for failure?") And if the Catholic Church is under attack from its liberal members (on birth control, for example) it is also alienating the traditionalists who liked their minor saints (even if they didn't actually exist) and were perfectly content with the Latin Mass. For the alienated Catholic liberal there are other places to go; for the lower-middle-class parishioner in Chicago or Boston there are none.

Perhaps, in some measure, it has always been this way. Perhaps none of this is new. And perhaps it is also true that the American lower middle has never had it so good. And yet surely there is a difference, and that is that the common man has lost his visibility and, somehow, his claim on public attention. There are old liberals and socialists—men like Michael Harrington—who believe that a new alliance can be forged for progressive social action:

> From Marx to Mills, the Left has regarded the middle class as a stratum of hypocritical, vacillating rear-guarders. There was often sound reason for this contempt. But is it not possible that a new class is coming into being? It is not the old middle class of small property owners and entrepreneurs, nor the new middle class of managers. It is composed of scientists, technicians, teachers, and professionals in the public sector of the society. By education and work experience it is predisposed toward planning. It could be an ally of the poor and the organized workers—or their sophisticated enemy. In other words, an unprecedented social and political variable seems to be taking shape in America.
>
> The American worker, even when he waits on a table or holds open a door, is not servile; he does not carry himself like an inferior. The openness, frankness, and democratic manner which Tocqueville described in the last century persists to this very day. They have been a source of rudeness, contemptuous ignorance, violence—and of a creative self-confidence among great masses of people. It was in this latter spirit that the CIO was organized and the black freedom movement marched.

There are recent indications that the white lower middle class is coming back on the roster of public priorities. Pucinski tells you that liberals in Congress are privately discussing the pressure from the middle class. There are proposals now to increase personal income-tax exemptions from $600 to $1000 (or $1200) for each dependent, to protect all Americans with a national insurance system covering catastrophic medical expenses, and to put a floor under all incomes. Yet these things by themselves are insufficient. Nothing is sufficient without a national sense of restoration. What Pucinski means by the middle class has, in some measure, always been represented. A physician earning $75,000 a year is also a working man but he is hardly a victim of the welfare system. Nor, by and large, are the stockholders of the Standard Oil Company or U.S. Steel. The fact that American ideals have often been corrupted in the cause of self-aggrandizement does not make them any less important for the cause of social reform and justice. "As a movement with the conviction that there is more to people than greed and fear," Harrington said, "the Left must . . . also speak in the name of the historic idealism of the United States."

The issue, finally, is not *the program* but the vision, the angle of view. A huge constituency may be coming up for grabs, and there is considerable evidence that its political mobility is more sensitive than anyone can imagine, that all the sociological determinants are not as significant as the simple facts of concern and leadership. When Robert Kennedy was killed last year, thousands of working-class people who had expected to vote for him—if not hundreds of thousands—shifted their loyalties to Wallace. A man who can change from a progressive democrat into a bigot overnight deserves attention.

30
Organized Labor in Electoral Politics:
Some Questions for the Discipline

Harry M. Scoble

ORGANIZED LABOR AS A SYSTEM OF ELECTORAL POWER

The CIO's Political Action Committee was created under and largely by Sidney Hillman in 1943 for the purpose of "nonparty, nonpartisan" politics. The American Federation of Labor hesitated just long enough, in its traditional reluctance to turn away from "business-unionism," to witness the failure of organized labor to defeat the Taft-Hartley Act in 1946; then it, too, took the path of electoral action, patterning its Labor's League for Political Education on the earlier PAC. (Since 1955 and the merger of the AFL and CIO, these political-action arms have slowly been merged into the joint Committee on Political Education.) These

From *Western Political Quarterly*, 16 (September 1963), 666–685. Reprinted by permission of the University of Utah, copyright owners. The author says: The present article is the result of a broader research on ideology and electoral action in American politics. That research has been made possible by grants from The Maurice and Laura Falk Foundation through the Eagleton Institute of Politics, Rutgers, The State University; from the Social Science Research Council of New York City; and from the Graduate Research Committee, University of Wisconsin. Obviously, no one of these is to be considered the author, publisher, or proprietor of the present publication; nor are they to be understood as endorsing by virtue of their grants or aid any of the statements made or views expressed herein.

facts, which every politically oriented student of America ought to know, are repeated here to underscore the major point that the most fundamental postwar change in the structure and process of political parties has been the entrance of organized labor into electoral activity at the precinct level and on up.

But when one searches the literature of social science for a full description of what it is in fact that labor unions *do* in elections and for systematic analysis of such activity, one finds primarily pronouncements and sentiments instead of facts and science. For example, Blaisdell concluded in 1957 that "pressure groups do practically everything in political campaigns that the parties do expect the nominating of candidates for office"—but he can cite no studies to show that this is so.[1] Ranney and Kendall also recognized that change had occurred; but their recognition, in 1956, is again couched in general terms and is focused on the *legal* reasons why unions (like corporations, the NAM, and the Chamber of Commerce) continue to insist that the money they spend in elections goes only into propaganda and educational activity.[2] Clinton Rossiter, meanwhile, having apparently reviewed the empirical studies that have, however, not been made, concluded in 1960 that organized labor's political-potential had now been maximized.[3] And where the Schattschneider of 1955 noted generally that the growth of "ancillary organizations" such as PAC and LLPE had introduced a functional parallelism which had "greatly modified the behavior of the regular party organizations," the Schattschneider of 1960 was able to conclude that the impact of such electoral activity must be small because "the largest special-interest group in the country can swing only about one million votes."[4]

Lest the purpose of the preceding paragraph be misunderstood—I am not jousting with particular individuals. When a political scientist sets out to illuminate his students' minds on the subject of unions and politics, he necessarily resorts to "generalization without the inconvenience of observation," in Key's felicitous phrase, because the textbooks are no good; and the textbooks are no good because political scientists have done no research (*vide* index and contents of the *American Political Science Review* since 1945). Nor are political scientists alone in this failing. A recent bibliography of 314 titles, in political science, sociology, and economics, on the subject of "power and democracy in America" reveals per-

[1] Donald C. Blaisdell, *American Democracy under Pressure* (New York: Ronald Press, 1957), p. 115. The book is written as if we were still in the midst of the Depression, with labor only just beginning to organize.

[2] Austin Ranney and Willmoore Kendall, *Democracy and the American Party System* (New York: Harcourt, Brace, 1956), pp. 373–374. At p. 268 the almost inevitable reference to the *exclusive* control of nominations is made. Presumably this is a consequence of the fact that political scientists became relatively fixated upon the presidency during the Roosevelt years and even after; but even here they did not do their homework—as will be shown in discussion of national conventions in the text.

[3] Clinton Rossiter, *Parties and Politics in America* (Ithaca: Cornell University Press, 1960), pp. 57–58, 94–95, 164–165, and 167. Surely the 1950's evidenced first a stabilization and then a decline in union membership numerically; but equally surely the witticisms of Parkinson should bring political scientists up short: until we know something about the rate and the efficiency of resource expenditure, no inferences about political power may be derived from changes in the magnitude of the raw resource itself.

[4] The first conclusion may be found in Sigmund Neumann (ed.), *Modern Political Parties* (Chicago: University of Chicago Press, 1956), p. 214. The second quotation from E. E. Schattschneider may be found in his *The Semisovereign People* (New York: Holt, Rinehart and Winston, 1960), p. 52. An assessment of the electoral impact of organized labor will be made in the text below.

haps 15 which might possibly touch in any empirical way on the subject of organized labor in electoral politics.[5]

Therefore, the purpose of this article is to attempt to pull together the few facts that exist on the subject. For tentative organization of the factual matter, it is convenient to look at organized labor from the standpoints of the following areas of electoral behavior: the national conventions and legislative recruitment; the party apparatus itself; and vote mobilization in terms first of registration drives, get-out-the-vote drives, and the direction of the vote, and then in terms of labor money in elections. These categories are convenient only; it should be clear that they are not mutually exclusive.

THE NATIONAL CONVENTIONS AND LEGISLATIVE RECRUITMENT

The available facts are pitifully few. Why should this be so? The area of national conventions and legislative recruitment provide illustrations. If one takes the date of the creation of the PAC as the proper starting point of the entrance of unions into elections, it is clear that nine national elections have now passed in which organized labor has participated; four of these were presidential elections. It seems not unreasonable to hypothesize that mass-membership interest groups will seek to seat their officers-members in the state delegations to the national nominating convention of that party with which the overwhelming majority of the interest group members identify. For example, Key noted that "around 200 unionists attended the Democratic National Convention as delegates or alternates in 1952";[6] and anyone attending to his television set in 1960 could learn that there were 42 officers-members of the United Steel Workers alone among the total Pennsylvania delegation to the Democratic Convention. Furthermore, it is common knowledge among political scientists that the Brookings Institution has expended large sums of money and has produced several massive descriptions of national party conventions and of presidential elections; and in all that body of description, it is possible to learn that in 1948 labor union representatives constituted 2.1 percent of the total Democratic delegations as against 0.2 percent of the total Republican delegations while 1962 data include information on the annual income, the education, and so on of the delegates (one may even discover the races of the ministers who prayed for those conventions)—but one cannot find information on the *occupations* or the *interest group memberships* of the delegations for 1952, or for 1956, or for 1960.[7] This suggests that sheer description is not enough; the product amounts only to a dated edition of the *New York Times*. The conclusion is inescapable: if teams of political scientists are to describe complex political behavior such as a national convention or a presidential campaign, some organizing principles other than mere chronology must first be decided upon. It is my con-

[5] See William V. D'Antonio and Howard J. Ehrlich (eds.), *Power and Democracy in America* (Notre Dame: University of Notre Dame Press, 1961), "Selected Bibliography."
[6] V. O. Key, Jr., *Politics, Parties and Pressure Groups* (4th ed.; New York: Crowell, 1958), p. 73, quoting Max M. Kampelman.
[7] Paul T. David *et al.*, *The Politics of National Party Conventions* (Washington: Brookings Institution, 1960), p. 177, and *Presidential Nominating Politics in 1952* (Baltimore: Johns Hopkins Press, 1954), I. See also Charles A. H. Thomson and Frances M. Shattuck, *The 1956 Presidential Campaign* (Washington: Brookings, 1960) and Ralph M. Goldman, "The National Party Conventions," in Alfred Junz (ed.), *Present Trends in American National Government* (New York: Praeger, 1961).

tention that group theory can provide organization and meaning where none now exist.

Candidate-recruitment presents another enigma. Labor's League for Political Education announced in 1949 that it would henceforth subsidize labor members of those state legislatures in which salaries were extremely low.[8] The proposal was patterned on the long-standing practice of the British Labour party; its purpose was to increase the availability of labor union candidacies by organized compensation for social-structural processes noted at least as long ago as the time of Max Weber.[9] Within the limits of the institutional and demographic gerrymander against the union vote in all state politics, the LLPE proposal *might, if carried out*, have had some measurable counterbalancing effect. But what political scientist in America even knows whether the policy was attempted, much less effective? One may, of course, suppose that the LLPE activists were somewhat naïve in their public announcement: the reader may easily imagine the editorial reaction to such a "radical" proposal in the pages of the *New York Times*, the *Wall Street Journal*, and almost every other newspaper in the land.[10] It is not inconceivable that labor leaders might have decided that such policies are best carried out away from the glare of flashbulbs and klieg lights. But who in the political science profession is carrying out trend analyses to find out whether, regardless of labor propaganda, labor ideology is in fact being advanced by increasing union representation in state legislatures? It was like pulling teeth to find out that "laborers and craftsmen" constituted 5.5 percent of all lower-house members and 2.5 percent of all state Senate members in 1949; the combined percentage was 5.0, and such *possibly* union legislators were most *numerically* frequent in the legislatures of Rhode Island, Minnesota, Connecticut, and Pennsylvania, in descending order; on the other hand, in the most heavily industrialized states of Massachusetts, Michigan, New York, and New Jersey "representatives of labor were so few that in numerical terms they were of little significance, although in these states there were more labor leaders." [11] That summarizes what is known.

LABOR AND THE PARTY APPARATUS

Suppose that one asks what is known concerning organized labor and the party apparatus, again with relation to the Democratic party. If it could be demonstrated that organized labor *is* sometimes the political party at city, county, and/or state levels, political scientists could finally turn away from the foolish distinction about nominations and begin to ask the more important questions: Under what conditions, with what tactics, and with what consequences do mass-mem-

---

[8] See John P. Roche and Murray S. Stedman, Jr., *The Dynamics of Democratic Government* (New York: McGraw-Hill, 1954), p. 70.
[9] See "Politics as a Vocation," in H. C. Gerth and C. Wright Mills (eds.), *From Max Weber: Essays in Sociology* (New York: Oxford University Press, 1958).
[10] If newspapers ever train labor correspondents instead of converting unsuccessful sports writers to this chore, both editorials and news columns should become more accurate and therefore, from labor's viewpoint, more fair. As things stand now, labor leaders and ordinary members alike apparently are finding truth—and thus allies—in the most unlikely places, viz., the *New Yorker* magazine. See A. J. Liebling, *The Press* (New York: Ballantine Books, 1961), pp. 119–122.
[11] Belle Zeller (ed.), *American State Legislatures* (New York: Crowell, 1954), p. 72.

bership interest groups become the party apparatus? The trend questions also then become appropriate.

To illustrate: in Rockford, Illinois, the CIO-PAC organized to elect precinct captains in order successfully to swing the election of the Democratic chairman for Winnebago County.[12] Concerning *local* elections, the evidence—such as it is—is an odd mixture. In New Haven, Connecticut, the city itself is the fifth largest employer; most of its employees are now unionized and, along with other union members and union families, now constitute about 36 percent of the electorate; these people have apparently voted as a bloc in at least one important election (1945)—but unionist activity has not become the apparatus for local nominations and elections, and the trade union leadership's activity and involvement is largely that of traditional lobbying "only on questions of the wages, security, and working conditions of city employees." [13] A survey of the politics of education in Massachusetts also suggests that labor union leaders and members have not yet perceived local electoral activity as a means to their ends, relying instead on ineffectual traditional lobbying to promote the addition of pro-labor courses to the public school curriculum, to protest the politico-economic views of teachers, and to protest the use of NAM-supplied "educational materials" in the school system.[14] In Madison and Kenosha, Wisconsin, on the other hand, evidence exists of direct and increasing union activity in local educational elections.[15] The best available survey of New York City politics suggests the following: The Central Trades and Labor Council (AFL and representing about three-quarters of a million unionists) had initially de-emphasized its political purpose, but had "an almost unbroken history of endorsing the major candidates of the Democratic Party for city office" (with, however, an occasional split to a Republican candidate for Borough President and City Council in the last decade). Its electoral activity locally was directed primarily toward a broad concern for personnel and policy in the limited interests of the building trades, teamsters, and longshoremen's unions. Meanwhile the authors expected that the 1959 merger (with a million-and-a-half unionists) would lead to slow change in the direction of "greater and more unified influence" because of the CIO's greater concern for electoral action and also because of the 400,000 votes quadrennially mustered by the Liberal party (largely ILGWU).[16]

The evidence that is available thus suggests that organized labor has not yet become the party apparatus of the community with regard to community or local politics; on the other hand, lacking "community political systems" analyses of Akron, Cicero, Gary, or Pittsburgh, it is wisest to suspend judgment on this point.

At least the study of organized labor with regard to nationally oriented party machinery has been a little more thorough and slightly more revealing. Recent studies of the successes of the Democratic party in such widely separated states as Maine and Wisconsin provide brief generalized descriptions of union activity;

---

[12] Cited in Hugh A. Bone, *American Politics and the Party System* (New York: McGraw-Hill, 1955), p. 113.
[13] Robert A. Dahl, *Who Governs?* (New Haven: Yale University Press, 1961), pp. 76 and 253–254.
[14] Neal Gross, *Who Runs Our Schools?* (New York: Wiley, 1958), pp. 50, 52, and 53.
[15] Unpublished material of the author.
[16] Wallace S. Sayre and Herbert Kaufman, *Governing New York City* (New York: Russell Sage Foundation, 1960), pp. 508–514.

at the lowest level of analysis, therefore, one may infer some effect.[17] More directly descriptive of the relations between organized labor and the growth of successful party organization are recent studies of the Minnesota and Michigan Democratic parties. Mitau indicates the present importance of union-member identification with the Democrat-Farmer-Labor party in the former state [18] while the studies of the Michigan Democrats by Calkins, by the Sarasohns, and by Eldersveld and his associates [19] particularly highlight the role of unions in creating a party apparatus. In Michigan, for example, it is estimated that 821 of 1000 members filing in 1948 for Wayne County precinct delegate were stimulated to action by their union-membership; shortly after that (the year of the first Williams victory) it was estimated that 64 percent of all money donated to the Democratic State Central Committee and directly to statewide candidates came from United Auto Worker and other CIO-union funds. And, by the mid-1950s, evidence existed for concluding that CIO-PAC electoral action not only exceeded that of the regular Democratic organization in much of Wayne County but that "in fact, in a few of the Detroit Congressional Districts the regular organization has been largely supplanted by the CIO-PAC." [20] More broadly, Heard has cited evidence indicating that in 1952, somewhere in the neighborhood of 1000 unionists were active as full-time campaign workers in the closing weeks of the election in California, while in 1956 in the Detroit area 1549 UAW temporary election workers were hired with dues money paid to local unions.[21] Additional evidence of the integration of union structure and Democratic party structure comes from a study of precinct committeemen in Gary, Indiana; for the study by Rossi and Cutright indicates the importance of membership in and identification with the union, particularly the United Steel Workers, in leading into precinct political work. In the sample, 20 percent of the white Democratic and 23 percent of the Negro Democratic precinct committeemen gave union (or class-interest) responses as the "self-activating motive" for entering political work. Among Republican precinct workers the comparable percentages were zero.[22] From such facts one may infer

[17] See John C. Donovan, *Congressional Campaign: Maine Elects a Democrat* (New York: Holt, 1958), and Leon D. Epstein, *Politics in Wisconsin* (Madison: University of Wisconsin Press, 1958).
[18] G. Theodore Mitau, *Politics in Minnesota* (Minneapolis: University of Minnesota Press, 1960).
[19] Fay Calkins, *The CIO and the Democratic Party* (Chicago: University of Chicago Press, 1952); Stephen B. and Vera H. Sarasohn, *Political Party Patterns in Michigan* (Detroit: Wayne State University Press, 1957); and Samuel J. Eldersveld et al., *Political Affiliation in Metropolitan Detroit* (Ann Arbor: Bureau of Government, University of Michigan, 1957). Arthur Kornhauser et al., *When Labor Votes* (New York: University Books, 1956), also provides useful information on the political activities of the United Auto Workers.
[20] Eldersveld et al., *Political Affiliation in Metropolitan Detroit*, p. 87.
[21] Alexander Heard, *The Costs of Democracy* (Chapel Hill: University of North Carolina Press, 1960), p. 205 and n. 108. Heard did not identify the California labor leader source, nor did the latter indicate whether these election workers were union-paid. The 1956 data derive from the 1957 report of the Senate Special (McClellan) Lobby Committee.
[22] Peter H. Rossi and Phillips Cutright, "The Impact of Party Organization in an Industrial Setting," in Morris Janowitz (ed.), *Community Political Systems* (New York: Free Press, 1961), p. 88. These union, class-motivated Democratic committeemen were also reported to be the most issue-oriented—at both local and national levels—of all their fellows. Curiously, in their report, Rossi and Cutright do not trace out the specific

that since World War II union leaders and members alike have in large numbers come to the conclusion that political activism within—and public identification with—the Democratic party is an efficient means to personal and organization goals.

VOTE MOBILIZATION

Vote-mobilization is the third area of inquiry in this review of the scant factual material available about organized labor in electoral politics. Labor unions have carried out registration drives and get-out-the-vote drives in both primary and general elections and have done everything else that a political party does, including provision of free baby-sitting service on election day. At the level of description, facts abound; but at the level of analysis, knowledge remains fragmentary, shadowy, and highly unsystematic. For example, the New Jersey CIO-PAC carried on a self-appraisal of its early-registration drive; and at least one political scientist, having read this, stated that "convincing evidence is available to show that the CIO did a relatively better job in 1950 in registering its members than the general public"; while Heard more generally cites a Connecticut CIO Council report, "Voter Registration Survey—1954," to the effect that it revealed "startlingly low registration among union members, and the rewarding effects of attempts to raise it" [23]—the sole references available in political science literature today that constitute anything close to evaluations of the effectiveness of such political action. This raises a series of interrelated questions: Have union political activists stopped attempting to appraise their activities since 1951? If not, have they "clamped a lid of secrecy" on such analysis? Again if not, then have political scientists been remiss in not asking the right questions of the right people? A second comment must be made about the meager data: the correct baseline for the measurement of effect of any union political activity—registration or get-out-the-vote or directional-impact—is other unorganized workers and not "the general public." Thus when Jack Kroll wrote in 1951, estimating that roughly the first five years of labor voter-registration drives had resulted in "about 55 to 60 percent of labor union members" having been registered and that this constituted "only a slight edge on the general population," [24] the political scientist

---

nature of the organizational ties of their respondents (see their Table IV and related text, pp. 91–92).

[23] Bone, *American Politics and the Party System*, p. 114, citing *The Effectiveness of CIO-PAC in New Jersey in 1950* (Newark: New Jersey State CIO Council, 1951). The report claimed a net gain of 12,000 CIO members registered in September 1950 in four key counties of the state. Union registration is considered in Heard, *The Costs of Democracy*, p. 205 and n. 108. In discussing "the biggest election upset since Harry Truman's 1948 victory," John H. Fenton does not directly discuss registration and get-out-the-vote drives by unions in Ohio in 1958; but one might infer this as related to the defeat of an incumbent Republican senator, an incumbent Republican governor, and of the "right-to-work" proposition. See his "The Right-to-Work Vote in Ohio," *Midwest Journal of Political Science*, 3 (1959), 241–253.

[24] Jack Kroll, "Labor's Political Role," in *Annals*, 274 (1951), 118–122, at p. 121. (Kroll had succeeded Hillman to the chairmanship of the CIO-PAC in 1946.) Avery Leiserson, "Organized Labor as a Pressure Group," in the same issue of *Annals*, 108–117, is also worth reading.

ought to have been skeptical: organized labor has a vested interest in appearing efficient-but-not-too-efficient in American politics.

This is an exceedingly important point—what does activity mean?—and one on which, despite the repeated injunctions of Lasswell in favor of trend analysis [25] and despite the welcome work of the Survey Research Center,[26] it is apparently impossible to obtain relevant data for comparison over more than three successive elections in a time-series. For example, do union members vote (including register) more frequently than relevant others? Campbell and Cooper present data for 1948, 1952, and 1954 indicating that unionists voted 6.7 percent more frequently than others—but the comparison is with the general population; [27] but when union members are correctly compared only with non-union workers of comparable occupation, education, income, and status—for the two presidential elections on which data are available the unionists voted at an average of 16.0 percent more.[28] Both of these figures suggest that important differences in volume of political activity are associated with labor unions and that these differences between unionists and non-unionists (whether generally or specifically compared) *increased* between 1945 and 1955.

This brings us to the second point of inquiry. It is hardly esoteric social science knowledge that organized labor, at least since 1936, has consistently voted more Democratic than have other sectors of society. But all knowledge beyond this seems to be highly esoteric in the sense that it is extremely difficult to find intelligent appraisals of *how much* more Democratic and of trends. Illustratively, union families in Elmira, New York, whether of skilled workers or unskilled, were at least 24 percent more Democratic than non-union families in both categories in the 1948 election; [29] but that was an unusual election, as Dr. George Gallup and other commercial pollsters have revealed. Its uniqueness is evident in the 1948 "Iowa Poll" of the *Des Moines Register and Tribune,* which indicated that union members were 9 percent more likely to report having had conversations concerning the election and were 18 percent more "certain of vote" than the general Iowa sample *even with education controlled.*[30] It is appropriate, therefore, to turn away from the "unique event" which plagues social science just as much as it

[25] For recent reiteration of a thirty-year theme, see Harold D. Lasswell, "Strategies of Inquiry: The Rational Use of Observation," in Daniel Lerner (ed.), *The Human Meaning of the Social Sciences* (New York: Meridian, 1959).
[26] For the reconstruction attempted in the text, I have drawn on publications of the Survey Research Center, all of which may be cited as Angus Campbell *et al.: The People Elect a President* (Ann Arbor: Survey Research Center, University of Michigan, 1952); *The Voter Decides* (New York: Harper & Row, 1954); *Group Differences in Attitudes and Votes* (Ann Arbor: Survey Research Center, University of Michigan, 1956); and *The American Voter* (New York: Wiley, 1960).
[27] Campbell and Cooper, *Group Differences in Attitudes and Votes*, Table III–11 at p. 31.
[28] Campbell and Kahn, *The People Elect a President*, for 1948 (an observed difference of 15 percent); and Campbell and Cooper, *Group Differences*, for 1952 (17 percent).
[29] Bernard R. Berelson *et al., Voting* (Chicago: University of Chicago Press, 1954), pp. 46–47. Their analysis also indicated that CIO members were most Democratic, IAM next, and AFL least. Such intra-union differences also show up in Eldersveld *et al., Political Affiliation in Metropolitan Detroit,* p. 99.
[30] This was also revealed too late. I infer from this that PAC and LLPE activity had some effect. See Norman C. Meier and Harold W. Saunders (eds.), *The Polls and Public Opinion* (New York: Holt, 1949).

does Dr. Gallup, although in somewhat different ways. Gallup data for the entire period 1936 through 1960 have recently been published [31] indicating that "union families" voted an average of 6.7 percent more Democratic than "all manual-worker families." An earlier Gallup analysis, covering only 1936 through 1948 *but more directly* comparing "non-union labor" with "union members," indicated that the latter were on the average 12 percent more Democratic than non-union labor.[32] Furthermore, if in the depressing discontinuities of social science research it is permissible to consider four successive data points as constituting trend data, the spread between unionist and non-union has increased with the political activity of organized labor; for the 1936 and 1940 differences are the same (8 percent) and only half the 1944 and 1948 differences. My belief that an *increasing* differential has occurred simultaneously with increasing electoral activity by unions is supported by the most recently published Survey Research Center data, in that a comparison of union members in 1956 with "a '*control*' group of non-members that matches the '*test*' group of members on all important aspects of life situation save the fact of membership" [33] indicated that the unionists were more than 20 percent more Democratic than the control group, while union families were 17 percent more Democratic than the matched control group.

These figures have been patiently reconstructed, and the bases of choice and comparison perhaps laboriously verbalized, in order to test the assumption of E. E. Schattschneider that the net electoral impact of organized labor is just under one million votes.[34] My estimate is presented in Table 1. It suggests that the net gain of the Democratic party in presidential elections as a consequence of the existence of unions is perhaps as much as 2,800,000 votes; furthermore the *gross* impact of unionization may be estimated by alternatively hypothesizing what the Democratic vote would be if *all* 31,000,000 workers were unionized (over 16,-000,000 votes) and what it would be if *none* of them were (just under 10,500,000 votes)—that is, the total variation for the relevant labor force could be as much as

---

[31] In V. O. Key, Jr., *Public Opinion and American Democracy* (New York: Knopf, 1961), p. 523. As usual, the academic social scientist must have some reservation concerning the precision of comparative analyses by the Gallup organization; that is, the data reported in the text constitute a comparison of "union families" with "all manual-worker families," and there is no indication that the latter category is *exclusive* of the former. I suspect that it is not and that, for the reasons given in the text and drawn from SRC data, it unnecessarily deflates the extent of Democratic-orientation of unionists.

[32] George Gallup, "How Labor Votes," in *Annals*, 274 (1951), 124. Heard, *The Costs of Democracy*, p. 205, n. 110, cites unpublished Survey Research Center data from 1956 indicating that among Stevenson-voters, members of union families more frequently indicated having engaged in actual campaign work than did members of non-union families (the reverse was true for Eisenhower-voters). Furthermore, 21 percent of union members reported having used campaign buttons or car stickers, whereas this figure was only 13.5 percent for non-union respondents. Stricter controls would undoubtedly reveal greater spreads in rates of "higher forms" of political action as well as in the act of voting alone.

[33] Campbell *et al.*, *The American Voter*, pp. 301–306, at p. 304, original emphasis. A less rigorous comparison with "the residual, non-member portion of the total sample" revealed the following Democratic deviation in the two-party vote division percentage: for union families, + 35.8 (1948), + 19.8 (1952), and +18.1 (1956); for union members only, no separate comparison was available for 1948, but 1952 showed + 24.9 and 1956, + 21.4 deviation.

[34] Schattschneider, *The Semisovereign People*, pp. 49–52.

TABLE 1

Probable Net Democratic Vote Impact of Electoral Action of Organized Labor in Late 1950s and Early 1960s

	Organized Labor	Unorganized Labor
Total numbers	15,000,000	16,000,000
Mean voting rate	75%	59%
Probable turnout	11,250,000	9,440,000
Mean Democratic percent of the two-party vote	70%	56%
Probable Democratic vote	7,875,000	5,381,000
Probable Democratic vote with assumptions reversed:		
1. if organized labor behaved politically like unorganized labor	5,044,500	—
2. if unorganized labor behaved politically like organized labor	—	8,400,000
Democratic gain as consequence of unions	2,830,500	—
Republican avoidance of loss as consequence of lack of unionization	—	3,019,000

Note: This table is based on probable Presidential vote; the 1960 Labor Force figures have been approximated; the turnout rates and the party-vote rates for union members have been averaged from Survey Research Center data cited in footnote 26 previously; the differentials between union member and non-union member have been averaged between the SRC (higher) and the Gallup (lower) data.

5,848,700 votes at the present time and under projections of available data as to both turnout and Democratic-preference. And this is why my estimate is almost three times what Schattschneider's was: he assumed that the voting rate was "only about half of the membership" (i.e., for unionists); he assumed that there was *no* spread between unionists and non-unionists (the data available indicate it is about 16 percent); and he lastly assumed a party-preference differential of only 10 percent (whereas the conservative estimate used here is only 13 percent, to compromise the differences between Survey Research Center and Gallup data).

Now, my point in all this is not to attack a single individual—Schattschneider's reputation was long ago established and at a deservedly high level—but rather to underline unmistakably how damningly difficult it is for *any* political scientist to obtain relevant and reliable data for comparative analysis, because individually and collectively we have failed our profession. We have been anecdotalists and not empiricists; we have been individualistic librarianists and not field-oriented team- or group-researchers; and we have not as yet learned the inestimable quality and capacity for collective self-appraisals that appear regularly and usefully in sociology, psychology, and other social sciences. The only thing we have that I would not grant the other social sciences is a superior personal (and therefore modal-collective) political ideology, but in this we are not much different from members of labor unions; and, however superior the ideology for personal (and collective) action, it is not the basis upon which a social *science* can be founded.

MAGNITUDE AND METHOD OF FINANCIAL INVOLVEMENT

The analysis of voter-mobilization by labor unions in the preceding section leads to the conclusion that the *net* gain to Democratic presidential candidates during the 1950s was something under one-eleventh of the total popular vote necessary for election.[35] But voter-mobilization is also the end-purpose of the flow of money into elections; therefore it is appropriate to examine in this section what is known concerning the extent, methods, and impact of labor money in politics.

To begin with, it is extremely difficult to obtain any reliable and comparable data that span more than two elections—as Alexander Heard, the author of the most exhaustive treatment of money in politics, has carefully noted.[36] However, it is possible to examine a variety of alternative data presented by Heard in an attempt to establish the upper limit of the extent of spending in elections by labor unions. A first, and perhaps the best, measure is that of direct expenditure (for goods and services consumed during a campaign) by national-level campaign groups. For 1952, labor money constituted 15 percent of all direct expenditures in behalf of Democrats, and in 1956 this proportion was 11 percent.[37] At a second and quite different level, Heard estimates that the *voluntary* political giving by some 17,000,000 unionists in 1956 constituted about $2,000,000 which in turn just about balanced the voluntary contributions in amounts of $500 or more recorded by 742 officials of the 225 largest business concerns in the nation.[38] Approximately one union member in eight contributed voluntarily during this period, with the average contribution something less than $1.00 and with considerable variation: in highly politicized unions such as the UAW or the ILGWU, both the rate and the average amount of contribution were considerably higher (e.g., one in two members and an average of $2.57 in the latter union). But voluntary contribution is only part of the process, as Heard notes; for dues-money may flow into election campaigns through one or more of a wide variety of activities: donations (e.g., the ILGWU donated an average of $15,500 annually to the ADA in 1953–1956); the maintenance of political departments, such as the "political shop-steward" program of the ILGWU; the creation of special "Citizenship Funds" (in the UAW, 5 percent of the member's dues goes into such a fund maintained by the international and another 5 percent into a local fund); the development of "education and information" programs, such as the IAM training classes on the relation between legislation and political activity; or undertaking communications and public service activities (e.g., the AFL-CIO sponsors Edward P. Morgan on ABC nationally, while the UAW sponsors the radio-television newscasts of Guy Nunn in the Detroit metropolitan area). In addition, it should be obvious that electoral purposes may be served through union expenditures on: public relations and research; union legal departments; union-executive expense accounts; general administrative costs; and, of course, salaries. All of these account for some hard-to-measure but nonetheless real methods for organized investment in the electoral process by unions. In an effort to provide some estimate of the dollar magnitude of such investment, Heard has taken organized labor's numerical membership as a proportion of the potential electorate—roughly 17

[35] Based on an assumption of an average of 33,000,000 popular votes to win, derived from the last three presidential elections.
[36] Heard, *The Costs of Democracy*, chaps. i and ii especially.
[37] Heard, *The Costs of Democracy*, p. 20.
[38] Heard, *The Costs of Democracy*, pp. 195–196. Heard estimates this to be 0.3 percent of annual union dues; the significance of such money does not, however, lie solely in its magnitude but in its legal status as well; i.e., opponents of organized labor have sought to restrict the use of union-dues by a variety of legal controls; for example, the Taft-Hartley Act of 1947 sought to prohibit unions from *expenditures* as well as contributions in *nominations* as well as general elections for federal offices.

percent—and concludes that "labor money in politics from all sources pays *a much smaller share* of the nation's campaign-connected costs than union members constitute of the population of voting age."[39] However, such an estimate may unintentionally conceal the significance of such labor money to the Democratic party. For example, one might arbitrarily take 10 percent as labor's actual share of the roughly $165,000,000 in cash-and-kind costs for financing all the electoral activities entailed in a presidential election year; but that 10 percent of the *total* would be highly significant in Democratic party finance for two reasons: very close to 100 percent of all labor money goes to the Democractic side (see below) *and,* for the period under review, the two-party division of resources and expenditures was roughly 60–40 in favor of the Republicans; therefore the 10 percent over-all share of labor actually would constitute close to 25 percent of all Democratic funds. Whether the empirical basis for testing this tentative conclusion will ever be unearthed seems highly problematical; such a project would require even more time, money, and effort than were put forth in the heroic labors of the University of North Carolina (Heard) project. Meanwhile one may infer that the apparent autonomy, decentralization, and disarray of the organizational structure of unions provide national labor leaders with a convenient excuse for saying that they simply do not and cannot know all the facts;[40] and one might equally suppose that some, perhaps many, Democratic (and Republican) candidates also prefer not to know too much about the entire process of money in elections.

When one turns from the *magnitude* of labor's financial involvement in elections to the *method* of its involvement, three additional aspects of Heard's analysis of labor money become relevant. Heard's available evidence on the geography of labor support in 1956 indicated that such support was concentrated within the ten states whose populations include two-thirds of all organized labor.[41] His next analysis, focused on the partisan recipients of funds transferred by labor committees, showed the almost exclusive support of Democrats. In 1952, for example, $833,000 could be traced, and $5450 had been transmitted to one senatorial and five House Republican candidates (an average of $908 each); the analysis for 1956 of $1,616,000 of national-level and of $430,000 of state-local-level labor committee transfers showed a total of $3925 going to eight House Republican candidates (about $491 each).[42] A final aspect of the method of labor's financial involvement as depicted by Heard is contained within the data of Table 2. The major point of interest in the table is the clear indication that labor union leaders desire to, and primarily do, deal directly with Democratic *candidates* (or

---

[39] Heard, *The Costs of Democracy*, pp. 196–208, at p. 208; my emphasis. The estimate of others occasionally runs higher than this. See for example Ivan Hinderaker, *Party Politics* (New York: Holt, 1956), p. 585. The evidence is sketchy; but to judge from data assembled from the *Congressional Quarterly* and Heard, it seems likely that longer-term analyses will show that organized labor—unlike most party and non-party groups—is able to sustain its level of operation from one election to the next, i.e., it does not suffer post-presidential atrophy.
[40] See Heard, *The Costs of Democracy*, pp. 183–184, on the Gore Committee experience in 1956. Furthermore, as seems true in almost all aspects of the study of American politics, information is most full and accurate at the national level and least at the local level—yet six-sevenths of all electoral expenditures are incurred at the state, district, and local levels.
[41] Heard, *The Costs of Democracy*, pp. 173–175 and 187–188.
[42] Heard, *The Costs of Democracy*, recomputed from footnotes to Table 23, p. 185, and text at p. 187.

TABLE 2
Types of Recipients of Transfers of Labor Funds from National-Level and State-Local-Level Committees in 1952 and 1956

	Election Year, Type, and Number of Labor Committees Transferring Funds					
	1952 14 N-L		1956 17 N-L		1956 155 S-L	
Types of Recipients	Amount	Per Cent	Amount	Per Cent	Amount	Per Cent
At national level		26		25		9
Labor and other non-party committees	$119,000		$297,000		$ 34,000	
Democratic party committees	98,000		109,000		3,000	
At state-local level		74		75		91
Labor committees	268,000		236,000		95,000	
Democratic candidates or their committees						
for the Senate	100,000		326,000		43,000	
for the House	80,000		334,000		136,000	
Other (non-party) and miscellaneous	101,000		272,000		27,000	
Democratic party committees	67,000		42,000		24,000	
State-local candidates or their committees	—		—		68,000	

Source: Simplified and recomputed from data presented in Heard, *The Costs of Democracy,* p. 185, Table 23.

their personal committees); they deliberately bypass the established Democratic party committees at both national and state-local levels. Heard also indicates the obverse of this, in that there is evidence that union leaders have frequently sought to prevent Democratic party solicitation within and among their local memberships.[43] In the broader context of my analysis, these data on voter-mobilization are further indications of the tendency of interest groups to expend such potential resources as exist within the electoral process and to expend them at such a rate and with such efficiency that the group takes over *all* of the *relevant* functions of the political party.

This last broad generalization unfortunately creates more intellectual problems than it solves, for it begs three additional questions: How much in fact has organized labor committed its potential resources to electoral politics? How efficiently in fact has it exploited these committee resources? And what in fact have political scientists done by way of systematic analysis to answer these first two questions?

At several points in the preceding sections I have pointed out the lack of both data and analysis; consequently I recommend the following specific questions for focusing disciplined inquiry into the increasing electoral action of organized labor. Does a strongly held and economically based ideology—for business or for labor —lead to efficiency in electoral action? Does a left-oriented *labor* ideology incorporate, ignore, or conflict with the central cultural concept and value of "efficiency" in the first place? Furthermore, to what extent is organized labor activity confined to *general* elections? Are the electoral practices of organized labor similar in disbursement and endorsement to those of the party groups and of other non-party political groups? Does organized labor in its electoral action normally aid established incumbents, or do its major efforts go into support of non-incum-

[43] Heard, *The Costs of Democracy,* p. 193, n. 58.

bent challengers? Lastly, to what extent has political science analysis provided intelligible answers to these questions?

Before surveying the substantive material available for answering such questions, several explanatory comments are required. To begin with, as one committed to group theory I am acutely aware of gross inaccuracies in the monolithic assumption implied by speaking of "organized labor" or, conversely, "the business community." In my usage of "organized labor," therefore, let it be understood that I believe that sufficient evidence already exists to justify working upon the assumption that in political behavior a unimodal (rather than a bi- or multi-modal) tendency exists and that political science can advance only by working out from this initial primitive—yet empirically based—assumption. After that, the necessary refinements can be made. Secondly, it should be clear from the particular phraseology of the questions posed in the last two paragraphs that I believe that the scheme of analysis framed by these questions is appropriate to the study of *all* interest groups that engage in electoral action. Finally, I am knowingly taking on the unpopular but necessary task of bringing to the threshold of consciousness the very perplexing question of just how much we political scientists really know.

What precisely have political scientists stated about the electoral impact of organized labor? One text [44] notes that organized labor spoke of Election Day 1946 as "Black Tuesday" because only 73 of 318 House candidates and only 5 of 21 Senate candidates endorsed by labor won—but it is impossible to learn whether these were Democrats or Republicans, incumbents or non-incumbents, or how well labor did relative to, say, the Democratic party itself in that Republican year. One author has taken the analysis of 1946 somewhat further, however, in noting that California Republicans uniformly centered their campaign attack on CIO-supported Democratic congressional candidates; that this attack on "CIO-PAC package" candidates became a campaign theme for Republicans almost everywhere in the nation; and that CIO-PAC endorsement of some congressional candidates proved to be a "kiss of death" under certain circumstances.[45] That is, in a number of constituencies the PAC leaders made only a public announcement of endorsement of the candidate and either did not think it important to, or in fact could not, commit labor to any other campaign activity; as a consequence, the labor endorsement in those constituencies provided an issue to opponents of the candidate and permitted them to activate their members and sympathizers with no offsetting gains for the labor-endorsee. As for 1948, which was critical in many ways, slightly more information and analysis are available. Hugh A. Bone pointed out that after the 1948 election the new Labor's League for Political Education (AFL) claimed 172 "friends" of labor elected and 106 "enemies" retired (i.e., now ex-incumbent). Interestingly the most sophisticated analysis of 1948 is to be found in Truman's book—published eleven years ago.[46] Noting generally that the CIO-PAC had endorsed 215 House candidates in 1948 and that 144 of these were elected, the author breaks down the 144 victories in several ways: first, 64 were of incumbents, 74 involved defeating incumbents, while the remain-

---

[44] Roche and Stedman, *The Dynamics of Democratic Government*, p. 71.
[45] Hugh A. Bone, "Political Parties and Pressure Group Politics," in *Annals*, 319 (1958), 73–83; also Bone, *American Politics and the Party System*, pp. 146–149.
[46] David B. Truman, *The Governmental Process* (New York: Knopf, 1951), pp. 315–316, citing his earlier data and the analysis in Frederick Mosteller *et al.*, *The Pre-Election Polls of 1948* (New York: Social Science Research Council, 1949).

ing 6 were in non-incumbency situations; next, 57 of the labor-endorsed incumbents re-elected had voted against the Taft-Hartley Act of 1947 while all 74 of the incumbents defeated had voted for it; and finally, a partial analysis of such factors as the two-party division of the popular vote at the last election and the partisan control of the constituencies leads to the conclusion that "the changes in 1948 were of major importance. Presumably the CIO-PAC efforts had something to do with them."

Despite the fact that a tentative scheme for analysis has been in existence for at least a decade,[47] neither textbook writers nor the researchers they cite have done anything further on this subject. To be sure, one can find conclusions that, for example, in 1950 "the labor-endorsed candidates took a fearful drubbing," [48] or that "in California, following the 1958 elections, labor's power emerged as a great part of the substance behind the Democratic Party's victory." [49] What one finds is unrelieved anecdotalism, and not very good anecdotes at that. This may be partly a result of the combined tendency of politicians (including labor politicians), news media, and the political scientist audience alike to personify the issue of labor's electoral activity in one key race at a time, viz., Taft and Ohio in 1950 or Goldwater and Arizona in 1958. And there is some evidence that labor, especially in its allocation of funds, may be inefficient in such races. For example, organized labor *reported* expenditures of $180,880, Senator Taft *reported* expenditures of $243,740, and probably more than $2,000,000 was spent in that one 1950 contest.[50] As for 1958, the close reader of the *New York Times* found that "Rumor has it that the national COPE organization has been pouring money—as much as $400,000—and political workers into Arizona to defeat Senator Goldwater. . . ." [51] COPE officials and Arizona labor leaders immediately denied this, of course, indicating that labor's financial involvement would be about the same as the $33,000 expended in Arizona in 1956; but when the battle had ended, labor's reported contributions to McFarland (Goldwater's opponent) interestingly totaled only $3500.[52] Meanwhile, Goldwater's re-election effectively obscured the fact that two other COPE-endorsed Arizona candidates had been elected with impressive vote-margins.[53] The focus upon one great personalized contest at a time may also result from the facts that organized labor, even the AFL-CIO, has no centralized endorsement machinery and that it is therefore difficult, though hardly im-

---

[47] In some ways, for almost twenty years. See V. O. Key, Jr., "The Veterans and the House of Representatives: A Study of a Pressure Group and Electoral Mortality," *Journal of Politics*, 5 (1943), 27–40.
[48] Roche and Stedman, *The Dynamics of Democratic Government*. It is only fair to point out that their book was published in 1954; on the other hand, the sole reference they make is to the re-election of Republican Senator Robert Taft of Ohio.
[49] William Goodman, *The Two-Party System in the United States* (2d ed.; New York: Van Nostrand, 1960), p. 355.
[50] The labor figure is given in the *New York Times*, November 25, 1950, p. 8, and includes $74,470 reported by the secretary-treasurer for the Ohio CIO-PAC; the Taft figure may be found in the *New York Times*, November 17, 1950, p. 30. The over-all estimate is that of the Senate Committee on Rules and Administration, Subcommittee on Privileges and Elections, 82nd Cong., 1st and 2nd sess., *Hearings on Investigation into the 1950 Ohio Senatorial Campaign* (1951 and 1952). The *New York Times*, November 8, 1950, p. 1, characterized Taft's re-election as "the worst labor defeat since 1932" and most readers, political scientists included, probably agreed.
[51] October 15, 1958, p. 1, article by Gladwin Hill.
[52] *Congressional Quarterly Almanac*, 15 (1959), 809.
[53] *New York Times*, November 6, 1958, 22.

possible, as indicated below, to learn what the state, district, and local political units of labor are doing; and as a general rule in this country, that which it is difficult to learn normally goes unreported and necessarily unanalyzed.

But at least one political scientist has provided interesting clues concerning the behavior of organized labor in endorsements. In a tentative survey of CIO-PAC activity in the Detroit area, Nicholas Masters has generalized that "the PAC attempts to endorse the candidate who most nearly meets the claims of the group and who commands the greatest prestige, but it will endorse the mediocre or weak candidate if he is opposed by a candidate who is closely identified with business groups." [54] Thus there is evidence of the push and pull of ideological stereotypes in electoral behavior. Furthermore, Masters has noted that the Democratic partisanship of the candidate is the primary criterion for PAC endorsement in Wayne County, with liberal position coming next in importance; and—

> The term "liberal" does not puzzle PAC leaders as it does academicians. A candidate may prove his liberalism by allowing the PAC to evaluate his stand on ten or twelve key and current issues with which the CIO is concerned. The *usual method for evaluation of a candidate, however, is to tabulate his recorded votes on such issues. Thus the incumbent has the inside track for endorsement.* . . .[55]

This in turn is evidence—if tentative and subject to further testing—that the influence of organized labor, even in a labor-dominated area, may be inoperative or ineffectual until *after* the candidate has established himself; it may also mean that organized labor operates as a conservative force in the limited sense of freezing out challengers and preventing intraparty conflict; at the minimum Masters' evidence suggests that repeated endorsements of incumbents is the major factor in explaining the high rate of success of the CIO-PAC in the 1946–1955 period.[56]

More information is available concerning the national level of politics and especially concerning the 1960 election. For example, that election is the first in which data both on the Senate campaign committees and on labor endorsements and disbursements are readily available to the political analyst. Using such data, then, Table 3 compares the Democratic Senate Campaign Committee and the AFL-CIO. Labor made only approximately half as many major-support decisions (defined as allocations of $5000 or more) [57] as did the DSCC in 1960; sight inspection of this figure also shows that the order of preference varied considerably between the two groups; and a rank-order correlation coefficient (Kendall's *tau*) of the candidates appearing commonly in both the DSCC and the AFL-CIO

[54] Nicholas A. Masters, "The Politics of Union Endorsement of Candidates in the Detroit Area," *Midwest Journal of Political Science*, 1 (1957), 136–150.
[55] Masters, "The Politics of Union Endorsement," p. 149; emphasis added.
[56] Masters, "The Politics of Union Endorsement," p. 149, ". . . the PAC endorsement average was 67.5 percent in the primary elections and 91.2 percent in the general elections for Congressional, state, and county offices."
[57] The assumption is that a contribution of less than $5000 is considered to be relatively insignificant by most senatorial candidates. This cut-off is unrealistically low for states like New York and probably too high for states like Vermont or New Hampshire; presumably electoral costs bear some observable relation to numbers of constituents. Thus when political scientists get about their proper business, the analyst will finally be able to make class discriminations of senatorial constituencies similar to those the Senate itself makes with regard to allocation of office expenses.

See George B. Galloway, *The Legislative Process in Congress* (New York: Crowell, 1953), pp. 391–394.

TABLE 3

Rank-Order Comparisons of Major-Support Decisions (of $5000 or More) Made by the DSCC and by the AFL-CIO Respectively in 1960 Senate Elections

\multicolumn{3}{c}{DSCC}	\multicolumn{3}{c}{AFL-CIO}
Rank	Name	State	Rank	Name	State
1	Frear (Delaware)		1	Kefauver (Tennessee)	
2	Anderson (New Mexico)		2	Humphrey (Minnesota)	
3	Bartlett (Alaska)		3	Douglas (Illinois)	
4	Humphrey (Minnesota)		4	McNamara (Michigan)	
5	Whitaker (Wyoming)		5	Neuberger (Oregon)	
6	Neuberger (Oregon)		6	O'Connor (Massachusetts)	
7	Pell (Rhode Island)		7	Pell (Rhode Island)	
8	Metcalf (Montana)		8	Knous (Colorado)	
9	McLaughlin (Idaho)		9	Metcalf (Montana)	
10	McNamara (Michigan)				
11	Burdick (North Dakota)				
12.5	Knous (Colorado)				
12.5	Kerr (Oklahoma)				
14	Randolph (West Virginia)				
15.5	Long (Missouri)				
15.5	McGovern (South Dakota)				
17	Douglas (Illinois)				

Source: *Congressional Quarterly Almanac*, 17 (1961).

lists was only +.143—quite close to full independence—for the particular election.

We may also compare the disbursement practices of the AFL-CIO with those of the political party Senate campaign committees (in Table 4). These data for 1960 show several interesting behavioral differences. First, as many political scientists have long suspected, the DSCC in 1960—at least—operated to the distinct advantage of incumbent members of The Club—by a mean difference in excess of $2400. The Republican National Campaign Committee, secondly, contested the greatest number of races at the level of major-support and, also presumably reflecting the mathematical decline of Republicans in the Senate since 1952, the party allocation policy actually worked to the slight advantage of their non-incumbent candidates. In between these two, the AFL-CIO concentrated its activity—disbursing a much higher mean contribution to a much reduced total number of candidates. Furthermore, for an established electoral interest group such as organized labor, 1960 must be regarded as a year of consolidationist effort. That is, the AFL-CIO devoted its major efforts to helping re-elect five preferred incumbents,[58] disbursing to them almost three times the mean amount contributed to non-incumbent Democratic candidates.

The question of electoral efficiency (and power) can be dealt with least satisfactorily here. At best, until comparable data for a sequence of elections become available, I can only illustrate the types of assumptions that seem immediately relevant to this question. The crudest measure of efficiency, of course, is whether the endorsed-supported candidates of the electoral interest group in fact win their elections. By one form of this measure—examining the proportion of all

---

[58] Because of the recent history of the Oregon constituency and the Neuberger-Lusk-Neuberger sequence during 1960, I have classified the 1960 Oregon contest as the re-election of a Democratic incumbent.

TABLE 4

Major-Support Decisions (of $5000 or More) of Senate-Oriented Party and Labor Political Groups in 1960 Elections—Analyzed by Incumbency and Non-Incumbency Situations

	All Major Support		Incumbent Support		Non-Incumbent Support	
Political Group	Mean Amount	No. of Races	Mean Amount	No. of Races	Mean Amount	No. of Races
DSCC	$ 9,880	17	$10,876	10	$8,457	7
AFL-CIO	14,511	9	20,980	5	6,425	4
RNCC	8,327	22	8,119	10	8,500	12

Source: Congressional Quarterly Almanac, 17 (1961).

disbursements (not just major-support allocations) according to the final division of the two-party total vote in the constituency—Table 5 indicates that the AFL-CIO was more efficient than either party campaign committee, for it allocated 81 percent of all 1960 disbursements to winning candidates whereas its closer competitor (the DSCC) could claim only 61 percent here. But the data previously given, regarding incumbencies, suggest that this very primitive assumption on which Table 5 is based is appropriate only where one has a very limited number of cases with which to deal. When the number of cases has increased significantly, the analyst would do well to invoke a second assumption here, already implied by the construction of Table 5, that devoting group efforts to "close" contests is more efficient—in terms of the psychology of indebtedness—than either winning too easily (presumably by backing only incumbents) or losing too badly. As the number of cases becomes truly adequate, a third and more important assumption is necessary: that it is more efficient to help a non-incumbent challenger defeat an incumbent than it is merely to aid an already-incumbent candidate win

TABLE 5

Relative Efficiency of Senate-Oriented Party and Labor Groups in 1960 Elections—Measured in Terms of Proportion of Disbursements to "Close" and "Not Close" Races

Senate Races: Division of Two-Party Total Vote	Party and Labor Political Groups		
	DSCC	AFL-CIO	RNCC
"Not close"—more than 55 percent	39	52	23
"Close"—50+ through 54 percent	22	29	27
"Close"—46 through 50 percent	23	8	25
"Not close"—less than 46 percent	16	11	25
Total	101[a]	100	100

[a] Errors due to rounding.
Source: Congressional Quarterly Almanac, 17 (1961).

re-election. Furthermore, in this context, efficiency is a function of *net* impact on the distribution of legislative seats (i.e., victories minus losses) rather than of *gross* (victorious) behavior alone. But such more sophisticated and, it is believed, realistic analysis clearly requires detailed information on individual constituencies not now available in any numbers.[59]

[59] I have been able to obtain sufficient data to permit invoking these assumptions in the case of the National Committee for an Effective Congress. The analysis of the efficiency

To conclude this section, then, one must presently fall back upon fragmentary and discontinuous *aggregate* data such as have been brought together in Table 4. This table provides a framework for summary analysis of four aspects of the electoral activity of organized labor. A first cluster is indicated in Table 6: for example, the magnitude of organized labor's electoral involvement in House races has significantly diminished in the past fifteen years; and I infer from this that labor strategists have acquired experience in limiting labor money to the lesser number of constituencies in which it can make a difference. (When the post-1960 Census redistricting is completed, probably by the 1964 election, the number of House seats that labor can hope to contest should increase.) As for the Senate, analysis of the geography of endorsements indicates that labor now participates in virtually the full 100 percent of contested general elections, reflecting the greater advantage of statewide constituencies for labor's electoral resources. And, lastly, labor's electoral efficiency—measured solely by percentage of victories—has closely paralleled the ebb and flow of Democratic party fortunes in the past fifteen years.

TABLE 6

Type, Number, and Frequency of Victory of Organized Labor Endorsements in Selected Congressional General Elections

	House of Representatives			Senate		
Year	Contests	Victories	Per Cent	Contests	Victories	Per Cent
1946 (CIO-PAC)	318	73	23	21	5	24
1948 (CIO-PAC)	215	144	67	—	—	—
1954 (CIO-PAC)	256	126	49	26	16	61
(AFL-LLPE)	—	154	—	30	18	60
1956 (AFL-CIO)	288	159	55	29	12	41
1958 (AFL-CIO)	199	—	—	34	24	71
1960 (AFL-CIO)	193	106	55	21	12	57

Note: This table has been pieced together from the sources previously cited in this section plus *Congressional Quarterly Almanac*, 15 (1959), and 17 (1961).

A related aspect, not revealed by Table 6, is the fact that labor money is almost wholly concentrated within the Democratic party, probably more so recently than Heard's earlier figures indicated. For example, of 199 money-endorsements for House seats in 1958, only 6 were of Republican candidates. In 1958 senatorial races, only 2 of 34 candidates supported by labor were Republicans; one of these (Knight of California) received less than one-twenty-fourth the sum contributed to his Democratic opponent, while the other (North Dakota's Langer) was noted as a domestic Democrat. In 1960's Senate races, 3 of 21 labor-endorsed candidates were Republicans; 2 of these received relatively token contributions of $500 each (incumbent Cooper of Kentucky and successful challenger Boggs of Maryland) while in the third contest, in New Jersey, incumbent Case received $2500 to the $1000 given to his Democratic opponent.

The influence of incumbency may be treated as a third aspect of analysis, in that endorsements of incumbents seem to account for a greater proportion of labor victories in the House than in the Senate. The data are not extensive, but they indicate the following: 10 of the 24 Senate victories in 1958 and 7 of the 12

of that electoral interest group is presented in my *Ideology and Electoral Action* (San Francisco: Chandler Publishing Company, 1967).

in 1960 involved support of a successful incumbent, while in the case of the House, 95 of the 106 victories claimed in 1960 were of re-elected incumbents.

A final point may be gleaned from the available data, namely the fact that labor-money activity is *not* confined, as the limited data that Heard had available seemed to indicate, to those seventeen states in which three-quarters of all unionists reside. In 1960, for example, a full half of labor's major financial efforts for the Senate fell outside those seventeen states; despite the artificialities of federalism, money is a highly mobile political resource, and the recent extension of this activity by both business and labor would seem both a cause and a reflection of the nationalization of electoral politics in America.

Between the Depression and the end of World War II, business unionism essentially achieved its three major goals of union recognition, shorter hours and higher wages, and control of the job market. The Employment Act of 1946 should be viewed as symbolic of the transition from business unionism to political unionism—in the sense that unions have been able to survive as a social movement in America by the development of a logical succession of goals. Since 1946, labor's goals have been employment, security, and peace.[60] But business unionism could not directly contribute to the achievement of such goals. Each of these new goals was significantly affected by what the national government would or would not do. Therefore business unionism has now been replaced by a political unionism based upon the realistic and realizable premise that political action is necessary to control the government that in such a major way conditions achievement of the newer and broader goals of organized labor.

From the sketchy evidence available, political unionism—consciously undertaken within the framework of the existing national two-party system—has meant that organized labor acts as a party-within-a-party. But the descriptions available *are* fragmentary and discontinuous. Lacking adequate descriptive bases, we are necessarily precluded from experimentation with logical methods for evaluating the efficiency of power-oriented action. Lacking both description and evaluation, there can be no political *theory* as distinct from political philosophy. Therefore, at numerous points in this article I have referred to the sins of omission of political scientists. But guilt is not ours alone, for no one else has yet attempted systematic appraisal of organized labor's role in American politics. For example, respected research organizations—such as the National Bureau of Economic Research, Incorporated—have neither conducted nor sponsored research on organized labor in electoral politics. The social scientists who control client-oriented educational institutions—such as the University of Wisconsin's School for Workers—have apparently lacked inclination, resources, and/or ability for research into labor's political activities and power. The modern myriad of corporate-financed "educational" foundations—such as the American Enterprise Association or the Foundation for Economic Education—publish only unreliable polemics on this subject. And organized labor itself understandably is no more anxious scientifically and publicly to appraise its efficiency and power than any other group in the political arena. In this sense—but in this only—the future is bright: it now remains to be seen which of the sectarian fields of social science will contribute to understanding of a major political phenomenon.

[60] See the anticipation of this change from business to political unionism in Eli Ginzberg, *The Labor Leader* (New York: Macmillan, 1948), pp. 173–187.

31
The Pluralist Period: The AFL until the New Deal

J. David Greenstone

Marx developed so forceful and penetrating an interpretation of working-class politics under capitalism that his categories continue to affect our political and scholarly discourse. Even in the 1960s, such terms as "proletariat," "consciousness," "ideology," and even "working class" retain ideological, radical, anticapitalist connotations. The Marxist impact on our political vocabulary has had unfortunate consequences for the analysis of union political behavior in the United States. Most American unions have always vigorously rejected even the most moderate social doctrines. Many American scholars have reacted to this distaste for socialism by maintaining a pluralist group-politics interpretation of American labor politics. But in the 1960s pluralism explains the behavior of American organized labor with respect to either national elections or to the important welfare-state issue no better than Marxism. The increasing moderation of most contemporary European trade unions hardly confirms Marx's socialist prophecies, of course, even in those countries from which he drew the evidence for his analysis. But it is equally true that, as many European unions lose their socialist militancy, American unions have increasingly, though still far from completely, come to resemble them on at least two counts. In the policy process, the American labor movement

From *Labor In American Politics*, by J. David Greenstone. Copyright © 1969 by Alfred A. Knopf, Inc. Reprinted by permission of the publisher.

supports the continuous expansion of welfare-state measures. In national electoral politics, the unions have assumed many of the functions of the political campaign apparatus for the Democrats, the dominant party in the United States since 1930.

A decline in industrial employment together with the emergence of more liberal Republican candidates may someday reduce labor's partisan activity on behalf of the Democrats. Nevertheless, the American labor movement's political development through the mid-1960s remains important if we are to gain a theoretical understanding of the range of possible relationships between American parties and pressure groups and of the connection between political and social change. Significantly, labor's partisan campaign role emerged in conjunction with a political revolution that produced a class or at least an income-group partisan alignment resembling that of many Western European nations.[1] As a result, although this study focuses on an organizational elite of paid union officials, elected local union officers, and the small proportion of politically active union members, the efforts of these groups to elect mainly Democratic candidates have been paralleled in the voting behavior of union members. V. O. Key's reanalysis of 1936 to 1948 survey data, for example, showed a high correlation between prounion issue attitudes and Democratic partisanship.[2] The authors of *The American Voter* confirmed earlier findings of Democratic leanings among AFL union members and suggested that there was (by a relatively constant margin of about 10 percent) a still stronger Democratic preference in the industrial unions formerly in the CIO. Their analysis showed that these party affiliations reflected the intensity of the unions' own efforts to activate their rank and file politically.[3]

THE GROUP INTERPRETATION OF LABOR IN AMERICAN POLITICS

These facts may conform to Marx's prophecy but they hardly validate it. His analysis did not primarily concern worker and union support in a capitalist system for welfare programs that constituted only "immediate demands" short of socialism. For Marx, the decisive questions were instead the workers' passions, beliefs, and self-consciousness as manifested by their loyalty to their own specifically socialist and working-class organizations. American and European labor politics have always differed from the Marxist expectation. American unions have only infrequently represented class-conscious workers loyal to their own at least formally socialist party. Instead, they have traditionally acted as much more narrowly based economic interest groups that displayed no recognition of a historical mission to end capitalism. Given these inadequacies of the Marxist analysis, pluralism has seemed to many a highly attractive alternative explanation.

As a social theory, pluralism refers to the overlapping social-group member-

---

[1] See Seymour Martin Lipset, *Political Man* (Garden City, N.Y.: Doubleday, 1960), p. 303.
[2] V. O. Key, Jr., *The Responsible Electorate* (Cambridge, Mass.: Harvard University Press, 1966), chap. 3, esp. p. 55.
[3] Angus Campbell, *et al.*, *The American Voter* (New York: Wiley, 1960), p. 312. In 1956, a Republican year, members of the most politically committed unions were 67 percent Democratic, but this figure "fell to 55%, then to 51% [in still less political oriented unions] and finally to 44% where standards were least clear." P. 315. Equally important, almost the entire variation could be accounted for by differences among the most loyal union members. P. 316.

ships that supposedly prevent any one group from pursuing extremist goals that would threaten the entire regime. In this discussion, however, the term "pluralism" will primarily refer to a *political* pattern of behavior in which the major actors are self-interested groups, representing relatively narrow and usually homogeneous constituencies. Because these groups' political demands are relatively limited, the major parties try to build alliances on particular issues with as many interests as possible, rather than make broad programmatic commitments that might alienate possible supporters. The pressure groups tend to move between the parties, bargaining for the best arrangement.

As we shall see, this pluralist pattern did dominate trade-union politics until the New Deal, and it cannot be too strongly emphasized that it persists in most local communities and in many state political systems. A number of traditional unions with highly skilled members have adhered to this pluralist tradition even in national politics with considerable success, although their activities are not the main concern of this study. The central thesis of this book concerns instead the emergence particularly at the state and national levels of the American Federation of Labor–Congress of Industrial Organizations (AFL-CIO) as a Democratic party campaign organization. This partisan involvement cannot be reconciled with pluralism because it has taken from the labor movement much of its freedom to bargain with each of the major parties. In addition, the union's effective *political* constituency in national politics has been widened far beyond that anticipated by pluralist theory and now includes most of the welfare-state oriented supporters of the Northern Democratic party.

A pluralist interpretation has, nevertheless, proved so persuasive that it is accepted by radical and even Marxist critics who are dissatisfied with American labor's political activities. Marc Karson points out organized labor's Democratic party and welfare-state inclinations, but concludes, "The top men running America's unions are called labor leaders, but . . . politically they follow the methods of the pressure groups." [4] According to Paul Jacobs:

> In Israel, in the Scandinavian countries, in England and in many other foreign lands unions are an integral part of the political system, not onlookers as they are in America, where the simplistic AFL tradition of rewarding friends and punishing enemies in the political arena is still dominant.[5]

In the late 1940s, C. Wright Mills described the CIO's Political Action Committee (PAC) as "an appendage of the Democrats," but still argued that the New Deal "left no durable instrument for liberal, much less radical activity . . . its effect on the political development of labor in America was essentially to put it aside." [6] American labor leaders viewed politics "as a pluralist system of interests which balanced each other in shifting compromise." [7]

As this study will attempt to demonstrate, however, the radical critique of American unions since the New Deal as simply pluralist is fatally overstated despite the AFL's and CIO's undeniable opposition to socialism. In their support of the Democrats as a mass pro-welfare-state party, American trade unions have

---

[4] Marc Karson, *American Labor Unions and Politics* (Carbondale: Southern Illinois University Press, 1958), p. 305.
[5] Paul Jacobs, *The State of the Unions* (New York: Atheneum, 1963), p. 293.
[6] C. Wright Mills, *The New Men of Power: America's Labor Leaders* (New York: Harcourt Brace Jovanovich, 1948), pp. 184, 209.
[7] Mills, p. 163.

forged a political coalition with important—although hardly complete—structural and behavioral similarities to the socialist party–trade union alliances in Western Europe. The radical critics have made the valid point that the New Deal, which forged the contemporary alliance of the Democratic party and the American unions, advocated modest reforms rather than spurred the working class on to social revolution. These reforms were significant enough to help the working class adjust to, rather than overthrow, the existing system of corporate capitalism, as much of the data and interpretations offered here will show. I would only add that the social democratic parties of Western Europe have been similarly—although not identically—conservative in function. They have left undisturbed a very large proportion of their countries' capitalist economies.

The validity of their insight, in other words, does not obscure the fact that at another level these radical writers share the empirical view of avowed pluralists. Without excepting organized labor, Donald Blaisdell argues, for example, that group leaders operate inside parties, but he believes that the groups themselves "work autonomously, but in cooperation with [parties] . . . throwing their weight first to one party then to the other depending on which party seems to offer more." [8] Two other analysts of interest-group behavior, Harmon Zeigler and Abraham Holtzman, both point out organized labor's affinity for the Democrats. Zeigler, however, concludes that labor "is not a unified and reliable basis of support for the Democratic Party," basing the statement on the voting behavior of individual union members. Holtzman observes that

> there is nothing [in the United States] comparable to the ideological ties between interest groups and parties which exist in Italy. Groups forge temporary alliances with other interest groups in the absence of ideological inhibitors, and groups cooperate with members and leaders of both parties.[9]

Significantly, although the ostensible focus of these writers is pluralist, that is, they emphasize the behavior of organized interest groups, they assert the pluralist character of American labor by citing attitudinal factors. In Zeigler's analysis it is the presumably uncertain partisan preferences of union members as voters and, in Holtzman's, the weak ideological affinity between parties and such groups as trade unions.

This view of labor as "basically" nonpartisan has been bolstered by some of labor's own spokesmen, partly to minimize the break with earlier nonpartisan doctrines, partly to placate Republican union members, and partly to avoid embarrassing the Democrats. Mary Goddard Zon, research director for the AFL-CIO's Committee on Political Education (COPE), explicitly denied and then implicitly conceded labor's partisan involvement in two consecutive sentences.

---

[8] Donald Blaisdell, *American Democracy Under Pressure* (New York: Ronald Press, 1957), p. 63. He also points out, "Pressure groups do practically everything in political campaigns that the parties do except the nominating of candidates. . . . They endorse candidates . . . raise money and spend it on behalf of particular candidates . . . ring door bells, make telephone calls . . . and use all the devices of propaganda." But on the next page he makes clear that "Both experience and observation reinforce the truth of the rule that success in pressure politics turns on neutrality as between the parties." Pp. 115–116.
[9] Harmon Zeigler, *Interest Groups in American Society* (Englewood Cliffs, N.J.: Prentice-Hall, 1964), p. 246. Abraham Holtzman, *Interest Groups and Lobbying* (New York: Crowell-Collier-Macmillan, 1966), p. 57.

While COPE is non-partisan, and supports liberal candidates of both parties, it is a simple fact that many more Democrats than Republicans qualify for COPE support. The success of liberal legislation in the immediate future will depend on the ability of the Democrats to hold the seats they have and, if possible, to increase their margin.[10]

A Democratic bias is conceded, but the unions are also depicted as operating independently of either party. When they endorse candidates, the unions are thought to be "as free as before" they made their alliance with the Democrats. V. O. Key makes the same assumption with his characteristic caution.

Those critics who deplore [labor's apparently recent Democratic allegiance] . . . make too much of the new practice of the formal endorsement of presidential candidates. . . . In 1916, Sam Gompers, in his "private" capacity, asserted "If the men of labor have to depend on what is promised by the Republican Party in this campaign, God save them. That is all." The non-partisan policy makes of labor, as one of its leaders has remarked, "non-partisan Democrats." [11]

AN ALTERNATIVE PARTISAN INTERPRETATION

Even as revised by Key, this pluralist interpretation views the largest of our economic interest groups as pro-Democratic but still outside the party in terms of political organization and activity. Key was entirely right in stressing the continuity of Democratic partisan preference and the steadfast rejection of the rhetoric and emotion of European socialism. As a result of the New Deal, however, a distinct break did occur when American unions emerged as a *party* campaign organization. And organized labor's formal endorsements of Democratic Presidential candidates accurately symbolized this major alteration in its political *behavior* rather than any change in partisan *attitudes*. The difference of interpretation is qualitative. In my view, labor is not simply at one end of a continuum of organizations distributed according to their Democratic versus Republican partisanship, but in many cases is a valued and integral part of the Democrats' normal campaign apparatus.

This thesis is supported by an impressive number of observers who have focused on the specific content of the labor–Democratic party alliance rather than uncritically invoking pluralism as a universally valid explanation for the political behavior of all American economic interest groups. As early as 1945, Richard Rovere, in an article on the Democrats' 1944 victory, described the CIO's Political Action Committee, as

a national machine, and although it will use local issues to advantage where that can be done, its principle concern is with national policy.
This has never been true of our regular party machines. Neither major party is really a national organization.[12]

[10] Mary Zon, "Labor in Politics," *Law and Contemporary Problems*, 27 (Spring 1962), 241. For a similar statement of a decade earlier see Jack Kroll, "Labor's Political Role," *The Annals of the American Academy of Political and Social Science*, 274 (March 1951), 120.
[11] V. O. Key, Jr., *Politics, Parties, and Pressure Groups* (New York: Crowell, 1964), p. 63.
[12] Richard Rovere, "Labor's Political Machine," *Harper's Magazine*, 190 (June 1945), 601.

Labor's activity, of course, is not tantamount to effectiveness in winning elections. In fact, the assessment of such effectiveness requires extensive survey techniques beyond the scope of this research. The unions' contributions, however, are valued by experienced politicians. Rovere, for example, questioned labor's actual assistance to the Democrats in 1944. "But all this scarcely matters now," he wrote a year later. "PAC today has the prestige of association with victory. Most of the men it marked for defeat were defeated; most of those it sought to elect were elected." [13] Four years later, Max Kampelman, counsel to Senator Hubert Humphrey, asserted, "The labor movement was unmistakably, though perhaps unofficially, considered an essential arm of the Democratic Party." By 1948, he noted, labor had come to realize the "importance of local Party organization." [14] In periods of Democratic success (e.g., 1960) this was a common verdict.[15]

Political scientists studying party and electoral politics have also tended to recognize labor's partisan role. Ralph Goldman observes, "Union officials and members found that they could perform many of the activities—registering voters, helping candidates campaign, raising funds, getting voters to the polls—ordinarily left to the parties. . . . Often, union locals served the Democratic cause in the absence of party locals." [16] "In many parts of the country," adds Clinton Rossiter, "it is more correct than misleading to describe the Democrats as a 'labor party.' " [17] E. E. Schattschneider, writing in 1955 with the labor-Democratic alliance explicitly in mind, provided an epigraph for this volume:

> . . . a shift in the locus of power or a revision of party functions may leave the formal structure untouched, or new structures may arise without being recognized as parts of the party system. Thus pressure groups may become so partisan that they might properly be described as ancillary organizations of one or the other of the major parties.[18]

[13] Rovere, p. 593.
[14] Max M. Kampelman, "Labor in Politics," in George W. Brooks *et al.* (eds.), *Interpreting the Labor Movement* (Madison, Wisc.: Industrial Relations Research Association, 1952), pp. 171, 172.
[15] A labor spokesman, for example, was able to quote Republican leaders, who told both *The New York Times* and the Washington *Daily News* that labor's role in the 1960 election was the single most important factor in Richard Nixon's defeat. Zon, p. 246.
[16] Ralph M. Goldman, *The Democratic Party in American Politics* (New York: Crowell-Collier-Macmillan, 1966), p. 21.
[17] Clinton Rossiter, *Parties and Politics in America* (Ithaca, N.Y.: Cornell University Press, 1960), p. 95.
In *Politics in Wisconsin*, Leon Epstein found that almost as many Democratic state legislators had been helped in political campaigns by labor (37.1 percent) as by the party organization (40.0 percent). (Madison: University of Wisconsin Press, 1958), p. 207. See also John Hutchinson, "Labour in Politics in America," *Political Quarterly*, 32 (April–June 1962), 140.
[18] E. E. Schattschneider, "The United States: The Functional Approach to Party Government," in Sigmund Neuman (ed.), *Modern Political Parties* (Chicago: University of Chicago Press, 1956), p. 213. For his references to labor see pp. 209–214. As Harry Scoble has pointed out, even Schattschneider resorted to a pluralist, empirical interpretation of labor in national politics when he specifically addressed himself to pressure politics. He calculated that labor could deliver relatively few of its members' votes so that "*it is nearly impossible to translate pressure politics into party politics.*" E. E. Schattschneider, *The Semisovereign People* (New York: Holt, Rinehart and Winston, 1960), p. 53. (Schattschneider's emphasis.) See Harry M. Scoble, "Organized Labor in Electoral Politics: Some Questions for the Discipline," *Western Political Quarterly*, 16 (September 1963), 674 [p. 354 of this text—EDITOR]. See also Hugh Bone's com-

This view has been further substantiated by several writers who have focused on organized labor in national politics. In his suggestively titled article "The Organized Labor Bureaucracy as a Base of Support for the Democratic Party," Nicholas Masters argues:

> The AFL-CIO has been able to provide for the Democratic Party one thing business interests have been unable to supply for the Republicans . . . namely organization. The most fundamental point to emphasize is the sheer muscle union workers can provide in a campaign.[19]

Fay Calkins concluded the first comparative study of unions and the Democratic party in several locales by describing industrial unions as "party pressure groups" that "give life and direction to the party mechanism." [20]

The most comprehensive evidence supporting the thesis of labor's organizational integration into the Democratic party has been assembled by Harry Scoble. "The most fundamental post-war change in the structure and process of political parties," he writes, "has been the entrance of organized labor into electoral activity at the precinct level and on up." [21] Scoble not only rejects Schattschneider's low estimate of labor's contribution to the Democratic vote but also calculates that labor accounted for a fourth of the party's total financial support and contributed almost nothing to the Republicans.[22] In addition, labor used this money to support Democrats from rural areas with few unions and concentrated its contributions in close races so that "labor's electoral efficiency—measured solely by percentage of victories [of candidates it has supported]—has closely paralleled the ebb and flow of the Democratic Party fortunes in the past fifteen years." [23] Scoble concludes, "Organized labor acts a party-within-a-party," although he admits that "the descriptions available [on which to base this judgment] are fragmentary and discontinuous." [24]

If these views are accurate, they force us at least to qualify the pluralist notion that both American parties, save for the vestiges of urban machines, have elite or "cadre" structures. Except perhaps in Detroit, American unions did not provide the Democrats with the branch structures comparable to those of some European working-class parties in which rank and file party activists are organized on a permanent basis to mobilize the party's supporters.[25] Organized labor's campaign organizations in the United States, however, have provided a significantly closer equivalent to the monetary support and electoral work of European branch or-

---

ments on pressure group activities as a party campaign organization. "Political Parties and Pressure Group Politics," *The Annals*, 319 (September 1958), 77. He subsequently flatly asserted that "Labor bargains with both major parties, often striking an identity with the Democrats." *American Politics and the Party System*, 3rd ed. (New York: McGraw-Hill, 1965), p. 566.

[19] Nicholas Masters, "The Organized Labor Bureaucracy as a Base of Support for the Democratic Party," *Law and Contemporary Problems*, 27 (Spring 1962), 258.

[20] Fay Calkins, *The CIO and the Democratic Party* (Chicago: University of Chicago Press, 1952), p. 147.

[21] Scoble, p. 666. Scoble reviews many of the sources on labor politics, pp. 669ff.

[22] Scoble, p. 674. Scoble argues that Schattschneider based his estimate on too low a turnout rate and too small an estimate of differentials in the percentages of union and nonunion Democratic votes.

[23] Scoble, p. 684.

[24] Scoble, p. 685.

[25] See, for example, Maurice Duverger, *Political Parties* (New York: Wiley, 1963), pp. 21ff.

ganizations than is usually recognized.[26] The behavioral equivalence of American union campaign organizations and the European party branches is suggested by the fact that unions have been less important for the party in the United States where branch electoral activities are still performed by regular patronage organizations.

British trade unionists, to take just one example, have, of course, been tied to the Labour party by much stronger class feelings than those that bind American workers to the Democrats, although both groups are committed to welfare-state programs. British unions also have had a much more important role in the Labour party with respect to holding formal party offices, informal influence, financial contributions, and campaign work than the AFL-CIO has enjoyed in the Democratic party.[27] But if the Democrats regularly seek but much less regularly follow the advice of AFL-CIO leaders, the Labour party's increasingly middle-class, moderate leaders had by the 1960s also begun to disregard some important union demands. In sum, the partial approximation of party branch structures increasingly permits meaningful comparisons and contrasts between European and American party systems.

It is possible, of course, that a sufficiently broad pluralist interpretation could account for these developments within a group-politics framework. As Schattschneider suggests, however, a definition of pluralism broad enough to cover almost every conceivable relationship between parties and pressure groups and to explain all possible outcomes in general explains nothing in particular. Propositions built on such an interpretation of pluralism are almost impossible either to refute or to verify empirically.[28] Scoble and Calkins, for example, seem inclined to interpret party behavior as the consequence of the interests and activities of its constituent groups. As this study will show, however, the labor movement lost much of its independent bargaining position vis-à-vis the party when it began to function as a party campaign organization. It actually became subject to many of the external constraints that limit the party itself.[29] A broad definition of pluralism, then, prevents us from making relevant theoretical distinctions between the clearly pluralist behavior of the early AFL described in this chapter and its present role as a Democratic electoral organization and finally as a potential bulwark of consumer class politics. . . . Such a definition also makes it more difficult to compare—and contrast—the American party system with those in Western Europe and deprives us of the opportunity to treat American politics as a standard subject for comparative political analysis rather than as a unique area to be studied by area specialists.

TOWARD A PARTIAL THEORY OF GROUP POLITICS

If American free-enterprise rhetoric has tended to disguise, as well as to retard, our acceptance of collectivist welfare-state programs, the pluralist rhetoric of group politics has disguised the nonpluralist alliance between our largest party and our largest economic interest group. The admittedly real differences between

[26] Duverger, pp. 24ff.
[27] Samuel Beer, *British Politics in the Collectivist Age* (New York: Knopf, 1965), esp. part 2.
[28] Schattschneider, pp. 21–22.
[29] Compare Schattschneider, pp. 42–43.

American and European politics have thus been exaggerated and the considerable differences between the contemporary situation and our own political past have been understated. Pluralism thus obstructs development of a new partial theory that distinguishes politics in the 1920s from politics in the 1960s. Such a theory should account not only for the remaining important differences between American and European politics, especially in the legislative and administrative processes, but also for the growing similarities, especially in the party system. It should indicate not only the effect of group behavior on parties but also the effect that the AFL-CIO's alliance with the Democrats has had on labor's own political goals and activity. This partial theory would thus avoid reducing political behavior either to the pluralist politics of largely economic interest groups or to a Marxist conflict among classes generated entirely out of economic relationships. It would expect that when two political organizations cooperate intimately for a long period of time, their patterns of activities begin to fuse. It would prepare us, in other words, to find that the large formal organizations that have dominated pressure politics for most of this century have begun to operate inside at least one of the major American parties.[30]

Three Analytical Approaches to Labor Politics

In order to contribute toward such a partial theory, this book draws on three overlapping dimensions of analysis. The first, the social stratification approach, which is derived from European sociology, looks at politics in terms of the interaction of particular social strata, like that between the industrial working class and their employers. This view can be directly traced to Marx, who viewed politics as a struggle between social classes, regulated by the values and world view of the ruling class. But it is also related to that part of Aristotle's analysis in which he empirically classified different regimes according to the social groups and values that controlled them. The social stratification approach has the merit of concentrating on the substantive character of the political regime. It examines the distribution of influence and power among social and economic groups and the prevailing system of philosophical values, standards of excellence, and patterns of prestige or deference. This orientation then considers the differential policy outputs of the system to various social groups.

A second approach, the analysis of political systems and roles, tends to emphasize the causal importance, or autonomy, of the polity. It must be stressed that this view is not logically incompatible with predominantly economic and social explanations. Nevertheless, this approach turns our attention to the differentiation and variation among political roles such as citizen ruler, statesman and broker of interests, and institutions such as parties, legislatures, and administrative bureaucracies. In one version of this approach politics is conceptualized as a differen-

---

[30] For discussions of the emergence of such organizations earlier in the century and in the late nineteenth century, see Grant McConnell, *Private Power and American Democracy* (New York: Knopf, 1966), chap. 3; Blaisdell, p. 61, who identifies the term "pressure group" as coming into general use after 1924; and Theodore J. Lowi, "Toward Functionalism in Political Science," *American Political Science Review*, 57 (September 1963), 579–580.

tiated system of behavior with its own complex inputs and outputs handled by political actors in ways that contribute to or detract from system maintenance.[31]

A related concept sees politics as a constellation of actors and interests that the system creates, combines, controls, and serves through a basic set of functions.[32] Behind this concentration on political systems and roles appears to be a basic assumption, powerfully formulated by Max Weber, that since the Middle Ages the Western polity has become increasingly independent of social relationships, and is therefore capable of the creative alleviation of societal strain.[33]

The third analytic dimension, perhaps the most fruitful yet employed in the interpretation of American political behavior, focuses on the size of the relevant political unit. This unit can be the *constituency* of the particular group or political leader or the *scope* of political conflict (the ratio of active participants to the uninvolved audience). We can also consider the *type of government policy*, conceptualized as the size and number of benefits distributed, ranging from a few large disbursements to social classes to more numerous smaller ones intended for individuals and small groups. Finally, the analyst may also focus on the political *incentives* that organizational leaders dispense to induce political activity. These vary from such small and divisible incentives as patronage jobs and monetary payments appealing to individual self-interest to larger and collective incentives, that is, ideal benefactions appealing to a wider group loyalty.[34] Like the mode of analysis that focuses on political systems and roles, the size-of-political-unit approach stresses patterns of political behavior and political structures. Both approaches, for example, treat the different methods that politicians use to build coalitions as significant research questions in their own right. But the size-of-political-unit focus is less directly concerned with the consequences for the American political system as a whole than for the particular individuals and groups within it. System maintenance and even relief of societal strain have seemed less pressing empirical questions for the highly stable American polity than are the questions of alternative methods of allocating values among competing public and private interests. This concern with specific interests and actors is obviously shared by the stratification approach. But the size of a political unit like a constituency is a formal attribute not logically or necessarily connected to particular economic or social groups. It is not directly and overtly relevant, for example, to American workers or to unions. The urban machine could thus appeal to

---

[31] See in particular, David Easton, *A Systems Analysis of Political Life* (New York: Wiley, 1965).

[32] Gabriel Almond, "Introduction," *The Politics of the Developing Areas.* (Princeton: Princeton University Press, 1960.)

[33] The analysis in these pages follows the observations of Morris Janowitz in "Political Sociology," in *The International Encyclopedia of the Social Sciences* (New York: Crowell-Collier-Macmillan, 1968).

[34] For a discussion of constituency, see McConnell, chap. 4. On scope of conflict, see Schattschneider, chaps. 1, 2. On types of issues, see Theodore J. Lowi, "American Business, Public Policy, Case Studies and Political Theory," *World Politics*, 16 (July 1964), 677–693. On incentive systems, see Peter B. Clark and James Q. Wilson, "Incentive Systems: A Theory of Organizations," *Administrative Science Quarterly*, 6 (September 1961), 129–166 and Edward C. Banfield and James Q. Wilson, *City Politics* (Cambridge, Mass.: Harvard University Press, 1963), chaps. 9–11. McConnell refers to the relationship between constituency and other units of political analysis like ideology, tactics, and policy, pp. 113ff.

both business groups and poor immigrants by promising relatively small divisible material payoffs. Peculiarly American conditions may also explain this characteristic of the size-of-political-unit approach, for the predominance of middle-class values and perspectives provide little stimulation to focus on such European social categories as aristocrats, bourgeoisie, and proletarians.[35]

Each of these three analytic modes is compatible with a pluralist interpretation of American politics. In terms of the analysis of political systems and roles, the American polity is said to maintain itself securely through reliance on political brokers who skillfully assemble different interests through ingenious compromises that reduce strain and avoid deep political cleavages. Small political units, like compact, relatively homogeneous constituencies, private-regarding incentives, individualist and group rather than class issues, and narrow rather than broad conflict are said to dominate the American scene and thus be appropriate subjects for the size-of-political-unit analysis. Unions themselves play this particularistic role.[36] Social stratification theorists can also pluralistically characterize American politics as dominated by business and entrepreneurial rather than by working-class and collectivist values. Even the purportedly progressive income and inheritance taxes appears to be only a moderately effective attempt at redistributing wealth.[37]

A Nonpluralist Interpretation

The interpretation of labor politics offered here, however, asserts a substantial modification of pluralism on all three dimensions of analysis. The emergence of labor as a Democratic party electoral organization is likely to alter the political balance among social classes. This change will rarely mean that the union pressures or controls the party. The complex labor-party coalition instead often operates on the basis of shared decisions and a division of labor and responsibilities in the political struggle. But simply because labor functions as a vital element in the Democrats' entire campaign operation, party leaders are likely to anticipate the reaction of their labor campaign workers and thus to cater to some of their wishes. For this reason, class as a political category must refer not only to objective economic position or to subjective awareness of social status but also to organizational structures through which collective interests and perspectives are expressed.

Given the importance of interest groups and parties, this labor-party fusion has equally important consequences for the analysis of political systems and roles. Labor's position within the party enables it to share in and to strengthen the process of aggregating the many labor and nonlabor interests by which the party builds its majority coalition. In turn, this concern for successfully assembling a majority coalition to elect Democratic candidates has transformed labor's own political role. As the arm of a political party, the unions' behavior is no longer simply a reflex of their own economic position and constituency; they also consider the entire political constituency that the party seeks to mobilize. In Easton's terms, the pattern of labor's inputs into the political system includes relatively more support and fewer demands than a typical interest group's inputs and is

[35] Louis Hartz, *The Liberal Tradition in America* (New York: Harcourt Brace Jovanovich, 1955).
[36] See, for example, McConnell, chap. 9.
[37] Gabriel Kolko, *Wealth and Power in America* (New York: Praeger, 1962), chap. 2.

thus far closer to the pattern of a major party.[38] This process moderates labor's demands and broadens labor's political constituency to include relatively deprived groups who do not happen to belong to trade unions.

Finally, in terms of size-of-political-unit analysis, the incorporation of organized labor as a functioning partner in a partisan coalition is likely to increase the prevailing size of constituency and scope of conflict. At the same time it is likely to reduce the relative importance of narrow and particularistic (as opposed to public-regarding or class-oriented) policies and incentives. In general, the party will be influenced to favor class legislation whereas labor will have to pay greater attention to interests larger than its own.

Measured on all three dimensions of analysis, then, European and American politics have, by the 1960s, appreciably converged in the area of party and interest group behavior as well as in the more widely recognized areas of welfare policies and voter alignment. . . .

[38] Easton, pp. 256–257.

CHAPTER ELEVEN

THE AFFLUENT MIDDLE CLASS

32
Politics and Reform in American Cities

James Q. Wilson

TYPES OF REFORM MOVEMENTS

The principal theme in the study of local politics has always been the checkered history of reform in the major American cities. Long before Lincoln Steffens wrote *The Shame of the Cities*, the fundamental problem of local government was viewed in terms of a contest between rascals and reformers. Our federal government has only occasionally been seen from this perspective; usually, the national administration has been evaluated in terms of the substance of the policies it has carried out. Corruption and conflict of interest have always been discovered in Washington, but these unsavory incidents have rarely provided the leitmotif for the study of national politics.

It is by no means obvious why this discrimination against local government should persist. It is not enough to say that local affairs are seen in terms of corruption simply because there is more corruption to be found there, for corruption could coexist (and, in fact, has coexisted) with substantive policies which are in the public interest. Nor have local machines always encouraged waste and corruption. The Memphis organization of Boss Edward Crump, for example, was reputedly an efficient and relatively honest administration of city government. A

From pp. 41–44 and 48–52 of "Politics and Reform in American Cities" by James Q. Wilson, from *American Government Annual 1962–1963*, edited by Donald G. Herzberg. Copyright © 1963 by Holt, Rinehart and Winston, Inc. Reprinted by permission of Holt, Rinehart and Winston, Inc.

municipal government which practiced corruption could at the same time keep the streets clean, the water pure, the citizenry safe, and the children educated. Indeed, in some large, complex cities, corrupting at least some officials may be essential if those ends are to be attained.

There are, of course, several reasons why our attention to big-city politics is so often absorbed by reports of graft and impropriety. One may be a result of the generally accepted belief that local government is, or ought to be, that level of government "closest to the people" and thus most expressive of widely shared sentiments and fundamental principles. Dishonesty in local government is "close to home" and disturbing, while rascality in Washington or abroad is remote and, in a way, expected. Cities, after all, educate our children and police our streets. But this reason, while it may have some merit, is not completely convincing. Although local government may be close to the people in small cities and towns, it is doubtful whether the people feel that the government of a vast metropolis such as New York, Chicago, or Los Angeles is any "closer" to them than the local representatives of the federal government who collect taxes, draft soldiers, or pay benefits.

A more general reason might be that, in most cases, the activities of local government are not intrinsically interesting, at least not in the way the great, national issues of peace and war, prosperity and depression, are interesting. Local government, if it is to attract attention at all, can usually do so only when evidence of wrongdoing is brought forward. Most cities do little more than provide certain minimal, essential, public services. And, for most people most of the time, these services are provided adequately, or at least not so inadequately as to call for anything more than routine complaints. The politics and policies of big cities rarely implicate the most important interests of many powerful individuals or organizations. City politics are peripheral to the major concerns of most organized groups. This fact has several implications for the study of local government.

First, it means that local politics is rarely studied systematically by first-rate scholars. Although there are several intellectually interesting questions to be found in municipal affairs, there are—or seem to be—relatively few questions of great practical interest. Thus, we know little of a general nature about city government; we are left, as a consequence, with what the newspapers choose to tell us about the more picaresque aspects of city hall life.

Second, concern over municipal affairs is usually precipitated by a real or apparent interruption in the flow of essential public services, rather than stimulated by a debate over new policies or the larger ends of government. Congress discusses whether to raise or lower tariffs, pay farmers more or less, or build bigger or smaller missiles. City councils discuss complaints about uncollected garbage, unpoliced neighborhoods, or unpaved streets. Debates about missiles can be carried on without raising questions of corruption or malfeasance; complaints about a breakdown in garbage collection naturally—and often reasonably—lead to suggestions of dishonesty or incompetence as explanations for a failure in such a basic service.

Third, reform efforts in city politics have typically been aimed, not so much at altering the ends of government—reformers have usually assumed that most people were in agreement on what public services ought to be performed—but at altering the personnel of government and eliminating dishonesty and inefficiency. In this, of course, they may have been fundamentally wrong, for there are many people in big cities who prefer less, rather than more, police supervision and who care little about public education. But reform efforts have usually been led by persons with a commitment to a high level of certain "noncontroversial" public services; it is the high cost or low quality of these services, rather than the services themselves, that the reformers have typically wanted to change.

Finally, organized support for reform has typically come from groups which had some stake in the level and price of municipal services. Downtown department stores, public utilities, and banks need local customers, and thus they need those local services that are a prerequisite to attracting and holding those local customers—good streets, good police, efficient bureaucrats, and a "good business climate." (In an earlier era, of course, such firms, particularly utilities, needed franchises from the city in order that they could *become* a business. Franchises could be, and were, purchased from political bosses. Once the franchises were obtained, however, such firms gradually became more interested in maintenance than in entrepreneurship, and thus lost interest in what bosses could deliver and became more interested in what "good government" could deliver.) Local firms and local elites have been the backbone of most reform efforts, at least until recently. National firms—big manufacturers, wholesalers, and investment houses—which occupy local real estate but do not serve a local market are often absent from local reform movements.

TABLE 1
Major Types of Civic Reform Organizations

Relation to Parties	Goals		
	Policies	Candidates	Organizations
Extraparty	Citizens' leagues; municipal research bureaus	Screening committees; nonpolitical elites	Independent local parties
Intraparty	[Residual category, no major examples]	"Blue-ribbon" leadership factions, and candidates	Intraparty reform clubs or factions

Reform movements are not identical, however. Although most of them have certain common features, there are local differences and, what is even more important, some have undergone a radical transformation in recent years. Generally speaking, there have been five kinds of local political reform efforts: citizens' leagues, candidate screening committees, blue-ribbon candidates, independent local parties, and intraparty factions. One variant type could be added, although it is only called into being on an ad hoc basis—the informal group of nonpolitical community notables who coalesce before elections, usually in nonpartisan cities, to select and raise money for local candidates. These five kinds can be conveniently categorized on the basis of whether they operate within or outside the regular political parties and whether they are interested primarily in suggesting policies and programs, selecting candidates, or winning office.

These kinds of reform efforts can be briefly identified:

1. *Citizens' leagues* Citizens' leagues are voluntary associations, often with a

paid staff executive or research director, which scrutinize local government structure, programs, and expenditures and recommend changes and reforms. The New York Citizens' Budget Commission, the Chicago Civic Federation, the Detroit Citizens' League, the Pennsylvania Economy League, the Seattle Municipal League, and the Boston Municipal Research Bureau are all examples of extra-party, policy-oriented, citizens' committees which have been the vehicle for various kinds of reform efforts. The League of Women Voters is probably the largest single organization of this kind.

2. *Candidate appraisal committees* Created outside the political parties, the committees are organizations, permanent or ad hoc, which recommend or evaluate candidates for public office. Where the parties are weak or nonexistent (as in certain nonpartisan cities, Los Angeles, for example), these committees may be informal groups of the most influential businessmen, lawyers, and publishers who, in the absence of party control, actually select a candidate for mayor and raise the funds to hire a public relations firm to conduct his campaign. In such a case, the group will almost never be formally organized; it will usually have no name, staff, or office; and its membership will be carefully limited. Where, on the other hand, the parties are strong (as in New York, for example), no outside group can dictate the choice of candidates. Whatever committee may exist in this area will, typically, be composed of lesser business and professional people (there is too little at stake to attract top men); it will be formally organized with an office, budget, and staff; and it will confine itself to evaluating candidates for office, often by ranking them, "endorsed," "preferred," "qualified," or "unqualified." The Citizens' Union of New York City is an example of such an organization, although it also is active in other aspects of government, such as evaluating proposed legislation and scrutinizing the conduct of public officials.

3. *Independent local parties* Under certain circumstances, reform-minded people will enter the elective process directly by creating a local political party, independent of the major parties, which will run slates of candidates for municipal and other local offices. The City Charter Committee in Cincinnati and the Citizens' Association in Kansas City, Missouri, are perhaps the two most important examples. The Liberal Party in New York City is an independent party of a special kind: unlike most organizations of this kind, it was formed by certain strong, Jewish-led labor unions committed to a New Deal ideology, rather than by business and professional men (often conservatives on national issues) interested in efficiency and economy in local government. The Citizens' Union of New York, which is now primarily a candidate screening committee, began in 1897 as an independent political party which ran Seth Low for mayor, unsuccessfully in 1897, and successfully in 1901. Among its founders were Carl Schurz, Nicholas Murray Butler, Jacob Schiff, J. Pierpont Morgan, Elihu Root, and R. Fulton Cutting. It failed to sustain itself beyond its initial victories, however, and by 1918 had been transformed into a nonpartisan civic group. Other examples of independent, "good government" parties include the San Francisco Volunteers for Better Government, the San Antonio Good Government League, the Phoenix Charter Government Committee, the Minneapolis Citizens Organized for Responsible Government, the Independent Voters of Illinois (in Chicago), and the Cambridge (Massachusetts) Civic Association. Sometimes, such local parties are formed to contest school board elections, as is the case with the Boston Citizens' Schools Committee.

4. *"Blue-ribbon" leadership factions* Comprised of leaders of a regular political party, these factions seek to induce the party to nominate "good government" or "blue-ribbon" candidates for local offices. Sometimes such a leadership faction is a minority, composed of dissident reformers who happen to occupy party posts; just as often, blue-ribbon candidates may be slated at the instigation of regular party leaders who have no personal commitment to reform at all. Examples of the former would be Richardson Dilworth and Joseph S. Clark who have attempted to reform the Democratic party in Philadelphia from the top down, by fighting both to retain party support for themselves and to obtain it for like-minded men whom they endorse. Examples of the latter would be Col. Jacob Arvey and Mayor Richard J. Daley in Chicago who, although not at all interested in party reform, have, from time to time, recognized the electoral advantages to be obtained from nominating men such as Paul Douglas and Adlai Stevenson for posts at the top of the Democratic ticket. James Finnegan of Philadelphia, who before his death was an ally of Clark and Dilworth, was also a regular party man who thought "good government was good politics."

5. *Intraparty reform factions* Of late, reformers have not been content with forming extraparty civic groups or with seeking nominations for blue-ribbon candidates; instead, they have entered the regular party (usually the Democratic) at its lowest levels, in the wards and assembly districts, to capture control of party posts and the party organization. The clubs associated with the New York Committee for Democratic Voters have had considerable success with this tactic in Manhattan, coming close to winning a majority of the votes on the executive committee of the party, popularly known as Tammany Hall. In California, local political clubs have been formed, under the aegis of the California Democratic Council, which have sought to create machinery for endorsing Democratic candidates for public office that will guarantee that these nominees will be liberal, good government types.

All of these kinds of reform or good government efforts have existed for many years. With the exception of certain of the larger, better established ones, however, most are fairly short-lived. So little systematic research on city politics has been done that we know little, except in a few cities, about any causal factors which may be associated with the rise and fall of reform efforts. We have little general knowledge concerning the conditions under which one rather than another reform strategy is likely to be employed. Nor can anything be said with confidence about the relationship between the type of local political system, as described in the preceding section, and the type of reform effort which appears. What appears below, therefore, is of a very speculative nature.

First, a shift has probably begun from extraparty to intraparty reform efforts. Early in this century, there were civic groups, research bureaus, and independent local parties in many large cities. All represented efforts to reform government and politics with the power of publicity and research and by electing a few good men to top offices on independent slates. Very few made more than a momentary impression on their cities. The reasons for their limited value are well-known: their inability to sustain volunteer interest in political campaigning; their failure to create permanent political organizations which could defend the reform candidates who were elected to office; and their willingness to contest only the prestigious higher offices, leaving the minor—but often politically more important—

offices in the hands of the machine. Research bureaus, of course, did not contest any offices; their decay began with the realization that the majority of the voters did not automatically respond to "objective" facts about municipal expenditures and administrative procedures by spontaneously organizing themselves in order to throw the inefficient or dishonest politician out of office. In fact, some citizens, for reasons the early reformers never really understood, seemed to prefer waste and favoritism so long as somebody in the machine was willing and able to look after a distressed voter's personal needs.

Further, except in the genuinely nonpartisan cities, the allegiance of the voters continued to be to the traditional party labels—particularly the allegiance of the lower-income, less educated voters who, in most cases, made up a majority of the electorate. Creating an independent local party led by upper-middle-class lawyers and housewives was often an excellent means for attracting the support of "independent" voters; unfortunately, these usually happened to be a distinct minority. Although exposures of shocking examples of graft and malfeasance could often give the independent party a temporary majority, these never endured as vote-getting devices when matched against the lasting power of the words "Democratic" or "Republican."

Thus, after World War II, certain young reformers in various cities and states began to think seriously of the possibility of taking over one of the major parties —of shifting from an extraparty to an intraparty strategy. This would give them the best of both worlds—reform leadership combined with control of a traditional party label. Such a strategy, of course, would be far harder to pursue, at least in its initial stages, because the regular party leaders would fight bitterly any attempt to wrest control of the organization from them. But if that battle could be won, the reformers reasoned, maintaining a reform movement would be far easier, for they would then have at their disposal the resources of the regular party, including the patronage on which conventional politicians often depended.

A second, and related, trend has been a shift from conservatives to liberals, or at least from Republicans to Democrats, as the backbone of reform efforts. The earliest independent local parties, research bureaus, and citizens' committees were often founded and financed by some of the wealthiest men in town, mostly Republicans. The New York Citizens' Union, as noted above, had J. P. Morgan as an earlier backer. The New York Municipal Research Bureau, the first of its kind, was heavily financed by John D. Rockefeller, Andrew Carnegie, and Mrs. Edward H. Harriman; the bureau in Rochester was backed by George Eastman; the Boston bureau for many years was underwritten by Henry L. Shattuck. The Civic Federation of Chicago was founded by Marshall Field, Cyrus McCormick, Jr., and Mrs. Potter Palmer, among others. A 1957 survey showed that 72 percent of the directors of the Seattle Municipal League described themselves as Republicans. In heavily Democratic Boston, Republicans outnumber Democrats on the board of the Municipal Research Bureau by three to one. The Cincinnati Charter Committee was begun by a small group of young Republican lawyers and insurance men, although few of the wealthiest, most conservative Republicans gave it much support.

The new, postwar group of young reformers shares the mentality of older reformers—a belief in good government and efficiency, a dislike of machines and patronage, and a desire to see public policies set as a result of deliberate action (ideally, by "planning") rather than as the unintended consequence of struggles for power—but the difference in political strategy has meant that the new reform leaders have been drawn from a different ideological background. If one decides to be an intraparty rather than extraparty reformer, it means one must be willing to enter politics at the lowest level and spend much time and effort in the menial chores of politics—forming organizations, circulating petitions, ringing doorbells, and speaking on street corners. Such a strategy is rarely congenial to an affluent, middle-aged businessman with a secure position in society. The older reformer preferred to write a check and allow his name to be used on a letterhead; staff men were hired to do the rest, with the businessmen merely attending periodic luncheon meetings to approve high policy and hear evangelical speeches.

The intraparty reformer, therefore, tends to be young, usually under thirty-five and often under thirty and in the early years of his career. Further, the laborious nature of the work requires a high level of motivation on the part of the activist. Intraparty reform offers one inducement which is identical to that provided by extraparty reform: the opportunity to do good and throw the rascals out. But it also provides an additional incentive: the opportunity to gratify personal political ambitions. Older reformers concentrated on one or a few major offices—usually the mayor and perhaps a few city councilmen—and they were suspicious of persons who offered themselves as candidates for these posts. They preferred men who were reluctant to take on such assignments and who had to be talked into leaving lucrative law practices to serve the public. The new reformers, dedicated to taking over the entire party and all the offices it controls, can offer many opportunities for exercising power and acquiring prestige; far from being reluctant to run for such offices, the reformers often compete among themselves for the nominations.

The Democratic party dominates the politics of most major cities and, thus, intraparty reform means entering and taking over the Democratic party. As a result, the young men and women with sufficient ideological or personal motivation to undertake the difficult task are usually people who feel strongly (or who act *as if* they feel strongly) about the policies of the Democratic party, and these, of course, are usually the members of the party's liberal—sometimes even "extreme" liberal—wing. The new strategy of reform and the organizational problems it creates, therefore, virtually insure that the new reformers will be liberal Democrats while the older group were middle-of-the-road or, at best, Progressive Republicans.

If the new strategy of intraparty reform promises to be more enduring and, for young liberals, more attractive, it also has a profound disadvantage. The young reformers, although not necessarily the sons and daughters of the well to do, are at least middle class: thus, their political strength is to be found only where the middle class lives, not primarily in the central city, but in its suburbs. Where it does live in the central city, it is usually in relatively small neighborhoods, often surrounded by lower-class slums. In New York City, for example, the Democratic reformers live, by and large, in districts where they are outnumbered by Republicans. This is not a handicap so long as the reformers are struggling for control of the party in that district, for party leadership fights are waged in primary elections in which only enrolled Democrats can vote. The problems arise when these reformers attempt to extend their influence in the party; then they must contend with the fact that many, if not most, central city party officials are chosen in districts in which the middle class—and, hence, in which middle-class reformers—do not live: Negro Harlem, Puerto Rican East Harlem, the Jewish Lower East Side, and so forth.

This ecological obstacle is encountered again when reformers attempt to make their weight felt in general elections—in, for example, the election of a mayor. Here, members of all parties can vote, and in most cases the Democratic votes in reform-controlled districts are overwhelmed by the Republican votes. In the November 1961 New York mayoralty election, for example, the reform-backed Democratic candidate, Robert F. Wagner, got his strongest support from lower-income districts where the regular Democratic leaders had fought him in the primary, and little or no support from the middle-class districts where the reform Democratic leaders had backed him in the primary. Although the reformers had helped him win the nomination in the primary, the nonreform districts helped him win the general election against the Republican opposition. The reformers, as a result, could not lay full claim to Wagner's loyalties. . . .

Intraparty Reform

The history of the New York City Fusion party—its short-lived successes, its lack of permanent impact—led the generation of reformers, who came of age politically after World War II, to consider a new strategy: entering the regular party organization and capturing it from within. This process, which began in 1949 with the formation of the Lexington Democratic Club on Manhattan's East Side, culminated in 1961 with the defeat of Tammany Leader Carmine G. De Sapio and the re-election of Mayor Robert Wagner on a reform platform.

Simultaneously with the New York reform effort, liberals were creating in California an organization composed of political clubs which sought to become the extralegal backbone of the Democratic party. Since the cities of California are nonpartisan, with hardly any examples of what could be called a political machine, the California clubs directed their attention to the state party organization and state-wide elections. Further, because of legal restrictions on formal party activity which, among other things, prevented the parties from having any kind of permanent, grass roots organization, there was no party hierarchy based on precinct and ward committees which a reform group could take over. Thus, the California liberals became intraparty reformers of a sort different from those found in New York: they were preoccupied with *creating* a club structure which could then be used to influence—ideally, control—the primary elections and thus determine the nature of the party's nominees.

The young men and women who joined the club movement in New York and California were initially attracted, not so much by evidence of municipal waste and corruption or by a felt need to reform the city, as by the appeal of a powerful national personality, Adlai E. Stevenson, whom they were eager to support in his 1952 and 1956 presidential campaigns. At first, the club members simply wanted to help elect their idol. In New York, the regular Democratic organization seemed more interested in local contests and, in 1956, had tried to win the Democratic presidential nomination for Governor Averell Harriman, fighting Stevenson's bid for a second chance. In California, there seemed to be, in 1952 and 1956, no organization at all either to help or hinder Stevenson.

Whatever the reason the clubs were formed, they quickly found themselves in conflict with professional politicians. In New York, of course, the conflict was inevitable, once the reform clubs began to enter candidates in the Democratic primaries for district leader, the basic unit of the party hierarchy. In California, with no such posts to compete for, the struggle was between liberal clubs and Democratic elective officials (assemblymen and Congressmen) who saw in the movement a threat to their autonomy and a rival force seeking to influence the choice of candidates.

The amateurs who made up the rank and file of the club movement were more or less generally aware of the failures of reform in the past. In New York, they were convinced that attempting to elect reform public officials without first capturing the party on which these officials would ultimately have to rely was meaningless; indeed, they pointed to the blue-ribbon reform efforts of Dilworth and Clark in Philadelphia as a contemporary example of the wrong reform strategy. In California, the club leaders argued that not only had the reforms of the Progressive era (the initiative and referendum, the restrictions on party activity, and civic nonpartisanship) not achieved their announced ends, they had, in fact, raised a major obstacle to the creation of an effective party and thus lessened the ability of the clubs to make their weight felt against elective officials.

In each case, a coordinating organization was created to bring the clubs together. The New York Committee for Democratic Voters (CDV) was formed in 1959 under the sponsorship of former Senator Herbert Lehman, Mrs. Eleanor Roosevelt, Thomas Finletter, Irving Engle, Lloyd Garrison, and Frank Adams, and set about raising funds and providing elder statesman prestige and professional staff assistance for the New York reform clubs which, by late 1961, numbered 36. Of these, 15, all in Manhattan, actually controlled the Democratic party leadership in their districts and sent representatives to the party's county executive committee, Tammany Hall. The California Democratic Council (CDC) was created in 1953 to bring together and expand the spontaneously growing club movement which had mushroomed since 1952. The CDC was not an antiregular or antiboss group; instead, it was intended to be a semiofficial umbrella organization in which all elements of the party—clubs, elective officials, Young Democrats, and state and county committee members—would be represented. In fact, representation was heavily weighted in favor of the liberal clubs; the president of CDC is generally considered to be a club spokesman and the conventions of the CDC are regarded as the voice of the issue-oriented, liberal wing of the party.

The CDV and the CDC club members have in common at least two goals: intraparty democracy and committing the party to issues. These are the newer and, to their exponents, more sophisticated versions of such old reform slogans as "throw the rascals out" and "efficiency and honesty." Intraparty democracy means creating institutional constraints on party leaders such that party members—which usually means reform-minded, liberal, party members—can exercise a significant measure of control over them in such matters as the selection of candidates for office, campaigns, the allocation of patronage, party finance, and relations with public officials. Issue commitment means changing the party from a more or less ideologically neutral broker of competing interests into a source of positive programs; the party is to profess principles and policies, not because they are useful in winning votes, but because they are, in the eyes of the party activists, the "right" policies. The party would thus become a radically different kind of organization. Conventional local parties, based on machines, social clubs, personal followings, or interest groups, can induce their workers to contribute time and effort because of material, social, or personal interests; this leaves the party a rather considerable freedom in adopting whatever "principles" seem most expedient for winning votes. The reform-controlled party, by contrast, can only induce its intellectually oriented, liberal volunteers to work by committing itself on a wide range of issues, whether or not such positions are politically expedient.

In New York, the CDV has paid relatively little attention to substantive issues thus far, being more preoccupied with the intraparty struggle against the regular clubs—particularly those which had looked to former Tammany chief De Sapio for leadership. The club members have, until now, been galvanized into action largely with cries of "bossism" and descriptions of De Sapio as the archvillain of New York politics. In the 1961 primary, however, a reform club defeated De Sapio as leader of the Greenwich Village district. This was followed by the re-election of Mayor Wagner after he had broken, not only with De Sapio, but with the Democratic county leaders of the Bronx and Brooklyn as well. Having beaten the "devil" and helped elect a mayor, the CDV had lost a valuable enemy and gained a reluctant friend.

Success will probably prove to be as mixed a blessing for the CDV as it has been for the CDC. Both organizations seek to elect liberal, good government Democrats to office. In both cases, such candidates have often found club support a valuable asset in Democratic primaries, but a liability in general elections. Reformers, as mentioned before, tend to be influential precisely in those areas where few Democratic votes are to be found. Democrats who have won their primaries usually discover that they must appeal to a broad range of voters in a way which an overly close identification with ultraliberal clubs can embarrass. And, once safely in office, they are anxious to avoid any commitments which will inhibit their ability to maintain good relations with the wide variety of interest groups and political forces which can affect their prospects for re-election.

Becoming intraparty reformers can bind the clubs equally with the party. Before the great Democratic victory of 1958, the California clubs did not need to fear embarrassing Democratic public officials with their policy statements, for almost all the public officials in Sacramento were Republicans. And there was always something to do: select candidates to oppose Republican incumbents. After 1958, there was little to do except help re-elect Democratic incumbents, since the clubs are rarely willing to risk challenging a Democratic incumbent in a primary. However, some of these Democratic officials are no longer so certain they want club help—after all, some voters think the CDC clubs are too left-wing. In New York, the CDV endorsed Mayor Wagner as part of its campaign against "bossism" only to discover that the Mayor believed that he had done more for the reformers than they had for him and that he ought to be the undisputed party leader with complete control over legislation, appointments, and party organization. The semantics which distinguish leaders from bosses are complex indeed.

The strategy of intraparty reform, were it successful, might solve one of the dilemmas of the reformers. If they captured control of their party, they would not have to choose—as leaders of independent local parties do—between attacking the local machine and thereby risk hurting liberal national candidates, or helping the national candidates even if these choose to accept support, as they almost inevitably do, from the machine. But no group of intraparty reformers is in command of the party in any big city or state. And, in the 1960 Presidential campaign, the reformers were vexed to discover that Kennedy placed his reliance in California on Assemblyman Jesse Unruh and State Chairman Roger Kent rather than the CDC, in Philadelphia on William Green rather than Dilworth or Clark, and in Chicago on Mayor Daley. Only in New York City did the Kennedy organization bypass, to some extent, the regular party and create a special "citizens' committee" which brought regulars and reformers together in an uneasy alliance for the campaign. And for this Kennedy had good reason, even apart from the existence of a reform faction: De Sapio had only supported Kennedy's nomination under duress (he is believed to have been for Stuart Symington originally); De Sapio's ally, State Chairman Michael Prendergast, had publicly snubbed Herbert Lehman (who wields great influence with a large number of Jewish voters); and the regular organization, particularly in Manhattan, seemed unable to get out the vote. Even so, Kennedy's administration continued to be on friendly terms with Bronx Democratic leader Charles Buckley, a politician whose qualifications for the title "boss" were far more impressive than any of which De Sapio could boast.

Nonpolitical Elites

The nonpolitical elites who tend to dominate politics in the genuinely nonpartisan big cities are not necessarily pursuing a particular kind of civic reform strategy; they are, more correctly, the heirs of an earlier strategy which was based on the dubious premise that the ills of the city could be cured by eliminating politics. Advocates of nonpartisanship frequently repeated their argument that there is no Democratic or Republican way to pave a street or collect the garbage and that, therefore, parties were not only unnecessary but pernicious. Nonpartisanship, together with many of the reforms which often accompanied it, such as the city manager form of government, small city councils based on elections at large, and the merit system, were often based on an analogy between city government and business. The council should be like a board of directors, the mayor or city manager similar to a corporation president; the "best man" would win and the most "efficient" policies would be carried out without partisan interference.

These reforms were popular in the early decades of this century and the movements which sponsored them were often business-led or business-backed municipal research bureaus and citizens' leagues. With the structural reforms established, some of these groups decided to remain in being as independent local parties to safeguard the gains and keep the rascals from coming back in. Such were the origins of the Kansas City Citizens' Association and, to some extent, the Cincinnati Charter Committee.

In other nonpartisan cities, however, no independent party was formed; election campaigns were conducted instead by ad hoc groups which came into being, often only on an informal basis, before each contest. In Los Angeles, such a group would come together for lunch at the University Club and consist of representatives (often the top executives) from the *Los Angeles Times*, the major utilities, banks, and insurance companies, and some high-powered attorneys. They would agree on a mayoral candidate, raise a war chest, hire a public relations firm, and disband.

Although *every* "reform" is a redistribution of power in the community which benefits some groups at the expense of others, the costs and benefits are partially concealed when politics is conducted by a citizens' association which, because of its permanent and public character, must make some effort at attracting to it representatives of the various elements of the community. But when politics is in the hands of a cozy, nameless caucus of notables, and campaigning in the hands of PR men, it is almost inevitable that there will be charges made that the city is run by a "power elite" of Republican businessmen interested only in their own profits—even though, as may very likely be the case, the substantive policies of government in the two instances are nearly identical. Detroit, Los Angeles, and Cincinnati are all "good government" cities, with few scandals and with laws reflecting a middle-class ethos; elections in the first two have been dominated by nonpolitical elites and in the last by the Charter and Republican parties.

In Detroit, the elites were responsible for keeping Mayor Albert E. Cobo in office for four terms; in Los Angeles, they kept Norris Poulson in office for two terms. But both Poulson and Cobo's successor, Louis Miriani, lost in 1961 despite complete support from the elites.

Even more perplexing is that Miriani and Poulson had not only the backing of big businessmen and the metropolitan newspapers, but, in addition, the support of most of the major labor unions and most of the leading Democratic and Republican party officials. Miriani had the endorsement of both the Detroit *Free Press* and the *News* as well as of the United Auto Workers (which thereby extended its astonishing record of never having backed a winner in a Detroit mayoralty contest). Poulson, although not the official candidate of a party, had the personal endorsement of most leading Democrats and Republicans, as well as heavy financial backing from businessmen and newspaper editorial support.

Because the elections were nonpartisan, no party slates were entered and thus the defeat of incumbent mayors was not necessarily accompanied by the advent of an entirely new government. In Los Angeles, Mayor Poulson was defeated, but with one exception, all other incumbents running were re-elected easily. In Detroit, the changes were somewhat more extensive: in addition to a new mayor, the city acquired three new members of the nine-man city council.

The similarities between the Detroit and Los Angeles elections may suggest some general observations about the conditions under which nonpolitical elites can be defeated in nonpartisan cities, although upsets in only two mayoral elections are hardly grounds for predicting any fundamental change in the political institutions of these cities.

In both cities, the votes of minority groups were important factors in the defeat of incumbents. Negroes voted heavily for the victors—Samuel W. Yorty in Los Angeles, and Jerome P. Cavanagh in Detroit. An issue which observers felt was particularly important in arousing Negro voters was allegations of police mistreatment. Both cities have substantial Negro populations—in Los Angeles, about 13.5 percent and in Detroit about 26.4 percent of the total. Both also have highly professionalized, "good government" police forces which work diligently and efficiently at keeping crime rates down. Since the crime rates are highest in Negro areas, this means heavy police activity there. It can also mean police harassment of Negroes—stopping cars with Negro drivers, searching Negroes on the street, confiscating weapons, and generally treating Negroes with suspicion—which whites tend to describe as "good police work" but which Negroes describe as "police brutality." Both Yorty and Cavanagh appealed strongly for Negro votes, stressing the brutality theme. Public arguments between police chiefs and Negro leaders on this subject have been frequent in both cities for some time. Detroit's only Negro city councilman, William T. Patrick, had submitted a measure which would have given the Detroit Community Relations Council power to investigate charges of police brutality. All councilmen who voted for it were re-elected; those defeated had voted against it.

Television apparently played an important part in the upsets. Both Cavanagh and Yorty made effective use of television programs, while their incumbent opponents did little. Further, TV commentators in Los Angeles—an influential group of men with wide audiences—were far more sympathetic to Yorty than to Poulson. The victors based their campaigns on hard, personal attacks on the opposition and the state of civic affairs generally. Cavanagh attacked the "forces" behind Mayor Miriani, criticizing *by name* the two daily newspapers, the banks, General Motors and the Ford Motor Company, the Michigan Consolidated Gas Company, and several important Democratic politicians. Yorty similarly attacked the "downtown interests" backing Mayor Poulson, and criticized the latter for almost every aspect of his administration—the Bunker Hill urban renewal project, the baseball park "give away" to the Los Angeles Dodgers, the trash collection program, harbor oil leases, a proposal for a new zoo, and so forth. Both incumbents relied largely on their "record" and the endorsements of their powerful backers.

An additional factor in Los Angeles was the role of the many strong suburban newspapers, which frequently opposed downtown Los Angeles and the projects and candidates favored by the downtown newspapers, principally the *Times*. The community press was almost solidly behind Yorty, who easily carried those parts of the city, such as the San Fernando Valley, furthest from downtown.

Both winning candidates appealed to a wide range of possible popular discontents. In Detroit, continued unemployment and widespread discussion (including an article in *Time* just before the election) of the economic weaknesses of the city probably contributed to the number of issues about which voters may have felt strongly. In both cities, the mayor—whatever his actual powers—seems to be the person against whom grievances and the complaints of minority groups are directed. City council contests offer a more confused picture, for in Los Angeles the councilmen are selected by districts (15 in all) while in Detroit all nine are elected at large. In the former city, the incumbents, many—if not most—of whom identified themselves closely with local community loyalties and neighborhood newspapers, were re-elected. In the latter, three "conservative" councilmen were defeated by three "liberals," and liberals on the council generally gained strength over previous elections.

Although such a generalization can scarcely be supported by the available data, it is worth speculating whether the system of elections at large, discouraging neighborhood-legislator identification, produces, in a period of general discontent, a reliance on ideological distinctions as a basis for expressing that discontent. With nonpartisanship common to both cases, the district system of Los Angeles may have more conservative tendencies than the at large system of Detroit, because of the ability of the local councilman to distinguish himself from the "downtown forces" to which voters impute responsibility for undesirable conditions.

CONCLUDING OBSERVATIONS

The most general theme which appears again and again in this cursory sketch of the politics of large American cities is the importance of the class structure of the community in determining at least the broad outlines of political conflict. Although narrow conceptions of "class conflict" are—quite properly—disappearing from most of the literature of political science, the extent to which differences in income and ethnicity continue to provide the raw material of city politics is, nonetheless, striking.

In partisan cities, the perennial contests between professional and reform politicians are, in large part, the political expression of fundamental differences between the conceptions of the public interest held by lower- and lower-middle-class voters on the one hand, and upper-middle and upper-class voters, on the other. The former have a political ethic which places a high value on personal friendships, tangible needs, family and ethnic loyalties, and the exchange of favors; the latter an ethic which stresses the need for enacting general principles, serving city-wide rather than neighborhood interests, making policy by planning rather than by political bargaining, and rationalizing politics with law.

The organizational expression of the former ethic has been the political machine or its factional variants; of the latter, the civic associations, newspapers, reform movements, and committees of elites. The struggle between these two kinds of organizations has been surprisingly even, with the advantage shifting back and forth with pendulumlike regularity. The identity of the followers of each set of leaders has changed: in an earlier era, Irish Democrats fought Yankee Republicans; today, Italian and Negro leaders fight Yankee and Jewish Democrats. Only in those cities which have fundamentally changed their governing institutions have the reformers scored permanent gains: nonpartisanship and patronage-free administrations have largely prevented the political organization of the lower classes. Only when, as has recently happened in Los Angeles and Detroit, a widespread sense of grievance provides an issue which can activate large minorities do the community elites suffer a reverse. Otherwise, Negroes—the natural source of strength for new machines—are excluded from a share in the governing of these cities; the men who "represent" them in city hall can only be men who are acceptable to moderate white sentiments.

Shifting from an extraparty to an intraparty reform strategy has not solved this problem. Although some reformers hope that it may lessen the gulf between them and Negroes by creating the possibility of an alliance within a single party—the Democratic—it should not be forgotten that in the interwar period, reformers and many minority groups were also of the same party—the Republican. The difference, of course, is that previously the reformers sought power with leadership caucuses or independent parties, while today they seek it within the regular organization. The elimination of this organizational distinction, however, is not likely to eliminate the real grounds for the lack of rapport between lower-class voters and upper-class reformers, for that difference is far more profound than one of organizational allegiance—it is a difference in class, rhetoric, style of life, and social purposes.

33
Wallace and the Middle Class: The White Backlash in Wisconsin

Michael Rogin

Preliminary reports suggest that the white backlash did not play a great role in the Johnson-Goldwater presidential contest.[1] Yet only a few months before the Johnson landslide many political observers believed that significant proportions of normally Democratic working-class and ethnic groups, angered over Negro advances and civil rights militancy, would desert the Democratic Party and vote for Goldwater. There was speculation that this white backlash might elect Goldwater; certainly it was thought to be his best chance of victory.

The success of Alabama's Governor Wallace in the presidential primaries of three Northern states gave substance to this analysis. Running in the spring of 1964, Wallace received 33.8 percent of the Democratic primary vote in Wisconsin, 31.6 percent in Indiana, and 42.7 percent in Maryland. His showing in the large cities of these states was even better. In Milwaukee County, Lake County (Gary), and Baltimore (city and county)—all traditionally Democratic, Polish working-class centers—Wallace received 38.4, 50.8, and 42.1 percent of the Dem-

From *Public Opinion Quarterly* (Spring 1966), pp. 98–108. Reprinted by permission of publisher and author.

[1] Cf. "GOP Seeks Clues to Party Future in Study of Vote," *New York Times*, Nov. 8, 1964, 1.

ocratic vote, respectively. To scholars and journalists alike these results demonstrated a white backlash located predominantly among workers and ethnic minorities. Lipset, for example, wrote:

> In the Democratic presidential primaries in Wisconsin, Indiana, and Maryland, Governor Wallace (who campaigned against President Johnson in opposition both to civil rights and to increased federal powers) generally received his highest vote in the predominantly Catholic, working-class areas of Milwaukee, Gary, Baltimore, and other cities.[2]

This apparent racist sentiment among workers would be predicted by survey data and recent social science analysis. Workers are less educated than members of the middle class, and surveys have shown that prejudice, like a host of other anti-democratic attitudes, declines as education increases. On most questions measuring anti-Negro feeling, workers are more likely to reveal prejudice than are middle-class respondents. Workers tend to score higher than members of the middle class on scales measuring authoritarian predispositions. Workers, many social scientists argue, are culturally deprived, prone to the use or acceptance of violence, less committed to the democratic rules of the game. True, workers are liberal on socio-economic issues; but where civil rights and civil liberties are involved, social scientists place greater trust in the economically more conservative urban middle class.[3]

However, a closer look at the more politically relevant attitudes toward Negroes suggests quite different conclusions. On many issues, controlling for education, the lower class is *less* discrimination-minded than the upper class. With education controlled, for example, lower-class members are more likely to favor educational and job equality, and not to object to Negroes going where whites go. Of course, among the lower class the poorly educated predominate, and there are more well-educated in the middle and upper classes. On the other hand, consider the following: Within the lower class, 27 percent of the grade-school-educated, 26 percent of those with some high school, and 29 percent of those who completed high school would accept Negroes as next-door neighbors. This compares in the upper class with 14 percent of the college-educated and 20 percent of those who completed high school; and with 24 and 19 percent of those categories in the middle class. Similar results obtain when respondents are asked if they would move if substantial numbers of Negroes moved into their neighborhood.

---

[2] Seymour Martin Lipset, "Beyond the Backlash," *Encounter*, 23 (November 1964), 22.

[3] Cf. Samuel A. Stouffer, *Communism, Conformity, and Civil Liberties* (New York: Doubleday, 1955), pp. 26–57, 119–123; Seymour Martin Lipset, *Political Man* (New York: Doubleday, Anchor Books, 1963), pp. 87–126; James W. Prothro and Charles W. Grigg, "Fundamental Principles of Democracy," *Journal of Politics*, 22 (Spring 1960), 276–294; G. H. Smith, "Liberalism and Level of Information," *Journal of Educational Psychology*, 39 (1948), 65–82; G. H. Smith, "The Relationship of 'Enlightenment' to Liberal Conservative Opinions," *Journal of Social Psychology*, 28 (1948), 3–17; Bernard Berelson *et al.*, *Voting* (Chicago: University of Chicago Press, 1954), pp. 184–206; H. J. Eysenck, *The Psychology of Politics* (London: Routledge & Kegan Paul, 1954); W. J. McKinnon and R. Centers, "Authoritarianism and Urban Stratification," *American Journal of Sociology*, 61 (1965), 618; Melvin M. Tumin, *Segregation and Desegregation* (New York: Anti-Defamation League of B'nai B'rith, 1957); Charles Herbert Stember, *Education and Attitude Change* (New York: Institute of Human Relations Press, 1961).

Moreover, at every educational level the lower class is more willing than the upper or middle class to accept Negroes as fellow workers.[4]

Do authoritarian and racist politicians gain suport from economically liberal working-class voters or rather from more traditional right-wing sources? Is "middle-class authoritarianism" a more fruitful political concept than working-class authoritarianism? Wisconsin is a good state to examine for preliminary answers to such questions. Not only was it one of the three states in which Wallace campaigned, but a decade earlier it was also Senator McCarthy's home base. Earlier research has demonstrated that, contrary to the main body of social science theorizing, McCarthy's electoral support came primarily from traditionally conservative Republican areas (ethnically German-American) plus east-European ethnic groups particularly concerned over communism, Catholics, rural voters, and people living in or near McCarthy's home county.[5] To determine the core of the white backlash sentiment it was possible to (1) compare the Wallace vote with the normal party vote; (2) compare the social characteristics of counties or smaller jurisdictions most favorable and most opposed to Wallace; (3) compare the Wallace vote with the McCarthy vote. (The relative stability of the Wisconsin population aided the reliability of comparison over time.)

The Wallace vote in Wisconsin reveals a very different picture from the one predicted by social science research and popularly accepted. In Wisconsin, a state where Republicans can vote in the Democratic primary, Wallace's vote closely resembled the normal Republican vote.[6] The center of racist strength was not in working-class areas, but in the wealthy upper-middle-class suburbs of Milwaukee.

The evidence is remarkably clear-cut. Milwaukee County contains eighteen suburbs, nine strongly Democratic and nine Republican. In the 1960 gubernatorial race, Democrat Nelson received 59 percent or more of the vote in each of the Democratic suburbs, and from 23 to 46 percent of the vote in the Republican suburbs. The nine Democratic suburbs are working-class centers: between 44 and 63 percent of the employed population works in manufacturing industries. Professionals, managers, and wealthy businessmen live in the Republican suburbs: the percentage of the employed population in manufacturing in these suburbs varies from 21 to 41 percent.

In each of Milwaukee's Democratic, working-class suburbs Wallace received less than 42 percent of the Democratic primary vote. In each Republican, middle-class suburb he received 44 percent or more of the vote. He actually carried over half these suburbs, receiving 66 percent of the Democratic vote in River Hills, where the average home value is over $35,000.[7]

Product-moment correlation coefficients, measuring the relationship between the percentage in each suburb for Wallace and various demographic variables,

[4] Cf. Stember, *Education and Attitude Change*, pp. 81–82, 129–136, 168–173.
[5] Cf. Michael Rogin, *Intellectuals and McCarthy: The Radical Spectre* (Cambridge: M.I.T. Press, 1969).
[6] Wallace himself, like other observers, felt otherwise. "The primary votes I received in Wisconsin, Indiana, and Maryland," he said, "startled the leaders of both parties and scared plenty of them, for that tremendous vote which I rolled up was just from Democrats; no Republicans were permitted to express their feelings." Cf. the interview with Wallace in *Playboy*, 11 (November 1964), 62.
[7] Note that the four Milwaukee wards that gave Wallace more than 40 percent of their vote comprise the north and northeast corner of the city, which borders on the pro-Wallace middle-class suburbs.

clearly locate the Wallace vote among middle-class Republicans. The correlation between the percentage employed in manufacturing and the Wallace vote was −.767, that between the percentage of male professional and managerial employees and the Wallace vote .653.[8] Since those of Polish extraction live predominantly in the working-class areas ($r=.852$), the higher the percentage of the population of Polish stock, the *lower* the Wallace vote ($r=.669$). The most important single determinant of the Wallace vote was party. The correlation between the vote given the Republican candidate for governor in 1960 and the vote given Wallace in 1964 was .848.[9]

If one compares the five suburbs that Wallace carried with the five in which he did worst, the picture is equally striking (see the bottom section of Table 1). The Wallace suburbs average 47 percent of their employed males in professional and managerial positions, the anti-Wallace suburbs average 21 percent. Thirty-one percent of the employed population in the Wallace suburbs works in manufacturing compared with 52 percent in the anti-Wallace suburbs. The median family income in the Wallace suburbs is $3000 higher than in the anti-Wallace suburbs—$10,027 compared to $7246. The homes are valued almost $10,000 higher in the Wallace suburbs—$24,500 compared to $15,896. In the Wallace suburbs the average person has had a year of college; in the anti-Wallace suburbs he has not graduated from high school. The suburbs which opposed Wallace have twice as many Poles as those which supported him.[10]

Wallace's vote, then, was strikingly concentrated in the middle- and upper-class, native-stock, suburbs.[11] Apparently, Republican voters in these suburbs

[8] Adding women and clerical and sales workers slightly lowers the correlation. This was an upper-class white-collar vote for Wallace, not simply a lower-middle-class one.
[9] Demographic variables are even more strongly related to the traditional party vote than to the Wallace vote. For example, the percentage of male professional and managerial employees correlated .653 with the Wallace vote, .900 with the Republican vote for Governor in 1960. This suggests that much of the contrast between middle- and working-class support of Wallace was the consequence of party loyalty.
[10] The two middle groups of suburbs do not fall as consistently between the most pro- and anti-Wallace suburbs as one might expect. This is primarily because Wallace failed to carry Bayside and Fox Point, the two wealthiest Milwaukee suburbs, with the highest median education and the greatest proportion of professional and managerial employees. Apparently, there was somewhat more resistance to him at the top of the upper class than in the upper-middle and middle classes—although not so much as in the working class.

Among the working class, there is some suggestion that home ownership made a Wallace vote more likely. In the two most working-class of the nine Wallace suburbs (the only two with 40 percent of their population engaged in manufacturing), 90 percent and 85 percent of the homes are owned by their occupants. This is higher than the percentage in most of the more middle-class suburbs, and far higher than that in most working-class suburbs. The correlation between the Wallace vote and home ownership in the eleven suburbs with more than 40 percent of their population engaged in manufacturing is .386. Were it not for the sizable Wallace vote in West Milwaukee, where the percentage of the homeowners is by far the lowest in the country, the correlation would be .798. Survey data suggest that home ownership decreases willingness to live next to Negroes at all educational levels (cf. Stember, *Education and Attitude Change*, p. 134).
[11] There is, however, another issue. The middle-class suburbs may have supported Wallace more than the working-class suburbs, but that does not necessarily mean that most of Wallace's vote came from the middle class. In fact, the middle-class suburbs are smaller than the working-class suburbs—containing only 40 percent of the suburban

TABLE 1
The Wallace Vote in Ten Milwaukee Suburbs

	Percent for Wallace	Percent for Dem. Gov. in 1960	Percent in Manu-facturing	Percent Males in Professional Managerial	Percent Polish	Median Family Income	Value of Homes	Percent Owner Occupancy	Median School Years
Pro-Wallace suburbs									
Brown Deer	51	46	40	29	2	$ 7,836	$18,931	91	12.2
Glendale	54	42	36	54	2	8,752	22,568	80	12.2
River Hills	66	23	21	52	2	12,622	35,000+	80	13.0
Whitefish Bay	51	31	29	56	1	12,103	25,129	83	14.2
Wauwatosa	56	33	31	43	2	8,821	20,900	76	12.3
Anti-Wallace suburbs									
Greendale	32	59	46	38	3	7,711	17,600	71	12.4
Oak Creek	38	67	50	16	5	6,980	15,704	76	10.7
St. Francis	35	71	52	12	7	7,358	14,899	77	11.5
South Milwaukee	33	65	63	21	7	7,216	16,475	66	11.1
West Allis	37	65	48	17	4	6,966	14,800	70	11.0
Four groups of suburbs									
Top 5	55	35	31	47	2	10,027	24,500+	82	12.8
Second 4	46	40	29	51	4	12,538	27,300+	80	13.3
Third 4	40	65	49	20	6	7,237	16,112	68	10.8
Bottom 5	37	65	52	21	5	7,246	15,896	72	11.3

crossed over into the Democratic primary to vote for the Alabama governor. Crossover is common in Wisconsin primaries when, as in the present case, the primary of only one party is contested. Congressman Byrnes, running as a favorite son in the Republican primary, received 24 percent of the total suburban primary vote—half that given to Republican gubernatorial candidate Kuehn in 1960, when both primaries were uncontested. However, this difference alone does not demonstrate crossover, since it may be accounted for by increased Democratic turnout rather than by Republican crossover. Thus Byrnes received a higher total number of votes than Kuehn—24,441 to 18,299. Population growth and the more general interest in the 1964 primary probably explain the greater Byrnes vote.[12] Nevertheless, while Kuehn failed to outpoll Byrnes in any of the nine anti-Wallace suburbs, he did receive more votes in six of the nine pro-Wallace suburbs. In addition, the Wallace suburbs averaged a drop of 36 percent from 1960 to 1964 in the Republican percentage of the two-party vote, compared with an average drop of 7 percent in the anti-Wallace suburbs. (In every Wallace suburb the drop was more than double what it was in any anti-Wallace suburb.) [13] Perhaps most significant, in thirteen of the eighteen suburbs (and eight of the nine most strongly for Wallace) more people voted in the Democratic *primary* than voted Democratic in the gubernatorial *general election* four years before.[14]

Although middle-class Republicans supported Wallace far more than working-class Democrats, the vote for Wallace in the working-class areas of Milwaukee County was high. In each of the Milwaukee working-class suburbs, and in seventeen of Milwaukee's nineteen wards, Wallace received better than 30 percent of the Democratic vote. The unpopularity of Wisconsin's Governor Reynolds may have been partly to blame. One of the very few Democratic incumbents to lose office in the Johnson landslide, Reynolds had opposed Wallace in the primary. Still, one should not underestimate the anti-Negro component in the working-class Wallace vote.

To find areas where Wallace ran badly one must leave the Milwaukee metropolitan area. Of all the wards and suburbs of Milwaukee County, only those with

population. But they contributed 49 percent of the Wallace vote. This does not mean that the other half of the Wallace vote came from the working class. There are many middle-class residents in the more working-class suburbs, and our aggregate analysis suggests that middle-class people were more likely than workers to vote for Wallace. Therefore, a sizable percentage of the vote for Wallace even in the working-class suburbs probably came from the middle class.

[12] Wisconsin presidential and gubernatorial primaries occur in different months, so there were no presidential candidates as well as no contests in the 1960 gubernatorial primary.

[13] Since crossover is the rule in contested Wisconsin primaries, to compare the Wallace primary with previous Democratic contests is not of great significance. Thus, in the 1960 Humphrey-Kennedy primary contest, Nixon received about as high a percentage of the state-wide two-party vote as did Byrnes in 1964. (The turnout was also roughly the same.) Nevertheless, in the strong Wallace counties there was apparently more Republican crossover than in 1960. Consider the ten Republican counties among the twelve counties most strongly for Wallace. Turnout in these counties was about the same in the two years. But in seven of the counties the Republican percentage of the two-party vote declined from 1960 to 1964 (by an average of 7 percent). In one county it increased, and in the remaining two it remained the same.

[14] In a competitive, two-party state, a party almost always receives less votes in the primary than in the general election. Cf. V. O. Key, Jr., *American State Politics* (New York: Knopf, 1956), pp. 105–106, 134–140.

a substantial Negro population gave Wallace less than 30 percent of the Democratic vote; but he did this badly or worse in half of Wisconsin's seventy-one counties.

Wallace did best in the Republican counties of Wisconsin, just as he did in the Republican suburbs of Milwaukee. The correlations between his vote and that given recent Republican candidates are fairly high—.491 with the Republican candidate for Senator in 1958, .600 with the Republican gubernatorial candidate in 1960, and .522 with the Republican gubernatorial candidate in 1962. Wallace ran worst in the poor, rural, generally Scandinavian counties of northern Wisconsin. These counties, where La Follette progressivism was once strong, now tend to support the Democrats. Only one of the twelve most anti-Wallace counties was in southern Wisconsin, compared to nine of the twelve most pro-Wallace counties (with five of these in the wealthy, industrialized southeastern tip of Wisconsin). Seven of the twelve Wallace counties can be classified as strongly Republican on the basis of their electoral behavior since World War II. Three more were moderately Republican. None of the anti-Wallace counties was strongly Republican, and only two were even moderately Republican. (Two more were inconsistent; the rest were Democratic.) The pro-Wallace counties were heavily German, the anti-Wallace counties Scandinavian.[15] In half the anti-Wallace counties more than 30 percent of the population lives on farms; this was true in only two of the pro-Wallace counties. Half the Wallace counties have more than 30 percent of their population engaged in manufacturing, compared with one-quarter of the anti-Wallace counties.

Many have sought to explain Wallace's strong Wisconsin showing in terms of McCarthy's strength there, but to say that Wallace and McCarthy got the same support is only half true. Both were strong in Republican areas and weak in Democratic counties. But McCarthy did well in rural East European counties, whose residents were probably upset about communism, and in Catholic counties. Neither of these groups of counties was attracted to Wallace. McCarthy also received strong support in the northeastern counties surrounding his home. Of these nine counties, three were among the top twelve Wallace counties, and three more were included in the top third of Wallace strength. But the nine northeastern counties are traditionally Republican. Although they gave McCarthy more than their normal Republican support, they supported Wallace about as heavily as they support the typical Republican.

Of most significance, McCarthy attracted rural voters, rich and poor, and repelled urban residents. Wallace had the opposite effect. The five counties in southeastern Wisconsin that supported Wallace had been among the ten that most heavily deserted the GOP in order to vote against McCarthy.[16]

The relation between the support given Wallace and McCarthy is the key to understanding the appeals of both men. Each was strong among conservative Republicans—people who could not defect from the Democratic Party over race

[15] At the time of the 1930 census, more than 20 percent of the population of nine of the twelve Wallace counties was of German stock, compared with four of the anti-Wallace counties. In only one of the Wallace counties was more than 7 percent of the population of Scandinavian stock, compared with seven of the anti-Wallace counties. (Because most of those of German and Scandinavian stock are not immigrants or their children, more recent censuses than 1930 give a less accurate picture of the ethnic composition of the counties.)

[16] Cf. Rogin, *Intellectuals and McCarthy: The Radical Spectre.*

or communism because they were never in it. Insofar as the white backlash is confined to these groups—and the evidence is that it is strongest among them—it posed no threat to a Johnson landslide. But Wallace also got more working-class support than McCarthy was able to attract, while McCarthy obtained the backing of rural voters impervious to Wallace's appeal.

To understand Wallace's appeal and how it differed from McCarthy's one must examine the particular relevant issues, not the general level of education or the abstract attitudes of the individuals involved. The Wallace vote in the North repeats the black-belt pattern long familiar in the South, where whites in counties with large numbers of Negroes vote more for racists than do other Southern whites.[17] Rural voters were probably attracted to McCarthy by his anti-cosmopolitan tone. But the rural areas of northern and western Wisconsin have no Negroes, and the race issue is an abstraction there. Anti-Negro sentiment is much more salient in the urban centers. For workers, like other urban residents, race has a reality that the Communist issue lacked.[18]

But anti-Negro feeling is even more salient in the urban middle class. There are several possible reasons for this. Suburban middle-class whites have sought to create homogeneous communities;[19] the potential presence of Negroes terrifies them, as they perceive a threat both to property values and life styles. In voting for Wallace, these suburbanites could express their general resentment against outside interference in their lives—from government as well as Negroes. They could include a vote for Wallace in their generally conservative politics—and it should be pointed out that these suburban Republicans in no sense represent the *declining* values and life styles often said to explain support for right-wing extremists.[20] Without individual survey data we cannot know for sure, but these Wallace voters would appear to be educated, successful, upwardly mobile professional men and corporate executives. Extremist behavior may be more integrated into modern American institutions and social life than many commentators would like us to believe.

One must also consider the impact of the political structure on the Wallace vote. Middle-class Republicans may have voted for Wallace to embarrass the Democrats as well as to express support for the actual positions Wallace represented. There was, however, no organized Republican campaign to encourage crossovers.

---

[17] Cf. V. O. Key, Jr., *Southern Politics in State and Nation* (New York: Knopf, 1949), pp. 10–12, 319, 344, 666–667, *et passim*.

[18] Two recent referendums in California provide an interesting parallel. In 1962 the so-called "anti-subversive" Francis amendment to the state constitution, although it led in the public opinion polls prior to the election, was defeated by the voters in November. Two years later Proposition 14, outlawing anti-discriminatory housing legislation, passed by a 2 to 1 margin. To most Americans, Negroes have a physical, immediate presence; Communists do not. In terms of salient attitudes, people may well fear Negroes more than Communists. Racism, therefore, would seem to hold more potential than anti-communism for building a mass-based right-wing movement.

[19] The impressionistic literature here is immense. An excellent treatment is Robert C. Wood, *Suburbia* (Boston: Houghton Mifflin, 1959), pp. 3–53, 289–302.

[20] For example, Lipset, "Beyond the Backlash," p. 11, finds backlash politics throughout American history when declining social groups strike out against the changing social structure. Cf. also Richard Hofstadter, *The Age of Reform* (New York: Knopf, 1955); Daniel Bell, *The End of Ideology* (New York: Free Press, 1960); Daniel Bell (ed.), *The Radical Right* (New York: Doubleday & Company, 1963).

Workers lack many of the motivations that might have produced middle-class support for Wallace. They may have prejudiced and antidemocratic attitudes, but the relevant questions for political *behavior* are the saliency of those attitudes and the conditions under which they will become operational. In general, workers are more politically apathetic and difficult to mobilize. Members of the middle class are more likely to be frightened by distant and abstract threats; workers live a more concrete, present-oriented existence. They were probably less likely to have heard of Wallace, and perhaps local Democratic Party activists played a role in keeping them in line.

There was speculation that workers voted for Wallace out of fear of losing their jobs to Negroes, but journalistic reports and some limited statistical evidence indicate that fear of Negroes taking over neighborhoods rather than jobs was crucial.[21] And survey data suggest that middle-class residents want to keep Negroes out of their neighborhoods at least as much as workers do. Many workers voted for Wallace, but members of the middle class, in spite of their greater verbal commitment to democratic values and Negro rights, voted for him in greater numbers.

The Wisconsin primary alone cannot tell us how many white workers voted for Goldwater in November. But it does suggest that much of the political expression of white prejudice is concentrated among middle- and upper-class conservatives. If the Wisconsin results are typical,[22] then to locate the white backlash among ethnic minorities and workers both overestimates and understimates its significance. It exaggerates the immediate political consequences of the backlash, because it overlooks the fact that the most powerful antipathy toward the Negro in the North is expressing itself among already convinced Republicans. But, on the other hand, to see only the prejudice of white workers and ethnic minorities is to minimize the pervasiveness of anti-Negro feeling—particularly among the educated and cosmopolitan—in America's urban centers.

[21] Cf. "Gary, Ind.: Supposed Center of Backlash Appears to be Heavily for Johnson," *New York Times*, Sept. 9, 1964, p. 40; and note 10 above.
[22] Further research on support for Wallace and Goldwater is in progress. Examination of electoral behavior *within* states, however, does not always tell the whole story. Analysis of Goldwater's strength on public opinion polls indicates that regional differences overshadow all others in accounting for Goldwater supporters and opponents. Southerners were much more likely to support Goldwater than Easterners, with Westerners and Midwesterners falling in between. (Cf. Irving Crespi, "The Structural Basis for Rightwing Conservatism: The Goldwater Case," *Public Opinion Quarterly*, 29 (1965).)

34
The Scar of Wallace

Edward Schneier

In 1964 George Corley Wallace, in his words, "shook the eye teeth of the liberal establishment" by polling more than one-third of the primary vote in Maryland, Indiana, and Wisconsin. This year Wallace's American Independent Party will be on the ballot in all fifty states; and if the Gallup and Harris Polls prove accurate, the liberal establishment will be shaken right back to its wisdom teeth this November. Even if he polls but half of the 22 percent recently predicted, George Wallace will receive more popular votes than any third-party candidate since Theodore Roosevelt.

Wallace is not running for show; he believes he has an outside chance of being elected President in his own right, or failing that, of playing a major role in deciding who will be elected and how. With solid support in Alabama, Louisiana, Mississippi, and South Carolina, Wallace could win the electoral votes of as many as eleven Southern states. Even in Texas, with its prize of twenty-five electoral votes, Wallace is considered a strong contender. In the North, however, he is unlikely to receive the 35 or 40 percent needed to carry many states in a three-man race, so that even if he wins all 120 Southern electors, he will be far short of the 270 he needs to win.

From *The Nation* (November 4, 1968), pp. 454–457. Reprinted by permission of publisher and author.

But whatever the outcome in 1968, Wallace will have left his mark. His candidacy has already altered dramatically the calculations and strategies of both Democrats and Republicans. It is he more than Nixon, McCarthy, Humphrey, or Johnson who has set the tone of this campaign. It is his issue—"law and order"— that has dominated the campaign dialogue, not just in the race for the Presidency but in countless Congressional, state, and local contests. It is to his followers, not to those of McCarthy, Kennedy, or Rockefeller, that the major-party candidates have made their pitch. And whatever its impact in 1968, the Wallace movement may be still more formidable by 1972. For unlike the Dixiecrats of 1948, the American Independent Party cannot be dismissed as a regional phenomenon. Nor, at this point, does it appear to be an ephemeral puff of popular passion. On the contrary, Wallace has tapped streams that run deep in American society, and has won the allegiance not just of a radical fringe but of a solid cross section of a disaffected electorate. More than any popular uprising of this century, the Wallace movement threatens to reshape the American political system. For all that Left talk about a new politics, it is the Right that now threatens to produce it.

Given its now obvious political significance, the Wallace movement has received remarkably little serious attention. The press has learned that Wallace cannot be ignored (until September his campaign entourage included only one full-time reporter), but it still tends to view his candidacy as a quaint bit of political exoticism, somewhat on the order of the World Flatists, Vegetarianism, or Technocracy. Political scientists, perhaps because we have been so well sold by our own arguments about the stability of the two-party system, have tried to pretend that Wallace doesn't exist. But ignoring George Wallace has not caused either him or his followers to go away. What it has caused is some rather serious distortions of fact and interpretation. Seldom has so significant a political phenomenon been so underestimated and misunderstood.

When Wallace tells his supporters that "there are more of us than there are of them," the "them" are not difficult to identify. Negroes, implicitly, and more directly intellectuals, beatnicks, *The New York Times,* student demonstrators, and federal bureaucrats are the bogy men. The "us" are not so easily defined. For all the speculative essays written in the long wake of the 1964 primaries, we still know very little about the kinds of people who voted, and who will again vote, for the former Governor of Alabama. Indeed, a close look at the 1964 returns, as well as at data gathered earlier this year by the Gallup organization, indicates that many of the most common assumptions about the constituency that has grown up around George Wallace are quite wrong.

Foremost among these erroneous assumptions is the myth of ethnic revolt. Comforting as it may be to charge one minority group with discriminating against another, the white backlash was not basically an ethnic phenomenon. Wallace in 1964 did not make his best showings in foreign-stock areas. In Baltimore, for example, thirteen census tracts are more than 40 percent foreign stock (first- or second-generation immigrants). These districts gave Wallace an average of 16 percent of the vote. The twelve white neighborhoods with less than 10 percent foreign stock gave the Alabama Governor a whopping 68 percent. Many of the high-foreign-stock neighborhoods are Jewish, and Jews were second only to Negroes in their hostility to Wallace. But even in the distinctively Polish areas of southeast Baltimore, Wallace ran less well than he did among suburban WASPs.

Similarly, in both Gary and Milwaukee, among comparable socio-economic groups, native-born, native-stock whites were at least as inclined as Poles or Italians to vote for Wallace.

The most telling factors associated with support for Wallace in 1964 were home ownership and income. In all three states where he took part in primary contests, middle-income, suburban home owners were the backbone of the backlash. Thus Wallace carried Baltimore County but not the city; he carried the Washington suburbs of Prince Georges County and won majorities in more than half of the suburban communities surrounding Milwaukee, Gary, and Indianapolis. He carried Lake County by 2600 votes, but lost the city of Gary by 3500. In all three states, Wallace won a majority in the suburbs, trailed in the cities, and ran poorly in rural areas. He did well with ethnic voters because he did well in the kinds of neighborhoods where ethnic voters now live.

The Wallace vote in 1964 was generally highest in middle-income areas. In Gary, for example, he carried all fourteen of the all-white census tracts, but in doing so he averaged 10 percent better in middle-income ($6000 to $8000) than in either high- or low-income areas. His best showing (79 percent) was in a district with a median family income of $7093, his worst (58 percent and 59 percent) in districts with median incomes respectively of $9703 and $5910. Poll figures for 1968 show a similar pattern: Wallace supporters in the North have numbered from 8 to 12 percent of those with incomes of less than $5000; 14 to 15 percent in the $5000 to $7000 bracket; and 5 to 8 percent of those with incomes of $7000 or more.

Finally, housing is a key variable. In 1964, Wallace voters were a majority in 64 percent of the urban and suburban white areas where home ownership was high (more than half); he carried only 40 percent of the other white districts. Thus if there was a typical Wallace voter in 1964, he was a suburban, white, middle-income home owner, of no particular ethnic group (though not Jewish). Contrary to widespread assumptions, he was as likely to be a clerk as a steelworker, a Methodist as a Catholic, an Anglo-Saxon as a Pole, or to live in a securely all-white suburb as in an increasingly Negro central city area.

In many parts of the country it takes courage to display a Wallace button or bumper sticker; in other areas it takes courage not to. Both pollsters and politicians have been careful to hedge their bets, believing that many people are lying about, or have not yet faced, their real preferences. And of course the returns from 1964 cannot be taken at face value if only because votes in a primary do not have the same meaning as votes in a general election. Nevertheless, it is possible to predict what some of the short-run consequences of the Wallace candidacy will be and, more important, to evaluate the long-range meaning and significance of the movement.

In the short run, the Wallace candidacy hurts Nixon more than Humphrey. Despite the oft publicized defections of such normally Democratic groups as union members and ethnic minorities, the polls have consistently shown that there are only slightly more Wallace Democrats than Wallace Republicans. And when one considers that many Southerners who call themselves Democrats seldom vote the Democratic ticket nationally, the overall picture is one that, if the tide of opinion were less strongly anti-Administration, would seriously worry Mr. Nixon. One recent poll of union members showed Wallace with 49 percent. Humphrey with 39 percent, and Nixon with 12 percent. This and similar polls have been widely interpreted as being most damaging to Humphrey; but when one considers that Nixon won 36 percent of the union vote in his 1960 campaign against Kennedy, it appears that both major parties have lost about equally. Similarly, an erroneous tendency to regard the South as solidly Democratic has led some analysts to conclude that Humphrey has more to lose than Nixon from Wallace's Dixie drive. Nixon, however, trailed Kennedy by less than 1 percent in the South, and Republican strength there has grown in the intervening eight years. With Wallace in the race, Nixon will do well to match Barry Goldwater's total of forty-five Southern electoral votes, or even his own 1960 total of thirty-three.

What this suggests is that Wallace is helping Humphrey by siphoning off protest votes that might otherwise go to Nixon. In 1964 Wallace ran best in Wisconsin's Republican areas. As Michael Rogin wrote in the *Public Opinion Quarterly:* "Wallace's vote . . . was strikingly concentrated in the middle- and upper-class, native stock, suburbs. Apparently, Republican voters in these suburbs crossed over into the Democratic primary to vote for the Alabama Governor." Ironically, however, similar neighborhoods gave Wallace his biggest margins in Indiana and Maryland, where cross filing was not permitted. Democrats who voted for Wallace were, it would seem, demographically marginal Democrats: that is, they were registered Democrats whose economic, social, and ethnic characteristics are normally associated with Republicanism. In this autumn of discontent, most of them could have been expected to vote Republican or not at all. The Wallace candidacy allows them to express their hostility to national policies without severing their traditional party ties.

One of the most interesting questions in this year of surprises is what such voters will do with the rest of their ballots. "Franklin Roosevelt is like a ferry boat," local Democratic candidates were assured in 1936, "he'll bring in a lot of garbage in his wake." In this sense, Wallace is like a scow—his candidacy may carry a lot of garbage out to sea. For whatever else it proves to be, 1968 is likely to tumble many incumbents out of office, particularly those from suburban areas where Wallace is strongest. The structure of committee power in the House of Representatives is thus almost certain to be significantly altered this November.

Much as Wallace may unsettle us in 1968, it is the long-range effect of his candidacy that is most interesting and perhaps most significant. Wallace has built his campaign on a politics of pure status. It is, indeed, the clearest manifestation of status politics that this country has witnessed since the temperance crusade of fifty years ago. Joseph Gusfield, in his study of the American Temperance Movement, defines status politics as those in which

> what is at issue is the position of the relevant groups in the status order of the society. Such issues polarize the society along lines of status group differentiation, posing conflicts between divergent styles of life. They are contrasted with class issues, which polarize the society along lines of economic interests.

Gusfield describes the drive for Prohibition as a "symbolic crusade," a culturally sanctioned means of expressing deeper social, ethnic, and religious hostilities. Passage of the Eighteenth Amendment symbolized the "superior power and prestige of the old middle class in American society."

Similarly, the Wallace vote is a symbol of the power and prestige of the new middle class. It provides a culturally sanctioned means of expressing hostilities, not just toward Negroes but toward a wide range of social groups and values. The Negro, in fact, is not the principal scapegoat. "The real target ain't race," Wallace says in almost every speech. "The real problem is all these intellectual liberals, who can't even park their bicycles straight, trying to run people's lives." To his detractors this is hokum: to them Wallace's cries for law and order and States' rights are euphemisms for keeping blacks in line. For his followers, however, the equation is not so simple. Indeed, in a society permeated by the rhetoric of equality, few of Wallace's supporters consider themselves bigots, and Wallace's vulnerability to the charge of racism probably hurts rather than helps his campaign.

Instead of race, what exercises the typical Wallace supporter is a sense of remoteness from government. The major issues of the past three decades seem irrelevant to his concerns. Wallace offers a new politics, a politics of conviction, of limited interference in people's lives. It is a politics that will not trouble people with issues like poverty, urban renewal, or rent subsidies that are irrelevant to their day-to-day lives; a politics that will keep such troublesome phenomena as narcotics, crime, peace demonstrations, and college protests out of sight. In this context it is significant that Gallup found voters in the 21 to 29 age group considerably more likely than older voters to be Wallace supporters. For older voters, memories of the Great Depression, or even of the recession of 1958, are too strong to enable them completely to abandon class politics. Issues like the minimum wage, Medicare, Social Security, and right-to-work laws still agitate those who have lived through the battles. After a decade of prosperity, however, today's young worker takes the security of his job almost for granted—he has never been through a recession and he doesn't expect to see one. And if he should be laid off—well, there's always unemployment compensation.

This, in short, is the politics of prosperity: the politics of those who can afford to use their vote not to achieve economic objectives but to express moral indignation. This kind of politics has not displaced the old politics of economic and class issues, but it has been laid down on top of it to produce a confusing, sometimes contradictory pattern.

In every previous era of American political history, the emergence of a fully developed system of status politics has been checked by the emergence of a new and overwhelming class conflict. As Gusfield has said of Prohibition:

> The most significant element in the repeal of the Eighteenth Amendment was not directly related to the cultural conflicts and struggles for status that had precipitated the Prohibition issue. It was the change in the tone of political life brought about by the Great Depression that killed the Eighteenth Amendment.

Such a change of tone is unlikely in our times. Our growing ability to manage economic affairs in such a way as to avoid economic catastrophes effectively precludes the dominance of class politics. Class conflicts exist and will continue to exist, but in the political arena they will be forced as never before to compete with status issues for the attention of the electorate. The Wallace campaign has demonstrated the appeal that such issues have for a large segment of the American voting public.

Political commentators will interpret the 1968 election as a turn to the right in the attitudes of the American people. But even if Hubert Humphrey finishes third, it may not symbolize that at all. Lyndon Johnson's landslide victory in 1964 was based primarily on voter reactions to two issues: nuclear war and economic policies. The fear of Goldwater's positions on Social Security, Medicare, and nuclear weapons buried him in an avalanche of "leftist" votes. In 1968, attitudes on these issues have not changed; they have simply become irrelevant. Hubert Humphrey has tried desperately to resurrect them; thus far, he has failed, and his failure may be the handwriting on the wall for the future of American politics.

Lyndon Johnson once said that a great society would be one which asked not just "how much?" but "how good?" Many Americans cannot yet afford to raise this second question—their stakes in the economic services of the government are too high. What sets the Wallace supporters apart from the rest of the community is that they see themselves as sufficiently affluent to raise this question, and they are in fact raising it.

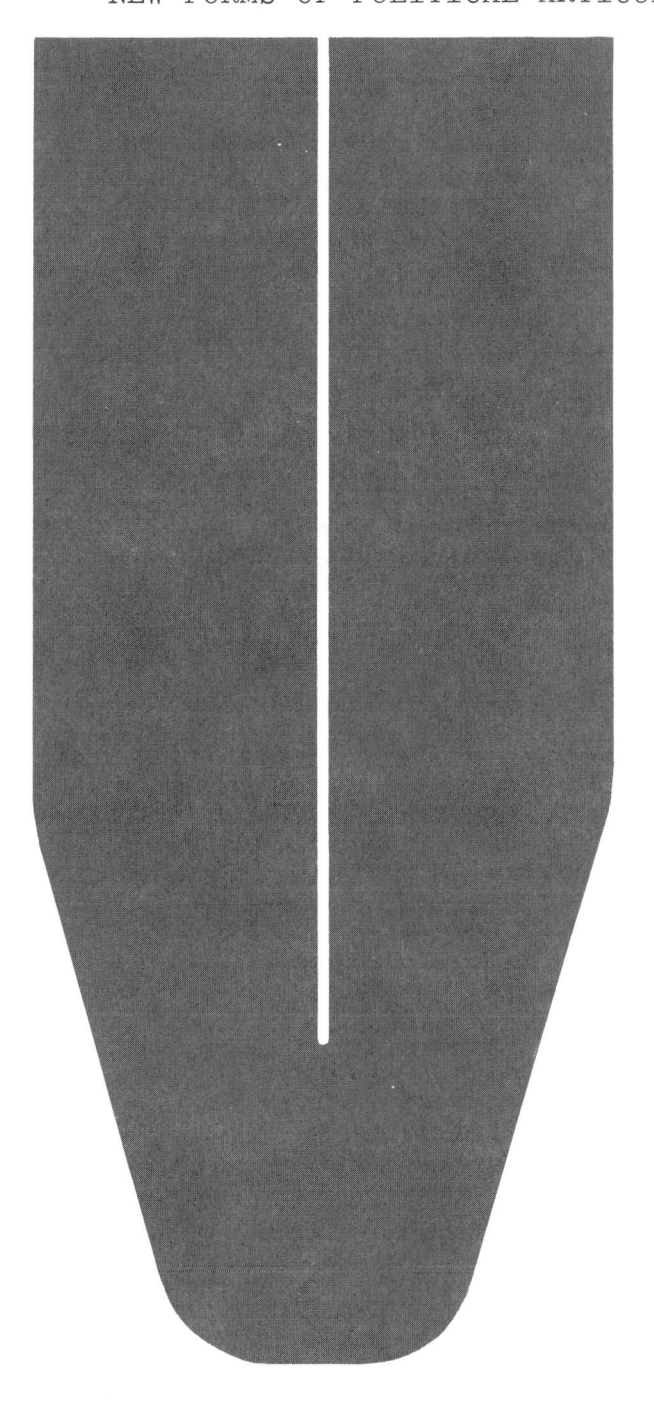

NEW FORMS OF POLITICAL ARTICULATION

Since the traditional process of coalition and compromise is slow, and disadvantaged groups appear to have little to offer prospective allies (for example, access to decision makers, votes, or financial resources) while requiring much from them, it often has appeared that the two party system and the pluralistic system of pressure group politics have provided few meaningful rewards for disadvantaged groups. Thus, some individuals have been seeking to develop new forms of political organization to replace existing politican mechanisms by substituting direct democracy via community participation for the traditional system of representative democracy. Their aim has been to foster active, broad-based participation in the political process, often by stressing conflict and confrontation rather than consensus politics. New techniques for the expression of political demands have been utilized—from the calculated use of group violence to the creation of locally initiated and operated community projects. Two outcomes to group protest and locally initiated conflict appear possible. First, the American political system may react by admitting these newer groups into established decision-making processes. This may lead the newly aggregated groups into the "mainstream" of American politics and result in a modification of their demands and tactics. The second alternative appears to be the development of a more enduring political polarization which could culminate in the use of repressive techniques to suppress minority group dissent.

The articles in Chapter Twelve, discuss the successes and failures of one new political technique—community organization. Saul Alinsky, the "father of community action," sets forth the importance of community participation in an advanced technological and urban society. Daniel Moynihan indicates why "the war on poverty"—which sought to institutionalize the concept of community organization—did not achieve major results; and David Cohen presents a critique of a newer variant on the theme of community organization—"community control."

In Chapter Thirteen the calculated use of protest politics, as an alternative to traditional political mechanisms, is assessed. Graham and Gurr, in excerpts from the conclusion of the official report of the National Commission on the Causes and Prevention of Violence, conclude that violence is deeply embedded in American life and history, and attempt to determine whether violence can "succeed." Henry Specht discusses the variety of disruptive tactics that can be used to achieve change, while Michael Lipsky examines the problems inherent in protest leadership.

CHAPTER TWELVE

COMMUNITY ORGANIZATION

35

Reveille for Radicals

Saul Alinsky

The fundamental issue that will resolve the fate of democracy is whether or not we really believe in democracy. Democracy as a way of life has been intellectually accepted but emotionally rejected. The democratic way of life is predicated upon faith in the masses of mankind, yet few of the leaders of democracy really possess faith in the people. If anything, our democratic way of life is permeated by man's fear of man. The powerful few fear the many, and the many distrust one another. Personal opportunism and greedy exploitation link the precinct captain, the mayor, the governor, and the Congress into one cynical family. It is difficult to find the faintest flicker of faith in man, whether one scours the Democrats, from the Southern racist politicians to the Northern corrupt city machines, or one scrutinizes the decayed reactionaries of the Republicans. On the contrary, it will be found that with few exceptions all of these leaders, regardless of their party labels or affiliations, share in common a deep fear and suspicion of the masses of people. Let the masses remain inert, unthinking; do not disturb them, do not arouse them; do not get them moving, for if you do you are an agitator, a trouble maker, a Red! You are un-American, you are a radical!

The past, the glorious past with all of its comfortable familiarity, was rooted in

From pp. 192–204 of *Reveille for Radicals,* by Saul D. Alinsky. Copyright 1946, © 1969 by Saul D. Alinsky. Reprinted by permission of Random House, Inc.

a general surrender of everyday democratic rights and responsibilities of the people. It was founded on masses of people who were and still are denied the opportunity to participate; who are frustrated at every turn and who have been mute for so long that they have lost their voices. Only at rare intervals did this quiet, peaceful, seemingly dead foundation stir and move. These upheavals were the revolutions of men fighting for the opportunity to play a part in their world, for a chance to belong, to live like men.

These masses of people were and are the substance of society. If they continue inarticulate, apathetic, disinterested, forlorn and alone in their abysmal anonymity, then democracy is ended. It has been stated and restated throughout these pages that substance determines structure and that the form of economy and politics will be and always has been a reflection of either the active desires of a democratically minded citizenry or the passive torpor of a people whose innate dignity and strength have atrophied from disuse, and who will follow slavelike after a dictator. It is irony worthy of the gods that here in the greatest democracy on earth is found the least concern over the prime element of democracy—citizens who shoulder obligations and stand up for their rights. A people's democracy is a dynamic expression of a living, participating, informed, active, and free people. It is a way of life that belongs to the people, that draws its very life blood from popular participation. Democracy is alive, and like any other living thing it either flourishes and grows or withers and dies. There is no in-between. It is freedom and life or dictatorship and death.

Human beings do not like to look squarely into the face of tragedy. Gloom is unpopular and we prefer the "out of sight, out of mind" escape. But there comes a time when issues must be recognized as issues—and resolved. The democratic way of life is at stake. You cannot meet today's crisis tomorrow. You cannot pick and choose when and what you will do at your personal convenience. You cannot dawdle with history.

We must face the bitter fact that we have forsaken our great dream of a life of, for, and by the people; that the burning passions and ideals of the American dream lie congealed by cold cynicism. Great parts of the masses of our people no longer believe that they have a voice or a hand in shaping the destiny of this nation. They have not forsaken democracy because of any desire or positive action of their own; they have been driven down into the depths of a great despair born of frustration, hopelessness, and apathy. A democracy lacking in popular participation dies of paralysis.

There are many conditions in America which we are unable to see in their correct perspective. To a significant extent the old saying that "we cannot see the woods for the trees" holds true of the vast majority of us Americans. Gunnar Myrdal in a survey of the American scene that is strongly reminiscent of Tocqueville's classical analysis a hundred and ten years earlier, bluntly stated:

> Political participation of the ordinary citizen in America is pretty much restricted to the intermittently recurring elections. Politics is not organized to be a daily concern and responsibility of the common citizen. The relative paucity of trade unions, cooperatives, and other civic interest organizations tends to accentuate this abstention on the part of the common citizens from sharing in the government of their communities as a normal routine of life.[1]

[1] Gunnar Myrdal, *An American Dilemma* (New York: Harper & Row, 1944), p. 717.

There are other bitter truths that must be faced. The stifling of opportunities for mass participation in America has inevitably meant the throttling of interest in America as such. Social interests have been displaced by selfish interests. The people no longer think as Americans for America. They no longer speak as Americans for America. They speak for their interest cliques. The welfare of their narrow groups completely overshadows any thoughts of national welfare. They speak for "Organized Labor," for "Business," and for the "Farm Bloc." Even assuming that they do speak for all of their membership, which is an erroneous assumption, the total membership of organized labor, organized business, and the farm blocs would certainly not exceed a maximum of twenty million people. Twenty millions organized with the machinery to articulate their desires, but *many more millions of Americans* who do not speak, have no collective tongue, have no voice, are silent.

It is not the fault of the legislators that they must listen to the twenty million who are organized, for those are the loudest and, with minor exceptions, the only voices in America. It is not the Constitution of the United States that renders the rest of the population inarticulate; what we have is an evil combination of circumstances and conditions that deny and denounce popular participation. It is true that one day every four years Americans can cast their ballot in an election, but it is also true that for more than 1400 days that intervene between major elections they are blocked from articulating or carrying on the functions and responsibilities of American citizenship.

These are bitter facts and they have embittered millions of Americans. That is the main reason for the appalling lack of desire on the part of masses of Americans for self-education. The hope for democracy lies in not only a participating *but an informed people.* This already deplorable condition continues to deteriorate steadily.

> The diverse activities collectively known as "adult education" in America are often laudable strivings to disseminate education among the common people by universities, philanthropic organizations, state and federal agencies, radio companies, or groups of enlightened community leaders. There is still little concerted drive for self-education in civic affairs. There is no spontaneous mass desire for knowledge as a means of achieving power and independence.[2]

Education must be presented to our people in a way that they will find meaningful. But educators must first educate themselves in the art of democratic teaching in a democracy. They must learn to teach and work with people. The enormous importance of the function of educators in the fulfillment of a democratic destiny is second to nothing.

The job ahead is clear. Every conceivable effort must be made to rekindle the fire of democracy while a few embers yet glow in the gray ashes of the American dream. Once it goes out it may take generations before a new fire can be started. The fire, the energy, and the life of democracy is popular pressure. Democracy itself is a government constantly responding to continuous pressures of its people. The only hope for democracy is that more people and more groups will become articulate and exert pressure upon their government. It is short-sighted to attack

---

[2] Myrdal, *An American Dilemma*, p. 713.

the few major pressure groups in this country as "dangerous lobbyists" or "un-American," for although these pressure blocs are seeking primarily to further their own interests, their organizing and bringing pressures to bear upon the government is participation and democratic activity which is infinitely more American, more democratic than the dry, dead rot of inactivity, of refusing to become involved in pressure groups. When we talk of democratic citizenship we talk and think in terms of an informed, active, participating, interested people—an interested and participating people is popular pressure!

A people can participate only if they have both the opportunity to formulate their program, which is their reason for participation, and a medium through which they can express and achieve their program. This can be done only through the building of real People's Organizations in which people band together, get to know one another, exchange points of view, and ultimately reach a common agreement which is the People's Program. This is the reason for participation: their reason—their lives and the lives of their children. The universal premise of any people's program is, "We the people will work out our own destiny." This is the cardinal basis of democracy, and various specific issues are not too important in comparison with the main issue. *Can there be a more fundamental, democratic program than a democratically minded and participating people?* Can man envisage a more sublime program on earth than the people having faith in their fellow men and themselves? A program of co-operation instead of competition?

Faith without hope is short-lived. The People's Organization is the machinery through which the people can achieve their program. The People's Organization carries within it the overwhelming power generated by the people fighting for themselves. Even their leadership is their own, their natural leaders. In their unity they find the strength to break down all of those restrictions of opportunities which have hitherto prevented participation. It is the most invincible army known to mankind—the people on the march. To the people ultimate triumph may be delayed but it cannot be denied.

It is in an all-inclusive People's Organization that people fight and think as people, as Americans, and not as businessmen, workers, Catholics, Protestants, Jews, whites, or colored. A People's Organization inevitably smashes all artificial barriers, sectarian interests, religious, nationality, and racial distinctions. It is made up of people, its program is a people's program, and they think together, work together, fight together, hope together, achieve together, as people.

The issue to be resolved is the creation of a world for the little people, a world where the millions instead of the few can live in dignity, peace, and security. By a little people's world we mean that way of life that is best for the millions of little people who cluster about the thousands of little crossways of America. The final judgment will not be rendered by the few on Madison and State streets in Chicago, but by the thousands who cluster about Forty-seventh and Ashland. It will not come from one of the busiest crossroads of America at Rockefeller Center in New York, but from the little crossroads of St. Mark's Place and Second Avenue. The coming world for the little people will be shaped by the millions of little people who live around the thousands of these little crossways.

Some sincere intellectual believers in democracy voice two major objections to the building of People's Organizations. First, they fear that it is revolution. They forget that democracy is one of the greatest revolutions in the history of man.

They forget that the American government was born out of the Revolutionary War and they forget that the birth certificate of these United States, known as the Declaration of Independence, proudly proclaims as a human right, "That whenever any Form of Government becomes destructive of these ends, it is the Right of the People to alter or to abolish it, and to institute new Government, laying its foundation on such principles and organizing its powers in such form, as to them shall seem most likely to effect their Safety and Happiness."

Those who fear the building of People's Organizations as a revolution also forget that it is an orderly development of participation, interest, and action on the part of the masses of people. It may be true that it is revolution, but it is *orderly revolution*. To reject orderly revolution is to be hemmed in by two hellish alternatives: disorderly, sudden, stormy, bloody revolution, or a further deterioration of the mass foundation of democracy to the point of inevitable dictatorship. The building of People's Organizations is orderly revolution; it is the process of the people gradually but *irrevocably* taking their places as citizens of a democracy.

The second objection voiced by those who fear the building of People's Organizations stems from distrust of power in the hands of the people. They fear that the development and building of People's Organizations is the building of a vast power group which may fall prey to a fascistic demagogue who will seize leadership and control and turn an organization into a Frankenstein's monster against democracy. Those who fear this possibility have learned very little from our present historic period. The road to fascism and dictatorship is paved with apathy, hopelessness, frustration, futility, and despair in the masses of people. It is this fear and complete hopelessness on the part of the masses which ultimately make them relinquish all control over their lives and turn the power over to a dictator.

Fascism does not have a chance of establishing itself over a people who are active, interested, participating, co-operating, informed, democratically minded, and who above all have learned through their experiences to have confidence in themselves and their fellow men. They have learned to become self-reliant, and this feeling of self-respect, respect for their fellow men, and confidence in the power of the people which comes out of a People's Organization is actually the strongest barrier and safeguard against fascism which a democracy can possess.

The critics in this case continue to think of democracy only in terms of its form and structure. It is easier to think of democracy in those terms; it is neat and orderly. The other kind of democracy, real democracy, is as disorderly as life itself—it does not hold to a form; it grows, expands, and changes to meet the needs of the people.

The enormous power necessary for the development of democracy and the resolving of those issues which make life unhappy and insecure can come only from an organization of all of the People's Organizations, institutions, and the people themselves. Only through this kind of People's Organization can we secure the invincible strength that flows from the pooling of all the popular pressures inherent within the people and their organizations.

Among all of the life-and-death lessons we can learn from the 1930s and World War II, none is more important than the lesson that no single people's institution, regardless of its strength or size, can resolve the issues facing mankind. The failure of the institutions of the people to solve basic issues is the result not only of their jealous isolation from one another but of the same mental isolationist policy concerning their objectives. They have forgotten that there is no such thing as a single problem, that all problems are interrelated, that all issues are part of a chain of human issues, and that a chain is no stronger than its weakest link.

The labor unions have concerned themselves primarily with their own problem of bettering working conditions within the industrial areas of their nations. They have placed other issues in a very secondary position and frequently concentrated their all on getting higher wages and shorter hours. They have neglected to recognize that political and social action are as important to their ultimate objective as their economic ends; that money is only meaningful in terms of the kind of life, the kind of housing, the kind of security and health which a people can purchase with it.

Organized business has assumed that greater profits would be pretty much of a cure-all, and it has to a major extent ignored the fact that the welfare of business rests upon the welfare of the consumers of a nation; that business or free enterprise will function in a democracy only so long as the democracy functions.

Organized religion has too often followed the road of other people's institutions. It has made adjustments, compromises, and surrenders to a materialistic civilization for the benefit of material security in spite of occasional twinges of conscience and moral protests. The result has been that today much of organized religion is materialistically solvent but spiritually bankrupt. Laski, the philosopher of the British Labour Party, commented:

> It is not enough for them to profess the acceptance of the Christian ethic. In its operation, that ethic has accommodated itself to slavery at its ugliest, to capitalism in its most ruthless form, to every war that has been waged since Constantine made Christianity the official religion of the Empire.[3]

Sectarianism and the pursuit of particular objectives without recognition that life cannot be approached in terms of individual parts have brought havoc to those people's institutions which persist in accommodations, compromises, and surrender on all issues except those which they interpret as their own particular spheres of activity. These practices have insured their survival in structure, but if continued will insure the demise of their substance. Jacques Maritain stated that: "It was not given to believers faithful to Catholic dogma but to rationalists to proclaim in France the rights of man and of the citizen, to Puritans to strike the last blow at slavery in America, to Atheistic Communists to abolish in Russia the absolutism of private profit." [4]

This statement implicitly asks the fearful question, Why? Why was not the Catholic Church in the forefront of the French Revolution for the rights of man and of the citizen? Why was it not a leader in the attack on slavery in America? Why was the Russian Orthodox Church not only absent in the revolt against tyranny and the absolutism of private profit; why was it not in the vanguard of the Revolution? These questions keep recurring.

There is one lesson that came out of the catastrophe of World War II which we had better remember, for if we do not, a recurrence of the catastrophe will not leave a sufficient number of us alive to relearn and profit by this lesson. The

---

[3] Harold J. Laski, *Faith, Reason, and Civilization* (New York: Viking, 1944), pp. 122–123.
[4] *Christianity and Democracy* (New York: Scribner's), p. 38.

words of this lesson were written in the bombed-out buildings and the broken hearts and bodies of Europe. Europe possessed a militant labor movement far stronger than that of America—yet fascism and war came to Europe. Thirty-three million people were involved in the co-operative movement in Europe—yet fascism and war came to Europe. The organized Christian Church is much older and much more entrenched in Europe than in any other part of the world—yet fascism and war came to Europe.

Organized religion, organized labor, and all other organized institutions of the people were completely impotent in preventing fascism and war. We must learn from this, and learn it now, that only in the united effort of all People's Organizations working together in concert lies hope of peace, security, and happiness. Only in the pooling of all the strength of every people's institution and in the awakening of our people to participation lies hope of salvation on earth!

This, then, is the job ahead. It is the job of building broad, deep People's Organizations which are all-inclusive of both the people and their many organizations. It is the job of uniting, through a common interest which far transcends individual differences, all the institutions and agencies representative of the people. It is the job of building a People's Organization so that people will have faith in themselves and in their fellow men. It is the job of educating our people so that they will be informed to the point of being able to exercise an intelligent critical choice as to what is true and what is false. It is the job of instilling confidence in men so that they are sure they can destroy all of the evils which afflict them and their fellows, whether unemployment, war, or other man-made disasters. It is the greatest job man could have—the actual opportunity of creating and building a world of decency, dignity, peace, security, happiness; a world worthy of man and worthy of the name of civilization. This is the job ahead.

The building of these People's Organizations and the achievement of popular participation cannot and will not be done by denouncing the present deplorable condition of democracy. It will not be done by wailing self-recriminations. It can be done only by setting ourselves to the dirty, monotonous, heart-breaking job of building People's Organizations. It can be done only by possessing the infinite patience and faith to hang on as parts of the organization disintegrate; to rebuild, add on, and continue to build.

It can be done only by those who believe in, have faith in, and are willing to make every sacrifice for the people. Those who see fearlessly and clearly; they will be your radicals. The radical will look squarely at all issues. He will not be so weighted down with material or malignant prejudice that he can only look upward with a worm's-eye view. He will not look down upon mankind with the distorted, unrealistic, ivory-tower bird's-eye view, but will look straight ahead on the dead level, seeing man as a man. Not from a long distance, up or down, but as a man living among men.

Let it sound, then. Let it come, clear, strident, ringing, and heart-stirring. Let it come, the rallying cry of America. From the historical "Don't tread on me" to the grim "Tyranny, like Hell, is not easily conquered," to "John Brown's soul goes marching on," to "You shall not crucify mankind on a cross of gold," to "Solidarity Forever!"

These are a few of the past battle cries of the American dream. Let the cry sound again, clearly, boldly, shattering the deathlike silence of decay. Let it reach every corner of America and let its echoes go beyond and shake the hearts of oppressors everywhere. Let it come so that the Western plowman will stop, wipe the sweat from his brow, and, looking up into the bright skies, see the same American vision that will come to the eyes of the millions who dwell in dingy New York tenements, to the sharecroppers of the South, to the rubber workers of Akron, to the shipbuilders and lumber workers of the Northwest, to the packinghouse workers of the Midwest, and to all the people of these United States. Sound it now. Whether it be the hoarse voice, the bell, the written word or the trumpet, let it come. Sound it clear and unwavering. REVEILLE FOR RADICALS!

36
Social Science and Social Policy
Daniel Patrick Moynihan

The essential problem with community action was that the one term concealed at least four quite distinct meanings: organizing the power structure, as in the Ford Foundation programs of Paul Ylvisaker; expanding the power structure, as in the delinquency program of Cloward and Ohlin; confronting the power structure, as in the Industrial Areas Foundation program of Saul Alinsky; and finally, assisting the power structure, as in the Peace Corps of Sargent Shriver. The task of government, in this case of the President's advisors, was first to discern these four different meanings, to make sure they were understood by those who had to make decisions about them, and to keep all concerned alert to the dangers of not keeping the distinctions clearly enough in mind. Which is not to say that policy had to choose between the various approaches: government no less than life is suffused with ambiguities and internal contradictions. But to be surmounted they must be perceived. *And there were warnings.* At a conference on Community Development held in San Juan in December 1964, while there was still time, the British social scientist Peter Marris outlined the contradictions between three of these views of community action. He proposed not to exclude any. He proposed

Reprinted with permission of The Macmillan Company from *Maximum Feasible Misunderstanding* by Daniel P. Moynihan, pp. 168–171, 177–190. Copyright © 1969 by The Free Press, a Division of The Macmillan Company.

that there be established in each community two organizations: one, close to city hall, for the purpose of studying and analyzing the local social structure, another for organizing the poor to bring their own strength to the bargaining table. It was abundant good sense, but ignored.[1]

Just possibly one reason is that the key decisions in the White House and the Executive Office of the President were made by lawyers and economists. None was especially familiar with the social science theory on which the various positions were based and, if an impression may be permitted, few were temperamentally attuned to the frame of mind of the reformers. Very possibly, a matter of professional style is involved here. William C. Mitchell has noted that "The political sociologist tends to view a political system as a place of *struggle* for power or influence, while the economist tends to see it as an essentially *cooperative* division of labor within which various forms and degrees of competition may take place for the various roles and rewards that constitute the system."[2] Order and efficiency are the passions of lawyers and economists, and properly so. It may be that the presence is needed in the Executive Office Building of persons trained to other disciplines who can more readily give credence to the thought that there are those who with even greater passion seek disorder and destruction.

But this risks the tendentious: it was not social science competence that was missing in the conception and management of this program; it was intellect. By and large the political actors come off best. Their sensibilities quickly alerted them to the probability that the community action activists would cause more trouble than could be contained. Unfortunately, there was no creative political response forthcoming once this had actually begun to occur. The poorest performance was that of the high-level staff aides, some nominally political, some nominally in the career service, but far more like one another than otherwise, who busied themselves with the details of community action but never took time to inform themselves, much less their superiors, that the government did not know what it was doing.

This is the essential fact: *The government did not know what it was doing.* It had a theory. Or, rather, a set of theories. Nothing more. The U.S. Government at this time was no more in possession of confident knowledge as to how to prevent delinquency, cure anomie, or overcome that midmorning sense of powerlessness, than was it the possessor of a dependable formula for motivating Vietnamese villagers to fight Communism. At any time from 1961 to 1964 an afternoon of library research would have established that the Cloward-Ohlin thesis of opportunity structure, though eminently respectable, was nonetheless rather a minority position, with the bulk of delinquency theory pointed in quite a different direction. Nor would it have been necessary to have spent an afternoon to ascertain this not unimportant fact. Ohlin would have been pleased to make it explicit in the course of half an hour's conversation. Two practical considerations would have emerged from such a revelation. First, that most theorists in the field, because of their emphasis on early family socialization, would be much less optimistic concerning rapid social change than were Cloward and Ohlin and their sup-

---

[1] Peter Marris, "The Strategies of Reform," Conference on Community Development, San Juan, Puerto Rico, December 1964, mimeographed. Marris probably would not see the "Peace Corps model" as a distinct variety of community action.
[2] William C. Mitchell, "The Shape of Political Theory to Come," *American Behavioral Scientist* (November–December 1967), 16.

porters. Much the same would be said of the Ford Foundation theory of institutional gymnastics: nothing seems to move that rapidly, at least in the view of most students of organizational behavior. Second, the divergence of the various theories was such that what would serve to cure in the one case would exacerbate in the other. A *big* bet was being made. No responsible persons had any business acting as if it were a sure thing. . . .

Hypotheses: some developed very close to the subject at issue, others at some remove, all intelligent, well argued, well intended, but at very most only a tentative grasp on a fantastically elusive reality. Why then, it will be asked, did the social scientists involved in these events not insist on the limits of their knowledge and methodology? The answer would seem to lie in part in the essentially dual nature of the American social scientist. He is an objective "seeker after truth." But he is also very likely to be a passionate partisan of social justice and social change to bring it about. Herman Kahn has described the United States as "a white, Anglo-Saxon, Protestant, middle class, Christian-Fundamentalist country run by a coalition of minorities, which these terms do not describe." [3] By and large, social scientists would seem to have much more in common with those minorities than otherwise. Indeed increasingly they are not only personally drawn from them, in an ethnic and cultural sense, but make up a minority in their own right. During the 1960s, in particular, they have had quite extraordinary access to power. And they have used this access in considerable measure to promote social change in directions *they* deem necessary and desirable.

Noting the rise of the ideology of "participation" and "social conflict," major themes in community action as it worked in practice, Irving Kristol observes that although its origins are complex, "obviously, it had more to do with an initial animus against the status quo than with any ripe sagacity about the difficulties of public administration in a large democracy." [4] This may be no more than to state that social scientists tend to be politically liberal or left, especially when they are young. Economists would seem to be rather an exception to this: as the discipline gets "softer," the radicalism grows more pronounced. Doubtless for the great bulk of sociologists and the like "extremism" takes no more extraordinary form than believing in civil rights for Negroes, but there is a gloss to these attitudes that in the circumstances of the 1960s would seem to have had enormous consequences. Social scientists love poor people. They also get along fine with rich people. (Not a few are wealthy themselves, or married to heiresses. In any event, in the 1960s, persons of great wealth have been a major source of support not only for social science research, but for radical political activity.) But, alas, they do not have much time for the people in between.

In particular, they would appear to have but little sympathy with the desire for order, and anxiety about change, that are commonly enough encountered among working-class and lower middle-class persons. . . . In the 1960s, the typical urban resident was himself growing more and more concerned about a "failure of community." But conceived not in the abstractions of a conservative philosopher such as Nisbet or an existential anarchist such as Goodman, but perceived in the same terms as the cop-on-the-beat: disorder. For whatever reasons, fundamen-

[3] Herman Kahn, "Truce or More War?" *U.S. News & World Report* (June 3, 1968).
[4] Irving Kristol, "Decentralization for What?" *The Public Interest* (Spring 1968), 20.

tal or transitory, justified or unjustified, "other" people did not seem to be behaving properly any longer, and the "typical" American grew more and more upset. During the 1960s, for the first time in the history of public opinion surveys, crime emerged as the principle issue of domestic concern.

The reaction among many of the more activist social scientists (obviously this risks labelling a vast number of persons from a smallish number of incidents) was not to be appalled by disorder, *but almost to welcome it.* How grand to live in interesting times! This began in earnest with the Negro riot in Watts in 1965, which was promptly declared not to have been a riot at all, but rather a revolt, an uprising, a manifesto, any term that suggested that the masses were on the move. For that love affair is still unrequited. Earlier, Midge Decter observed that the whole MFY [Mobilization for Youth] enterprise reeked of the notion of the proletariat. This was especially to be seen in MFY's insistence that the "real" leaders of the people would not be the ostensible ones, that behind the institutional facade of political party committeemen, locality "mayors," vice lords, and parish priests, there was to be found an echelon of uncorrupted men who, given opportunity, would assume leadership and . . . what? Change the world.[5]

The presumption of superior empathy with the problems of the outcast is surely a characteristic, and a failing, of this liberal mindset. Thus in an otherwise helpful abstract on the "maximum feasible participation" clause Lillian Rubin writes that many of those involved in drafting the legislation seemed not to have understood its full meaning.

> A lifetime spent in an atmosphere dominated by racism and the casework emphasis of modern rehabilitation philosophy infects even the most sophisticated and sympathetic. It is difficult indeed to fully penetrate the stereotype—to envision and comprehend a poor man grasping abstract concepts of participation, a Negro asserting his manhood.[6]

In illustration she cites a communication from James N. Adler, a young lawyer who worked with the Shriver task force.

> I had never really conceived [he writes] that it (participation) would mean control by the poor of the community action represented on the community action organization but that organization itself. . . . I expected that the poor would be such representation would be something in the order of 15 to 25% of the board. . . . *Moreover, I don't think it ever occurred to me, or to many others, that the representatives of the poor must necessarily be poor themselves.* [Her italics.][7] [*Sic*—exactly as quoted—EDITOR.]

One might think this a candid and helpful statement, coming, as it happens, from an unusually attractive and productive young political executive. But it was cited by Miss Rubin as a failure of imagination. In contrast with whom? Is a female graduate student in sociology at the University of California, Berkeley, better able to grasp the meaning of "a Negro asserting his manhood"?

All this might have been innocent enough, save that as the 1960s passed, signs increased that the various forms of public disorder either sanctioned, induced, or

---

[5] See Daniel P. Moynihan, "Three Problems in Combatting Poverty," in Margaret S. Gordon (ed.), *Poverty in America* (San Francisco: Chandler Publishing Company, 1965).
[6] Lillian Rubin, "Maximum Feasible Participation, The Origins, Implications, and Present Status," *Poverty and Human Resources* (November–December 1967).
[7] Rubin, "Maximum Feasible Participation."

led by middle-class liberal-radicals had begun to acquire an ominous, even sinister cast in the mind of the public at large. At the necessary risk of oversimplification, it may be said that crime in the streets as a political issue began to assume the role that Communists in government had played in the 1940s and early 1950s. The parallels were striking: on the one hand an élite-proletarian axis, in which the proletarians played rather a passive role, or at least a largely nonideological one, despite the interpretations to be read in the *Nation* or wherever. In between were the mass of fundamentalist citizens increasingly concerned, puzzled, and alarmed. The élite were in power; the fundamentalist *mass* out of power, save in institutions such as the Congress, the influence of which was largely negative. In particular, the élite controlled the major national institutions, such as the State Department in one era and the Department of Justice in the other, contrasted with the "mass" custody of such popular institutions as the police. In each instance the insistence by the fundamentalists was that something immediate be done; the response by the élite was that root causes must be attended to first. There was ethnic conflict: Catholic cops vs. Jewish radicals. There was regional conflict: New York and San Francisco vs. the Great Void, as the regions in between tend to be regarded at the extremities; the South, an ever-willing ally of the conspiracy hunters. There was the emergence of élite figures such as the Secretary of State and the Attorney General as symbols either of conspiracy or acquiescence in it. There was the control or near control of the national media by élitist journalists convinced that ultimate issues of liberty were at stake, and taking a not inconsiderable satisfaction in relating the ways of the Yahoos. There was the romanticization of the proletariat. Finally, the ambiguous role of the FBI, to which, mindlessly, the élite in both situations turned over custody of its most serious political problems. Deep wounds were inflicted by both sides as the tempo and intensity of conflict mounted, and community declined.

In both eras a distinctive posture of altogether too many members of the intellectual-academic world was to reject the legitimacy of the issue either of subversion or violence on grounds that those who raised it either were not intelligent enough to comprehend fully any complex issue or else had something other in mind than their putative concern for the public safety. The plain fact is that in both instances the intellectual group had acquired an *interest* in the political turmoil of the moment and came very near to misusing its position to advance that interest. In the first period the intellectual-academic community seemed filled with persons who, in Kristol's description, "prefer to regard Whittaker Chambers and Elizabeth Bently as pathological liars, and who believe that to plead the Fifth Amendment is the first refuge of a scholar and a gentleman." [8] In the second period the apologetics for violence were not less curious. The community action ideology became in ways more, not less, extreme in the face of evident failures. *Complete* community control, usually meaning black control, of *all* community-affecting institutions became the demand of the more militant whites. On the surface a reasonable enough position, in reality this took the form of denying the legitimacy of those institutions of electoral representation that had developed over the years—indeed, the centuries—and which nominally *did* provide community control. Of a sudden the city councilman was not enough, the state assemblyman not enough, the Congressman not enough, the mayor and the gov-

---

[8] Irving Kristol, "The Web of Realism," *Commentary* (June 1964), 610.

ernor and the President but tools of the power structure. Plebiscitory democracy, the people-in-council, became the seeming nonnegotiable demand of many. The institutions of representative government, imperfect as they may be, have the singular virtue of defining who speaks for the community in certain set circumstances. Thus the elected (black) representatives of the Harlem community had several times ratified the construction by Columbia University of a gynmasium in Morningside Park. But the black students of the University decided that the assemblymen and senators, councilmen and borough presidents did not speak for the community, and that *they* did. This quickly enough becomes government, as one observer has noted, by a process of private nullification, which has never been especially good news for democracy. It would be absurd to blame the community action programs of the war on poverty for this *reductio ad absurdum,* but the legitimation of something called "community control," in opposition to the established system of electoral representation; the assumption that established systems were somehow not meeting the needs of the people, was certainly much encouraged by the community action movement. It is altogether natural that more conservative citizens became alarmed.

Nor is it to be wondered at that representatives of local government became concerned. In New York City the Republican John V. Lindsay had succeeded Wagner after a vigorous election campaign in which, generally speaking, he had adopted the radical critique of the antipoverty program, promising more participation, less control by City Hall. But in office, Lindsay, if anything, tightened control over such programs as he could get his hands on and evinced less and less enthusiasm for protesting welfare mothers and rampaging teen-age antipoverty program employees. Even the director of MFY indicated a measure of disenchantment. Far from insisting that the cure for participation was more participation, Beck and others like him became revisionists of sorts. The results of the "poverty elections" held in such places as Philadelphia and Los Angeles for representation on the local community action agency boards had been, as Wofford allows, pitiful. They appear to have made an impression on some persons at least. Early in 1968, Bertram Beck, Executive Director of MFY, spoke almost bitterly on the subject:

> To me, the great sell-out of the antipoverty program was the invention of these elections of community corporations. There is a meager amount of money available. And where does it end up? It ends up with groups of poor people fighting one another over an inadequate, paltry sum of money that can do nothing. . . . It looks liberal. It looks great. It looks like a forward step. I say it's a regressive step.[9]

Beck said more than that: in his view "too much antipoverty activity has been strictly agitational."

At this time, Lindsay proposed that community action agencies turn to more visible, tangible projects if they were to retain the confidence of the public and the Congress. In February 1968, he told a news conference, "Community action work in the past has tended to be in the field of community organization. But this must give way to the higher priority of public works type activity, particularly in the area of rehabilitation of physical structures." Mitchell Ginsberg, the City Human Resources Administrator, and an original board member of MFY, put it

[9] Bertram Beck, Remarks, New York Report, WOR-TV, February 11, 1968.

even more bluntly: "In the first stages all of the emphasis of the community action programs was on organization, but how many times can you organize the same people. You have to organize them to do something." Again, the flaws of the original antipoverty legislation were having their belated consequences: so much of the "hard" program having gone elsewhere, OEO and the community action programs were left with too little to do, and too much tendency to talk. Lindsay's private judgment may have slipped out six months later when, objecting to a Congressional move to transfer the Head Start program to the Department of Health, Education and Welfare, he said, "Head Start has been one of the few real successes of OEO." [10] But little came, at least in the short run, of his proposed redirection of community action. The City's Council Against Poverty would have to agree, and he indicated at the time that he was not sure it would. Many thought it was "demeaning" for the poor to work at such things as cleaning buildings, sidewalks, and vacant lots. Bertram Beck was appalled: "I don't see how we can expect the Mayor to run a city and an antipoverty program when he has such limited influence over it."

Thus the director of MFY was proposing powers for City Hall in 1968 that his predecessor had fiercely opposed in 1965. A learning process is to be observed: when the Johnson Administration put forth its Model Cities Program, it was provided that the communities involved would participate in the planning process, but strictly in association with the institutions of local government. "Somehow it has seemed easier," remarked H. Ralph Taylor, Assistant Secretary of Housing and Urban Development in May 1967, at a time the antipoverty program seemed almost lost, "to set up competing institutions than to make existing institutions work together more effectively." The political executives at HUD had no intention of letting happen to them what had happened to Shriver and his associates, and to their respective programs. Mayor Naftalin's quiet counsel was finally getting through.

The blunt reality is that sponsors of community action programs who expected to adopt the conflict strategy of Saul D. Alinsky and at the same time expected to be the recipients of large sums of public money, looked for, to paraphrase Jefferson, "what never was, and never will be." Alinsky emerges from the 1960s a man of enhanced stature. His influence on the formulation of the antipoverty program and its predecessors was not great. Indeed it was negligible, in that a primary motive of these efforts was to *give* things to the poor that they did not have. Alinsky's law, laid down in *Reveille for Radicals,* which appeared in 1946,[11] was that in the process of social change there is no such thing as give, only take. True or not, by the time the community action programs began to be funded, he had behind him some three decades of organizing poor or marginal neighborhoods (*white* at well as black) and in every instance this process had taken the form of inducing *conflict* and fighting for *power*. Was there not something to be learned here? Could it be that this is somehow the normal evolution once such an effort is begun? Was it not possible, for example, that MFY had to move towards disruption if those in charge of the program were to elicit any response from the neighborhood, and in that way acquire some feeling that they were having an impact? Alinsky's view was nothing if not explicit and public: social stability is a

---

[10] *New York Times,* July 27, 1968.
[11] Saul D. Alinsky, *Reveille for Radicals* (Chicago: University of Chicago Press, 1946).

condition reached through negotiated compromise between *power organizations*. (His origins, of course, are in the trade union movement, specifically the United Mine Workers.) The problem of the poor is not only that they lack money, but that they lack power. This means they have no way of threatening the status quo, and therefore that there can be no social change until this organizational condition is changed. Organization first; antipoverty program second. Early in the life of the Office of Economic Opportunity, Alinsky was willing to contemplate that Federal funds, bypassing City Hall and channeled directly to indigenous organizations, might be used to bring such organizations into being. But his own experience and practice belied any such possibility. Throughout his career he had begun his organizing campaigns with cash in hand, completely independent of the power structure with which he wished to bargain. His entire analysis of the process of social change argued that official community action programs would soon fall under the direction of City Hall, as indeed they did.

Just as importantly, Alinsky (a "professional radical") posed a serious challenge to the concept of professionalism in reform. Speaking early in 1965, he used the analogy of the Foreign Aid program that had followed World War II. Why had the United States undertaken the program? From some moral principle? Nonsense. Foreign aid was begun because the Russians threatened. Precisely the same dynamics, he argued, would determine the outcome of the then barely begun war on poverty: "under present circumstances a poverty program based on a moral dynamism is not going to carry the thrust which comes from the threat" of an organized poor. The whole affair, he declared, was "political pornography," the first war ever launched on a balanced budget. He did not expect it would last long:

> Unless there are drastic changes in direction, rationale and administration, the anti-poverty program may well become the worst political blunder and boomerang of the present administration. If ever a program demanded an aggressive, partisan, unafraid-of-controversy administration it is the antipoverty program. It must be a program which contends that poverty involves poverty of power as well as poverty of economy.[12]

Whether or not his analysis was correct, his prognosis was near to perfect. It ought to have been attended to, but was not. One reason for this was the absence of persons within the administration attuned to such modes of thought, capable of assessing their validity, at very least, alert to the possibility that what such a man says might just be so.

The long-run effectiveness of Alinsky's organizing programs remains to be documented: the long-run has not yet occurred. But in the near-term, none can fault his insistence that social radicalism is not a civil service calling. Would it not, then, have been wiser for the antipoverty program to direct its efforts to the creation, for example, of trade union organizations in minority groups, using the contracting powers of the government and the protective sanctions of the National Labor Relations Board to create units of economic and political power, which, once established, would thereafter have an independent life of their own? Was it that trade unionism had lost its glamor for the youth of the upper middle class who flocked to Shriver's OEO in the heady months of 1964 and 1965?

---

[12] Saul D. Alinsky, "The War on Poverty—Political Pornography," *The Journal of Social Issues* (January 1965).

Similarly, would it not have been wise to seek ways to support and expand the activities of the small fundamentalist churches of the Negro community and the Pentacostal sects of the Puerto Ricans? Are these not the single incontrovertibly indigenous and independent institutions created by these minority slum dwellers in the present age? And are they not singularly vigorous and tough in the capacity to survive and to grow? Do they not *really* reflect the energies and personal styles of the poor? Or was it that hymn-shouting and bible-thumping somehow does not elicit in the fancies of the white radical quite the same fascination as does the black demi-monde? Difficult questions to answer, but ones appropriate to the calling and method of social science.

In sum, it must be insisted that the opportunity theory behind Mobilization for Youth is and was no more than that. Evidence to support it exists, but nothing like final agreement. To the contrary the theory of participation as therapy is much disputed. Bernard J. Frieden and Robert Morris write, in the context of the general problem of alienation:

> Least convincing have been those analyses which have asserted that the fact of participation by the poor, in itself, will significantly alter the conditions deplored, as for example the belief that civic participation in itself leads to a reduction in deviant behavior.[13]

The failure of the social scientists, the foundation executives, the government officials lay in not accepting—not insisting upon—the theoretical nature of their proposition. As a matter for speculation, even for experiment, various forms of government-sponsored community action had much to commend themselves. The problems of community were properly a matter of concern at this time. But to proceed as if that which only *might* be so, in fact was so, was to misuse social science. It is the necessary condition of politics that action be based on insufficient knowledge. That is the responsibility of persons who get themselves elected as representatives of the people. They are expected, required, to act as if they know more than they do. Regularly they pay the price for turning out to have been wrong. Life in American politics is singularly solitary, nasty, brutish, and short—the exceptions only contrast with the generality—and those who with Hobbes would seek a "quiet corner" from which to observe it all, must deny themselves some of the excitements of the fray, or else not complain when bashed. One of the least attractive qualities of some of the early middle-class practitioners of conflict-oriented community action was the tendency to cry "Foul" when the animal defended itself. Chazen, certainly a sympathetic commentator, writes:

> The theoreticians were often unprepared for the enemies they acquired when their opinions of the public aid bureaucracy moved out of the professional journals and on to the picket signs. For an experienced labor or civil rights organizer there would be nothing unsettling about the political entanglements of militant social action. But social action enthusiasts came from an entirely different organizing tradition. Many of them arrived at their current welfare theories while organizing teenagers for juvenile delinquency projects which enjoyed the cooperation of city authorities. This preparation was not adequate for the political problems the social action theoreticians

[13] Bernard J. Frieden and Robert Morris, *Urban Planning and Social Policy* (New York: Basic Books, 1968), p. 178. But see also Erdman B. Palmore and Phillip E. Hammond, "Interacting Factors in Juvenile Delinquency," *American Sociological Review* (December 1964), 848–854.

encountered when they obtained older constituencies in places like New York's Lower East Side.[14]

Yet even he refers to Screvane as "Mobilization's executioner."

It is difficult to avoid the conclusion that in all these goings on social science was being misused. Professional persons were too willing by half to see public funds, and tax-free private funds, employed on a vast scale to further what was in effect a political agenda of a fairly small group of intellectuals. At just that time when their colleagues, and students, were raising the utmost rumpus about the intrusion of Federal money, and *therefore* influence into universities via national security and space programs, these professors were enthusiastically pressing for ever more public money to be expended in urban and rural neighborhoods in such a way as to change the political and social attitudes of the residents thereof. The precedent in either case is a questionable one. The next President of the United States, as I write, will not be Lyndon Johnson. It could be George C. Wallace. How much public money would American liberals be willing to see President Wallace expend for the purpose of increasing the participation in public affairs of those elements in the population he regards as simultaneously deprived and underorganized? But this is an obvious point and need not be pressed, save to note that what is involved, in a word, is integrity. And common sense. If a populist, illiberal conservatism began swelling to ominous proportions in the late 1960s, the middle-class advocates of expressive violence and creative turmoil had something to answer for. Indeed it is directly to them, the professors and "pseudointellectuals," that Governor Wallace and others like him, addressed *their* critique of the power structure, and *their* challenge to the forms of civility and social stability that liberal academic America had seemingly thought so secure as not to need defending. . . .

[14] Leonard Chazen, "Participation of the Poor: Section 202 (a)(3) Organizations Under the Economic Opportunity Act of 1964," *Yale Law Journal,* 75 (March 1966), 608.

37
The Price of Community Control
David K. Cohen

Like everything else in the cities, education seems to defy both management and comprehension. The struggle over urban schools has in recent years grown progressively more ferocious, with the casualties mounting accordingly. Discussions of underachievement and psychological damage have given way to cries of genocide. No longer are anger and criticism confined to the malfeasance of an occasional superintendent; the arena of contention now includes entire educational programs—integration, school improvement, community control—each designed in its own way to remedy conditions in slum schools. Meanwhile, the schools remain segregated, student achievement shows no sign of change, and the distribution of power is no different from what is used to be. Yet while we appear to have been on a treadmill with respect to basic educational reform, the ideological scenery has been going by at a furious rate; at present, the main issue no longer appears to be whether segregation should be eliminated, or more money allocated to schools, but who shall control what exists.

How has this change come about? Until about a year ago, most people would have agreed that the main purpose of school reform was to eliminate racial disparities in educational achievement; this, in turn, was regarded as the best way to

Reprinted from *Commentary*, by permission; Copyright © 1969 by the American Jewish Committee.

reduce racial disparities in jobs and income. The debate, by and large, centered on the question of how the schools should go about accomplishing that task. Many Negroes and white liberals supported an emphasis on integration, arguing that segregated schools impaired motivation and achievement, and thereby damaged Negroes' chances for occupational success and full citizenship. Educators, on the other hand, typically located the problem not in the racial organization of public education but in the intellectual and cultural "deprivation" of Negro children; hence, they advocated educational programs aimed at compensating for those deficiencies.

Recently, two new educational proposals have been advanced—decentralization and community control. In the form in which they were initially made, these proposals did little to disturb the assumptions underlying earlier efforts at reform. Thus, increased accountability to the local community was presented as another way of unlocking a school's potential for raising the educational attainment of its pupils. Although other issues have since arisen, the original claims for decentralization rested on the belief that the traditional "liberal" approaches to school reform—integration and/or compensatory education—had been tried and had failed.

Behind this notion lay three major assumptions. One was that government had in fact redistributed resources—in the form of students, teachers, dollars, or whatever—in order to eliminate the racially unequal distribution of results in schooling. A second was that the programs of integration and compensatory education had been evaluated, and it had been demonstrated that they did not work: i.e., test scores had not changed. Finally, the reason for this failure was perceived to be administrative or political in nature: the school bureaucracy was opposed to reform, the teachers were racist, or the entire structure was hopelessly unresponsive. From these assumptions flowed the conclusion that any new policy proposal —be it bloc grants, administrative decentralization, or community control—must center on transforming fundamental political relationships.

Before taking up the merits of these new proposals, I should like to discuss the assumptions on which they rest. For it is by no means self-evident: a) that liberal programs of educational reform were in fact tried on a significant scale; b) that where they were tried, they failed; or c) that political and administrative change is necessarily a precondition for change in the distribution of educational achievement.

II

Hard evidence on the effectiveness of educational strategies has never been easy to come by. Until 1966, for example, when the Coleman Report was published,[1] virtually no direct evidence existed on the relationship between a school's racial composition and how well its student performed. What the Coleman Report revealed turned out to be at some variance with integrationist ideology: Negro students in mostly white schools were indeed higher achievers than those in mostly Negro schools, but this apparently bore no intrinsic relation to a particular school's racial composition. Rather, in those mostly white schools where Negroes performed well, the white students were typically from more advantaged homes; Negro students in a middle-class white school would do no better than Negro students in an equally middle-class Negro school. As a practical matter, integra-

[1] James S. Coleman et al., *Equality of Educational Opportunity* (Washington, 1966).

tionists could reassure themselves that the relative lack of a Negro middle class meant that social-class integration would inevitably entail racial integration as well, but in view of this finding they could no longer embrace the notion that a school's racial composition *per se* affected achievement.

Of course, the absence of unequivocal evidence on achievement was never the main obstacle to school integration, and in many communities where integration was tried, achievement gains seem indeed to have followed. In most communities, however, the attempt was never even made. The blame for this may be placed primarily on the indifference, inertia, and opposition of school officials, and on the general political sentiment which they reflected. Although committed educational leadership in places like Berkeley, Evanston, and Syracuse showed that organized white resistance could be overcome, most school systems—in the hundreds of communities whose size and demography put integration within easy reach— never reached that stage. Even fewer efforts were made in the large cities, where national attention was riveted.

Integrationists responded to this situation by devising a strategy which promised to reduce white opposition by coupling integration with a variety of beguiling educational attractions: educational parks, magnet schools, special education centers, and the like. If most white parents, the reasoning went, were forced to choose between inferior all-white schools and educationally superior integrated facilities, they would not hesitate to choose the latter. The problem was that educational innovations are as expensive as school budgets are tight; the strategy required new legislation which would allocate much more money to city schools.

In any event, the strategy was never really tried, since most professional educators chose a different response altogether. They saw that Negro parents wanted better schools and higher achievement, and therefore offered programs of remedial and compensatory education in the existing segregated schools. When this counter-strategy was embodied in local programs, and in Title I of the Elementary and Secondary Education Act of 1965, it put a premium on the perpetuation of segregated schools. It paid educators to maintain schools in the slums rather than create the integrated, educationally superior facilities envisioned in integrationist rhetoric.

Thus it is incorrect to say that school integration failed; what failed was the politics required to bring it about. Like most liberal strategies for social change, integration is politically viable only on the assumption that it is in the interest of whites to reduce the status disparity between themselves and Negroes. Inducing whites to choose integration by creating educationally irresistible schools was a clever effort to create such an identity of interest. The only flaw was that before white parents could be presented with the choice, vast new funds would have had to be appropriated, with the explicit proviso that they would be used to create these schools. And naturally the money itself could not be obtained without substantial white support. In political terms this meant that in order to make the strategy work one had to presume the prior existence of that very identity of educational interests which the strategy was designed to bring into being. In this case, circular reasoning proved to be as deadly in politics as it usually is in logic: only a few of the integrationists' schools have ever been created.

The concept of compensatory education favored by most educators represented an effort to avoid this fatal circularity. Since compensatory programs operated only in slum schools, they seemed indeed to offer a happy political alternative. Whites could assume a progressive stance by supporting improved ghetto education—and better schools for poor whites, too—while opposing or remaining neutral on demands for busing, Princeton plans, and other politically volatile integration tactics. For these reasons—to say nothing of the substantial Negro support the remedial programs enjoyed—a powerful coalition of moderate and liberal reformers and schoolmen came together behind such legislation as Title I of the Elementary and Secondary Education Act.

How did these programs fare? Over the past two years a succession of evaluations has been unable to find much evidence of improved achievement. To be sure, their sponsors have proclaimed the programs a success: the litanies of praise that have been issued cite improved school conditions, brighter attitudes, better attendance, reduced vandalism, happier teachers, etc. Nonetheless, to judge by the main criterion the programs were designed to satisfy, the general absence of gains in achievement makes all these claims seem trivial or disingenuous.

What accounts for this unhappy record? In a strict sense the question cannot be answered, for as long as we don't know what works, it is impossible to make the comparisons which might suggest the reasons for failure. Comparisons aside, however, one *can* assess in a general way the actual impact on slum schools of the millions of federal dollars that have been appropriated for their improvement. Title I increased instructional expenditures for each participating child by about $60 a year in 1966–1967, and last year by about $65. Since the nation annually spends an average of about $450 per pupil for instruction, the increment (10 to 15 per cent) from Title I can only be described as modest. The simplest way to figure the amount of educational improvement that an increase like that can buy is in terms of the time a teacher devotes to her children. If a teacher has thirty students and works a five-hour day (and if we imagine that she divides the day into a series of tutorials), then each student receives a ten-minute daily tutorial. An increase of 10 per cent in the teaching staff would add one minute to the daily individual attention a student receives. That does not exactly constitute an educational revolution.

There is more. For one thing, the compensatory moneys have often been used to make up for existing differences between black and white schools, rather than for creating better-than-equal black schools. For another, the funds made available under Title I frequently have been so dispersed that their budgetary impact —which is clear enough on a balance sheet—is undetectable in the target schools themselves. As a result, in many cases the infusion of money has had the opposite effect from the one intended. If, on the one hand, the funds are concentrated only on the neediest children, a noticeable change does occur in these children's school program, but only for an hour or so a day, or a day a week. Teachers who work in the school but not in the program often become hostile or jealous, and those who do work in the program, since their colleagues are unfriendly and their students unsuccessful, grow frustrated and discouraged. They explode and leave, or somehow adjust cynically to the situation; neither reaction is particularly productive. If, on the other hand, the funds are diffused widely over a variety of children and schools, intense frustration on the part of a few teachers is traded off for a more generalized low level of despondency or indifference. Then there is the added problem of turnover in both teaching staff and in the programs themselves, which occurs partly as a result of the conditions I have just outlined, partly for political or administrative reasons. Continuity is rare and knowledge noncumulative: the same basic lessons are often learned over and over again, either by new teachers in the same program, or by the same teachers in new programs. No one benefits perceptibly.

There have been a few experiments which involved rather larger sums than those provided by Title I, but here too one would be hard put to say unequivocally that they resulted in improved achievement. Some interpretations of evidence from the More Effective Schools program in New York City, for example, suggest that there may have been achievement gains for children who were exposed to the program over long periods of time, but other interpretations suggest the opposite; similarly with the tutoring program conducted by New York's Mobilization for Youth and a few other programs. In all cases, reports of improvement are open to serious question.

Finally there are pre-school programs, which vary in content and direction from traditional classroom situations, to parent-training programs, to programs giving individual attention to two-years-olds. A number of these programs have reported substantial gains. Two things, however, should be noted about them. The first is that the gains appear to dissipate quickly if things are allowed to return to normal; the second is that those programs which are school-centered are very expensive, costing between $1000 and $1500 per child per annum. Now, research on pre-school education seems to indicate that it is indeed possible, although it is by no means easy, to affect patterns of intellectual development if pervasive changes in a child's environment are instituted a good deal earlier than the age at which schooling now begins, and if they are continued on into the elementary school years. But the prospect of undertaking such a course of action raises many problems in its turn. One of these relates to the political and cultural implications of further extending the schools' dominion over children; I will take this up later. Another is suggested by the price that is likely to be exacted for such reform: if the cost of improving achievement will be an additional one or two thousand dollars per pupil per year, and if our main goal is to eliminate racial disparities in adult income and occupation, then why not spend the money directly on family income maintenance, or on creating socially useful and important jobs? Perhaps the best way to change existing inequalities in income and occupation is to change them, not to use schooling as a means of deferring reform.

The costliness of programs of intensive education in early childhood is politically crucial in another way, too, for a ghettoized approach to school improvement assumes that whites will trade off the programs' cost for the maintenance of segregation. Although to some extent that is doubtless true, there is no guarantee that the commitment of whites to existing patterns of segregation will stretch to the point where they would be willing to spend on black children two or three times what is typically spent on whites. It is precisely here that the "failure" of compensatory education resides. As a recent publication of the U.S. Office of Education dolefully pointed out, a really serious effort in compensatory education would ". . . require a mobilization effort more far-reaching than any now envisioned by any community." It would, in other words, imply a level of white support for ghetto development which—in light of the past eight years' experience—is as difficult to conceive as the amount of white support that would be required for integration.

III

What has failed, then, is not the traditional "liberal" educational technologies—whether of the integrationist or compensatory variety; these technologies have been tried too sporadically and haphazardly to permit of careful assessment. Rather, the deficiency lies in the absence of operational political strategies which would bind up the interests of blacks and whites in such a way as to elicit white support for programs that would improve the relative status of black children. That is a primitive political defect, an inability to apply what might be called the politics of common interest to basic social reform.

But if it is incorrect to say that integration and compensatory education have been tried and found wanting, politically it all seems to amount to the same thing: the relative educational status of Negro and white children in metropolitan areas is little different now from what it was in 1954. The persistence of this dreary contrast has in recent years provided a major impetus to movements for decentralization and community control.

Decentralization and community control refer to a variety of notions about schooling and school reform, not all of them related to the problem of disparities in achievement. One of these is that the potentially effective components of city school systems—parents, teachers, and inquisitive children—are walled off from each other by a Byzantine bureaucratic maze; before the elements can function to the children's best advantage, the argument runs, the walls must be broken down and the bureaucracy brought under control. Another view is that the entire educational system is racist, from the way it allocates resources, to the attitudes of its teachers and the character of its textbooks; according to this view the remedy is not to make the system more accessible but to transfer control of the enterprise altogether: until the schools are operated by the parents of their young black clients (or those who legitimately stand *in loco parentis*), they will not be responsive to the needs of Negro children. A third view is that the problem resides in the psychological consequences of powerlessness. As things now stand, it is argued, the central fact of life for black Americans is that they do not control their personal and collective destinies. All the significant ghetto institutions—schools, government, welfare, etc.—are controlled by whites. Unless these whites are replaced by Negroes, black children will lack a sense that the world will respond to their efforts, and their achievement will languish as a consequence. The last two ideas roughly comprise the meaning of community control, the first, decentralization.

Of the three, the notion that the root problem is bureaucracy probably has the broadest appeal. For one thing, the complexity and unresponsiveness of many big-city school systems is legendary; no client of any class or color happily accepts the reign of the clerk, and increasing numbers reject the inflexible style and pedagogy of the schools. For another, we have long been accustomed to the idea that the very size of institutions inevitably produces a kind of social arteriosclerosis, and assume that the remedy lies not in reaming out the conduits, but in reducing the distance between the vital organs and the extremities. Finally, the anti-bureaucratic critique is almost always couched in irresistible contrasts between extreme situations—Scarsdale as opposed to Bedford-Stuyvesant, or Winnetka as opposed to the West Side of Chicago.

Unfortunately, however, there is no evidence that the level of parent participation in schools is related to students' achievement. It is true that parents in suburban communities are somewhat more likely to participate in school affairs than those in central cities, but this seems to have more to do with the consequences of affluence than with anything else; analysis of the data in the Coleman Report fails to reveal any association between the level of parental participation and achievement. Nor is there any evidence that smaller school districts—which we all presume to be less bureaucratized and more responsive to parents and children—produce higher levels of achievement than larger ones. With a few outstanding exceptions, public education in the U.S. runs on the assumption that administrative decentralization, small and homey school districts, and local control are educational essentials; literally thousands of school jurisdictions stand as testimony to this creed, against only a handful of urban monoliths. Yet here again there appears to be no relation whatsoever between the size of a school district (or whether its board is elected or appointed) and the achievement of the students in its schools.

On the other hand, there is abundant evidence that parents who are involved in a direct way in their children's education tend to have children who achieve at higher levels. Involvement of this sort includes reading to children, taking them to libraries, talking to them, explaining things, and otherwise providing lots of cognitive stimulation and support for intellectual accomplishment. Thus, when poor parents are trained to behave toward their children in the way middle-class parents do, the children's level of achievement rises. This should not come as a surprise, except perhaps to those hardy souls who believe that the intellectual deprivation associated with poverty can be traced exclusively to genetic makeup. It does, however, argue for the establishment of parent-training efforts, like the one that has been operating in Ypsilanti, Michigan, rather than programs aimed at eliminating bureaucracy in schools.

Advocates of community control (as opposed to administrative decentralization) might raise the objection here that the source of underachievement is not bureaucratic inertia in the first place, but institutional racism. There is, in fact, no dearth of evidence that city school systems discriminate against the poor in general and Negroes in particular. Studies of resource allocation almost always reveal that predominantly black schools suffer by comparison with white schools, in terms of such things as teacher experience, tenure, and certification. In addition, the attitudes of many teachers are influenced by class and racial antagonisms; in the Coleman sample of Northern urban elementary schools, between 10 and 20 percent of teachers in ghetto schools overtly expressed a preference for schools with all or nearly all white student bodies. It should be noted, however, that Negro children whose teachers are as good as or better than the average for whites and have better than average racial attitudes, do not show higher achievement than their less fortunate counterparts in ghetto schools.

Here it may be countered that it is not a teacher's racial attitudes which affect performance, but his expectations of his students' academic success. And indeed, this idea appears to make intuitive good sense. It seems reasonable to believe that bigoted white teachers—or Negroes who accept white stereotypes—will somehow communicate to their students the sense that black children are academically less capable. If that is so, then it might well follow that the most efficient way to deal with such teachers, short of large-scale psychotherapy, would be to sharpen dramatically their responsibility to the parents of Negro children, on the theory that they would then have to shape up or ship out.

Let us assume for the moment that this hypothesis is correct.[2] Let us also grant that community control would transform academic expectations that have been distorted over the years by bigotry or brainwashing. Would it also eliminate underachievement in ghetto schools? The latter is unlikely, for most achievement differences appear to be related not to a student's race or to his school's racial composition, but to factors having to do with social class. Correcting the consequences of racist distortions in teachers' expectancies is not the same thing as correcting the vast class differentials which produce differences in achievement in the first place. The notion that bigoted teachers depress the academic performance of black children is based on the premise that these teachers fail accurately to perceive and/or to act upon the children's real potential, *because the children are black*. Yet it has been shown that differences in achievement are of roughly the same magnitude at grade six or nine as they are at the time children enter school, and are relatively insensitive to variations in *anything* about schools. All the research of the last four decades points to the conclusion that differences in nutrition, general health, and access to intellectual and cognitive stimulation—which, of course, vary widely by social and economic status, and therefore by race—are the chief environmental determinants of children's intellectual performance. Eliminating racial distortions in teacher expectations would improve ghetto education, but it would probably not eliminate disparities in achievement that are ultimately due to differences in social class.

Both of the theories that I have discussed so far suffer from the obvious defect of presuming that schools have an impact upon students' achievement, when most evidence on this point tends in the opposite direction. The third—the fate-control theory—does not so presume. Its premise is the notion that the central educational problem for black children is not poor pedagogy, but powerlessness, a political condition in the ghetto which is not at all unique to the schools. Now, it takes only a modicum of political insight to notice that Negroes do not control most of the institutions which directly affect their lives, and little ideological originality to argue that hence they are a subject people, dominated in colonial fashion by a foreign white ruling class. This argument has been advanced with increasing strength since World War II, but until publication of the Coleman Report there was no way to link the political fact of powerlessness with students' performance in school. One of that report's major findings, however, was that the extent to which black students felt they could master their destiny was a powerful determinant of their achievement, more important than all the measures of family, social, and economic status combined.

That provided the necessary link. If a student's sense of environment control

[2] It has been argued most persuasively by Robert Rosenthal and Lenore Jacobson in *Pygmalion in the Classroom* (New York: Holt, Rinehart and Winston, 1968). In a review published in the *American Educational Research Journal* (November 1968), Robert L. Thorndike cast serious doubt on the authors' research.

strongly influenced his achievement, black control of ghetto schools, it seemed to follow, would produce a sense of personal efficacy which would in turn lead to improved performance. The idea now enjoys enormous popularity, primarily because it seems entirely consistent with reality. First of all, political and cultural emasculation has been a dominant element of the black experience in America. Secondly, all the precedents of American ethnic history are supposed to demonstrate that group political and economic solidarity is the touchstone of personal status and mobility. Finally, it seems to make eminent sense that people who feel in control of their destiny will be high achievers; the sense of mastery leads to mastery.

But try it the other way: mastery leads to the sense of mastery; high achievers are more likely to have a stronger sense of environment control than low achievers. It sounds just as persuasive one way as the other, a perplexity which is amply reflected in research. Some studies suggest that the sense of efficacy causes achievement, some suggest that it works the other way around, and others find no association whatsoever. We have no studies of the relationship between parents' political efficacy (or their sense thereof) and their children's test scores; the few studies that relate parents' general sense of environment control to their children's achievement are inconclusive and contradictory. Here as elsewhere, the results of scientific research provide a firm basis for nothing but further research.

In summary: a good deal has been made of the various ways in which decentralization and community control will improve achievement, but a review of what we know turns up confused, contradictory, or discouraging evidence. This does not mean that greater participation, less bureaucracy, greater openness, and more accountability are not worthwhile goals; I happen to think they are crucial. In my view, however, these are essentially political and administrative issues, and one's assessment of their significance or desirability should be determined by theory and evidence particular to those realms of experience. The one thing my brief review of the educational evidence *does* mean is this: if one were guided solely by research on achievement and attitudes, one would not employ community control or decentralization as the devices most likely to reduce racial disparities in achievement.

IV

But the gathering momentum for community control and decentralization is unlikely to be diminished by this news. On the contrary, advocates of these policies argue that evidence derived from the existing situation is not simply inadequate but altogether inapplicable. More important, the major pressures for decentralization and community control now have less to do with the failure of educational strategies than with the failure of what I referred to earlier as the politics of common interest.

As a historical matter, it is of course true that one of the underlying causes of the movement for community control has been the persistence of racial disparities in achievement. Yet the nature of the current situation is best illustrated by the fact that within the last year, the persistence of these disparities has not simply produced more militant demands for higher achievement but has created a profound crisis of authority in ghetto schools, a sense that these schools lack legitimacy as educational institutions. This feeling is strongest among Negroes—especially the young, the activists, and the professionals—but it is reinforced by the many middle- and upper-middle-class whites who reject the public schools' regimentation and authoritarianism for other reasons. For some blacks and whites, the notion that only parents and community residents are legitimately empowered to operate schools rests on what is taken to be the objective inadequacy of those in authority; scarcely anyone with access to print denies that the schools have failed to correct ghetto educational problems. Repeated for years, this assertion has led effortlessly to the idea that the established agencies lack the special competence upon which most educational authority is assumed to rest.

There is, however, more to the crisis of authority than that. The illegitimacy of ghetto education is more and more often proclaimed to reside not in the failure of that education to produce achievement equal to that of white schools—had it done so, according to the earlier logic, the criterion of legitimacy need never have been challenged—but in the defective nature of the social contract between black and white America. One manifestation of this position is the attack that has been launched on the instruments—achievement test results, rates of college acceptance, etc.—typically used to determine if the older, "rational" criterion of authority was being satisfied; not only that, but the intellectual and cultural content of those instruments has been dismissed as irrelevant or antithetical to the black community's political and cultural aspirations. A second, and politically more explosive, manifestation of this view is the assertion that school officials and teachers whose ideas or activities suggest the absence of political and cultural identification with the black community therefore also lack the qualifications requisite to educate black children. This is entirely consistent with the new criterion of authority, which assumes that the task of educators in the ghettos is to establish the basis for a valid social contract between Negroes and the institutions in their communities. Hence it becomes not at all strange to substitute for the old, "rational" tests of educational competence a subjective test of political consensus, for in a sense the situation is presumed to have reverted to the precontract state of nature, wherein the main issue is one of defining the body politic that is about to come into being, and deciding who shall be its citizens.

This "anti-colonial" position is, in the technically correct sense of the term, revolutionary; it asserts that the established authorities and the principles upon which their dominion rests are fundamentally and irreparably illegitimate, and that the only way they can continue to command is by the use of naked power. In such a situation the minimum task of the revolutionary is to bring that fact into the open, to "expose" the illegitimacy by provoking the authorities to violence.

Although only a relatively few Negroes consciously hold this position, their political strength is multiplied enormously by the fact that there are *very* few who explicitly hold the opposite view. Most blacks have an acute sense of the injustice which white society has visited upon them, so that if white authorities should attempt to suppress an openly revolutionary cadre, the best response they could hope for from the general community would be one of sullen hostility. In the case of the struggle over the schools, this makes it functionally impossible to distinguish those who want community control as a means of fulfilling the achievement criterion from those who want it as the basis for a new social contract. The two groups will remain pretty much identical so long as the achievement criterion remains unsatisfied.

It is easy to see why the anti-colonial position is anathema to the established authorities. Among other things, in selecting school personnel advocates of this position seek to substitute what amounts to a test of political loyalty for a series of universalistic "professional" standards. In last year's school dispute in New York, for example, the Ocean Hill Board was accused of racism and of violating due-process guarantees for teachers, but whether or not this was true, the real issue was the Board's effort to apply a test of political consensus to educators. Since—as in Africa—there are always whites who can pass such a test, the Ocean Hill Board could maintain that it was not guilty of racism at the same time that it sought to expel teachers for what *it* called racism—i.e., non-consensus.

But whatever the local variations, the crucial fact is that the crisis in urban education is passing into a phase in which only a change in the locus of authority will bring peace. How long the present transition period will last is hard to say, but the main elements of the domestic political situation appear to favor an increase rather than a diminishing of the anti-colonial impulse. Those elements include: the inability of the liberal/labor/civil-rights coalition to secure legislation that would mount a broad and basic attack upon black-white disparities in income and occupation; an unprecedented (but hardly unheralded) upsurge of black nationalism; the emergence of a black professional class in Northern cities as a political force.

Since the collapse of the Johnsonian consensus on domestic affairs, which can be roughly dated to the 1966 White House Conference "To Fulfill These Rights," these three elements have come into high relief, reinforcing one another. After the White House Conference, it became increasingly clear that Congressional liberals were light-years away from the political strength required to legislate fundamental change in the economic and social status of Negroes. The resources lost to the war effort in Vietnam were of course partly to blame, but there was more to it than that: as the White House Conference report suggested, fundamental change would require social spending on an absolutely unprecedented scale. Even without a war in Vietnam the Congressional struggle would have been titanic in its proportions; it was clearly impossible under conditions of large-scale defense spending.

In the cities, therefore, where no real effort has been made to deal with the underlying problems of jobs and income, attention remains where it has been since 1954. The schools are visible and accessible, in the sense that the political nexus of employment and housing is not; their performance has been obviously out of harmony with the ideology of education expounded by all moderates and liberals since *Brown* vs. *Board of Education;* and the inability in the last decade to effect widespread educational reforms has insured that existing frustrations would grow as performance fell farther and farther behind expectations.

As a result, the primary urban activity since late 1967 has been a struggle for the division and control of what already exists. Although one may argue that this is a rational response if one believes there is no hope for new social legislation, it has the notable drawback of creating political divisions which even further diminish the likelihood of such legislation. The greatest division of this kind has occurred between Negroes and white liberals. (To be sure, the peace between them had never been easy. Aside from the inevitable element of paternalism—whites in the movement were cooperating to solve what was typically seen as "the Negro problem"—there was the problem generated by rivalry for jobs and leadership once the movement began to score some successes.) In the recent disasters in New York City, many of the same white liberals who had championed the cause of civil rights suddenly found themselves under attack because they happened to inhabit those institutions toward which urban Negroes were now turning with hungry eyes. In a sense, the social-welfare bureaucracies—schools, welfare, anti-poverty programs—were the least strategic places to attack. They have, after all, been among the most liberal institutions, they have a common interest with blacks in the expansion of social-welfare legislation, and they are typically populated by whites who are noticeably more liberal than the average. But they were close at hand, they were the institutions Negroes knew about, they were (or seemed) easier to approach than others more remote and conservative, they were located in the ghettos rather than downtown, and they were even sympathetic to the situation which produced the movement for black control.

Add to this the politicization of the cultural and psychological upsurge known as black nationalism, which began in the mid-1960s and was well underway long before black power became a political and ideological reality. Renewed interest on the part of blacks in Afro-American culture and "Negritude" produced basic and legitimate demands upon white America, in the schools and elswhere. The written materials of education are typically bigoted, and there is virtually no important aspect of public education in the cities, from the distribution of money to the attitudes of teachers, which is untouched by discrimination or racial antagonism. These problems, however, are as amenable to remedy by integration as by black separatism.

But in the absence of genuine integration, or of much evidence of fundamental economic and social change, nationalism became wedded to the demand for a piece of the action, and was forged into a program for change. This is not the place to argue the merits of the position as a general matter; what is important is that black nationalism offered a system of ideas which seemed to correspond with the interests of the emerging class of black professionals, and to explain the need for black community control. Even in itself integration is a difficult path: it promises strain, tension, and unfamiliarity to black and white administrators and teachers equally, and hence it has never inspired real enthusiasm except among a few. Community control, on the other hand, avoids these pitfalls. It offers concrete gains long overdue—jobs and promotion to administrative and supervisory positions, without the accompanying discomfort of venturing into foreign schools and neighborhoods—under the ideological aegis of assisting in the development of one's own community. A more perfect coincidence of ideology and self-interest can hardly be imagined.

The coming-of-age of the black professional class, a potent aspect of the struggle for community control, may turn out in the end to be the most important element in the battle over the schools, more significant than the substitution of parent for citywide boards, or community for bureaucratic control. The enfranchisement of a black elite, long overdue, should indeed help to improve education. In the short run, however, it has poured fuel on an already raging fire. Frustration, hostility, ambition, and concern for children long neglected is a potent combination, especially when applied generously to the complicated gear-works of big-city civil-service labor relations. The results have been spread depressingly over more editions of the New York *Times* than one cares to contemplate. As the struggle continues—and it surely will—the Lindsays of the world will seek to maintain civil peace—and their positions—by accommodating as many black demands for a slice of the action as they find possible, while the Albert Shankers will seek to maintain life by holding on to what they have. In so doing, the Lindsays will find themselves alienating lower-class and sometimes liberal white constitutents, and the Shankers will find themselves making alliances with and concessions to conservative elements. The liberals will find themselves in the position of having to defend those portions of the social-welfare bureaucracies they control against black demands; all they can do, aside from hanging on for dear life, is to assume a principled position against segregation and for the application of vastly greater resources. However one may sympathize with that position, it is no more likely to be useful in the next day's struggle to keep afloat politically than it is either to reduce segregation or to increase the available resources.

V

Is there a way out of our present morass? The difficulty here is twofold. One might still imagine that a massive assault on status disparities would shift attention away from the question of legitimacy, but it is hard to conceive of such an assault being mounted. Producing the needed legislation would require sustained political mobilization of blacks and whites, a prospect which seems remote so long as: a) they are so fatally preoccupied with each other; b) new money cannot be found to reduce the competition and allow recruitment of a broader constituency; and c) many powerful whites and ambitious blacks, for their separate reasons, prefer a political settlement to economic and social justice.

I do not mean to imply, however—and this is the second difficulty—that the way out would be clear if only more resources were available. That, unfortunately, is only the converse of the argument for decentralization: it makes no more sense to pretend that removing social and economic disparities will solve all the problems of city schools than to argue that political rearrangement will eliminate achievement disparities. The point can be conveniently illustrated: the liberal ideology of educational improvement tells us that since schooling is the least divisive and best way to insure equal chances for jobs and income, we should provide more of it for Negroes. School reforms based on this notion typically include heavy doses of those disciplined activities which are thought to yield high scores on achievement tests. But the same middle-class liberals who advocate this medicine for the poor often cannot stomach administering it to *their* children; they enroll them instead in more open, permissive, and pedagogically diversified private schools. This paradox suggests in practice what many advocates of school reform cannot admit as a matter of principle: that there exists presently a fundamental tension between the sorts of educational changes which are thought to improve achievement, and those designed to diversify pedagogy, reduce routine, and allow for individual and cultural creativity.

As an ideological matter, school reformers have dealt with this tension by placing exclusive stress on either diversity or achievement; the practical political consequence has been to behave as though solving one problem would solve the other. Many liberals have therefore supported programs designed to extend the dominion of the schools over children's lives, and have advocated such things as twelve-month school years, pre-schools and kindergarten for all, afternoon school centers, and the like. Under any circumstances serious questions could be raised about the desirability of a further intrusion of state institutions into a child's cultural and intellectual development; given the current circumstances—in which the institutions in question suffer from an advanced form of political, cultural, and pedagogical atrophy—the problems are terrific. Although one can easily imagine a program of extended schooling being executed well, with concern for diversity and individuality, there is a big difference between what one can imagine and what one can actually do with the materials at hand. The extension of schooling means the extension of the schooling that happens to exist, as the history of Head Start and Title I—to say nothing of the compulsory education movement—makes abundantly clear. Thus, liberals who advocate such measures run the risk of overtly or covertly subverting other educational values they hold dear.

In the case of decentralization—as the recent events in New York reveal—the same insistence on unitary solutions to separate problems has led to the widespread idea that political and administrative change will remedy racial achievement differences, an idea which, as I have tried to show, flies in the face of all past experience and knowledge concerning the determinants of achievement. As for the aim of creating diversity in the schools, decentralization and community control can be described only as half-hearted and incomplete attempts in that direction.

Consider the various proposals for decentralizing the New York City schools. All, from the Bundy plan to the most radical proposals for community control, assume that the necessary and sufficient condition for producing diversity is the imposition of new control on existing institutions and resources. But this amounts to nothing more than a system of educational laissez-faire, which is hardly the same thing as diversity, especially when schools are segregated by race and class. In the competition for school resources, the net effect of such a system would be to institutionalize the political disadvantages of blacks and poor people, isolate them in the competition for money, and thereby establish in custom, law, and administrative code those failures of the politics of common interest which led to the demands for control in the first place.

More important, however, is the fact that the need for diversity—for alternative cultural and pedagogic styles in schooling—cannot be satisfied by racial division or changes in administrative structure alone. Diversity and excellence in schools are qualities not likely to appear unless a premium is put upon them. Creating such diversity would entail the recruitment of new people to education, and new institutions to schooling: not just neighborhood boards, but universities, labor unions, churches, and voluntary associations formed for the purpose of education. The business of attracting, organizing, funding, and maintaining such institutions cannot be accomplished by further provincializing the existing structure, any more than regulating it can be left to essentially free competition.

Real diversity would be costly both politically and fiscally, and would require a somewhat different view of the relationship between the state and the schools from the one now regnant. At the moment we think of the state not only as the sole regulator of public education, but as exclusive operator of the schools; this greatly restricts, for political and constitutional reasons, the extent to which the schools can be diverse. Were the state to continue its role as regulator but take less of a hand in actually running the schools, greater diversity might be possible; under such conditions the state would concern itself with maintaining essential principles of interest regulation, civil liberties, civil rights, and educational standards.

The form that such an arrangement would take is uncertain. There have been proposals to put money on the heads of children—or in the pockets of their parents—but they raise problems related to segregation, and to the well-known fact that the poor usually exercise choice in a less strategic fashion than do the affluent. Another proposal has been to create alternative *institutions;* this might obviate the problem of choice to a certain extent, but like the tuition proposals, it raises questions about the interests of parties that are presently involved in the educational enterprise.

All these alternative proposals deserve careful consideration, whether one is concerned with pedagogy, political participation, or the possibilities for a democratic culture. They deserve consideration not only as to their intrinsic merits, but because they serve as a counterbalance to the idea that diversity and openness in the schools can be produced solely through political arrangements designed to settle an authority crisis arising from long-standing grievances of quite another sort. One might also hope that a discussion of these issues would contribute to repairing some of the deep political divisions within the democratic Left. These fissures have sprung in part from the fact that organizations and individuals that would in a more civilized atmosphere have tended to take different stands on different issues—racial identity, pedagogic diversity, political participation, reduction of racial disparities in income and occupation—have in the current climate been forced to take a single stand on all at once. The resulting schizophrenia has been widely displayed in the columns of all serious publications which either originate in or recognize the existence of New York City.

Finally, attention to alternative forms of education might help to set in clear relief another idea currently simmering at the edges of the liberal political consciousness, namely that the best way to reduce racial disparities in children's school achievement might be to reduce the disparities in their parents' social and economic status. Support for this notion, as I pointed out earlier, arises from a variety of considerations: the dependence of achievement on parental status; the potential political, cultural, and emotional dangers of extending the system of schooling that now exists; the inherent risks of presuming that profound social change can be purchased cheaply with a bit of improved schooling.

VI

It should be plain by now that I myself am persuaded by the soundness of this analysis, yet I am also aware that its intellectual cogency is strongly and negatively related to its chances for political life and prosperity. We are presently at an important crossroad, both in education and in race relations, and the path we take will probably influence the shape of things for many, many years. Roughly speaking, the issue is how to settle an increasingly severe crisis of authority. On the one hand, by carving up existing institutions and resources in such a way as to arrange a viable contract between blacks and the institutions in their neighborhoods, we can work out a political settlement of the tensions that have arisen from a longstanding failure to remedy basic social and economic injustice. Thereby, perhaps, we can purchase peace, or, if not peace, at least the confinement of the conflict and noise within the ghetto. On the other hand, we can resolve the authority crisis by attacking the fundamental disparities which produced it.

It would be easy to overestimate in alarmist fashion the consequences of choosing the easier path; a good deal of this has unfortunately already been done. It would be silly, or worse, to argue that educational disaster will ensue from whatever decentralization and community control can be politically arranged. There will be problems, but there are problems now. It seems to me much more likely that under community control the basic disparities would remain more or less intact, while the atmosphere and conduct of the schools would show improvement.

A good deal has also been said to the effect that the movements for decentralization and community control are provoking a general rightward trend in American politics. That such a trend exists is clear, and it also seems reasonable to believe that it feeds upon the wilder and more vociferous elements in the movement for community control. But we should remember that this trend was first noticed years ago as a reaction to the movement for *integration,* and that it probably manifests the underlying reality of white attitudes in a limited-resource situation, not a response to particular strategies. It is unhappy and frustrating to witness the present spiral of distrust, and the struggle for control of what exists; these contribute their share to the general poisoning of the political atmosphere. But they are symptoms of the underlying political weakness, not its primary cause.

Of the two alternatives, it takes no great vision to see where the political chips lie. The second alternative is costly, whether we measure cost in dollars allocated, status lost, stereotypes shattered, or political effort expended. The first has a certain political price—as the convulsions in New York revealed—but it gives the appearance of costing little otherwise. In addition to this enormous political advantage, it has behind it the gathering momentum of profound changes in black politics, culture, and society. Although the politicization of these forces, and their arrangement behind the banner of community control, results chiefly from the failure of the society at large to deal directly with social and economic inequality, political facts cannot be wished away, either by dreams of what might have been or strategies on paper about what might be: unless the inequalities are swiftly attacked, these forces will not be denied.

CHAPTER THIRTEEN
PROTEST AND VIOLENCE

38
Violence in America

Hugh Davis Graham
Ted Robert Gurr

THE COMMONALITY OF COLLECTIVE VIOLENCE IN THE WESTERN TRADITION

Future historians may marvel at the ostensible "rediscovery" of violence that has both fascinated and bemused contemporary observers. That the recent resurgence of collective nonmilitary violence in Western society is widely regarded as anomalous probably reflects both a cultural and a contemporary bias. We have tended to assume, perhaps unconsciously, that such violence was an uncivilized practice of more primitive societies that the civilized and affluent West had largely outgrown. Our historians have themselves been guilty of contributing to this popular illusion; while they have retained their fascination for military exploits, they have tended either to ignore the persistence of domestic turmoil except when it reached revolutionary proportions, or to minimize its significance by viewing it from the perspective of established authority. When viewed from the top down, violence was understandably regarded as an abnormal and undesirable breach of the public order.

"Conclusion" from *Violence in America—Historical and Comparative Perspectives*. A Report to the National Commission on the Causes and Prevention of Violence, June 1969. Prepared under the direction and authorship of Hugh Davis Graham and Ted Robert Gurr (Washington, D.C.: Government Printing Office, 1969).

On the contrary, Tilly concludes, "collective violence is normal."

> Historically, collective violence has flowed regularly out of the central, political processes of western countries. Men seeking to seize, hold, or realign the levers of power have continually engaged in collective violence as part of their struggles. The oppressed have struck in the name of justice, the privileged in the name of order, those in between in the name of fear.

In Tilly's analysis, collective violence in the European experience was fundamentally transformed but not foredoomed by the processes of industrialization and urbanization. The old "primitive" forms of violence in feudal Europe—such as communal feuds and religious persecutions—were characterized by small scale, local scope, communal group participation, and inexplicit and unpolitical objectives. The subsequent evolution of the nation-state prompted such "reactionary" disturbances as food riots, Luddite destruction, tax revolts, and anticonscription rebellions. Although industrialization and urbanization muted such disorders by disrupting their cohesive communal base, the metropolitan society these forces forged gave rise to "modern" forms of protest—such as demonstrations and strikes —which involved relatively large and specialized associations with relatively well-defined and "forward-looking" objectives and which were explicitly organized for political or economic action.

Tilly's model suggests that modern collective protest, owing to its broader associational base, is more likely to occur on a large scale. But modern protest is less likely to become violent because the associational form gives the group a surer control over its own actions, and thus permits shows of force without concomitant damage or bloodshed. Moreover, the historic shift from communal to associational bases for collective protest brought into being a number of modern nonviolent mechanisms for the regulation of conflicts: the strike, the demonstration, the parliament, and the political campaign. Collective violence, then, historically belongs to political life, and changes in its form tell us that something important is happening to the political system itself.

What is happening to the political system in contemporary America? Preliminary to such an inquiry is the historical task of surveying the patterns of group violence that have accompanied the development of the United States. Brown has traced an overview of American collective violence, and his organizational categories of "negative" and "positive" violence in some ways parallel Tilly's analytical distinctions between reactionary disturbances, which center on rights once enjoyed but now threatened, and modern disturbances, which center on rights not yet enjoyed but now within reach. It might be more appropriate in this conclusion to discuss the American historical legacy of violence in relation to the contemporary relevance of the various categories Brown employed. Brown catalogued as "negative" forms of American violence that associated with feuds, lynching, political assassination, free-lance multiple murder, crime, ethnic and racial prejudice, and urban rioting. "Positive" forms were associated with the American Revolution and Civil War, agrarian uprisings, labor protests, vigilantism, Indian wars, and police violence.

Perhaps the historically violent episode that is least relevant to our contemporary concerns is the family feud. The famous and colorful clan feuding seems to have been triggered by the Civil War in border areas where loyalties were sharply divided and where the large extended family of the 19th century provided both a locus for intense loyalties and a ready instrument of aggression. But this tradition has waned with the fading of the circumstances that conditioned its birth. It is arguable, however, that the brutalizing traditions associated with the Indian wars have left their callous imprint on our national character long after the estimated 850,000 American Indians had been ruthlessly reduced by 1950 to 400,000. Similarly, the violence associated with the American Revolution, the Civil War, and Reconstruction has surely reinforced the ancient notion that the ends justify the means, and clearly the defeat of the Confederacy and the failure of Reconstruction has convinced generations of white Southerners that Negro political participation and Federal efforts at reform are irrevocably linked with corruption and subversion.

Whether the long association with violence of agrarian uprisings and the labor movement has permanently faded with changing modern circumstances is fervently to be hoped, but by no means certain. Employer acceptance of unions during and after the New Deal suggests that that long and bloody conflict is largely behind us. But the stubborn persistence of rural poverty constitutes a latent invitation to a resurgence of latter-day populism.

Two other sordid American traditions that have largely waned but that recently have shown some signs of revival are vigilantism and lynching. Although vigilantism is associated in the popular mind with such frontier and rural practices as antirustler and antihorsethief popular "justice" in areas largely devoid of regular enforcement agencies, the largest local American vigilance committee was organized in San Francisco in 1856. If vigilantism is defined more broadly to include regional and even national movements as well as local organizations, then America's preeminent vigilante movement has been the Ku Klux Klan—or rather, the Ku Klux Klans, for there have essentially been three of them. The original Klan arose in the South in response to radical Reconstruction, and through terror and intimidation was instrumental in the "redemption" of the Southern state governments by white conservatives. The second Klan, by far the largest, was resurrected in Atlanta in 1915 and boomed nationally in the 1920s. Strong in the Midwest and Far West as well as the South, and making inroads even in the cities, the Klan of the 1920s—despite its traditional racist and xenophobic rhetoric—focused its chastisement less upon Negroes, Catholics, and Jews than upon local white Protestants who were adjudged guilty of violating smalltown America's Victorian moral code. The third Klan represented a proliferation of competing Klans in the South in response to the civil rights movement of the 1950s. Generally lacking the prestige and organizational stength of the earlier Klans, these groups engaged in a period of unrestrained terrorism in the rural and smalltown Black Belt South in the 1950s and early 1960s, but have belatedly been brought under greater control.

Lynching, vigilantism's supreme instrument of terror and summary "justice," has been widely practiced in America certainly since the Revolutionary era, when miscreant Tories were tarred and feathered, and worse. Although lynching is popularly associated with racial mob murder, this pattern is a relatively recent one, for prior to the late 19th century, white Americans perforce lynched one another —Negro slaves being far too valuable to squander at the stake. But lynching became predominantly racial from 1882 to 1903, when 1985 Negroes were murdered in the tragic but successful effort of those years to forge a rigid system of biracial caste, most brutal and explicit in the South but generally reflective of national attitudes. Once the point—that this was a white man's country—was made, lynching gradually declined. Its recent resurgence in response to the civil rights movement is notorious, but it nowhere approximates its scale at the turn of the century.

The contemporary relevance of political assassination and free-lance multiple murder needs no documentation to a nation that has so recently witnessed the murders of John and Robert Kennedy, Dr. Martin Luther King, and, on television, Lee Harvey Oswald—in addition to the chilling mass slaughtering sprees of Charles Whitman in Austin, Texas, and Richard Speck in Chicago. Historically, political assassination has become a recurrent feature of the political system only in the South during (the first) Reconstruction and in New Mexico Territory. Although four American Presidents have been assassinated since 1865, prominent politicians and civil servants occupying the myriad lesser levels of government have been largely immune. Whether the current spate of public murder is an endemic symptom of a new social malaise is a crucial question that history cannot yet answer, other than to observe that precedents in our past are minimal.

Similarly, historical precedents are few regarding massive student and antiwar protests. American students have historically succumbed to the annual spring throes of the panty-raid syndrome, but the current wave of campus confrontations is essentially an unprecedented phenomenon—as is the massive and prolonged opposition to the war in Vietnam. As Professor Brooks has observed, "unfortunately the past does not have much to tell us; we will have to make our own history along uncharted and frightening ways."

But the past has much to tell us about the rioting and crime that have gripped our cities. Urban mobs are as old as the city itself. Colonial seaports frequently were rocked for days by roving mobs—groups of unruly and often drunken men whose energies were shrewdly put to political purpose as Liberty Boys in the American Revolution. Indeed, our two principal instruments of physical control evolved directly in response to 19th-century urban turmoil. The professional city police system replaced the inadequate constabulary and watch-and-ward in response to the rioting of the 1840s and 1850s, largely in the Northeast. Similarly, the national guard was organized in order to control the labor violence—or more appropriately, the antilabor violence—of the 1880s and 1890s.

Probably all nations are given to a kind of historical amnesia or selective recollection that masks unpleasant traumas of the past. Certainly Americans since the Puritans have historically regarded themselves as a latter-day "Chosen People" sent on a holy errand to the wilderness, there to create a New Jerusalem. One beneficent side effect of our current turmoil may be to force a harder and more candid look at our past and at our behavior in comparison with other peoples and nations.

CONTEMPORARY AMERICAN VIOLENCE IN HISTORICAL PERSPECTIVE

Our current eruption of violence must appear paradoxical to a generation of Americans who witnessed the successful emergence from depression to unparalleled affluence of a nation they regarded as the world's moral leader in defense of freedom. Only a decade ago America's historians were celebrating the emergence of a unique society, sustained by a burgeoning prosperity and solidly grounded on a broad political consensus.[1] We were told—and the implications were reassuring—that our uniqueness was derived from at least half a dozen historical sources which, mutually reinforcing one another, had joined to propel us toward a manifestly benevolent destiny. We were a nation of immigrants, culturally enriched by the variety of mankind. Sons of the frontier, our national character has grown to reflect the democratic individualism and pragmatic ingenuity that had conquered the wilderness. Our new nation was born in anticolonial revolution and in its crucible was forged a democratic republic of unparalleled vitality and longevity. Lacking a feudal past, our political spectrum was so truncated about the consensual liberal center that, unlike Europe, divisive radicalism of the left or right had found no sizable constituency. Finally, we had both created and survived the great transformation from agrarian frontier to industrial metropolis, to become the richest nation of all time.

It was a justly proud legacy, one which seemed to make sense in the relatively tranquil 1950s. But with the 1960s came shock and frustration. It was a decade against itself: the students of affluence were marching in the streets; middle-class matrons were besieging the Pentagon; and Negro Americans were responding to victories in civil rights and to their collectively unprecedented prosperity with a paradoxical venting of outrage. In a fundamental sense, history—the ancient human encounter with poverty, defeat, and guilt as well as with affluence, victory, and innocence—had finally caught up with America. Or at least it had caught up with white America.

Historical analysis of our national experience and character would suggest that the seeds of our contemporary discontent were to a large extent deeply embedded in those same ostensibly benevolent forces which contributed to our uniqueness. First, we are a nation of immigrants, but one in which the original dominant immigrant group, the so-called Anglo-Saxons, effectively preempted the crucial levers of economic and political power in government, commerce, and the professions. This elite group has tenaciously resisted the upward strivings of successive "ethnic" immigrant waves. The resultant competitive hierarchy of immigrants has always been highly conducive to violence, but this violence has taken different forms. The Anglo-Americans have used their access to the levers of power to maintain their dominance, using legal force surrounded by an aura of legitimacy for such ends as economic exploitation; the restriction of immigration by a national-origin quota system which clearly branded later immigrants as culturally undesirable; the confinement of the original Indian immigrants largely to barren reservations; and the restriction of blacks to a degraded caste. But the system was also conducive to violence among the latter groups themselves—when, for instance, Irish-Americans rioted against Afro-American "scabs." Given America's unprecedented ethnic pluralism, simply being born American conferred no automatic and equal citizenship in the eyes of the larger society. In the face of such reservations,

---

[1] Exemplary of the "consensus school" of American historians are Daniel Boorstin, *The Genius of American Politics* (Chicago: University of Chicago Press, 1953); David Potter, *People of Plenty* (Chicago: University of Chicago Press, 1954); and Louis Hartz, *The Liberal Tradition in America* (New York: Harcourt, Brace & World, 1955). These scholars did not deny that the American past was replete with violence. Rather, they emphasized that America lacked the feudal past that had led to acute class animosity in Europe, that virtually all Americans shared the liberal ideology of Locke and Jefferson, and that Americans were highly pragmatic and did not take any ideology seriously enough to be fundamentally divided by it.

ethnic minorities had constantly to affirm their Americanism through a kind of patriotic ritual which intensified the ethnic competition for status. As a fragment culture based on bourgeois-liberal values, as Hartz has observed, yet one populated by an unprecedented variety of immigrant stock, America's tightened consensus on what properly constituted "Americanism" prompted status rivalries among the ethnic minorities which, when combined with economic rivalries, invited severe and abiding conflict.

Most distinctive among the immigrant minorities was the Negro. The eternal exception in American history, Afro-Americans were among the first to arrive and the last to emerge. To them, America meant slavery, and manumission meant elevation to the caste of black pariah. Comer has seen in the psychological legacy of slavery and caste a psychically crippling Negro dependency and even self-hatred which is largely immune to mere economic advance. The contemporary black awareness of this tenacious legacy of racial shame is abundantly reflected in the radical rhetoric of black power and "Black-is-Beautiful," and goes far toward resolving the paradox of black rebellion against a backdrop of general—albeit uneven, as Davies suggests—economic improvement. Meier and Rudwick have charted the transformation of racial violence from white pogrom to black aggression—or, in the analysis of Janowitz, from "communal" to "commodity" rioting. While emphasizing that the transformation has led to violent black assault less against white persons than against white property, and while Janowitz speculates that the summer of 1968 may have been yet another turning point, we are reminded that history, even very recent history, is an imperfect guide to the future.

The second major formative historical experience was America's uniquely prolonged encounter with the frontier. While the frontier experience indubitably strengthened the mettle of the American character, it witnessed the brutal and brutalizing ousting of the Indians and the forceful incorporation of Mexican and other original inhabitants, as Frantz [Fanon] has so graphically portrayed. Further, it concomitantly created an environment in which, owing to the paucity of law enforcement agencies, a tradition of vigilante "justice" was legitimized. The longevity of the Ku Klux Klan and the vitality both of contemporary urban rioting and of the stiffening resistance to it owe much to this tradition. As Brown has observed, vigilantism has persisted as a socially malleable instrument long after the disappearance of the frontier environment that gave it birth, and it has proved quite congenial to an urban setting.

Similarly, the revolutionary doctrine that our Declaration of Independence proudly proclaims stands as a tempting model of legitimate violence to be emulated by contemporary groups, such as militant Negroes and radical students who confront a system of both public and private government that they regard as contemptuous of their consent. Entranced by the resurgence of revolution in the underdeveloped world and of international university unrest, radical students and blacks naturally seize upon our historically sacrosanct doctrine of the inherent right of revolution and self-determination to justify their rebellion. That their analogies are fatefully problematical in no way dilutes the majesty of our own proud Declaration.

The fourth historic legacy, our consensual political philosophy of Lockean-Jeffersonian liberalism, was premised upon a pervasive fear of governmental power and has reinforced the tendency to define freedom negatively as freedom *from*. As a consequence, conservatives have been able paradoxically to invoke the doctrines of Jefferson in resistance to legislative reforms, and the Sumnerian imperative that "stateways cannot change folkways" has historically enjoyed a wide and not altogether unjustified allegiance in the public eye (witness the debacle of the first Reconstruction, and the dilemma of our contemporary second attempt). Its implicit corollary has been that forceful and, if necessary, violent local and state resistance to unpopular federal stateways is a legitimate response; both Calhoun and Wallace could confidently repair to a strict construction of the same document invoked by Lincoln and the Warren court.

A fifth historic source both of our modern society and our current plight is our industrial revolution and the great internal migration from the countryside to the city. Yet the process occurred with such astonishing rapidity that it produced widespread socioeconomic dislocation in an environment in which the internal controls of the American social structure were loose and the external controls were weak. Urban historian Richard Wade has observed that—

> The cities inherited no system of police control adequate to the numbers or to the rapid increase of the urban centers. The modern police force is the creation of the 20th century; the establishment of genuinely professional systems is historically a very recent thing.
>
> Throughout the 18th and 19th century, the force was small, untrained, poorly paid, and part of the political system. In case of any sizeable disorder, it was hopelessly inadequate; and rioters sometimes routed the constabulary in the first confrontation.[2]

Organized labor's protracted and bloody battles for recognition and power occurred during these years of minimal control and maximal social upheaval. The violence of workers' confrontations with their employers, Taft and Ross concluded, was partly the result of a lack of consensus on the legitimacy of workers' protests, partly the result of the lack of means of social control. Workers used force to press their grievances, employers organized violent resistance, and repeatedly state or federal troops had to be summoned to restore order.

The final distinctive characteristic—in many ways perhaps our most distinctive —has been our unmatched prosperity; we have been, in the words of David Potter, most characteristically a "people of plenty." Ranked celestially with life and liberty in the sacrosanct Lockean trilogy, property has generated a quest and prompted a devotion in the American character that has matched our devotion to equality and, in a fundamental sense, has transformed it from the radical leveling of the European democratic tradition into a typically American insistence upon equality of opportunity. In an acquisitive society of individuals with unequal talents and groups with unequal advantages, this had resulted in an unequal distribution of the rapid accumulation of abundance that, especially since World War II, has promised widespread participation in the affluent society to a degree unprecedented in history. Central to the notion of "revolutions of rising expectations," and to Davies' J-curve hypothesis as well, is the assumption that unproved economic rewards can coincide with and often obscure a degree of relative deprivation that generates frustration and can prompt men toward violent protest despite measurable gains.

Our historical evolution, then, has given our national character a dual nature: we strive, paradoxically, for both liberty and equality, which can be and often in

[2] See Richard Wade, "Violence in the Cities: An Historical View," *Urban Violence* (Chicago: University of Chicago Press, 1969), pp. 7–26.

practice are quite contradictory goals. This is not to suggest that American society is grounded in a fatal contradiction. For all the conflict inherent in a simultaneous quest for liberty and equality, American history is replete with dramatic instances of the successful adjustment of "the system" to the demands of disparate protesting groups. An historical appraisal of these genuine achievements should give pause to contemporary Cassandras who bemoan in self-flagellation how hopelessly wretched we all are. These radically disillusioned social critics can find abundant evil in our historical legacy: centuries of Negro slavery, the cultural deracination and near extinction of the Indians, our initiation of atomic destruction—ad infinitum. Much as the contemporary literary Jeremiahs have, in Lynn's view, libeled the American character by extrapolating violence from its literary context, these social critics in their overcompensations have distorted the American experience in much the same fashion, although in an opposite direction, as have the more familiar superpatriotic celebrants of American virtuosity. While a careful and honest historical appraisal should remind us that violence has been far more intrinsic to our past than we should like to think—Brooks reminds us, for example, that the New York Draft Riot of 1863 vastly exceeded the destruction of Watts—our assessment of the origins and dimensions of contemporary American violence must embrace the experience of other societies.

COMPARISONS OF PROTEST AND VIOLENCE

Whether the United States is now a "violent society" can be answered not in the abstract but only by comparison, either with the American past or with other nations. The historical evidence, above, suggests that we were somewhat more violent toward one another in this decade than we have been in most others, but probably less violent in total magnitude of civil strife than in the latter 19th century, when the turmoil of Reconstruction was followed by massive racial and labor violence. Even so, in contemporary comparison with other nations, acts of collective violence by private citizens in the United States in the last 20 years have been extraordinarily numerous, and this is true also of peaceful demonstrations. In numbers of political assassinations, riots, politically relevant armed group attacks, and demonstrations, the United States since 1948 has been among the half-dozen most tumultuous nations in the world.[3] When such events are evaluated in terms of their relative severity, however, the rank of the United States is somewhat lower. The Feierabends and Nesvold have used ranking scales to weigh the severity and numbers of such events during the years from 1948 to 1965, rating peaceful demonstrations as having the least serious impact, civil wars the most serious impact on political systems. In a comparison that gives greatest weight to the frequency of violent events, the United States ranks 14th among 84 nations. In another comparison, based mainly on the severity of all manifestations of political instability, violent or not, the United States stands below the midpoint, 46th among 84 nations. In other words, the United States up to 1965 had much political violence by comparison with other nations but relative stability of its political institutions in spite of it. Paradoxically, we have been a turbulent people but a relatively stable republic.

[3] These absolute comparisons are from Michael Hudson, "Violence and Political Institutionalization in the United States: A Comparative Analysis," a working paper prepared for the National Commission on the Causes and Prevention of Violence, 1968.

Some more detailed comparisons are provided by a study of the characteristics of civil strife in 114 nations and colonies in the 1960s. The information on "civil strife" includes all reported acts of collective violence involving 100 or more people; organized private attacks on political targets, whatever the number of participants; and antigovernment demonstrations involving 100 or more people. Three general kinds of civil strife are distinguished: (1) *Turmoil* is relatively spontaneous, partially organized or unorganized strife with substantial popular participation and limited objectives. (2) *Conspiracy* is intensively organized strife with limited participation but with terroristic or revolutionary objectives. (3) *Internal war* is intensively organized strife with widespread participation, always accompanied by extensive and intensive violence and usually directed at the overthrow of political regimes.

The comparisons of the strife study are proportional to population rather than absolute, on grounds that a demonstration by 10,000 of Portugal's 9 million citizens, for example, is more consequential for that nation than a demonstration by the same number of the United States' 200 million citizens is for ours. About 11 of every 1000 Americans took part in civil strife, almost all of it turmoil, between mid-1963 and mid-1968, compared with an average of 7 per thousand in 17 other Western democracies during the 1961–1969 period. Six of these 17 had higher rates of participation than the United States, including Belgium, France, and Italy. About 9500 reported casualties resulted from American strife, most of them the result of police action. This is a rate of 48 per million population, compared with an average of 12 per million in other Western nations, but American casualties are almost certain to be overreported by comparison with casualties elsewhere. Strife was also of longer duration in the United States than in all but a handful of countries in the world. In total magnitude of strife, taking these three factors into account, the United States ranks first among the 17 Western democracies.

Despite its frequency, civil strife in the United States has taken much less disruptive forms than in many non-Western and some Western countries. More than a million citizens participated in 370 reported civil-rights demonstrations and marches in the 5-year period; almost all of them were peacefully organized and conducted. Of 170 reported antiwar demonstrations, which involved a total of about 700,000 people, the participants initiated violence in about 20. The most extensive violence occurred in 239 recorded hostile outbreaks by Negroes, which resulted in more than 8000 casualties and 191 deaths. Yet the nation has experienced no internal wars since the Civil War and almost none of the chronic revolutionary conspiracy and terrorism that plague dozens of other nations. The most consequential conspiratorial violence has been white terrorism against blacks and civil-rights workers, which caused some 20 deaths between 1963 and 1968, and black terrorism against whites, mostly the police, which began in 1968.

Although about 220 Americans died in violent civil strife in the 5 years before mid-1968, the rate of 1.1 per million population was infinitesimal compared with the average of all nations of 238 deaths per million, and less than the European average of 2.4 per million. These differences reflect the comparative evidence that, from a worldwide perspective, Americans have seldom organized for violence. Most demonstrators and rioters are protesting, not rebelling. If there were many serious revolutionaries in the United States, or effective revolutionary organizations, levels of violence would be much higher than they have been.

These comparisons afford little comfort when the tumult of the United States is contrasted with the relative domestic tranquillity of developed democratic nations like Sweden, Great Britain, and Australia, or with the comparable current tranquillity of nations as diverse as Yugoslavia, Turkey, Jamaica, or Malaysia. In total magnitude of strife, the United States ranks 24th among the 114 larger nations and colonies of the world. In magnitude of turmoil alone, it ranks sixth.

Though greater in magnitude, civil strife in the United States is about the same in kind as strife in other Western nations. The antigovernment demonstration and riot, violent clashes of political or ethnic groups, and student protests are pervasive forms of conflict in modern democracies. Some such public protest has occurred in every Western nation in the past decade. People in non-Western countries also resort to these limited forms of public protest, but they are much more likely to organize serious conspiratorial and revolutionary movements as well. Strife in the United States and other European countries is quite likely to mobilize members of both the working class and middle classes, but rarely members of the political establishment such as military officers, civil servants, and disaffected political leaders, who so often organize conspiracies and internal wars in non-European nations. Strife also is likely to occur within or on the periphery of the normal political process in Western nations, rather than being organized by clandestine revolutionary movements or cells of plotters. If some overt strife is an inevitable accompaniment of organized social existence, as all our comparative evidence suggests it is, it seems socially preferable that it take the form of open political protest, even violent protest, rather than concerted, intensively violent attempts to seize political power.

One evident characteristic of civil strife in the United States in recent years is the extent to which it is an outgrowth of ethnic tensions. Much of the civil protest and collective violence in the United States has been directly related to the nation's racial problems. Comparative studies show evidence of parallel though not identical situations in other developed, European, and democratic nations. The unsatisfied demands of regional, ethnic, and linguistic groups for greater rights and socioeconomic benefits are more common sources of civil strife in Western nations than in almost any other group of countries. These problems have persisted long after the resolution of fundamental questions about the nature of the state, the terms of political power and who should hold it, and economic development. It seems ironical that nations that have been missionaries of technology and political organization to the rest of the world apparently have failed to provide satisfactory conditions of life for all the groups within their midst.

THE SOURCES OF VIOLENCE

Is man violent by nature or by circumstance? In the Hobbesian view, the inescapable legacy of human nature is a "life of man solitary, poor, nasty, brutish, and short." This ancient pessimistic view is given recent credence by the ethologists, whose study of animals in their natural habitats had led them to conclude that the aggressive drive in animals is innate, ranking with the instinctive trilogy of hunger, sex, and fear or flight.[4] But most psychologists and social scientists do not regard aggression as fundamentally spontaneous or instinctive, nor does the

[4] See Konrad Lorenz, *On Aggression* (New York: Harcourt Brace Jovanovich, 1966), and Robert Ardrey, *The Territorial Imperative* (New York: Dell, 1966).

weight of their evidence support such a view. Rather they regard most aggression, including violence, as sometimes an emotional response to socially induced frustrations, and sometimes a dispassionate, learned response evoked by specific situations.[5] This assumption underlies almost all the studies in this volume: nature provides us only with the capacity for violence; it is social circumstance that determines whether and how we exercise that capacity.

Man's cultural diversity offers concrete evidence that this essentially optimistic view of human nature is justified. Man can through his intelligence so construct his cultural traditions and institutions as to minimize violence and encourage the realization of his humanistic goals. Cultural anthropologists have identified societies, such as four contiguous language groups in the remote Eastern Highlands of New Guinea, in which the rhythms of life were focused on a deadly and institutionally permanent game of rape and cannibalism. But they have also studied such gentle societies as those of the Arapesh of New Guinea, the Lepchas of Sikkim, and the pygmies of the Congo rain forest, cultures in which an appetite for aggression has been replaced by an "enormous gusto for concrete physical pleasures—eating, drinking, sex, and laughter." [6] Revealingly, these gentle societies generally lack the cultural model of brave, aggressive masculinity, a pervasive model that seems so conducive to violence. Evidence that culture is a powerful if not omnipotent determinant of man's propensity for violence is the melancholy contemporary fact that Manhattan Island (population 1.7 million) has more murders per year than all of England and Wales (population 49 million). We need not resolve the interminable hen-and-egg debate over the primacy of nature versus nurture to conclude that man has the cultural capacity to minimize his recourse to violence.

One general approach to the explanation of the nature and extent of collective violence, supported by considerable evidence in this report, begins with the assumption that men's frustration over some of the material and social circumstances of their lives is a necessary precondition of group protest and collective violence. The more intense and widespread frustration-induced discontent is among a people, the more intense and widespread collective violence is likely to be. Several general attitudinal and social conditions determine the extent and form of consequent violence. People are most strongly disposed to act violently on their discontent if they believe that violence is justifiable and likely of success; they are likely to take violent political action to the extent that they regard their government as illegitimate and responsible for their frustrations. The extent, intensity, and organization of civil strife is finally determined by characteristics of the social system: the degree and consistency of social control, and the extent to which institutions afford peaceful alternatives to violent protest.[7]

[5] See Leonard Berkowitz, *Aggression: A Social Psychological Analysis* (New York: McGraw-Hill, 1962), and Ashley Montagu (ed.), *Man and Aggression* (New York: Oxford University Press, 1968).
[6] See Geoffrey Gorer, "Man Has No 'Killer' Instinct," *The New York Times Magazine*, Nov. 17, 1966.
[7] "Frustration" interpretations of the impetus to collective violence are proposed by Davies, the Feierabends, and Nesvold, and, in somewhat different guises, by Comer and Carstairs. Gude considers some effects of legitimacy and force, Janowitz social control generally. Gurr's analysis deals with motivational, attitudinal, and institutional variables that lead to violence. Siegel examines the kinds of external stresses on a group and group attitudes that lead it to defensive institutional responses which minimize external violence.

If discontent is a root cause of violence within the political community, what kinds of conditions give rise to the widespread discontents that lead to collective violence? All societies generate some discontent because organized social life by its very nature frustrates all human beings, by inhibiting some of their natural impulses. Socialized inhibitions and outlets for such discontents are provided by every society, though their relative effectiveness is certainly an underlying factor in national differences in rates of aggressive crimes. Another fundamental factor may be the ecological one. Carstairs summarizes evidence that overcrowding of human populations may lead to aggressiveness. On the other hand, Tilly shows that high rates of immigration to French cities in the 18th and 19th centuries was, if anything, associated with civil peace rather than rising disorder. Lane also finds that increasing urbanization in 19th-century Massachusetts was accompanied by a decline in violent crime rates. Neither culture stress nor population concentrations per se seem to be consequential causes of upsurges in collective violence, though they probably contribute to the "background noise" of a violence common to almost all cultures. Probably the most important cause of major increases in group violence is the widespread frustration of socially deprived expectations about the goods and conditions of life men believe theirs by right. These frustratable expectations relate not only to material well-being but to more intangible conditions such as security, status, freedom to manage one's own affairs, and satisfying personal relations with others. Men's rightful expectations have many sources, among them their past experience of gain or loss, ideologies of scarcity or abundance, and the condition of groups with which they identify. In any case, men feel satisfactions and frustrations with reference to what they think they ought to have, not according to some absolute standard.

New expectations and new frustrations are more likely to be generated in times of social change than social stasis. The quantitative comparisons of the Feierabends and Nesvold suggest, for example, that nations undergoing the most rapid socioeconomic change also are likely to experience the highest levels of collective violence. Large-scale socioeconomic change is ordinarily accompanied by changes in peoples' values, by institutional dislocations that affect people on top as much as people "on the way up," and even by the temporary breakdown of some social institutions. Rapid social change is thus likely to add to the discontents of many groups at the same time that it improves the conditions of some. In addition, it may contribute to the partial breakdown of systems of normative control, to the collapse of old institutions through which some groups were once able to satisfy their expectations, and to the creation of new organizations of the discontented. Under these conditions the motivational and institutional potential for collective violence is high.

Some specific patterns of social change are directly indicted as causes of collective violence. One is a pattern of rising expectations among people so situated that lack of opportunity or the obdurate resistance of others precludes their attainment of those expectations. American society is especially vulnerable to the frustration of disappointed expectations, for we have proclaimed ourselves the harbinger of a New Jerusalem and invited millions of destitute immigrants to our shores to partake of its fulfillment. "Progressive" demands by such groups that have felt themselves unjustifiably excluded from a fair share of the social, economic, and political privileges of the majority have repeatedly provided motivation and justification for group conflict in our past, as they have in the history of

Western Europe. Demands of workers for economic recognition and political participation were pervasive and chronic sources of turmoil in the United States and Europe. The aspirations of the Irish, Italians, Slavs, and—far most consequentially—Negroes have also provided repeated occasion for violence in America. Demands for an end to discriminatory privilege have not been confined to minorities or ethnic strata either. The struggle for women's suffrage in the United States was not peaceful, and America has not heard the last of women's claims for effective socioeconomic equality with men. Although the current resurgence of protest by many groups testifies to the continued inequity in the distribution of rewards, it also reflects the self-sustaining nature of social adjustment in this most pluralistic of nations. The same process through which Americans have made successive accommodations to demands for equity encourages the regeneration of new demands.

Protective resistance to undesirable change has been a more common source of collective violence in America than "revolutions of rising expectations," however. For example, most ethnic and religious violence in American history has been retaliatory violence by groups farther up the socioeconomic ladder who felt threatened by the prospect of the "new immigrant" and the Negro getting both "too big" and "too close." As Taft and Ross have demonstrated, most labor violence in American history was not a deliberate tactic of working-class organization but a result of forceful employer resistance to worker organization and demands. Companies repeatedly resorted to coercive and sometimes terroristic activities against union organizers and to violent strikebreaking tactics. The violence of employers often provided both model and impetus to counterviolence by workers, leading in many situations to an escalating spiral of violent conflict to the point of military intervention or mutual exhaustion.

Aggressive vigilantism has been a recurrent response of middle- and working-class Americans to perceived threats by outsiders or lesser classes to their status, security, and cultural integrity. The most widely known manifestations have been the frontier tradition of citizens' enforcement of the law and Ku Klux Klan efforts to maintain class lines and the moral code by taking their version of the law into their own hands. Brown has traced the emergence of such vigilante groups as the "Regulators" of pre-Revolutionary South Carolina and the Bald Knobbers of the Missouri Ozarks in the late 1800s. There are many other manifestations of aggressive vigilantism as well; no regions and few historical eras have been free of it, including the present. A contemporary one is the sporadic harassment of "hippie" and "peacenik" settlements in rural and smalltown America, and the neovigilante organizations of urban Americans, white and black, for "group defense" that often have aggressive overtones. There also is a vigilantism of a somewhat different sort, an aggressive and active suppression of deviancy within an otherwise-cohesive group. An historical example was the White Cap movement of the 1880s and 1890s, a spontaneous movement for the moral regulation of the poor whites and ne'er-do-wells of rural America. Such vigilantism also is apparent in the internecine strife of defensive black organizations, which have occasionally used violence to rid themselves of innovative "traitors" like Malcolm X.

Agrarian protests and uprisings have characterized both frontier and settled regions of the United States since before the Revolution. They have reflected both progressive and protective sentiments, including demands for land reform, defense against more powerful economic interests, and relief from onerous political restrictions. Among them have been Shays' Rebellion in Massachusetts, 1786–1787; Fries' Rebellion in eastern Pennsylvania, 1799; some of the activities of the Grangers, Greenbackers, and Farmers' Alliance after the Civil War; and the "Green Corn Rebellion" of Oklahoma farmers during World War I.

Antiwar protest in American history also has a predominantly protective quality. The nation's 19th-century wars, especially the Civil War, led often to violent resistance to military conscription and the economic impositions of war. The 20th century has seen the development of a strong, indigenous strain of pacifism in the United States. The goals of those who have promoted the cause of peace, during both World War I and the Vietnam war, have been protective in this sense: they adhere to a set of humanitarian values that are embodied in the basic social contract of American life, and see that contract threatened by those who regard force as the solution to American and foreign problems. The evidence of American history and comparative studies suggests no exact relationship between the occurrence of war and domestic protest against it, however. In the United States it appears to be the pervasive sense that a particular war and its demands are unjust or illegitimate that leads to protest and, occasionally, to violent resistance.

Davies identifies a third general pattern of change that is frequently associated with the outbreak of rebellion and revolution: the occurrence of a short period of sharp relative decline in socioeconomic or political conditions after a prolonged period of improving conditions. A period of steady progress generates expectations that progress will continue. If it does not continue, a pervasive sense of frustration develops which, if focused on the government, is likely to lead to widespread political violence. It is not only economic reversal in this pattern that leads to violence. People whose dignity, career expectations, or political ambitions are so frustrated are as likely to rebel as those whose pocketbooks are being emptied.

This specific pattern is identified in Davies' studies of socioeconomic and political changes affecting various groups before the outbreak of the French Revolution, the American Civil War, and the Nazi revolution. It may also be present in data on relative rates of white and Negro socioeconomic progress in the United States during the last several decades. From 1940 to 1952, nonwhite family income relative to educational attainment appears to have increased steadily and substantially in comparison with white income. In 1940 the average Negro with a high school education was likely to receive 55 percent of the earnings of a white worker with comparable education. This figure increased to 85 percent in 1952—but then declined to a low of 74 percent by 1962. These data call into question simplistic notions to the effect that unsatisfied expectations of black Americans increased to the point of violence simply because of "agitation," or because of unfulfilled promises. Rather it may have been real progress, judged by the firsthand experience of the 1940s and early 1950s, and probably also by reference to the rise of the black bourgeoisie, which generated expectations that were substantially frustrated by events of the late 1950s and early 1960s.

Discontent is only the initial condition of collective violence, which raises the question of the extent to which the actualization of violence is determined by popular attitudes and institutional patterns. A cross-national study by Gurr was designed to provide preliminary answers to this question, by relating differences among nations in economic and political discontent, apparent justifications for violence, and institutional strength to differences in magnitudes and forms of civil strife. The results are that more than a third of the differences among contemporary nations in magnitudes of strife are accounted for by differences in the extent and intensity of their citizens' discontent, even though measured imprecisely. Attitudes about politics and violence are almost as important. Nations whose political systems have low legitimacy are likely to have extensive strife; nations with a violent past—and, by implication, popular attitudes that support violence—are likely to have a violent present and future. Institutional patterns can meliorate or magnify these dispositions to violence. If physical controls are weak, and especially if they are inconsistent in application, strife is likely to be high. Similarly the weakness of conventional institutions, and the availability of material and organizational support for rebellion, lead to high levels of strife, particularly in its most intensive and violent forms.

The experience of the United States is consistent with this general pattern. For all our rhetoric, we have never been a very law-abiding nation, and illegal violence has sometimes been abundantly rewarded. Hence there have developed broad normative sanctions for the expression or acting out of discontent, somewhat limited inhibitions, and—owing to Jeffersonian liberalism's legacy of fear of central public authority—very circumscribed physical controls. Public sympathy has often been with the lawbreaker—sometimes with the nightrider who punished the transgressor of community mores, sometimes with the integrationists who refused to obey racial segregation laws. Lack of full respect for law and support for violence in one's own interest have both contributed to the justifications for private violence, justifications that in turn have helped make the United States historically and at present a tumultuous society.

On the other hand, the United States also has characteristics that in other countries appear to minimize intense revolutionary conspiracies and internal wars. Thus far in our history the American political system has maintained a relatively high degree of legitimacy in the eyes of most of its citizens. American political and economic institutions are generally strong. They are not pervasive enough to provide adequate opportunities for some regional and minority groups to satisfy their expectations, but sufficiently pervasive and egalitarian that the most ambitious and talented men—if not women—can pursue the "American dream" with some chance of success. These are conditions that minimize the prospects of revolutionary movements: a majoritarian consensus on the legitimacy of government, and provision of opportunity for men of talent who, if intensely alienated, might otherwise provide revolutionary cadres. But if such a system is open to the majority yet partly closed to a minority, or legitimate for the majority but illegitimate for a minority, the minority is likely to create chronic tumult even though it cannot organize effective revolutionary movements.

Some consequences of patterns of social control, legitimacy, and institutional development for the processes of collective violence are examined more fully below.

SOME CONSEQUENCES OF VIOLENCE

Does violence succeed? The inheritors of the doctrines of Frantz Fanon and "Ché" Guevara assert that if those who use it are sufficiently dedicated, revolution can always be accomplished. Many vehement advocates of civil order and strategists of counterinsurgency hold essentially the same faith: that sufficient use of public violence will deter private violence. This fundamental agreement of "left" and "right" on the effectiveness of force for modifying others' behavior is striking. But to what extent is it supported by theory and by historical evidence?

The two most fundamental human responses to the use of force are to flee or to fight. This assertion rests on rather good psychological and ethological evidence about human and animal aggression. Force threatens and angers men, especially if they believe it to be illegitimate or unjust. Threatened, they will defend themselves if they can, flee if they cannot. Angered, they have an innate disposition to retaliate in kind. Thus men who fear assault attempt to arm themselves, and two-thirds or more of white Americans think that black looters and arsonists should be shot. Governments facing violent protest often regard compromise as evidence of weakness and devote additional resources to counterforce. Yet if a government responds to the threat or use of violence with greater force, its effects in many circumstances are identical with the effects that dictated its actions: its opponents will if they can resort to greater force.

There are only two inherent limitations on such an escalating spiral of force and counterforce: the exhaustion of one side's resources for force, or the attainment by one of the capacity for genocidal victory. There are societal and psychological limitations as well, but they require tacit bonds between opponents: one's acceptance of the ultimate authority of the other, arbitration of the conflict by neutral authority, recognition of mutual interest that makes bargaining possible, or the perception that acquiescence to a powerful opponent will have less harmful consequences than resisting to certain death. In the absence of such bases for cooperation, regimes and their opponents are likely to engage in violent conflict to the limit of their respective abilities.[8]

To the extent that this argument is accurate, it suggests one kind of circumstance in which violence succeeds: that in which one group so overpowers its opponents that they have no choice short of death but to desist. When they do resist to the death, the result is a Carthaginian peace. History records many instances of successful uses of overpowering force. Not surprisingly, the list of successful governmental uses of force against opponents is much longer than the list of dissident successes against government, because most governments have much greater capacities for force, provided they keep the loyalty of their generals and soldiers. Some dissident successes discussed in this volume include the French, American, Nazi, and Cuban Revolutions. Some governmental successes include, in Britain, the suppression of the violent phases of the Luddite and Chartist movements in the 19th century; in Venezuela the Betancourt regime's elimination of revolutionary terrorism; in the United States the North's victory in the Civil War, and the quelling of riots and local rebellions, from the Whiskey Rebellion of 1794 to the ghetto riots of the 1960s.

Governmental uses of force are likely to be successful in quelling specific outbreaks of private violence except in those rare circumstances when the balance of force favors its opponents, or the military defects. But the historical evidence also suggests that governmental violence often succeeds only in the short run. The government of Imperial Russia quelled the revolution of 1905, but in doing so intensified the hostilities of its opponents, who mounted a successful revolution 12

---

[8] This discussion is drawn from arguments and evidence in Ted Robert Gurr, *Why Men Rebel* (Princeton: Princeton University Press, 1969), ch. 8. The survey datum is from Hazel Erskine, "The Polls: Demonstrations and Race Riots," *Public Opinion Quarterly* (Winter 1967–1968), 655–677.

years later, after the government was weakened by a protracted and unsuccessful war. The North "won" the Civil War, but in its very triumph created hostilities that contributed to one of the greatest and most successful waves of vigilante violence in our history. The 17,000 Klansmen of the South today are neither peaceable nor content with the outcome of the "War of Northern Aggression." [9] State or federal troops have been dispatched to quell violent or near-violent labor conflict in more than 160 recorded instances in American history; they were immediately successful in almost every case yet did not significantly deter subsequent labor violence.

The long-range effectiveness of governmental force in maintaining civil peace seems to depend on three conditions identified by the papers in this volume: public belief that governmental use of force is legitimate, consistent use of that force, and remedial action for the grievances that give rise to private violence. The decline of violent working-class protest in 19th-century England was predicated on an almost universal popular acceptance of the legitimacy of the government, accompanied by the development of an effective police system—whose popular acceptance was enhanced by its minimal reliance on violence—and by gradual resolution of working-class grievances. The Cuban case was quite the opposite: the governmental response to private violence was terroristic, inconsistent public violence that alienated most Cubans from the Batista regime, with no significant attempts to reduce the grievances, mostly political, that gave rise to rebellion.

We have assumed that private violence is "successful" in those extreme cases in which a government capitulates in the face of the superiority of its opponents. This is not the only or necessarily the best criterion of "success," though. A better criterion is the extent to which the grievances that give rise to collective protest and violence are resolved. Even revolutionary victories do not necessarily lead to complete success in these terms. The American Revolution returned effective political control to the hands of the colonists, but eventually led to an expansion of state and federal authority that diminished local autonomy to the point that new rebellions broke out in many frontier areas over essentially the same kinds of grievances that had caused the revolution. The Bolshevik revolution ended Russia's participation in World War I, which was perhaps the greatest immediate grievance of the Russian people, and in the long run brought great economic and social benefits; but the contingent costs of the subsequent civil war, famine, and totalitarian political control were enormous. The middle-class political discontents that fueled the Cuban revolutionary movement, far from being remedied, were intensified when the revolutionary leaders used their power to effect a basic socioeconomic reconstruction of society that favored themselves and the rural working classes.

If revolutionary victory is unlikely in the modern state, and uncertain of resolving the grievances that give rise to revolutionary movements, are there any circumstances in which less intensive private violence is successful? We said above that the legitimacy of governmental force is one of the determinants of its effectiveness. The same principle applies to private violence: It can succeed when it is widely regarded as legitimate. The vigilante movements of the American frontier had widespread public support as a means for establishing order in the

---

[9] On Klan membership in 1967, see U.S. Congress, House Un-American Activities Committee, *The Present-Day Ku Klux Klan Movement* (Washington, D.C.: Government Printing Office, 1967), p. 62.

absence of adequate law enforcement agencies, and were generally successful. The Ku Klux Klan of the Reconstruction era similarly had the sympathy of most white Southerners and was largely effective in reestablishing and maintaining the prewar social and political status quo. The chronicles of American labor violence, however, suggest that violence was almost always ineffective for the workers involved. In a very few instances there was popular and state governmental support for the grievances of workers that had led to violent confrontations with employers, and in several of these cases state authority was used to impose solutions that favored the workers. But in the great majority of cases the public and officials did not accept the legitimacy of labor demands, and the more violent was conflict, the more disastrous were the consequences for the workers who took part. Union organizations involved in violent conflict seldom gained recognition, their supporters were harassed and often lost their jobs, and tens of thousands of workers and their families were forcibly deported from their homes and communities.

The same principle applies, with two qualifications, to peaceful public protest. If demonstrations are regarded as a legitimate way to express grievances, and if the grievances themselves are widely held to be justified, protest is likely to have positive effects. One of the qualifications is that if public opinion is neutral on an issue, protest demonstrations can have favorable effects. This appears to have been an initial consequence of the civil-rights demonstrations of the early 1960s in the North. If public opinion is negative, however, demonstrations are likely to exacerbate popular hostility. During World War I, for example, pacifist demonstrators were repeatedly attacked, beaten, and in some cases lynched, with widespread public approval and sometimes official sanction. Contemporary civil-rights demonstrations and activities in the South and in some northern cities have attracted similar responses.

The second qualification is that when violence occurs during protest activities, it is rather likely to alienate groups that are not fundamentally in sympathy with the protesters. We mentioned above the unfavorable consequences of labor violence for unions and their members, despite the fact that violence was more often initiated by employers than by workers. In the long run, federally enforced recognition and bargaining procedures were established, but this occurred only after labor violence had passed its climacteric, and moreover in circumstances in which no union leaders advocated violence. In England, comparably, basic political reforms were implemented not in direct response to Chartist protest, but long after its violent phase had passed.

The evidence supports one basic principle: Force and violence can be successful techniques of social control and persuasion when they have extensive popular support. If they do not, their advocacy and use are ultimately self-destructive, either as techniques of government or of opposition. The historical and contemporary evidence of the United States suggests that popular support tends to sanction violence in support of the status quo: the use of public violence to maintain public order, the use of private violence to maintain popular conceptions of social order when government cannot or will not. If these assertions are true—and not much evidence contradicts them—the prolonged use of force or violence to advance the interests of any segmental group may impede and quite possibly preclude reform. This conclusion should not be taken as an ethical judgment, despite its apparent correspondence with the "establishmentarian" viewpoint. It represents a fundamental trait of American and probably all mankind's character, one which is ignored by advocates of any political orientation at the risk of broken hopes, institutions, and lives.

To draw this conclusion is not to indict public force or all private violence as absolute social evils. In brief and obvious defense of public force, reforms cannot be made if order is wholly lacking, and reforms will not be made if those who have the means to make them feel their security constantly in jeopardy. And as for private violence, though it may bring out the worst in both its practitioners and its victims, it need not do so. Collective violence is after all a symptom of social malaise. It can be so regarded and the malaise treated as such, provided public-spirited men diagnose it correctly and have the will and means to work for a cure rather than to retaliate out of anger. Americans may be quick to self-righteous anger, but they also have retained some of the English genius for accommodation. Grudgingly and with much tumult, the dominant groups in American society have moved over enough to give the immigrant, the worker, the suffragette better—not the best—seats at the American feast of freedom and plenty. Many of them think the feast is bounteous enough for the dissatisfied students, the poor, the Indians, the blacks. Whether there is a place for the young militants who think the feast has gone rotten, no historical or comparative evidence we know of can answer, because absolute, revolutionary alienation from society has been very rare in the American past and no less rare in other pluralistic and abundant nations.

SOME ALTERNATIVES TO VIOLENCE

Political leaders faced with outbreaks or threats of collective violence can respond in the two general ways that we discussed above: they can strengthen systems of forceful social control, or they can exert public effort and encourage private efforts to alleviate conditions leading to discontent. Primary reliance on force has indeterminate outcomes at best. If popularly supported, public force will contain specific outbreaks of private violence, but is unlikely to prevent their recurrence. At worst, public force will so alienate a people that terrorist and revolutionary movements will arise to challenge and ultimately overthrow the regime. The teaching of comparative studies is that governments must be cautious in their reliance on force to maintain order, and consistent in the exercise of the modicum of force they choose to use. These are policies that require both appropriate leadership and well-trained, highly disciplined, and loyal military and police forces.

The effort to eliminate the conditions that lead to collective violence may tax the resources of a society, but it poses less serious problems than increased resort to force. American labor violence has been mitigated in the past 25 years partly by growing prosperity, but more consequentially because employers now have almost universally recognized unions and will negotiate wage issues and other grievances with them rather than retaliate against them. The movement toward recognition and negotiation was strongly reinforced when workers in most occupations were guaranteed the right to organize and bargain collectively in the National Labor Relations Act of 1935. Taft and Ross judge the act to have been effective not just because it established procedures but because of the concerted effort to enforce them by the National Labor Relations Board and the willingness of both employers and unions to recognize the Board's authority. Their willingness may be a testimony also to their own and public dismay at the destructiveness of earlier conflicts. It is worth emphasizing that in this situation the long-range consequences of conciliatory response was a decrease not increase in violent conflict. In fact, violence was chronic so long as union recognition was denied. The outcome suggests the inadequacy of arguments that concessions necessarily breed greater violence.

The history of English working-class protest supports these interpretations. In the 19th century, when England was transformed by an industrial revolution in which a highly competitive, laissez faire market economy disrupted traditional employment patterns and led to sweatshop conditions for many urban workers, violent public protest then became chronic. Several conditions averted to what many Englishmen then feared as a threat of working-class revolt. One was economic growth itself, which led to a significant improvement in the standard of living of urban workers and to hopeful prospects shared by all classes. A second was the acceptance by upper-class political leaders of demands for political reform, and acceptance dictated by both principle and practicality that led to the enfranchisement and assimilation of the working classes into the English body politic. A third was a trend toward grudging toleration of, and ultimately the acceptance and encouragement of, working-class organization. Recognition of the right of workers to organize and bargain led to a flourishing not only of unions but of self-help organizations, cooperatives, and religious and educational groups, all of which together provided British workers with means to work toward the resolution of their discontents.

There were and are characteristics of English society that had no direct American parallels. Expectations of English workers were less high than those of ambitious immigrants to the United States. The English class structure, though more stratified and complex than the American, was generally accepted by all classes, seldom directly challenged. The laissez faire sentiments of British employers were tempered by an acceptance of civic responsibilities that developed more quickly than it did in the United States, and as one consequence English labor violence never reached the intensity that it did in the United States. Working-class demands for political reform were predicated on the common assumption that governments could be changed and the power of the state used to ameliorate the economic grievances of workers. Though the parallels are not exact, the English experience seems to suggest some general lessons for the contemporary United States: civil peace was established through a judicious, perhaps fortuitous, combination of governmental and political reform, and institutional development among the aggrieved classes of society.

Intensely discontented men are not will-less pawns in a game of social chess. They also have alternatives, of which violence is usually the last, the most desperate, and in most circumstances least likely of success. Peaceful protest, conducted publicly and through conventional political channels, is a traditional American option. As one of the world's most pluralistic societies, we have repeatedly albeit reluctantly accommodated ourselves to discontented groups using interest and pressure-group tactics within the political process as a means of leverage for change. But it also is an American characteristic to resist demonstrative demands, however legal and peaceful, if they seem to challenge our basic beliefs and personal positions. Public protest in the United States is a slow and unwieldy instrument of social change that sometimes inspires more obdurate resistance than favorable change.[10]

Another kind of group response to intense stresses and discontents is called "defensive adaptation" by Bernard Siegel. It is essentially an inward-turning, nonviolent response motivated by a desire to build and maintain a group's cultural integrity in the face of hostile pressures. The defensive group is characterized by centralization of authority; attempts to set the group apart by emphasizing symbols of group identity; and minimization of members' contacts with other groups. It is an especially common reaction among ethnic and religious groups whose members see their social environments as permanently hostile, depreciating, and powerful. Such adaptations are apparent, for example, among some Pueblo Indians, Black Muslims, and Amish, and many minority groups in other nations. This kind of defensive withdrawal may lead to violence when outside groups press too closely in on the defensive group, but it is typically a response that minimizes violent conflict. Although the defensive group provides its members some, essentially social and psychological, satisfactions, it seldom can provide them with substantial economic benefits or political means by which they can promote their causes vis-à-vis hostile external groups.

A third general kind of response is the development of discontented groups of positive, socially integrative means for the satisfaction of their members' unsatisfied expectations. This response has characterized most discontented groups throughout Western history. In England, social protest was institutionalized through the trade unions, cooperative societies, and other self-help activities. In continental Europe, the discontent of the urban workers and petit bourgeoisie led to the organization of fraternal societies, unions, and political parties, which provided some intrinsic satisfactions for their members and which could channel demands more or less effectively to employers and into the political system. In the United States the chronic local uprisings of the late-18th, the 19th, and the early-20th century—such as the Shay, Whiskey, Dorr, and Green Corn Rebellions—have been largely superseded by organized, conventional political manifestations of local and regional interests. Labor violence similarly declined in the United States and England once trade unions were organized and recognized.

The contemporary efforts of black Americans to develop effective community organizations, and their demands for greater control of community affairs, seem to be squarely in this tradition. So are demands of student protesters for greater participation in university affairs, attempts of white urban citizens to create new neighborhood organizations, and the impulse of middle-class Americans to move to the suburbs where they can exercise greater control over the local government.

The initial effects of the organization of functional and community groups for self-help may be increased conflict, especially if the economic and political establishments attempt to subvert their efforts. But if these new organizations receive public and private cooperation and sufficient resources to carry out their activities, the prospects for violence are likely to be reduced. The social costs of this kind of group response seem much less than those of public and private violence. The human benefits are likely to be far greater than those attained through private violence or defensive withdrawal. . . .

[10] Kenneth E. Boulding makes the same point in a discussion of the possible consequences of antiwar protest, in "Reflections on Protest," *Bulletin of the Atom Scientists*, 21 (October 1965), 18–20.

39
Disruptive Tactics

Harry Specht

There is both confusion and uncertainty about the use of disruptive tactics to bring about planned change in American communities. The confusion, in part, grows out of a major problem the United States faces today—violence, its causes and resolution. Indeed, it is the major problem throughout the world, which we have succeeded so little in dealing with. In addition, in the social sciences as in social work there is neither extensive knowledge about the dynamics of either disruption or violence nor systematic processes the practitioner can use to deal with them.[1]

The idea of government by and through elected officials is being seriously questioned on all sides. Many have lost confidence in the viability of established democratic political structures—students and other young people, minority groups, and the political left. But today, the ubiquity of violence and legal behavior in American communities is only a reflection of the violence and lawless behavior supported by many of the country's leaders. Thus, the mayor of a large city castigated his police force for not "shooting to kill or to maim" young arsonists and looters; the governor of a large state called rioters "mad dogs"; and the former President lost his credibility when the deception, corruption, and violence of the country's foreign policy became evident.

Reprinted with permission of the author and the National Association of Social Workers, from *Social Work*, 14, no. 2 (April 1969), pp. 5–15.

[1] Raymond C. Mack, "Components of Social Conflict," *Social Problems*, 12, no. 4 (Spring 1965), 388–397.

It seems that Fanon's belief in the cleansing force of violence and the need to use violence as an agent of change is gaining wide support as many white families buy guns to defend themselves against blacks, black action groups arm to protect themselves against the police, and the police increase their arsenals to defend the cities against black insurgents. It is as though the whole country is caught by Fanon's ideas:

> For if the last shall be first, . . . this will only come to pass after a murderous and decisive struggle between the two protagonists. That affirmed intention . . . can only triumph if we use all means to turn the scales, including, of course, that of violence.[2]

It is only in a climate of unreason that this mixture of "blood and anger," which can lead to insurrection, becomes thoroughly confused with legitimate dissent and political radicalism. We should not talk of crime in the streets or violence on the campus in shocked dismay when the larger part of the nation's resources are being used to fashion this country into the world's greatest instrument of violence.

A discussion of the moral and ethical, as well as the programmatic, consequences of disruptive tactics used in efforts at planned change presupposes the existence of some organized system of available tactical choices. This paper will first distinguish different kinds of tactics that constitute the spectrum of choices and then discuss disruptive tactics in detail. This order is necessary if the use of disruptive tactics is to be understood as a consciously planned choice made on the basis of moral and ethical considerations as well as strategic objectives. The author uses "strategy" to refer to an over-all plan of action and "tactics" to indicate the more specific actions of moving and directing resources to attain goals. Strategy requires a long-term plan of action based on some theory of cause and effect, while tactics are the somewhat more constant methods of action.

WHY DISRUPTION?

What is it about issues that makes them subject to one or another set of tactics? Warren describes the association between different modes of intervention and different responses to issues.[3] (Modes of intervention are categories of tactics.) The range of responses to issues he describes are the following: (1) *issue consensus*, when there is a high possibility of agreement between the action and target system; (2) *issue difference*, when for one reason or another the parties are not in complete agreement but there is a possibility of agreement; and (3) *issue dissensus*, when there is no agreement between the parties. Consensus is associated with collaborative modes of intervention; difference with campaigns of a competitive, persuasive, or bargaining nature; and dissensus with contests in which there is a high degree of conflict between the parties. (Conflict may be considered as an element in all modes of intervention to some degree.) In this paper, disruptive and contest tactics will be associated with dissensus.

The question still remains: Why these responses? The response to an issue,

---

[2] Frantz Fanon, *The Wretched of the Earth* (New York: Grove Press, 1963), p. 37.
[3] Roland L. Warren, *Types of Purposive Social Change at the Community Level*, University Papers in Social Welfare, No. 11 (Waltham, Mass.: Florence Heller Graduate School for Advanced Studies in Social Welfare, Brandeis University, 1965).

whether rational or not, indicates how the issue is *perceived* by the different parties; perception determines response. By extending Warren's typology, the associations among different perceptions of change, responses to the change, and the kinds of intervention these responses command may be suggested. Table 1 combines these elements but adds violence as a fourth mode of intervention based on a perception of change that aims at "reconstruction of the entire system" to which the response is "insurrection."

PERCEPTIONS, RESPONSES, INTERVENTIONS

Collaboration is based on consensual responses to planned changes that are perceived as a rearrangement of resources. For example, the parties to the change are in essential agreement about the co-ordination or reorganization of services. No one thinks they will lose a great deal in the change. Until only recently, there had been a rather narrow concentration on this kind of intervention in social work, based on work with homogeneous and elitist types of community action systems. For the most part, the action system (that undertaking change) and the target system (that being changed) are identical, and the client system (on whose behalf change is sought) is probably not involved at all. The role of the worker is most frequently that of enabler and educator.

Redistribution of resources is a qualitatively different perception of a change. One of the parties expects he will end up with more or less of something (money, facilities, authority) but, because they perceive the need to remain within the rules of the game—the institutionalized system of competition—the contending parties utilize campaign tactics to persuade, negotiate, bargain, and, eventually, compromise and agree. The action, target, and client systems might be expected to appear as separate entities, with the action system serving as mediator or arbitrator between the other two. The role of the professional change agent is most likely to be that of advocate.

Contest or disruption is generated by a challenge to existing status relationships and this view of change creates an entirely different type of discourse than any of the others mentioned. Contest or disruption is rooted in the competition for power in human relations. Status relationships refer to the social arrangements (the institutionalized system) by which promises, expectations, rights, and responsibilities are awarded, and the social arrangements always give more to some than to others. A threat to the system of relationships in which some people have power over others is the basis for this kind of response whether it involves parents and children, welfare workers and clients, students and teachers, or blacks and whites. None surrenders power voluntarily. The ability to perpetuate these patterns of varied and complex relationships long after the historical conditions that gave rise to them cease to exist is a human quality but also creates conflict.

When community issues are perceived by one group as eliminating or diminishing its power over others, the response will be dissensus; contest and disruption, the result. "To carve out a place for itself in the politico-social order, a new group may have to fight for a reorientation of many of the values of the old order" is the way Key states this proposition.[4] In these kinds of change efforts, the action and target systems are distinctly separate and the client system is

[4] V. O. Key, Jr., *Politics, Parties and Pressure Groups* (5th ed.; New York: Thomas Y. Crowell, 1964), p. 48.

closely aligned or identical with the action system. The role of the community worker is that of partisan or organizer.

A change perceived as intended to overthrow the sovereign power of the state is responded to as insurrection. The mode of intervention associated with it—violence—is not part of the arsenal of tactics available to professional social workers and, therefore, the author will not comment on the relative positions of the action, target, and client systems or the worker's professional role. However, these tactics do pose serious dilemmas for community change agents, which will be discussed in the final section of the paper.

TABLE 1

Change: Perceptions, Responses, and Modes of Intervention

Perception of Change	Response	Mode of Intervention
Rearrangement of resources	Consensus	Collaboration
Redistribution of resources	Difference	Campaign
Change in status relationships	Dissensus	Contest or disruption
Reconstruction of the entire system	Insurrection[a]	Violence

[a] Insurrection is used here because the word "revolution" can only be applied to a successful insurrection.

However, it should be said here that the major overriding objective of community organization is to enable communities to create a strategy of reconciliation, to move from insurrection to contest, to campaign, to collaboration. It is necessary for the professional change agent who utilizes the tactics described in this paper to operate with goals that will, as Cloward puts it, "eventually heal, not further disrupt." [5]

EXAMPLES

The following examples will illustrate the interplay of the three elements that comprise Table 1: perceptions, responses, and modes of intervention.

Objectively, fluoridation should present a good case for collaborative modes of intervention. It is said to be sensible, scientific, and not only inexpensive, but money-saving. Many health officials and community organizers have approached it with exactly that logical frame of mind because superficially fluoridation would appear to be a rather simple rearrangement of resources that calls for an educational mode of intervention. Yet the issue of fluoridation has been the basis for harsh, vindictive social conflicts in hundreds of communities in the United States.[6]

There appear to be two major sets of reasons for the resistance. First, there are those people who question the effectiveness of the proposed change or who fear that fluoride may be poisonous. This type of resistance does yield to collaborative modes of intervention.[7] But the second basis for resistance does not respond to such methods at all. This is resistance based on the belief that fluoridation in-

[5] Richard A. Cloward, "A Strategy of Disruption," *Center Diary*, 16 (January–February 1967), 34.
[6] "Trigger for Community Conflict," entire issue of the *Journal of Social Issues*, 17, no. 4 (October 1961).
[7] Benjamin D. Paul, "Fluoridation and the Social Scientist: A Review," in the above issue, p. 5.

fringes on the rights of individuals, that "compulsory medication" usurps the rights of free men. Green supports this contention with concrete findings. His research indicates that indignation over the *presumed* violation of personal freedom is more fundamental than the danger of poisoning. The fear of poisoning symbolizes a disposition to see fluoridation as an insidious attack by a vague constellation of impersonal social forces bent on usurping the powers and prerogatives of the common citizen, and the root cause of this feeling of being victimized experienced by active opponents of fluoridation is the increasing remoteness and impersonality of the sources of power and influence affecting the daily life of the individual.[8] In short, the issue of fluoridation becomes a contest when it is perceived to be a threat to status.

Another example of the delicate balance between perceptions of change as a redistribution of resources and an alteration in status is provided by Marris and Rein in their analysis of community action programs. They pose this question: If community planners had larger grants of money available to them, would it have been easier for them to move the bureaucracies along the lines of the change they desired? This is their answer:

> If the funding agencies had offered more money, they would . . . have given communities a greater incentive to meet the criteria of concerted action. But they would also have raised the stakes in the competition for control of the project's resources. . . . A marginal addition to the city's resources stood at least a chance of insinuating an influence for change, without intruding a challenge to bureaucratic authority too obvious to overlook.[9]

This suggests that an increase in the amount of resources may convert a perception of change from one of a rearrangement or a redistribution to a change in status.

The civil rights movement seems to have shifted in the last five years from a major focus on the rearrangement and redistribution of resources to a greater concern with change in status. Of course, all along, the demands being made by the movement may have *required* change in status for success, but the movement has increasingly recognized that the power of whites over blacks is the issue, as is pointed out in the following statement by Hamilton:

> While there are masses of poor, powerless whites, they do not *perceive* [italics added] their condition as a result of deliberate policy. . . . Many blacks do have such a view.[10]

Memphis, Tennessee, in the events preceding the assassination of Martin Luther King, was not confronting a simple question of the redistribution of resources as in an ordinary labor dispute. That the striking workers recognized the question of status was quite evident in their signs that read: "I Am a Man!" for indeed it was their manhood they perceived to be at stake. That the mayor of Memphis saw it the same way is clear from his statement that he would be damned if he would be the first southern mayor to bargain collectively with a black union.

---

[8] Paul, "Fluoridation and the Social Scientist," p. 7.
[9] Peter Marris and Martin Rein, *Dilemmas of Social Reform* (New York: Atherton Press, 1967), p. 158.
[10] Charles Hamilton, "The Meaning of Black Power," reprinted from the *New York Times* in the *San Francisco Chronicle*, "This World," April 21, 1968, p. 25.

TACTICS

Modes of intervention comprise sets of tactics. While the purpose of this paper is to discuss disruptive tactics, the idea that there is a dynamic relationship between tactics used for different modes of intervention is helpful in understanding their use. Table 2 suggests what this relationship may be.

TABLE 2

The Relationship between Tactics and Modes of Intervention

Mode of Intervention	Tactics
Collaboration	Joint action Co-operation Education
Campaign	Compromise Arbitration Negotiation Bargaining Mild coercion
Contest or disruption	Clash of position within accepted social norms Violation of normative behavior (manners) Violation of legal norms
Violence	Deliberate attempts to harm Guerilla warfare Deliberate attempts to take over government by force

These behaviors constitute a continuum of interventive modes rather than discrete actions. A strategy for change might utilize tactics from one or more modes of intervention simultaneously, depending on the goals of the action system and the organizational context within which it operates.[11] For example, in *A Manual for Direct Action*, a handbook of action for civil rights and other nonviolent protests, the authors instruct organizers in the use of bargaining and educational tactics along with disruptive tactics, and sometimes all three are directed at the same system.

> Poor negotiation . . . can bring a return to open conflict. . . . [In work with the target system] describe the results of change as *less* threatening than the opponents suppose, and . . . describe the results of not changing . . . as *more* threatening than . . . change. . . . Bring illustrations of successes in other places.[12]

What is meant by disruptive tactics? They are used by one or both parties to a contest. Their purpose has been described as preventing an opponent from continuing to operate, to neutralize, injure, or eliminate him.[13] Warren describes tac-

---

[11] For an interesting discussion of the relationship between these variables *see* Martin Rein and Robert Morris, "Goals, Structures, and Strategies for Community Change," in Mayer N. Zald (ed.), *Social Welfare Institutions* (New York: Wiley, 1965), pp. 367–382.

[12] Martin Oppenheimer and George Lakey, *A Manual for Direct Action* (Chicago: Quadrangle Books, 1964), p. 24. An interesting related question that cannot be considered in this paper is how the structure of an action system is related to these modes of intervention. All action systems expand and contract throughout their history and one might predict the relationship between organizational structure and tactical choices. For example, movement to insurrection would be accompanied by narrowing the action system and movement from campaign to collaboration by its expansion.

[13] Lewis Coser, *The Functions of Social Conflict* (New York: Free Press, 1956), p. 8.

tics as "processes where deliberate harmful activity is directed toward an opposing party."[14] However, in the strategic viewpoint outlined in this paper, disruptive tactics are considered those that aim in different ways to move the other party toward some acceptable reconciliation. The term "disruptive" seems most appropriate for these tactics because their major objective is to *prevent* the target system from continuing to operate as usual, i.e., to disrupt, but *not* to injure, harm, or destroy. The latter are the goals of the tactics of violence.

DISRUPTIVE TACTICS

Clash of Position

This tactic is used within accepted social norms and essentially involves such actions as debate, legal disputes, written statements of intent, or public speeches. The objective of this tactic is to bring the issue to the attention of the public, usually in such a way as to mobilize sympathy from the larger community as well as to stir discontent among the "oppressed."

The way in which Gandhi's philosophy of nonviolence has been popularized in the United States often causes Americans to overlook many of the subtle meanings of the elaborate system Gandhi developed, which he called *satyagraha* (search for truth). *Satyagraha* is a complicated and difficult term to define because it embraces both a philosophy of life as well as a methodology of social action and, therefore, is certainly a more developed system than the one described in this paper. It is a refined technique for social and political change that transcends the simple concepts of civil disobedience, nonviolence, or disruptive behavior.

In the Gandhian view, clash of position comes at quite an advanced stage in dealing with an issue, and a number of other steps are required before a *satyagrahi* makes use of this tactic, such as negotiation, arbitration, reasoning, and other methods designed to win over the opponent. Civil disobedience is, of course, one of the final stages of this action system.[15]

Oglesby and Shaull, in analyzing the process by which the oppressed become revolutionaries, describe a clash of position as the tactic of "mass-based secular prayer." This appeal to a higher power, they say, sometimes results in change. More often, it shows the victim-petitioner that change is more difficult to achieve than he imagined, and this may become "the spiritual low point of the emergent revolutionary's education," for he learns that "the enemy is not a few men, but a whole system."[16]

Violation of Normative Behavior

This tactic refers to actions that might be viewed as a moving away from what may be deemed good manners and involves activities like marches, demonstrations, boycotts, protests, vigils (extended demonstrations), rent strikes, dropping out, haunting (following one's opponent for long periods), renouncing honors,

[14] Warren, *Types of Purposive Social Change*, p. 29.
[15] Joan V. Bondurant, *Conquest of Violence* (Berkeley: University of California Press, 1965), pp. 40–41.
[16] Carl Oglesby and Richard Shaull, *Containment and Change* (New York: Macmillan, 1967), p. 145.

hartals (having large masses of people stay at home, a sort of spiritual variation of a general strike), fasts, and interjection (having large masses of people congregate in an area, as, for example, 10,000 Japanese did in 1956 to prevent successfully the use of the site for a U.S. Air Force base). The objectives of these actions are the same as those listed under the heading "clash of position" as well as to generate conscience, discomfort, and guilt in the oppressors and an *esprit de corps* among the oppressed.

This tactic, more than any others, demonstrates the effects of changing social and legal definitions of behavior. Rent strikes and boycotts, for example, lie in a gray area between violation of normative behavior and violation of law. The increased number of protests by citizens over the last decade has elevated demonstrations and marches to a tactic that is more like a clash of position than anything else. One can hardly announce a grievance today without a public demonstration of some sort. Furthermore, the tactic of choice is, to some degree, specific to the group. For example, only those who have been included in society can drop out; that tactic is available to middle-class college students, not to the hard-core unemployed of the ghetto. Fasting, a technique used with enormous success by Gandhi, is reserved for situations in which there is a rather special relationship of mutual respect between the opposing parties.

Moreover, tactics are *patterned* group behaviors. Whether used consciously or not, the styles of action in different action systems are based on numerous group and organizational variables, such as social class, ideology, resources, and values.

Violation of Legal Norms

This tactic includes techniques like civil disobedience and nonco-operation, tax refusal, sit-ins, draft resistance, and other violations of law. Carried to its final stages in *satyagraha*, this tactic includes usurping the functions of government and setting up a parallel government. The objectives of this tactic include all those listed for the other types of disruptive tactics and, in addition, they aim to demonstrate that people feel strongly enough about an issue to expose themselves to the danger of punishment by legal authorities for violating the law.

Civil disobedience presupposes an absence of, or inadequacy in, established law that morally justifies violation of it. The difficult moral question with which action systems must deal is whether they can find it morally correct to disobey an unjust law to protest its injustice or a morally just law to protest another injustice. Based on a philosophical anarchism and the concept of "natural rights," these acts have quite an honorable tradition in American life—a tradition that recognizes that the legal system is and always will be imperfect; the majority, whose wishes the laws (at least theoretically) are supposed to reflect, is itself imperfect; and all moral values have not been and never will be enacted into law.[17]

There are specific requirements of actions classified as nonviolent civil disobedience. They are only utilized after all other remedies have been exhausted and are used openly and selflessly. (That is, the actions have a public character and are carried out with public explanations of the reasons for the action in the name of some higher morality.) Furthermore, they are utilized with an awareness of the

---

[17] Vernon Louis Parrington, *Romantic Revolution in America, 1800–1860*, "Main Currents in American Thought" (New York: Harcourt Brace Jovanovich, 1930), pp. 271–460.

consequences for the participants.[18] These tactics are exemplified by the nonviolent resistance to police enforcement of laws. Indeed, the major tenet of those who have committed themselves to these actions expresses a profound faith in the value of the existing legal-political system and it is the absence of this faith that characterizes changes perceived as insurrection. While rebellion may claim moral justification, unlike civil disobedience its aim is to overthrow the social order, not to change and reconcile. This separation between the legality and the morality of the social order was precisely the distinction Socrates made in recognizing the right of his judges to condemn him to death.

OBJECTIVES AND EFFECTIVENESS

It should be noted that the direction of issues can be from consensus to violence or the reverse, but, as Simmel pointed out in his still relevant seminal work on conflict written in the early 1900s, "the transitions from war to peace constitute a more serious problem than does the reverse." [19] Certainly, the use of disruptive tactics has the potential for great harm to the group in whose interests they are used. It allows the oppressor to put increasingly fewer limits on himself, freeing him to act disruptively or violently when he might otherwise have been constrained to avoid such behavior. For example, the police in many cities have attacked demonstrators with obvious relish when they used what the police perceived to be tactics of violence, as was the case in the antidraft demonstrations of October 1967 when some student groups attempted to shut down draft centers by violent means. In just this way, Mayor Daley attempted to justify the attacks on demonstrators by the Chicago police during the 1968 Democratic Convention.

Violent tactics can provide the other party with the opportunity to "change the subject," so that the public's concern switches from the issue to the illegal behavior of the demonstrators. Both King and Gandhi always consciously sought to use nonviolent techniques as a rein on the violence of the established ruling class —"to keep the conversation open and the switchblade closed" [20]—and the correctness of their views is borne out by the fact that there were fewer deaths in ten years of nonviolent direct action in the South than in ten days of northern riots.

Stinchcombe asserts that the resort to violent tactics is related to the strengths of social norms governing the use of violence in society. In particular, his comments point up that nonviolent methods are viable only as long as civil authorities continue to accept the responsibility for carefully controlling their own use of violence in dealing with civil disputes. He says:

> The crucial question . . . about the violent organizations of a society [i.e., the police and the army] is how far their entry into politics is governed by an understood set of limiting norms. For if the army and police enter the conflict unconditionally on one or another side of the conflict, supplying a ruling group or a revolutionary group with unlimited power to dispose of its enemies, then competition for place among organizations tends to become unlimited. Because the opposition to currently ruling powers is equally pun-

---

[18] John de J. Pemberton, Jr., "Is There a Moral Right to Violate the Law?" *Social Welfare Forum, 1965* (New York: Columbia University Press, 1965), pp. 194–195.
[19] Georg Simmel, "On Conflict," in Talcott Parsons (ed.), *Theories of Society* (New York: Free Press, 1961), p. 1325.
[20] Oglesby and Shaull, *Containment and Change*, p. 149.

ished, whether it uses speech or riot, opponents are likely to choose the most effective means . . . of combatting government terror [which] are not always peaceful. And a government or revolutionary group supported by the army and police in an unlimited fashion is likely to undertake to root out its opposition, rather than to limit the opposition to approved means of conflict.[21]

To use disruptive tactics, several questions must be considered by the action system: Is the stress that stimulated the use of these tactics recognizable to the opponent? Is there support and reassurance to the opponent whose change is desired that the extent of change is not unlimited? Have encounters opened or closed communication between contending parties? Has there been an adequate process of inquiry and exploration prior to the disruption? In the Gandhian use of disruptive techniques, the major question asked of the *satyagrahi* is whether he had engaged the opponent in a manner designed to transform the complexity of relationships so that new patterns may emerge.[22] When all these attempts fail, violent tactics become a likely alternative.

TACTICS OF VIOLENCE

Insurrection differs from disruption both in the tactics used and the ends sought. It is not a call to resist the immoral acts of legitimate authority, but the withdrawal of legitimacy from the sovereign authority. It ties up the conflict over status relationships with something much larger, whereby the entire system is viewed as impossible to reform.

> The leap into revolution leaves "solutions" behind because it has collapsed and wholly redefined the "problems" to which they referred. The rebel is an incorrigible absolutist who makes the one grand claim that the entire system is in error.[23]

The tactics of violence are not available for use by the professional social reformer for several reasons. Quite practically, he cannot practice social work if he is a fugitive from justice, in jail, or dead. But, more important, a professional receives his sanction for practice from the larger society he serves and its legal and political systems. Morally, he may reach the conclusion that the framework is no longer worthy of legitimacy, and it is certainly difficult to argue that the moral basis for that choice does not exist in today's society. But it should be clear that this is the choice that must be made, and the professional should not be confused about what he is undertaking when he commits himself to violence.

This confusion is often encountered among students who think their protest actions should lead to a reversal of policy even if their behavior is violent. But to be a revolutionary requires that one believe that policy *cannot* be changed without replacing the government by force.

The social worker's authority stems from his knowledge, values, skills, and sanction to deal with social welfare institutions and to use social work methods. Although he may give his personal commitment to rebellion, it is improper to use his authority to give legitimacy to the destruction of institutions. This is when the

---

[21] Arthur L. Stinchcombe, "Social Structures and Organizations," in James G. March (ed.), *Handbook of Organizations* (Chicago: Rand McNally Co., 1965), p. 97.
[22] Bondurant, *Conquest of Violence*, p. viii.
[23] Oglesby and Shaull, *Containment and Change*, p. 146.

larger strategy that directs a professional's work is especially important because it forces him to test his choice of a specific tactic in relation to its historical perspective. Is the choice of tactics dictated by his view of the long-range struggle and within a professed area of competence? Disruption used without some strategy for change is unlikely to achieve anything but escalation to violence; it certainly will not provide a means for changing the structure of American society.

The task of the intellectual leaders of any community undertaking is to help community action systems maintain freshness and vigor in moving toward goals by elucidating the legal, political, and historical relationships that underlie their efforts.[24] Invariably, revolutionary movements develop with strong, narrow ideologies that monopolize the conduct of the struggle over issues and bind the rebels in a united contempt for all other solutions. Social workers should expect neither support nor quarter from revolutionary groups because, as a rule, they consider others who are struggling on the same side to be more dangerous than the oppressor since they must disallow any who would offer an appealing alternative. They represent the other side of oppression, "killing their way to power." [25] They believe, with Fanon, that "no gentleness can efface the marks of violence; only violence itself can destroy them." [26]

The question for the professional is whether his objective is to enable people to make choices or to assert *his* choice and cast his lot with those who have arrived at *the* solution. Social work operates in a framework of democratic decision-making, and if one decides that the framework is no longer viable, then there is no profession of social work to be practiced.

DILEMMA

As long as this country participates in unjust wars of conquest and does not provide the resources needed to deal with domestic crises of racism, poverty, and other social injustices, all professionals will face the dilemma of either working through institutions they believe may be unable to overcome social rot or participating in their destruction. But that awful choice should be made with clarity about the consequences for professional status as well as the objectives to be served.

Guevara was extremely clear about the preconditions for choosing revolutionary tactics:

> It must always be kept in mind that there is a necessary minimum without which the establishment and consolidation of the first center . . . [of guerrilla warfare] is not practicable. People must see clearly the futility of maintaining the fight for social goals within the framework of civil debate. . . . Where a government has come into power through some form of popular vote, fraudulent or not, and maintains at least an appearance of constitutional legality, the guerrilla outbreak cannot be promoted, since the possibilities of peaceful struggle have not yet been exhausted.[27]

[24] Harry Specht, *Urban Community Development*, Publication No. 111 (Walnut Creek, Calif.: Council of Community Services, 1966), 44.
[25] Robert Pickus, "Civil Disobedience But Not Violence," *Dissent*, 15, no. 1 (January–February 1968), 21.
[26] Fanon, *The Wretched of the Earth*, p. 21.
[27] Ernesto Ché Guevara, *Guerrilla Warfare* (New York: Monthly Review Press, 1961), pp. 15–16.

These clear guides notwithstanding, many young people attempt to impose the strategies of Fanon, Debray, and Guevara on the American society. Given Guevara's preconditions for revolution, these philosophies of social change in the "Third World" can provide vicarious pleasures for American radicals but not realistic action strategies. Moreover, as Lasch warns:

> While violence as a meaningful strategy is tactically premature in the United States, without other strategic perspectives militancy will carry the day by default and is dangerous because it may support the development of an American fascism.[28]

The New Left and student politics should not be dismissed out of hand. Surely they have created a valuable training ground in which a new generation can test its solutions to social and political problems. However, other persons who are committed to radical social change are often caught between two worlds. They have spent much of their lives working to reform the established order and find their perspective inadequate and their strategy ineffective—or at least they are viewed that way by young people. It is like the dialogue between mother and son in a poem by Aimé Césaire:

> THE MOTHER: My race—the human race. My religion—brotherhood.
> THE REBEL: My race: that of the fallen. My religion . . . but it's not you that will show it to me with your disarmament. . . . 'tis I myself, with my rebellion and my poor fists clenched and my wooly head. . . .[29]

CONCLUSION

Perhaps, though, new ways may be found to define the roles of reformer and revolutionary despite their seemingly irreconcilable divergence. For example, Shaull, in coming to grips with this dilemma, suggests that it may be oversimplified. He proposes a "political equivalent" of guerrilla warfare and suggests that greater attention be given to the question of the relationship of those working for radical change and the institutions of the established order. He says: "Service in the framework of a particular institution does not necessarily demand complete subservience to it." [30] In Shaull's view, revolutionaries can contribute to the renewal of institutions by being in but not of these structures, by living as exiles within their own society. Whether this alternative is a viable one or simply Utopian cannot be decided without some exploration but, given the size of this society's institutions and the enormous concentration of power within them, it is certainly an important alternative to consider.

Ultimately, choice of tactics must rest on our beliefs about this society. If we believe it is possible to move the community, we can continue to work for change through its institutions. If it is not possible, then God help us all, for then we must either continue to act in a drama that has lost its purpose or join in the destruction of society. Disruption and violence can contribute to change, but more than that will be required for reconciliation—more than that is required to transform America.

---

[28] Christopher Lasch, "The Trouble With Black Power," *New York Review of Books*, 10, no. 4 (February 29, 1968).
[29] Quoted in Fanon, *The Wretched of the Earth*, p. 86.
[30] Oglesby and Shaull, *Containment and Change*, pp. 196–197.

40
Protest as a Political Resource

Michael Lipsky

The frequent resort to protest activity by relatively powerless groups in recent American politics suggests that protest represents an important aspect of minority group and low income group politics.[1] At the same time that Negro civil rights strategists have recognized the problem of using protest as a meaningful political

From *American Political Science Review* (December 1968), pp. 1144–1158. Reprinted by permission of publisher and author. The author says: This article is an attempt to develop and explore the implications of a conceptual scheme for analyzing protest activity. It is based upon my studies of protest organizations in New York City, Washington, D.C., Chicago, San Francisco, and Mississippi, as well as extensive examination of written accounts of protest among low-income and Negro civil rights groups. I am grateful to Kenneth Dolbeare, Murray Edelman, and Rodney Stiefbold for their insightful comments on an earlier draft. This paper was developed while the author was a Staff Associate of the Institute for Research on Poverty at the University of Wisconsin. I appreciate the assistance obtained during various phases of my research from the Rabinowitz Foundation, the New York State Legislative Internship Program, and the Brookings Institution.

[1] "Relatively powerless groups" may be defined as those groups which, relatively speaking, are lacking in conventional political resources. For the purposes of community studies, Robert Dahl has compiled a useful comprehensive list. See Dahl, "The Analysis of Influence in Local Communities," in Charles R. Adrian (ed.), *Social Science and Community Action* (East Lansing, Michigan, 1960), p. 32. The difficulty in studying

instrument,[2] groups associated with the "war on poverty" have increasingly received publicity for protest activity. Saul Alinsky's Industrial Areas Foundation, for example, continues to receive invitations to help organize low income communities because of its ability to mobilize poor people around the tactic of protest.[3] The riots which dominated urban affairs in the summer of 1967 appear not to have diminished the dependence of some groups on protest as a mode of political activity.

This article provides a theoretical perspective on protest activity as a political resource. The discussion is concentrated on the limitations inherent in protest which occur because of the need of protest leaders to appeal to four constituencies at the same time. As the concept of protest is developed here, it will be argued that protest leaders must nurture and sustain an organization comprised of people with whom they may or may not share common values. They must articulate goals and choose strategies so as to maximize their public exposure through communications media. They must maximize the impact of third parties in the political conflict. Finally, they must try to maximize chances of success among those capable of granting goals. The tensions inherent in manipulating these four constituencies at the same time form the basis of this discussion of protest as a political process. It is intended to place aspects of the civil rights movement in a framework which suggests links between protest organizations and the general political processes in which such organizations operate.

"PROTEST" CONCEPTUALIZED

Protest activity as it has been adopted by elements of the civil rights movement and others has not been studied extensively by social scientists. Some of the most suggestive writings have been done as case studies of protest movements in single southern cities.[4] These works generally lack a framework or theoretical focus which would encourage generalization from the cases. More systematic efforts

---

such groups is that relative powerlessness only becomes apparent under certain conditions. Extremely powerless groups not only lack political resources, but are also characterized by a minimal sense of political efficacy, upon which in part successful political organization depends. For reviews of the literature linking orientations of political efficacy to socioeconomic status, see Robert Lane, *Political Life* (New York, 1959), chap. 16; and Lester Milbrath, *Political Participation* (Chicago, 1965), chap. 5. Further, to the extent that group cohesion is recognized as a necessary requisite for organized political action, then extremely powerless groups, lacking cohesion, will not even appear for observation. Hence the necessity of selecting for intensive study a protest movement where there can be some confidence that observable processes and results can be analyzed. Thus, if one conceives of a continuum on which political groups are placed according to their relative command of resources, the focus of this essay is on those groups which are near, but not at, the pole of powerlessness.

[2] See, e.g., Bayard Rustin, "From Protest to Politics: The Future of the Civil Rights Movement," *Commentary* (February 1965), 25–31; and Stokely Carmichael, "Toward Black Liberation," *The Massachusetts Review* (Autumn 1966).

[3] On Alinsky's philosophy of community organization, see his *Reveille for Radicals* (Chicago, 1945); and Charles Silberman, *Crisis in Black and White* (New York, 1964), chap. 10.

[4] See, e.g., Jack L. Walker, "Protest and Negotiation: A Case Study of Negro Leadership in Atlanta, Georgia," *Midwest Journal of Political Science*, 7 (May 1963), 99–124; Jack L. Walker, *Sit-Ins in Atlanta: A Study in the Negro Protest*, Eagleton Institute Case Studies, No. 34 (New York, 1964); John Ehle, *The Free Men* (New York, 1965)

have been attempted in approaching the dynamics of biracial committees in the South,[5] and comprehensively assessing the efficacy of Negro political involvement in Durham, N.C. and Philadelphia, Pa.[6] In their excellent assessment of Negro politics in the South, Matthews and Prothro have presented a thorough profile of Southern Negro students and their participation in civil rights activities.[7] Protest is also discussed in passing in recent explorations of the social-psychological dimensions of Negro ghetto politics [8] and the still highly suggestive, although pre-1960s, work on Negro political leadership by James Q. Wilson.[9] These and other less systematic works on contemporary Negro politics,[10] for all of their intuitive insights and valuable documentation, offer no theoretical formulations which encourage conceptualization about the interaction between recent Negro political activity and the political process.

Heretofore the best attempt to place Negro protest activity in a framework which would generate additional insights has been that of James Q. Wilson.[11] Wilson has suggested that protest activity be conceived as a problem of bargaining in which the basic problem is that Negro groups lack political resources to exchange. Wilson called this "the problem of the powerless." [12]

While many of Wilson's insights remain valid, his approach is limited in applicability because it defines protest in terms of mass action or response and as utilizing exclusively negative inducements in the bargaining process. Negative inducements are defined as inducements which are not absolutely preferred but are preferred over alternative possibilities.[13] Yet it might be argued that protest designed to appeal to groups which oppose suffering and exploitation, for example, might be offering positive inducements in bargaining. A few Negro students sitting at a lunch counter might be engaged in what would be called protest, and by their actions might be trying to appeal to other groups in the system with positive inducements. Additionally, Wilson's concentration on Negro civic action, and his exclusive interest in exploring the protest process to explain Negro civic ac-

[Chapel Hill]; Daniel C. Thompson, *The Negro Leadership Class* (Englewood Cliffs, N.J., 1963) [New Orleans]; M. Elaine Burgess, *Negro Leadership in a Southern City* (Chapel Hill, N.C., 1962) [Durham].
[5] Lewis Killian and Charles Grigg, *Racial Crisis in America: Leadership in Conflict* (Englewood Cliffs, N.J., 1964).
[6] William Keech, "The Negro Vote as a Political Resource: The Case of Durham" (unpublished Ph.D. Dissertation, University of Wisconsin, 1966); John H. Strange, "The Negro in Philadelphia Politics 1963–65" (unpublished Ph.D. Dissertation, Princeton University, 1966).
[7] Donald Matthews and James Prothro, *Negroes and the New Southern Politics* (New York, 1966). Considerable insight on these data is provided in John Orbell, "Protest Participation among Southern Negro College Students," *American Political Science Review*, 61 (June 1967), 446–456.
[8] Kenneth Clark, *Dark Ghetto* (New York, 1965).
[9] *Negro Politics* (New York, 1960).
[10] A complete list would be voluminous. See, e.g., Nat Hentoff, *The New Equality* (New York, 1964); Arthur Waskow, *From Race Riot to Sit-in* (New York, 1966).
[11] "The Strategy of Protest: Problems of Negro Civic Action," *Journal of Conflict Resolution*, 3 (September 1961), 291–303. The reader will recognize the author's debt to this highly suggestive article, not least Wilson's recognition of the utility of the bargaining framework for examining protest activity.
[12] "The Strategy of Protest," 291.
[13] "The Strategy of Protest," 291–292.

tion, tend to obscure comparison with protest activity which does not necessarily arise within the Negro community.

Assuming a somewhat different focus, protest activity is defined as a mode of political action oriented toward objection to one or more policies or conditions, characterized by showmanship or display of an unconventional nature, and undertaken to obtain rewards from political or economic systems while working within the systems. The "problem of the powerless" in protest activity is to activate "third parties" to enter the implicit or explicit bargaining arena in ways favorable to the protesters. This is one of the few ways in which they can "create" bargaining resources. It is intuitively unconvincing to suggest that fifteen people sitting uninvited in the Mayor's office have the power to move City Hall. A better formulation would suggest that the people sitting in may be able to appeal to a wider public to which the city administration is sensitive. Thus in successful protest activity the *reference publics* of protest *targets* may be conceived as explicitly or implicitly reacting to protest in such a way that target groups or individuals respond in ways favorable to the protesters.[14]

It should be emphasized that the focus here is on protest by relatively powerless groups. Illustrations can be summoned, for example, of activity designated as "protest" involving high status pressure groups or hundreds of thousands of people. While such instances may share some of the characteristics of protest activity, they may not represent examples of developing political resources by relatively powerless groups because the protesting groups may already command political resources by virtue of status, numbers or cohesion.

It is appropriate also to distinguish between the relatively restricted use of the concept of protest adopted here and closely related political strategies which are often designated as "protest" in popular usage. Where groups already possess sufficient resources with which to bargain, as in the case of some economic boycotts and labor strikes, they may be said to engage in "direct confrontation." [15] Similarly, protest which represents efforts to "activate reference publics" should be distinguished from "alliance formation," where third parties are induced to join the conflict, but where the value orientations of third parties are sufficiently similar to those of the protesting group that concerted or coordinated action is possible. Alliance formation is particularly desirable for relatively powerless groups if they seek to join the decision-making process as participants.

The distinction between activating reference publics and alliance formation is made on the assumption that where goal orientations among protest groups and the reference publics of target groups are similar, the political dynamics of peti-

---

[14] See E. E. Schattschneider's discussion of expanding the scope of the conflict, *The Semisovereign People* (New York, 1960). Another way in which bargaining resources may be "created" is to increase the relative cohesion of groups, or to increase the perception of group solidarity as a precondition to greater cohesion. This appears to be the primary goal of political activity which is generally designated "community organization." Negro activists appear to recognize the utility of this strategy in their advocacy of "black power." In some instances protest activity may be designed in part to accomplish this goal in addition to activating reference publics.
[15] For an example of "direct confrontation," one might study the three-month Negro boycott of white merchants in Natchez, Miss., which resulted in capitulation to boycott demands by city government leaders. See *The New York Times*, December 4, 1965, p. 1.

488 Protest and Violence

tioning target groups are different than when such goal orientations are relatively divergent. Clearly the more similar the goal orientations, the greater the likelihood of protest success, other things being equal. This discussion is intended to highlight, however, those instances where goal orientations of reference publics depart significantly, in direction or intensity, from the goals of protest groups.

Say that to protest some situation, A would like to enter a bargaining situation with B. But A has nothing B wants, and thus cannot bargain. A then attempts to create political resources by activating other groups to enter the conflict. A then organizes to take action against B with respect to certain goals. *Information concerning these goals must be conveyed through communications media* (C, D, and E) to F, G, and H, which are B's *reference publics*. In response to the reactions of F, G, and H, or in anticipation of their reactions, B responds, *in some way*, to the protesters' demands. This formulation requires the conceptualization of protest activity when undertaken to create bargaining resources as a political process which requires communication and is characterized by a multiplicity of constituencies for protest leadership.

A schematic representation of the process of protest as utilized by relatively powerless groups is presented in Figure 1. In contrast to a simplistic pressure group model which would posit a direct relationship between pressure group and pressured, the following discussion is guided by the assumption (derived from observation) that protest is a highly indirect process in which communications media and the reference publics of protest targets play critical roles. It is also a process characterized by reciprocal relations, in which protest leaders frame strategies according to their perception of the needs of (many) other actors.

FIGURE 1

Schematic Representation of the Process of Protest by Relatively Powerless Groups

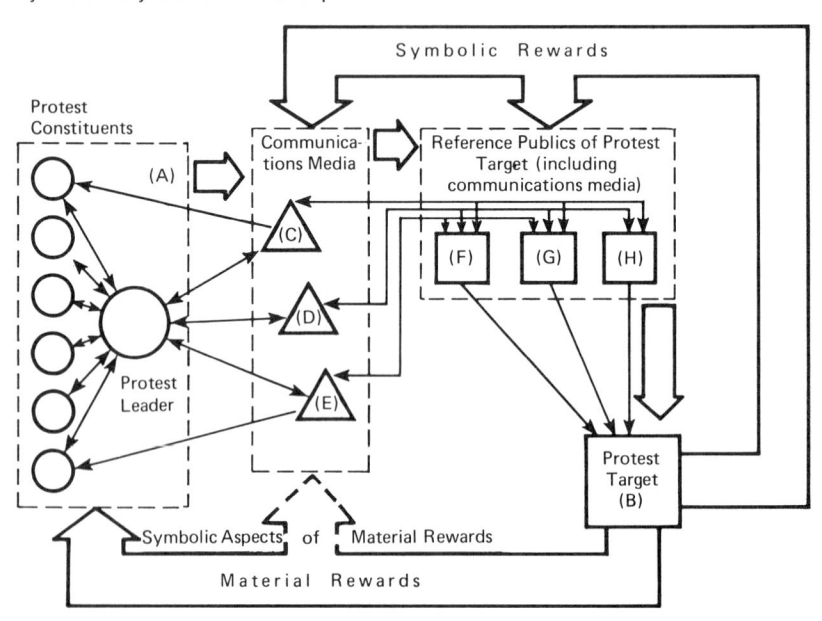

In this view protest constituents limit the options of protest leaders at the same time that the protest leader influences their perception of the strategies and rhetoric which they will support. Protest activity is filtered through the communications media in influencing the perceptions of the reference publics of protest targets. To the extent that the influence of reference publics is supportive of protest goals, target groups will dispense symbolic or material rewards. Material rewards are communicated directly to protest constituents. Symbolic rewards are communicated in part to protest constituents, but primarily are communicated to the reference publics of target groups, who provide the major stimuli for public policy pronouncements.

The study of protest as adopted by relatively powerless groups should provide insights into the structure and behavior of groups involved in civil rights politics and associated with the "war on poverty." It should direct attention toward the ways in which administrative agencies respond to "crises." Additionally, the study of protest as a political resource should influence some general conceptualizations of American political pluralism. Robert Dahl, for example, describes the "normal American political process" as "one in which there is a high probability that an active and legitimate group in the population can make itself heard effectively at some crucial stage in the process of decision." [16] Although he agrees that control over decisions is unevenly divided in the population, Dahl writes:

> When I say that a group is heard "effectively" I mean more than the simple fact that it makes a noise; I mean that one or more officials are not only ready to listen to the noise, but expect to suffer in some significant way if they do not placate the group, its leaders, or its most vociferous members. To satisfy the group may require one or more of a great variety of actions by the responsive leader: pressure for substantive policies, appointments, graft, respect, expression of the appropriate emotions, or the right combination of reciprocal noises.[17]

These statements, which in some ways resemble David Truman's discussion of the power of "potential groups," [18] can be illuminated by the study of protest activity in three ways. First, what are the probabilities that relatively powerless groups can make themselves heard effectively? In what ways will such groups be heard or "steadily appeased"? [19] Concentration on the process of protest activity may reveal the extent to which, and the conditions under which, relatively powerless groups are likely to prove effective. Protest undertaken to obstruct policy decisions, for example, may enjoy greater success probabilities than protest undertaken in an effort to evoke constructive policy innovations.[20]

Second, does it make sense to suggest that all groups which make noises will receive responses from public officials? Perhaps the groups which make noises do not have to be satisfied at all, but it is other groups which receive assurances or

[16] *A Preface to Democratic Theory* (Chicago, 1956), pp. 145–146.
[17] *A Preface to Democratic Theory*, pp. 145–146.
[18] *The Governmental Process* (New York, 1951), p. 104.
[19] See Dahl, *A Preface to Democratic Theory*, p. 146.
[20] Observations that all groups can influence public policy at some stage of the political process are frequently made about the role of "veto groups" in American politics. See Truman, *The Governmental Process*, pp. 104 ff. See also David Reisman, *The Lonely Crowd* (New Haven, 1950), pp. 211 ff., for an earlier discussion of veto-group politics. Yet protest should be evaluated when it is adopted to obtain assertive as well as defensive goals.

recognition. Third, what are the probabilities that groups which make noises will receive tangible rewards, rather than symbolic assurances? [21] Dahl lumps these rewards together in the same paragraph, but dispensation of tangible rewards clearly has a different impact upon groups than the dispensation of symbolic rewards. Dahl is undoubtedly correct when he suggests that the relative fluidity of American politics is a critical characteristic of the American political system.[22] But he is less precise and less convincing when it comes to analyzing the extent to which the system is indeed responsive to the relatively powerless groups of the "average citizen." [23]

The following sections are an attempt to demonstrate the utility of the conceptualization of the protest process presented above. This will be done by exploring the problems encountered and the strains generated by protest leaders in interacting with four constituencies. It will be useful to concentrate attention on the maintenance and enhancement needs not only of the large formal organizations which dominate city politics,[24] but also of the ad hoc protest groups which engage them in civic controversy. It will also prove rewarding to examine the role requirements of individuals in leadership positions as they perceive the problems of constituency manipulation. In concluding remarks some implications of the study of protest for the pluralist description of American politics will be suggested.[25]

PROTEST LEADERSHIP AND ORGANIZATIONAL BASE

The organizational maintenance needs of relatively powerless, low income, ad hoc protest groups center around the tension generated by the need for leadership to offer symbolic and intangible inducements to protest participation when immediate, material rewards cannot be anticipated, and the need to provide at least the promise of material rewards. Protest leaders must try to evoke responses from other actors in the political process, at the same time that they pay attention to participant organizational needs. Thus relatively deprived groups in the political system not only receive symbolic reassurance while material rewards from the system are withheld,[26] but protest leaders have a stake in perpetuating the notion

[21] See Murray Edelman, *The Symbolic Uses of Politics* (Urbana, Ill., 1964), chap. 2.
[22] See Dahl, *Who Governs?* (New Haven, 1961), pp. 305 ff.
[23] In a recent formulation, Dahl reiterates the theme of wide dispersion of influence, "More than other systems, [democracies] . . . try to disperse influence widely to their citizens by means of the suffrage, elections, freedom of speech, press, and assembly, the right of opponents to criticize the conduct of government, the right to organize political parties, and in other ways." *Pluralist Democracy in the United States* (Chicago, 1967), p. 373. Here, however, he concentrates more on the availability of options to all groups in the system, rather than on the relative probabilities that all groups in fact have access to the political process. See pp. 372 ff.
[24] See Edward Banfield, *Political Influence* (New York, 1961), p. 263. The analysis of organizational incentive structure which heavily influences Banfield's formulation is Chester Barnard, *The Functions of the Executive* (Cambridge, Mass., 1938).
[25] In the following attempt to develop the implications of this conceptualization of protest activity, I have drawn upon extensive field observations and bibliographical research. Undoubtedly, however, individual assertions, while representing my best judgment concerning the available evidence, in the future may require modification as the result of further empirical research.
[26] As Edelman suggests, cited previously.

that relatively powerless groups retain political efficacy despite what in many cases is obvious evidence to the contrary.

The tension embraced by protest leaders over the nature of inducements toward protest participation accounts in part for the style adopted and goals selected by protest leaders. Groups which seek psychological gratification from politics, but cannot or do not anticipate material political rewards, may be attracted to militant protest leaders. To these groups, angry rhetoric may prove a desirable quality in the short run. Where groups depend upon the political system for tangible benefits, or where participation in the system provides intangible benefits, moderate leadership is likely to prevail. Wilson has observed similar tendencies among Negro leaders of large, formal organizations.[27] It is no less true for leadership of protest groups. Groups whose members derive tangible satisfactions from political participation will not condone leaders who are stubborn in compromise or appear to question the foundations of the system. This coincides with Truman's observation: "Violation of the 'rules of the game' normally will weaken a group's cohesion, reduce its status in the community, and expose it to the claims of other groups." [28] On the other hand, the cohesion of relatively powerless groups may be strengthened by militant, ideological leadership which questions the rules of the game and challenges their legitimacy.

Cohesion is particularly important when protest leaders bargain directly with target groups. In that situation, leaders' ability to control protest constituents and guarantee their behavior represents a bargaining strength.[29] For this reason Wilson stressed the bargaining difficulties of Negro leaders who cannot guarantee constituent behavior, and pointed out the significance of the strategy of projecting the image of group solidarity when the reality of cohesion is a fiction.[30] Cohesion is less significant at other times. Divided leadership may prove productive by bargaining in tandem,[31] or by minimizing strain among groups in the protest process. Further, community divisions may prove less detrimental to protest aims when strong third parties have entered the dispute originally generated by protest organizations.

The intangible rewards of assuming certain postures toward the political system may not be sufficient to sustain an organizational base. It may be necessary to renew constantly the intangible rewards of participation. And to the extent that people participate in order to achieve tangible benefits, their interest in a protest organization may depend upon the organization's relative material success. Protest leaders may have to tailor their style to present participants with tangible successes, or with the appearance of success. Leaders may have to define the issues with concern for increasing their ability to sustain organizations. The poten-

---

[27] *Negro Politics*, p. 290.
[28] *The Governmental Process*, p. 513.
[29] But cf. Thomas Schelling's discussion of "binding oneself," *The Strategy of Conflict* (Cambridge, Mass., 1960), pp. 22 ff.
[30] "The Strategy of Protest," p. 297.
[31] This is suggested by Wilson, "The Strategy of Protest," p. 298; St. Clair Drake and Horace Cayton, *Black Metropolis* (New York, 1962, rev. ed.), p. 731; Walker, "Protest and Negotiation," p. 122. Authors who argue that divided leadership is dysfunctional have been Clark, p. 156; and Tilman Cothran, "The Negro Protest Against Segregation in the South," *The Annals*, 357 (January 1965), 72.

tial for protest among protest group members may have to be manipulated by leadership if the group is to be sustained.[32]

The participants in protest organizations limit the flexibility of protest leadership. This obtains for two reasons. They restrict public actions by leaders who must continue to solicit active participant support, and they place restraints on the kinds of activities which can be considered appropriate for protest purposes. Poor participants cannot commonly be asked to engage in protest requiring air transportation. Participants may have anxieties related to their environment or historical situation which discourages engagement in some activities. They may be afraid of job losses, beatings by the police, or summary evictions. Negro protest in the Deep South has been inhibited by realistic expectations of retribution.[33] Protests over slum housing conditions are undermined by tenants who expect landlord retaliation for engaging in tenant organizing activity.[34] Political or ethical mores may conflict with a proposed course of action, diminishing participation.[35]

On the other hand, to the extent that fears are real, or that the larger community perceives protest participants as subject to these fears, protest may actually be strengthened. Communications media and potential allies will consider more soberly the complaints of people who are understood to be placing themselves in jeopardy. When young children and their parents made the arduous bus trip from Mississippi to Washington, D.C. to protest the jeopardizing of Head Start funds, the courage and expense represented by their effort created a respect and visibility for their position which might not have been achieved by local protest efforts.[36]

Protest activity may be undertaken by organizations with established relationship patterns, behavior norms, and role expectations. These organizations are likely to have greater access to other groups in the political system, and a demonstrated capacity to maintain themselves. Other protest groups, however, may be

[32] This observation is confirmed by a student of the Southern civil rights movement:
> Negroes demand of protest leaders constant progress. The combination of long-standing discontent and a new-found belief in the possibility of change produces a constant state of tension and aggressiveness in the Negro community. But this discontent is vague and diffuse, not specific; the masses do not define the issues around which action shall revolve. This the leader must do.

Lewis Killian, "Leadership in the Desegregation Crises: An Institutional Analysis," in Muzafer Sherif (ed.), *Intergroup Relations and Leadership* (New York, 1962), p. 159.
[33] Significantly, southern Negro students who actively participated in the early phases of the sit-in movement "tended to be unusually optimistic about race relations and tolerant of whites [when compared with inactive Negro students]. They not only *were* better off, objectively speaking, than other Negroes but *felt* better off." Matthews and Prothro, *Negroes and the New Southern Politics*, p. 424.
[34] This is particularly the case in cities such as Washington, D.C., where landlord-tenant laws offer little protection against retaliatory eviction. See, e.g., Robert Schoshinski, "Remedies of the Indigent Tenant: Proposal for Change," *Georgetown Law Journal*, 54 (Winter 1966), 541 ff.
[35] Wilson regarded this as a chief reason for lack of protest activity in 1961. He wrote: "... some of the goals now being sought by Negroes are least applicable to those groups of Negroes most suited to protest action. Protest action involving such tactics as mass meetings, picketing, boycotts, and strikes rarely find enthusiastic participants among upper-income and higher status individuals": "The Strategy of Protest," p. 296.
[36] See *The New York Times*, February 12, 1966, p. 56.

ad hoc arrangements without demonstrated internal or external relationship patterns. These groups will have different organizational problems, in response to which it is necessary to engage in different kinds of protest activity.

The scarcity of organizational resources also places limits upon the ability of relatively powerless groups to maintain the foundations upon which protest organizations develop. Relatively powerless groups, to engage in political activity of any kind, must command at least some resources. This is not tautological. Referring again to a continuum on which political groups are placed according to their relative command of resources, one may draw a line somewhere along the continuum representing a "threshold of civic group political participation." Clearly some groups along the continuum will possess some political resources (enough, say, to emerge for inspection) but not enough to exercise influence in civic affairs. Relatively powerless groups, to be influential, must cross the "threshold" to engage in politics. Although the availability of group resources is a critical consideration at all stages of the protest process, it is particularly important in explaining why some groups seem to "surface" with sufficient strength to command attention. The following discussion of some critical organizational resources should illuminate this point.

Skilled professionals frequently must be available to protest organizations. Lawyers, for example, play extremely important roles in enabling protest groups to utilize the judicial process and avail themselves of adequate preparation of court cases. Organizational reputation may depend upon a combination of ability to threaten the conventional political system and of exercising statutory rights in court. Availability of lawyers depends upon ability to pay fees and/or the attractiveness to lawyers of participation in protest group activity. Volunteer professional assistance may not prove adequate. One night a week volunteered by an aspiring politician in a housing clinic cannot satisfy the needs of a chaotic political movement.[37] The need for skilled professionals is not restricted to lawyers. For example, a group seeking to protest an urban renewal policy might require the services of architects and city planners in order to present a viable alternative to a city proposal.

Financial resources not only purchase legal assistance, but enable relatively powerless groups to conduct minimum programs of political activities. To the extent that constituents are unable or unwilling to pay even small membership dues, then financing the cost of mimeographing flyers, purchasing supplies, maintaining telephone service, paying rent, and meeting a modest payroll become major organizational problems. And to the extent that group finances are supplied by outside individual contributions or government or foundation grants, the long-term options of the group are sharply constrained by the necessity of orienting group goals and tactics to anticipate the potential objections of financial supporters.

Some dependence upon even minimal financial resources can be waived if organizations evoke passionate support from constituents. Secretarial help and block

---

[37] On housing clinic services provided by political clubs, see James Q. Wilson, *The Amateur Democrat: Club Politics in Three Cities* (Chicago, 1962), pp. 63–64, 176. On the need for lawyers among low-income people, see, e.g., *The Extension of Legal Services to the Poor*, Conference Proceedings (Washington, D.C., n.d.), esp. pp. 51–60; and "Neighborhood Law Offices: The New Wave in Legal Services for the Poor," *Harvard Law Review*, 80 (February 1967), 805–850.

organizers will come forward to work without compensation if they support the cause of neighborhood organizations or gain intangible benefits based upon association with the group. Protest organizations may also depend upon skilled nonprofessionals, such as college students, whose access to people and political and economic institutions often assist protest groups in cutting across income lines to seek support. Experience with ad hoc political groups, however, suggests that this assistance is sporadic and undependable. Transient assistance is particularly typical of skilled, educated, and employable volunteers whose abilities can be applied widely. The die-hards of ad hoc political groups are often those people who have no place else to go, nothing else to do.

Constituent support will be affected by the nature of the protest target and whether protest activity is directed toward defensive or assertive goals. Obstructing specific public policies may be easier than successfully recommending constructive policy changes. Orientations toward defensive goals may require less constituent energy, and less command over resources of money, expertise and status.[38]

PROTEST LEADERSHIP AND COMMUNICATIONS MEDIA

The communications media are extremely powerful in city politics. In granting or withholding publicity, in determining what information most people will have on most issues, and what alternatives they will consider in response to issues, the media truly, as Norton Long has put it, "set . . . the civic agenda." [39] To the extent that successful protest activity depends upon appealing to, and/or threatening, other groups in the community, the communications media set the limits of protest action. If protest tactics are not considered significant by the media, or if newspapers and television reporters or editors decide to overlook protest tactics, protest organizations will not succeed. Like the tree falling unheard in the forest, there is no protest unless protest is perceived and projected.

A number of writers have noticed that the success of protest activity seems directly related to the amount of publicity it receives outside the immediate arena in which protest takes place. This view has not been stated systematically, but hints can be found in many sources. In the literature on civil rights politics, the relevance of publicity represents one of the few hypotheses available concerning the dynamics of successful protest activity.[40]

When protest tactics do receive coverage in the communications media, the way in which they are presented will influence all other actors in the system, in-

---

[38] An illustration of low income group protest organization mobilized for veto purposes is provided by Dahl in "The Case of the Metal Houses." See *Who Governs?*, pp. 192 ff.
[39] Norton Long, "The Local Community as an Ecology of Games," in Long, *The Polity*, Charles Press (ed.), (Chicago, 1962), p. 153. See pp. 152–154. See also Roscoe C. Martin, Frank J. Munger, *et al.*, *Decisions in Syracuse: A Metropolitan Action Study* (Garden City, N.Y., 1965) (originally published: 1961), pp. 326–327.
[40] See, e.g., Thompson, *The Negro Leadership Class*, p. 134, and *passim*; Martin Oppenheimer, "The Southern Student Movement: Year I," *Journal of Negro Education*, 33 (Fall 1964), 397; Cothran, "The Negro Protest," p. 72; Pauli Murray, "Protest Against the Legal Status of the Negro," *The Annals*, 357 (January 1965), 63; Allan P. Sindler, "Protest Against the Political Status of the Negroes," *The Annals*, 357 (January 1965), 50.

cluding the protesters themselves. Conformity to standards of newsworthiness in political style, and knowledge of the prejudices and desires of the individuals who determine media coverage in political skills, represent crucial determinants of leadership effectiveness.

The organizational behavior of newspapers can partly be understood by examining the maintenance and enhancement needs which direct them toward projects of civic betterment and impressions of accomplishment.[41] But insight may also be gained by analyzing the role requirements of reporters, editors, and others who determine newspaper policy. Reporters, for example, are frequently motivated by the desire to contribute to civic affairs by their "objective" reporting of significant events; by the premium they place on accuracy; and by the credit which they receive for sensationalism and "scoops."

These requirements may be difficult to accommodate at the same time. Reporters demand newsworthiness of their subjects in the short run, but also require reliability and verifiability in the longer run. Factual accuracy may dampen newsworthiness. Sensationalism, attractive to some newspaper editors, may be inconsistent with reliable, verifiable narration of events. Newspapers at first may be attracted to sensationalism, and later demand verifiability in the interests of community harmony (and adherence to professional journalistic standards).

Most big city newspapers have reporters whose assignments permit them to cover aspects of city politics with some regularity. These reporters, whose "beats" may consist of "civil rights" or "poverty," sometimes develop close relationships with their news subjects. These relationships may develop symbiotic overtones because of the mutuality of interest between the reporter and the news subject. Reporters require fresh information on protest developments, while protest leaders have a vital interest in obtaining as much press coverage as possible.

Inflated reports of protest success may be understood in part by examining this relationship between reporter and protest leader. Both have role-oriented interests in projecting images of protest strength and threat. In circumstances of great excitement, when competition from other news media representatives is high, a reporter may find that he is less governed by the role requirement of verification and reliability than he is by his editor's demand for "scoops" and news with high audience appeal.[42]

On the other hand, the demands of the media may conflict with the needs of protest group maintenance. Consider the leader whose constituents are attracted solely by pragmatic statements not exceeding what they consider political "good taste." He is constrained from making militant demands which would isolate him from constituents. This constraint may cost him appeal in the press.[43] However, the leader whose organizing appeal requires militant rhetoric may obtain eager

[41] See Banfield, *Political Influence*, p. 275.
[42] For a case study of the interaction between protest leaders and newspaper reporters, see Michael Lipsky, "Rent Strikes in New York City: Protest Politics and the Power of the Poor" (unpublished Ph.D. dissertation, Princeton University, 1967), pp. 139–149. Bernard Cohen has analyzed the impact of the press on foreign policy from the perspective of reporters' role requirements: see his *The Press and Foreign Policy* (Princeton, N.J., 1963), esp. chaps. 2–3.
[43] An example of a protest conducted by middle-class women engaged in pragmatic protest over salvaging park space is provided in John B. Keeley, *Moses on the Green*, Inter-University Case Program, No. 45 (University, Ala., 1959).

press coverage only to find that his inflamatory statements lead to alienation of potential allies and exclusion from the explicit bargaining process.[44]

News media do not report events in the same way. Television may select for broadcast only thirty seconds of a half-hour news conference. This coverage will probably focus on immediate events, without background or explanatory material. Newspapers may give more complete accounts of the same event. The most complete account may appear in the weekly edition of a neighborhood or ethnic newspaper. Differential coverage by news media, and differential news media habits in the general population,[45] are significant factors in permitting protest leaders to juggle conflicting demands of groups in the protest process.

Similar tensions exist in the leader's relationships with protest targets. Ideological postures may gain press coverage and constituency approval, but may alienate target groups with whom it would be desirable to bargain explicitly. Exclusion from the councils of decision-making may have important consequences, since the results of target group deliberations may satisfy activated reference publics without responding to protest goals. If activated reference publics are required to increase the bargaining position of the protest group, protest efforts thereafter will have diminished chances of success.

PROTEST LEADERSHIP AND "THIRD PARTIES"

I have argued that the essence of political protest consists of activating third parties to participate in controversy in ways favorable to protest goals. In previous sections I have attempted to analyze some of the tensions which result from protest leaders' attempts to activate reference publics of protest targets at the same time that they must retain the interest and support of protest organization participants. This phenomenon is in evidence when Negro leaders, recognized as such by public officials, find their support eroded in the Negro community because they have engaged in explicit bargaining situations with politicians. Negro leaders are thus faced with the dilemma that when they behave like other ethnic group representatives they are faced with loss of support from those whose intense activism has been aroused in the Negro community, yet whose support is vital if they are to remain credible as leaders to public officials.

The tensions resulting from conflicting maintenance needs of protest organizations and activated third parties present difficulties for protest leaders. One way

---

[44] This was the complaint of Floyd McKissick, National Director of the Congress of Racial Equality, when he charged that ". . . there are only two kinds of statements a black man can make and expect that the white press will report. . . . First . . . is an attack on another black man. . . . The second is a statement that sounds radical, violent, extreme—the verbal equivalent of a riot. . . . [T]he Negro is being rewarded by the public media only if he turns on another Negro and uses his tongue as a switchblade, or only if he sounds outlandish, extremist or psychotic." Statement at the Convention of the American Society of Newspaper Editors, April 20, 1967, Washington, D.C., as reported in *The New York Times*, April 21, 1967, p. 22. See also the remarks of journalist Ted Poston, *The New York Times*, April 26, 1965, p. 26.

[45] Matthews and Prothro found, for example, that in their south-wide Negro population sample, 38 percent read Negro-oriented magazines and 17 percent read newspapers written for Negroes. These media treat news of interest to Negroes more completely and sympathetically than do the general media. See *Negroes and the New Southern Politics*, pp. 248 ff.

in which these tensions can be minimized is by dividing leadership responsibilities. If more than one group is engaged in protest activity, protest leaders can, in effect, divide up public roles so as to reduce as much as possible the gap between the implicit demands of different groups for appropriate rhetoric, and what in fact is said. Thus divided leadership may perform the latent function of minimizing tensions among elements in the protest process by permitting different groups to listen selectively to protest spokesmen.[46]

Another way in which strain among different groups can be minimized is through successful public relations. Minimization of strain may depend upon ambiguity of action or statement, deception, or upon effective intergroup communication. Failure to clarify meaning, or falsification, may increase protest effectiveness. Effective intragroup communication may increase the likelihood that protest constituents will "understand" that ambiguous or false public statements have "special meaning" and need not be taken seriously. The Machiavellian circle is complete when we observe that although lying may be prudent, the appearance of integrity and forthrightness is desirable for public relations, since these values are widely shared.

It has been observed that "[t]he militant displays an unwillingness to perform those administrative tasks which are necessary to operate an organization. Probably the skills of the agitator and the skills of the administrator . . . are not incompatible, but few men can do both well." [47] These skills may or may not be incompatible as personality traits, but they indeed represent conflicting role demands on protest leadership. When a protest leader exhausts time and energy conducting frequent press conferences, arranging for politicians and celebrities to appear at rallies, delivering speeches to sympathetic local groups, college symposia and other forums, constantly picketing for publicity and generally making "contacts," he is unable to pursue the direction of office routine, clerical tasks, research and analysis, and other chores.

The difficulties of delegating routine tasks are probably directly related to the skill levels and previous administrative experiences of group members. In addition, to the extent that involvement in protest organizations is a function of rewards received or expected by individuals because of the excitement or entertainment value of participation, then the difficulties of delegating routine, relatively uninteresting chores to group members will be increased. Yet attention to such details affects the perception of protest groups by organizations whose support or assistance may be desired in the future. These considerations add to the protest leader's problem of risking alienation of protest participants because of potentially unpopular cooperation with the "power structure."

In the protest paradigm developed here, "third parties" refers both to the reference publics of target groups and, more narrowly, to the interest groups whose regular interaction with protest targets tends to develop into patterns of influence.[48] We have already discussed some of the problems associated with activating the reference publics of target groups. In discussing the constraints placed upon protest, attention may be focused upon the likelihood that groups seeking to create political resources through protest will be included in the explicit bargain-

[46] See footnote 31 above.
[47] Wilson, *Negro Politics*, p. 225.
[48] See Wallace Sayre and Herbert Kaufman, *Governing New York City* (New York, 1960), pp. 257 ff. Also see Banfield, *Political Influence*, p. 267.

ing process with other pressure groups. For protest groups, these constraints are those which occur because of class and political style, status, and organizational resources.

The established civic groups most likely to be concerned with the problems raised by relatively powerless groups are those devoted to service in the public welfare and those "liberally" oriented groups whose potential constituents are either drawn from the same class as the protest groups (such as some trade unions), or whose potential constituents are attracted to policies which appear to serve the interest of the lower class or minority groups (such as some reform political clubs).[49] These civic groups have frequently cultivated clientele relationships with city agencies over long periods. Their efforts have been reciprocated by agency officials anxious to develop constituencies to support and defend agency administrative and budgetary policies. In addition, clientele groups are expected to endorse and legitimize agency aggrandizement. These relationships have been developed by agency officials and civic groups for mutual benefit, and cannot be destroyed, abridged or avoided without cost.

Protest groups may well be able to raise the saliency of issues on the civic agenda through utilization of communications media and successful appeals or threats to wider publics, but admission to policy-making councils is frequently barred because of the angry, militant rhetorical style adopted by protest leaders. People in power do not like to sit down with rogues. Protest leaders are likely to have phrased demands in ways unacceptable to lawyers and other civic activists whose cautious attitude toward public policy may reflect not only their good intentions but their concern for property rights, due process, pragmatic legislating or judicial precedent.

Relatively powerless groups lack participation of individuals with high status whose endorsement of specific proposals lend them increased legitimacy. Good causes may always attract the support of high status individuals. But such individuals' willingness to devote time to the promotion of specific proposals is less likely than the one-shot endorsements which these people distribute more readily.

Similarly, protest organizations often lack the resources on which entry into the policy-making process depends. These resources include maintenance of a staff with expertise and experience in the policy area. This expertise may be in the areas of the law, planning and architecture, proposal writing, accounting, educational policy, federal grantsmanship or publicity. Combining experience with expertise is one way to create status in issue areas. The dispensing of information by interest groups has been widely noted as a major source of influence. Over time the experts develop status in their areas of competence somewhat independent of the influence which adheres to them as information-providers. Groups which cannot or do not engage lawyers to assist in proposing legislation, and do not engage in collecting reliable data, cannot participate in policy deliberations or consult in these matters. Protest oriented groups, whose primary talents are in dramatizing issues, cannot credibly attempt to present data considered "objective" or suggestions considered "responsible" by public officials. Few can be convincing as both advocate and arbiter at the same time.

---

[49] See Wilson, *The Amateur Democrats*, previously cited. These groups are most likely to be characterized by broad scope of political interest and frequent intervention in politics. See Sayre and Kaufman, *Governing New York City*, p. 79.

Michael Lipsky 499

PROTEST LEADERSHIP AND TARGET GROUPS

The probability of protest success may be approached by examining the maintenance needs of organizations likely to be designated as target groups.[50] For the sake of clarity, and because protest activity increasingly is directed toward government, I shall refer in the following paragraphs exclusively to government agencies at the municipal level. The assumption is retained, however, that the following generalizations are applicable to other potential target groups.

Some of the constraints placed on protest leadership in influencing target groups have already been mentioned in preceding sections. The lack of status and resources that inhibit protest groups from participating in policy-making conferences, for example, also helps prevent explicit bargaining between protest leaders and city officials. The strain between rhetoric which appeals to protest participants and public statements to which communications media and "third parties" respond favorably also exists with reference to target groups.

Yet there is a distinguishing feature of the maintenance needs and strategies of city agencies which specifically constrains protest organizations. This is the agency director's need to protect "the jurisdiction and income of his organization [by] . . . [m]anipulation of the external environment."[51] In so doing he may satisfy his reference groups without responding to protest group demands. At least six tactics are available to protest targets who are motivated to respond in some way to protest activity but seek primarily to satisfy their reference publics. These tactics may be employed whether or not target groups are "sincere" in responding to protest demands.

1. Target groups may dispense symbolic satisfactions. Appearances of activity and commitment to problems substitute for, or supplement, resource allocation and policy innovations which would constitute tangible responses to protest activity. If symbolic responses supplement tangible pay-offs, they are frequently coincidental, rather than intimately linked, to projection of response by protest targets. Typical in city politics of the symbolic response is the ribbon cutting, street corner ceremony or the walking tour press conference. These occasions are utilized not only to build agency constituencies,[52] but to satisfy agency reference publics that attention is being directed to problems of civic concern. In this sense publicist tactics may be seen as defensive maneuvers. Symbolic aspects of the actions of public officials can also be recognized in the commissioning of expensive studies and the rhetorical flourishes with which "massive attacks," "comprehensive programs," and "co-ordinated planning" are frequently promoted.

---

[50] Another approach, persuasively presented by Wilson, concentrates on protest success as a function of the relative unity and vulnerability of targets. See "The Strategy of Protest," pp. 293 ff. This insight helps explain, for example, why protest against housing segregation commonly takes the form of action directed against government (a unified target) rather than against individual homeowners (who present a dispersed target). One problem with this approach is that it tends to obscure the possibility that targets, as collections of individuals, may be divided in evaluation of and sympathy for protest demands. Indeed, city agency administrators under some circumstances act as partisans in protest conflicts. As such, they frequently appear ambivalent toward protest goals: sympathetic to the ends while concerned that the means employed in protest reflect negatively on their agencies.
[51] Sayre and Kaufman, *Governing New York City*, p. 253.
[52] See Sayre and Kaufman, *Governing New York City*, pp. 253 ff.

City agencies establish distinct apparatus and procedures for dealing with crises which may be provoked by protest groups. Housing-related departments in New York City may be cited for illustration. It is usually the case in these agencies that the Commissioner or a chief deputy, a press secretary and one or two other officials devote whatever time is necessary to collect information, determine policy and respond quickly to reports of "crises." This is functional for tenants, who, if they can generate enough concern, may be able to obtain shortcuts through lengthy agency procedures. It is also functional for officials who want to project images of action rather than merely receiving complaints. Concentrating attention on the maintenance needs of city politicians during protest crises suggests that pronouncements of public officials serve purposes independent of their dedication to alleviation of slum conditions.[53]

Independent of dispensation of tangible benefits to protest groups, public officials continue to respond primarily to their own reference publics. Murray Edelman has suggested that: "Tangible resources and benefits are frequently not distributed to unorganized political group interests as promised in regulatory statutes, and the propaganda attending their enactment." [54] His analysis may be supplemented by suggesting that symbolic dispensations may not only serve to reassure unorganized political group interests, but may also contribute to reducing the anxiety level of organized interests and wider publics which are only tangentially involved in the issues.

2. Target groups may dispense token material satisfactions. When city agencies respond, with much publicity, to cases brought to their attention representing examples of the needs dramatized by protest organizations, they may appear to respond to protest demands while in fact only responding on a case basis, instead of a general basis. For the protesters served by agencies in this fashion it is of considerable advantage that agencies can be influenced by protest action. Yet it should not be ignored that in handling the "crisis" cases, public officials give the appearance of response to their reference publics, while mitigating demands for an expensive, complex *general* assault on problems represented by the cases to which responses are given. Token responses, whether or not accompanied by more general responses, are particularly attractive to reporters and television news directors, who are able to dramatize individual cases convincingly, but who may be unable to "capture" the essence of general deprivation or of general efforts to alleviate conditions of deprivation.

3. Target groups may organize and innovate internally in order to blunt the impetus of protest efforts. This tactic is closely related to No. 2 (above). If target groups can act constructively in the worst cases, they will then be able to preempt protest efforts by responding to the cases which best dramatize protest demands. Alternatively, they may designate all efforts which jeopardize agency reputations as "worst" cases, and devote extensive resources to these cases. In some ways extraordinary city efforts are precisely consistent with protest goals. At the

---

[53] See Lipsky, "Rent Strikes in New York City," chaps. 5–6. The appearance of responsiveness may be given by city officials *in anticipation* of protest activity. This seems to have been the strategy of Mayor Richard Daley in his reaction to the announcement of Martin Luther King's plans to focus civil rights efforts on Chicago. See *The New York Times*, February 1, 1966, p. 11.
[54] See Edelman, *The Symbolic Uses of Politics*, p. 23.

same time extraordinary efforts in the most heavily dramatized cases or the most extreme cases effectively wear down the "cutting-edges" of protest efforts.

Many New York City agencies develop informal "crisis" arrangements not only to project publicity, as previously indicated, but to mobilize energies toward solving "crisis" cases. They may also develop policy innovations which allow them to respond more quickly to "crisis" situations. These innovations may be important to some city residents, for whom the problems of dealing with city bureaucracies can prove insurmountable. It might be said, indeed, that the goals of protest are to influence city agencies to handle every case with the same resources that characterize their dispatch of "crisis" cases.[55]

But such policies would demand major revenue inputs. This kind of qualitative policy change is difficult to achieve. Meanwhile, internal reallocation of resources only means that routine services must be neglected so that the "crisis" programs can be enhanced. If all cases are expedited, as in a typical "crisis" response, then none can be. Thus for purposes of general solutions, "crisis" resolving can be self-defeating unless accompanied by significantly greater resource allocation. It is not self-defeating, however, to the extent that the organizational goals of city agencies are to serve a clientele while minimizing negative publicity concerning agency vigilance and responsiveness.

4. Target groups may appear to be constrained in their ability to grant protest goals.[56] This may be directed toward making the protesters appear to be unreasonable in their demands, or to be well-meaning individuals who "just don't understand how complex running a city really is." Target groups may extend sympathy but claim that they lack resources, a mandate from constituents, and/or authority to respond to protest demands. Target groups may also evade protest demands by arguing that "If-I-give-it-to-you-I-have-to-give-it-to-everyone."

The tactic of appearing constrained is particularly effective with established civic groups because there is an undeniable element of truth to it. Everyone knows that cities are financially undernourished. Established civic groups expend great energies lobbying for higher levels of funding for their pet city agencies. Thus they recognize the validity of this constraint when posed by city officials. But it is not inconsistent to point out that funds for specific, relatively inexpensive programs, or for the expansion of existing programs, can often be found if pressure is increased. While constraints on city government flexibility may be extensive, they are not absolute. Protest targets nonetheless attempt to diminish the impact of protest demands by claiming relative impotence.

5. Target groups may use their extensive resources to discredit protest leaders and organizations. Utilizing their excellent access to the press, public officials may state or imply that leaders are unreliable, ineffective as leaders ("they don't really have the people behind them"), guilty of criminal behavior, potentially guilty of such behavior, or are some shade of "left-wing." Any of these allegations may serve to diminish the appeal of protest groups to potentially sympathetic third parties. City officials, in their frequent social and informal business interaction with leaders of established civic groups, may also communicate derogatory information concerning protest groups. Discrediting of protest groups may be undertaken by some city officials while others appear (perhaps authentically) to remain

[55] See Lipsky, "Rent Strikes in New York City," pp. 156, 249 ff.
[56] On the strategy of appearing constrained, see Schelling, *The Strategy of Conflict*, pp. 22 ff.

sympathetic to protest demands. These tactics may be engaged in by public officials whether or not there is any validity to the allegations.

6. Target groups may postpone action. The effect of postponement, if accompanied by symbolic assurances, is to remove immediate pressure and delay specific commitments to a future date. This familiar tactic is particularly effective in dealing with protest groups because of their inherent instability. Protest groups are usually comprised of individuals whose intense political activity cannot be sustained except in rare circumstances. Further, to the extent that protest depends upon activating reference publics through strategies which have some "shock" value, it becomes increasingly difficult to activate these groups. Additionally, protest activity is inherently unstable because of the strains placed upon protest leaders who must attempt to manage four constituencies (as described herein).

The most frequent method of postponing action is to commit a subject to "study." For the many reasons elaborated in these paragraphs, it is not likely that ad hoc protest groups will be around to review the recommendations which emerge from study. The greater the expertise and the greater the status of the group making the study, the less will protest groups be able to influence whatever policy emerges. Protest groups lack the skills and resource personnel to challenge expert recommendations effectively.

Sometimes surveys and special research are undertaken in part to evade immediate pressures. Sometimes not. Research efforts are particularly necessary to secure the support of established civic groups, which place high priority on orderly procedure and policy emerging from independent analysis. Yet it must be recognized that postponing policy commitments has a distinct impact on the nature of the pressures focused on policy-makers.

CONCLUSION

In this analysis I have agreed with James Q. Wilson that protest is correctly conceived as a strategy utilized by relatively powerless groups in order to increase their bargaining ability. As such, I have argued, it is successful to the extent that the reference publics of protest targets can be activated to enter the conflict in ways favorable to protest goals. I have suggested a model of the protest process which may assist in ordering data and indicating the salience for research of a number of aspects of protest. These include the critical role of communications media, the differential impact of material and symbolic rewards on "feedback" in protest activity, and the reciprocal relationships of actors in the protest process.

An estimation of the limits to protest efficacy, I have argued further, can be gained by recognizing the problems encountered by protest leaders who somehow must balance the conflicting maintenance needs of four groups in the protest process. This approach transcends a focus devoted primarily to characterization of group goals and targets, by suggesting that even in an environment which is relatively favorable to specific protest goals, the tensions which must be embraced by protest leadership may ultimately overwhelm protest activity.

At the outset of this essay, it was held that conceptualizing the American political system as "slack" or "fluid," in the manner of Robert Dahl, appears inadequate because of (1) a vagueness centering on the likelihood that any group can make itself heard; (2) a possible confusion as to which groups tend to receive satisfaction from the rewards dispensed by public officials; and (3) a lumping together as equally relevant rewards which are tangible and those which are symbolic. To the extent that protest is engaged in by relatively powerless groups which must create resources with which to bargain, the analysis here suggests a number of reservations concerning the pluralist conceptualization of the "fluidity" of the American political system.

Relatively powerless groups cannot use protest with a high probability of success. They lack organizational resources, by definition. But even to create bargaining resources through activating third parties, some resources are necessary to sustain organization. More importantly, relatively powerless protest groups are constrained by the unresolvable conflicts which are forced upon protest leaders who must appeal simultaneously to four constituencies which place upon them antithetical demands.

When public officials recognize the legitimacy of protest activity, they may not direct public policy toward protest groups at all. Rather, public officials are likely to aim responses at the reference publics from which they originally take their cues. Edelman has suggested that regulatory policy in practice often consists of reassuring mass publics while at the same time dispensing specific, tangible values to narrow interest groups. It is suggested here that symbolic reassurances are dispensed as much to wide, potentially concerned publics which are not directly affected by regulatory policy, as they are to wide publics, comprised of the downtrodden and the deprived, in whose name policy is often written.

Complementing Edelman, it is proposed here that in the process of protest symbolic reassurances are dispensed in large measure because these are the public policy outcomes and actions desired by the constituencies to which public officials are most responsive. Satisfying these wider publics, city officials can avoid pressures toward other policies placed upon them by protest organizations.

Not only should there be some doubt as to which groups receive the symbolic recognitions which Dahl describes, but in failing to distinguish between the kinds of rewards dispensed to groups in the political system, Dahl avoids a fundamental question. It is literally fundamental because the kinds of rewards which can be obtained from politics, one might hypothesize, will have an impact upon the realistic appraisal of the efficacy of political activity. If among the groups least capable of organizing for political activity there is a history of organizing for protest, and if that activity, once engaged in, is rewarded primarily by the dispensation of symbolic gestures without perceptible changes in material conditions, then rational behavior might lead to expressions of apathy and lack of interest in politics or a rejection of conventional political channels as a meaningful arena of activity. In this sense this discussion of protest politics is consistent with Kenneth Clark's observations that the image of power, unaccompanied by material and observable rewards, leads to impressions of helplessness and reinforces political apathy in the ghetto.[57]

Recent commentary by political scientists and others regarding riots in American cities seems to focus in part on the extent to which relatively deprived groups may seek redress of legitimate grievances. Future research should continue assessment of the relationship between riots and the conditions under which access to the political system has been limited. In such research assessment of the ways in

[57] Clark, *Dark Ghetto*, pp. 154 ff.

which access to public officials is obtained by relatively powerless groups through the protest process might be one important research focus.

The instability of protest activity outlined in this article also should inform contemporary political strategies. If the arguments presented here are persuasive, civil rights leaders who insist that protest activity is a shallow foundation on which to seek long-term, concrete gains may be judged essentially correct. But the arguments concerning the fickleness of the white liberal, or the ease of changing discriminatory laws relative to changing discriminatory institutions, only in part explain the instability of protest movements. An explanation which derives its strength from analysis of the political process suggests concentration on the problems of managing protest constituencies. Accordingly, Alinsky is probably on the soundest ground when he prescribes protest for the purpose of building organization. Ultimately, relatively powerless groups in most instances cannot depend upon activating other actors in the political process. Long-run success will depend upon the acquisition of stable political resources which do not rely for their use on third parties.